Settlement in Rom

Archaeological excavatio

London Underground Limited Jubilee Line

Extension Project

MoLAS Monograph Series

1 Excavations at the Priory and Hospital of St Mary Spital, London,
Christopher Thomas, Barney Sloane and Christopher Phillpotts
ISBN 1 901992 00 4

2 The National Roman Fabric Reference Collection: a handbook,
Roberta Tomber and John Dore
ISBN 1 901992 01 2

3 The Cross Bones burial ground, Redcross Way, Southwark,
London: archaeological excavations (1991–8) for the London
Underground Limited Jubilee Line Extension Project,
Megan Brickley and Adrian Miles with Hilary Stainer
ISBN 1 901992 06 3

4 The eastern cemetery of Roman London: excavations 1983–90,
Bruno Barber and David Bowsher
ISBN 1 901992 09 8

5 The Holocene evolution of the London Thames: archaeological
excavations (1991–8) for the London Underground Limited,
Jubilee Line Extension Project, Jane Sidell, Keith Wilkinson,
Robert Scaife and Nigel Cameron
ISBN 1 901992 10 1

6 The Limehouse porcelain manufactory: excavations at 108–116
Narrow Street, London, 1990, Kieron Tyler and Roy Stephenson,
with J Victor Owen and Christopher Phillpotts
ISBN 1 901992 16 0

7 Roman defences and medieval industry: excavations at Baltic
House, City of London, Elizabeth Howe
ISBN 1 901992 17 9

8 London bridge: 2000 years of a river crossing, Bruce Watson,
Trevor Brigham and Tony Dyson
ISBN 1 901992 18 7

9 Roman and medieval townhouses on the London waterfront:
excavations at Governor's House, City of London, Trevor Brigham
with Aidan Woodger
ISBN 1 901992 21 7

10 The London Charterhouse, Bruno Barber and Christopher Thomas
ISBN 1 901992 23 3

11 Medieval 'Westminster' floor tiles, Ian M Betts
ISBN 1 901992 24 1

12 Settlement in Roman Southwark: archaeological excavations
(1991–8) for the London Underground Limited Jubilee Line
Extension Project, James Drummond-Murray and Peter Thompson
with Carrie Cowan
ISBN 1 901992 28 7

Settlement in Roman Southwark

Archaeological excavations (1991–8) for the London Underground Limited Jubilee Line Extension Project

James Drummond-Murray and Peter Thompson with Carrie Cowan

MoLAS Monograph 12

Museum of London Archaeology Service

Published by the Museum of London Archaeology Service
Copyright © Museum of London 2002

A CIP catalogue record for this book is available from the British Library

Production and series design by Tracy Wellman
Typesetting and design by Susan Banks, Vanessa Bunton
and Jeannette van der Post
Reprographics by Andy Chopping
Copy editing by Simon Burnell
Series editing by Sue Hirst/Susan M Wright

Printed by the Lavenham Press

*Front cover: 4th-century mosaic from London Bridge Station; intaglio of Achilles or
Alexander the Great from Borough High Street; excavation for new ticket hall on
Borough High Street*

*Back cover: 1st-century oil lamp shaped like a sandalled foot from Borough High
Street; 2nd-century masonry building from Borough High Street; painted wall plaster
showing Hercules and the Nemean lion from Redcross Way*

CONTRIBUTORS

Principal authors	James Drummond-Murray, Peter Thompson, with Carrie Cowan
Building materials	Susan Pringle, Ian M Betts (painted wall plaster)
Roman pottery	Louise Rayner, Fiona Seeley, with Kay Hartley (stamped mortaria), Joanna Bird (samian ware), Brenda Dickinson (samian stamps), Robin P Symonds (amphorae overview)
Accessioned finds	Angela Wardle, with Martin Henig (intaglio)
Glass	Angela Wardle and John Shepherd
Roman coins	Michael Hammerson
Iron smithing	Lynne Keys
Botanical remains	Lisa Gray
Animal bone	Charlotte Ainsley
Eggshell	Jane Sidell
Conservation	Elizabeth Goodman, with Virginia Neal, Kirsten Suenson-Taylor (mosaic)
Graphics	Susan Banks, Kikar Singh, David Bentley, Jeannette van der Post, Sophie Lamb
Photography	Andy Chopping, Maggie Cox, Edwin Baker
Project managers	Al Green, Mike Hutchinson, Gordon Malcolm
Editor	Simon Burnell

CONTENTS

FIGURES

TABLES

SUMMARY

The construction of the Jubilee Line Extension provided an opportunity for archaeologists from the Museum of London Archaeology Service to investigate the archaeology of the areas of London through which the new Underground line passed. The tunnels themselves were well below the level of any archaeological deposits, but every connection between the tunnels and the surface – escape shafts, escalator shafts, vent shafts, new stations – posed a potential threat. Each was investigated between 1991 and 1996.

This volume deals with the results from work in and around London Bridge Station which date to the Roman period. The main excavation concerned the new Ticket Hall on Borough High Street and took place over six months in 1995. In the prehistoric period the topography of north Southwark consisted of a series of low sand islands projecting out of the tidal reaches of the Thames. The layout of the northernmost island, on which stood the southern end of the first London Bridge built by the Romans, was further elucidated. In particular a previously unknown inlet of Guy's Channel on the eastern side of the island was recognised.

The earliest Roman features were a series of large quarry pits and drainage ditches. The former were to extract gravel for building the road to the bridge, the latter for draining land that was prone to flooding. The alignment of the road to the bridge was confirmed and the first timber-framed buildings along its eastern side were excavated. One may have been a blacksmith's workshop. A narrow alley ran off to the east of the main road.

All the eight buildings alongside the road (a stretch of 60m) were burnt down c AD 60. This was almost certainly part of the sacking of Londinium in the Boudican revolt of AD 60/1. Small areas of destruction of that date had previously been recorded in Southwark, suggesting that the settlement to the south of the river had also been sacked, but the large scale of the Jubilee Line excavations provided more conclusive evidence of this.

The roadside buildings were rebuilt shortly after the fire. One masonry building was constructed at the north end whilst timber-framed buildings lined the rest of the road. A blacksmith's forge was located with several phases of use, and a butcher's shop was also excavated. Narrow alleys running east from the main north–south bridge road were uncovered as well as a series of timber roadside drains. In the early part of the 2nd century a colonnade was built alongside the road and a complex of masonry buildings may have formed a small market hall. In the latter part of the century a building with large amounts of grain found within it – possibly a baker's shop – was located alongside the road. Behind the buildings was an open area containing yard surfaces and wells.

Away from the road to the east a large masonry building erected in the late 1st century may have been a warehouse. There was also evidence for extensive land reclamation on the marginal eastern fringes of the island. This area may then have become a residential area, as a 2nd-century building with high-status associations was excavated, and later, in the 3rd century, a building with a mosaic was constructed.

To the west of the road a further part of the mansio excavated earlier (Cowan 1992) was revealed with high quality painted wall plaster. Further information on the Southwark Street channel, which divided the north and south islands of Roman Southwark, was also recorded as well as a scattering of burials, though nothing that could be termed a cemetery was uncovered.

The entire archaeological programme through to publication was funded by London Underground Limited (Jubilee Line Extension Project).

ACKNOWLEDGEMENTS

The analysis and publication of this volume has been entirely funded by London Underground Limited (Jubilee Line Extension Project – JLEP), to whom the authors, on behalf of MoLAS, would like to extend their grateful thanks. Particular thanks should go to Paul Chapman and Marcus Karakashian of the Jubilee Line Extension Project who have worked closely with MoLAS throughout the archaeological project. In addition the following JLEP staff were of invaluable assistance during the site work: Chris Field, Martin Gamble, John O'Connor, Dave Wass, Brendan Hunt and Barry Mathers. Natalie Beeson and Simon Kaye are due particular thanks for their help during the publication phase.

The authors would also like to thank John Dillon, then the Archaeology Officer for the Borough of Southwark, and his successor Sarah Gibson. Mark Hassall is due thanks for his comments on the graffiti. Robin Symonds wishes to thank Armand Desbat for his comments on the stamped Dressel 2-4 amphora from BGH95 [1753], as well as Fanette Laubenheimer and her CNRS/CNRA research group for numerous conversations on the quantification of amphorae. Charlotte Ainsley extends her thanks to Kevin Rielly and Alan Pipe for their help and comments during the recording and analysis of the animal bone.

Thanks also to the numerous field staff who worked on the project in north Southwark during the five years when fieldwork was taking place. Special mention must be made of Adrian Miles, Tony Mackinder, Aidan Woodger, Julian Bowsher, Robin Nielsen, Portia Askew, Kieron Heard, Oona Wills, Helen Jones, Dick Bluer, Simon Stevens and Steve Tucker who supervised some of the individual sites that made up the project and undertook the initial post-excavation work.

Thanks are also due to the team who worked under the Borough High Street road deck in difficult conditions: Simon Askew, Raoul Bull, Phil Carstairs, Jay Carver, Pat Connolly, Jessica Cowley, Andy Daykin, Mark Dunkley, Mike Edwards, Helenka Jurgielewicz, Dave Mackie, Peter Price, John Roberts, Niall Roycroft, Nick Sambrook, Jo Sturgess, Chris Swain, Jez Taylor, John Taylor, Jo Thomas, Andy Thomson, Richard Turnbull, Jo Wainwright and Dave Wicks. Thanks also to Dick Malt for his help during the post-excavation process.

The post-excavation programme was managed by Penny Bruce, Gordon Malcolm and Barney Sloane. Editorial comment was provided by Sue Hirst with Peter Rowsome. Academic advice was furnished by Martin Millett.

1

Introduction

1.1 The Jubilee Line Extension

Since the end of the Second World War there have been plans for a new Underground line linking the south and east of London to the centre of the city. The regeneration of Docklands and the new Canary Wharf development gave these plans new impetus and, as a result, the Jubilee Line Extension Project was conceived in 1989 to improve communications between central London and Docklands. In August 1989 an environmental assessment of the route was commissioned from the independent consulting group Environmental Resources Limited. This was produced in March 1990. The assessment recognised the importance and potential of the archaeological remains likely to lie along the route and in 1991 the Museum of London, through its archaeological service, was contracted to undertake the excavation of any archaeological deposits threatened by the construction work associated with the project.

Between 1991 and 1998 a series of evaluations, excavations and watching briefs were carried out. These were centred on three areas of known historic and archaeological interest – Westminster, London Bridge and Stratford – but included all sites where ground disturbance was to take place. The archaeological work at Westminster and London Bridge was carried out by the Museum of London Archaeology Service. The work at Stratford was undertaken by the Newham Archaeology Service and the Oxford Archaeology Unit under the project management of MoLAS.

As well as paying for the fieldwork, the Jubilee Line Extension Project also agreed to fund publication of the results of the excavations. These will appear in a series of monographs and articles. The work at London Bridge has produced this volume on the Roman remains uncovered (Fig 1; Fig 5) and another volume on the medieval and later remains is forthcoming. A third, on the post-medieval cemetery at Redcross Way, has already been published (Brickley and Miles 1999).

In addition a 44-page colour booklet, entitled *The Big Dig*, has been produced (Drummond-Murray et al 1998) featuring the highlights of the archaeology along the whole line, and was launched by Glenda Jackson, Minister for Transport in London and Dennis Tunnicliffe, Head of London Transport, at the Museum of London in July 1998.

1.2 Circumstances of fieldwork

The Borough High Street Ticket Hall excavation (site code BGH95) was the largest undertaken for the Jubilee Line Extension Project in Southwark, and there were several phases of archaeological work associated with the Ticket Hall between 1992 and the main excavation in 1995. In January and February 1992 two trenches were excavated in Borough High Street to gain access to the Battlebridge sewer for

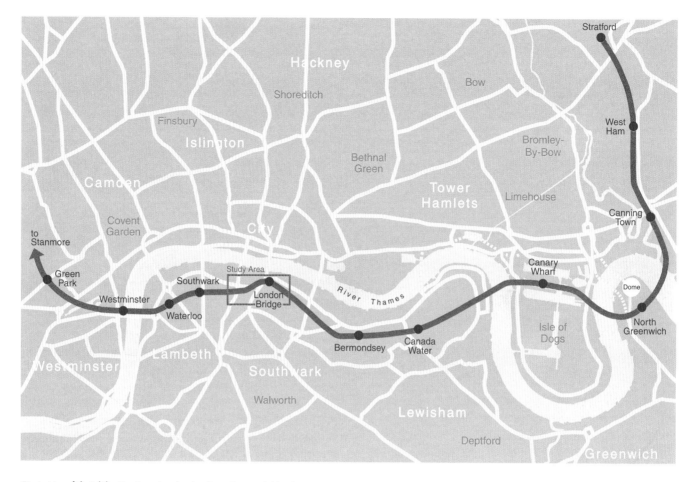

Fig 1 *Map of the Jubilee Line Extension showing the study area of this volume*

preparatory works for its diversion later in the project (JSS92). In March and April 1992 preparatory work for the re-routing of certain services and utilities entailed the digging of three separate trenches in Southwark Street and St Thomas Street (STU92). In March and April 1993 work was carried out around a British Telecom junction box in Borough High Street prior to the diversion of telecom services (BTJ93).

Three phases of work were undertaken on the site of 31–37 Borough High Street in 1994. An evaluation took place in January, excavation of underpinning pits for adjacent buildings in June and a watching brief in November (BUG94). In March and April 1994 monitoring work associated with the construction of the pile wall around the Ticket Hall site and associated utility diversion was carried out (BSE94). A further phase of this work took place in early 1996 during the construction of a heading around the west of the Ticket Hall and outside the pile wall to take the diverted Battlebridge sewer.

Over the Easter weekend 1995 (14–17 April) the surface of Borough High Street was dug up and replaced by a temporary road deck made of steel (Fig 2). This was because this main route south of London Bridge could not be closed for the two and a half years required to build the new Ticket Hall. Once the road deck was in place, ground reduction took place beneath it while the traffic flow continued uninterrupted above. As the numerous services (water, electricity, telecom)

were exposed in the process, they were suspended from the bottom of the road deck. A watching brief took place during this process, until archaeological deposits were reached, generally about 2.0m beneath the road deck, at c 2.5m to 2.7m OD. The site was divided into five areas for engineering purposes (hereafter areas A–E) and the whole site was bisected by the Victorian-built Battlebridge sewer which ran down the centre of the road at such a depth that all archaeological deposits in its path were removed during the cut-and-cover method of construction. The cut for the sewer was c 2.5m wide and caused extensive truncation. In addition there were a series of smaller feeder sewers joining the main sewer from individual buildings alongside both sides of the main road, and these too caused extensive truncation of archaeological deposits.

Areas A, B and D lay under the road deck and together measured c 60m north–south by 13m east–west. Area C extended east into St Thomas Street and measured 11m x 70m. Area E occupied the site of 31–37 Borough High Street, to the east of the road deck, and measured c 15m x 15m.

The excavation itself (BGH95) took place between July and November 1995 with up to 25 staff on site, and with a large number of labourers employed by the main contractor, Costain Taylor Woodrow, in attendance. Spoil was removed by a network of movable conveyor belts and lighting was provided by a large number of halogen lamps. Despite this, conditions

Fig 2 *View of the Borough High Street excavation, which took place beneath an artificial road deck*

were difficult under the road deck, and the success of the excavation was only achieved thanks to the dedication of the archaeological team and the cooperation of the contractors working alongside the archaeologists, and the assistance of the JLEP engineers.

A large number of sites were located beneath London Bridge Station. As a result much of the work took place under the railway arches originally constructed in the 1830s. The initial work began in 1991 as part of a watching brief of the preparatory works west of Joiner Street. In January 1992 the first of five phases of work began on a series of test pits (MSA92). Archaeological deposits were recorded at the base of a total of 11 investigative shafts all located on the western side of Joiner Street.

Between 1992 and 1995 a watching brief was conducted on the preparatory works including sewer and service diversions under railway arches either side of Joiner Street. From the end of 1994 a watching brief and subsequent excavation took place ahead of the construction of an escalator machine chamber immediately south of Tooley Street, on the east side of Joiner Street (LBH94).

A large escalator shaft for three sets of escalators linking the underground and surface transport systems was constructed west of Joiner Street, immediately in front of London Bridge Station. An archaeological excavation (LBE95) was carried out in two phases ahead of the engineering works in March

and then again between November and December 1995. The two phases of excavation were located within the 30m long and 10m wide concrete pile box. At the south end of Joiner Street the east vent shaft required archaeological excavation prior to the ventilation shaft being sunk to its full depth (Fig 3). The excavation (LBC95) during August and September 1995 took place within the confines of the rectangular shaft. A circular vent shaft, 15m in diameter, was located in the middle of Joiner Street, now closed to traffic. This was subject to large-scale truncation due to deep foundations, but excavation of undisturbed areas took place during April 1995 (LBD95).

At the northern limit of the station, at Station Approach, two phases of excavation (LBI95) were carried out. The first was between February and April 1995 for an escalator shaft for the London Underground Northern Line. The second phase in April 1996 was immediately to the east and preceded the construction of a Ticket Hall. The first phase was complicated by the extensive grouting that had taken place prior to excavation. This had not only stabilised the underlying natural gravels but had also leaked onto parts of the site, turning some of the archaeology into the consistency of concrete, and making it impossible to excavate. In particular some post-medieval skeletons were fused together (Fig 4).

Outside London Bridge Station two shafts were excavated on the north side of London Bridge Street. The first (LBB95),

Fig 3 View of the Joiner Street vent shaft during excavation

Fig 4 Grouting caused problems on the Northern Line escalator shaft excavation

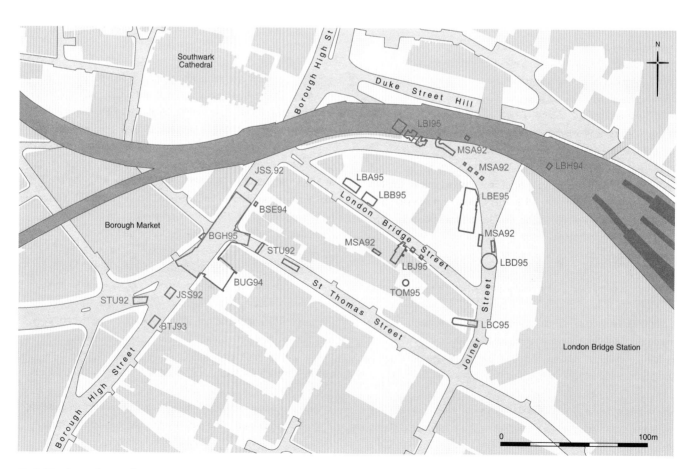

Fig 5 Map showing location of excavations in the London Bridge area

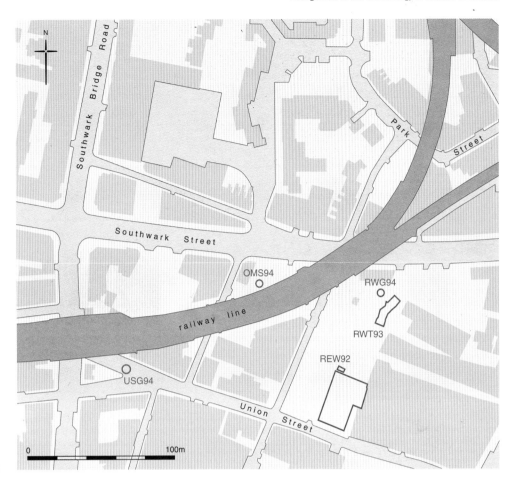

Fig 6 Map showing location of
excavations in the Redcross Way area

a rectangular vent shaft, was excavated in July and September
1995. Excavation within an escape shaft, situated just to the
north (LBA95), followed in September and October 1995.

Other archaeological recording, beneath 20–26 London
Bridge Street (LBJ95) and behind the same address (TOM95),
was carried out during 1995. The former was required for
underpinning works as the new Tube line was to run directly
underneath the standing building, and the latter was a grouting
shaft so that the underlying gravels could be stabilised.

A long-running watching brief was carried out to the east
of Joiner Street in the Bonded Bottlers arches on the site of
escalator shafts linking London Bridge Station concourse with
the Jubilee Line platforms (LBG95).

The third main area of work in north Southwark lay to the
west of Borough High Street and was centred on the Redcross
Way worksite (Fig 6). In November 1992 an evaluation was
carried out at Redcross Way (REW92) on the site of an
electricity substation (Miles 1992), and this was followed up
by two further phases of work on the site in April 1993 and
February 1996. A cable trench linking the electricity substation
to the access shaft on Southwark Street was excavated in
February 1993 (RWT93), while a grouting shaft adjacent to
the cable trench was excavated in May and June 1994 (RWG94).
Another grouting shaft to the south on Union Street (USG94)
was dug in September 1994 (Mackinder 1994), and a final
grouting shaft to the west on O'Meara Street was investigated
in October 1994 (OMS94).

1.3 Background to the archaeology of Roman Southwark

Southwark has only slowly taken its place in the study of
Roman London. For many years maps of Londinium stopped
somewhere in the middle of the Thames. Despite the efforts
of the Southwark and Lambeth Archaeological Excavation
Committee, and the publication of two volumes of excavations
in 1978 (Bird et al 1978) and 1988 (Hinton 1988), Southwark
has remained very much the poor relation of its more glamorous
northern neighbour. However, the recent publication of a
complex sequence of masonry buildings in Southwark Street
(Cowan 1992) and a timber warehouse from the Courage's
Brewery site (Brigham et al 1995), coupled with the
forthcoming publication of the important Winchester Palace
site (Yule in prep), two further volumes on the Courage's
Brewery site (Cowan in prep; Hammer in prep), the results
of the JLEP excavations and an English Heritage funded volume
on Roman backlog excavations, will enable Southwark to
assume its rightful place as an important suburb of Londinium,
with serious discussion of its function and role.

North Southwark was certainly occupied in the prehistoric
period. On Fennings Wharf a Bronze Age ring barrow with
associated cremations was uncovered. Further to the east in
Bermondsey, on the Horsleydown eyot, Bronze Age plough
marks provide evidence of agriculture. A scattering of Iron Age

burials and other features shows that occupation continued up until the Roman invasion. However, no settlement sites have been discovered to date on the sandy islands of north Southwark.

Any study of Roman Southwark must start with the bridge and the road running up to it – Southwark Road 1. This road has long been recognised as the continuation of Watling Street and Stane Street which, according to their known alignments, should meet at the northern limit of the mainland near the modern Borough Tube station before crossing the sand and gravel islands of north Southwark. The exact topography of these islands is still not entirely clear but enough information has now been collected to enable detailed models to be built of their layout. The picture that has developed of the south bank of the Thames is of a series of low-lying islands, little more than one metre above OD level, with abraded channels and marshland surrounding them (Fig 7). The road across the islands follows the line of modern Borough High Street, albeit running very slightly to the west of it.

Brigham (in Watson et al 2001, 12) has established the presence of an early (pre-AD 60) embankment on the Toppings Wharf site as a flood defence – the first Thames barrier? – enabling the sand island to be occupied safely. Revetments of a similar date along the edges of the channel have also been found, for example at 64–70 Borough High Street (Graham 1988b).

Early Roman occupation was concentrated alongside the main road until the settlement was destroyed in the Boudican revolt (see Chapter 5). Rebuilding and substantial expansion followed in the latter part of the 1st century AD, so that by the middle of the 2nd century a considerable settlement of at least 45 acres had grown up with large masonry buildings performing a variety of functions, including public and administrative duties (Heard et al 1990). The use of the channels for navigation continued, as attested by the finding of a river barge at Guy's Hospital (Marsden 1994).

A cemetery was excavated at 103–167 Great Dover Street in 1996 (Mackinder 2000) where a mortuary complex alongside Watling Street revealed both inhumations and cremations dating from the middle of the 2nd to the middle of the 3rd century. This conforms to the general Roman pattern of burying their dead alongside the main roads leading from settlements, and this is the first coherent cemetery group from south of the river.

Contraction seems to have occurred in the 3rd and 4th centuries, with some areas that were previously occupied now

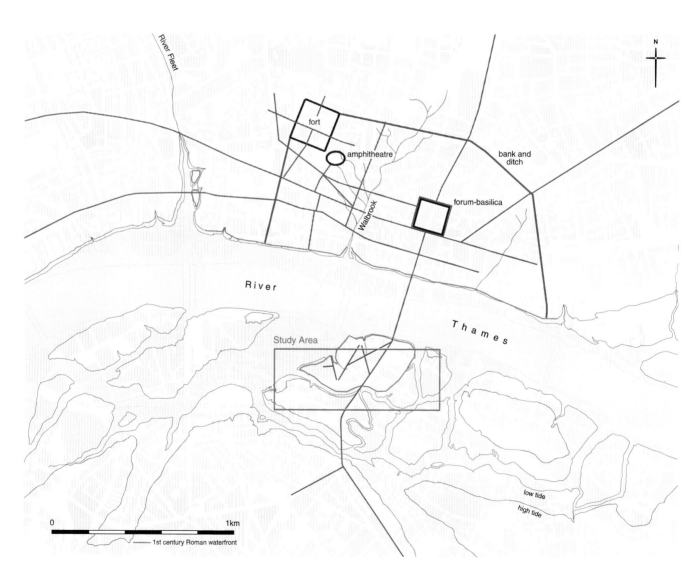

Fig 7 Map showing location of the study area in relation to the rest of Londinium

being given over to burials, for example at 15–23 Southwark Street (Cowan 1992). However, this did not represent complete abandonment as masonry buildings continued in use at Winchester Palace (Yule 1989), and it was noted in the *Gentleman's Magazine* in 1840 that during the demolition of the south wing of St Thomas's Hospital adjacent to Borough High Street '...a Roman pavement of the common red tesserae, surrounded by walls of flint and rubble, with courses of Roman tiles, has been discovered, at a depth of 20 feet from the level of the High Street.' In 1842 the Victorian antiquarian Charles Roach Smith recorded that: '... on the tessellated floor itself were picked up several of the small brass coins of the Constantine family, which shew that this house was occupied at least as late as the period when they were in circulation.' This building is probably a continuation of the complex of 3rd- to 4th-century buildings excavated at 1–7 St Thomas Street in 1974 (Dennis 1978).

1.4 Organisation of the report

Following the lead established in the first MoLAS monograph (Thomas et al 1997), this report will integrate the different strands of evidence into a coherent narrative. The individual chapters will have the relevant finds and environmental information available in the main text. Technical supporting data has been placed in appendices at the end of the volume (see Chapter 11). Likewise, specialist reports and discussions relating to the research questions will appear in the most relevant chapter (for example, the main smithing report will be included in the chapter where the blacksmith is discussed).

The use of colour will make plans and drawings easier to interpret and more accessible, whilst the experiment of combining graphic and photographic elements in the pottery illustrations is intended to enhance the report without compromising academic integrity. The graphical conventions used are shown in Fig 8.

Methodologies

Methodology for stratigraphy

The stratigraphy was analysed using a mixture of traditional methods and more modern techniques. The archaeological sequence for each site was built up by collecting contexts together in subgroups, which were then put into groups of related activity given a land use. Periods were established by grouping together contemporary land uses. Period plans were generated electronically by digitising all the plans and analysing them using GIS. Seven periods were established for the Roman sequence on Borough High Street:

Period 1   AD 55
Period 2   AD 55–61
Period 3   AD 61/2
Period 4   AD 62–100
Period 5   AD 100–20
Period 6   AD 120–60
Period 7   AD 160+

These periods form the basis of Chapters 3–9 respectively. The sequences from the other sites are discussed in relation to the relevant Borough High Street period.

Methodology for animal bones

The faunal remains discussed within this report were collected by hand-retrieval and from the processed bulk samples.

Period plans at 1:200

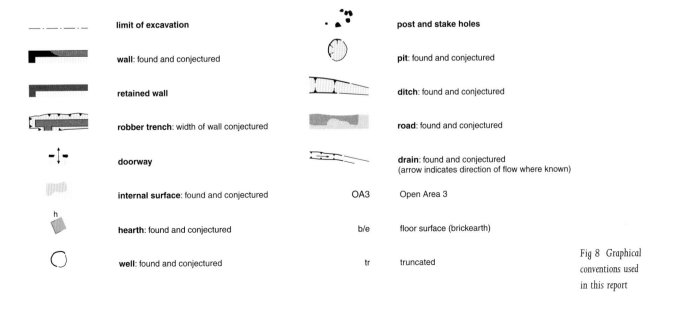

limit of excavation		post and stake holes	
wall: found and conjectured		pit: found and conjectured	
retained wall		ditch: found and conjectured	
robber trench: width of wall conjectured		road: found and conjectured	
doorway		drain: found and conjectured (arrow indicates direction of flow where known)	
internal surface: found and conjectured		OA3 Open Area 3	
hearth: found and conjectured		b/e floor surface (brickearth)	
well: found and conjectured		tr truncated	

Fig 8 Graphical conventions used in this report

Identifications were made using the MoLSS Environmental Archaeology Section reference collection in conjunction with a range of faunal identification manuals. Where it was impossible to determine exact identifications to species, approximate classifications based on size were employed, for example 'cattle-sized', 'sheep-sized' and 'chicken-sized'. Wherever possible, the utmost information for each bone was recorded, including species, element, side, age, butchery evidence, burning, pathologies, gnawing and measurements. For full listings of reference methodologies see the animal bone appendix (Chapter 11.8).

Methodology for plant remains

The plant remains discussed here came from a range of sites and features, and were identified using a modern seed reference collection and seed identification manuals. They have been interpreted on two levels, ecological and economic. Reconstructions of the local natural environments have been based on the assumption that the ecological preferences of plants for certain habitats are the same today as they were in the past. This means that modern floras are used to define habitat ranges for each plant type recovered while considering the level of identification made possible by the quality of preservation of the plant tissue. Economic interpretations have been based on archaeological and documentary evidence where appropriate and, in the case of cereal processing, ethnographic observations of pre-industrial farming communities have been employed. Habitat and plant use codes are given in the tables. Reconstructions of activities and the uses of features and areas have been carried out by examining the context-related variation of the botanical assemblages.

Methodology for building materials

The building materials from all the sites in the project were quantified by fabric, form and context using the standard Museum of London recording sheet and fabric codes. The fabrics which are referred to in the text are described in the specialist appendix (see Chapter 11.1) and samples are held at the Museum. The data were computerised to facilitate the correlation of the building materials with the stratigraphic periods, and to assist with the interpretation of the archaeological features. The results of this analysis have been integrated as far as possible with the main body of the report, and an overview of the range, quality and source of the building materials is given in the specialist appendix. The post-Roman material from the Jubilee Line Extension sites is not included in this report.

Methodology for Roman pottery

The Roman pottery in this report is presented within the integrated site narrative on two levels. The first level presents a brief summary of the pottery recorded from key buildings or features, where this was considered worthwhile, above all for dating purposes. This data is presented by sherd count and/or count of records or 'rows'. The second level presents key assemblages as quantified groups using weight (in grams) and estimated vessel equivalent (EVEs). These groups are illustrated and the full catalogue is provided in Chapter 11.2. For the BGH95 assemblage the pottery has been examined by period and discussed in comparison with the Roman Ceramic Phases (RCPs) published in *A dated corpus of early Roman pottery from the City of London* (Davies et al 1994) (abbreviated to ERC in the text). This overview is presented in Chapter 11.2.

All codes used in the text are current in the Museum of London Specialist Services. These consist of common name fabric codes, numeric-alpha form codes and decoration codes. A key to the codes is provided in the form of Tables 39–41 in Chapter 11.2.

Further discussion of the methodology and all data tables can be found in Chapter 11.2. The catalogue of decorated samian, samian stamps and mortarium stamps examined for this publication is also provided there.

2

The topography of north Southwark

Britain is triangular in shape, rather like Sicily
Diodorus Siculus, 1st century BC

2.1 Archaeological background

Over the years, and in particular in the course of excavation work carried out between 1970 and 1990, the principal elements of the prehistoric and early Roman topography of north Southwark have been established (Fig 9). The evidence for the wider, braided channels of the River Thames and the series of sand and gravel eyots making up the background topography for Roman Southwark has been described elsewhere (Yule 1988) and will be summarised below.

Even since the model put forward in *Antiquity* (Heard et al 1990), enough new information has been forthcoming to significantly refine and reinterpret this picture using data and evidence from more recent work and borehole studies. The Southwark Street Channel between the north and south islands has been investigated recently by Pre-Construct Archaeology (Killock 1997) and revealed revetting on the south side. The northern edge of the island has been discussed by Brigham (in Watson et al 2001) after re-examination of the evidence from the Toppings Wharf excavation, and post-excavation analysis of the Courage's Brewery excavation (Cowan in prep) has elucidated the north-west area of the north island.

However, it was the construction of the Jubilee Line Extension, running west to east across north Southwark, that has recently contributed most to the knowledge of the topography of the northern island of Roman Southwark, particularly the eastern side. Here comparatively little work has been done in the past because the majority of archaeological remains beneath London Bridge Station have not been disturbed since the construction of the extensive foundations. The brick-built railway arches and station were largely constructed between 1836 and 1849. The fact that the Victorian engineers founded the bases of the arches on the consolidated gravels required the removal of large quantities of made ground and overburden during a period when very limited recording of archaeological deposits took place.

It is likely that further refinements will be made as a result of the English Heritage publication programme for prehistoric and Roman Southwark, where the emphasis is on areas away from Borough High Street and London Bridge, particularly on the southern island.

Various excavations to the north of Tooley Street have helped to establish the northern limits of the island, or rather have demonstrated that large-scale erosion in the medieval period removed the north edge of the island. On Toppings Wharf a large east–west ditch may have formed part of early flood defences (Brigham in Watson et al 2001). Just to the east, on Cottons Wharf, various natural and revetted channels were recorded (*London Archaeol* 5, 1985, 65).

On Tooley Street itself the District Heating Scheme (Graham 1988a) recorded the east edge of the island with a creek or inlet running north–south and mudflats beyond that. This creek was probably the mouth of Guy's Channel.

The Winchester Palace excavations revealed the early Roman riverfront and late 1st-century dumping on the foreshore to reclaim land from the river (Yule 1989).

Fig 9 North Southwark in the late Iron Age

To the south of London Bridge Station work in and around Guy's Hospital has elucidated the limits of the north and south islands as well as Guy's Channel, where the remains of a Roman barge were recorded (Marsden 1994). In 1989 drainage ditches and a timber quay on the west side of the channel were located (Wilson 1990). Further work on the west side of Guy's Channel has recently been carried out by Pre-Construct Archaeology (R Wilson pers comm).

At 21–27 St Thomas Street excavations revealed an area of low-lying, open ground which was subject to regular flooding. A series of ditches were dug in the 2nd and 3rd centuries AD to aid drainage (Cowan et al in prep).

The north bank of the Southwark Street Channel crossed the site of 52–54 Southwark Street and the line of two 1st- and 2nd-century timber revetments was revealed (Wilson 1990). At 64–70 Borough High Street (Graham 1988b) Road 1 crossed the eastern edge of the site and the southern bank of the Southwark Street Channel was revealed. A sequence of revetments was constructed along the edge of the stream channel.

2.2 The Jubilee Line excavations

The centre of the island

The local topography in the immediate vicinity of the Borough High Street Ticket Hall site (BGH95) may have included a ridge of higher ground at c 1.0m OD associated with the centre of the northern sand and gravel island (Fig 10). This slightly higher ground would have dictated to, and been utilised by, the road builders and by those constructing the earliest buildings.

The top of natural sands was generally recorded at between 0.8m and 1.1m OD (Table 1). This represents the top of the eyot with the ground level slightly lower to the east of the road corridor. This slight drop in level may have been the start of the slope down towards the eastern edge of the island at Guy's

Fig 10 East-facing section through the natural gravel forming the bridgehead island

Hospital. The northern bridgehead island had been subject to inundation in the early or pre-Roman period. These inundation events occurred across all the eyots and caused the deposition of silts and clays. The flood clays cover most of the site and were present at approximately 1.2m OD. This inundation is considered as a loose division between the prehistoric and Roman periods in north Southwark.

Eastern edge of the island and Guy's Channel

The channel referred to as Guy's Channel, after being recorded on excavations at Guy's Hospital (Marsden 1965), was anticipated to run along the line of Joiner Street. Channel deposits and the western edge of the channel at GHL89 (Wilson 1990; Cowan et al in prep) indicated that four sites along the approximate course of the channel afforded the opportunity to investigate it. The waterlain deposits recorded at LBC95, LBD95, LBE95 and LBH94 all reflect the frequency of seasonal or tidal flooding along the edge of the eyot. These deposits covered low-lying ground as well as filling the channels themselves.

Clays and silts which accumulated at LBC95, just to the north of St Thomas Street (Fig 5), may belong to the 1st-century flooding. However, by the 2nd century similar flooding and rubbish dumping was still taking place. On LBC95 there were also attempts at raising the contemporary ground level by dumping gravel.

An excavation in the middle of Joiner Street – LBD95 (Fig 5) – was located very close to the eastern edge of the island, some 175m to the east of Southwark's Road 1. Natural sand here was recorded between 0.5m and 0.3m OD, sloping gently down from north-west to south-east. There were some ephemeral prehistoric features, which were sealed by a waterlain silt layer. This was either a single episode of flooding or a period of more extensive inundation over the site. Further evidence for subsequent flooding of the site reflected the marginal nature of the area, for example the lack of any traces of Roman occupation in the 1st century AD. No revetments were recorded or the channel edge itself, but the marginal nature of the land suggested that it is unlikely to have been far to the east.

Approximately 50m due east of LBD95 on LBG95 only marsh and waterlain deposits were observed in a watching brief. As the most easterly of the London Bridge sites, LBG95 was most likely located beyond the limits of the eyot and within a low-lying area of running water during the Roman period. This was most probably within Guy's Channel, although the watching brief was unable to confirm this. Evidence for peat/stagnant water points to changes in the course of the channel at different times.

Open Area 2 at LBE95 (Fig 5) indicated the lack of any significant activity at the eastern margins of the eyot during the 1st century AD. Some small-scale dumping of domestic debris took place probably into a wet environment subject to periodic flooding. Abraded pottery represents the surviving element of household rubbish deposited at or beyond the limit of the settlement. This may have originated from the building and occupation at LBI95 (see Chapter 6).

Small keyhole excavations between foundations at LBH94 (Fig 5) revealed some highly truncated elements of the Roman landscape. Natural alluvial silts were recorded at −0.2m OD and Open Area 2 on LBH94 included a small segment of ditch and a part of a channel.

The early stratigraphy at LBH94 was poorly represented, but included partial evidence of a large channel which would represent one of possibly numerous naturally shifting channels occupying the line of Guy's Channel. A small segment of ditch was uncovered, which had begun to silt up during the 2nd century AD. Active channels and channel deposits may therefore have covered the site during the 1st and early 2nd centuries AD.

During the trial work in Mayor Sworder's Arches (MSA92) (Fig 5), a series of test holes revealed the edge of the sand island sloping off from +0.73m OD in the west to −0.31m OD in the east where natural sand was sealed by Roman foreshore deposits. These, in turn, were sealed by an alluvial deposit c 0.5m thick which was cut by a north–south channel forming part of the Guy's Channel sequence.

Fifty metres to the west of Joiner Street on LBJ95 (Fig 5) a series of shafts were dug to allow for the underpinning of 20–26 London Bridge Street. Natural sands were recorded sloping down from 0.9m in the west to c 0.2m OD in the east. An east–west V-shaped ditch was excavated, and was found to have a sticky waterlain silt forming the primary fill, but no dating evidence was recovered. However, it is likely to be of early Roman date and dug to drain into Guy's Channel to the east.

A test pit in the adjacent Telephone House basement, 10m to the west of LBJ95, revealed the edge of a channel dipping down sharply to the south-east with natural sand at a height of 0.85m OD.

Table 1 Natural deposits on the JLE sites

Site code	Height of natural	Deposit	Comment
BGH95	+0.9m–+1.1m OD	sand	north island
BSE94	+0.9m	sand	north island
BTJ93	+1.0m OD	sand	north island
STU92	+1.2m OD	sand	north island
LBA95	+0.7m OD	sand/foreshore	low lying/marginal
LBB95	+0.4m OD	sand/foreshore	low lying/marginal
LBC95	+0.34m–+0.28m OD	sand	Guy's Channel
LBD95	+0.5m–+0.3m OD	sand	low lying/marginal
LBE95	+0.6m–+0.1m OD	sand/alluvial	low lying/marginal
LBG95	?+0.5m max	alluvial	Guy's Channel
LBH94	+0.5m–−0.2m OD	alluvial	Guy's Channel
LBI95	+0.8m–+0.7m OD	sand	north island
LBJ95	+0.9m–+0.2m OD	sand	low lying/marginal
MSA92	+0.7m–−0.31m OD	sand/foreshore	E edge of north island
TOM95	+0.5m OD	sand	low lying/marginal
RWG94	+1.25m OD	sand	north island
RWT93	+1.3m–+0.8m OD	sand	S edge of north island
OMS94	+0.6m–−0.6m OD	sand/alluvial	S edge of north island
USG94	+1.35m OD	sand	south island
REW92	+0.37m–+0.08m OD	alluvial	Southwark Channel

A similar pattern was noted just to the south on TOM95 (Fig 5) where natural sand was recorded at 0.5m OD. This sealed an extensive sequence of sands and silts reflecting a series of inundations on the site before natural glacial river gravels were reached at −0.9m OD. Little Roman activity was recorded in the first two centuries AD.

Further to the north, on LBI95 (Fig 5), natural sands and gravels were recorded between 0.8m OD in the west and 0.7m OD in the east. These were sealed by a layer of river silt c 0.25m thick representing a substantial inundation, and similar to the deposit found elsewhere in Southwark in the immediate pre-Roman period. This layer was not present in the central and eastern trenches of the site, where it may have been stripped off prior to gravel quarrying in the early Roman period.

Many of the waterlain deposits represent the environment of the eyot during the 1st century AD. The eastern limit of the island does not suggest any evidence of Roman occupation or significant activity before the Boudican rebellion of AD 61. During the period of initial occupation in Southwark this area would have been highly marginal land, with the focus of activity located to the west alongside Road 1. There is certainly little evidence to suggest that any early attempts were made to affect the environment close to the edge of the channel.

Taking into account all the new evidence for the JLE sites around London Bridge Station, it points to the presence of a previously unknown area of lower, more marginal land to the east of the main road. This seems to form a shallow inlet between higher ground recorded to the north on LBI95 and extending southwards towards the Joiner Street and St Thomas Street junction. Natural here was recorded at c 0.5m OD or lower and therefore was probably unsuitable for immediate occupation with available land elsewhere. No attempt was made to reclaim it until the 2nd century AD, when pressure on land necessitated more marginal land being brought into occupation (see Chapter 7).

South-western edge of the island and the Southwark Street Channel

A series of excavations in the Southwark Street and Redcross Way area (Fig 6) were located at the south-western limit of the eyot. Here further information was recorded about the Southwark Street Channel dividing the north and south sand islands. The surface of natural gravel in the Southwark Street channel area was generally too low to be reached during open area excavation on the sites, but small sondages at RWG94 showed the surface of the gravel at −0.8m OD, while at REW92 the natural gravel was recorded at −0.72m OD and at OMS94 at −0.73m OD.

Above the gravel were layers of sand deposition which indicated the natural surface of the northernmost island of Southwark. At RWG94 the surface of this sand was at a height of 1.25m OD and was overlain by a weathered sand with roots and charcoal flecks at 1.4m OD. At RWT93 a series of holes drilled with an auger revealed natural sands sloping down gradually to the south, from a height of 1.3m OD at the north

end of the excavation down to 0.8m OD at the south end, thereby indicating the natural slope of the northernmost island down to the margins of the channel. At OMS94 overlying the gravel was a fine sand with a surface in the northern part of the site at +0.6m OD sloping down to −0.6m OD in the south, which indicated the north bank of the Southwark Street Channel. The southern side of the channel in the west of the study area was not firmly located but excavations at USG94, on the south sand island, recorded the natural sand at 1.35m OD sealed by the weathered sand with root disturbance at 1.6m OD. The channel was situated to the north of this land surface and the south side was recorded, due north of USG, at 51–55 Southwark Street (Killock 1997).

Alluvial deposits within the Southwark Street Channel

Above the gravel at REW92 was a sequence of clean, banded sands, above which were silt/clay deposits, the top of which varied between 0.37m OD in the east down to 0.08m OD in the west.

A monolith sample was taken for sedimentological assessment in order to provide a detailed analysis of these deposits (Wilkinson 1996). The large variation found within the sample – which mainly consists of a succession of sand and silt/clay deposits – suggests rapid and cyclical alteration in deposition, perhaps on a seasonal basis. However, on an even shorter time scale, the laminations present in certain of the deposits indicate deposition during a single event such as a flood. All the deposits within the sample are likely to have accumulated either within a river or stream channel, or as a result of overbank flooding, with the large amounts of sand found perhaps favouring the former. There appears to be a trend in the sampled deposits for increasing iron staining towards the base of the sequence as well as manganese oxide stained sediments. This could be due to periodic drying during the deposition of these sediments (which would have allowed iron minerals contact with oxygen).

Alluvial deposits also collected in the channel at OMS94. An organic silt/clay layer developed at −0.3m OD in the south rising to +0.2m OD in the north. It eventually thinned out towards the north of the site leaving an area of foreshore sand exposed.

One monolith sample showed a degree of sand present in the units to indicate that scouring from the edge of the island had taken place as a result of high-energy conditions or fast-flowing water within the channel.

2.3 Discussion of topography and conclusions

The active nature of a fluvial regime such as that affecting 1st-century AD north Southwark was probably represented by shifting river channels, formation of smaller creeks, and varying points of erosion and deposition. This environment became increasingly controlled as early attempts to manage

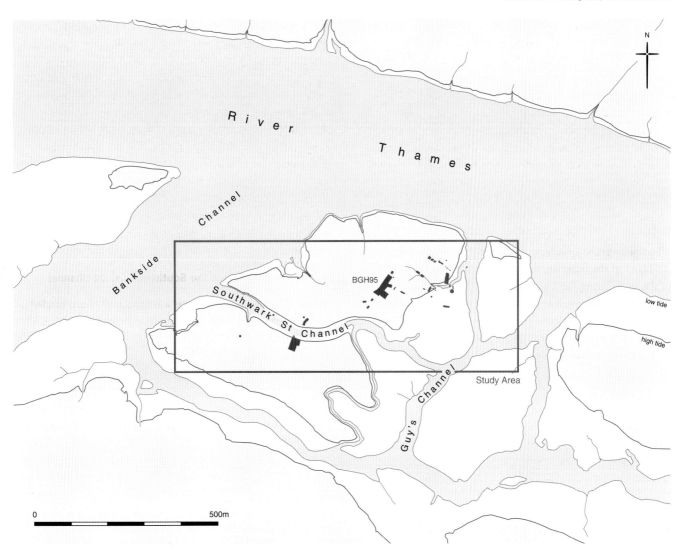

Fig 11 Plan of the natural topography of north Southwark revised in the light of the JLE excavations

the river channels by canalisation, revetting, banks and backfilling began to take effect. A revised topographical survey based on the new data from JLE excavations provides a topographical map of the islands prior to any canalisation (Fig 11).

Previous work established the likely limits of the north and southern eyots, including refining the positions of the various channels. However, knowledge of the eastern edge of the larger bridgehead island has previously relied largely on data from the north and south of London Bridge Station. This was a consequence of the nature of the railway arches and the consistent function of the station, and as a result little archaeological work had been carried out under the station.

The eastern JLE sites (LBC95, LBD95, LBE95, LBG95, LBH94, LBJ95 and MSA92) provided details of the marginal nature of the eastern edge of the island. This was subject to depositional episodes, including tidal and seasonal floods.

Alluvial deposits may also indicate previous positions of earlier versions of Guy's Channel or smaller creeks.

No conclusive evidence for revetments or quays came from the JLE sites on the east side of the island, corresponding to that at Guy's Hospital further south (Wilson 1990). Such structures may have been situated further east at the edge of a main channel or may not have been built due to lack of use of adjacent marginal land. It is now clear that in the 1st century the main focus of activity was more to the west of the main road. Apart from the immediate eastern roadside frontage, the eastern area was largely ignored, whilst to the west efforts were made to control the Southwark Street Channel in order to make the area fit for occupation. The eastern reaches of the island were left unoccupied throughout the 1st century as suitable building land was available elsewhere. Only in the north-east corner, on LBI95, is any significant occupation to be found (see Chapter 6).

3

The arrival of the Romans

As the best place for gaining this [a proper triumph],
Claudius chose Britain, which no-one had attempted
to invade since the deified Julius
Suetonius, 2nd century AD

3.1 Period 1: early Roman activity

The currently accepted date for the founding of Londinium is
c AD 50, seven years after the invasion led by Claudius brought
Britain into the Roman Empire. The impetus for Londinium's
birth and development is generally accepted as having resulted
from the selection of this location for the first permanent
Thames crossing point. Prior to this, a crossing point further
upstream at Westminster has been suggested from early road
alignments in Southwark (Sheldon 1978). Certainly the Thames
was shallower there, but there has been no definitive evidence
proving the existence of an early Roman crossing point, despite
the best efforts of the Time Team (Sloane et al 1995).
However, the Thames at Westminster was not suitable for a
port – the shallowness that encouraged the location for a ford
precluded large ships from approaching to dock. The deeper
water further downstream provided a much more inviting site.

Southwark Road 1

The exact construction date for the road linking Stane Street
and Watling Street to the river crossing is not precisely defined
(Fig 12). However, all indications from previous work suggest
that the road would have been one of the first Roman projects
carried out in Southwark and may well have been the work of
army engineers. The new Thames crossing may originally have
been by ferry (Milne 1995, 42) as there is no evidence for a
bridge at this early date. Indeed there is no evidence for a
bridge at all on the south bank, medieval erosion having
removed the bank where the southern bridgehead would have
been located. However, its location can be inferred from the
road alignment of Southwark's Road 1 as being slightly
downstream from the existing London Bridge on the site of
Fennings Wharf, where excavations in 1984 revealed Peter de
Colechurch's medieval successor to the original Roman bridge.
Brigham (in Watson et al 2001, 32–6), however, favours an
early date for the construction of the first bridge, of around
AD 50–2, and places it further to the south and west after
re-examining the evidence from Fennings Wharf and the
excavation at Toppings Wharf (Sheldon 1974). This has the
advantage of putting the bridge and the road running north
from it, to the Forum, on the same alignment.

The construction of the main approach road required a
timber corduroy base to act as a solid foundation when the
road approached the marginal land at the edges of the island.
This was overlain by sand and gravel agger and surfaces
(Fig 13). The whole process would have required land clearance,
gravel quarrying and timber clearance. Southwark's Road 1 itself
was not uncovered during the main excavation of the Borough
High Street Ticket Hall. The alignment of the road should
have taken it across the south-west corner of the site, but
this area was completely truncated down to natural and no
archaeological deposits were present. However, the road was
revealed in section during a post-excavation watching brief on
a heading to divert the Battlebridge sewer around the west of

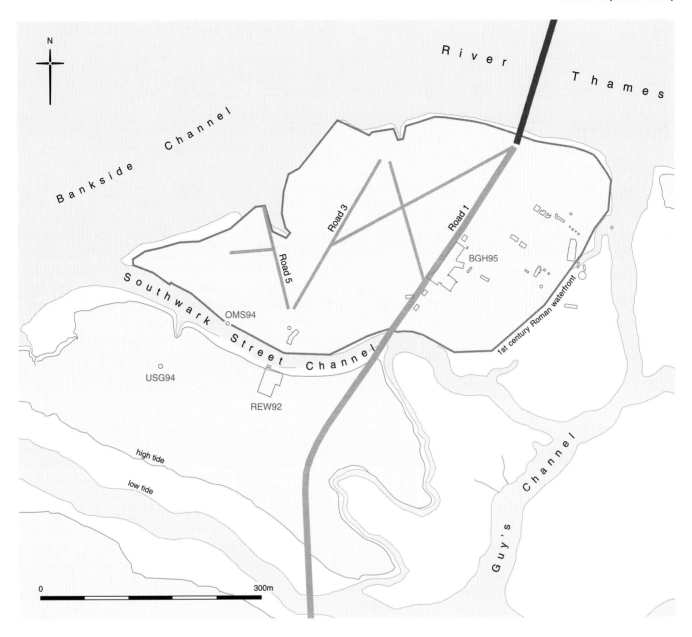

Fig 12 *Plan of Roman roads in Southwark*

the site (BSE94). Despite heavy truncation a series of gravel surfaces were recorded, but no dating evidence was recovered to establish a date for the initial construction of the road.

The road here was of simple construction with none of the elaborate timber foundations that were present further south, for example at 106–114 Borough High Street (Schwab 1978), where the edge of the island was approached. A more extensive stretch of the road was uncovered in an excavation immediately to the west of the site at 2 Southwark Street in 1985 (Graham and Hinton 1988) which, combined with the watching brief evidence, enables it to be said with a reasonable degree of certainty that the main Roman road in Southwark was between 6.0m and 7.0m wide at this point and its eastern edge was immediately to the west of the western limit of the Ticket Hall excavation.

Other JLE sites close to the likely alignment of the road were the series of small excavations at BTJ93, STU92 and the south trench of JSS92. These were located around the junction of Borough High Street and Southwark Street (Fig 14). These

Fig 13 *South-facing section through Southwark Road 1 revealed in the sewer diversion tunnel*

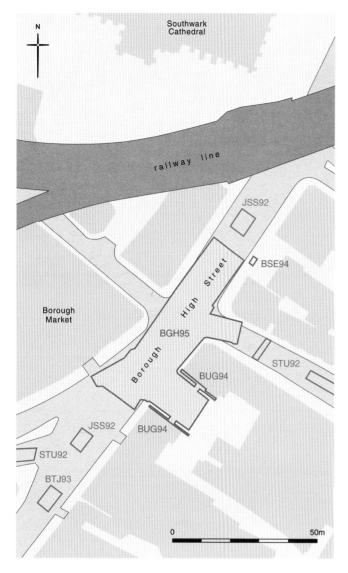

Fig 14 Map of location of JLE sites on and around Borough High Street

excavations were carried out at the outset of the project during work to divert main services. The archaeological remains in these trenches were partly truncated by the original sewer, water and gas pipes.

Road 1 was not located in these trenches. Gravel deposits recorded at 1.7m OD on JSS92 and STU92 may have originally derived from the road itself. The lack of evidence for a definite roadside drain or the limits of the road agger at these sites does not allow for the exact position of the road to be located nor for the function or origins of the gravel spreads to be definitively interpreted. It seems certain that the line of the road must run immediately between these sites. The alignment of the road may be further inferred from the complementary alignment of building and boundary evidence on STU92 and BTJ93 as well as the buildings on BGH95 itself.

Since the Roman engineers were expending considerable energy on constructing a road, it seems more probable that a bridge was built as well, a comparatively simple task, rather than having an elaborate road terminate at a ferry crossing. This would particularly be so if a large settlement was planned on the north bank and this was a major junction in the communications network.

In conclusion, the evidence from the JLE sites tends to confirm the basic alignment of Southwark Road 1 established by previous work (Graham and Hinton 1988) but goes no further towards settling the question of the construction date because of the lack of dating evidence. It is possible to suggest minor variations in its alignment over time from the position of various roadside features that were recorded (see subsequent Chapters) including building frontages and drains. However, these also tend to confirm the general location and direction of the road.

Early Roman activity alongside the road

Quarry pits

The earliest evidence of Roman occupation on the Borough High Street site consists of a series of large quarry pits in the western half of the site, close to the line of the main road, and, further to the east, two ditches. The quarry pits, it can reasonably be assumed, were for the extraction of the gravel needed in the construction of the road, and most were almost immediately backfilled with sand, though peat formation in one indicated that it stood open for a period of time (Fig 15).

The gravel itself was only c 0.2m below the sand capping and therefore easy to exploit. The almost immediate backfilling of the quarry pits means that the date of their assemblages can be used to support a construction date for Southwark Road 1 early in the AD 50s.

The pits, from the environmental evidence they contained, were dug in an area of (or backfilled with soil from) disturbed ground and scrub or woodland as well as semi-aquatic ground. The pits were generally at least 2.0m in diameter and 1.0m deep but no one pit was completely within the excavation, several being half-sectioned by the Battlebridge sewer, and some may have been considerably larger. The pits occupied an area (OA2) c 3.0–4.0m to the east of the main north–south road at the nearest point and continued to the east. A small number of pondweed seeds recovered from two of the pits may mean that pools of water were temporarily present before they were backfilled.

Pottery came from at least three of the pits. The condition of the sherds and number of joining sherds or partially complete vessels suggests that the material was backfilled into the features as a primary deposit.

QUARRY PIT 1

From the first quarry pit an assemblage with three individual vessels was recovered. The most complete vessel is a SHEL jar with a diamond-shaped rim <P1> (Fig 16). The jar is handmade, although the rim may have been wheel-finished. There is black pitch or resin on the rim, both externally and internally. The vessel is rilled from the shoulder to cover the whole of the body; the fabric is hard-fired with fine shell inclusions, and the surface is mottled due to burning, but is primarily dark grey to brown in colour.

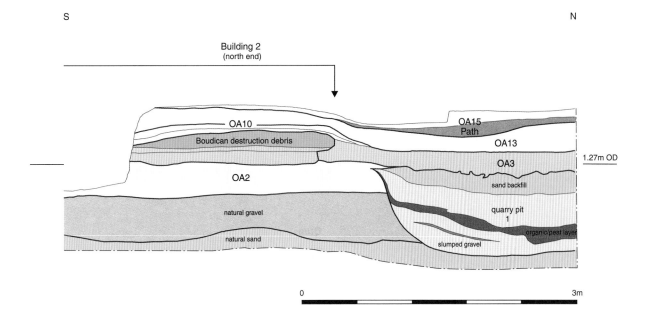

S   N

Fig 15 *East-facing section through quarry pit 1*

A very similar vessel was recovered from a pre-Flavian ditch at 201–211 Borough High Street (Bird et al 1978, 110, fig 37, no. 108). The published vessel is described as dark grey, with light horizontal combing on the exterior, with a hard, fine shell temper, and handmade. The source of these vessels is unknown, but it is of interest that two very similar examples have been found at sites along the line of Southwark Road 1. Vessels with horizontal rilling or combing on the body are a distinctive trait of late Iron Age assemblages from Hertfordshire and west Kent, and other vessel types from Kent also have black pitch or resin on the rims and shoulders.

QUARRY PIT 2

The assemblage from the second quarry pit consists of large, frequently joining sherds. Four vessels were substantially complete and these have been illustrated (<P2>–<P5>, Fig 16). Included is a SAND dish, loosely imitating Gallo-Belgic prototypes. The vessel has a dark grey burnished interior and the external surface is mottled from burning, black to pale orange-brown in colour. A SHEL bead-rimmed jar has a complete profile; the vessel is sooted on the exterior and has an organic residue on the interior base, indicating that it was used for cooking. The fabric has poorly sorted

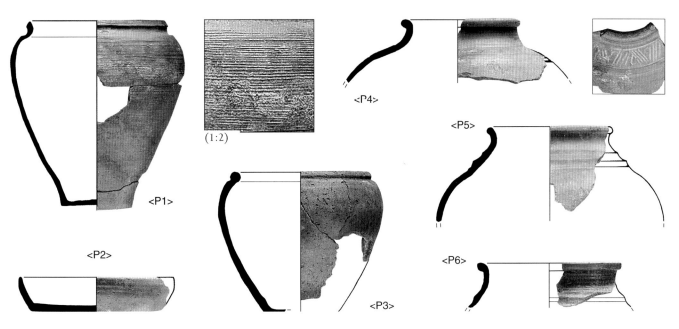

Fig 16 *Pottery <P1>–<P6> from the quarry pits (1:4)*

moderate quartz and shell inclusions. The surfaces range from mid brown to dark grey. The Alice Holt/Surrey ware (AHSU) narrow-necked jar with burnished decoration is comparable to Lyne and Jefferies class 1A, a type which forms a relatively minor component of this industry (Lyne and Jefferies 1979, 24, fig 9). The GROG necked jar fits broadly into Thompson type B3-1 with bulges on the shoulder between cordons (Thompson 1982, 139–42). The fabric has an oxidised silty matrix with occasional grog and sparse quartz inclusions. The internal surface is light grey, the external surface mid grey and lightly burnished.

QUARRY PIT 3

A third quarry pit produced one sherd from another GROG jar (<P6>, Fig 16) with pre-Roman or 'Belgic' influences. The necked jar has a ripple on the shoulder, similar to Thompson type B2-1, but has a more upright neck and a thicker, beaded rim than the published examples (Thompson 1982, 117–21). These types are often wheel-made and this example appears to have a wheel-finished rim. The jar has highly burnished surfaces and black paint or resin on the rim, neck and shoulder. The mid grey fabric contains moderate black and light grey finely crushed grog and sparse organic inclusions.

DATING OF QUARRY PITS IN OPEN AREA 2

The types in these assemblages suggest a date of c AD 50–5 (Table 2). The GROG necked jars <P5> and <P6> are related to Thompson (1982) type B3-1 and B2-1 respectively, which date from the pre-Conquest period but continue into the 1st century, with other examples found in post-AD 43 contexts.

AHSU is one of the few sourced reduced wares found in the City in Roman Ceramic Phase (RCP) 1A, usually present in small quantities (Davies et al 1994, 168). The narrow-necked storage jar is not well dated, but is seen by Lyne and Jefferies (1979, 24) to appear only post-Conquest. The dominance of handmade, unsourced SHEL and GROG tempered vessels, the single example of AHSU and the absence of Verulamium White ware (VRW) supports a date prior to the influx of wares from Romanised industries such as the kilns at Verulamium, Highgate Wood and Alice Holt, Surrey, which evidence from the City suggests occurred by c AD 55/60. BAETE Dressel 20 is the most common amphora type in RCP1A from the City and an equally early date for its presence in Southwark seems likely. Two examples of BAETE are present in the pre-Flavian ditch assemblages from 201–211 Borough High Street (Bird et al 1978, 112, fig 39, nos 170–1).

Ditches

The ditches were located further to the east of the road and were probably initially dug for drainage during road construction, given the evidence for inundation and proximity of channels and tidal high water, but may also have had other functions. Ditch 1 ran north-east to south-west almost parallel to the line of the road and 11.0m to the west of it, and was

Table 2 Dating table for period 1

Land use	Feature	Grp/sgrp/context	Material	Date
OA2	quarry pit 1	6/17/[940]	Rpot	50–100
		6/18/[920]	BM	50–80
			Rpot	50–100
	quarry pit 2	04/10/[5102]	coin	50–140
	quarry pit 3	42/183/[6051]	Rpot	40–100
		42/183/[6048]	coin	45–200
	quarry pit 4	5/1100/[5036]	BM	50–80
			Rpot	50–100
		5/1100/[5038]	BM	50–80
			Rpot	50–70
	ditch 1	42/181/[6039]	BM	50–80
		42/182/[6040]	BM	50–80
			Rpot	50–70
	external dumps	5/14/[918]	Rpot	50–70
		5/14/[921]	Rpot	50–70
		7/21/[5098]	Rpot	50–70
		8/22/[873]	BM	50–80
			coin	45–100
			Rpot	60–70
		43/184/[6041]	Rpot	50–70
		179/1001/		
		4125	Rpot	60–70

traced on and off for nearly 9.0m. The ditch was just over 1.0m wide and 0.5m deep. There was evidence both for re-cutting of the ditch and possible revetting, represented by a line of stakes on the east side of the ditch or channel. The presence of extensive peat deposits in the ditch suggests that it stood open and stagnant for a considerable period.

Part of another ditch, ditch 2 (or just possibly a continuation of the same one), ran north–south, further to the south and immediately to the east of the Battlebridge sewer. It survived to a width of 1.5m and a depth of 0.9m and was traced for c 25.0m in separate stretches. The bottom of the ditch contained an organic peaty deposit. The remainder of the ditch was filled with waterlain silts or dumped material. The ditch would have been approximately 7.0–8.0m east of the edge of the road and may have been dug during the construction of the road to drain the immediate area.

A 2.0m long segment of a V-shaped gully or ditch and a small pit formed evidence of early Roman activity on the western side of Road 1 and was recorded on STU92. The 0.4m wide gully was aligned north-west to south-east with the pit on its southern side, possibly respecting the gully. There is no obvious structural evidence and this feature may be associated with early land allotment, the ditch possibly forming a property boundary. The boundary line was retained after the infilling of the ditch by a line of stakeholes; four stakeholes formed a fence line running adjacent to the western side of the backfilled ditch.

If the ditches were not performing their primary function of drainage, and the absence of extensive deposits laid down by flowing water suggests they were not, it is possible that they had a secondary function. This might have been as boundary markers to demarcate the road corridor and its alignment but, with their alignment deviating slightly from parallel to the road, this cannot be regarded as certain. Alternatively the ditches may simply have been abandoned, perhaps because other measures, not recorded on site, were taken that rendered them unnecessary. It is possible that they were only ever intended as temporary drainage features during road construction and were replaced after the construction of the road by a more formal roadside drain. However, the evidence for reuse of ditch 1 indicates that it was in use for a reasonable period of time.

Further to the west, in area C, a large feature, which may have been a pond or channel or even a large pit, with minimum dimensions of 3.0m x 3.0m, exhibited peat formation at least 0.7m deep. This peat deposit was similar to peat filling the bottom of ditches running across Open Area 2. It is possible that the ditches were dug to drain into this feature, which might have acted as a large sump. A similar depth of peat was recorded in section at the north end of area D and may have been part of the same feature, which may merely have been a low-lying area prone to flooding.

Monolith samples were taken and examined from one of the ditches. Wilkinson (1996) has reported that the primary fills were laid down by fluvial action, but that the secondary fills indicate a period when there was no water flow through the ditch, although it was damp/waterlogged with occasional flood episodes, the degree of peat formation indicating that the ditch was open but not functioning for some time. Analysis of the seeds and pollen from the peat and the quarry pits revealed an area of open scrubland and uncultivated damp ground. This would tend to confirm that this particular sand island had not been extensively occupied before, presumably because of its tendency to flood.

The general composition of the pottery assemblage from the ditches is comparable to that recovered from the quarry pits, although wares from the Verulamium region, both VRW and BHWS <P8> (Fig 17), are recorded for the first time.

Also present are sherds of OXID butt beaker in a silty fabric with black iron-rich inclusions. This fabric has been identified at a number of sites in Southwark, including the published example from Toppings Wharf (Sheldon 1974, 42–3, fig 22.1; Marsh and Tyers 1978, 568–9, fig 239), and is the subject of more detailed discussion in the forthcoming Roman Southwark publication (Cowan et al in prep). The example from Toppings Wharf was recovered from ditch fill dated to the Flavian period and preliminary analysis of the recently identified examples suggests a similar date range.

Of interest is a GROG flat-footed pedestal base <P11> (Fig 17) similar to Thompson type A8. The flat-based type, although originating in the Iron Age, continues into the Roman period, and other examples have been recovered along with 1st-century Roman wares and produced in Roman fabrics (Thompson 1982, 75). Pedestal-based jars or urns are generally rare in Southwark and the City, although a trumpet-type base was recovered from Park Street, Southwark (PRK90) (Groves in prep; Tyers 1996, 144, fig 17.3).

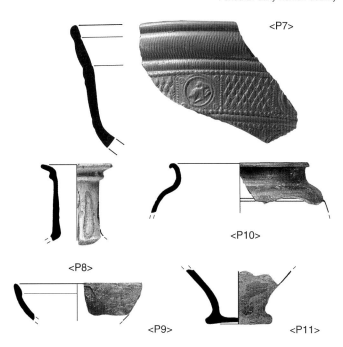

Fig 17 Pottery <P7> (1:2), <P8>–<P11> (1:4) from the ditches

DATING OF DITCHES IN OPEN AREA 2

The range of types in this assemblage is wider than the quarry pit assemblage and includes examples of pre-Flavian fabrics from known sources such as HWB, HOO, VRW and BHWS (Table 2). The appearance of Verulamium region wares may indicate that the group dates from nearer AD 55, as evidence from London and Verulamium suggests that products from this region are common by AD 55/60 (Davies et al 1994, 168). The decorated samian bowls have both been assigned a date range of c AD 50–70 (for example <P7>). The environmental evidence suggests that these ditches were left open for some time and underwent re-cutting and revetting, which may account for the slightly later overall date for the assemblage.

Dumped deposits

The ditches and quarry pits were probably only open for a relatively short time, since this early activity was sealed by extensive dumping of varying thickness over much of the area of the excavation, up to 0.4m thick, raising the ground level from 1.2m to 1.6m OD in places and from 1.1m OD to at least 1.35m OD more generally. The dumps were mainly of relatively sterile sand and gravel, though some included a higher proportion of domestic waste. This lack of inclusions might suggest that the make-up was quickly redeposited and the dumping may have utilised displaced sand from gravel extraction, road construction or sands specifically recovered for the purpose. Some of the quarry pits and ditches were backfilled with this sand. The raising of the ground level was presumably a countermeasure against potential flooding and provided a suitable platform for initial building construction.

A small quantity of building stone was noted in the dumps, including chalk rubble and knapped flint. Also present was a piece of red ferruginous sandstone. This is an unexpected find for this date, as this type of stone, which probably comes from the Folkestone Beds in the Weald of Kent, has not been found in the City in securely dated contexts earlier than the late 2nd century. This points to an earlier exploitation of this stone than had hitherto been thought.

As already mentioned, there were areas with more domestic refuse in them. One dump in particular in the north-west of the site was particularly productive and contained several finds of interest. A simple British Nauheim derivative wire bow brooch <R1> (Fig 18) belongs to a class that dates from the early to the mid/late 1st century; its form and context suggest that here it should be dated to the middle part of the century. The same dump also produced an imported lamp <R13> made at Lyon in southern Gaul. An Eros with alabastron and shell, depicted on the discus, is a motif common throughout the Roman Empire (Fig 19). Other finds from this dump comprised corroded fragments of copper alloy, from now unidentifiable objects, and scraps of sheet lead as well as two coins of Claudian date (AD 41–54), one irregular.

An Aucissa brooch <R2> (Fig 18) from another dump in the same area is likely to be of mid 1st-century date, and is a form of Gaulish origin, often although not exclusively associated with military activity during the Conquest period.

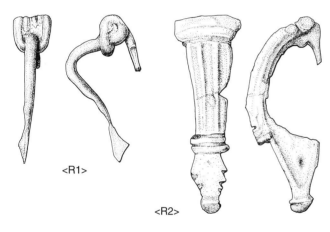

Fig 18 Copper alloy brooches <R1> and <R2> from Open Area 2 (1:1)

The environmental evidence was still dominated by seeds of spike-rush and sedge, though there was one charred barley (*Hordeum* sp) grain in one of the quarry pits and 13 charred barley grains in one of the ditches.

The dumped deposits above the ditches and quarry pits produced a large assemblage of pottery with a wider range of fabrics, including wares from non-local sources such as COLEC and COLWW, and shell-tempered wares NKSH and SESH. For the first time imported fine wares other than SAMLG are recorded, including both PRW3 and LYON.

Part of this dump contained a quantity of domestic refuse. This included a pottery assemblage with mortaria appearing for the first time. A COLWW early wall-sided mortarium <P18>, similar to Symonds and Wade type 33, is present (Fig 20).

Fig 19 Ceramic oil lamp <R13> from Open Area 2 (1:1)

The earliest examples of this type at Colchester are recorded from group 4, which has an end date of AD 60/1 (Symonds and Wade 1999, 165–71, fig 4.1, no. 7). A second example of this type is present in an unsourced OXID fabric and both vessels fall within Hartley's group III, being generally confined to Neronian groups (Hartley 1985, 92–3).

An unusual mortarium <P19> is also recorded as OXID (Fig 20), with granular, well-sorted quartz and red iron-rich inclusions, similar to VRW but with more abundant white clay pellets. The mortarium is very worn and no evidence of the grits remains. The vessel is also burnt. The form is a very simple, early wall-sided one with only one external beaded moulding, similar to Cam. form 194. The vessel is poorly finished. Two holes had been drilled post-firing, one into the wall just below the rim and the second into the base; the holes are *c* 5mm and 3mm in diameter respectively. These holes were possibly drilled for a repair or may have been used to suspend the vessel. Despite similarities to VRW the fabric cannot confidently be assigned to this ware, although it seems likely that the vessel is a product of the Verulamium region. The form cannot be paralleled in any of the published kiln assemblages from the region or from the occupation assemblages at Verulamium. The simplicity of the form, the poor finishing and the more mixed fabric may indicate that this vessel is an early product of that region and not part of the main production.

A small jar or beaker with a short neck and flat rim <P21> is in an oxidised fabric with moderate quartz inclusions, creating a pimply surface (Fig 20). There is a single groove on the shoulder. The fabric is relatively coarse for a form of this type, which is more commonly found in either RDBK or FMIC wares.

One of the bead-rimmed jars <P22> (Fig 20) is in a sandy fabric, densely packed with well-sorted quartz grains and sparse burnt organic inclusions. Mica is clearly visible on the pale brown surfaces. The jar has a cordon at the shoulder and slight internal thickening at the rim. Between the cordon and the rim are traces of black resin or paint. The surface is

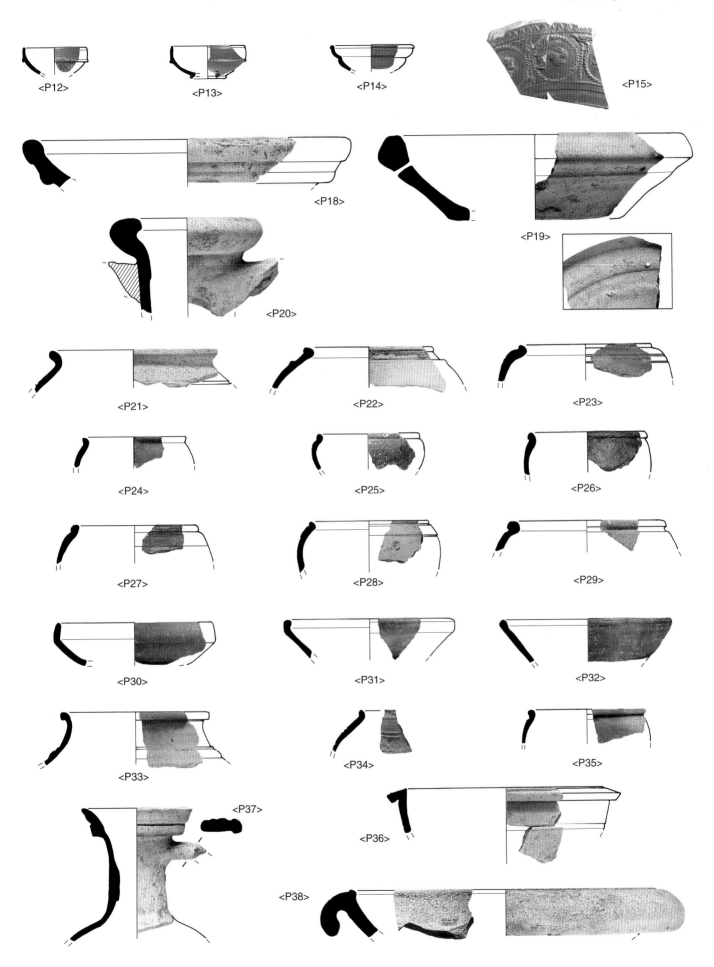

Fig 20 Pottery <P12>–<P14> (1:4), <P15> (1:2), <P18>–<P38> (1:4) from the dumped deposits in Open Area 2

lightly burnished. This form is possibly a Kentish type, as
black pitch on the rim and shoulder is a common feature
of the storage jars from this region (Davies et al 1994, 102).
Sherds from this vessel are also present in contexts [918]
and [5038], which are an external surface and a quarry pit
respectively, both sealed by the dump [873].

ERSI appears in this deposit for the first time. The bead-
rimmed jar <P23> (Fig 20) is predominantly handmade with
a poorly executed, double groove on the shoulder and a lightly
burnished zone between the rim and groove.

A probable AHSU bead-rimmed jar <P35> is an unusual
form, unlike the 2A12–13 typically recorded and more similar
to 2A14 (Marsh and Tyers 1978, 554–6, fig 234). The jar has
a small bead and sloping shoulder, delineated by a cordon.
Burnished decoration occurs on the shoulder, in the form of
rough crosses.

DATING OF DUMPED DEPOSITS IN OPEN AREA 2

All of the fabrics and forms present are indicative of a pre-
Flavian date (Table 2). The samian cup form Drag. 24/25
(<P12> and <P13>) is a good indicator of a pre-Flavian date
and the decorated samian from contexts [873] <P15> and
[6053] has been assigned a date of AD 50–65. In the City, ERSI
is seen as particularly diagnostic of pre-Boudican groups, and
the evidence from Open Area 2 suggests that it was in
circulation in the same period in Southwark.

Early activity away from the main road

Channel revetments in the Southwark Street Channel

Efforts were made to control the edges of the channel and
protect the low-lying land from flooding. The mid 1st-century
AD Mean High and Low water spring tidal levels probably
ranged from −0.5m to +1.0/1.25m OD (Brigham 1990, 2).

There was evidence from two sites, REW92 and OMS94, for
channel management in the 1st century AD within the Southwark
Street Channel. This consisted of three timber structures,
Structures 1 and 2 at REW92 and Structure 1 at OMS94.

A series of 18 posts at REW92 (REW92 Structures 1 and 2),
in two rows aligned approximately north–south, were cut
into the top of the silty clay fills of the channel. These had
survived only as voids as most of the timber had decayed.
The eastern alignment, Structure 1, consisted of 14 posts in
two groups while the western alignment, Structure 2, had
four posts evenly spaced 0.6m apart. Structure 1 consisted
of sub-rectangular voids measuring 0.12m x 0.06m and
0.3–0.45m deep. Structure 2 consisted of slightly larger,
approximately square voids measuring 0.14m x 0.12m,
which were slightly deeper at between 0.4m and 0.7m in
depth. Most of the posts penetrated into the sands, but not
into the gravel below.

The slight variation in alignment of the two rows was
nevertheless sufficient to indicate separate structures; their
interpretation is discussed below, but they may not be revetments
as they appear to have been placed within and across the

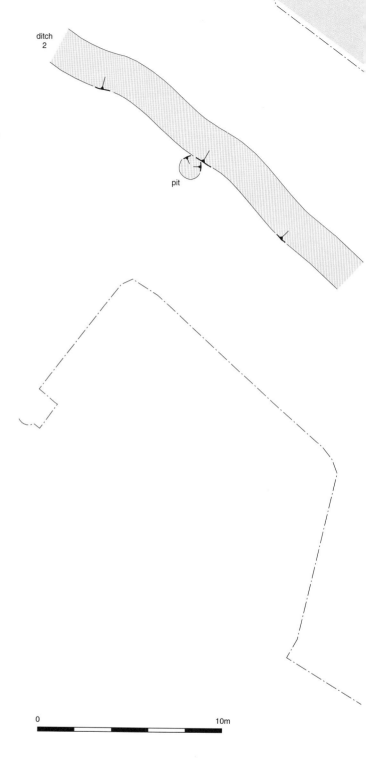

Fig 21 Plan of principal archaeological features, period 1

channel itself. The tops of the posts were truncated, perhaps by
inundations (see below), at a height of 0.18–0.31m OD.

Driven into the channel silts at OMS94, but not reaching into
the sand below, was an east–west alignment of timber stakes
representing Structure 1, which was parallel to the edge of
the channel. Five stakes were recorded which were partially
decayed, their tops rotted, although they still retained some
sapwood. They were mostly circular, although one was wedge-
shaped, and their bases had been sharpened to a point. The

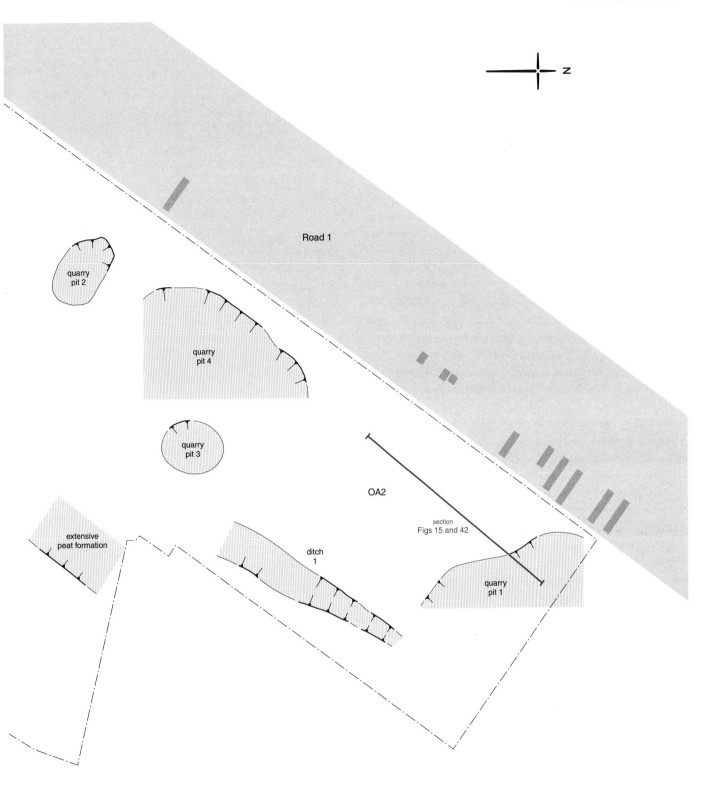

diameter of the stakes was between 0.05m and 0.1m, with that of the longest being 0.55m. Their tops were truncated at a height of 0.35m OD.

Of the identifiable stakes, one was oak and another alder. There was no evidence of planks, so it was not certain if this was a post-and-plank revetment, but their position parallel to and at the edge of the channel and their regular spacing of 0.8m apart would suggest that they were part of a revetment.

It is possible that Structure 1 at OMS94 could have been part of the same waterfront as that revealed during excavations at 52–54 Southwark Street (52SOS89) further to the west (Cowan in prep).

Discussion

A rise in the river level in the late pre-Roman period was responsible for deposits of river clay over the natural gravel and over the prehistoric peat and alluvial deposits where these occurred. In some places in north Southwark the clay covered the natural gravel up to a height of 1.3m OD.

There is a difficulty, in the absence of dated peat deposits underlying the clay or dated timbers or features cutting into the clay, in recognising whether the clay deposits in REW92 Open Area 1 or OMS94 Open Area 1 could have belonged to this period. Neither group contained any dating evidence.

The size, depth and uniformity of spacing of the timbers, together with their similarities to other Roman waterfronts in Southwark, would suggest, however, that the timber structures on both sites were of Roman date. OMS94 Structure 1 was similar to Waterfront 4 at 52SOS89. The stakes at OMS94 were only a little smaller but were spaced slightly further apart. There was no dating evidence from OMS94 Structure 1 but Waterfront 4 at 52SOS89 was dated to around AD 70–100 by pottery within channel deposits and dumps behind the waterfronts.

REW92 Structures 1 and 2 showed many similarities to Roman revetments at 64–70 Borough High Street (64BHS74) and 52 Southwark Street (52SOS89). The spacing of the Structure 2 posts was not dissimilar to those of revetment 2 at 64BHS74 (Graham 1988, fig 21) and the spacing of the REW92 Structure 1 posts could be interpreted as similar to revetment 1 at 64BHS74. The absence of wattlework, as encountered in revetment 1, or collapsed planking, as in revetment 2, could be explained by the truncation of the REW92 structures.

It has been suggested that the REW92 structures could constitute part of a causeway or bridge (D Bentley pers comm). This suggestion is based on their position relative to a minor road (Road 3) (Yule in prep), which may have crossed the channel at this point, and the apparent position of the two alignments of REW92 stakes in the centre of the channel; the structures were aligned obliquely across the projected channel in this area. It is possible that the edges of the channel loop round here or that the area is more complex, perhaps with smaller streams feeding into the channel, although none were visible in the area of excavation. The edges of the channel are not firmly fixed in this area; Fig 11 shows the areas of high ground above 1.0m OD, that is, ground which would have been habitable above the high water mark.

There do not appear to be enough posts to support a bridge, nor do Structure 1 and Structure 2 appear to be on the same alignment. Furthermore, it is not known if Road 3 would have crossed here; it may have continued no further than Road 2 or only as far as the buildings at 15–23 Southwark Street.

It is likely, therefore, that the REW92 and OMS94 timber structures were part of channel revetments having much in common with the waterfronts from 64BHS74 and 52SOS89, and which would have been constructed in the period AD 50–70.

Overbank flooding

Overlying Structures 1 and 2 at REW92 was silty clay (0.49m OD). This was a thicker deposit than the others below, and there appeared to have been some truncation of the underlying deposits. Perhaps the clay recorded at REW92 represented a major flood that was partly responsible for the truncation and the destruction of the post structures.

Similarly overlying the revetment of OMS94 Structure 1 was a deposit of clay with sand. This contained occasional degraded organics, root traces and freshwater mollusc shells, and was thought to have been a high-energy deposit. It is possible that this deposit resulted from an inundation which could have destroyed the revetment, as this clay also covered the previously exposed foreshore area. The surface of the clay was at 0.8m OD in the northern part of the site, sloping down to 0.4m OD in the south.

The uppermost part had been exposed and had started forming into a ground surface. Perhaps a new revetment had been built at that time to the south (beyond the limits of excavation) thus allowing the land behind to be reclaimed for building. At both sites dumping as reclamation within the channel followed the inundations.

Summary of period 1

The dumps in Open Area 2 mark the end of period 1 at BGH95 and signify a change in land use with the construction of clay and timber buildings (Fig 21). The sequence of quarry pits, ditches and the extensive dumped layers that sealed them are thought to span a period of around five years, and the assemblages recovered from them are certainly pre-Boudican in date (Table 2). Whether there was always an intention to have a settlement on the south side of the river is not clear. Southwark may have been a transit point until the construction of the first bridge, as opposed to a ferry, encouraged the development of a community around the southern bridgehead. However, the presence of dumps with domestic refuse in them indicates that there was some occupation taking place nearby to produce this refuse, so building activity may have been going on even during this period. This may have taken place nearer the river initially, and only now stretched back as far as the Borough High Street site as the buildings spread out alongside the road.

It is also probable that measures to prevent the Southwark Street Channel flooding would have been taken early in the post-Conquest period, but the dating cannot be refined enough to give other than a date of AD 50–70.

4

The pre-Boudican settlement

There is no problem of greater historical importance than the origin of London itself
Merrifield 1983

4.1 Period 2: the first buildings in Southwark

Timber-framed buildings alongside the main road

The first buildings on the Borough High Street Ticket Hall site (BGH95) were constructed sometime after AD 50 along the eastern frontage of the main road. They were all of timber-framed construction and were typical of the strip buildings recorded throughout Londinium at this period (Milne and Wardle 1993). These buildings were generally long and thin with narrow frontages onto the prime land alongside the road, but with a range of rooms stretching back from the road, usually to a yard at the rear.

The development at Borough High Street matches this pattern. The east side of the main road was intensively occupied in this early phase. Two much smaller excavations from the 1980s, not covered in this volume, indicate that there was similar occupation on the west side, though less work has been carried out on this side of the road (Cowan et al in prep).

The frontages of most of the buildings lay just to the west of the excavation and the width of the excavated area (c 12.5m) was not sufficient for the rear of the buildings to be present on site – strip buildings up to 30m long have been recorded in Londinium (Milne and Wardle 1993).

To the north of the Ticket Hall site, on JSS92, an east–west side road (Alley 1) was laid out. Two short stretches were present on either side of the Battlebridge sewer cut, revealing this road as being at least 2.6m wide. The south end was not within the limits of excavation, but from the angle of the camber the whole would have been c 3.0m wide with external occupation to the north of it. There was one possible resurfacing of the road. It is not clear where this road was going. The area to the east of the island was marginal at this time and there is no evidence for any occupation to the east of the roadside buildings. The road may simply have been designed to give access to the rear of the buildings where there may have been yards or other open areas. However, the back walls of the buildings lay beyond the limit of excavation so it was not possible to confirm this (Fig 31).

Building 1

At the north end of the site was Building 1. This building was heavily truncated and no walls survived. The surviving area was 3.5m wide by 6.0m long, though even this had several later features cut through it. However, a complex hearth or oven feature was recorded in a room with a brickearth floor, close to a narrow linear feature that may have been a robbed out wall.

A continuation of Building 1 was found to the north-east on BSE94, where parts of a brickearth floor were uncovered (BSE94 B1). Some fragments of moulded stone from a masonry building were used as part of the make-up dumps for this building. Petrological analysis of this stone has shown that it was Reigate/Merstham stone (Blows 1998). It is unusual to find Reigate stone in Roman contexts in London, and this is the earliest recorded instance.

It is likely that Building 1 would have continued up to Alley 1 to the north, forming a clay and timber building of similar size to Building 2 to the south of it. To the west of the building was an open area that contained domestic rubbish and hearth rakings, though these may have derived from Building 2 as the suggested entrance to the building opened out onto this area (OA3). The only find of note was a small lead weight <R25> (Fig 22). This was originally conical, but had the upper part cut away or fractured; the top is irregular in contrast to the neatly made lower half.

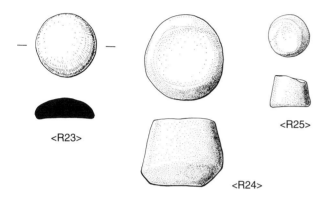

Fig 22 Finds group from period 2: glass counter <R23>; lead weights <R24> and <R25> (all 1:1)

Building 2

To the south of Building 1 there was another range of clay and timber buildings. There was no gap between the buildings, which formed a continuous block. Building 2 was located immediately north of Alley 2 (see below) and was recorded on both sides of the Battlebridge sewer (Fig 31). To the west a shallow cut of 0.1m was dug, into which was laid a brickearth slab which formed the initial floor surface. The cut measured 2.6m east–west by 2.1m north–south (truncated), which was similar to Building 3 to the south. There were several alignments of stakes and posts indicating external walls and internal partitions. An area of scorching on the brickearth floor points to the location of a hearth. An entrance into the building was suggested by an area of extensive wear on the floor at the west end of the north side of the building, with a line of postholes and a robbed out beamslot to the east. There were also traces of a brickearth wall. The western frontage of the building was just inside the western limit of excavation. There were also a series of stakeholes indicating some internal features. The southern limit was truncated by a feeder of the Battlebridge sewer. On the southern side of the truncation the building continued, though it is not clear if this was the same room.

There was a very fragmentary collection of internal features, possibly including a north–south beamslot forming

a partition wall with a further room to the east (though this was heavily truncated and only c 0.3m wide) which probably continued to the east of the Battlebridge sewer. There was a series of floors and occupation layers, the floors being mainly brickearth but including one gravel surface.

To the east of the Battlebridge sewer, a further stretch of Building 2 was uncovered (Fig 23). More substantial parts of the building survived here and its construction technique differed from the section of the building to the west. Two rooms were defined by upstanding brickearth walls and decayed timber beams. A narrow strip of room C measuring 0.75m x 4.2m was recorded to the east with a series of stakeholes cutting a brickearth floor. The south and west walls were recorded and consisted of brickearth 0.2m wide, with a series of robbed posts and stakes visible in the walls, which survived to a height of 0.2m. The western limit of room B was either truncated by the Battlebridge sewer or was represented by the beamslot from Building 3 above. If the latter is correct then the room measured 9.0m east–west by 6.0m north–south. The northern limit was defined by a decayed beamslot and the southern by an upstanding brickearth wall with posts and stakes visible in it. A substantial hearth (1.5m x 0.7m) was present in the northern half of the room. No evidence of industrial activity was found so the hearth was probably domestic. The floors were of brickearth. It is likely that the building was occupied for some time as the original floor was replaced at least once. One of the floors had a BAETE Dressel 20 amphora inserted into the surface. Large sherds, probably from the lower part of the globular body, were recovered, but no handles or fragments of rim were present; this may suggest that they were removed when the amphora was reused. The position of the amphora inside Building 2 suggests that it was reused for storage, probably of foodstuffs, rather than as a water butt or urinal, but there was no direct evidence for its contents.

A study of the building material noted the similarity of the material in the make-up for Buildings 1 and 2, which suggests that they were constructed at the same time, probably as a single building. It also suggests that tile may have been used for paving, which is also likely for Buildings 1 and 2, though no in situ paved floors were recorded. A wall foundation in Building 2 also contained three blocks of Reigate stone (see Chapter 11.1 for fuller discussion).

Numerous charred grain and stem fragments were found in this building, suggesting that cereals were stored or processed here. Barley (Hordeum spp) and wheat (Triticum spp) were both present. A small number of wild or domesticated oat (Avena spp) grains were also recovered. Oats can grow as weeds of cultivation and may have been harvested with the main wheat or barley crop. The presence of straw and charred seeds means that some of this assemblage could have been coarse or fine sieving waste subsequently disposed of on the fire. A smaller number of seeds from semi-aquatic habitats, for example spike-rush, were present and may have entered these contexts as floor covering.

Fig 23 Building 2 under excavation

Alley 2

Alley 2 was a narrow east–west road that ran for the whole width of the site – some 15m – between Buildings 2 and 3 (except where truncated by the Battlebridge sewer) (Fig 31). It was of basic sand and gravel construction with none of the timber corduroy foundations seen elsewhere in Southwark, where the ground was less stable. Its width was up to 5.0m (the gap between Buildings 2 and 3) and there was a shallow roadside ditch to the south of the first surface, which was later sealed by a subsequent resurfacing. The date of its construction was no earlier than AD 50 and probably only shortly after that date. At the eastern end it slumped sharply into an earlier ditch which resulted in a slight realignment to the north. The width at any given time is hard to determine but it is possible that there were two phases of metalling, each *c* 3.0m wide and overlapping, the first phase being the more southerly until the slumping into the ditch enforced its moving to the north. An alley 5.0m in width would be rather wide at this early date, implying some major access route to a rather more substantial settlement than there is currently evidence for. There was also evidence for a fence on the north side represented by a line of robbed out stakeholes. A series of narrow linear features in the surface of the alley represent the ruts made by the traffic using the alley (Fig 24).

Some personal and domestic objects were found on the road. A poorly preserved fragment of rosette brooch <R3> of 1st-century date (not illustrated) came from its surface. A circular counter made of natural blue glass <R23> (Fig 22) would have been part of a set, used for the games of chance that were a popular way of passing leisure time. A fragmentary lamp <R17>, although of uncertain form, is probably of Spanish manufacture and is another example of the large number of imported goods entering London during this period, while a fragment of stand in dark purple glass is a further demonstration of the quality of some of the material found in the early settlement. Glass stands or 'coasters', also imported and more often found in Italy, are rare in Britain but there are now four known from Southwark (Shepherd 1992, 136). They would have been used as centrepieces at table, or placed under serving dishes.

Two pieces of pottery from a very intriguing object were recovered, one from a layer assigned to the alley, <P39> (Fig 25), and the second from Building 2. The fragments are very thick-walled (12mm to 31mm at the widest part of the rim) and have a diameter of over 600mm. The 'rim' is flat with a wide, square profile. The fragments have a thick grey core and oxidised orange-pink surfaces. The surfaces are roughly wiped and there are traces of a white wash or thin slip. The fabric is coarsely tempered with quartz and flint inclusions, and mica is also abundant on the surfaces. These fragments may come from a large storage container or transportation vessel, although the possibility that they belong to an unusual chimney or louver cannot be discounted. No parallels for these pieces have been found.

Fig 24 Detail of Alley 2 with evidence of wheel ruts

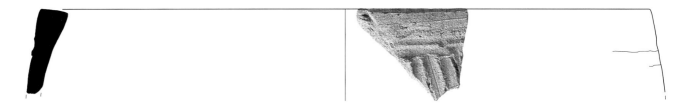

Fig 25 Ceramic container or building fitting <P39> (1:4)

Building 3

Building 3, to the south of Alley 2, has been interpreted as a blacksmith's workshop, because of the large quantities of hammerscale which covered the main floor of the building. Hammerscale is produced by the working of hot metal on an anvil and is a clear indication of the work of a blacksmith (see Chapter 11.6). The building was constructed on a substantial brickearth slab cut into the underlying deposits. This measured 4.75m north–south by 2.3m east–west. The north and west edges were real edges, the south and east being truncated. A line of posts and smaller stakes marked the west frontage and there were traces of wattling forming the west wall of the building (Fig 26). The brickearth slab was cut by a series of features, some of them also containing slag and other metalworking waste. It is not clear if these features were directly related to the smithing process but they were clearly not hearths. Slag was also present on a

gravel surface to the west of the building, representing an external surface between the building and the road. This building did not appear to continue in use up until the Boudican fire (see Chapter 5) as the southern edge of Alley 2 encroached over the northern wall line. It is not clear why the building went out of use, although traces of burning suggest that a fire was responsible. Such an event would not be uncommon in a timber building used for industrial purposes.

To the east of the Battlebridge sewer was a continuation of this timber building, though the walls were on a slightly different alignment (Fig 31). It is possible that the workshop was constructed separately from the domestic rooms to the rear, reflecting the different functions being carried out. Certainly the construction techniques were different. An east–west wall was identified on the north side with a series of occupation layers running to the south of it. However, these were mainly recorded in section because of a great deal of truncation caused by post-medieval and modern features. These layers consisted of a series of brickearth floors with occupation deposits accumulated over them. There did not appear to be a construction cut as there was for the brickearth slab to the west. Perhaps the blacksmith's working area needed a more substantial floor to support the forge and anvil, while this would have been unnecessary in the domestic rooms to the rear.

South of Building 3 was Open Area 4. This was a narrow open space between Buildings 3 and 4, measuring about 5.0m wide. The layers here were predominantly dump layers containing large amounts of ash, metalworking waste and hammerscale. This waste is likely to have come from Building 3 to the north. Further waste came from the continuation of the open area to the east of the Battlebridge sewer. This open area contained a small amount of charred grain and stem fragments. It is possible that this is waste from activities such as winnowing or coarse sieving which would have taken place outdoors.

Fig 26 View of Building 3, possibly a blacksmith's workshop

Building 4

Building 4 was a timber-framed building constructed over one of the earlier quarry pits, in the middle of the site, and was badly slumped into it as the underlying pit fills settled. Additionally a small east–west feeder trench for the Battlebridge sewer chopped the building in half. It is possible that the two halves were in fact adjacent and separate buildings but the alignment of walls suggests it was all one.

The surviving remains of the building measured 8.0m north–south by 3.0m east–west. To the east the Battlebridge sewer truncated the building. On the far side of the sewer a small area of clay floor was probably from this building, but there were no walls associated and this area was heavily truncated by a large British Telecom manhole. South of the Battlebridge sewer feeder, two large postholes 0.5m in diameter and 0.5m deep, connected by a robbed out beamslot 2.0m long and 0.3m deep, represented part of the west frontage of the building. A narrow internal beamslot divided this portion of the building into two rooms. The northern

room, room A, survived to 1.2m x 1.2m, and the southern room, room B, measured 2.0m x 1.6m. The floors of both rooms were of brickearth. Occupation over one of them produced an irregular Claudian coin, dated AD 54–64, whilst a cylindrical lead weight <R24> (Fig 22), intended for use in the scale pan of a balance, came from the make-up for a floor. It now weighs 64g, although lead is an unstable metal and it may originally have weighed three Roman ounces. Such an object could be suggestive of commercial activity, for which there is, however, no other evidence. The only other domestic item from this building is a badly corroded stud of copper alloy <R34>.

A linear feature at least 3.0m long running north–south to the west of Building 4 and at least 0.4m deep may have been the original roadside ditch, though it was not traced elsewhere on site.

North of the Battlebridge sewer feeder was either a continuation of room A or another room. In this room internal brickearth walls survived to a height of 0.1m. South of this partition may be a continuation of room A, giving a total width of the room of 4.0m. North of the wall remains of plank floorboards were recorded burnt *in situ* (room C). Only a small area of this room (0.8m x 1.0m) survived truncation by the Battlebridge sewer. To the west of room C, two robbed out beamslots indicate that Building 4 continued to the west. However, this takes the frontage of the building beyond that of the southern part of the building, indicating that this was in fact another building or formed a northern wing to the building. The latter possibility is currently preferred. The pottery is of a generally utilitarian and domestic nature and dates the building to the period AD 50–70 (see below).

Roof tile in the Eccles fabric and daub came from occupation levels in the building. This indicates that Building 4 probably had a tiled roof, although some of the tile was abraded and reused, which could mean that it was present in some other capacity. However, the presence of Kentish ragstone rubble from Open Area 4 suggests that somewhere in the vicinity was a building with rubble and mortar foundations, or possibly a wall or other structure faced with ragstone rubble.

DATING OF BUILDING 4
A total of 52 sherds (24 rows) were recovered from six contexts, with the majority recovered from make-up and floor levels. SLOW appears in this assemblage and SAMLG is accompanied by imported Gallo-Belgic wares TN and TNIM. The pottery is generally domestic in character and dated AD 50–70 (Table 5).

Buildings 5 and 6

Behind Buildings 3 and 4 was Open Area 5, where there was little sign that any substantial activity was taking place.

South of the Bedale Street and St Thomas Street axis were more fragmentary remains of a further four buildings. The walls and floors were truncated variously by the sewer cuts and other later intrusions. At the western side of the site an isolated area of stratigraphy included sandy make-up deposits and clay floor surfaces. The earliest building in this area was a clay and timber structure with a compacted floor laid on make-up dumps. This construction must have been contemporary with the creation of the first settlement soon after AD 50. However, no detailed picture of these earlier buildings was gained and the limited evidence in section suggested that elements of this building were quickly replaced by Buildings 5 and 6. This may have been a direct replacement or repair of the internal features, although there was some evidence of a brief period of dumping and occupation, represented by a pit (OA6). The activity associated with the pit may have separated the earlier activity and the construction of Building 5.

The remains of the two buildings survived within several isolated blocks of stratigraphy on either side of the Battlebridge sewer. The two buildings appeared to share an east–west wall division. Building 5 to the north was constructed first, using a series of levelling deposits which were dumped over a low-lying area. This area was previously crossed by an earlier drainage ditch and a single pit. Immediately prior to construction the ground must have been uneven and possibly wet. Redeposited sands and other clay dumps were deposited into the area of the building and north of the backfilled pit, and clay floors were then laid on top of the levelled ground. Despite these precautions, at an early stage of the building's history, possibly even during its construction, the building was subject to slumping into the earlier features. Further clay was deposited to level the area again and a repair thickened the clay floor. The southern limit of this part of the building was represented by a beamslot and a group of postholes and stakeholes. Many of the posts and stakes may belong to the construction or use of the building, although no coherent structure was suggested. At the eastern end of Building 6 a 2.0m long linear slot and a similar slot 1.2m long are both likely to have held timber baseplates. A group of postholes may also define fragments of the frontage of the building. A clay surface formed the internal floor of, at least, one room within a building some 6.0m wide. Elements of surfaces on the western side of the site suggest that the building extended to the road. The remains were heavily truncated, but a 2.0m long and 1.4m wide area with floor make-up and surface deposits occurred at the southern limit of this area. The corner of the room is indicated by the remains of a slot running 1.6m

west to east and 2.0m north to south along the western side of the room. These construction slots, originally holding sillbeams, also contained several postholes forming the frame of the building. The east–west slot may have been an internal division between two separate rooms to the north and south. Here a 3.0m long slot was associated with two postholes and 0.2m depth of clay foundation material. This 0.5m wide foundation trench may represent the western limit of the building. A 2.3m long and 1.3m wide area of clay floor survived adjacent to the wall foundation. This room was possibly utilised for industrial activities, as the floors were partially replaced in gravel and intervening occupation debris included charcoal and burnt debris.

Clay floor surfaces at the front of the building contained a small number of charred plant remains including wheat and cereal grains.

DATING OF BUILDING 5

Within Building 5 was a cut feature lined or packed with BAETE amphorae sherds. All of these sherds are burnt, including a rim dated AD 40–60 (Peacock and Williams 1986, fig 65, no. 9). The burning of these sherds does not appear to relate to the primary use of the vessel and is probably a result of the fire that destroyed the building. The assemblage is dated AD 50–70 (Table 5).

The destruction levels of Building 5 seem to include an element of in situ debris that contained well preserved vessels. These vessels, although very fragmentary, are largely complete and very badly burnt. Thirty-four sherds represent the greater part of a storage jar <P40> (Fig 27), with an upright neck, rough almond-shaped rim and notched decoration on the shoulder. The form is comparable to Cam. 273, which at Colchester is dated to the 1st and earlier 2nd century, declining in use after AD 125 (Symonds and Wade 1999, 447–51, fig 6.101–3).

The latest element in this group is a SAND fabric Marsh type 35 bead and flanged bowl <P41> (Fig 27). This vessel was recovered from context [5068], the primary layer in this floor sequence. This form occurs in a variety of fabrics, although in London it is predominantly associated with Romano-British fine wares, such as mica-dusted and eggshell wares, and dates from the Flavian period (Marsh 1978).

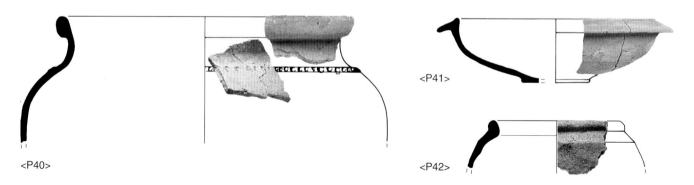

<P40>

<P41>

<P42>

Fig 27 Pottery <P40>–<P42> from Building 5 (1:4)

However, this vessel has a granular, quartz-rich fabric with oxidised surfaces, probably caused by burning. The external surface has traces of a white slip, but this may also have been discoloured. A similar, but slightly deeper, vessel was found in association with vessels dating to the 2nd century at 199 Borough High Street (Marsh 1978, fig 6.16, no. 35.17; Hinton 1988, 286, fig 121, no. 1036).

Open areas and Buildings 7–8

To the south of Building 6 was Open Area 6, a narrow opening less than 3.0m wide, between two ranges of buildings (Fig 31). Two features, a pit and linear cut – probably a ditch – may represent activity prior to the construction of Building 5. Alternatively, these features might have formed some part of the use and function of the buildings to north and south.

This open area included several dumped deposits, which were partially truncated by roadside drains. A sandalled foot-shaped ceramic oil lamp was recovered from the edge of one of these dumps. Lamps in the form of the human foot wearing a sandal were made in both ceramic and metal, and <R16> (Fig 28) is an exceedingly fine example. The motif might well have some symbolic significance not now apparent to us, and it is noticeable how many of the known ceramic lamps of this type have been found in the military areas of the north-west provinces, where this example apparently originated.

To the south of Open Area 6 was another timber-framed building, Building 7. Internal floors were represented by timber floorboards laid on small beams or joists. These survived as an area of charred timber and slight linear depressions. The floor was constructed on 0.3m of sand dumps or make-up deposits. Three separate areas 1.4m wide had evidence of the planked floor, which survived only as charred fragments and staining. The southern area included the best survival with two 0.7m long grooves which may indicate the position of supporting timbers. A single beamslot 1.4m long and 0.4m wide ran west to east. This foundation may represent the northern wall of the building.

The floor contained charred remains of many poorly preserved seeds. Those that were identifiable were identified to genus and included knotgrass (*Polygonum* sp), dock (*Rumex* sp), sedge (*Carex* sp) and brome (*Bromus* sp). These seeds came from plants of disturbed and damp ground, and would have been growing in the local environment.

Beyond a series of modern service pipes, a compacted clay floor may represent another room of the building, though no internal division survived. A hearth was located at the southern edge of an area of clay floor. This was a roughly square depression measuring 0.8m x 0.68m with large quantities of broken BAETE Dressel 20 amphorae. Amphorae fragments and pottery in the upper fills were probably originally used as lining. The hearth may have been situated against the southern wall of the building. No remains of this wall survived, however, and the dimensions of the building were only indicated by the extent of floors and occupation debris.

The occupation debris from the usage of the building was

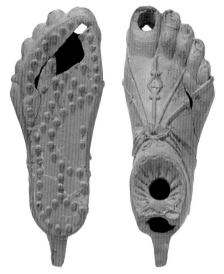

Fig 28 Oil lamp <R16> in the shape of a sandalled foot from Open Area 6 (2:3)

rich in charred plant remains and grains (Table 3). Cereal grains predominated and included 104 indeterminate grains, 33 barley grains, 133 wheat (*Triticum* sp) grains, 14 bread wheat (*Triticum aestivum* L) grains, 15 spelt (*Triticum spelta* L) grains, 24 emmer (*Triticum dicoccum* L) grains, 15 bread wheat/spelt (*Triticum aestivum/spelta* sp) grains, 34 spelt grains, 16 straight barley grains, one twisted barley grain and one oat (*Avena* sp) grain. The presence of large amounts of clean grain indicated that part of the building was used as a granary. The quantity of surviving grains present vastly outnumbered the amount of chaff and weed seeds, so it is clear that these remains represent a prime grain store. The grains may have been stored ready for processing or as a retail product and the building may have functioned as both bakery and granary.

Building 7 probably had several rooms, only one of which may have functioned as the grain store. It is possible that this is a store of material not yet put through the fine-sieving stage which would have removed the small weed seeds and chaff fragments. The presence of the nearby hearths or oven may indicate that grain was being dried here prior to storage. Charred chaff and weed seeds were present, including a small

Species		Building 7 % grains 1/64ss	Rear of B7 % grains 1/64ss	Floor of B7 % grains 1/64ss	Total %
		{397}	{314}	{311}	
Spelt	Triticum spelta L	15	30.7	0	**38.78**
Emmer/spelt	Triticum dicoccum L/spelta	34	32.3	85.45	**27.82**
Emmer	Triticum dicoccum L	24	5.34	0	**9.89**
Bread wheat/spelt	Triticum aestivum spelta	15	12.9	0	**13.04**
Bread wheat	Triticum aestivum L	14	0.08	0	**0.12**
Barley	Hordeum sp	49	0.17	0	**2.34**
Oat	Avena sp	1	0.27	0	**0.21**
Wheat	Triticum sp	133	18.24	14.55	**8.9**
Grain (indet)		104			

Table 3 Plant remains from Building 7

number of wheat glumes, seeds of brome, spike-rush (*Eleocharis* sp) and vetch (*Vicia* sp) which may represent sieving waste. Other charred remains may have derived from food waste, including hazelnut (*Corylus avellana* L) fragments and one stone pine (*Pinus pinaea* L) kernel. It may have been accidentally charred during storage or the destruction of the building, or else survived as a result of charring whilst being roasted or parched.

Open Area 7 was a strip of land approximately 3.0m wide situated between Buildings 7 and 8. The area remained open and may have been used as a pathway between the buildings. No metalling survived as several pits had been dug into the area. An east–west orientated ditch was suggested by a segment of linear cut, and this may define the northern limit of this yard area. Three pits occupied the area adjacent to the buildings. These pits were generally sub-rectangular, between 1.6m and 2.0m long, and approximately 1.0m wide and 0.5m deep; their function is not clear, but they represent the use of part of the yard area. Two of the pits may have been in use when the adjacent buildings were occupied and were used as rubbish pits. The pits were possibly only partly backfilled when the buildings were burnt as they also contained burnt demolition debris. The range of types of pottery present suggests that these pits were backfilled with domestic rubbish from the adjacent buildings.

To the south only a small fragment of Building 8 survived, represented by a 3.0m long stretch of a sillbeam forming the northern limit of the building, with a small area of clay floor to the south including evidence for an internal partition.

Activity behind the buildings

To the east of Buildings 7 and 8 (within the post-medieval basemented areas of 31–37 Borough High Street) was an area of external yards or open space (OA8). This part of the site had been subject to greater truncation due to medieval and post-medieval activities. The surviving evidence included a group of pits and ditches indicative of the continuity of land use of this open space during much of the history of the site.

The open area may have formed behind the buildings from the expanded open areas emerging from between buildings. The narrow open areas may have functioned as paths, though possibly short-lived ones, and as small yard areas adjacent to

buildings, such as Open Area 7. These were small areas, often subsequently built upon. Open Area 8 seems to have been much larger, extending across the rear of many buildings, and appears to have remained open and been repeatedly used for pitting and dumping of rubbish.

Pits in Open Area 8

A group of pits in Open Area 8 were situated between 4.0m and 12.0m to the rear of Building 7 (Fig 31). A 1.2m diameter circular pit (pit 3) included several fills containing domestic debris with large quantities of pottery. The upper fills of the 1.0m deep pit contained large amounts of burnt debris, and it may have functioned as a rubbish pit. A 0.8m wide segment of a possibly larger circular pit (pit 2) survived adjacent to the first. This also contained large quantities of pottery including mortaria and BAETE Dressel 20 amphorae fragments used as a lining around the upper edge of the pit. The fragments of amphorae were laid in an overlapping fashion forming a packed lining of the pit. The fills of the 0.4m deep pit also contained burnt material, and it may have been utilised as a fire pit or small furnace.

A circular pit lay at the eastern limit of the site. It produced a very unusual fragment of worked Wealden shale, as well as some brick in the red London fabric (fabric group 2815) and roof tile made in Radlett (3060). The shale fragment is of particular interest. It is part of a slab 15mm thick which had been sawn from a larger block of stone, and its surface is grooved with saw marks (Fig 29). It is almost certainly an offcut from the manufacture of shale objects, probably floor tiles. Its presence indicates that shale was being worked in the area, probably for use in a building of some importance. Similar cut stone was found at Fishbourne, in the mason's yard (Cunliffe 1971). The occurrence of this class of material in Southwark indicates that decorative work on the interior of a building was being undertaken at an early date.

The pits were open during the early years of the settlement. Their lower fills contained domestic debris, including many fragments of storage vessels and mortaria. This debris also included limited faunal remains, with cattle, sheep/goat, pig

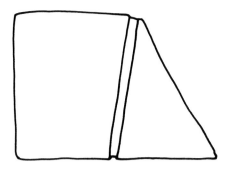

Fig 29 Offcut from manufacture of Wealden shale tiles (1:1)

and goose present. Pig and goose were each represented by a single fragment. The goose bone was a tarso-metatarsus that had been chopped transversely through the distal epiphysis to prepare the bird for the table. Knife marks located on the shaft of this bone indicate the removal of meat. The debris represented small-scale dumping of both domestic and initial butchery waste.

The upper fills were up to 0.6m thick and contained charcoal, burnt clay and daub, and represented the backfilling of the pits. This may have been derived from nearby industrial activity or more possibly resulted from clearance following the Boudican destruction.

The pits must have been in use within a yard or open space, and charred grain and stem fragments from dump layers may indicate that winnowing took place or that cereal processing waste was dumped in this area. The truncated elements of two other pits survived, cut by a medieval ditch, and display similar characteristics to those described above.

The pottery assemblages from the four pits in Open Area 8 were quantified and are presented together. The pottery is all closely dated to the pre-Flavian period, suggesting that at least some of the pits were in use at the same time and that they were backfilled over a relatively short period. A wide range of forms are identifiable in this assemblage, predominantly characteristic of domestic occupation, and including some unusual vessels. Several vessels were recovered partially complete and two vessels have been reconstructed. This, along with the condition of the sherds, suggests that they form part of the primary deposits in the pits as rubbish disposal.

There is no stratigraphic evidence of activity in this area prior to the pits and no fire horizon sealing these features either; therefore the dating of these features relies heavily on the ceramic evidence which contains no material that need date to the Flavian period (Table 5).

PIT 1

A total of 25 sherds (13 rows) were recovered from this pit. The quantified assemblage totalled 441g and 0.27 EVEs. From this small group 14 sherds of ERMS are recorded, probably coming from a single vessel. The decorated samian has been dated to AD 50–65 and AD 55–75; all the sherds are from Drag. 29 bowls.

PIT 2

A total of 172 sherds (16 rows) were recovered from this pit. The quantified assemblage totalled 14,608g and 1.39 EVEs. A number of vessels were substantially complete, including 18 sherds from a SHEL mortarium (2529g, 1.0 EVEs).

The SHEL mortarium <P44> (Fig 30) has been reconstructed and is complete with the exception of a few sherds of the base. It has a small bead and hooked flange, and the wall immediately beneath the flange is distinctively undercut, forming a slight ledge.

Two other occurrences of this type of vessel are also recorded from BGH95. A rim section from a second mortarium <P45> (Fig 30) (period 4, B12) is also a bead and hooked flanged type, although this example has a shorter flange and is not as strongly undercut. This vessel has a post-firing perforation drilled into the wall (interestingly this feature also occurs on an early wall-sided mortarium from BGH95). Two further sherds were recovered (period 5, OA20) consisting of a worn basal sherd and a sherd from the upper wall, with a small bead rim and the beginning of the flange, now broken. However, the wall is undercut and the ledge apparent.

Despite small typological variations, the vessels form a homogeneous group. All three examples are of a bead and flanged type; the bead is small and only demarcated by a shallow groove. The sherds all show signs of use; the internal surfaces are very worn and externally have patches of burning. None of these examples show evidence of the addition of extra trituration grits on either the base or flange, although it is not unlikely that these could have been completely worn away. In an attempt to put these vessels into a regional context, it became clear that although this is an unusual fabric to be used for mortaria production, it is not the first time it has been identified in Southwark.

The recent reassessment of 120 Borough High Street, Southwark (120BHS89) identified a further seven sherds of SHEL mortaria from three contexts, even though they appear to belong to one vessel. This vessel is typologically very similar to BGH95 <P45>, with a slight bead and shorter hooked flange (Cowan et al in prep).

A published example from the Bonded Warehouse, Montague Close, Southwark is more similar to BGH95 <P44>, with a longer, hooked flange and clear ledge beneath (Bird et al 1978, 279, fig 126, no. 821). There are two further examples published from 199 Borough High Street, which are described, with reference to the Bonded Warehouse example, as 'probably local and probably Neronian'. Hartley also notes the lack of additional trituration grits for these vessels and concludes that the examples from both sites may have been made in the same, probably local, workshop and that 'unusual mortaria in unknown fabrics are difficult to date, and this rim form could be any date up to c AD 120. However, small workshops producing mortaria in some very unusual fabrics and selling locally were more common in Britain in the Neronian period (c AD 55–70) than at any other time' (Hartley 1988, 271, fig 103, no. 456; fig 104, no. 497).

Only one example from the City is published (Davies et al 1994, fig 90, no. 585). This vessel is classified as NKSH and was

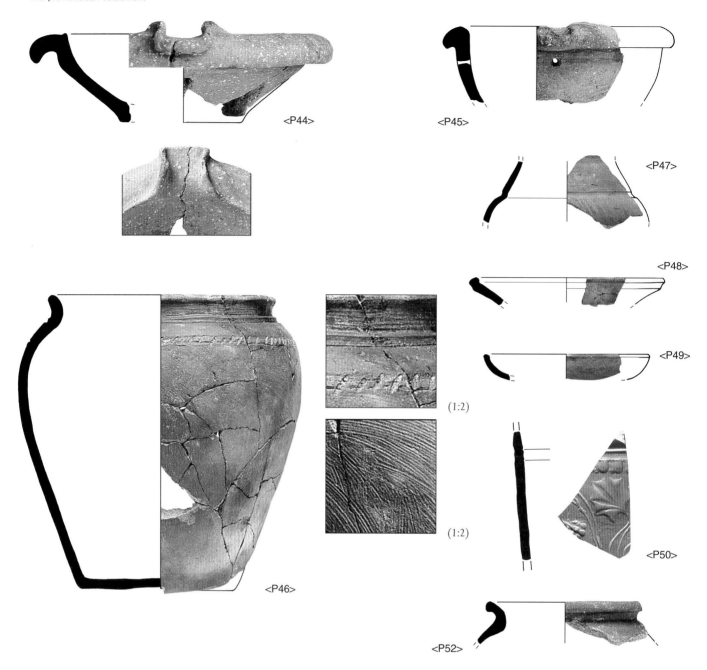

Fig 30 Pottery <P44>–<P49> (1:4), <P50> (1:2), <P52> (1:4) from Open Area 8

recovered from a Neronian/early Flavian context from 19–25 Birchin Lane, EC3 (BRL87). However, recently further examples from the City have been identified during the assessment of the Roman assemblage from No. 1 Poultry (ONE94).

Macroscopically, the fabric of the above vessels is very similar. The external surfaces fire to an orange-buff brown colour, although frequently the core remains mid grey. The fabric has dense shell inclusions, with common black, elongated, burnt organics and common, sub-rounded, red iron-rich inclusions visible in all examples. With the exception of the sherds from No. 1 Poultry, all of the above examples have been examined together by Mr John Cooper (Natural History Museum). He concluded that the density of fossil shell such as *Gryphaea* (oyster sp) and the carbon-rich nature of the clay suggests an Oxford Clay source, which extends across England from Lyme Regis to Whitby, outcropping mainly in the Oxford–Peterborough area of the East Midlands. Therefore it appears that the example from BRL87 has been wrongly classified when published as NKSH, and that the examples found in both the City and Southwark are from the same or associated workshops, sourcing the clay from the Oxford Clay Beds.

With the exception of the examples from the City and Southwark, very few other shell-tempered mortaria are recorded. There are only two published examples from Wookey Hole (Branigan and Dearne 1990) and Longthorpe (Frere and St Joseph 1974). These vessels are both very different typologically and are not comparable to the London vessels.

The earliest date for these vessels would appear to be Neronian/early Flavian, as confirmed by the published examples and the recent discoveries at BGH95.

PIT 3

An assemblage of 78 sherds (22 rows) was recovered, the quantified data totalling 4233g and 1.24 EVEs. Again several of the vessels were partially complete and have been reconstructed.

Two separate fills produced a substantially complete GROG storage jar <P46> (Fig 30). The everted, cordoned jar is handmade, with impressed decoration on the shoulder and combed or furrowed oblique lines on the body. The external surface is dark grey to orange, lightly combed in oblique bands. The cordon and shoulder are lightly burnished and covered in a black pitch or resin which continues over the top of the rim on the interior. The fabric is mid grey, hard with a hackly fracture and moderate quartz and pale grog inclusions.

This vessel fits broadly into Thompson type C6-1 (storage jars: large, heavy, coarse with everted rims, usually cordoned and sometimes decorated on the shoulder, and combed below) and is a common feature of late Iron Age to early Roman assemblages in the south-east of England. This vessel can be well paralleled in examples from Canterbury and Richborough, east Kent (Pollard 1988, fig 14, nos 28–29), but combed bodies also occur on vessels in Hertfordshire. However, the black pitch or resin on the rim is commonly found on other types of storage vessels from Kent (see discussion of the NKSH storage jars in Davies et al 1994), and this seems the most likely source for this vessel.

This type of storage jar is essentially late Iron Age in origin but continues in use into the Roman period, remaining unchanged to the end of the 1st century AD (Thompson 1982, 259). In the early to mid 1st century AD assemblages from Canterbury, the large, everted-rim necked jars, with cordons or corrugations on the neck, are one of the most common forms. Here these 'Belgic' style storage jars continued in use into the 2nd century (Pollard 1988, 42). Within Kent the distribution of these jars with the combed or furrowed bodies appears to be restricted to the east of the county; they are absent in assemblages from west Kent, which Pollard regards as evidence for the regionalisation of pottery styles in late Iron Age Kent (ibid, 31).

Also recovered from this pit was a SAND butt beaker with grooves <P47> (Fig 30) demarcating a zone of roughly burnished horizontal line decoration. Sherds of this vessel were also found in another fill.

An AHSU dish <P48> (Fig 30) was also recovered partially complete. This dish falls into Lyne and Jefferies (1979) class 6, although it is more angular than the published examples, with a flat rim. The rim is burnished but otherwise the surfaces are untreated. A TN dish <P49> (Fig 30) in Cam. form 16 (Rigby form GB 4) is present with a highly polished blue-black surface (Rigby 1989, 123).

The decorated samian includes a Drag. 30 <P50> (Fig 30) in the style of Mascius which has been dated c AD 50–65.

Open areas and buildings

The area to the east and rear of Building 8, Open Area 9, extended for at least 4.0m northwards and 2.3m eastwards.

No limits were defined for this area, but it is likely to have extended over a larger area before possibly merging into Open Area 8 to the east (Fig 31).

Two sunken hearths or 'fire pits' were present in the area, giving Open Area 9 a clearly separate function from that of the larger area. The hearths were constructed on clay dumps and a 0.15m thick layer of sand and gravel which could have served as a working floor surface. Both hearths were of similar construction and consisted of a bowl-shaped cut with amphora, tile and brick fragments set into the top edge and sides. The hearths were 1.1m wide and pear-shaped in plan. Another hearth is suggested by the presence of earlier rake-out deposits. The quantity of dumps suggests that this area was outside the building and that those working at the hearths may have utilised the rear wall of the building to create a partially open structure. The area was covered in extensive ash, charcoal and burnt clay, most probably rake-out from several hearths. The rake-out, up to 0.3m thick, included tile and brick fragments providing evidence for the structure of the hearths.

Hearth bricks were recorded from this area. Bricks up to 60mm thick were noted in fabric 2815 and up to 80mm thick in fabric 3070. The brick in fabric 3070 is of interest. Measuring 265mm across, it may have been a lydion, although this is not certain as only the ends were present. It appeared to have been specially made, with holes 10–15mm in diameter in two corners, one of which contained charcoal and the other mortar dust, which may have supported some sort of superstructure. It had a third, smaller, hole 8–10mm in diameter centred approximately 110mm from the end and side of the brick, and which may originally have perforated the tile, the top surface of which is now missing in that area. The upper surface of the brick is burnt and appears to have been heavily worn after burning. It may represent an oven or kiln base, which had been reused as flooring or for a step, or else the wear might have been caused during use as a hearth.

Further rake-out deposits and a small, 0.5m wide area of rough brickearth floor or working surface were associated with the hearths. No wall foundations or structural remains survived in the area from its initial use, which may be due to truncation by a feeder sewer cut. The concentration of dumped and reused hearth debris and the density of hearth use might suggest that the activity was conducted in the open or at least under a structure adjacent to and associated with Building 7. That this area was being utilised for industrial purposes is clear, and activity must have been fairly intensive. It is less certain, however, what industrial activity was being carried out. No metalworking or glass debris was associated with the hearths and it is possible that they were serving as small ovens. Several isolated stakeholes and the presence of hearth bricks indicate the possibility of the hearths having had superstructures.

The area remained in use for a considerable period with a timber post structure and a later hearth set up in the same area. The hearth is again of similar construction, an oval bowl shape 1.04m long and 0.88m wide with a lining of amphora and tile fragments.

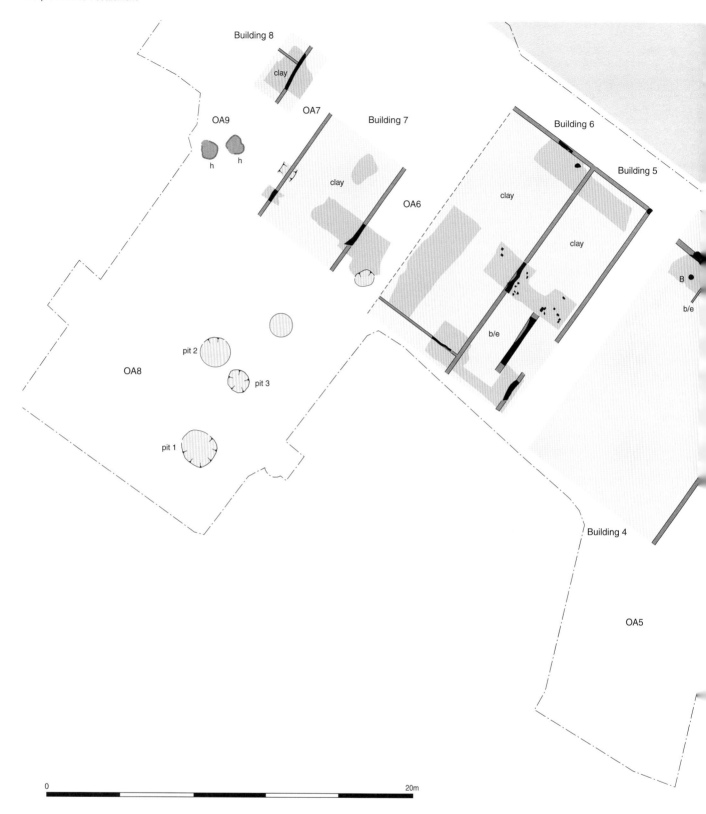

Fig 31 Plan of principal archaeological features, period 2

A further 40m south-west of BGH95, at BTJ93, a similar sequence was evident. Here a narrow strip of archaeological stratigraphy survived to the east of the Battlebridge sewer and a telecommunications junction box. The elements of further clay and timber structures built soon after AD 50 were recorded (Fig 33).

Two areas of clay floor may have been divided by a timber post-and-plank internal partition. No external wall foundations were present at the southern end of the building (BTJ93 B1) and its full extent can only be conjectured. The building is most likely to correspond to the range of buildings further north and to have formed a strip building extending to the eastern edge

of Road 1. This building went out of use after a short period and was replaced by a timber post structure and gravel dumps. The gravel dumping was a precursor to an intensive effort to raise the immediate ground level. This involved 0.5m to 0.6m of redeposited sand being brought onto the site, creating a newly established ground level of approximately 2.25m OD.

The new ground level presumably reflects the local requirement for protection against seasonal flooding.

The early building evidence is also reflected on the western side of the road at STU92, which is the only JLE site adjacent to the western edge of the road. Here there is only limited archaeological survival, but it includes floor surfaces and part of a timber building on the site.

A 2.0m long segment of a V-shaped gully or ditch and a small pit form the evidence of early Roman activity on the western side of Road 1 (STU92 OA2). The 0.4m wide gully was aligned north-west to south-east with the pit on its southern side, possibly respecting the gully. There is no obvious structural evidence and this feature may be associated with early land allotment, with the ditch possibly forming a property boundary. The boundary line was retained after the infilling of the ditch by a line of stakeholes; four stakeholes formed a possible fence line running adjacent to the western side of the backfilled ditch.

The composition of fabrics and forms in the pottery assemblage from Open Area 2 suggests a date very early in the sequence c AD 50–55 (Table 4).

The high presence of ECCW (such as <P53>, Fig 32) and unsourced OXID is comparable to the pattern in RCP1A. Interestingly, ERSI <P54> (Fig 32) is also present in this period at STU92 as it was at BGH95. In the City, ERSI is most common in pre-Boudican groups and was also identified in the pre-Flavian groups at 201 Borough High Street (Ferretti and Graham 1978, fig 35, no. 51). The proportion of GROG sherds is relatively high, and it is noteworthy that none was identified as HWB. Perhaps of more significance is the absence of wares from the Romano-British industries that dominate the supply to London in the later 1st and 2nd centuries, such as Alice Holt, Verulamium and Highgate Wood (Brown and Sheldon 1974). A low proportion of samian is present and there are no other imported fine wares from this group.

The forms present also support an early date for Open Area 2. The dominant form is jars, of which only bead-rimmed examples were identified, and a number of which were handmade <P55>–<P59> (Fig 32). Flagons are also well represented, mainly the collared, Hofheim type (for example <P53>). No cups are recorded at all and the only identifiable amphorae are BAETE.

Several dump deposits and make-up layers were deposited

prior to the construction of two foundation slots. The two beamslots may represent an internal division and a southern limit for the building (STU92 B1) respectively. A line of stakeholes follows the same alignment as the slot and may represent the frontage of the building. Little of the building survives, but it fronted onto the road and probably extended further west to form a small strip building (Fig 33).

The floor of Building 1 is the source of 464 of the 519 sherds of BAETE. The amphorae sherds appear to have been deliberately reused to provide a hard-wearing floor surface, a feature also seen at BGH95 where BAETE was reused for flooring and post packing. Clearly, sufficient discarded amphorae were available to be broken up and reused for this purpose. The floors, although undoubtedly rough and unlevelled, would have provided a solid and hard-wearing base, particularly useful for structures with industrial functions.

Floor surfaces constructed entirely of, or containing a high percentage of, amphora fragments occur in many examples in association with numerous buildings within the study area. The

Table 4 The breakdown by fabric of pottery from STU92 Open Area 2

Fabric	Shds	% shds	Wt	% wt	EVEs	% EVEs
AMPH	2	1.6	31	1.0	0.0	0.0
BAFTF	10	8.2	1565	48.7	0.2	8.9
ECCW	25	20.5	133	4.1	1.0	44.6
ERSI	4	3.3	35	1.1	0.2	8.9
FINE	4	3.3	8	0.2	0.0	0.0
GROG	26	21.3	317	9.9	0.47	21.0
NFSE	9	7.4	305	9.5	0.0	0.0
OXID	19	15.6	368	11.4	0.15	6.7
RWS	5	4.1	220	6.8	0.0	0.0
SAMLG	2	1.6	66	2.1	0.0	0.0
SAND	10	8.2	111	3.5	0.22	9.8
SHEL	6	4.9	56	1.7	0.0	0.0
Total	122		3215		2.24	

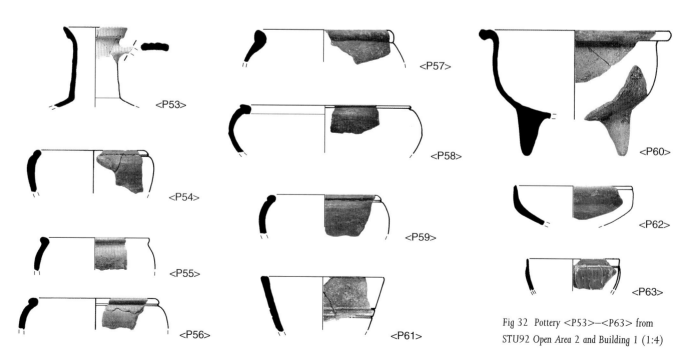

<P53>
<P57>
<P54>
<P58>
<P55>
<P59>
<P56>
<P61>
<P60>
<P62>
<P63>

Fig 32 Pottery <P53>–<P63> from STU92 Open Area 2 and Building 1 (1:4)

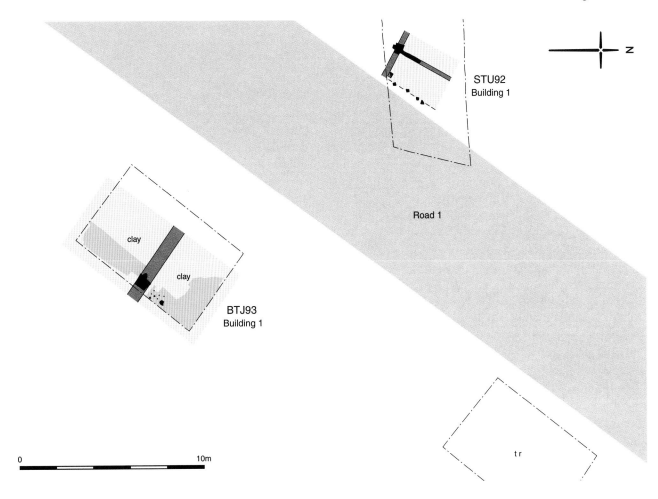

Fig 33 Plan of period 2: southern detail

floor surfaces or spreads are usually relatively thin, with amphorae fragments simply laid on top of make-up deposits or previous occupation. The amphorae fragments were usually irregular broken sherds, although in several examples apparently shaped or cut amphora pieces were used. The floors incorporating amphora and tile fragments may have been internal surfaces, although at STU92 the floor appears to straddle the likely threshold.

DATING OF STU92 BUILDING 1

A total of 698 sherds were recovered in association with Building 1, of which some 529 sherds (14,269g) were of BAETE amphorae (Table 70). The composition of the assemblage, in terms of fabric, has altered from Open Area 2, and the presence of wares from Alice Holt and Verulamium suggests a date of c AD 55–60 (Table 5). The assemblage is still very much pre-Boudican in character, but clearly has a more 'Romanised' appearance and includes a wider range of fabrics from known sources. Imported fine wares are also present, both Lyon colour-coated ware and Gallo-Belgic white ware, and there is a wider range of forms in SAMLG than were identified in Open Area 2. A Lyon hemispherical cup has vertical ridges of barbotine, a type of decoration not paralleled in Greene's survey of the industry (Greene 1979). Also of interest is a narrow, tapering base in VRW, which may come from a butt beaker. This form is not a common component of the VRW repertoire, but a previous example was recovered from the City (Davies et al 1994, 46).

Table 5 Dating table for period 2

Land use	Feature	Grp/sgrp/context	Material	Date
Building 1	occupation	46/201/[1970]	Rpot	50–100
	occupation	46/200/[1930]	BM	50–80
Building 2	floor	45/193/[6018]	BM	50–80
	floor	45/198/[1993]	Rpot	50–100
Building 3	occupation	13/41/[930]	BM	50–80
	posthole	203/202/[1877]	Rpot	50–70
Building 4	occupation	9/24/[5060]	Rpot	50–100
			coin	45–65
			BM	50–80
	make-up	11/31/[5121]	Rpot	50–70
	floor	11/33/[5106]	Rpot	60–80
Building 5	make-up	100/474/[5149]	Rpot	50–70
	floor	101/478/[5088]	BM	50–80
Building 6	occupation	126/575/[7095]	Rpot	50–70
			coin	45–65
			BM	50–80
	occupation	126/577/[7089]	Rpot	50–70
	floor	126/588/[7028]	Rpot	60–70
Building 7	hearth	123/565/[7115]	Rpot	50–100
Building 8	make-up	124/569/[3943]	Rpot	50–80
Road 1	make-up	18/67/[797]	Rpot	50–70
	occupation	18/70/[714]	Rpot	50–70
	occupation	44/1103/[1875]	Rpot	50–70
	surface	18/70/[727]	Rpot	60–80

39

5

The Boudican revolt in Southwark

A serious disaster was sustained in Britain
Tacitus, 2nd century AD

It is not yet clear if Southwark was also destroyed
Perring 1991

5.1 Period 3: destruction of the first settlement

Open Area 10

This first phase of settlement on BGH95 came to an abrupt end when a fire swept through the buildings leaving a thick layer of scorched and burnt brickearth, with patches of burnt daub, timber and charcoal, over much of the site (Open Area 10). The layer varied in thickness from 0.05m to 0.3m and was present over most of the 60m length of the site except where truncated by later activity (Fig 34). Considerable amounts of ash and burnt ceramic building material, particularly roof tile, were also recovered. Much of the layer appeared to be in *situ*, though in places, particularly in the open areas to the east, the burnt remains were dumped.

The timber-framed strip buildings, such as those occupying BGH95 and much of the settlement of Southwark from AD 50 onwards, would have been highly susceptible to fire. These buildings included large quantities of structural timbers, with wood and clay utilised internally, and possibly combustible roofs (thatch, shingle) alongside those with tile roofs. This is particularly true of those buildings that were used as light industrial workshops, such as the blacksmith's workshop in Building 3, or which included domestic hearths or ovens.

The remains of the destruction cover much of the Roman street including Buildings 1, 4, 5 and 6 (Fig 35). These all show evidence of the destruction which included the charred remains of in *situ* floors and wooden features, such as posts, the burnt daub and charcoal from clay wall foundations, and internal faces of walls. Whilst some of these structural elements were preserved in *situ*, the bulk of the damaged or destroyed buildings appear to have been razed to the ground or levelled during or after the event. There is also evidence of burnt domestic items and artefacts among the debris (Fig 36).

This layer was also recorded to the north (JSS92 Open Area 3) sealing the east–west secondary road, Alley 1. Here the debris was associated with large quantities (7kg) of fired clay mould <R39>. Stratigraphic evidence suggests that the deposit is well sealed and it is confined to a small area. There are occasional traces of copper alloy residues on the inner surfaces of the fragments, most of which are flat and heavily burnt, and there are several joining fragments (Fig 37). On several pieces the interior is rounded or curved and there are a very few fragments with a curved outer surface. It is possible that the mould represents some sort of structural hearth lining, but it is also a reasonable supposition that it is an investment mould, used for the production of a large copper alloy object, such as a large vessel, or even a statue, cast in a furnace sited above the ground which would leave no archaeological trace. There are insufficient remains for this question to be resolved.

The site also produced several small fragments of copper alloy waste, which could be casting residue, but there are no diagnostic fragments, such as sprues, dribbles, sheet metal or part-formed objects. Most fragments are irregular vesicular lumps, containing charcoal, copper alloy fragments and small pebbles, and seem likely to represent sweepings form a workshop floor, or perhaps from the edge of a furnace. Unlike the ceramic mould, the copper alloy waste is distributed throughout the sequence, although the most substantial fragments come from JSS92 Open Area 3, in the same area as the mould.

STU92 Building 1 was destroyed by fire, and charred timber, daub and brick fragments formed a 50mm thick destruction layer. On the eastern side of the road scorched clay floors and burnt daub in foundation slots indicated a similar destruction of BTJ93 Building 2 (Fig 38). These fire horizons, though much less extensive than that recorded on the Ticket Hall site (BGH95), are dated to a similar period of AD 60–70. As elsewhere there was evidence for some in situ scorching of floor surfaces and the subsequent levelling of the burnt buildings (Fig 39).

The burnt layer was also present in the open areas behind the buildings, although it was probably redeposited here.

A copper alloy key <R27> was discovered in these dumps. Keys of various types are among the most common finds on Romano-British sites, and this example is a slide key which operated a simple tumbler lock. It is of typical Roman form, as often found also in iron, with six teeth on a straight rectangular bit (Manning 1985, 91, no. 7, 93). The teeth corresponded to the number of tumblers in the lock, which were raised when the key was pushed up into the lock, thus freeing the bolt.

The tile from the destruction levels is, hardly surprisingly, very similar to that from earlier periods and dates to AD 50–80 (Table 7). Only two tile types were identified in the destruction deposits which did not appear earlier; both from Building 8, these are the earliest securely identified box-flue tile, with scored lattice keying and a rectangular vent, and a fragmentary opus spicatum paving brick. They are both in fabrics of the local London group.

Generally, the tile from the site up to and including the burnt destruction deposits is what would be expected from a group of clay and timber buildings. Roof tile is present in sufficient quantities to indicate that many of the buildings were tiled. Brick is present, but often in a burnt or worn condition, suggesting that it was being reused for flooring, paving in yard areas, or in hearths. Tegula mammata tiles would normally be expected in masonry buildings, and their appearance here probably demonstrates reuse.

Although the buildings on the site do not seem to be of particularly high status, ceramic items such as the flue tile, the reused tegulae mammatae, the opus spicatum brick, and stone items such as reused Reigate blocks and the worked shale, are evidence of masonry building somewhere in the vicinity.

A ligula <R10> came from the demolition layer over Building 4. Ligulae were long-handled small spoons and would have had a variety of uses, chiefly for extracting ointments, cosmetics or salves from jars or bottles. They are found in Roman settlements of all types from the earliest periods. This particular example is distinctive in having a flat lozenge-shaped spoon, instead of the more usual circular one, but it would have functioned in the same way.

Environmental samples from Open Area 10 contained a range of remains of charred economic plants, including lentil (Lens culinaris L) and waterlogged seeds from plants in the locality. Lentil is an exotic species native to the southern Mediterranean and Western Asia (de Rougemont 1989, 51) and would have been imported as a single commodity or as a contaminant of imported grain. The charred assemblages of both samples contained grains and seeds which could have come from a grain store. Abundant charred straw fragments were also recovered and could be the remains of thatched roofs.

In seeking a cause of the extensive destruction recorded on the Borough High Street site in the period c AD 55–70, one need look no further than the disaster that befell the settlement on the north bank at this time, the sacking of Londinium by Boudica.

5.2 Historical sources

The main source of information about the Boudican revolt is the historian Tacitus, who described events in Britain in some detail in his Annals (Grant 1971). Tacitus was born around AD 56/7 and the Annals were written early in the 2nd century. His account is thus separated by half a century or more from the events it describes, which means that not all of the details can necessarily be accepted at face value. However, it is unlikely that the general course of events he recounts is too far from the truth, though no doubt coloured by pro-Roman propaganda. Part of his account may have come from Agricola, governor of Britain in c AD 77–84, whose daughter Tacitus married. As a young man Agricola played a part in the suppression of the Boudican revolt. Tacitus outlines the reasons behind the uprising:

> Prasutagus, king of the Iceni [the tribe based in East Anglia], famed for his long prosperity, had made the emperor his heir along with his two daughters, under the impression that this token of submission would put his kingdom and his house out of reach of wrong. But the reverse was the result, so much so that his kingdom was plundered by centurions, his house by slaves, as if they were the spoils of war. First, his wife, Boudica, was scourged and his daughters outraged. All the chief men of the Iceni ... were stripped of their ancestral possessions, and the king's relatives were made slaves. Roused by these insults and the dread of worse ... they flew to arms and stirred to revolt the Trinovantes. (Annals, XIV.30–31)

After sacking Camulodunum (Colchester), Boudica marched on Londinium, which was abandoned to its fate by the governor, Suetonius, in order to protect the rest of the province. Again Tacitus describes what happened:

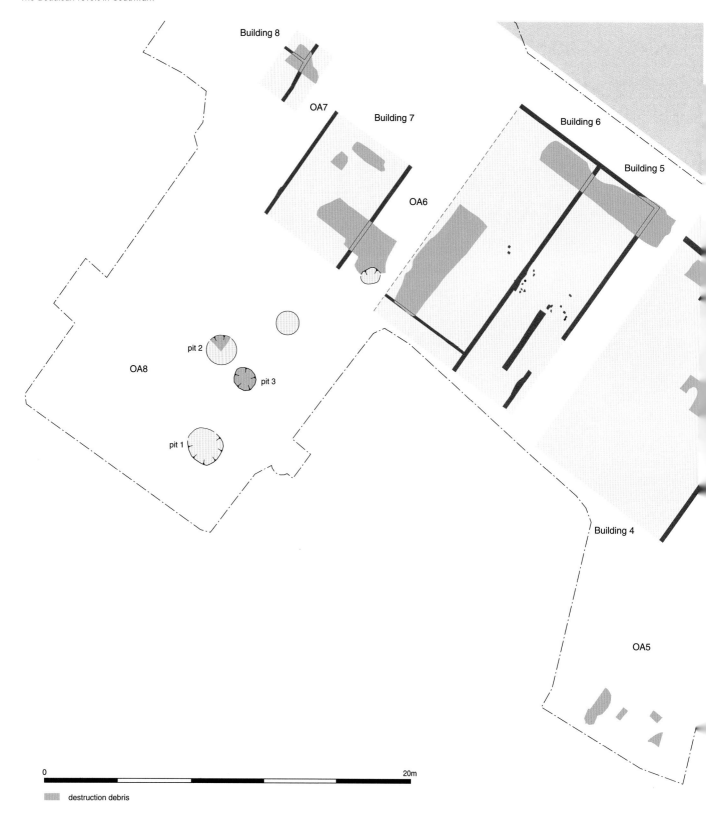

Fig 34 Plan of the destruction debris, which was widespread across the site

Suetonius, however, with wonderful resolution marched amidst a hostile population to Londinium, which, though undistinguished by the name of a colony, was much frequented by a number of merchants and trading vessels. Uncertain whether he should choose it as a seat of war, as he looked round his scanty force of soldiers ... he resolved to save the province at the cost of a single town. Undeflected by the prayers and tears of those who begged for his help, he gave the signal to move, and took into his column any who could join it. Those who were unfit for war because of their sex, or too aged to go, or too fond of the place to abandon it, were butchered by the enemy ... The Britons took

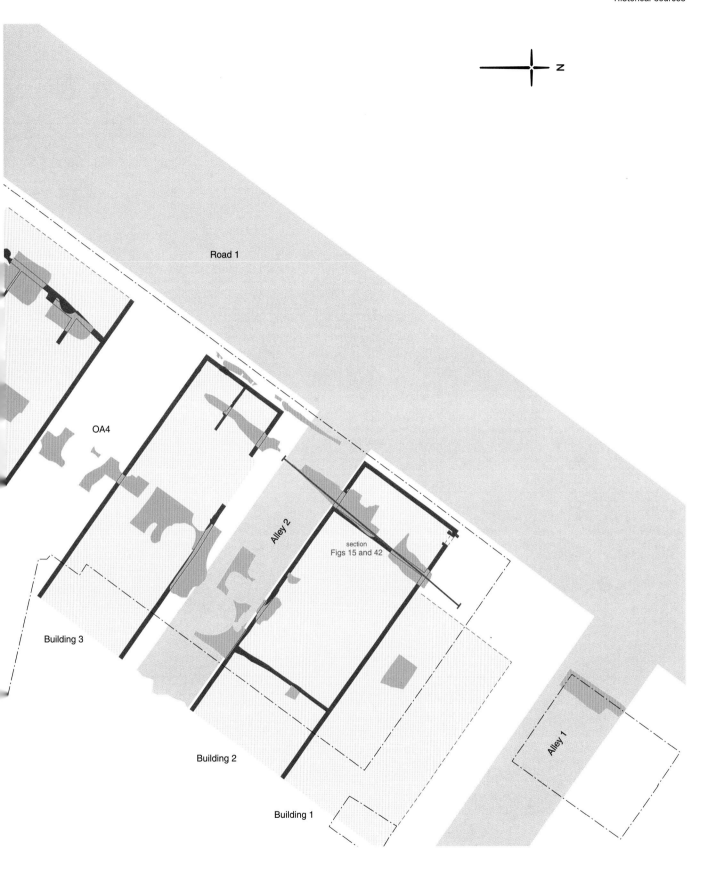

N

Road 1

OA4

Alley 2

section
Figs 15 and 42

Building 3

Building 2

Building 1

Alley 1

no prisoners, sold no captives as slaves, and went in for none of the usual trading of war. They wasted no time in getting down to the bloody business of hanging, burning and crucifying. (*Annals*, XIV.32–33)

Tacitus estimated that 70,000 people died in Londinium,

Camulodunum and Verulamium (St Albans) before the revolt was crushed and Boudica poisoned herself, though this figure is liable to Roman exaggeration. His version of events is paralleled by that of Dio Cassius, writing later and possibly using Tacitus as a source. A fuller account of the background to the revolt can be obtained elsewhere (Sealey 1997).

Fig 35 View of the destruction debris at the north end of the site

Fig 36 View of one of the burnt buildings under excavation

Fig 37 *Remains of the fired clay mould <R39> (1:2)*

Fig 38 *View of Boudican fire debris on BTJ93*

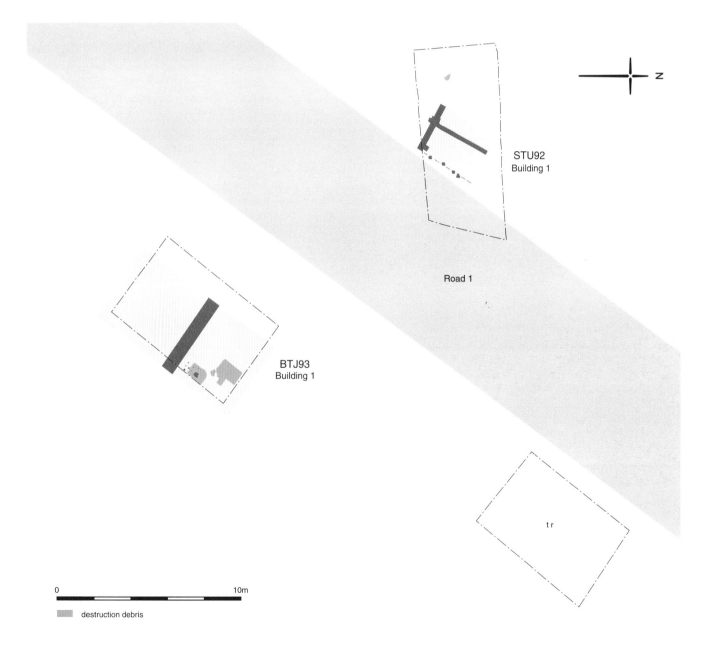

STU92
Building 1

Road 1

BTJ93
Building 1

t r

N

0   10m

destruction debris

Fig 39 *Plan of Boudican burning: southern detail*

5.3 Archaeological evidence from north of the river

Fire debris associated with the Boudican revolt has been found extensively north of the river (Table 6). The settlement was centred on the Cornhill area of the City, where an open market preceded the first Forum and extended west and east along the main Roman streets leaving the city, approximately along the lines of modern Cheapside and Fenchurch Street.

The pattern is clearly shown in Fig 40 and indicates the size and scale of the destruction at the time. It would not be surprising, therefore, if Southwark too were subjected to the same treatment, particularly if there was a bridge affording easy access.

Table 6 City sites with evidence of Boudican destruction (up to 1995)

Address	Site code
143–147 Cannon Street	GM33
55–60 Gracechurch Street	GM69
22–23 Lime Street/160–170 Fenchurch Street	GM95/GM297/FSE76
54–58 Lombard Street	GM100
80 Cannon Street	BLH73
76–80 Newgate Street	GPO75
10 St Swithin's Lane	SL75
130–131 Cheapside	WOW79
29–32 Clements Lane	CLE81
154–156 Fenchurch Street	CUL83
27–29 Eastcheap	EST83
8–12 Fenchurch Street	FEN83
27–30 Lime Street	IME83
25–26 Lime Street	LIM83
37–40 Fish Street Hill/16–20 Monument Street	FMO85
94–97 Fenchurch Street	FST85
36–37 King Street	KNG85
33–39 Gutter Lane	ABC87
DLR Bucklersbury	BUC87
1–7 Whittington Avenue	WIV88
72–75 Cheapside	CID90
76–80 Cheapside	BOL94
168 Fenchurch Street	FEH95
No. 1 Poultry	ONE94

5.4 Previous evidence from Southwark

Evidence from previous excavations in Southwark has been rather more circumstantial than that from north of the river. The sites that might provide evidence for such large-scale destruction have been very small-scale, keyhole excavations in basements (for example, at 2 Southwark Street (26), 22 Borough High Street (25), Southwark Cathedral (27) and observations from the District Heating Scheme) where it is very hard to extrapolate from a small area of burning to a Southwark-wide catastrophe. It has certainly been speculated

before (M Hammerson pers comm, D Sankey pers comm, M Millett pers comm) that Southwark suffered the same fate as the City north of the river, and the size of the BGH95 excavation does allow rather more general inferences to be drawn.

A pottery assemblage from the *in situ* destruction of Building 4 was selected for full quantification. A minimum of 12 individual vessels has been identified in this assemblage although the total EVEs value is only 0.87 (weight 2256g). The breakdown by fabric is detailed in the period overview (Table 56). Typologically the assemblage is dominated by jars, which account for 49.2% by sherd count. The jar types are restricted to bead-rimmed, necked and larger storage jars. Other form types identified are the Drag. 18 dish and Dressel 20 amphorae; sherds from a closed but otherwise indeterminate vessel are also recorded. The majority of the vessels are ascribed a kitchen or storage function, with small quantities of tableware and transport vessels, which supports the interpretation that Building 4 was primarily domestic occupation.

One of the GROG jars <P64> (Fig 41) was handmade, as are the lower parts of the HWB vessels <P65> and <P66> (Fig 41). These GROG jars have zones of burnished surfaces and decoration. The ERMS necked jar with burnished vertical lines <P67> (Fig 41) has a slightly longer neck than the standard ERMS jar 2B (Marsh and Tyers 1978, 557–8, fig 235, no. IIB.1).

There are two vessels which are not illustrated but are worthy of mention. The first is a fine reduced ware (FINE) jar or beaker with combed decoration. Several of the sherds from this vessel are burnt, but the fabric appears primarily oxidised with a fine silty matrix and rare larger quartz inclusions. The external surface is highly polished. The vessel has grooved cordons and two identifiable zones of decoration: one of burnished vertical lines and the second of oblique comb-impressed dots, the style of which suggests a loose attempt to imitate Gallo-Belgic beakers. The second vessel is a GROG cordoned jar with a slight bulge on the shoulder and burnished decoration (Thompson type B3-1). This is a widespread form type that begins pre-Conquest but continues in use into the 1st century AD, becoming increasingly Romanised in shape (Thompson 1982, 140).

Dating

This context is dated AD 55–60. The assemblage is dominated by HWB and unsourced GROG fabrics. The forms are not highly Romanised and can be seen to reflect aspects of pre-Roman or 'Belgic' influence. This assemblage is likely to be contemporary with the use of Building 4 before its destruction by fire.

5.5 Discussion

The destruction horizon present on the Ticket Hall site indicates a single disastrous event. A minimum of nine buildings were destroyed and a 0.3m thick destruction layer of burnt clay daub, charcoal and timber covered the majority of the site. This

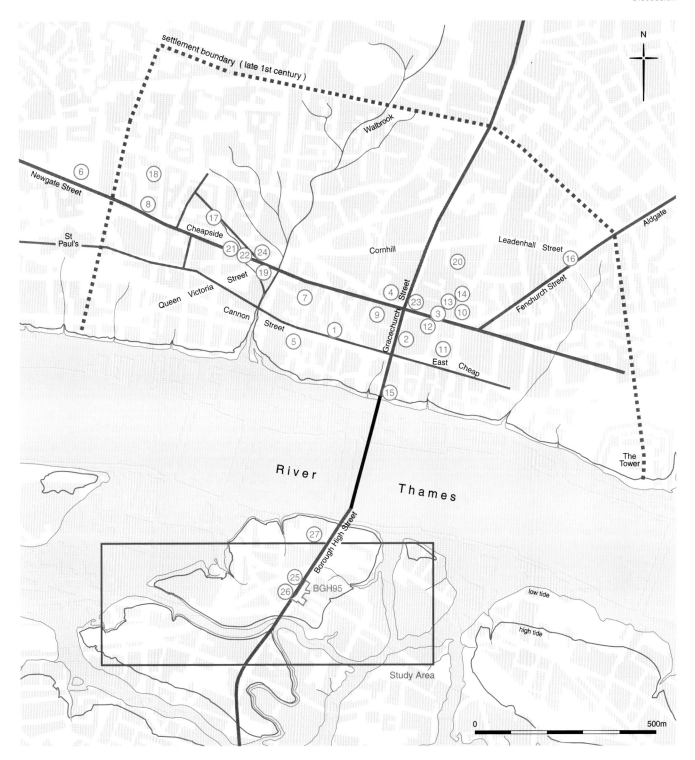

Fig 40 Plan of extent of Boudican destruction in Londinium

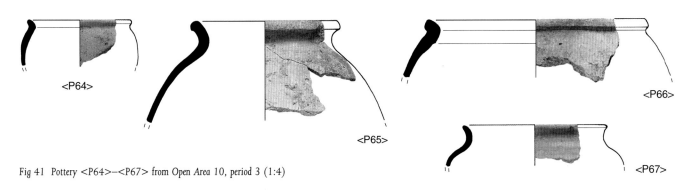

Fig 41 Pottery <P64>–<P67> from Open Area 10, period 3 (1:4)

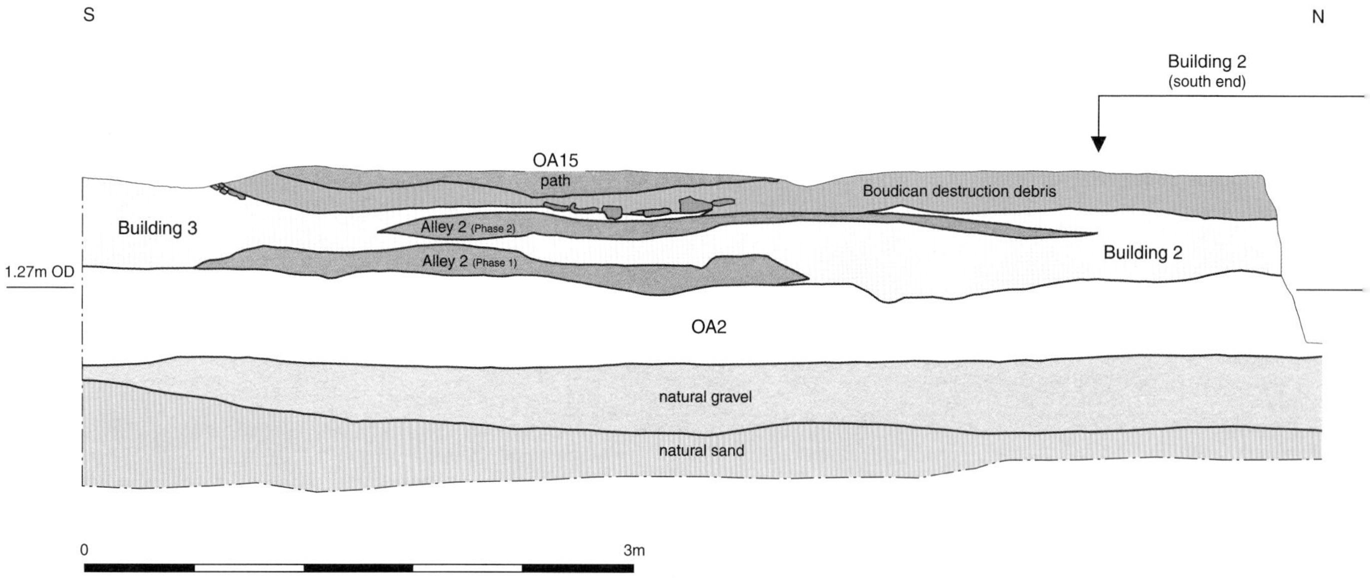

S   N

Fig 42 *East-facing section showing Alley 2 sealed by destruction debris*

suggests a large-scale destruction of much if not all of the early roadside settlement. Certainly evidence for the destruction of the primary Roman towns has been recorded in Colchester, Verulamium and in London north of the Thames. These sites have provided archaeological evidence for the attack on and destruction of Londinium. The evidence from the JLE sites may thus provide the first detailed evidence of the Boudican attack south of the river. If this is the case, it lends credence and further supporting evidence to the view recently put forward that the Boudican forces crossed and possibly destroyed the early military bridge over the Thames (Brigham et al 1995). However, there is no evidence surviving on the south bank for the destruction of the bridge.

On BGH95 a large fire destroyed at least a 60m stretch of the eastern frontage of the Roman main road in Southwark and is represented in the archaeological record by a distinctive red and black deposit (Fig 42). This layer was first noticed in 1993 in a British Telecom service tunnel running down the middle of the site during preliminary work diverting services (D Sankey pers comm). The western frontage, where excavated, shows a similar pattern from a much smaller sample. This fire took place between c AD 50 and 70 according to the dating evidence.

The extent and likely date of the demise of the first settlement provides a powerful argument for Boudican destruction. An alternative case can, however, be put forward for an accidental cause of the conflagration. It could have been the consequence of poorly supervised industrial activity (smithing) or domestic hearths resulting in correspondingly widespread damage. The archaeological remains associated with the destruction of these largely domestic buildings are likely to be indistinguishable in either case, and no definitive statements are possible in the absence of explicit epigraphic evidence. The JLE excavations have produced an expansion of the evidence, from the earlier small-scale excavations (for example 2SSBS85) where burnt

debris was present, to evidence of a much larger-scale and more securely dated event.

It is logical that after burning the City north of the river, the rebels would have crossed the bridge to the large suburb on the south side. Indeed, the destruction of the early settlement in Southwark provides an argument for the nature and importance of the settlement. If indeed destroyed in the course of the Boudican rebellion, the settlement would have been large enough to be included in the attack on Londinium. The devastation of the street was possibly sufficient at the time to cause the collapse and total destruction of many of the buildings. Alternatively, an official decision may have been taken to level all damaged buildings prior to settlement reconstruction.

5.6 Pre-Boudican Southwark

Location and extent of early settlement in pre-Boudican Southwark

The factors affecting the location of the early settlement must have included the local topography (see Chapter 2) and the position of the primary river crossing point. The construction of the road itself created a significant feature crossing the Southwark eyots and undoubtedly would have been a major influence on the location of early buildings. The construction of the road around AD 50 should have been followed soon after by the start of construction of the buildings. The course of the road would have followed the line of higher ground generally associated with the centre of the eyots. This higher ground, at 0.9–1.1m OD, was also of significance for the establishment of the settlement. In order to minimise the risk of flooding, the early buildings were located along this central 'spine', avoiding low ground and areas susceptible to flooding. From the outset, however, there is evidence for the raising of affected ground level and flood protection measures.

The arrangement and frequency of roadside buildings present on BGH95 and its adjacent sites suggest that these may have continued south to the edge of the northern eyot. The presence of early building evidence at BTJ93 marks the southerly limit of JLE site evidence for pre-Boudican buildings. The indications from sections investigated in the British Telecom tunnel (D Sankey pers comm) also indicated that building evidence occurred from BGH95 to the southern limit of the northern island. This distribution of buildings may well have been mirrored on the opposite, western side of Road 1. The building evidence from STU92 and Bedale Street (Cowan et al in prep) is limited, but supports this picture. This may, therefore, be indicative of the morphology of the early settlement, with the main approach road and buildings positioned along it. The evidence for the eastern side of the road would indicate a fairly dense set of buildings in a ribbon-style development from the crossing point onto the north island towards the main river crossing. It is very likely that this settlement extended as far north as the south bank of the Thames.

Thus, even at this comparatively early date, a street pattern was developing, indicating occupation away from the main road, though no evidence of this was recorded either on this site or indeed any other. Apart from the possible blacksmith's workshop, the clay and timber buildings were of a domestic nature – or at least it is not possible to assign any other industrial or commercial function to them.

The structural evidence on the western limit of the site most likely represented part of the street frontage of these early buildings; however, the direct stratigraphic link between the road frontage and the rear portion of the buildings has been lost. All of these buildings almost certainly took the form of long, narrow strip buildings.

The main street would have represented the major influence within the developing urban landscape, and the first buildings probably opened directly onto the street. At least eight buildings were recorded on BGH95 and most likely represent a significant sample of the roadside settlement in this part of the study area. It is possible to postulate a further four buildings in the 40m long gap between the southern limits of the BGH95 excavation area and further evidence revealed at BTJ93, where at least one additional building is suggested from the site.

This initial settlement development may not have extended far from the roadside and there is little evidence for occupation away from the central spine of the island.

The origins of Southwark

The origins of London and the role played by the army have been a much discussed topic (cf Milne 1995). A lot of the evidence for an early military presence in London has come from Southwark (Hammerson and Sheldon 1987), and Southwark has been compared to the pre-Flavian site of Sheepen, an industrial and commercial site outside, and supplying, the legionary fort at Colchester (Niblett 1985; Perring 1991).

It is generally thought that the army would have played a role in many of the larger engineering projects, such as the construction of the main road in Southwark. This may have involved a military presence in Southwark and points to the possibility that the army was involved in the early development of Southwark. However, by AD 50 the base of military operations had moved to the north and west. Very few coins or pottery dated to earlier than AD 50 have been recovered from either Londinium or its southern suburb, and by then the legions had moved away from the south-east of the country and were based further afield in the West Country and Wales.

If the road was built by the military, then the first buildings on BGH95 are not indicative of particularly strong army influence. There is nothing to contradict Perring's view that private enterprise took over the role of supplying the army, which could account for a continuing loss of artefacts with military associations on site, particularly of irregular coins to pay for the goods and services supplied. Evidence for an established army occupation in Southwark, in the form of a fort or camps, remains as yet unproven. Bird (1994) argues that the lack of evidence is indicative of the fact that there was no military base and 'no good reason to postulate one'. The Borough High Street excavation, the largest undertaken in the heart of Roman Southwark, has failed to find any overwhelming evidence for a strong military presence at this early date.

The 'military' character of Southwark

The presence of various items generally associated with military activity, comprising fragments of weapons and other equipment, is noted in several of the period summaries (see Chapter 11.3), but on its own this evidence adds little to the 'military' history of the settlement. It has been observed that in the 1st century deposits of military material are generally associated with early military bases (Bishop 1991) and this is true of both Britain and Germany. While no 1st-century base has yet been discovered in London, the early date of the settlement and the persistent evidence of early military equipment in Southwark attests a military presence, and it is not unreasonable to suppose that the army would have been involved in civil works before and after the Boudican revolt. The earliest items from the site at Borough High Street, found in period 2 groups, are a fragment of a buckle from a *lorica segmenta* and, more unusually for London, the terminal from a dagger chape made of copper alloy, which would have been mounted on the iron frame of the wood and leather scabbard. Two harness pendants of mid to late 1st-century type were also found in the London Bridge area, but in later contexts.

Two ring buckles of 3rd-century type were found in a period 7 deposit. Again, the presence of soldiers in the city as part of the resident or visiting population should be no surprise at this time. An unstratified pelta-shaped mount from REW92 is similar to 3rd-century equestrian equipment, for example from the Saalburg fort in Germany.

The Claudian coin copies: metric study

Probably all but one of the Claudian coin issues were of the copies now familiar in Southwark, the City of London and many other Romano-British sites. Thirty-four coins were identified as definitely and another five as possibly being of this type. Despite the fact that only a small proportion have been conserved, it was possible to determine the 'grades' (see Hammerson 1978) for 25 of the 34 as follows:

Grade I	6	(24% – cf 21% in Hammerson 1978)
Grade II	12	(48% – cf 53% in Hammerson 1978)
Grade III	6	(28% – cf 26% in Hammerson 1978)
Grade IV	–	(as in 21% in Hammerson 1978)

The grades refer to the standard of copying, ranging from I (good) to III (poor) and IV (image reversed); the system was proposed by Sutherland (1935) and employed by Hammerson (1978)

where it was tested on stratigraphic evidence, which suggested – albeit inconclusively – that it may have some validity. Clearly, comparable data from other localities would be desirable.

It is notable that the proportions of the various grades from BGH95 are closely similar to the overall Southwark trend. The hypothesis was put forward by Sutherland that the better the grade, the earlier the site, while more recent work by Robert Kenyon on the copies from Colchester indicates that copying started at that town and spread westwards through the province, and that production went through a series of weight reductions (Kenyon, cited in Reece 1987).

Study of the diameters of the Claudian copies from BGH95 shows that 23 of the 34 coins (68%) were within the range 25–30mm, which is close to the size of the official products. Though it is not at present possible to say where the Southwark coins were minted, this suggests that the Southwark issues are among the earlier of the Claudian copies, and that there is therefore no reason at present to revise the proposal made by

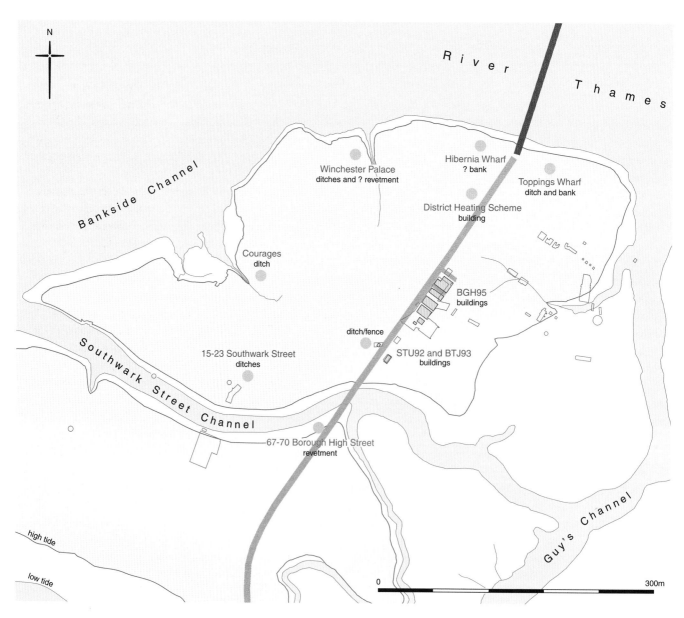

Fig 43 Plan of pre-Boudican Southwark

Hammerson (1978) that the Southwark coinage is typical of those sites which originated in the period *c* AD 50–5.

Development of Southwark

The picture that emerges of Southwark in the decade between the initial occupation and the Boudican revolt is one of a small settlement growing up along the main road. There appears to be little activity away from the road, apart from drainage measures (Fig 43).

The road itself would not appear to have been constructed before AD 50. Only the northern of the two sand islands was occupied, and this occupation is on a very small scale compared to the intensity of activity on the northern bank of the Thames.

Nevertheless, the level of occupation was sufficient to entice the Boudican rebels across the river in order to sack the settlement. There was almost certainly a bridge relatively soon after the establishment of the settlement (Watson et al 2001), and this left it more vulnerable than if a ferry had been the only method of crossing the river.

This density of occupation at such a comparatively early date raises the question of how large Roman Southwark was at this date. The north end of the site lies 225m south of the bridge and the south end 290m from it. If the whole of both sides of the road were occupied at this date, then London south of the river was a reasonable sized settlement, though still not comparable in scale to London north of the river. Indeed, D Sankey (pers comm) even suggests that the settlement extended to the south island at this early date, on the basis of section evidence in a British Telecom tunnel, though this cannot be corroborated for now. Alternatively, the centre of the island may have been settled first and the margins left alone until pressure on building land meant that the less suitable land next to the Thames itself to the north and the Southwark Street Channel to the south were occupied. Certainly excavations at Toppings Wharf to the north (Sheldon 1974) revealed no occupation by buildings until the Flavian period. If there was no bridge at this early date and a ferry was used for crossing the river, then it is more likely that the first occupation would have been in the dry centre of the island rather than the wet fringes, with no bridgehead to defend. However, if Brigham (in Watson et al 2001) is correct in suggesting an early date of *c* AD 50–2 for the construction of the first bridge, then it is unlikely that the southern bridgehead was left undefended or unoccupied. In any case, these are the earliest buildings yet discovered in Southwark, and they could mark the birth not just of Southwark but of Londinium itself, since the dates are comparable to those from the earliest buildings north of the river.

Prior to the Borough High Street excavations, there was little evidence for activity that could be firmly dated to the pre-Flavian period. Cowan (1992) reported on only six sites with building remains but only two of these, at 1a Bedale Street and the District Heating Scheme, yielded firm dating evidence. Both these sites lie alongside the main road, Road 1, as do two of the sites with less certain dating – 18 Southwark Street and Arcadia Buildings, the latter being alongside Watling Street

c 500m to the south. Extensive evidence for the Boudican fire has been recorded in the excavations (OA10), including destruction debris containing datable pottery and building material (Table 7)

Table 7 Dating table for Open Area 10

Context type	Number	Material	Date range
Open Area 10: layer of burnt demolition material			
Destruction debris	[999]	Rpot	50–60
Destruction debris	[687]	BM	50–80
Destruction debris	[576]	BM	50–80
		Rpot	50–80
Destruction debris	[509]	coin	45–65
		BM	50–80
Destruction debris	[753]	Rpot	60–80
Destruction debris	[1865]	BM	50–80
Destruction debris	[6077]	Rpot	50–70
Destruction debris	[2166]	Rpot	50–80
Destruction debris	[2077]	Rpot	50–70
Destruction debris	[7085]	Rpot	50–70

Away from the main road, there is little evidence of occupation. Ditches have been recorded at many sites alongside Borough High Street, for example at 64–70 and 106–114 Borough High Street, and quarry pits excavated at Montague Close and the District Heating Scheme. At Calverts Buildings, *c* 80m to the west of the main road, there was a fenced enclosure, and ditches were also recorded at Chaucer House.

However, the presence of at least two side roads running off to the east from the main road indicates that some activity was taking place away from the road. It could be that the side roads were only to gain access to open areas behind the street frontages. Certainly there is currently no evidence for any buildings.

The presence of large open areas away from the roads is also suggested by a study of the eggshells (see Chapter 11.9). Five deposits with eggshells can be dated with certainty to the 1st century. These are, with one exception, from features in a series of open areas. The final one comes from the Boudican fire debris. The nature of the features suggests that the deposits are generally rubbish tips which were utilised and accumulated in any available space. One sample from the fill of a well contains goose as well as chicken eggshell. Several of the fragments of chicken eggshell show signs of having hatched, which indicates that chickens were being kept in this area for breeding as well as for their eggs. The goose is the only non-chicken identification made from Borough High Street. Although this may be significant and suggest that goose was preferred in the earlier period of occupation, the sample size is rather low. A further possibility is that the area was less developed prior to the Boudican revolt, and more open space was available for keeping birds, geese requiring more room than chickens.

With the evidence from the Ticket Hall excavation it is now possible to suggest a large ribbon development along

Southwark Road 1 with extensive clay and timber buildings, but away from the road only drainage measures and possibly some evidence for animal husbandry to the west of the island. From new evidence from the JLE excavations the eastern side is now thought to be more marginal than originally believed.

However, one interesting aspect of the first buildings on BGH95 is the remains of a fragmentary masonry building in their make-ups, utilising the Reigate stone and Kentish ragstone already discussed, as well as other building features and fragments. The presence of such a building at such an early date may indicate an official function; it is not far from the road and is presumably contemporary with it. It must have been built *c* AD 50 and could only have been in use for five years at the most. A connection with the military or the civil administration is probable, perhaps serving some function that was rapidly assumed by a building north of the river, which would account for its brief life-span. This would indicate some connection with the port and docking facilities, which would initially have been on the south bank but rapidly transferred to the north bank. One possibility is a customs house to control commercial traffic into Londinium in its early years. A domestic function is equally plausible, though it is less easy to imagine circumstances where a domestic building is both abandoned and unable to be reused and hence demolished.

Discussion of the building materials used in period 2

The fabrics

In the pre-Boudican period, there were two main sources for the ceramic building material found in Southwark. The most abundant tiles, made with clays which fire to shades of red (fabric group 2815), came from a number of kilns situated within 30km of London (Betts 1987, 27–8), of which most of the known sites were situated along Watling Street between London and St Albans. As the tileries used very similar clays, it is not usually possible to attribute these red tiles to specific kiln sites, although the products of the tile kiln at Radlett in Hertfordshire are made from a distinctive clay which contains numerous small black iron oxide inclusions (fabric types 3023, 3060). Also likely to be of local production is a very coarse sandy fabric usually used for bricks (fabric 3070). These tiles were produced from *c* AD 50 to 160, although the Radlett kilns may have gone out of use by *c* AD 120.

The second important source of tile in the mid 1st century was the kiln site associated with the Eccles Roman villa on the Medway in north-west Kent. This site produced the distinctive yellow or white tiles (fabrics 2454, 3022) which are found

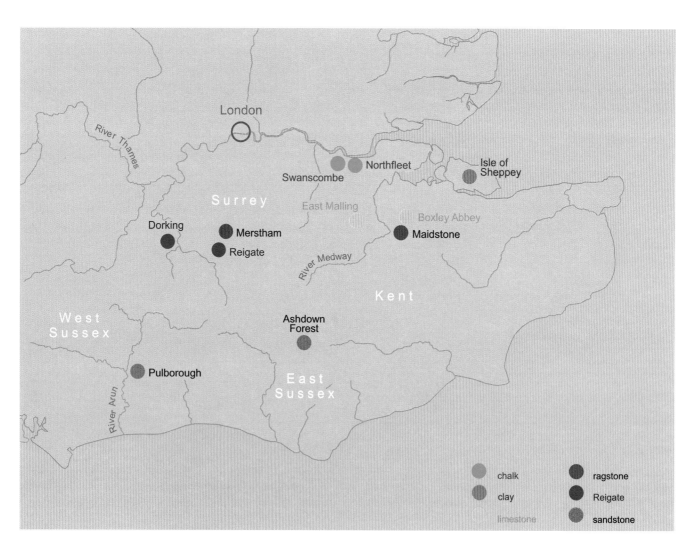

Fig 44 *Map of location of stone quarries in Roman Britain*

widely in Southwark between c AD 50 and 70–80. Tiles in other fabrics not local to London are occasionally found, but their sources are not known at present. The tiles used in Southwark in this early period are consistent with those from other parts of Roman London.

The tile types

The types of tile used in the buildings of period 2 are brick, including tegulae mammatae, and roof tile. It is likely that some of these simple timber-framed buildings had tiled roofs, and brick would have been used mainly for hearths and paving. The thicker bricks and tegulae mammatae, which are generally associated with substantial and hypocausted masonry buildings, are probably reused material taken from other buildings which had been altered or destroyed by fire. Their main interest for us is that their presence may be evidence for the existence in Southwark of one or more early masonry buildings of high status, possibly public buildings. This is supported by the finding of the shale offcut from the manufacture of floor tiles from a pit in Open Area 2. Such worked stone would have been incorporated only into important buildings, with similar material having been found at the 1st-century 'palace' at Fishbourne (Cunliffe 1971).

Other materials

Unfired clay building materials such as daub and mud brick were made from local clays, often with the addition of organic material such as straw, grass or dung. They were usually used in conjunction with wattle to form the walls of timber-framed buildings, but also in the construction of ovens and hearths, where the high temperatures would have adversely affected the strength of lime mortars.

Building stone

There is no local building stone available in Southwark, so all the stone found on the site was brought in from quarries outside London (Blagg 1990). Stone rubble from deposits in periods 1–3 included Reigate stone, Kentish ragstone, chalk, flint (possibly knapped) and ferruginous sandstone. The only decorative stone recorded from these early contexts was the Wealden shale. All these types of stone were available from Kentish sources (Fig 44).

There are features of interest in the stone assemblage, particularly the Reigate stone blocks from BSE94 Building 1 (which represents the northern extension of Building 1 on BGH95), and BGH95 Building 1 itself, which are the earliest recorded well stratified occurrences of Reigate stone in London. Although widely found in London in medieval contexts, there has been hardly any Reigate stone – which is quarried close to Reigate and Merstham in Surrey – recorded from Roman contexts in the City. Such early use, or in this instance reuse, of the stone indicates that it was exploited by the Romans for use in London at a much earlier date than was previously supposed. This, and the evidence for the presence of ferruginous sandstone – also rarely seen in Roman contexts before the late 2nd century – in Open Area 2, suggests that the materials used in early building activity in Southwark may have included stone from Kentish sources in a way that was not the case north of the Thames.

6

Late 1st-century reconstruction and expansion of the settlement

The winter oak is very useful in buildings
Vitruvius, 1st century BC

6.1 Period 4: reconstruction of the settlement

Reconstruction alongside the main road AD 60–70

Following the extensive destruction of the first settlement, the roadside buildings were completely levelled. This large-scale clearance operation appears to have been carried out shortly after AD 61 as there was time for a short-lived phase of activity before more substantial reconstruction c AD 70. This created a large open area (OA10, see Chapter 5) adjacent to Southwark Road 1. This may have been a systematic attempt to clear fire-damaged properties and partially destroyed buildings. The resultant open space would then have been available for rebuilding. The speed and layout of the new construction might allow speculation concerning the relative importance and administration of the Southwark settlement.

Temporary structures

However, in the immediate aftermath of the fire there appears to have been no strategic plan of reconstruction. Instead, there seems to have been a rather *ad hoc* approach, as some areas were redeveloped almost immediately and some were left open for a period. The first structures were most likely temporary in nature and built as emergency shelters in the immediate aftermath of the destruction. They were certainly not substantial buildings.

To the north of BGH95, on JSS92, external occupation continued immediately after the Boudican fire, but a timber-framed building, JSS92 Building 1 (not shown), was constructed around AD 65–70. No walls were recorded but a series of clay floors and occupation layers were present (Fig 56).

The west end of Building 2 was built over by BGH95 Building 9 (not shown). This was represented by a series of posts and stakes cutting through the Boudican destruction layer. The north wall of the building was represented by a 2.5m long line of rectangular postholes measuring c 0.25m x 0.15m and 0.2m deep. A collection of small stakes may be evidence of wattlework. A c 2.0m long line of smaller square posts may have formed an internal partition. No other walls were present but a large circular posthole 0.3m deep may have held up the roof. The south wall was removed by modern truncation but cannot have been more than 0.5m further to the south as there was no trace of the building on the other side of the truncation. There was no occupation associated with this building, and it appears to have had a brief life-span before being burnt down, the structure being sealed by a layer of burnt daub. This appears to have been a localised fire as the evidence of destruction does not spread very far. The building itself may have been little more than a temporary hut for shelter immediately after the Boudican fire.

The butcher's shop

In the north-east corner of the site was an open area, Open Area 11, that was related to Building 10 on its south side (Fig 46). The building occupied the line of the pre-Boudican road (Alley 2) which was not reinstated after the fire. The open area was full of dumps of butchered bone and also contained a pit filled with bones of similarly slaughtered animals. The building was of timber-framed construction with a decayed beamslot 2.9m long forming the northern wall. A series of internal pits also contained butchered bone, but this material differed from the bone from the external pits (see below). Heavy truncation made the southern limit of the building difficult to define. Situated 4.0m to the south was a truncated construction cut, but this was part of Building 11. It is also possible that it was the south wall of Building 10, but there was no direct evidence linking the two; however, the gap between them is consistent with this interpretation.

ANIMAL BONE FROM THE BUTCHER'S SHOP AND ASSOCIATED OPEN AREA

As can be clearly seen from Table 8, the species representation within Building 10 is very limited. It is exclusively cattle and 'cattle-sized' material except for a single fragment of 'sheep-sized' rib. Animal bones were recovered from two rubbish pits. Open Area 11 produced a much larger sample of faunal remains with slightly more species diversity; however, the non-domestic animals are never represented by more than two bones. The contexts were a range of external dumps, occupation layers and a pit; many of the bones were recovered from just one of the external dumps.

The composition of the cattle and 'cattle-sized' assemblages within Building 10 and Open Area 11 is clearly very different (see Fig 115 for cattle skeletal part representation).

Open Area 11 has a broad skeletal representation that encompasses a great percentage of the skeleton. There is, however, a noticeable bias towards the upper limb elements and a distinct lack of skull fragments and phalanges. Building 10, on the other hand, has a much more limited range with only metatarsals, horncores, mandibles and skull fragments

present, the majority originating from a large pit. The fragment counts of 'cattle-sized' material recovered from Building 10 and Open Area 11 echo this pattern: Building 10 contained only 8 vertebrae and 13 fragments of ribs whereas Open Area 11 contained 34 and 71 fragments respectively.

There is extensive butchery evident on the bones recovered from Open Area 11. Dressing of the carcass (that is, the removal of the skull and feet) was done to include the removal of the metapodials, the chop going transversely through the ankle joint. Occasionally this was missed and the chop went through the proximal epiphysis of the metapodial. This chop would have been most easy to execute successfully if the animal was lying on its side. Many of the metapodials were then further processed, chopped longitudinally to open the marrow cavity for use in stews and stocks and the like. The smashing of the metapodials for this purpose is one possible explanation for their under-representation. Unfortunately there is no evidence for the removal of the skull. However, three mandibles bear butchery marks, which are consistent with removal from the skull, most probably to allow access to the tongue.

Only a limited amount of butchery was recorded from the vertebrae. Despite this, the carcass clearly was halved either along the mid-line or to either side. The latter was more common on cervical vertebrae and the former on the thoracic vertebrae. A number of chops are transverse as a result of subdividing the carcass at some point into more manageable sections.

The removal of the rear leg was achieved either through the hip joint, with very few pelvises being intact due to chops through the acetabulum and corresponding chops through the proximal epiphysis of the femur, or on rare occasions by a chop through the mid shaft of the ilium. The removal of the forelimb was similarly through the shoulder joint. Further subdivision of the limbs was through the 'knee' and 'elbow' joints rather than through the bone shafts. There are a few marks on the proximal tibia and the distal femur, as evidence of the dismemberment through the 'knee joint'. It is possible that the butcher cut directly between the bones after trimming off the anterior section of the distal femur, which would have been achieved by laying the limb on its side. In contrast to this is the plentiful evidence for the separation of the radius and ulna from the humerus (the 'elbow' joint). There are only a few chops through the proximal end of the radius. This is because it was preferred to chop obliquely through the distal end of the humerus and the proximal end of the ulna, missing the radius. This chop would require less power but the joint has to be bent backwards.

As can be clearly seen from Table 9 the bone recovered from Open Area 11 then went through further processing. Instead of being sold on the bone the meat was removed. This was normally achieved by running a heavy blade along the shaft of the bone from the distal to the proximal end. The radius had fewer grazing chops, probably because the shaft is smoother with few areas on which to catch the blade, rather than because the meat was not being removed. Therefore the butcher was preparing meat of all quality: good meat from the upper limbs and the poorer meat such as the hind shank (removed from the tibia) and shin (from the radius and ulna).

Table 8 Species representation within Building 10 and Open Area 11

Species	Building 10		Open Area 11	
	No. of frags	Weight (g)	No. of frags	Weight (g)
Cattle	61	1712.95	305	9874.81
'Cattle-sized'	17	226.02	268	2504.97
Sheep/goat	0	0	7	42.1
'Sheep-sized'	1	6.64	41	122.53
Pig	0	0	11	101.7
Mouse/vole sp	0	0	2	0.02
Small passerines	0	0	1	0.01
Unidentified mammals	0	0	1145	1693.8
Unidentified birds	0	0	2	0.1
Total	79	1945.61	1782	14340.04

Table 9 *Absolute counts of butchery marks from Open Area 11*

Element	Cleaver marks		Knife marks
	Chops	Grazes	
Astragalus	3	2	1
Atlas	0	0	0
Axis	0	0	0
Calcaneum	1	0	0
Femur	27	30	2
Humerus	27	22	3
Mandible	2	0	0
Metacarpal	1	0	0
Metatarsal	4	0	1
Pelvis	0	0	0
Radius	14	2	0
Scapula	7	4	1
Skull	0	0	0
Tibia	17	37	2
Ulna	8	0	0
Total	111	97	10

The most frequent chop was through the axial plane; this was common on all the limb bones for the removal of marrow. The high number of unidentifiable mammal fragments probably results from breakage of the bones for the extraction of marrow for use in stews and broth.

One dump deposit contained a large volume of burnt material representing various degrees of burning. For example, one cattle mandible is burnt solely on the edge, showing that it was near to the fire and/or perhaps had a layer of protective meat still attached. Others are blue-white, indicating complete calcination. This only occurs at extreme conditions with temperatures in excess of 600°C (such as those at the centre of a fire) for a prolonged period.

The fusion information suggests that all the cattle were over 18 months old and that a small percentage of the cattle culled were aged between two and four years. The majority of the animals were older, suggesting that they had had a prior use, such as dairy or traction, and were not specifically bred for beef. A single mandible was sufficiently complete to allow it to be aged at approximately 36 months old. Again it appears that the butcher was catering for a range of customers, some of whom could afford young tender animals, but the majority of whom consumed meat from older animals that would have been tougher and thus cheaper. Yet both 'classes' were eating meat which had been removed from the bone.

In summary, it appears that Open Area 11 was rich in butchery waste, suggesting that the butcher either worked outdoors, or more probably disposed of his waste in the area immediately surrounding his premises. As noted above, the assemblage recovered from within Building 10 was unusual, being essentially composed of primary waste. It is conceivable that the differences between the assemblages reflect the waste derived from the initial division of the carcass (B10) and then that part of the carcass from which the majority of the meat was removed (OA11). It seems likely that the butcher would

have maintained a working relationship with the local tanner's, and it was common practice to leave the skull, horncores and feet attached to the hide in order to make it easier to handle and stretch out to dry. So the bones recovered from within the butcher's shop could represent hides that were intended for, but never reached, the tanner.

The location of the building also suggests that it was not just the dressing of carcasses that took place here but also the selling of meat to the public – the logical place for such a trade being alongside the high street. However, no trace of the internal layout of the building survived to support this contention. Marrow was also being utilised by the butcher, so this may have been sold as well. The question of what would have happened to the blood also arises. Carvings show bulls being sacrificed by having their carotid artery cut (Hodgson 1976, 8) and it is likely that cattle generally were dispatched in this way to remove the blood from the body by the action of the heart. Was the blood simply allowed to drain away? Was it collected and used in food by-products or for some other purpose, for example as fertiliser or as thickener in building materials? At least two of Apicius' recipes (Edwards 1984), those for *Bottellum Sic Facies* (small sausage) and small black pudding, mention blood as an ingredient, so this is likely to account for at least some of it.

Well in Open Area 11

A well in the open area to the north of Building 10 was sub-circular, *c* 1.0m in diameter and timber-lined. The well was dug down to *c* −0.5m OD. As it cut through the Boudican fire deposit it can only have had a very short time in use, since it was rapidly backfilled, and perhaps was dug for emergency water supplies in the immediate aftermath of the fire. The backfill contained an intact unguentarium <P68> (Fig 45). The vessel has a collared rim and rilling over the body. The pedestal base is flat, but poorly finished and not level, which does not allow the vessel to stand. The fabric is buff in colour with a smooth, slightly powdery feel. There are very few inclusions visible with the exception of rare quartz and silver and gold mica.

The source of this vessel is uncertain, but the fabric is comparable to COLWW and the form certainly finds parallels amongst the published examples from the kilns in Colchester (Hull 1963, 130–3, fig 72). The function of these vessels is debatable but interpretations include a use as unguent pots, candlesticks and amphorae stoppers (Symonds and Wade 1999, 39). Only a small amount of other pottery was recovered from the fills of this well, dated AD 50–100.

Further buildings and open areas

Building 11 to the south of Building 10 was another timber-framed building (Fig 46). It is possible that it was a continuation of the same building, and it was certainly part of the same range. The north wall was represented by a decayed beamslot, and the south wall was represented by a stub of brickearth wall 2.5m long with a series of decayed stakeholes up to 0.4m deep

Fig 45 The unguentarium <P68> from the well in Open Area 11

running along it. A brickearth slab sealing the wall was formed by the collapse of the wall. The two walls were 3.5m apart, making this building slightly less wide than Building 10. There were traces of a brickearth floor and a possible internal partition dividing the building in two. The more substantial nature of the south wall could be accounted for by this being an external wall with an open area (OA13) to the south, whilst the north wall was an internal wall dividing Buildings 10 and 11. The limited dating evidence recovered definitely indicated that it post-dated AD 60 (Table 10). A fragment of lamp <R129> was found as well as a stone hone <R172> and a pin <R255>. The small plain lamp, a south Gaulish import made in Lyon ware, is contemporary with the probable date of the building. The pin (Fig 47) has an unusual crozier-like terminal and its function is uncertain. It is too elaborate to have been used as a buckle or brooch pin, but is unlike any hairpins of the period. The hone (Fig 47) is well worn.

BGH95 Building 4 was replaced by Building 12 (not illustrated). This was a small clay and timber building measuring a minimum of 3.0m north–south by 1.8m east–west. No wall foundations were recorded and only one room, with a series of floors and occupation layers, was present within the excavation. A small hearth, oval in shape (1.0m x 0.5m) with a brickearth lining, was also recorded and was almost certainly domestic in nature. The floors were a mixture of fine gravel and brickearth.

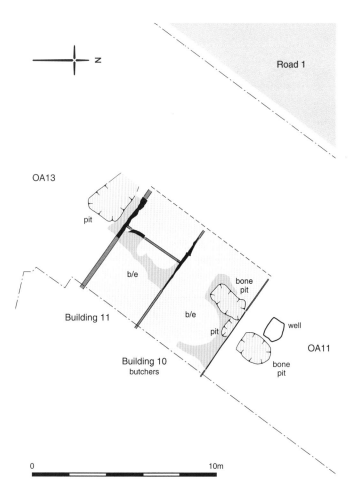

Fig 46 Plan of Buildings 10 and 11

Table 10 Dating table for period 4

Land use	Feature	Grp/sgrp/context	Material	Date
Building 9	demolition	27/112/[734]	Rpot	50–100
Building 10	make-up	50/220/[1902]	Rpot	50–100
	floor	50/221/[1901]	Rpot	50–100
	pit fill	50/221/[1808]	Rpot	50–100
Building 11	make-up	52/233/[1983]	Rpot	50–100
	make-up	52/234/[1931]	Rpot	60–100
Building 12	make-up	22/89/[878]	Rpot	70–100
	floor	22/89/[909]	Rpot	60–100
	make-up	22/89/[941]	Rpot	70–100
Building 13	occupation	49/214/[1789]	Rpot	70–100
	occupation	49/214/[1798]	coin	69–79
	make-up	49/215/[1838]	Rpot	70–100
	floor	54/243/[1758]	Rpot	70–100
	demolition	54/1106/[1716]	BM	70–120
	demolition	54/1106/[1705]	Rpot	70–100
Building 14	hearth	58/260/[1769]	Rpot	70–100
	posthole	58/260/[1806]	Rpot	70–100
	hearth	58/262/[1735]	Rpot	55–85
Building 15	dump	59/277/[1751]	Rpot	70–80
	floor	59/267/[1781]	Rpot	50–100
Building 16	floor	60/273/[1826]	Rpot	70–120
	occupation	60/273/[1827]	Rpot	70–160
	floor	60/273/[1828]	Rpot	90–160
Building 18	floor	139/639/[3795]	Rpot	70–100
	floor	130/644/[3793]	Rpot	70–160
	floor	133/622/[3250]	Rpot	70–100
Structure 2	floor	56/251/[1745]	Rpot	55–85
	occupation	56/254/[1623]	Rpot	50–100
			coin	69–79

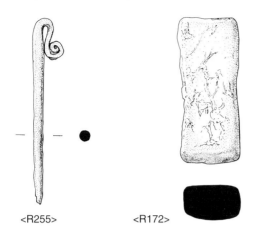

<R255>   <R172>

Fig 47 Copper alloy pin <R255> and stone hone <R172> from Building 11 (1:1)

Very little dating evidence was recovered so only a broad date of AD 60–100 was obtained (Table 10); however, the building certainly dates to the earlier part of that range. Like Building 9 to the north, this may have been merely a temporary structure built in the immediate aftermath of the Boudican fire to provide emergency shelter.

To the immediate north and south of this building was external occupation (OA12). This mainly consisted of dump layers although there were also traces of gravel surfaces. A small pit was provisionally interpreted as a cooking pit, but had traces of slag in it and may have had an industrial function. A line of postholes probably represented a fence line alongside the road but it only survived for a length of 2.0m.

Open Area 13, to the south of Building 11, consisted of a series of pits and other cut features and some desultory dumping (Fig 46). This open area ran to the east where Open Area 14 lay to the rear of the range of buildings. Here scrappy occupation included two external hearths and assorted post- and stakeholes as well as a cesspit (Fig 56).

The mineralised remains which were present in the environmental sample from the pit could have come from cess, floor covering, manure or any other circumstance in which mineralisation could occur. It needs to be stressed here that mineralised remains in the Borough High Street samples are rare. Since the area excavated was close to the line of the rear walls of the buildings, it is likely that general cess disposal would have taken place further to the east, away from the immediate vicinity of the buildings.

From an external surface in this open area a pottery assemblage was recovered, which included a number of interesting vessels, some of which are partially complete. The only imported fine ware present is SAMLG. The dominant ware type is tempered wares, while jars are overwhelmingly the most common form type present.

Nine sherds belong to a small, buff-coloured amphora <P69> (Fig 48). The amphora has a slightly flaring beaded rim with three grooves below; sherds from a sharply carinated shoulder and one fragment of slender oval handle without a groove are present. The length of the neck cannot be reconstructed. The fabric is identical to the Baetican Dressel 20

and Haltern 70 fabric, suggesting a similar source. Two examples of L555 rims have also been noted in BAETE fabric from London and Colchester, although the majority of L555 amphorae from London originate from a south Gaulish source (Sealey and Tyers 1989; Davies et al 1994, 16). Typologically, <P69> has points of comparison with both L555 and H70 types but, importantly, also shows marked differences, in particular the beaded rim, carinated shoulder and shape of the handle. The shape of the neck is similar to a type known as Ver. 1908, which has a long neck in a continuous curve and trumpet-shaped mouth (Wilson 1984, 202, fig 80, no. 1908; Sealey in prep). However, the type specimen for Ver. 1908 has handles joining the body at some distance down the neck, whereas on <P69> the handles start much higher up on the neck, curving up under the rim. Another noted feature of Ver. 1908 is an off-white slip on the surface, which is not apparent on <P69>.

Further, and more complete, examples are required before this amphora type can be clarified, but the typological differences are sufficiently marked that <P69> cannot be suitably fitted into the L555, H70 or Ver. 1908 amphorae types, and suggest that it should be regarded as a separate form also being produced in the Guadalquivir region.

The ECCW collared flagon <P70> (Fig 48) is a poorly made vessel, with an ill-defined collar and warped upper edge. Although possibly classed as a second, the vessel would function adequately and was probably still sold. Comparable vessels from kiln waste at Eccles are dated before AD 65 and groups from the City confirm that Eccles ware is largely confined to the pre-Flavian period (Detsicas 1977, 29; Davies et al 1994).

A large storage jar <P71> (not illustrated) is similar to examples from Colchester dated to the 1st and earlier 2nd centuries (Symonds and Wade 1999, 447–53). The reduced COAR fabric is very hard-fired with a surface densely pitted with voids, the shape of which suggests that the fabric was coarsely tempered with organic matter, probably straw or grass.

A SAND bead-rimmed jar <P72> (Fig 48) was recovered which has an offset shoulder and two zones of burnished decoration. The vessel has darkened surfaces due to burning, but retains an oxidised internal surface and rim. The rim is burnished to the shoulder and raised cordon. Two zones of decoration cover the upper part of the vessel separated by grooved lines. The upper zone has groups of three vertical lines and the second zone has single oblique lines.

A FMIC beaker <P73> (Fig 48) with everted rim and grooved cordons defining zones of rouletted decoration on the body is very similar to a published example from Exeter, which is classified as 'late imitation Terra Nigra'. The Exeter beakers are part of a group of vessel types thought to be local products imitating terra nigra forms and surface treatment; the beakers in particular are paralleled by products of kilns in Gallia Belgica. In Exeter the ware is most common in the late 1st-century levels and a similar date seems appropriate for <P73> (Holbrook and Bidwell 1991). Other industries producing FMIC wares, for example Upchurch, are also known to copy Gallo-Belgic type forms, and these have previously been identified in London (Davies et al 1994, 160–1, fig 139, no. 894).

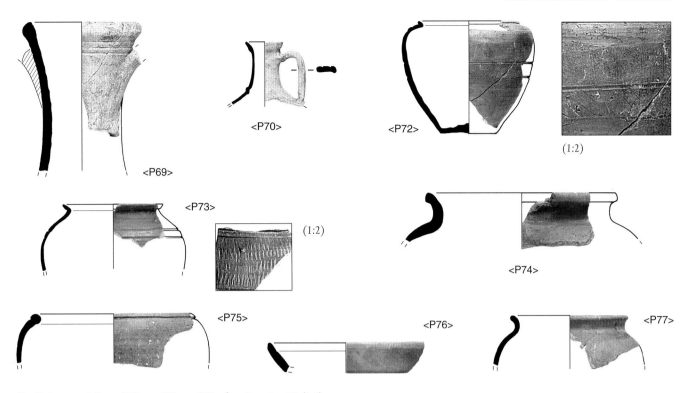

Fig 48 Pottery <P69>–<P70>, <P72>–<P77> from Open Area 18 (1:4)

DATING

The assemblage stratigraphically post-dates a fire horizon believed to be the Boudican fire of AD 60/1 (see Chapter 5). The composition of the assemblage suggests that it dates to the late Neronian to early Flavian period (c AD 60/5–75), which implies that activity was resumed in this area of the site within a few years following the conflagration.

Evidence for changes in activity in the immediate post-Boudican period

The finds groups from the relevant levels are too small to ascribe a function to specific buildings. The only immediately noticeable difference lies in the quality and preservation of the overall assemblage and in the relative scarcity of imported goods. For example, four copper alloy brooches from Open Area 14 are fragmentary examples of native British types which superseded the Aucissas and other imports in the second half of the 1st century, but they represent the continuation of the same Romanised style of dress. The basic paraphernalia of material culture remained the same, but the assemblages lack the more exotic imports that were a feature of the earlier groups.

Flavian reconstruction and development AD 70–100

Building 13

Around AD 70 the rather haphazard activity was replaced by a more formal approach to the post-fire reconstruction. A large masonry building, Building 13, was constructed at the north end of the site although the west frontage had been entirely

removed by the Battlebridge sewer. The south wall, measuring 6.0m, continued to the east of the excavation. Its foundations were of unworked ragstone and were 0.6m deep, indicating the need to support a substantial building. The surviving superstructure consisted of rough worked ragstone and tiles with random coursing. It stood 0.9m high above ground level and had traces of render on its north (internal) face. A north–south wall 1.75m long butted up against the south wall at the eastern edge of excavation and represented an internal partition wall (Fig 49). This wall continued to the north of the excavation, where a continuation of this building was recorded in BSE94 (BSE94 B3). Here a north–south ragstone wall 3.0m long (Fig 50) was recorded which continued to the north and south of the limits of excavation. This was 3.5m to the east of the north–south internal wall on BGH95 and parallel to it. There was also an east–west wall 1.7m long butting up to the wall on BSE94 and continuing to the west towards BGH95. By extrapolating these walls it is possible to build up a plan of a range of rooms. About 4.0m further north the foundations of another east–west masonry wall were recorded on JSS92 (JSS92 B2) with a parallel stub of wall a further 3.0m to the north. Both fragments were less than 1.0m long with unworked ragstone foundations 0.6m deep and 0.2m deep (truncated) respectively. The southern wall fragment had a rough worked ragstone superstructure surviving 0.5m high. Given that it is clear that Building 13 continued to the north, and the JSS92 fragments were of similar construction, it may be that these walls were also part of the same building. This suggests that there was one large masonry building with a frontage at least 14.0m long occupying the eastern side of the main road from the late 1st century onwards. Internally the floors of the building were plain brickearth, and there was no evidence for what functions were carried out within the rooms.

Fig 49 View of internal wall of Building 13

Fig 50 View of masonry wall of Building 13 from BSE94

DATING OF CONSTRUCTION OF BUILDING 13

An assemblage of 180 sherds (78 rows) was recovered from make-up layers for the construction of Building 13 (Table 10). The assemblage dates the construction and earliest use of Building 13 to the early Flavian period. There is no HWC present, a common indicator of a date of AD 70 or later, but HWB comprises 11.7% of the assemblage by sherd count (21 sherds/10 rows). VRW is also well represented, accounting for 17.2% by sherd count (31 sherds/10 rows). Amphorae comprise 31.7% by sherd count, with BAETE the dominant type present, accounting for 84.2% of all amphorae (48 sherds/5 rows). SAMLG (27 sherds/19 rows) and one sherd of MLEZ are the only imported fine wares.

Forms indicative of an early Flavian date include a ring-necked flagon (1B3), a Dechelette 67 beaker with barbotine decoration (3DE67) and a Drag. 33a cup (6DR33), although it must be noted that all of these vessels are only represented by a single sherd.

The pottery from the later part of the first phase of occupation formed an assemblage of 52 sherds (29 rows). This was recovered from contexts assigned to the use/disuse of Building 13 phase 1. In terms of composition, the assemblage is similar to the construction phase discussed above, but with some slight changes in proportions. Despite the small size of the assemblage, it is worth noting that HWC appears in this phase and that the quantity of HWB has declined (2 sherds/1 row). The amount of AHSU has risen and now represents 17.3% of the assemblage by sherd count, as opposed to 3.3% in the earlier construction phase. Therefore the end of phase 1 of Building 13 has been dated to AD 75–80+.

Despite the small number of sherds involved, the relative proportions of reduced wares are comparable to the pattern identified in the assemblages from periods 2, 3 and 4–5 at Leadenhall Court, which were examined in detail to refine the chronology of RCP2. It was concluded that the changing proportions of the reduced fabrics AHSU, HWB and HWC can be used as chronological indicators for the later 1st century. HWB was most common in period 2 (AD 65–70+), declining

over time in favour of AHSU and HWC. AHSU became increasingly common throughout the later 1st century and was the dominant reduced ware by period 4–5 (AD 85–95). HWC was present in small quantities from period 2 and had overtaken HWB by period 4–5 (Groves 1993, 123). Clearly these trends still require further validation from other quantified assemblages, but the comparable development observed with the qualitative data from Building 13 suggests that these trends are apparent in other Flavian assemblages.

FUNCTION OF BUILDING 13

The presence of such a large masonry building alongside the main road raises the question as to its function. It does not appear to be of high status, for the floors were generally of low quality brickearth and the finds of a utilitarian nature. It is unlikely to have been a private residence as this would have been located further away from the bustle of the main road, particularly since at this period there was no shortage of vacant land in Southwark. Moreover, a high-status building would be unlikely to have a blacksmith's immediately adjacent to it; this too would have been located away from the building. However, the building continued in use for some time, and around AD 120 a covered walkway was constructed along its roadside frontage and continued to the south, perhaps suggesting a more communal use for the building (see Chapter 8). One possible function could be that of a customs house, where tolls could be collected on goods entering the city. Another interpretation could be that of a market hall or *macellum*. The layout, particularly in the 2nd century, when the colonnade was added, is not dissimilar to that of a building at Cirencester (Wacher 1995, 64), although the Borough High Street building is very fragmentary. The location of the building, alongside the main road, would be a suitable one for such a building, and it is reasonable to assume that a settlement such as that in north Southwark would have had a centrally located local market to supplement the Forum north of the river. However, a purely domestic function cannot be ruled out, particularly in this early phase of the building.

Open Area 15 and Structures 1–2

To the west of Building 13 there was now an open area between the building and the main road (OA15) that consisted of compacted gravel surfaces (Fig 51). This sequence of gravel surfaces was also recorded to the north in JSS92 (JSS92 OA5). This would have formed a 'pavement' alongside the road for pedestrians to walk safely without going onto the road itself. A series of large postholes cutting one of the gravel surfaces may mark the introduction of a timber shelter, a precursor of later masonry structures along the road. Also noted was burnt and vitrified material which may be associated with the smithing activities taking place nearby.

The presence of a roadside drain, possibly a box-drain, is inferred from a linear feature robbed out in the early part of the 2nd century (see Chapter 7) so it is shown as being in use in this period.

A small circular structure, Structure 1, was constructed in front of Building 13, though later truncation cut away half of it. A semicircle of postholes with a diameter of *c* 2.5m enclosed a fine gravel floor. No walls were recorded but a midden or refuse dump formed a circle around the line of the posts,

indicating that there was a barrier to this layer. The dump provided a date of AD 60–70, though it is likely that the date is nearer the latter end of the range. There was no evidence at all from the floor to give any indication as to the function of the structure, though several almost complete pots were recovered from the surrounding layer. Included in the assemblage are two partially complete ERMS jars and carinated sherds of HOO ware, probably from a beaker or cup. In addition an enigmatic copper alloy object has been tentatively interpreted as a figurine; the cast fragment of copper alloy sheeting <R236> (Fig 52) has a ridged surface on one side, which could represent stylised drapery.

Overall it is not possible to be definite about the function of this small structure, but if the interpretation of a figurine is correct then a roadside shrine could be a possibility. In any case, it was not in use for long before being sealed by a gravel surface. Why the structure should have been in use for such a short period, particularly if it was a shrine, is not clear.

Abutting the south wall of Building 13 was Structure 2, a blacksmith's workshop, measuring at least 5.0m north–south by 5.8m east–west. The south side of the structure was confused by truncation caused by a Battlebridge sewer feeder trench. The first phase was a rather flimsy structure, possibly a lean-to attached to the south wall of the building. Sim (in Hammer in prep) outlines the requirements for smithing, which include good ventilation and subdued lighting. Thus it can be surmised that this early structure would have been open, possibly to the west where no evidence of a wall has been found. However, it would have had a roof to provide protection for the fire and create the necessary lighting environment for the blacksmith to determine the heat of the iron.

Two hearths cut a compacted brickearth floor, both surrounded by build-ups of ash and, crucially, hammerscale. One was aligned east–west and measured *c* 1.05m x 0.57m with a rake-out area to the west. This hearth was bowl-shaped, up to 0.24m deep and was lined with clay. The other hearth was heavily truncated and only survived as a semicircular bowl 0.35m in diameter which was also lined with clay. The floor

Fig 51 *View of gravel surface in Open Area 15*

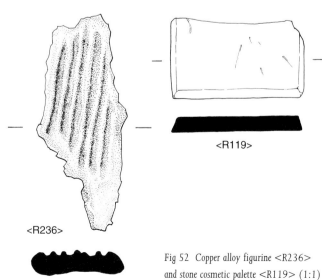

<R119>

<R236>

Fig 52 *Copper alloy figurine <R236>*
and stone cosmetic palette <R119> (1:1)

had a series of lenses of industrial deposits and charcoal. However, there are no iron finds of significance from the earlier phases of the smithy and its surrounding area, and indeed very little ironwork from any phase – a fact which is unsurprising, given the extensive corrosion of much of the ironwork and the practice of recycling and reworking the metal. Indeed the only iron objects, as opposed to nails, were found in the latest phase, where four unidentifiable fragments were associated with smithing waste within the building. In the construction and occupation levels were several fragments of lead waste, including sheet lead and an offcut. These could be associated with metalworking but could equally be structural debris, and there are no obvious concentrations. There will be a fuller discussion of smithing in Chapter 8.

Iron smithing produces micro-slags (hammerscale) of two types: flake and spheroidal. Flake resembles silvery fish scales and is the product of the ordinary hot working and hammering of a piece of iron where fragments of the oxide/silicate skin flake off from the iron and fall to the ground. Spheroidal are small solid droplets of liquid slag expelled from within the iron during the primary smithing of a bloom or the fire welding of two pieces of iron. Hammerscale is not visible to the naked eye when in the soil but is highly diagnostic of smithing activity, often remaining in the area around the anvil and near the hearth when macro-slags have been cleared out of the smithy and dumped elsewhere. Since it is generally highly magnetic, its detection with a magnet while excavating can allow the spatial relationship of the anvil to the hearth to be recorded and can pinpoint the smithing activity more precisely (Mills and McDonnell 1992).

Building 14

Building 14 (Fig 56) was either a new building on the same site or a secondary phase of Building 10. It was not quite on the same alignment, its north wall being further north, partially over Open Area 11. The south wall of the building has been tentatively identified by a beamslot 5.0m to the south, but this was separated from the rest of the building by later truncation. A timber shadow indicated that the building had a plank floor. However, towards the south was a hearth in a shallow cut surrounded by ash, suggesting that not the whole floor was wooden. The hearth contained a reasonable amount of animal bone, but overall the building did not contain anything like the quantity of bone yielded by Building 10. It remains possible, however, that this building continued in use as a butcher's shop, with bone now being disposed of off-site, possibly to the rear of the building. Alternatively, the butcher may have moved to Building 13 to the north.

Buildings 15 and 16

A narrow gravel path or alley, Alley 3, just over 1.0m wide and running east–west, divided Building 14 from Building 15. The surviving stretch was only 3.0m long and was not traced to the west of the Battlebridge sewer, though clearly it would have joined the gravelled area in front of the buildings. A coin of Vespasian dated to AD 71 was found on the path.

Just to the south of the path was Building 15 (Fig 56). The north wall was formed by a timber sillbeam, which survived for a length of 3.5m. An east west slot with a line of stakeholes associated with it may form the southern wall of the building c 6.5m to the south of the north wall. An internal wall running east–west was formed by a brickearth sill just under 3.0m long with a line of stakeholes in it, dividing the building into two rooms. The floors of the building were of brickearth and there was a series of internal features including a storage pit. A large cylindrical lead weight with an iron suspension loop was found on the floor of the building. The suspension loop makes it likely that it was used on a steelyard and its size, at a weight of 1054g (approximately 3.5 Roman pounds), suggests that it may have been for commercial rather than domestic use. There are, however, no other finds from the building that could indicate its function, although part of a stone cosmetic palette <R119> (Fig 52) was also recovered. Associated with the building was a well. Normally one might expect this to be in a yard or open area but it is directly south of the north wall of the building. Wells were not normally placed inside but, given that the building did not appear to continue to the west of the well, it is possible that the well was in a shelter or well house in front of the main part of the building. Alternatively, the well may have been an internal feature of the building as another similar well was located in Building 18 to the south.

To the south, between Building 15 and Building 16, was Open Area 16, which was c 2.8m wide though truncated. There was an external hearth with a tile base in this area. Whilst not an alley, it would have given access to Open Area 14 to the rear of the buildings.

Further to the south were several floors and occupation layers representing Building 16, including a timber plank floor (Fig 53). Only one possible beamslot was recorded. The greatest extent of the building as recorded was 2.5m x 2.0m. No south wall of the building was found because of later truncation but a ditch or gully to the south was clearly external. A fragment of gravel surface may represent an east–west alley but this could not be confirmed in this period.

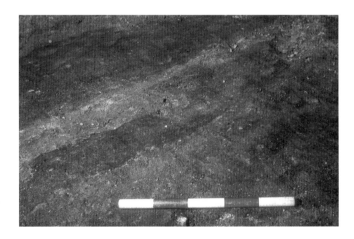

Fig 53 Detail of burnt floorboards in Building 16

Building 17 and Building 15 demolition dump

To the rear of the buildings Open Area 14 continued though now with two small external hearths in it. Neither were particularly large or contained anything to suggest that they were anything other than domestic in nature. To the east, a thin strip of clay and timber building was recorded on the east side of a north–south ditch. The ditch was 1.5m wide and was traced for 3.0m but presumably ran considerably further. The building, Building 17, consisted of a north–south robbed out beamslot with internal occupation to the east for 0.5–1.0m before the limit of excavation was reached. The ditch, which was retained in use and re-cut in later periods, would appear to be a property boundary marking the division between the roadside properties and the next block of properties extending to the east. Building 15 does not appear to have been occupied for long, and went out of use and was sealed by a large dump before the end of the 1st century. This dump contained a large quantity of pottery.

The quantified assemblage from the dump totals 266 sherds, 10,426g and 4.64 EVEs. The assemblage is dated AD 70–80 and is associated with a coin dated AD 64–5.

One of the latest elements in this context is a LOEG bowl <P78> (Fig 54) with a curved flange and slight bead, which falls within Marsh form type 34 (Marsh 1978, 166). Marsh proposes a date of c AD 90–130 for this fabric, although assemblages from the City have shown LOEG to first appear in late Neronian to early Flavian deposits (RCP1B), increasing into the Trajanic and Hadrianic periods (Marsh 1978, 199; Davies et al 1994, 146).

Other vessels of interest include a lid with a reddish-orange slip both internally and externally <P79> (Fig 54). The fabric has similarities to PRW3, being highly micaceous, but is not fine and soft. The slip is also different from classic PRW3, being thicker and denser on both surfaces. The lid form is very typical of the PRW repertoire with the distinctive concentric grooves on the upper surface.

Part of a coarse ware stamp is present on the base of a dish <P80> (Fig 54). The stamp is missing with the exception of the outline and the very corner of the initial character. A single notched wreath encircles the central stamp. The fabric has a white core and reduced mid grey surfaces, while the underside surface has discoloured to a pale orange colour. The main inclusions are well-sorted clear quartz up to 0.5mm with occasional white mica. No other inclusions are visible in the hand sample.

The source of this sherd is still questionable. The fabric bears strong similarities to Verulamium Grey ware (VRG) in both colour and inclusions. However, the stamping of non-mortaria forms is not common practice in this industry, although there are records of two RDBK vessels with stamps (Davies et al 1994, 165).

Alice Holt/Surrey products are well represented by <P81>–<P84> (Fig 54). Slightly more uncommon forms recorded include the top of a butt beaker or narrow-necked flask with tall narrowing neck and hint of a cordon <P83>.

A straight-sided dish <P84> with a single groove may be a variant example of a Surrey or Atrebatic bowl (4K).

Another example of a SAND imitation Gallo-Belgic dish <P85> (Fig 54) was recovered. The vessel has a smooth external profile and one poorly executed groove on the exterior, which runs parallel with the internal moulding. The plate is a poor imitation of Cam. form 12 (Thompson type G1-7). The fabric is dark grey throughout with moderately well-sorted medium quartz and the surfaces have obvious burnishing marks.

A flat-based, straight-sided dish with a flaring, everted rim <P86> (not illustrated) has burnished vertical lines on the exterior and a highly burnished surface on the interior of the rim. The rim itself is poorly finished. This vessel may be seen as a crude attempt to imitate the samian bowl form Drag. 29, with the carination at the rim. Dish <P86> has some similarities to a certain ERMS bowl (Davies et al 1994, 92, fig 77, no. 470). The fabric of <P86> is very similar to ERMS, with ill-sorted quartz, burnt organics and mica, which is most visible on the surface. The burnished vertical lines are also reminiscent of the decoration on ERMS vessels.

The Highgate Wood B ware vessels are common types from this industry (Brown and Sheldon 1974). The Building 15 dump included a cordoned necked jar, a storage jar with everted rim and incised decoration, and a flat-rimmed bowl <P87>–<P89> (Fig 54). The bowl is Southwark type 4F1, which is dated to the Flavian period. A SESH lid <P90> (Fig 54) is also present, which is an unusual form for this fabric.

A BAETE H70 amphora <P91> (Fig 54) has a distinctive collar rim, and the short length of handle remaining suggests a slender oval handle. There is no evidence of the deep groove commonly found on H70 amphorae, but the handle has broken off, possibly at a point before which this would be apparent. This vessel is similar, both typologically and in size, to a published example from Leadenhall Court (Davies et al 1994, 12, fig 4, no. 4). In the City, Haltern 70 is recovered from the earliest levels and dated from the 1st to early 2nd centuries.

Building 18

The evidence for the construction of buildings of the second settlement was again fragmentary at the southern end of the site. At least four separate buildings were identified. The buildings retained their previous form and construction style, and were identifiable as narrow strip buildings of clay and timber with clay or gravel floors. The burnt clay and timber buildings were replaced by similar structures. On the western side the small area of surviving stratigraphy south of Bedale Street did include structural evidence for rebuilding following the events of AD 61. The fragmentary remains were replaced by Building 18. A cleared area or open space may have existed as a result of the demolition of the earlier building. The pit and ditch representing this brief period could well have been associated with the use of Building 18.

The eastern part of the building lay directly beneath the suspended services running parallel with the eastern limit of excavation, making excavation and interpretation difficult. The

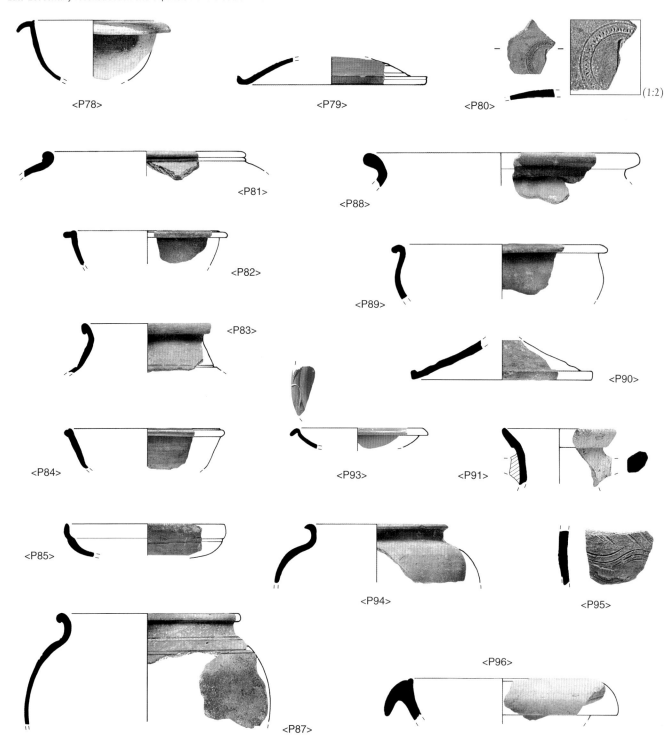

Fig 54 Pottery <P78>–<P85>, <P87>–<P91>, <P93>–<P96> from Building 15 demolition (1:4)

building had an east–west wall at least 2.9m long. Compacted yellow clay formed the foundation of the wall with evidence for several stakeholds within it. This wall was partially truncated and did not extend further westwards, and may have been the northern side of the building.

The western limit of the building was truncated by the latest phase of roadside drains, which represented the approximate line of street frontage for this building. Here a west–east slot 1.35m long and at least 0.6m wide had two

postholes inserted into its base. This slot, with a truncated north–south length of 1.7m, held timber baseplates for walls. An area of sandy gravel 3.8m long and 1.4m wide acted as a make-up deposit for a compacted clay floor. The floor had been subject to slumping on the northern and western edges. In these areas additional clay surfaces were recorded. The later floor repairs were covered with a layer of occupation debris containing tile fragments. This layer was used as a make-up deposit for a further clay floor.

A sequence of repairs and a new floor were constructed within Building 18, and part of the building may have been rebuilt. The earlier building may have been redesigned, with make-up deposit incorporating reused material from a higher quality building, including an *opus spicatum* brick and a tegula with *opus signinum* mortar adhering. The relaid floor contained several fragments of worn brick, which is likely to have formed the floor surface, and included a worn fragment of calcareous clay of the type known as septarian nodule or septaria.

A well with a square construction cut, but a circular shaft, was constructed within the footprint of the building against the southern wall. Later surfaces laid around the well may indicate that it was sunk inside the building, although by the date of construction the eastern 'room' may have been partially open to a rear yard area, as with Building 20. The well shaft could have been in the form of a reused barrel, though no organic evidence survived to indicate the exact construction. The well was dug approximately 0.5m into natural sands.

Building 19

To the south of Building 18, and immediately adjoining it, was Building 19. A narrow, 0.1m wide, slot or groove ran north–south for 1.2m. The southern end and its direct relationship with the northern wall were lost, but this was probably a setting for a partition or internal division within the building. A 0.6m diameter posthole at the northern end of the internal partition held a supporting vertical post for that setting. The posthole included evidence for a rectangular post pipe measuring 100mm x 50mm. Clay floor levels and lenses of occupation debris were present to the west of the partition, whilst within the eastern room occupation layers occurred with no fragments of floor. Structural features and the internal deposits slumped into earlier features and towards the tunnelled feeder sewer.

A sillbeam was probably set in a narrow, 1.4m long and 0.3m wide, east–west slot. This may have created an internal division or partition. If so, in the room or corridor to the south a shallow pit was dug. This 0.15m deep pit contained a large quantity of charcoal and charred remains, but it was greatly truncated and it is not possible to attribute a clear function.

The building continued in use during the later part of the 1st century AD. A line of shallow postholes was set in the earlier floor and a well-compacted clay floor with mortar patches was laid over occupation debris. A small hearth occurred to the north with a shallow oval scoop showing evidence of *in situ* burning.

The construction of a narrow alley or pathway, Alley 4, to the south of Building 19 was similar to other small lanes on the site: a shallow cut with a sand 'foundation' covered with gravel. It ran between Buildings 19 and 20 for 6.7m and was truncated to the west by the Battlebridge sewer and by modern intrusions to the east. The alley was approximately 2.0m wide, with limited evidence for an associated ditch or drain on its north side. It appeared to be relatively short-lived and was soon encroached on by new buildings.

To the south of the alley, gravel surfaces totalling 4.3m in width were truncated by a west–east feeder sewer, but these appear to have been laid down over the demolition layer Open Area 11 and form a yard area, Open Area 17.

At the western limit of this surviving area, well B was constructed. A roughly square construction pit was cut through the gravel and into the natural sand down to 0.3m OD. The construction pit was 1.65m wide and was truncated to the west by the effects of tunnelling carried out to insert extensive modern services. The well included no organic survival, but probably originally incorporated a timber frame (see Chapter 8).

This area may be indicative of the reorganisation of the settlement, which may have included the extension or realignment of buildings, but many areas continue to exhibit the same land use and function as before.

Building 20

To the south of Open Area 17 two foundation beamslots formed the northern wall of Building 20. The fragmentary remains indicate a multiple-roomed strip building, although the western end – the frontage of the building – was truncated. A short north–south slot may represent part of the eastern end of Building 20. The 2.3m long slot possibly formed an internal division and had three posthole settings within it. The southern post may have been part of a door fitting. The northern slot survived as a 1.5m length of upstanding clay wall foundation, while the second slot showed evidence for the robbing of the timber sillbeam.

Several areas of internal floor surfaces survived, but these were truncated by modern intrusions. The floors were constructed with broken amphora, reused roof tile, floor tile, and several reused high-status items, amongst which were fragments of marble slab, including Purbeck marble <1494> and Carrara marble <1533>, and a fragment of pink mudstone which has been identified as probably originating in the Mediterranean area, and probably came from an *opus sectile* tile. A third piece of exotic stone, an unidentified white marble with grey veining <1507>, was found in occupation deposits. The slab, which retains one original edge, had been re-cut and reused at least twice. It may originally have been used as wall veneer, but the degree of wear shows that it was subsequently used for paving.

A tile hearth was located centrally within the building. The rectangular hearth was composed of tiles approximately 0.3m by 0.42m in size. A fragment of lava quernstone <R136> (Fig 55) was recovered from the top of the hearth. This upper stone fragment was very worn.

The hearth contained two hearth bricks in the Radlett fabric (fabric 3060). Much of the residual brick and tile incorporated into this building showed the effects of burning (not unusual in Roman London). Other high-status materials, unlikely to be in their primary contexts, were an *opus spicatum* brick and a fragment of either scored wall tile or box-flue in the floor. The *opus spicatum* brick is the earliest in Eccles fabric from BGH95. Another context contained several pieces of brick, which had been reused as floor tiles, possibly in that room.

Additional clay floors and make-up deposits illustrate the continued occupation of the building, which was probably constructed fairly soon after the Boudican destruction.

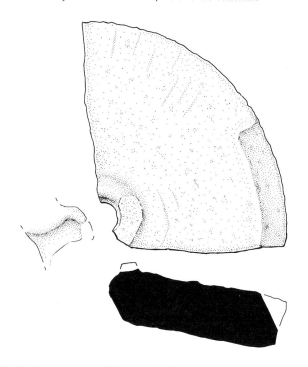

Fig 55 Lava quernstone <R136> from Building 20 (1:4)

DATING OF BUILDING 20

The total assemblage recovered from Building 20 amounts to 195 sherds (96 rows) and is dated to the early Flavian period *c* AD 70–5. The most diagnostic dating elements are a VRW ring-necked flagon (1B2) and the presence of HWC and LOMI, both of which also first appear in the City in RCP1B.

For imported fine wares both SAMLG and MLEZ are recorded. Also present is ITMO, a mortaria fabric rare in the City and occurring mainly in pre-Boudican levels or with later 1st- and early 2nd-century pottery (Davies et al 1994, 70).

Open Area 18 and Building 21

At the south-east end of the site, adjacent to 39 Borough High Street, in Open Area 18 (Fig 56), there was less obvious evidence of the extensive destruction of the settlement. This was particularly so in the area containing two hearths or ovens, and may be due to the presence of large quantities of industrial and hearth rake-out deposits. As a consequence of the burnt nature of these deposits the general destruction debris was not readily distinguished.

Two fire pits or hearths (not shown) were constructed in Open Area 18, which retained very similar characteristics to Open Area 9. An oval, bowl-shaped fire pit 1.15m long and 1.0m wide had several tile fragments set into the sides as a lining. Five small stakeholes may be associated with the hearth, though it was not clear whether these were part of the construction of the hearth; they may have formed part of a superstructure or a dividing screen. This was replaced by a 0.2m deep hearth, of similar proportions to the earlier fire pit. Layers of ash, burnt clay and sand occurred around the hearths. This material was most likely the debris removed directly from the hearths during or after firing and distributed in the

immediate area. Several fragmentary areas of compacted clay may have been remnants of attempts to cover these rake-out deposits with a temporary working surface. There was no particular evidence to suggest metalworking having been carried out around these hearths.

At the southern limit of the site and immediately west of Open Area 18 fragmentary remains of Building 21 survived. Building 21 was again of timber-framed construction. It was truncated to the west by modern basements, but a 3.3m long foundation trench may mark the southern wall of the building. An internal area of some 2.0m x 2.0m of occupation deposits was associated with it. The building was destroyed as a result of extensive fire damage. This has preserved the carbonised remains of at least four planks with the remains of a beam beneath them, proving that one room at least had a wooden floor-boarded floor. A mixture of barley (*Hordeum* spp) and wheat (*Triticum* spp) grains, very little chaff (just a few straw fragments) and charred remains of spike-rush, goosefoot (*Chenopodium* sp) and dock were found with the charred wood fragments. These may be the result of fine sieving, and residues may have been used as tinder.

Details of the eastern end of the building were not preserved, but it backed onto Open Area 18. It is indeed possible that the limited remains of Building 21 may, with Building 20, form a more complex building arranged around Open Area 18. However, the fragmentary nature of the two structures does not provide clear evidence for the exact extent or morphology of the buildings. The most probable interpretation suggests that the buildings conform to the pattern of the rest of the street and form parts of strip buildings.

Open Area 19

To the rear of Buildings 20 and 21 there remained a yard or area of rough ground, Open Area 19. The exact limit of the buildings and therefore the full extent of the open area was not certain, as much of the eastern part of the site was truncated by post-medieval cellars and late medieval cut features. This effectively removed the evidence for the rear of the buildings in this area. The dumping of domestic debris may have continued, but no well-defined features survived.

At the eastern limit of the site a square timber-lined well D occurred some 11m to the rear of the buildings. The upper part of the well was truncated by a later ditch, but showed evidence of a roughly oval construction cut into which was inserted the square wooden frame. A single fragment of an oak post included a vertical groove in each of two faces. These might have held horizontal planks in place to form a loose-fitting frame. Two fragmentary horizontal planks did survive and showed evidence of chamfering. No dates could be recovered from the elements of the frame. The well was cut into natural and redeposited sand, to a depth of approximately −0.3m OD.

The open area may have been crossed by a ditch which was identified in BUG94 and may be a continuation of the ditch in Open Area 14. No evidence of the ditch survived in the eastern area, having been removed by later truncation.

STU92 and BTJ93

Further south at STU92 and BTJ93 the pre-Boudican buildings and building plots continued to be redeveloped (Fig 57). On the western side of the road clay and amphorae fragments were deliberately laid down in a consolidation process or as a distinct floor surface. Above this deposit another compact, 0.1m thick floor was constructed by using sherds of amphorae and clay.

The only structural remains associated with the surface were two postholes. These may form elements of STU92 Building 2, as truncation might have caused the removal of additional posts and walls. The evidence does not suggest a very substantial building, although these remains may represent only a small part of the original structure.

A clay floor was laid over the eastern side of the site. This covered areas of slumping in the previous floor and accumulated occupation silts. No structural remains were identified as being associated with this internal surface.

STU92 Building 2 was constructed after the Boudican fire, but continued to have floors laid with large quantities of BAETE amphorae. Very little other pottery is associated with Building 2, with a total of only 60 sherds recovered. The fabrics present date from the late Neronian to early Flavian period, and the continued practice of laying amphorae sherds as flooring might suggest that the building continued under the same ownership and retained the same function as before the fire, and that rebuilding occurred fairly promptly.

Buildings were also reconstructed at BTJ93 during this period on the recently levelled ground and the demolition layer from the previous building. An area of clay floor and fragmentary remains of an amphorae sherd floor surface were divided by a single wall. These may be two rooms of the same building, BTJ93 Building 2.

These floors sometimes incorporated other tile fragments. The reuse of amphorae is a common feature of several sequences of buildings at STU92, BTJ93 and BGH95, where sherds form parts of internal floors. The reuse of amphorae sherds in this fashion has been identified before. These hard-wearing surfaces may have been used in connection with industrial activities at STU92 and BGH95, where slag and burnt debris have been found in association.

The frequent reuse of amphorae sherds as floors and packing material in many period 2 buildings may be indicative of the ready availability of those goods associated with amphorae in a domestic or retail context within the settlement at this time. The presence of these commodities at this time should not be a surprise given the intensity of activity in the settlement. The amphorae themselves may not have been reused intact before being put to use as flooring.

Discussion

The pattern of reconstruction of the settlement generally reflects that of the pre-Boudican one in many respects. The line of the road had become entrenched and did not change – no doubt because it remained the most direct route to the bridge. The cheaper, more readily available construction materials of timber and clay were used again despite the inherent risk of destruction by fire. The type of building and the functions carried out, where identifiable, also remained similar, for example the blacksmith's workshop. This indicates that the property was privately owned, so that the blacksmith could resume trade immediately after the Boudican fire on the same, that is, his, property. These decisions may reflect the nature of the population along the street and a primary desire for swiftly constructed, affordable properties from which small businesses could be conducted. There is no doubt that more 'desirable' building complexes, including public and private masonry buildings (Cowan 1992), were being planned and constructed elsewhere in the settlement.

The one exception was the masonry building at the north end of BGH95, where what might be Southwark's first *macellum* was established. With the growth of the settlement, it seems very likely that Londinium's southern suburb would have had its own market, rather than relying exclusively on the Forum on the north bank. The location, alongside the main road not far from the bridgehead, would also have been well situated for such a market hall.

The buildings were generally replaced, and the density of occupation and the industrial-based activity returned to its former level. There were, however, changes in layout and morphology of the roads and some buildings. Does this apparently organised rebuilding provide evidence of an administrative or organisational body? Is this a mercantile or craftsmen's guild arrangement, or does it reflect the central administrative body for Londinium encouraging such changes?

Flavian expansion of the settlement to the east of the main road

In the early years of the Roman occupation of Southwark the settlement was concentrated alongside the main road. Evidence for pre-Boudican occupation away from the main road is limited. Quarry pits close to the line of the main road have been found at Montague Close and in the District Heating Scheme (Graham 1988a). Revetments and ditches have been found in various places (Sheldon 1978) and these formed part of the early attempts to protect the islands from flooding and waterlogging. This process of protection and drainage was required, particularly at the peripheries of the eyots and prior to the construction of the first buildings. No buildings themselves have been found away from the line of the main road at this early period, before the Boudican fire.

The eastern half of the northern sand island does not appear to have been occupied until after the Boudican revolt at the earliest and probably not until AD 70 – rebuilding of the existing settlement, centred on Borough High Street, taking priority over expansion into new areas – both to the east and west of the main road.

The area under London Bridge Station was away from the main centre of the settlement, and appears to have been more marginal land (see Chapter 2) which would not have been taken into occupation until all the prime land was built on.

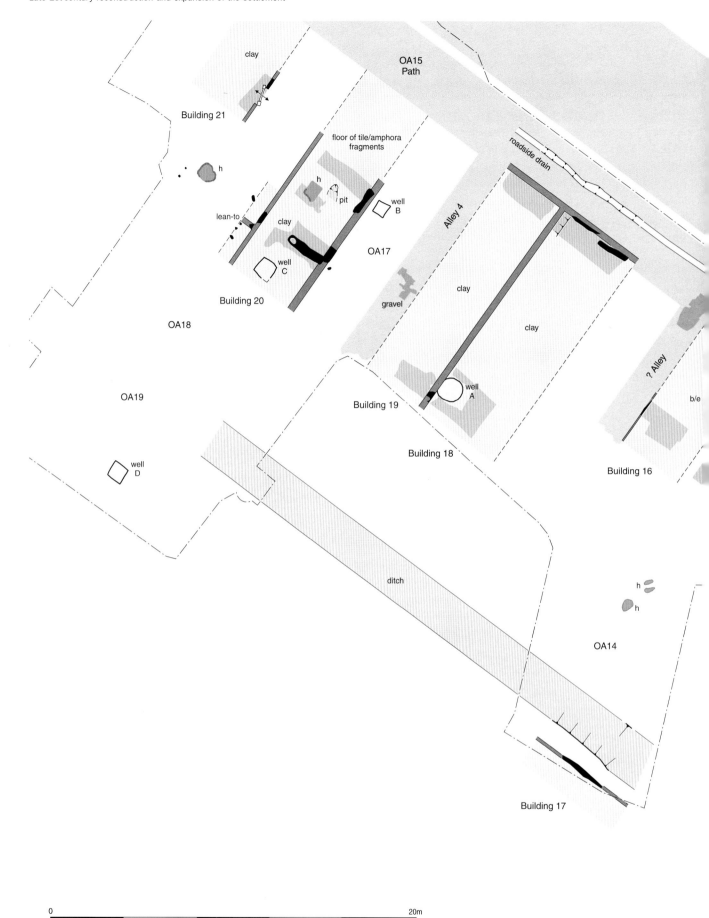

Fig 56 Plan of principal archaeological features, period 4

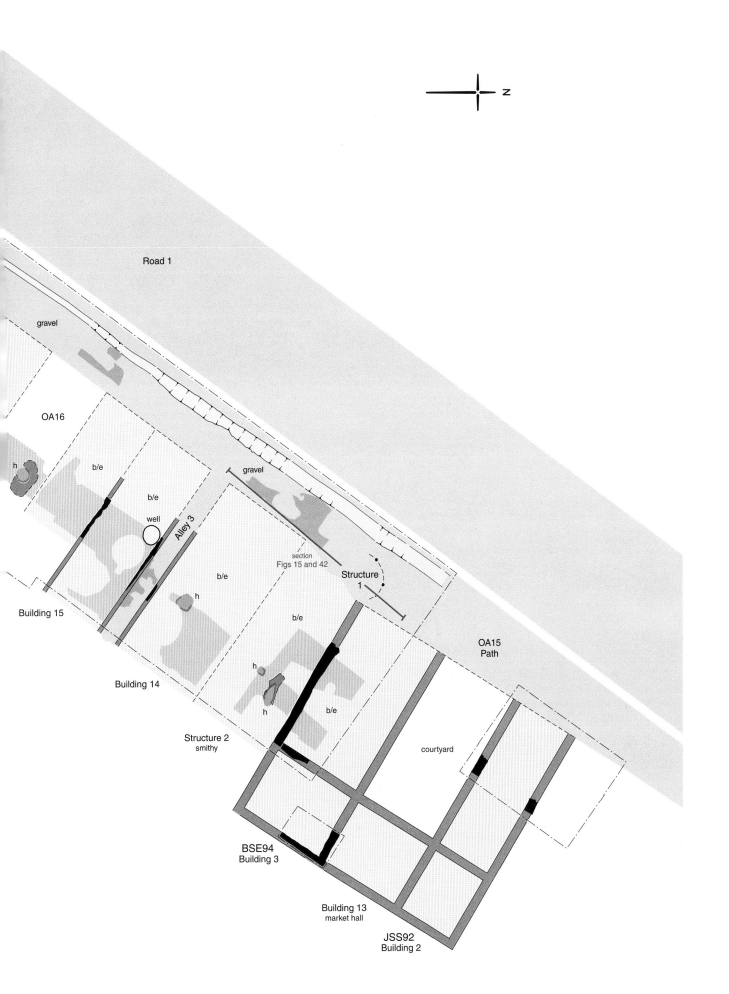

Road 1

gravel

OA16

h

b/e

b/e

well

Alley 3

b/e

h

Building 15

b/e

Building 14

h

h

Structure 2
smithy

b/e

gravel

section
Figs 15 and 42

Structure
1

OA15
Path

courtyard

BSE94
Building 3

Building 13
market hall

JSS92
Building 2

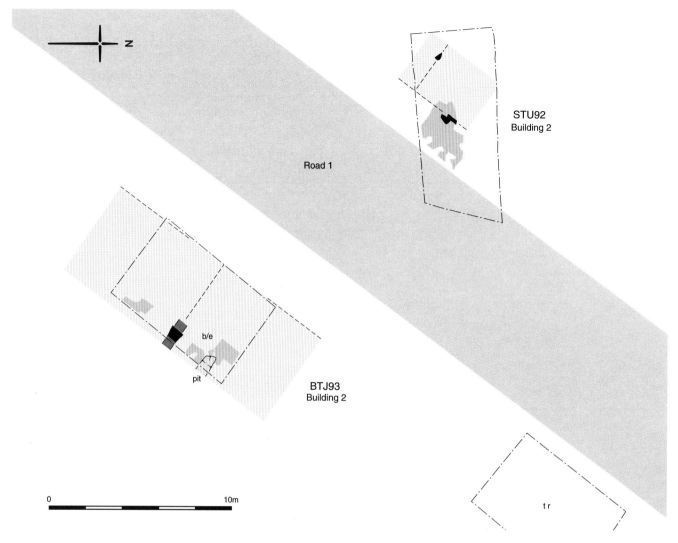

Fig 57 Plan of principal archaeological features, period 4: southern detail

LBI95 Open Area 3 and Building 1

The earliest activity in this area was evidence for gravel quarrying. This was recorded on LBI95 Open Area 3, consisting of a thick layer of sand that was probably left behind after the gravel was removed. This is 80m to the west of the main north–south road, and the quarrying may have been for a side road that has not yet been located. Since buildings appear in this area at this time, it is reasonable to assume that there was some form of access to them from the main road.

The dating suggests that this activity occurred in the period AD 50–70, though it is likely to have been in the latter part of the range and certainly after the Boudican revolt. A large quantity of amphorae was associated with this layer.

The assemblage has a total sherd count of 122, weighs 6877g and is dated c AD 50–70 on the absence of any fabrics or forms that post-date AD 70. The assemblage is unusual in being mostly comprised of amphorae, 71 sherds in total weighing 5946g (58.2% by sherd count and 86.5% by weight). As most of these are body sherds, all following comparisons are made by weight and sherd count rather than by EVEs. This group can be compared to assemblages in the City from the two Roman Ceramic Phases covered by the period, RCP1A

(c AD 50/5–60/1) and RCP1B (c AD 60/1–75). Amphorae represent 40% and 33% by weight respectively in these phases. Although imported wares are more common in pre-Boudican assemblages (Davies et al 1994, fig 143, 167), the figure for imported wares in Open Area 3 is exceptionally high at 78.7% by sherd count and 92.3% by weight. This is a result of the unusually high percentage of amphorae, which is greater than those from both corresponding RCPs (Table 11). Additionally, the types of amphorae that are present in Open Area 3 do not follow either pattern seen in the corresponding RCPs, where Dressel 20 (8DR20) is the dominant amphora form, representing over half the amphorae by weight. In RCP1A, in particular, the Dressel 20 represents almost 75% by weight of all amphorae in contrast to Open Area 3, where it represents just over 20%. The dominant amphora form in Open Area 3 is the London 555 (8L555), with at least three separate vessels identified during quantification; this type accounts for 43.7% by sherd count and 43.3% by weight. Although London 555 amphorae do occur in both RCP1A and RCP1B, their occurrence is so low as to be unquantifiable (ibid, 16, fig 8).

A small timber-framed structure, LBI95 Building 1 (Fig 58), was built in the western part of the site and may have been a

Table 11 *Percentages by sherd count and weight of amphorae from LBI95 Open Area 3*

Amph type	LBI95 OA3 % shds	LBI95 OA3 % wt	RCP1A % shds	RCP1B % wt
8L555	43.7	43.3	<1	<1
8C184	19.7	21.8	2.5*	<1*
8DR20	5.6	20.1	70	56
8G (PE47)	18.3	7.0	5	7.5
8DR2-4	7.1	5.5	8	13.5
8	5.6	2.3	-	-

* These figures relate to all amphorae in RHOD fabrics, which include not only Cam. 184 but also the rarer Dressel 43.

hut used by the workmen quarrying gravel. The building was represented by four postholes, a beamslot and a stakehole, and does not appear to have been very substantial. The beamslot was 3.9m long and 0.25m wide, and formed the southern wall of the building. Three postholes were up to 0.5m in diameter and 0.4–0.5m deep and formed an east–west alignment. The fourth posthole and the stakehole were not associated with any other feature, though the posthole may have been part of the west wall. The line of postholes was parallel to the beamslot and may have formed the north wall of the building. If it did, then the dimensions of the building would have been a minimum of 7.0m x 5.0m. There were no occupation levels associated with the building, but a demolition layer places the building no earlier than AD 70.

The building was truncated by a second phase of quarrying, LBI95 Open Area 4 (not shown). A large pit was only partially within the excavation but measured 3.4m x 3.1m x 1.2m deep. The pottery group from the pit in Open Area 4 is tentatively dated to *c* AD 70 based on the presence of two sherds of HWC,

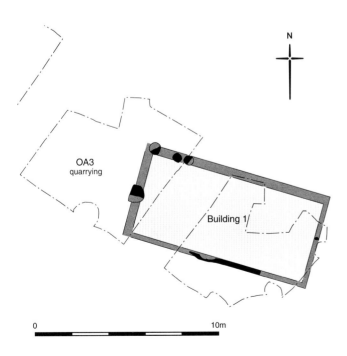

OA3
quarrying

Building 1

N

0   10m

Fig 58 Plan of LBI95 Building 1

a fabric which begins to appear in City assemblages around this date (Davies et al 1994, 82). Additionally, this pit cuts an external surface which contains a small sherd from a HWC beaker and other fabrics that are most common in the 1st century, such as HOO and ERSB. However, the pit group in Open Area 4 contains a high percentage of fabrics which dominate the pre-Flavian period, especially RCP1B assemblages, including HWB, GROG and ERMS. This pattern is also seen in the early jar types present such as bead-rimmed (2A) and necked round-bodied jars (2B) which again dominate RCP1B. Both the pit and surface contained ERSB, a fabric which, in the City, begins to appear in substantial quantities in the post-Boudican period (ibid 93, fig 78). The pit group also includes a Dressel 20 amphora with a rim that is dated *c* AD 50–70 (Peacock and Williams 1986, fig 66, no. 10). Overall the medium-sized assemblage from the pit suggests a late Neronian to early Flavian date.

Evidence of quarrying was also obtained from MSA92 to the east, where two intercutting quarry pits were recorded (MSA92 OA3). These pits could also have been for extracting gravel for an east–west road that has not yet been uncovered, probably further to the north. This quarrying is later than the quarrying that occurred alongside the main road to the west which was dated to *c* AD 55 (see Chapter 3).

LBI95 Building 2

Sometime shortly after AD 70 a large masonry building, LBI95 Building 2, was constructed (Fig 59). The alignment of this building was perpendicular to the main road to the west. Its distance from the road at a little over 60m suggests that a side road in the vicinity may be more directly dictating the alignment – perhaps built using the gravel from the earlier quarrying. A series of gravel surfaces, LBI95 Open Area 5, immediately to the north of the building, survived in too small an area (only 3.0m long by less than 0.5m wide) to be conclusively identified as a road, rather than a yard or other external surface.

Four rooms were identified in the building. Rooms A and B were separated from rooms C and D by the foundations of a Victorian railway arch. Room A was a minimum of 2.4m x 2.8m in area and had a brickearth floor with some repairs done to it. One floor was comprised of large quantities of amphorae sherds.

Room A produced a total of 127 sherds weighing 8293g and room B yielded 130 sherds weighing 5815g. The ceramic assemblages from the floors of rooms A and B of Building 2 contain high percentages of amphorae: 94% by weight and 71% by sherd count for room A, and 84% and 51% respectively for room B. The assemblage from room A is similar to the earlier assemblage from Open Area 3 in terms of the high percentage of London 555 amphorae, and there are numerous vessel and sherd links between these two pottery groups (Table 12). The percentages of amphorae from both rooms are unusually high when compared to early Flavian assemblages in the City (see above). One explanation for this high concentration of amphorae in the flooring levels of Building 2 and in Open Area 3 is that it had been used to raise and consolidate the ground level prior to and in the construction of Building 2. The deliberate selection

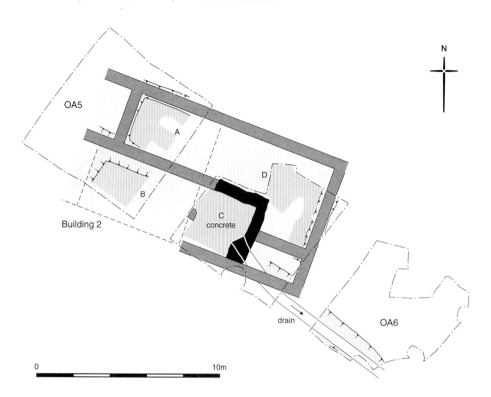

N

Fig 59 Plan of LBI95 Building 2

of amphora sherds (in particular body sherds) for this purpose is seen on several City sites including No. 1 Poultry (Rayner in prep) and Lloyd's Register of Shipping (Seeley, F in prep). The sherd links between the assemblages from the Building 2 construction levels and the stratigraphically earlier Open Area 3 rule out the possibility that the pottery is contemporary with the use of the building, and it therefore cannot be used in the interpretation of its function.

Room A is dated post-AD 70 by one sherd of HWC and room B is dated post-AD 60 by the presence of ERSB, although both these fabrics occur in rare instances before these dates, as discussed above. Apart from the presence of these fabrics, there is little ceramic evidence to distinguish the dating of these groups from the stratigraphically earlier assemblage in the Open Area 3 pit, especially in view of the sherd links and similarities in composition between the assemblages of room A and the aforementioned pit.

Table 12 Percentages by sherd count and weight of amphorae from LBI95 Open Area 3 and Building 2 rooms A and B

Amph type	OA3 % shds	OA3 % wt	B2RA % shds	B2RA % wt	B2RB % shds	B2RB % wt	RCP1B % wt
8L555	43.7	43.3	38.9	55.2	3.1	5.15	<1
8C184	19.7	21.8	1	0.43	-	-	<1*
8C186	-	-	2.2	3.68	10.76	36.41	16
8DR20	5.6	20.1	33.3	22.98	60	42.85	56
8G (PE47)	18.3	7.0	2.2	0.61	9.2	10.11	7.5
8DR2-4	7.1	5.5	6.6	9.8	-	-	13.5
8H70	-	-	4.4	2.68	-	-	1
8	5.6	2.3	11	4.58	16.9	5.47	-

The difficulty in dating these groups is that they are dominated by amphorae, most of which are broadly dated from the 1st to the mid 2nd centuries, and they contain few coarse wares and fine wares which would normally refine the dating of groups from this period. Due to the unusual composition of the assemblages it is not possible to rely on dating them on negative evidence, such as the absence of diagnostically early Roman fabrics and forms which normally occur in RCP1 assemblages, as the proportion of vessels other than amphorae is very small. But it should be noted that early fabrics and forms such as LYON, SLOW, butt beakers, Ritterling 12 bowls, Ritterling 9 cups and early wall-sided mortaria are a rare occurrence on the site as a whole. In room A there are small amounts of fabrics which are dated primarily to the 1st century, namely BHWS, HOO and SAMLG. Additionally, most of the BAETE sherds are from a single vessel that has been identified as a Dressel 20 amphora with a rim which is dated *c* AD 50–70 (Peacock and Williams 1986, fig 66, no. 10). In room B 1st-century fabrics include HWB, RDBK, SAMLG, HOO and a rare sherd of CGGW. The negative evidence of the absence of diagnostic RCP1A forms or fabrics and the comparative abundance of 1st-century fabrics, set against the lack of diagnostically post-AD 70 fabrics or forms (apart from the single sherd of HWC in room A) suggests a date of *c* AD 70 for these groups.

Room B measured a minimum of 2.5m x 2.5m and also had a brickearth floor. The location of the east walls of the rooms was not recorded, nor was the south wall of room B. Neither room was in use for long and the masonry walls were robbed out entirely in the mid-Flavian period (Fig 60).

The faunal assemblages from all the contexts relating to the usage of the rooms are very small (containing less than 10

Fig 60 View of LBI95 Building 2 rooms A and B

fragments of bone) except for one occupation layer. This
contained only a limited quantity of food waste from the three
main domesticates and chicken. In addition, it produced a small
number of 'background' species including mouse/vole and
frog/toad. It seems probable that these bones would have been
in the corners of the rooms and been easily missed if the room
had not been thoroughly swept before its abandonment.

However, the pattern was different in the next railway
arch to the east, separated by only 2.5m, where rooms C and
D were in use for considerably longer. Room C was a sunken
room with an impermeable concrete floor and a tile drain
leading out from its south-east corner (Fig 61). It measured
3.0m x 2.3m internally, and the floor was at c 0.3m OD,
approximately a metre lower than the other rooms. Its walls
were not as extensively robbed and were made of ragstone.
The north wall measured c 3.0m (the west end beyond the
limit of the excavation), the east wall measured 3.7m with the
tile drain at its south end, and the south wall returning to the
west for 1.0m before it too was robbed. The walls survived to
slightly over 1.0m high. The projected line of the west wall lay
to the west of the limit of excavation but a small block of
similar masonry 0.5m square in the west section may be part
of this wall. The function of this room is problematical. The
drain, located at the base of the room, must be for the removal
of water rather than the supplying of it. To the east of the
building the drain was timber-lined and ran south-east through
Open Area 6 for at least 7.0m. The cut for the drain was c 1.6m

wide and 0.6m deep and was presumably timber-lined (as
otherwise it would not have functioned) even though no
evidence for this survived. The walls of the room were not
rendered so as to make the room waterproof, thus ruling out
the possibility of a plunge bath. The primary occupation fills
from within the room were not 'cess-like', therefore making
it equally unlikely to have been a latrine block. A possible
function of the room is that of a cold store, possibly with ice
under the floor which would have flowed away through the
drain when it melted.

Room D lay to the north of room C and was L-shaped. It
measured at least 3.15m x 5.75m and had a clay floor. Neither
the north nor west walls were present within the excavation.
The clay floors were badly slumped into an underlying gravel
quarry pit. This entailed what appeared to be repair work
outside the room, where a series of posts may have been used
to support the wall. This area was also used for the dumping
of rubbish, and a midden started to develop there.

One particular group of pottery from this dump is worthy
of further discussion. The large assemblage consists of 173
sherds, 4.10 EVEs and weighs 9674g. It is dated c AD 90–110
on the presence of LOXI (1.7% sherds/ 3.9% EVEs/ 1.7%
weight) and two decorated samian forms, both of which are
dated to this period (<P97> and <P98>, Fig 62). LOXI is
dated from AD 90 on its first occurrence at Leadenhall Court
in the pre-Basilican period 4–5 which is dated c AD 85–100
(Groves 1993, 127). In the Leadenhall Court report, it is

Fig 61 View of LBI95 Building 2 room C

demonstrated that the key factor in defining early, middle and late Flavian assemblages is the changing patterns within local reduced wares (ibid, 122–7). Groves concludes that this is especially successful in defining late and early Flavian assemblages, and that among the defining characteristics of late Flavian assemblages are a high percentage of AHSU relative to HWB, a fairly high percentage of HWC, and a low percentage of ERSA/B and ERMS. These trends are seen in this assemblage, where the Early Roman Sandy fabrics (ERSA, ERSB, ERSA/B, ERMS) are absent, the dominant reduced ware is AHSU (11.6% sherds/ 30.2% EVEs/ 4.6% weight) and HWC is the most common product from the Highgate industry (6.4%/11.7%/ 3.3%), with only a small percentage of HWB present (1.7%/ 0%/0.2%). Additional dating evidence is provided by a VRW reed-rimmed bowl of type 4A3 <P99> (not illustrated), dated to c AD 80–110 (Marsh and Tyers 1978, 573).

The percentage of amphorae (37% sherds/ 11% EVEs/ 69.6% weight) is unusually high when compared with assemblages from RCP2, RCP3 and LCT84 period 4–5 (RCP2 2.0%/41.0%; RCP3 2.0%/30.0%; LCT84 period 4–5 3.81%/49.31%). The amphorae include three unsourced vessels from which there are a high number of large sherds, of which only one form has been identified, a Dressel 2-4. The other two amphorae both have cylindrical bodies and bead rims and could possibly be Dressel 2-4 or Cam. 184 amphorae. One is illustrated <P100> (Fig 62) and is in a dense, fine, hard pink fabric with light buff surfaces. The barbotine decoration on the Drag. 36 plate <P101>

(Fig 62) is unusual in that the ivy leaves are grouped together rather than in the more common pattern of flowing and intertwining leaves. The Drag. 35 cup <P102> (Fig 62) is also atypical in not having any barbotine decoration on its rim.

Additionally, from an MSA test pit that cut through room D came the first example of a Dressel 21-22 amphora <P106> (Fig 62) to be recorded from London or Southwark. A total of 43 sherds have been recovered, constituting the majority of the vessel although the foot is missing. The amphora weighs a total of 5172g and has a diameter of 140mm; 83% of the rim is present.

The fabric of this vessel has already been described in the National Roman Fabric Reference Collection (Tomber and Dore 1998, 104). The fabric is not the same as that described by Peacock and Williams (1986, 96–7) for this form but is attributed to the same region of Lazio or Campania.

This amphora represents a rare occurrence in Britain (it is only the fifth example found here), its main distribution area being the western Mediterranean, especially Italy (Peacock and Williams 1986, 96–7). Four vessels have been identified as Dressel 21-22 amphorae at Colchester (Symonds and Wade 1999, 138). On the evidence of the *tituli picti* its main contents were fruit, possibly waxed plums (Callender 1965, 13–14).

Dressel 21-22 amphorae are generally dated to the 1st century AD and this example comes from contexts dating from the late Neronian to early Flavian period. An occupation layer

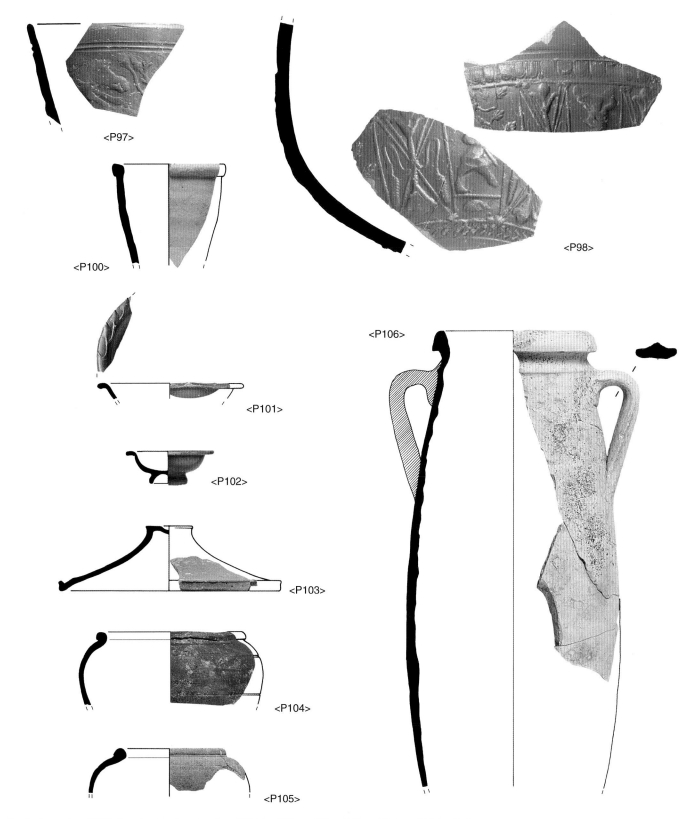

<P97>

<P98>

<P100>

<P101>

<P102>

<P103>

<P104>

<P105>

<P106>

Fig 62 Pottery from LBI95 Open Area 7 and amphora from MSA92 <P97>–<P98> (1:2), <P100>–<P106> (1:4)

over a brickearth floor from MSA92 Building 6 (= LBI95 B2) contains a small assemblage of 25 sherds dated c AD 60–75. This dating is based on the absence of any fabrics or forms which start after AD 70 and on the latest dated sherd of decorated samian, of c AD 60–75. A demolition layer sealing a brickearth floor had a medium-sized assemblage of 65 sherds and there are no fabrics that start post-AD 70. However, there

is a VRW ring-necked flagon which is closest in rim form to the type 1B2, and although this form does occur in the City in pre-Flavian contexts (Davies et al 1994, 42) it is more common after AD 70. Other notable forms in this context include a type 8 rim of a Dressel 20 amphora which is dated to c AD 40–70 (Peacock and Williams 1986, fig 65, no. 8). Overall the assemblage is dated to the early Flavian period.

The species represented in the animal bone assemblage within rooms C and D were more diverse than in the other two rooms, with goat, red deer, horse and teal also being present along with the three main domesticates, that is, cattle, sheep and pigs.

The assemblage from one particular occupation layer in room D was the most substantial (178 fragments) and also had a varied species range. A single red deer metatarsal was recovered, the substantial proportions suggesting that it possibly came from a buck. It is assumed that this is from a slaughtered animal despite the absence of butchery marks. Cattle and 'cattle-sized' bones dominate the assemblage, with the majority of the bones being those associated with initial slaughter waste: head, feet and vertebrae. The carcasses had been halved and subdivided through the vertebrae. A single atlas had been chopped transversely through the mid-shaft, representing decapitation either as the method of slaughter or during the dressing of the carcass. The fusion data show that the majority of animals were culled between 36 and 42 months old, but a single unfused pelvis indicates that at least one young bovine (below ten months) was also slaughtered. This may represent veal consumption but only on a limited scale. Also recovered from this context was a young adult horncore that had been chopped across the base to remove it from the skull. Horn is an exceptionally useful material, and once soaked becomes very easy to shape and work into a wide range of objects. This pattern of cattle skeletal representation is repeated in the other contexts.

Both sheep and goat were present, the latter represented by a single juvenile mandible and sheep by a horncore. Despite the very limited quantity of sheep/goat bones being identified within the layer (n=7), they are of interest. Of the five bones that could be aged, three were 'infant' (unfused at both ends): a humerus, a radius and a tibia, possibly from a single individual. The former had knife marks revealing its dismemberment from the radius and the ulna to make a 'shoulder' joint. The pig bones represented a mixture of elements from all areas of the skeleton, but in low frequencies. Of the four mandibles that could be sexed three were male. A pig mandible recovered from another occupation layer was pathological, with an incisor (I3) having erupted through the centre of the palate. The only bird remains were a single teal and seven chicken bones.

In summary, it appears that the contexts originate from a number of different sources, consisting largely of cattle slaughter waste but contained within this domestic waste as well. There is considerable evidence for the household(s) having a fairly rich and varied diet of young cattle, lambs and wild game including red deer and teal.

DISCUSSION OF BUILDING 2

The function of this large masonry building is problematical. The amphora assemblage is indicative of a dockside warehouse, yet the location is some 140m south of the Thames and nearly 100m west of Guy's Channel, which means that the amphorae cannot have been directly unloaded. If the amphorae had been reused as a flooring material it makes the warehouse interpretation less plausible. A secondary redistribution centre is a possibility but this still does not account for the design of

room C. It is also possible that this may have been a cool storage room, but this room had none of the concentrations of amphorae found in rooms A and B. However, if it had been for preserving fresh meat and produce there would not necessarily have been large quantities of amphorae present.

The subsequent use of the building after the initial phase of occupation ended (see below) shows a marked difference, but room C was still in use so its function, whatever it was, was still required.

Whilst rooms C and D continued in use, the walls of the western half of Building 2 were robbed out. The robber cuts were 1.2m wide and up to 1.0m deep, indicating a substantial structure. Large quantities of ragstone, chalk, tile and flint were found in the backfills, and the original walls were probably similar to those surviving in room C. After the robbing the area stood open for a period as Open Area 7. Here there was a collection of rubbish dumps and rubbish pits, contemporary with, and possibly originating from, the continued use of rooms C and D of Building 2.

Species representation within this area was diverse, but not as wide as within the earlier usage stages of Building 2. The faunal remains were recovered from a variety of pits and external dumps within the robbing stages of Building 2 and Open Area 7.

As can be clearly seen from Table 13, the majority of the animal bone was recovered from Open Area 7. Cattle and 'cattle-sized' material continued to dominate the assemblage, but pig remains were more common than sheep/goat.

Table 13 Species representation from the robbing phase of Building 2 and Open Area 7

Species	Robbing of Building 2		Open Area 7	
	No. of frags	Weight (g)	No. of frags	Weight (g)
Cattle	22	1916	61	2754
'Cattle-sized'	33	623	111	2222
Sheep/goat	1	5	7	52
Sheep	0	0	3	44
'Sheep-sized'	20	60	40	96.9
Pig	6	129	25	519.5
Hare	1	3	0	0
Mouse/vole sp	2	0.1	2	0.1
Chicken	1	1	11	18.9
Small passerines	1	0.05	0	0
Unidentified	8	11	7	1
Unidentified birds	1	0.05	2	0.6
Total	96	2748.2	269	5711.3

The fragment counts in Table 14 are misleading as the majority of limb bones were only waste fragments resulting from the dismemberment of the carcasses. Other limb fragments have indications of being chopped and/or smashed to allow access to the marrow. These two factors have combined to artificially inflate the fragment count of limb bones. The majority of the weight comes from metapodials, head fragments, vertebrae and ribs. Butchery on the metapodials was often found on the distal

Table 14 The combined cattle and 'cattle-sized' skeletal representation for the robbing phase of Building 2 and Open Area 7

Skeletal part	No. of frags
Head	28
Limb	23
Feet (tarsals and below)	22
Vertebrae and ribs	67

end of the shaft, showing that the butcher was filleting the meat off this low value element. Two bones were pathological: a naviculo-cuboid had become fused onto the proximal end of the metatarsal, which would have severely restricted movement in the 'ankle'. It may be an example of bovine spavin which occurs largely in the area surrounding the tarsals and carpals of draught animals (Baker and Brothwell 1980, 117). Just one bone could be sexed, a pelvis belonging to an adult cow.

Only a small quantity of bones of the other main domesticates was recovered, with no discernible skeletal preference. A single juvenile sheep horncore was recovered; it had been chopped across the base to remove it from the skull, thus allowing the horn to be removed from the core. Both the pig and sheep/goat bones had limited evidence for butchery, perhaps indicating a preference for the use of the knife rather than the cleaver. What was present indicated the dismemberment of the carcass through the joints, that is, the 'hip', 'ankle' and 'knee', rather than through the bone shafts.

There is a slightly greater representation of chicken, particularly within Open Area 7. Butchery was present on two femurs and one pathological tarso-metatarsus. The latter relates to the removal of the feet to prepare the bird for the table and the former to the removal of the meat from the bone. The tarso-metatarsus displayed extra bone growth on the distal shaft.

A hare radius was recovered from the same open area and despite the absence of evidence for butchery marks it is presumed to be food waste.

In summary, it can be seen that these features yielded mixed assemblages. The bulk of the material is represented by the primary butchery waste of cattle from Building 2, rooms C and D. It is noteworthy that the exploitation of the entire skeleton, particularly of the feet, demonstrates that both high and low quality meat was being produced. It was also observed that chicken and pigs were relatively more abundant than sheep/goat.

LBI95 Building 3

Open Area 7 was built over by a timber-framed building, LBI95 Building 3, which was probably constructed around AD 80. The walls of this building were also partially robbed, but stubs of brickearth survived to the north and south. The walls were aligned precisely the same as the previous walls but the settling of the robbing backfills caused considerable slumping of this building into the robber cuts. The north wall was c 3.35m long by 0.35m wide at a minimum, but had a gap of 1.0m in it which may have formed a doorway as the wall ends did not

appear to be truncated (Fig 63). There was also a possible post pit adjacent to the door. The south wall was only 0.7m long by 0.25m wide by 0.1m high. The lesser width may indicate that this was an internal wall while the north wall was the main external wall of the building on that side. The gap between the walls was 3.3m. There was a patchy brickearth floor and the pottery is dated to the early Flavian period, c AD 70–80. It is generally domestic in nature and bears more resemblance to the assemblages from the primary use groups of Building 2 room D than to the earlier assemblages in rooms A and B, which are dominated by amphorae. There is only a very small amount of HWC, which dates the groups from Building 3 to after AD 70. There is also a mortarium <P224> from northern France stamped by the potter Prasso and dated to AD 50–85 (see Chapter 11.2).

Fig 63 Detail of north wall of LBI95 Building 3, showing possible entrance

There was no east or west wall surviving on the site, though at the east end the clay and timber building must have butted up against the surviving masonry part of Building 2. There were two robber cuts, one immediately to the south of the south wall and a perpendicular one at its west end. This cut may have formed the west wall of the building or an internal wall (Fig 64). All the stratigraphy to the west had been removed by later intrusions or was badly affected by grouting and could not be excavated. However, one find of interest was a ceramic mould for a metal object. The incomplete fired clay investment mould <R249> (Fig 65) was used for the production of a single copper alloy object. It is probable that the surviving part is the channel into which the molten metal was poured and not the main body of the mould. Investment moulds, which are more typical of Iron Age technology, are not common in the Roman period and this is therefore an unusual, although possibly residual find.

To the south of the east–west robber cut later disturbance had removed any evidence for internal activity, but it is presumed that this was an internal area of Building 3.

A series of seven small contexts was recovered from the layers associated with Building 3, comprising make-up layers, occupation layers and floor surfaces. Unfortunately, only one context, an occupation layer, contained more than 10 bone

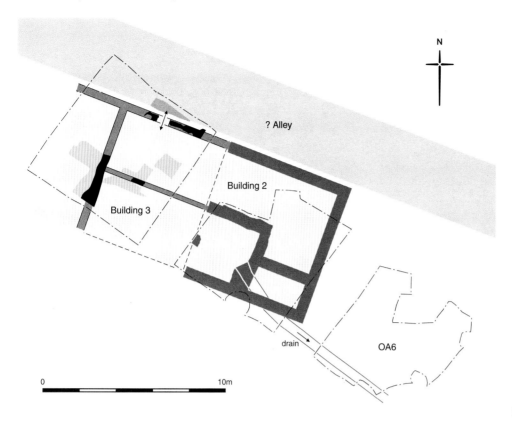

Fig 64 Plan of LBI95 Building 3

Fig 65 Ceramic mould <R249> from LBI95 Building 3 (1:2)

fragments. The majority of the bones are only fragments and identification is limited to only cattle- and sheep-sized. Also present was a single unidentified frog/toad species scapula and a fragment of non-specific mouse/vole long bone. It seems likely that this assemblage represents waste left inside the building, and which was missed when the floor was being swept; from this one can infer that it was not thoroughly cleaned, which has implications for the hygiene standard and use of the building.

At the eastern edge of the eyot there was little or no evidence to suggest that any occupation was occurring at this time. Three ditches were dug across LBE95 Open Area 2 and ran towards the edge of the island. These probably functioned from AD 70 onwards and served primarily for drainage before being backfilled.

Trade

The presence of such large quantities of amphorae, including rare types, gives an indication of the wide links with the Empire enjoyed by London at this period. The Guy's boat, found to the south in Guy's Channel, demonstrates that the channels were navigable, and the barge would have been ideal for the transfer of goods inland from sea- and ocean-going merchantmen moored in the river. The topographic information from the Jubilee Line sites shows that the land to the south and east of LBI95 was more marginal and low-lying than had previously been thought. It is not inconceivable that ships moored within a short distance of LBI95 Building 2, which could have been used as a warehouse where imports were stored before redistribution. Amphorae from Spain, Gaul and Italy were found here, including the rare fruit amphora from Campania-Latium discussed elsewhere (see Chapter 11.2).

The growth of the port on the north bank has been well documented (Milne 1985) but here the main development of riverside jetties and warehouses only occurs in the late 1st century, with more limited activity taking place in the first decades of the Roman occupation. It is possible that the channels of Southwark provided more natural landing places in the early history of Londinium before being superseded by the facilities on the north bank in the last quarter of the 1st century. This could explain the partial demolition of Building 2 and the change of use apparent in room D.

However, even into the 2nd century the channels of the southern suburb continued to be used for docking facilities. The timber quay on the Guy's Hospital site (Wilson 1990) could have been one such site, though it is a little far from the LBI95 warehouse. Dendrochronological dating indicates that it was constructed c AD 160 with alterations continuing into the 3rd century. A timber warehouse constructed c AD 152/3 has been located on the Courage's Brewery site (Brigham et al 1995) and it has been suggested from the cool conditions prevailing there that this was for the storage of fresh food and other perishables, possibly wheat and barley.

Links to BGH95

It is reasonable to assume that there was a road running to the east off the main north–south road crossing the north island, linking the large building to the heart of the settlement. Given the more marginal land to the south of LBI95, this road is postulated to have run to the north of LBI95 and been constructed with the gravels from the quarrying activity recorded on site. This road would have joined Road 1 in the area around modern Montague Close, not far to the south of the bridgehead. It could have continued to Guy's Channel to the east, though in this period the land to the east became increasingly marginal and there is no evidence of any further building work to the east of LBI95.

However, there are marked differences, as might be expected, in the occupation patterns for the two areas, that centred around the main road and that on the eastern half of the sand island.

Amphorae and the Southwark waterfront

One of most interesting questions that arises from examination of the pottery from the JLE Southwark sites is whether or not there were 'port-related' activities on the Southwark waterfront similar to the activities which took place in a very obvious manner at several sites on the north bank of the Thames. Many of the sites which ought to be considered in any general survey of activities associated with the Roman port have been discussed by Milne (1985), but few of these have been analysed in a manner which permits direct comparison with the JLE assemblage. It is fortunate, however, that this is not the case with the more recently excavated site at Regis House, which

lies at the north end of London Bridge. This site, excavated in 1994–6, lies just west of the putative northern end of the Roman bridge, and is characterised by very substantial quays with associated warehouses, which were probably first established in the earliest period of London's development, between AD 50 and 60. They were rebuilt as an integrated series of very solid timber structures from about AD 63 (Watson et al 2001, 32–3). The pottery recovered from recent excavations (Symonds in prep a) shows that the site was very much devoted to port-related activities between about AD 50 and 140. These activities began with the importation of goods including amphorae, but gradually became more specifically devoted to ceramics, especially samian ware. In the earliest period, however, it is amphorae which predominate, containing olive oil and fish sauce from southern Spain, and wine from southern France and (in small quantities) from eastern Spain, Italy and Rhodes.

It is in the nature of London and its development that the urban areas of the City and Southwark were among the most important destinations for many of the goods which arrived at the port. Although at Regis House there are quays and warehouses whose function is self-evident, it is also true that at many occupation sites there are high percentages of amphorae and samian ware in the 1st and early 2nd centuries.

The JLE Southwark site of LBI95 does, however, stand out as exceptional, with particular concentrations in Open Area 3 and the overlying Building 2 of early amphorae comparable to those found across the river at Regis House. The percentages are remarkably similar, as can be seen in Table 101 (see Chapter 11.2); the two assemblages are chronologically indistinguishable on the basis of the amphora types present. Most notable is the high percentage of amphorae in these pottery assemblages. At LBI95 amphorae comprise 27.5% of the assemblage by rows, and 41.8% by sherds; the figures are slightly higher at Regis House.

Reclamation of marginal land in the 1st century

Brigham (1990) has proposed a model for the tidal regime in London during the Roman period. In the 1st century High Tide was estimated at +1.25m OD, falling at Low Tide to −0.5m OD. This level would have caused daily flooding in north Southwark, as much occupation is recorded at lower levels than the high tide mark. Logically, therefore, there must have been flood defences in Southwark at this period. Evidence for embankments has been recorded near the bridgehead on Toppings Wharf (Brigham in Watson et al 2001, 12–13) and on the Courage's Brewery site (Hammer in prep). A revetment with a postulated top at 1.55m OD has been excavated at 64–70 Borough High Street (Graham 1988b).

There has also been considerable evidence for the reclamation of the more marginal areas and the infilling of the creeks and channels that separated the sand eyots of north Southwark. In particular there have been several excavations that revealed the progressive infilling of the Southwark Street Channel, dividing the main north and south islands, from the late 1st century onwards. Two east–west revetments on the north side of the channel were recorded at 52–54 Southwark Street (Heard 1989) and evidence for similar activity on the south side was uncovered at 55 Southwark Street (Killock 1997).

However, the north–south Guy's Channel to the east of the islands remained navigable until the end of the 2nd century, the date of the abandonment of the Roman barge discovered in 1958 (Marsden 1994). Indeed a substantial timber quay, dating to the 2nd century, was recorded on the west side of the channel in 1989 during redevelopment of Guy's Hospital (Wilson 1990).

1st-century reclamation within the Southwark Street Channel

On the other side of the island, some reclamation does start to take place in the latter part of the 1st century in the Southwark Street Channel separating the north and south islands of the Roman settlement (Table 15).

At OMS94 a layer of compact gravel metalling (OA3) was deposited over the clay of Open Area 2. It contained oyster shells towards the base of the layer and much pottery had been trampled into its upper surface (0.65m OD). This gravel appeared to have been deposited to level up the southern area within the Southwark Street Channel, as it was not seen to the north of the site. Pottery from this layer was dated to AD 50–100 and the samian to AD 45–80.

Similarly, at REW92 a series of dumps constituting Open Area 2 were laid over the alluvium. They were dated from AD 40–100 for the initial dumps and AD 70–80/100 for later dumps. These deposits represent deliberate dumping of demolition material and domestic rubbish over an extended period of time and into the 2nd century. In one of the REW92 dumps (REW92 OA2) was found a cup with scale decoration in Lyon ware; the type is probably pre-Flavian in date and mainly associated with military sites. Also from the same context is an unusual grog-tempered vessel.

The large assemblage from Open Area 2 consists of 183 sherds, 5.13 EVEs and weighs 3881g. The group is dated post-AD 70 on the presence of two sherds of HWC and a VRW ring-necked flagon with flaring mouth <P107> (Fig 66) although many of the forms and fabrics are typical of pre-Flavian assemblages.

The group includes a high percentage of imported wares (sherds 31.1%, weight 35.5%, EVEs 26.3). This is unusually high due to the presence of a single vessel, a LYON cup <P108>

(Fig 66) which is broken into 30 sherds (16.4%, 1.4%, 13.1%). SAMLG is the other significant import (8.2%, 4.9%, 13.3%). The other imported fabrics are all small quantities of amphorae (BAETE, RHOD2, GAUL1) although they dominate the group by weight (6.6%, 19.1%, 0%). Romano-British fine wares account for a small percentage of the total assemblage but include RDBK, TNIM and FMIC. The most common reduced ware is AHSU by weight (15.3%, 9.7%, 2.9%). Although Early Roman Sandy fabrics are present in small quantities they represent a high percentage of EVEs (3.8%, 3.6%, 10.9%) and the most commonly occurring tempered ware (13.7%, 10.6%, 15.6%) is HWB. Unsurprisingly, VRW is the most significant oxidised ware (15.8%, 29.5%, 27.3%).

The group includes two vessels which have been provisionally identified as lampholders or open lamps, one of which is especially unusual as it is handmade and in a grog-tempered fabric <P109> (not illustrated). This vessel has a flat base tapering at one end and terminating in two raised points of clay, and is sooted internally. If it is a lampholder it is of a type not previously identified in London. The TNIM dish <P110> (Fig 66) is loosely copying the form Cam. type 16 although there is no evidence for a footring (Hawkes and Hull 1947, 220, pl 49, nos 16A–B).

The LYON cup is of Usk type 3 (Greene 1979, 20, fig 5, no. 3). This hemispherical cup has quartz roughcasting on the interior, scale decoration on the exterior and a sharp cordon below the rim. LYON is most common in pre-Boudican assemblages in the City although examples do occur in Flavian contexts (Davies et al 1994, 126). LYON has been dated by Greene as having a main production period of c AD 40–70 (Greene 1979, 18). This would suggest that sherds occurring in the Flavian period are either residual or, in the case of more complete vessels, rare survivals. However, recent work on Roman military sites in northern Britain established after AD 70 suggests that LYON products continued being imported into the early Flavian period (Willis in prep, 3–5). If the terminal dates of LYON are extended forwards on this evidence, this vessel need not necessarily be an unusual survival in an early to middle Flavian assemblage but is possibly contemporary with the rest of the group.

At RWT93 a pelta-shaped mount <R232>, military in style, was found in an unstratified context. The mount, consisting of a single stud with footring on the reverse for attachment to a leather strap, is similar to 3rd-century equestrian equipment, for example from the Saalburg fort in Germany.

The revetting of the channel and the reclamation for building could have been a piecemeal development, but the presence of the Lyon cup and other military objects together with the early date might indicate early military involvement (Yule in prep).

OMS94 Building 1 was constructed over the gravel surface Open Area 3. Only a small corner of the building survived. It consisted of a make-up layer on which a brickearth floor (0.72m OD) had been laid. A corner of a brickearth wall 0.2m wide and 0.1m high rested on the floor. Pottery from the layers was dated AD 50–100. The building was then dumped over to create Open Area 4, which presumably represented further land

Table 15 *Dating of Southwark Street Channel deposits*

Land use	Feature	Grp/sgrp/context	Material	Date
OMS94 OA3	surface	5/51/[48]	Rpot	50–100
REW92 OA2	make-up	3/3/[230]	Rpot	70–100
	make-up	3/3/[231]	Rpot	70–80
	make-up	3/3/[231]	Rpot	40–100
OMS94 B1	construction	6/62/[44]	Rpot	50–100
	occupation	6/64/[39]	Rpot	50–70
OMS94 OA4	make-up	8/81/[37]	Rpot	60–100

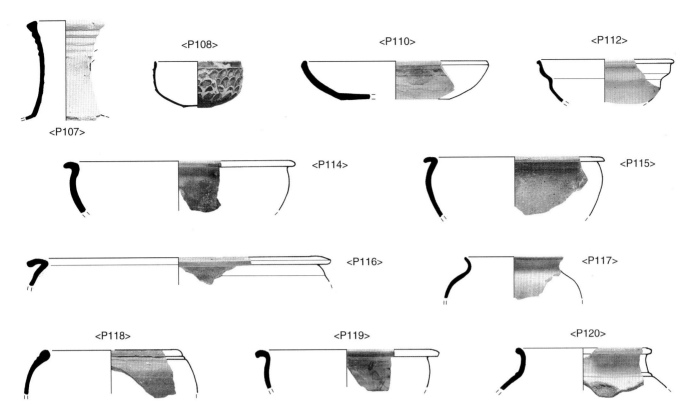

Fig 66 Pottery <P107>–<P108>, <P110>, <P112>, <P114>–<P120> from REW92 Open Area 2 (1:4)

reclamation. The only dating evidence was pottery dated AD 60–100. The dumps were truncated by a post-medieval burial ground. As mentioned previously, it is likely that the OMS94 revetment Structure 1 was contemporary with Waterfront 4 on 52SOS89, in which case Building 1 at OMS94 might be dated to AD 70+.

Laid over the natural sand at RWG94 was evidence for Building 1, a brickearth floor surface (1.5m OD) on which

was a deposit of grey brickearth overlain by charcoal and silt (1.58m OD). These could have been occupation deposits or destruction debris, but as so little remains it was not possible to be sure which. There was no dating evidence. It is possible that these deposits form part of the structures observed on the site of 15–23 Southwark Street, perhaps representing part of Building 1 there which was dated around AD 60–80 (Cowan 1992, 16–18).

7

Early 2nd-century continuity

The Britons were seduced into alluring vices
Tacitus, 2nd century AD

7.1 Period 5: 2nd-century consolidation

The early 2nd century in Southwark appears to be a period of consolidation and stability with no major changes to the general patterns of activity either along the main road or further afield.

Alongside the main road – a busy high street

On BGH95 timber-framed buildings remained the general rule with the exception of masonry Building 13 at the north end. They continued to develop or be replaced during the later part of the 1st and through to the early 2nd century. This development resulted in a fragmentary sequence of such buildings, which were constructed, repaired or even totally replaced on a regular basis (Fig 67).

The floors were frequently replaced, particularly those formed of compacted clay. When the build-up of occupation debris, including both domestic and industrial debris as well as other floor covering, such as straw, became excessive the floor was replaced, sometimes requiring further make-up deposits. This may indicate a consistent occupation and development of some buildings with repairs and possible extensions into yard areas. The structural aspects, including timber posts and clay wall foundations, would have remained intact whilst the usage of buildings stayed much the same.

Building 13

Alongside Southwark Road 1 on BGH95, Building 13 continued to be occupied. The first phase of activity ended with levelling dumps of brickearth, which contained demolition material. It is not clear where this material derived from, as the main structure of the building appeared to remain intact. Perhaps it came from internal restructuring not represented on the site, such as new internal walls or ceilings. There appear to have been attempts to repair the east (internal) wall, which was cracked. This cracking may have caused the end of the first phase of activity, resulting in the refurbishment of the whole structure. Some of the layers produced slag and waste, though it is possible that these derived from the blacksmith's immediately to the south as there is no evidence for this activity taking place within this building. The demolition layers involved the raising of the floor level quite substantially, so that by the end of this phase floor level was 0.5m higher than at the initial construction of the building some fifty years before. The rooms must have had high ceilings if there was still sufficient headroom in this and later phases. This was followed by a further sequence of brickearth floors and occupation layers. There were no layers that could be directly related to this phase from the continuation of the building in either BSE94 or JSS92, but it is reasonable to assume that the building continued to be occupied in these areas as well.

The 51 sherds of pottery (39 rows) from contexts assigned to the use of Building 13 phase 2 suggest a date of c AD 100 for the sequence of floor and occupation levels. North Kent

Grey ware appears for the first time in this phase and mica-dusted wares are also present, both of these being wares that become increasingly common in the 2nd century AD (Table 17).

Most of the brick and tile from Building 13 phase 2 is early, although Flavian tegulae in fabric 3028 were also recorded. One of the most interesting types from this phase of Building 13 is a curved brick, probably originally circular, in Radlett fabric 3060, which would have been used for the construction of *pilae* (context [1693]). Circular bricks in the same fabric were found in situ in the hypocaust of Building 6 on 15–23 Southwark Street (Crowley 1992, 144), and a further link between the buildings is the occurrence on both sites of the cross-combed Radlett box-flue tile, which occurs in period 4 deposits in BGH95 Buildings 13 and 14. Trajanic fabric 3019 occurs as roof tile in in situ destruction deposits [1705] and [1733], which perhaps should be dated later, particularly [1705] as it also contains Reigate brick which starts c AD 120–40.

Structure 2

The blacksmith's workshop, Structure 2, continued in use and it also seems to have been made rather more substantial, as a slot was recorded towards the south of the structure that would have supported a reasonably well-built wall, internal partition or other feature related to the work of the smith. It still ran up to the south wall of Building 13 and brickearth floors continued to be used. Little activity could be directly related to this phase in comparison with the previous and subsequent phases. It is possible that a clean-up occurred in the later phase which removed most of the evidence for activity in this phase. There is little reason to doubt that the smithy did continue in use during this period.

One interesting aspect of the use of the smithy came from an analysis of the eggshells from the site. This showed a high proportion coming from the blacksmith's shop. All the eggs were chicken eggs. One of the samples shows signs that eggs had hatched, and therefore indicates breeding as well as food production. A smithy is a rather unusual location for this, so it may simply be that rubbish deposits have accumulated here, in the occupation horizons. It is probable that the food waste derived from the occupants of the smithy, and was sufficiently small to be dropped on the floor and ignored. However, the hatched material cannot have come into the deposit via this mechanism. One possibility is that the hens were kept by the blacksmith as a sideline. However, this is unlikely to have been on a significant commercial scale and more probably involved little more than a hen or two. Most likely would be free-range hens using the smithy for shelter and warmth, and perhaps roosting in the rafters, out of the wet and the cold!

Building 14

Building 14 to the south of the forge also continued in use into the early part of the 2nd century. It was not possible to assign the remains of any walls to this phase. The building was represented by floor surfaces. One room had a heavily truncated brickearth floor which had the remains of a tile hearth associated with it and ashy deposits surrounding it. An iron knife with a bone handle <R170> was found in the occupation levels of Building 14 (Fig 68). The short length of the handle, which has crudely carved decoration on both sides, suggests that the blade – of which only a trace remains – was also short. A glass counter <R160> of the type used in board games was also found.

The area with the brickearth floor was adjoined by another with timber shadows on it and in this instance also iron nails holding the floorboards in place. There was no physical division visible between the two areas, but the abruptness of the change suggests that there might have been two rooms rather than one, with an insubstantial partition that left no trace in the archaeological record. This would have created two rooms c 3.0m wide rather than one large room 6.0m wide, so is quite plausible. The building appears to go out of use towards the end of the period and was sealed by a brickearth demolition deposit.

Building 22

Building 22 was a substantial brickearth building, located to the south of Building 14. It is possible that it was constructed slightly before the end of the 1st century but the main phase of activity was certainly in the first quarter of the 2nd century. The western frontage was truncated by the Battlebridge sewer. The northern wall was formed by an alignment of posts and stakeholes. The alley to the south of Building 14 was now overbuilt by the two buildings butting up against each other. At a distance of 4.0m to the south of the north wall a beamslot represented the southern limit of room A. A north–south line of stakes formed an internal partition on the west of room A, while another beamslot 5.0m to the east marked the eastern edge of the room.

A large stone and tile kiln or oven measuring 0.6m x 0.5m (truncated) was located in the north-east corner of the room, which had a brickearth floor. The superstructure then appears to have been sealed with brickearth. There was a large collection of amphora fragments in the hearth base which were probably reused as part of the construction of the structure. A sample of the oven contents gave no clue as to its function. The remains of a burnt beam did not appear to be in situ. This was associated with a layer of fire debris that marked the end of the first phase of the building.

This room contained brick and roof tile in London fabric group 2815 along with small amounts of Radlett and Eccles material. The hearths also contained tegulae in fabric 2815, some of which were fire-cracked, and a storage pit contained some Trajanic brick (fabric 3019).

Another room, room B, was situated to the south of room A. It was felt that this was part of the same building rather than a separate one. Room B also had a brickearth floor, and contained a small hearth with burnt tiles set in it and an internal storage pit. This room was less well defined apart from the northern partition wall with room A. No southern, eastern or western limits survived although it continued at least 2.75m to the south. The brick and roof tile assemblage is very similar in

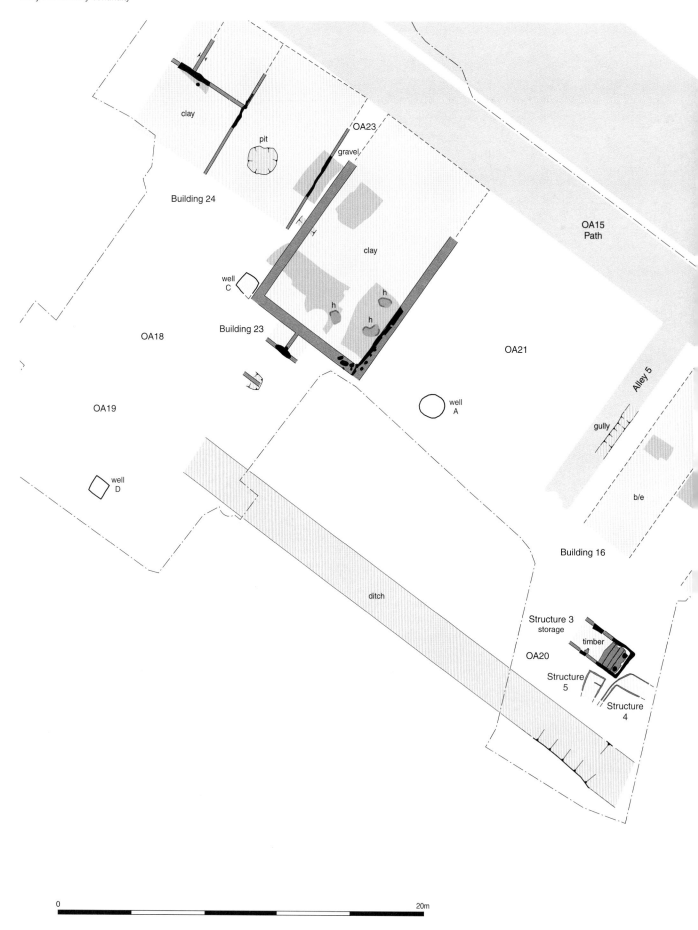

clay

pit

OA23

gravel

Building 24

OA15
Path

clay

well
C

h

h

OA18

Building 23

h

OA21

OA19

well
A

well
D

Alley 5

gully

b/e

Building 16

ditch

Structure 3
storage

timber

OA20

Structure
5

Structure
4

0   20m

Fig 67 Plan of principal archaeological features, period 5

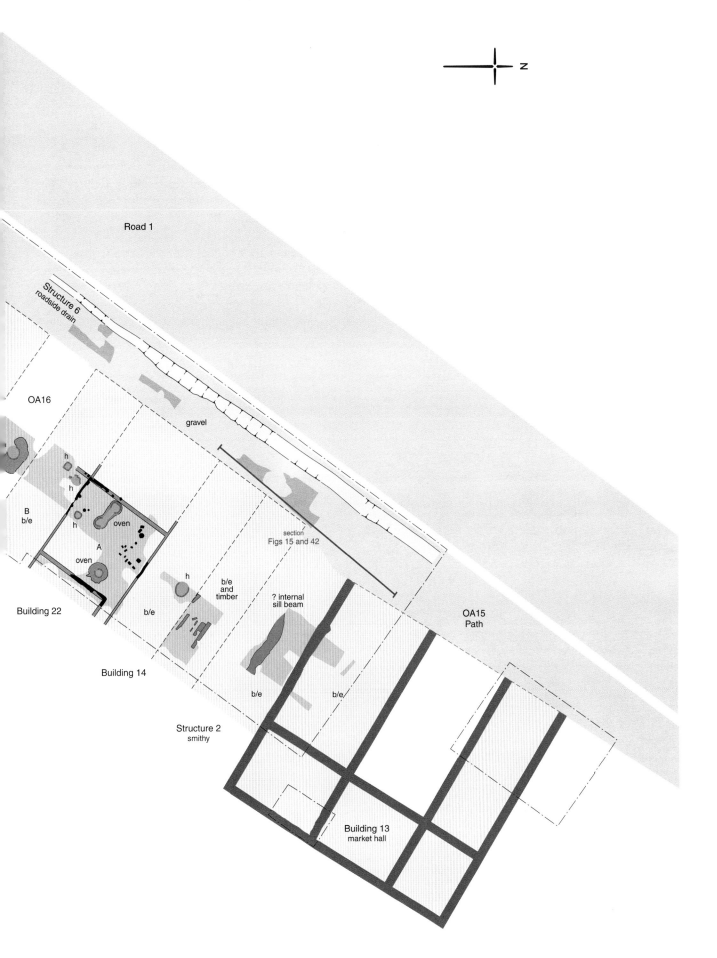

Road 1

Structure 6
roadside drain

OA16

gravel

h

h

B
b/e

h

oven

A

oven

Building 22

h

b/e

b/e

section
Figs 15 and 42

b/e
and
timber

? internal
sill beam

OA15
Path

Building 14

b/e

b/e

Structure 2
smithy

Building 13
market hall

N

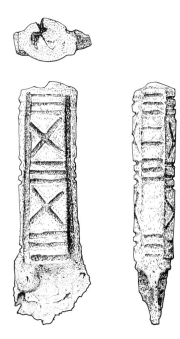

Fig 68 Bone knife handle <R170> from Building 14 (1:1)

composition to that from room A, with no diagnostic 2nd-century material. However, the local fabrics present (the Radlett and 2815 groups) probably continue in production until c AD 120 and 160 respectively, and so probably provided the roofing materials for Building 15. Decorative material includes a smoothly worn fragment of medium-grained laminated sandstone, which was probably reused as paving.

In its second phase of activity, room A may well have been external or at least partially open. A gravel surface was laid down and another large oven and a smaller hearth were constructed. The oven consisted of a circular chamber 0.65m in diameter to the west with a narrow shaft leading to a hearth of tile and clay. The smaller hearth had a circular base (c 0.5m in diameter) surrounded by a ring of stones and tile. This surround was originally encased in brickearth, suggesting that this hearth may also have been a small oven with a superstructure. The base of the hearth or oven contained large quantities of amphora fragments, probably as part of the structure rather than as residual contents. If this was an external area it must have formed a central courtyard within the building, perhaps a cooking or working area. The oven fills contained metal and slag suggesting some sort of industrial function, but these were not present in great quantities and could have been redeposited in a domestic setting.

Further eggshell fragments come from a range of samples associated with Building 22, again indicating general waste disposal. This may indicate that the building had people living, or at least eating, in it. All fragments were identified as chicken and none appear to be from hatched eggs, providing clear evidence that eggs continued to form part of the diet throughout the 2nd century.

These samples also contained a small number of glume wheat grains and seeds. The sample from one occupation layer included a buttercup seed head. This type of waste would have been produced during coarse sieving. The other sample is from

a hearth and contained ten cherry/plum (Prunus spp) stones, and small amounts of spelt and emmer grains, as well as seeds including a buttercup seed.

Open Area 16 and Building 16 continued in use to the south of Building 22, but both were heavily truncated with the building represented by only a small area of brickearth flooring. It is possible that there was still a hearth in the open area.

Open Area 20

To the east of the range of buildings, and probably as part of a yard area behind them, was Open Area 20. In the open area there was a small rectangular building, Structure 3, which might have been a dry storage shed. A construction cut was lined with clay and then a wooden floor was inserted, the floorboards surviving as decayed timber shadows. There was also a pair of large postholes. The south end was truncated but the surviving part of the structure measured 3.0m north–south by 1.5m east–west. There was little evidence from the finds for the function, but the construction clearly indicated that the internal area was meant to be kept dry.

Painted wall plaster came from one of the construction slots. This consists of a sandy mortar render, probably applied to a clay wall, with a white skim and grey spattered decoration; some fragments also have yellow and pink spatters. This decoration is typically used on the dado area of a wall. It is not clear whether this plaster had fallen from the surface of a wall in Structure 3, or if it was residual. However, given the nature of the structure it is more likely to have been the latter.

The structure was not in use for long as an extensive brickearth dump layer sealed it. Finds from these dumps included a copper-alloy chain which is part of the handle of a glass oil flask or aryballos, <R117> (Fig 69). Rings attached to the chain fitted through the dolphin-shaped handles set on either side of the neck of the vessel and the chain was attached to the owner's wrist. Bathing in elaborate public baths is always regarded as typical of the 'Roman' way of life, and although no such structures have been positively identified in this part of Southwark, their existence should not be doubted.

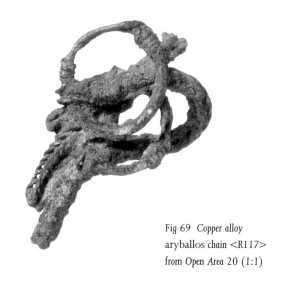

Fig 69 Copper alloy aryballos chain <R117> from Open Area 20 (1:1)

Indeed, a bath suite has been proposed at the Winchester Palace site some 160m to the north-west (Yule and Rankov 1998). Imposing bath buildings have been found north of the river, and it is highly probable that such facilities existed in the southern part of the town, although they may have been less elaborate. Larger houses could also have incorporated bath suites, as found on the north bank, for example at Billingsgate (Marsden 1980, 151–5). Bathing, as is well known, involved a progression through a series of heated rooms and a cold plunge bath. Bathers were rubbed down with oil which was scraped off with an iron strygil.

The vessel to which the handle was attached would date from the late 1st or early 2nd century, so the object from Open Area 20 could be residual, and there are indications of an as yet undiscovered hypocausted building in the area as early as the third quarter of the 1st century.

In Open Area 20 there were two elaborately constructed pits, Structures 4 and 5. Their proximity suggested that they were related, and the nature of their construction indicated some function beyond merely rubbish disposal or storage.

Structure 4 was a sub-rectangular pit with a channel leading off its south-east corner. Both the pit and channel were clay-lined with wooden bases, so were clearly intended to be waterproof to prevent any liquid escaping from them. The backfilling of Structure 4 produced a large pottery assemblage dated AD 90–120. The composition of this assemblage suggests that the backfill is probably derived from domestic refuse and does not appear to relate to the function or use of the pit.

Structure 5 was immediately to the south and was also a clay-lined pit, rectangular in shape and measuring 1.0m x 1.2m (truncated). There appears to have been a smaller chamber measuring 0.4m x 0.4m in the north-eastern corner of the pit sub-divided by a vertical band of clay. The backfill of Structure 5 produced pottery dated AD 100–20. As with Structure 4, the assemblage appears to be domestic refuse.

However, along with the household rubbish there was also a fragment of a small stone altar <R233> (Fig 70). The fragment survives to a height of 123mm and is 127mm wide. The upper corner is extant, with part of one scroll moulding and faint traces of a second to its left, defining the focus. Below this is a triple stepped moulding surmounting the narrower body of the altar, which is broken. There is no trace of any inscription. This is part of a miniature altar, suitable for use in a household or small public shrine. It was made from fine-grained oolitic limestone, probably from northern France (S Pringle, T Blagg pers comm).

This is an overtly religious item and may have come from a small shrine, possibly belonging to a private house. It is, however, interesting that Structure 1 (period 4), a building which produced a fragment of copper alloy figurine <R236>, is thought to have been a shrine, and one can therefore speculate about the altar's source. The fine-grained oolitic limestone from which the altar is made is a type of stone that was very likely to be reused, and it may be significant that only the upper part of the altar, with its distinctive moulding, had been discarded.

Fig 70 Stone altar <R233> (1:2)

The pits themselves may have served some sort of industrial function, perhaps related to the large ovens or hearths in Building 22. Unfortunately, analysis of the fills of these structures gave no clues to what this function might have been. As mentioned already, after its use Structure 5 was backfilled with domestic refuse and cess, but this is not likely to have been its primary function. Both features appeared to drain into the ditch to the east, which was continuing in use from the previous period.

Faunal remains were recorded from two contexts within Open Area 20, the ditch and one of the structural pits. The latter contained only three fragments of 'cattle-sized' rib, but the former was a very substantial context with a large quantity of animal bone in its backfill, consisting of 273 fragments of bone and weighing 5.1kg. The species range was slightly more diverse than in previous open areas (Table 16).

The distribution of anatomical parts for cattle shows practically all elements to be present. However, in contrast to many of the other large assemblages from this period there is a lack of skull fragments and this, combined with the low phalange counts, suggests their removal to the tanneries. Two cattle first phalanges exhibited butchery marks, which were consistent with the removal of the hide. Further butchery

Table 16 Species representation from Open Area 20

Species	No. of frags	Weight (g)
Cattle	87	3092.25
'Cattle-sized'	102	1482.64
Sheep/goat	17	173
Sheep	1	11.29
'Sheep-sized'	14	82.97
Pig	48	306.64
'Chicken-sized'	1	2.6
Duck	1	2.5

marks were identified on the metapodials which relate to the removal of the lower limbs, and jointing chops particularly on the femurs and humeri. Many of the butchery marks on the lower value limb bones indicate that the meat was removed and then the bone split longitudinally to enable marrow extraction. The single horncore present was aged to a 'sub-adult' (following Armitage 1982). It had been chopped through the base, which is suggestive of hornworking on a very small or individual scale.

The ageing evidence for the cattle is very limited but all fusion information points towards adults older than 36 months composing the bulk of the culled animals. There were only two exceptions to this, a metatarsal and a radius, both unfused, indicating that at least one individual younger than 18 months was present. Unfortunately no butchery was evident on either bone.

The distribution of the sheep/goat and pig elements is very much tilted towards 'dressing' waste. Butchery marks reveal a mixture of implements being employed, with removal of the feet through the proximal end of the metapodials being done by knife and the removal of the upper limbs by cleaver. A single skull fragment bore indications of butchery directly related to the splitting of the skull along the sagittal line to remove the brain.

The evidence from this period does not permit any building to be definitely identified as a butcher's premises, but the likelihood remains that there was such a shop nearby.

Alley 5

A new east–west alley, Alley 5, was inserted in the middle of the site over Building 12 and Open Area 13 to the west and south of Building 16 to the east (Fig 71). There was insufficient dating evidence to establish an accurate date for its construction, but it was certainly in use by this period. The surviving stretch of alley was only c 2.0m long and 1.0m wide and difficult to trace to the east of the Battlebridge sewer because of later truncation, but it must be presumed to have continued to the east and therefore been at least 15.0m long. There were a series of gravel surfaces with ruts made by wheeled vehicles visible on some of them. A copper alloy stud <R202> was found on one of the road surfaces; it has a thick circular head and may be a furniture fitting. Other finds from the road surfaces included fragmentary copper alloy tweezers <R115> from a manicure set, a stone hone <R174> used for sharpening metal tools, fragments of glass vessels and (residual) coins of 1st-century date.

Structure 6: the roadside drain

To the north of the alley at the west of the site was a linear feature, Structure 6, at least 23.0m long by 0.75m wide and 0.25m deep (maximum) with a large number of post- and stakeholes in it. Since there were two similar features later in the sequence, all with large numbers of stakeholes in them and on an almost identical alignment, it is very hard to assign the

Fig 71 View of Alley 5

stakes to the correct feature. The fills of the first feature, and indeed the subsequent ones, appeared to be backfills after robbing of the stakes rather than accumulations over time, and indicate that the structures had gone out of use before the backfilling. They were certainly not waterlain, as might have been expected from roadside ditches, and the features all run parallel to the main road at a distance of less than 1.0m. However, a timber-lined ditch or drain, subsequently robbed out and backfilled, remains the most likely interpretation, possibly with a fence along the east side. Remains of an elaborate timber box-drain have been recorded on the west side of the road at 2SSBS85 (Cowan et al in prep) where there was also evidence for a masonry structure straddling the drain, and it is entirely possible that there was something similarly complex on the east side. Since the robbing of the feature dates from this period it is reasonable to assume that it was in use as a drain in the preceding period, and should be interpreted as such.

In Open Area 21, to the south of the St Thomas Street junction, a 1.8m wide ditch crossed the site from the eastern limit of excavation into the central excavation area where it was truncated, although the bottom of the cut survived. The ditch was partially recorded in section in the Battlebridge sewer, but was not observed further west. A sub-circular pit was cut into the ditch and additional dumping took place in the area to the southern edge of the ditch. The ditch may have been primarily a drainage channel running eastwards to the rear of the roadside settlement. Well A remained open and probably in use on the east side of this yard area.

Building 23

Building 23 represents a redevelopment and change of land use of part of the southern area, where the gravel alleyway, Alley 3, and former open area were encroached upon and built over. A box-flue tile roller-stamped with die 85 was found in the make-up for Building 23. This die type has a fairly wide distribution, extending from Richborough and Canterbury in Kent westwards to Cirencester, and with find spots in Oxfordshire. In London it has been found in several locations, including Winchester Palace, Cheapside baths and Huggin Hill baths (Betts et al 1994).

The area of the site adjacent to 31 Borough High Street included truncated remains divided into three separate areas of occupation, but several areas of clay floor and a 2.8m slot with seven postholes form the northern wall foundation of the building. A southern return was again represented by a slot and postholes, and this may have been an eastern wall. An additional north–south line of postholes probably represents an internal division between two rooms. A central hearth, 0.7m in diameter, was set in a compacted clay floor at the east end of the building; half of the sunken hearth was truncated.

A further area of occupation debris 1.7m to the south indicated the extent of other internal rooms. Structural remains did not survive in this area. The fragmentary floor remains all show evidence of being replaced or resurfaced with an additional two clay floors. Another pair of hearths possibly

replaced the earlier version, with both of these again being sunken pits. One was positioned against the northern wall and was 1.0m long and a maximum of 0.4m wide. The hearth, though truncated, had two chambers with a larger oval bowl and a shallow oval flue. A second sunken hearth was situated centrally within the eastern room. This 0.7m long and 0.45m wide, oval-shaped hearth also had a lining of reused tile.

The building may have been extended eastwards where a north–south slot and a truncated robber trench represent a small room or structure, possibly a small storage room at the rear of the building. No internal surfaces or occupation survive in association with this part of the building, although a copper alloy weight <R163> weighing only 3g was recovered. This would have been used in a scale pan, perhaps for weighing more expensive but relatively light commodities.

Building 23 may have been fairly long-lived or was subject to a series of repairs and extensions, including the cutting of new beamslots which indicates that part of the building was replaced. In this later phase of activity the floor deposits contained a large amount of charred stem fragments which could be the remains of floor covering or hay. Greig's work on the types of wild plant present in hay (Greig 1984, 224–5) lists some of the plant types present in sample {702}, which include large quantities of rush and buttercup seeds. A deposit used as make-up for a further floor contained a large amount of domestic debris including fragments from a circular hand-mirror <R108> (Fig 72) and a nail cleaner.

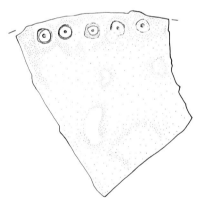

Fig 72 Copper alloy mirror <R108> from Building 23 (1:1)

A total of 590 sherds of pottery were recovered from the construction and use phase of Building 23 in period 5. Some of the assemblage may be redeposited from the previous phase, but dating evidence for the construction of the building suggests an early 2nd-century date (Table 17). The use/disuse phase of Building 23 continues in period 6 and includes the backfill of a pit containing mid 2nd-century material.

The composition of the assemblage from Building 23 compares well with the Leadenhall Court group of periods 4 and 5 (AD 85–95 and AD 95–100) (Groves 1993, 123). The quantities of reduced wares from Building 23 are very similar

Table 17 Dating table for period 5

Land use	Feature	Grp/sgrp/context	Material	Date
Building 13	pit fill	55/249/[1628]	Rpot	100–150
Building 22	pit fill	204/283/[1767]	Rpot	100–140
	occupation	204/285/[1759]	Rpot	100–120
Building 23	structure	149/953/[3139]	Rpot	50–120
Building 24	occupation	158/837/[3393]	Rpot	100–140
	floor	158/840/[3430]	Rpot	100–120
	floor	158/848/[3429]	Rpot	100–120
Alley 5	surface	23/1102/[698]	BM	50–120
Structure 3	make-up	206/416/[2192]	Rpot	100–120
	wall	206/1104/[2122]	Rpot	100–160
Structure 4	pit fill	207/426/[2092]	BM	50–160
Structure 5	pit fill	208/428/[2188]	Rpot	100–120
	pit fill	208/430/[2153]	Rpot	100–120
Open Area 20	pit fill	86/427/[2076]	Rpot	100–120
	ditch fill	89/438/[2011]	Rpot	100–120
Open Area 21	dump	128/718/[7014]	Rpot	100–120

to the pattern published; AHSU is the dominant fabric with 149 sherds (20.3%), HWB has declined to just one sherd (0.1%) and HWC has increased to 75 sherds (10.2%). ERMS has also fallen to a low count of just one sherd (0.1%). The assemblage records the introduction of LOXI (6 sherds, 0.8%), also reflected in the latest phases at Leadenhall Court.

Another group with a total of 446 sherds was recovered from a make-up layer for the building, with a total weight of 13,540g and constituting 15.83 EVEs. The dominant fabrics from this layer are (by percentage of weight and EVEs): AHSU (12.9; 16.3), FMIC (6.0; 10.8), BAETE (24.9; 10.7), SAMLG (7.0; 16.9) and VRW (22.4; 10.3). By form type, flagons and jars have the highest EVEs value with 19.9 and 20.1 respectively. Ring-necked flagons are present <P121>–<P123> (Fig 73) alongside the less common disc-mouthed type <P124> (Fig 73). The only identifiable amphorae recorded are BAETE <P125> and <P126> (Fig 73) and CADIZ, whilst the imported fine wares consist solely of SAMLG and PRW3.

The figures for FMIC are inflated by the presence of two very smashed but complete double cordoned vessels (for example <P127>, Fig 73). These vessels are paralleled by Monaghan class 4J Fine cordoned bowls (Monaghan 1987, 132, fig 133, 4J1). The bowls, in a very fine, reduced micaceous fabric, have very thin walls and double cordons on the shoulder. Vessels of this type were produced at Cliffe and Upchurch in Kent, and the fabric of the BGH vessels is comparable to Monaghan N2/1b (ibid, 252) so that it seems likely that these are north Kent products. Monaghan dates these vessels from the Conquest to the early 2nd century AD.

Another relatively uncommon FMIC form present in this context is a carinated cup imitating Drag. 27 <P128> (Fig 73). One example is published in the ERC and dated to the Flavian period (RCP2, AD 75–100).

Also of interest from this context is the high number of PRW3 lids (for example <P129> and <P130>, Fig 73). At least five individual vessels are recorded, totalling 340g and 0.88 EVEs. In the ERC the quantified data shows that PRW3

is common in the Hadrianic period and it has been found in Hadrianic fire deposits across the City.

The appearance of LOXI in this context suggests that it appears at a similar date here as in the City. The form is a plain rim dish, Marsh type 25.5 (Marsh 1978, 159, fig 6.12). LOMI is also recorded in this context in Marsh form 36 (ibid, 171, fig 6.16).

A VRW wide-mouthed jar <P131> (Fig 73), with a moulded bead rim folded back to form a collar, is a distinctive vessel, uncommon in either Southwark or the City. A similar example was found amongst kiln material from Brockley Hill, also in the VRW fabric (Suggett 1954; Castle 1972, 257, fig 4, no. 26). These wide-mouthed jars were probably used for storage.

The decorated samian includes a Drag. 37 and a Drag. 30 <P132> (Fig 73), both of which have been dated to the period c AD 70/5–85/95.

Other open areas and buildings

An external gravel surface, Open Area 23, may have formed between Buildings 23 and 24. This may have served as a pathway before it was used to deposit domestic debris in pits and as external dumps. The eastern end probably opened out into the space behind the buildings, which remained unchanged as rough ground.

Parts of another building, Building 24, were indicated at the south end of the site by a linear trench and several postholes. These features may be part of the northern wall foundation of the building. No building plan was revealed, but the rear of the building does not extend over the previous Open Area 18 and hearth area.

Open Area 18 continued to be used for industrial activity with further evidence for hearths and hearth use. This industrial activity from the late 1st century onwards certainly involved the use of hearths and heat, but it is less certain what function was being carried out. Only single fragments of lead waste and a copper alloy sprue <R239> occur, and there was no significant evidence of metalworking in these hearths.

The changes in building and land use which occurred in the roadside settlement were not uniform across the area of the site. This is most apparent in the alterations to construction at the north end, where masonry buildings replaced the clay and timber strip buildings. At the south end of this stretch of street there is no evidence of such a change in this period, but instead a continuation of the sequence of timber-framed buildings. This contrast may be the result of variation in settlement and land use, but it might also reflect a significant difference in the two parts of the street in terms of function, status and ownership of the buildings. The sequence at the south end appears to show a gradual replacement of buildings. This may have been due to the need for routine repair and rebuilding following accidental destruction (by fire, for instance).

Occupation to the east of the island

The area to the east of the sand island continued to be occupied, although at this stage no concerted attempts had been made to

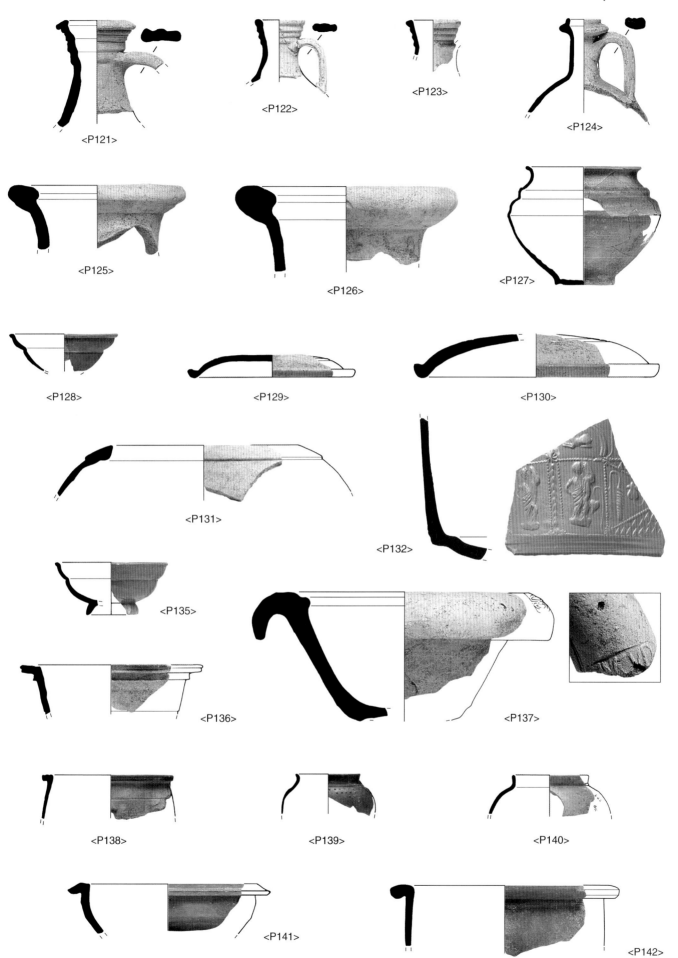

Fig 73 Pottery <P121>–<P131> (1:4), <P132> (1:2), <P135>–<P142> (1:4) from Building 23

reclaim any of the marginal land. That would occur later in the 2nd century (see Chapter 8).

Open Area 8

LBI95 Building 3 appears to have been destroyed by a fire, to judge from the large quantity of burnt demolition material sealing it and its immediate surroundings (LBI95 OA8). This would seem to have been a localised blaze as rooms C and D of Building 2 continued in use to the east. The area was left open for a short period during which a series of dumps accumulated. A flagstone in fine-grained laminated sandstone was found. It had a very worn surface from being part of a larger block, subsequently split off and reused for paving with the fresh face uppermost. The source of this is not clear, though Building 3 must be a possibility.

A large quantity of animal bone came from these external dumps. A total of 156 fragments of animal bone (approximately 2.7kg) was recovered. The species included cattle, sheep/goat, pig, hedgehog and roe deer. Chicken and heron were the only bird species present. Fourteen chicken bones were recovered including femurs, tibias, an ulna and a furcula. Knife marks commonly observed on these elements were consistent with the jointing of the birds and meat being removed from bones, both actions probably occurring at the table. A single femur had medullary bone present, which is the calcium reserve laid down by female birds prior to egg-laying. A single adult roe deer mandible was also recovered from one of the external dumps. The recovery of only a single bone is problematic and strongly suggestive of the reworking of the assemblage. Although no butchery marks were present on it, it too is presumed to be food waste. The cattle and 'cattle-sized' bones are from all areas of the skeleton, although with a distinct bias towards heads and feet (Table 18).

The butchery evidence suggests that the carcasses had been halved along (or just to either side of) the sagittal line of the vertebrae. A humerus and a scapula showed that the carcass had been divided into smaller, more manageable, sections. A single radius had been chopped along the axial plane to allow marrow extraction. Also present was a classic example of the removal of the feet, a clean transverse chop through the very distal end of a metacarpal. The fusion data clearly point towards all the animals being adult, except for a single distally unfused metatarsal that suggests that the animal was younger than 36 months old when it was culled. Two mandibles could be aged, one to approximately 36 months and the other as an 'old adult'.

Table 18 Cattle and 'cattle-sized' skeletal representation from LBI95 Open Area 8

Skeletal part	No. of frags
Head	22
Limbs	15
Feet	12
Vertebrae and ribs	27

Pigs continued to be more plentiful than sheep/goat, the former predominantly represented by primary waste, mandibles and metapodials. The ageing information is very limited. Most of the pigs were killed while still young. There was also a single infant scapula and just one discernible adult pig. Evidently the pigs were being culled at an age of less than 2.5 years.

An adult heron tarso-metatarsus was recovered from another external dump. It has been suggested that a heron may have been associated with ritual activities during the Roman period in the eastern cemetery of London (Rielly 2000). However, in the eastern Roman cemetery the heron was represented by an entire skeleton recovered alongside a dog skeleton and with a noticeable lack of 'normal' domestic refuse. Heron bones have been found within other London deposits dating to this period (West n d). In each case, as here, they were associated with general dumps of food waste.

A single adult metatarsal of a hedgehog was also recovered but is not considered to be food waste.

This assemblage would seem to have originated from a variety of sources. The remains of the cattle and pigs were heavily biased towards, and dominated by, primary waste. The chicken remains are all table waste. The presence of the individual roe deer mandible and the single hedgehog bone suggests the reworking of the assemblage. The age of the cattle (approximately three years) shows that good quality meat was being exploited with the animals being bred solely for this purpose. This differs from Borough High Street (BGH95), where the animals were substantially older and clearly had had another use prior to their slaughter. The roe deer, the heron and the young age of the pigs also suggest that good quality (possibly high-status) meat was being consumed in the vicinity.

LBI95 Building 4

After a short period of mixed dumping LBI95 Building 4 was built on exactly the same alignment. Its dimensions on site and construction mirrored that of Building 3. However, its walls survived in a better condition, the south wall in particular, which was 2.0m in length and had a series of posts and stakes in it, indicating its construction (Fig 74; Fig 75). Additionally there were fragments of painted wall plaster present in situ on its northern face, though retrieval of them was difficult as they had been thoroughly grouted. There was also a series of brickearth floors and occupation layers to the west with no associated walls, which represent either a further part of this room or an adjacent room to the west. At the west end of the south wall there was a threshold represented by in situ tiles, giving access to another room to the south. In this room there was a tile hearth up against the wall. The only decorative stone recorded was a fragment of Wealden shale – probably inlay – and tesserae, one in hard chalk, the other in fine-grained laminated sandstone.

Painted wall plaster decorated the northern room of clay and timber Building 4. The southern room of this building was also probably decorated, although no evidence of decoration was found. Only a relatively small quantity of plaster was

Fig 74 View of south wall of LBI95 Building 4

recovered, comprising mainly small fragments of plain white, grey and red coloured plaster, the latter probably from a panel. There are two border areas, one in grey and red and the other in yellow and black. Only one fragment with decoration survives; this is a yellow and blue border area with a trace of red and pink decoration in the yellow area.

The species representation within the animal bone from Building 4 (Table 19) is different from any previous assemblage.

Unusually, chicken is the most common species within this assemblage, followed by pig, cattle and then sheep/goat. The chicken bones represent a mixture of preparation waste (head and feet) and table waste (limb bones and vertebrae/ribs), the most common element being the tibio-tarsus (n=6). All of the bones are adult, except for one juvenile tibio-tarsus. Butchery is indicated by the removal of the feet. Knife marks on the meat bones were probably made while the birds were being consumed. The other bird species, teal, is represented by a single metatarsus.

Pig bones again increased, with sheep/goat being reduced to a negligible level, and with a new preference for pork over beef and lamb/mutton. The pigs are represented by a mixture of pelvises, skulls, lower limbs and feet. Only one butchery mark was present: a third metatarsal had three chop marks on the proximal end showing that the trotters had been removed. Cattle bones were all from the skull and metapodial regions except for a single fragment of humerus. The latter had been chopped so as to dismember the forelimb. Only four sheep/goat bones were present, two adult mandibles and two juvenile metapodials, and a single lamb jaw was also recovered.

Two hare bones were present in this assemblage (a pelvis and an ulna). Both were adult and probably from the same

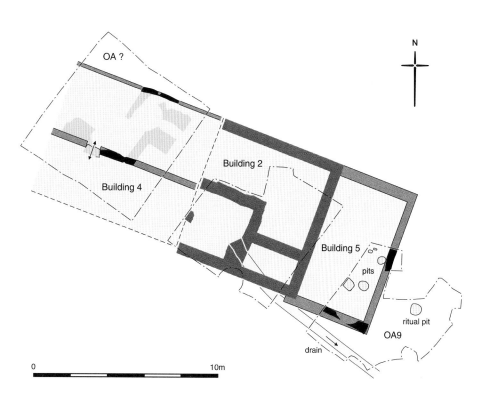

Fig 75 Plan of LBI95 Buildings 4 and 5

Table 19 Species representation from LBI95 Building 4

Species	No. of frags	Weight (g)
Cattle	9	347
'Cattle-sized'	32	245.6
Sheep/goat	4	25
Sheep	1	16
'Sheep-sized'	62	104.1
Pig	14	216.8
Hare	2	5.75
Mouse/vole	1	0.05
Rats	1	0.1
Chicken	37	23.1
Passerine	2	0.2
Teal	1	0.2
Total	**166**	**983.9**

individual. Despite the absence of butchery marks it is assumed that this animal had been consumed.

Three fragments of bone had been burnt to very high temperatures. These probably represent accidental burning on a hearth, with the fragments becoming incorporated and being swept out with the rest of the rubbish.

It is possible that this assemblage, with a mixture of preparation and table waste, represents the waste from one feast or meal. This is a very interesting assemblage, showing a movement towards an increase in the consumption of the smaller animals, such as chickens and pigs, rather than cattle. It is also important to note that the quantity of sheep/goat is again at a very low level, almost disappearing from the diet.

LBI95 Building 2

Building 2 continued in use, though undergoing changes. The function of room D was altered as it appears to have been used for an industrial purpose. The original floors had slumped into an underlying quarry pit and, after some levelling-up and possible shoring-up of the external wall to the north, two tile hearths were inserted into the room. These hearths measured 0.26m by 0.2m by 0.2m deep and 0.2m by 0.16m by 0.15m deep, and did not appear to be cooking hearths. Some slag was recovered from associated layers. There was not enough evidence to ascribe any particular function to the hearths and, indeed, a major industrial function would be at odds with the residential nature of the rest of the occupation evidence. This may just have been the small workshop of a local craftsman.

Room C continued unaltered although its final occupation layer was silty. There was still no clear evidence for what was taking place in this unusual room. The drain was re-cut and re-lined with timber before going out of use, pointing to the continuing importance of this feature to the room as a whole.

LBI95 Building 5

To the east of Building 2 a clay and timber building, Building 5, was constructed in c AD 100. This was not a substantial

structure and was represented by a series of postholes, stakeholes and a beamslot. The building may have been a small hut or lean-to attached to the east end of Building 2. However, the high quality of the painted wall plaster suggests a rather more substantial structure and an integral part of the building. The clay (daub) walls of this building were clearly keyed, as some of the wall plaster associated with Building 5 has clear keying impressions in the base. Such marks are absent from the plaster believed to have come from the masonry walls of Building 2.

Most of the plaster from Building 5 is plain white and very fragmentary, although at least certain areas seem to have been elaborately decorated. There are small fragments of white plaster with a decorative design in green, black, brown, yellow, pink, red, cream and purple, which may have been bordered by red and pink bands. There are also a few small fragments of plain dark red plaster. From the same building come fragments of white plaster decorated with pink, brown and yellow streaks, the streaks imitating marble veining. This is somewhat reminiscent of the streaked dado decoration found in situ in an early 4th-century building in York (Davey and Ling 1981, 207, pl 124).

Open Area 9

To the east of Building 5 was Open Area 9. In this open area was a small pit with an unusual assemblage of animal bones. They included a large volume of highly fragmented burnt material (approximately 180 fragments weighing 0.066kg). Despite the level of fragmentation, it was possible to deduce that the bulk of the fragments originated from two very juvenile pig skulls. The remainder of the assemblage was composed of a few unburnt fragments of pig (including fragments of an adult pelvis), sheep/goat (a juvenile tibia), some unidentified fish remains and a small quantity of 'sheep-sized' ribs. The bone had become completely calcinated, suggesting that it had been burnt at an extremely high temperature (in excess of 600°C) for a prolonged period of time. This may happen occasionally to small individual fragments of bone that have accidentally fallen into a hearth. In this case, where such a large volume of bone had been reduced to this state, it can only be assumed that it was intentional. The conditions required are very similar to those found in a cremation pyre. It seems highly likely that the 'cooking pit' actually represents a ritual offering of two very juvenile pigs' heads and unidentified fish remains. The unburnt bones probably represent material that was deposited on top of or mixed with the burnt pig bone during deposition. It is apparent from the lack of burning in this feature that the pigs were cremated elsewhere and then deposited in the pit.

This pit also contained a charred plant assemblage reminiscent of those found in the buildings and structures of Borough High Street. The mixture of wheat grains and weed seeds, including a lentil and pea (Pisum sativum L) seed, suggests the use of sieving waste as fuel. But seven other mineralised peas are also present, so it is possible that peas were part of a dish cooked or disposed of in this pit. The lentil could also have entered the samples as food waste rather than sieving waste. Lentils and peas can also be indicative of ritual and funerary practices and have been recorded in the eastern Roman cemetery of London (Barber and Bowsher 2000). However, there is no known cemetery nearby in Southwark at this date, the recently located one at Great Dover Street (Mackinder 2000) half a mile away being the nearest. It may be that this pit represents the remains of a meal held in Building 2 or 3 to the west in memory of a member of the family, after which the remains of the meal were buried in the garden as an offering. Alternatively, the offering may have been to appease the gods because of illness or bad luck afflicting the house.

Dumping in Open Area 9 sealed the drain running from Building 2. It appears to have been used mainly for dumping domestic refuse, although the drain backfill also contained three dog skeletons. There were also two structural postholes, though relating to what is not certain. A 12mm thick slab of Kentish ragstone, which may have been a stone roofing tile, was recovered and may have originated from Building 2.

8

Mid 2nd-century redevelopment

Hadrian set out for Britain

Scriptores Historiae Augustae, 4th century AD

8.1 Period 6: Southwark's market hall

Reconstruction of the settlement alongside the main road

There was a marked change around AD 120–40 when there was extensive reconstruction on the eastern frontage of the main road (Fig 76). There was no clear reason for this (for instance a disaster on the scale of the Boudican destruction) and it probably came about as a result of the continuous development of the settlement with the passage of time in response to a variety of factors, perhaps economic.

Southwark's market hall complex

Building 13

At the north end of the Ticket Hall site (BGH95), Building 13 continued to be occupied. The remains were very heavily truncated in this phase by later pitting. However, there were two hearths containing traces of metal and slag and a shallow linear east–west feature *c* 4.0m long also containing industrial debris, as well as an internal pit. It is possible, though unlikely, that some industrial activity was now taking place, perhaps in conjunction with the smithy to the south. Alternatively, this part of the building may have become a workshop for a craftsman. It is more probable, however, that this was chance deposition. It is presumed that the parts of the building traced in BSE94 and JSS92 continued in use as well, as there is no evidence for their demolition, though admittedly no evidence of activity datable to this period survived. The floors continue to be of utilitarian brickearth and there was no firm evidence from this phase either to confirm or discount the hypothesis that this might be a part of an expanded *macellum* complex.

Structure 2

Structure 2, the smithy, also continued in use with further new hearths and widespread ash and hammerscale deposits. The floors continued to be of brickearth. The first smithing hearth of this phase measured 0.8m long by 0.3m wide by 0.15m deep. It was aligned north–south with depressions in its centre interpreted as crucible settings (Fig 77). There was a rake-out area to the south. Layers surrounding the hearth and anvil area contained large quantities of ash, clinker, and micro- and macro-slag remains.

This was followed by the construction of a classic lozenge-shaped hearth, 1.2m long by 0.7m wide by 0.25m deep, with two stakeholes at the western, rake-out, end, which may have formed part of a superstructure over the hearth.

A fire pit was surrounded by a circle of stakeholes forming some sort of superstructure over the hearth. It has been suggested (L Keys pers comm) that these stakeholes could have supported the bellows used to heat the forge, but there was no clear pattern to them and this could not be confirmed. Another pit is thought to have contained fuel. A small hearth or burnt area was also recorded. The brickearth floor beside it was covered in hammerscale with a strong concentration in one area. Such a concentration of hammerscale in one particular area suggests that this may have been the location of the anvil. A copper coin of Hadrian came from this smaller hearth, and also associated with it was a possible cut for an anvil.

The larger hearth described above had no hammerscale around it, so it is possible to suggest a layout for the forge with the blacksmith standing to the north and heating the iron in the large forge, then transferring the hot metal to the anvil immediately to one side and beating it, causing the tell-tale hammerscale to form a layer around the anvil. A large number of stakeholes to the east of the smithy may have formed an internal partition or been part of an internal feature related to the smith's activities, as the surrounding area was very strongly magnetic and severely scorched.

Smithing in Southwark

The confirmed presence of a smithy alongside Southwark Road 1 should come as no surprise, for various finds over the last thirty years in the locality have suggested as much. At 1–7 St Thomas Street (Dennis 1978) a well (F30, Fig 78), dated to the late 2nd century, produced a 'smith urn', a ritual vessel associated with the Celtic smith-god and decorated with a hammer, pincers and anvil. This well lies approximately 20m to the east of the smithy excavated on the Borough High Street excavation. The remains of 20 dogs were also found in this well and two adjacent pits (F28 and F29), dogs being sacred to the Celts and also associated with the 'mallet' or 'striker' god Sucellos. These pits were timber-lined and divided into compartments.

Additionally, fragments of iron smithing slag were found in four adjacent 2nd-century pits (F9, 10, 11 and 23) and under the foundations of later buildings on the site. The layers in another pit (F14) were heavily concreted with iron. A fragment of crucible used in bronze working came from one pit (F17). Dennis (1978) concluded that these pits may have had an industrial function and when they went out of use may have had ritual deposits placed in them.

One possible interpretation is that these pits were in the open area behind the smithy and contained the waste and other objects associated with it. However, the pits would have been on the other side of the ditch in Open Area 20 (see below), if it continued to the north, and therefore may have been associated with another property, though this perhaps would have been too coincidental.

There is also a marked continuity apparent in the location of the smithy. The pre-Boudican smithy was replaced after the blaze by the new structure only 15m to the north-east. This could suggest that property ownership was respected during the new layout of the settlement after the fire. The ritual associations with a Celtic god in the St Thomas Street pits indicate that the family of smiths – for there is evidence of smithing over a period of a hundred years at least, covering several generations – is more likely to have been of British origin than Roman settlers.

Alternatively there could be an element of central control, with the smith possibly operating in an area designated for such activities. It is certainly a logical site for a blacksmith to operate from, alongside the main access road from the south and on the margin of the settlement.

However, the smithy stands alone as an industrial location on the site and there does not appear to be an industrial core like that at the Courage's Brewery site (Hammer in prep). Here various industrial activities, including copper working, were pursued over a long period of time. The smithy takes its place among a variety of different functions for buildings along the main road, including, at various times, a butcher's and a baker's.

Iron in Roman Southwark

Iron was required for the tools of virtually all craftsmen, for the large hooks, chains and other lifting equipment used to transfer cargo from ship to quay and vice versa, for the enormous number of nails and clamps needed in building and for ships, and for the weapons and armour of the military, to mention but a few uses. All of these objects were made by smiths but some could only be manufactured by specialist smiths, since among the Roman ironwork and tools found in London are types which, even today, cannot easily be made and must be ordered from particular firms (Morris 1982, 274).

The London smiths probably received their iron as roughly shaped blooms produced by the smelting industry of the Weald. If these were transported by road, Southwark would have been of some importance since this was the first part of Londinium they would reach. It may be that it was easier to have a great deal of the town's ironworking taking place in Southwark, not only to dispense with the need for transportation of iron back and forth across the river by boat or bridge, but also to spare the City the noise and dirt which must have characterised large ironworking districts at that time. If the military, perhaps the legionary fort, or the many ships on the river needed servicing and supplies Southwark would have seemed an obvious choice, since here smiths might be free of some of the constraints which the more formal City across the river would impose on its craftsmen. Hence, there must have been many different types of smith, including resident specialists, catering to the needs of the City and the military, and we ought to find much more evidence for their workshops than we have hitherto in London. There is a considerable amount of iron from the City, much of it dumps in the Walbrook, but the waste evidence from Southwark certainly supports the view that ironworking was an important craft in the area, and when specifically looked for, as in the case of BGH95, the smithies are there to be found.

There are numerous pictorial representations of the Roman smith from all over Europe and Britain, all furnishing information on his most important tools, and sometimes the layout of his smithy. Most smiths appear to have used a raised hearth, sometimes with a hood (as in a graffito scene from the Catacomb of Domatilla), which would leave no trace archaeologically except, perhaps, part of a square base of brick or stone. Building 3 probably had such a raised hearth because, despite

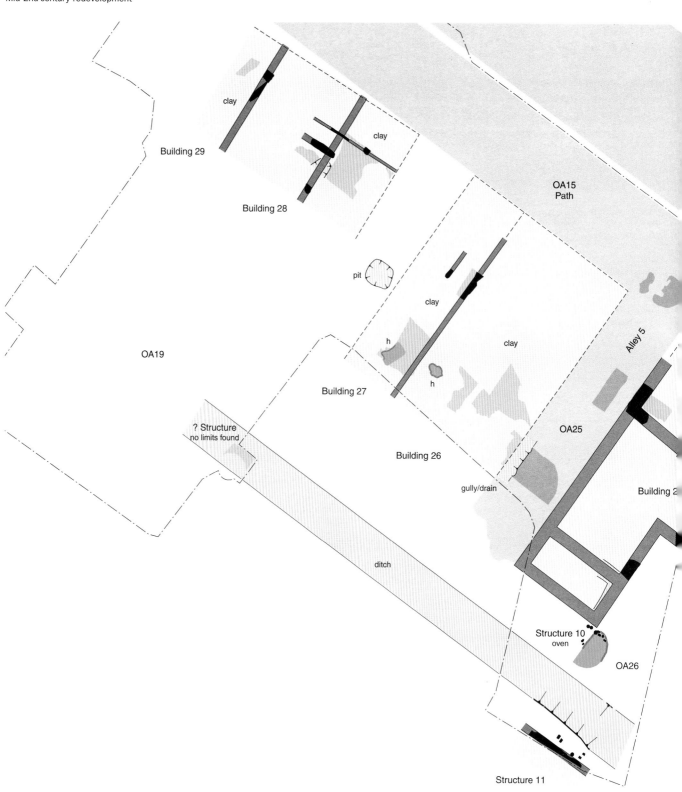

Fig 76 Plan of principal archaeological features, period 6

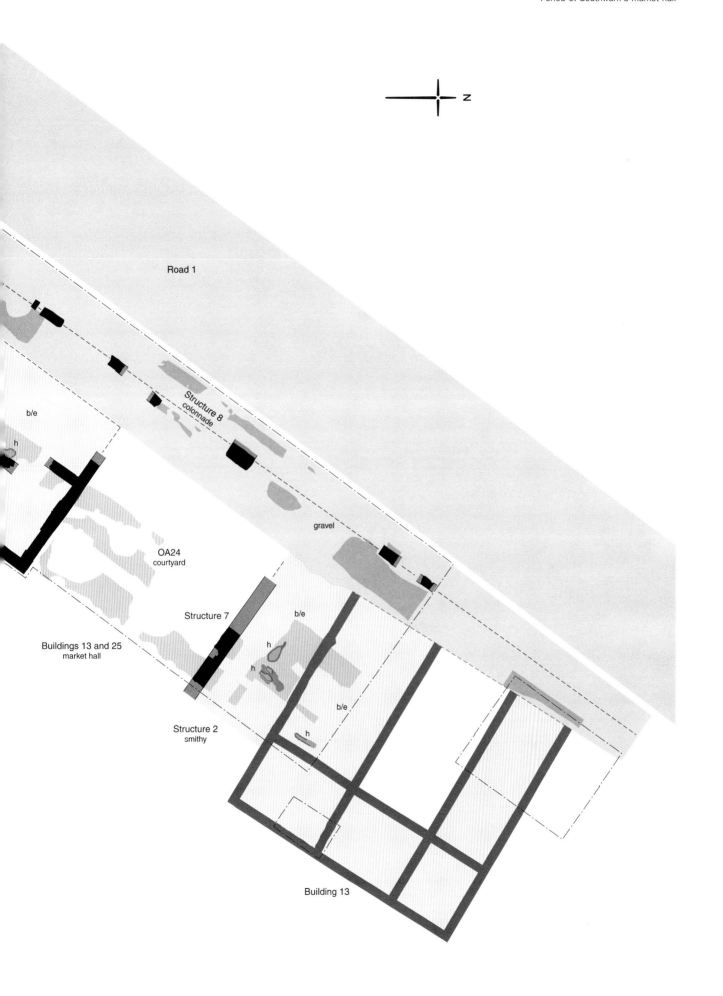

N

Road 1

b/e

h

Structure 8
colonnade

gravel

OA24
courtyard

Structure 7

b/e

h

h

Buildings 13 and 25
market hall

Structure 2
smithy

b/e

h

Building 13

Fig 77 View of blacksmith's hearth

the lack of ground level burning (a hearth in the conventional archaeological sense), the amount of hammerscale in and around the building indicates that it did function as a smithy. Two fragments of vitrified Roman brick were found along with iron slag in the area of Building 3 and could lend support to the supposition that the raised hearth was built of these. The Structure 2 sequence of hearths were, or appeared to be, ground level hearths – one with a low clay superstructure – and may imply a completely different type of smith and smithing activity from that of Building 3. It is also later in date and, whereas Building 3 could represent the traditional Roman smithy, Structure 2 may be representative of a re-emerging British tradition or a poorer smith.

The 'smith urn' found nearby at St Thomas Street (Dennis 1978, fig 166, no. 1273) bears representations of hammer, tongs and (possibly) a small anvil of the type which would have been inserted into a large anvil block of wood. On the appliqué sherd from the neck of a large jar from Corbridge (Toynbee 1962, pl 256), the 'smith god' holds a hammer and tongs and also appears to be using a small anvil set into a wooden anvil block. Tools and anvils rarely survive because they were too valuable to be abandoned or thrown away, and would have been recycled when no longer serviceable. In most representations of the Roman smith he is shown standing at his anvil, but in the relief on the gravestone from Aquileia and on the gravestone of L. Cornelius Atimetus (in the Vatican Museum) both smiths sit in front of their anvils, the latter having another raised block between his knees (a work surface?) as he faces the anvil. During the excavation of Structure 2, the possible site of the anvil block or stone anvil was located. It was a shallow circular depression, which had no hammerscale within it, located close to the mouth of the ground level hearth.

Where a representation shows another figure besides the smith, there is often an assistant working the bellows behind the hearth. Sometimes the bellows are quite large and would have required some structural support. Structure 2 had a number of stakeholes leading up to the back of its hearth, and these may be related to a bellows support. Also, to the north of the hearth in the same building, there was an almost perfect square of

charcoal staining (visible during excavation) on the floor next to the wall, implying that a box may have been used to store the fuel used in the hearth. In the case of both smithies the evidence is that charcoal was the smith's fuel: in samples from the smithies and amongst the slag it was ubiquitous, mostly as tiny fragments but sometimes as larger pieces.

Nails were found with the slag from both smithies but it is not known whether these were products, were gathered for recycling, or were old ones that had been discarded. Possibly both smithies were capable of producing nails if required, but they may not have been their only products.

Structure 7

The south side of the smithy was now marked by a large tile wall with pink mortar, Structure 7 (Fig 79). This wall runs east–west and was extremely well made with fine coursing and rendering. It was 3.5m long by 0.75m wide and was truncated at its west end by modern activity. Its east end ran beyond the limit of excavation. It survived to c 0.5m above ground level with relatively shallow foundations only 0.3m deep. The tiles are of a fabric not generally recognised in London before AD 140. There is nothing else of similar construction on the site. It is possible that there was a return of this wall to the north to form a more substantial smithy on the south side of Building 13. However, it is more likely that the west side of the smithy was left open for reasons already explained (see Chapter 6). The wall seems rather too well made to have been a simple property boundary. However, if it was doubling as the north side of an open market area (see below) then its high quality makes more sense. There was a low quality mortar render on the north internal face (that is, inside the smithy) but the south external face showed no sign of any decoration.

The wall was well constructed with courses of bonding bricks in two distinctive related fabrics (3050 and 3061), probably from kilns at Reigate in Surrey. These fabrics were definitely in use by AD 140 in the City, but on this site seem in several contexts to occur with Hadrianic pottery, which may mean that they start earlier in Southwark, possibly between AD 120 and 140. The bonding courses in the wall consisted of complete lydion bricks, the dimensions of which are approximately 1.5 Roman feet x 1 Roman foot (444mm x 296mm). The brick samples from Structure 7 fall into two distinct size groups: a) the smaller bricks are in the size range 355–380mm in length and 270–290mm in breadth (6 examples), with an average size of 368.3mm x 274.5mm; b) the larger bricks are in the size range 437–472mm in length and 288–309mm in breadth (7 examples), with an average size of 459.7mm x 299.9mm. Tile courses utilised bricks in both sizes, laid in different arrangements. Built into the same wall was a large fragment of reused *sesquipedalis* (a thick brick approximately 1.5 Roman feet square, usually used in hypocausts), also in fabric 3050 (Fig 104, <T7>). The mortar used was a fine, pink *opus signinum* containing charcoal flecks. It is not clear why a waterproof mortar was used in this structure. The Reigate lydion bricks used in Structure 7 are similar to those used in Structure 8, although in the latter they are more fragmentary.

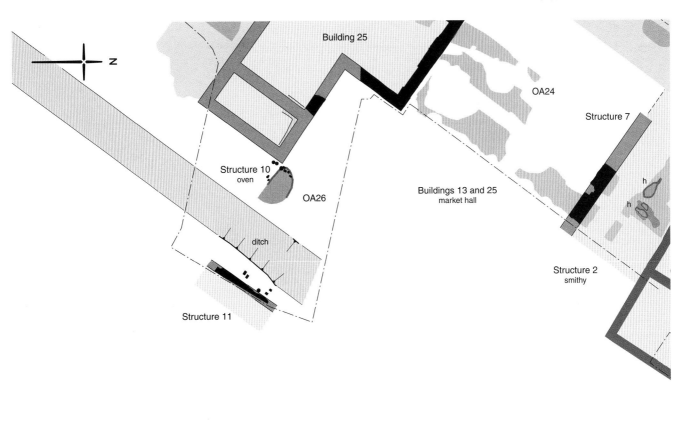

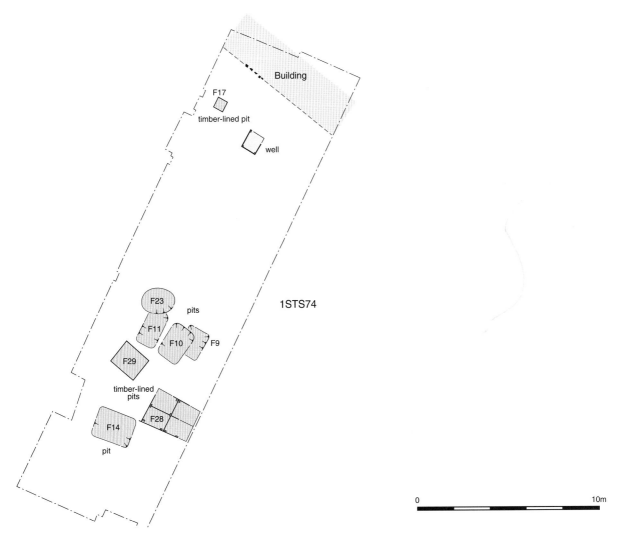

Fig 78 Plan of features associated with smithing

Fig 79 View of Structure 7

The wall, as well as delineating the northern edge of the central open area to the south, may also have been used to support a roof over this area as its size was certainly sufficient to have been load-bearing.

Open Area 24

To the south of Structure 7 was Open Area 24, where there were a series of external dumps and brickearth surfaces. A pit contained a lead waste droplet and there were also lumps of iron slag, presumably deriving from the smithy. A dump of domestic refuse contained a residual fragment of lamp <R131> made in a central Gaulish workshop, a stone hone <R178> and a gaming piece cut from a potsherd, together with glass vessel fragments, none of identifiable form, as well as large quantities of pot and bone. The sample also produced slag and metal waste. Further to the south there was a dump of brickearth, up to 0.3m thick, marking preparation and ground levelling for Building 25. The brickearth probably derived from the previous building in this area, Building 22. One of the dumps produced a stone weight <R166> made from an aluminium-rich clay found in the Thames estuary, which is often used as building rubble in the Roman period (Fig 81). Although the object is of the triangular form often ascribed to loom weights, it is possible that it was general-purpose or even a steelyard weight. It has a single suspension hole which had been drilled from both sides and there are wear marks around the hole caused by the friction of a cord on the relatively soft stone. Other finds from the dump included a bone needle <R121> (not illustrated) and a plain but well made bone hairpin with a conical head <R73> (Fig 81). In addition there was a little domestic glassware and coins of 1st-century date.

Painted wall plaster was again found in these dumps, and would appear to have come from the walls of Building 22. The plaster falls into two groups based on the thickness of the backing layer. In the first it measures 11–14mm while in the second it is up to 50mm; there is no obvious difference in the composition of the backing used in the two groups.

The thinner plaster comprises a red panel area bordered by a white band (6mm) followed by a green border (49mm) which in turn is bordered by a further white band (c 7mm) and black (Fig 80). This part of the colour scheme is very similar to that used to decorate part of Building 2 at LBI95. There is also a plain white fragment with a dark red band (5mm), probably part of a white panel. A number of plain white fragments recovered from context [1722] may be part of a panel or, more probably, from a wall area of plain white plaster.

The thicker fragments comprise both dado and border areas. The dado fragments are white with dark red and yellow splashes bordering both yellow and grey (not illustrated). The latter also has a grey vertical line (11mm thick) separating two areas of the dado. There are a number of panel fragments in white bordered by a thin grey band (3–6mm) and then red. One of the thicker fragments is part of a doorway or window opening. This is a border area painted in dark red, white (6mm band) and grey. The curved surface is painted grey and has a red paint splash at the edge, although it is not certain if this marks the start of a dado.

Animal bone associated with Structure 7

A total of 164 fragments of bone were recovered from two external dumps built up against the south side of Structure 7 (Table 20) and should be considered as related to the bone from Open Area 24.

Fig 80 Painted wall plaster from
demolition of Building 22 (1:2)

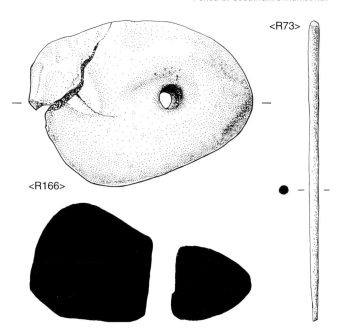

Fig 81 Stone weight <R166> (1:2) and bone hairpin <R73> (1:1) from Open Area 24

Table 20 Cattle and 'cattle-sized' skeletal representation from Structure 7

Skeletal part	No. of frags	Weight (g)
Head	44	1064.89
Feet	2	29.88
Limbs	83	2812.33
Ribs and vertebrae	24	862.07

The species range was dominated by cattle and 'cattle-sized' bones, both in terms of fragment counts and weight. The only other species present were minimal quantities of sheep/goat and pig, with a mere three bones indicating the presence of the latter.

Again the feet were poorly represented, implying that they were left attached to the hide for removal off the site to the tanner's, although this is not consistent with the high number of skull fragments present.

The cattle and 'cattle-sized' skeletal representation shows all elements represented, with a clear dominance of limbs. Butchery

marks were from a range of processes involved in the preparation of the carcass. A limited quantity of vertebrae (n=9) demonstrate that the carcasses had been halved but in an inconsistent manner: some along the central line and others to either side. One cervical vertebra had been chopped transversely across the anterior aspect to divide the carcass further. One skull fragment had been chopped transversely across the occipital condyles as evidence that the animal had been decapitated. An interesting example of butchery was a number of knife marks identified on a hyoid, which may indicate that the method of slaughter was by slitting the throat. Alternatively they may have been inflicted during the removal of the tongue. The carcasses were then further subdivided with chops through the girdle and the shoulder region. Meat was removed from the bones prior to cooking, as shown by the high proportion of grazing chops on the femur and humerus shafts. The lower value meat bones were commonly divided along the axial plane for marrow extraction. A cattle humerus and a tibia show evidence of gnawing by dogs, which might imply that the dogs had been fed from the table.

There is little data on the age of the animals present, but fusion evidence suggests that the majority of the cattle were older than 36 months, except for a single distally unfused metatarsal which represents an individual aged less than 36 months. A single ageable mandible was recovered and classified as 'senile' on the basis of tooth wear.

Animal bone from Open Area 24

The faunal remains for this area were recovered from a series of pits and external layers. Thirteen contexts produced a total of 1491 fragments (approximately 32kg). The majority of the contexts were small, containing less than 30 fragments of bone. The assemblage from one external dump [1265] weighed just over 11kg and contained 525 fragments of bone. Over 83% of these were cattle and 'cattle-sized' while sheep/goat and pig combined only accounted for 5%.

As can be seen from Table 21, the majority of the material comes from the vertebrae, rib, skull and feet regions, with once again a noticeable absence of phalanges. A small quantity of food waste was also present. Butchery was mainly focused on the vertebrae; some had been chopped along the central line but in the majority of cases it was to either side of this. The angle of the butchery marks implies that this was performed with the animal lying on its back. Chops through the pubic shaft of the pelvis (also directly related to the halving of the carcass) were also identified. A number of pelvises additionally had transverse chops through either the posterior or anterior aspects, dividing the carcasses into smaller, more manageable sections. Butchery on the meat-bearing elements is associated with dismemberment and partition into joints. A single chop on a mandible is consistent with the removal of the tongue.

Three cattle metatarsals from this deposit were indicative of working waste. They had been worked in a very consistent manner, each being finely sawn 35mm from the proximal epiphysis, in two directions: firstly, from the anterior, an attempt was made to break the rest off, and if this failed it was sawn slightly from the posterior face and then snapped. On the posterior face of one metatarsal there is an extra saw cut that had been abandoned. The bone could have been worked into any of a wide range of products including pins, buttons, beads, dice, knife handles and so forth. The smashed remains of an 'old adult' horncore (following Armitage 1982) were also recovered from this deposit. These two examples indicate that some craft activities were taking place in the near vicinity, even if it was only on an individual basis.

Scope for ageing the cattle present is severely limited. Fusion information indicates that all the cattle were older than 36 months. Only five mandibles were sufficiently complete to allow ageing; three were aged as old adult (including one 'senile') while the others were at least adult. The majority of the animals that were being processed here were mature, suggesting a former use as dairy cattle or draught animals.

A single loose, worn, cattle deciduous premolar was recovered. It is possible that this was a shed tooth from an animal that was bred on site or from a young animal that was culled. In the absence of any more evidence it is impossible to speculate further.

Other animals recovered from this context include a pair of chicken bones and a goose humerus. Three dog bones were recovered, possibly coming from one individual. Calculations on the humerus gave a stature of approximately 40cm to the shoulder. Besides these a partial skeleton of a house mouse (Mus musculus) was recovered, an animal which eats almost any form of grain or stored food. Lawrence and Brown (1973) state that a likely habitat for this creature is dirty corners of neglected buildings, so it is reasonable to believe that a small proportion of this context came from floor sweepings.

The other large single assemblage from this area came from an external dump deposit. The assemblage was dominated by cattle and 'cattle-sized' fragments, plus small quantities of sheep/goat and pig.

The cattle skeletal representation is largely composed of head, vertebrae and rib fragments (Table 22). All the limb elements are very fragmentary. This assemblage is clearly weighted towards primary butchery waste, although it also includes a large collection of food waste, dominated by vertebrae and ribs.

To judge from the lack of non-domestic species, and the incidence of dog gnawing on only a single bone, it is probable that the bones were dumped directly into an enclosed deposit.

The other pits in the area contained a wider range of species including dog (a single phalange), horse (a single third phalange) and unidentified chicken and goose in addition to cattle, sheep/goat and pigs. Unfortunately, the quantities are very limited. A single fragment of red deer antler tine was recovered from a pit; it is possible that this was working waste.

The presence of the primary butchery waste in this open area suggests that the butcher noted in Building 10 (see Chapter 6) may have relocated to the building to the north (Building 13) or to Building 25 to the south, and was disposing of his butchery waste here. The animal bone evidence from Building 25 (see below) suggests that this may have been the new location for the butcher's; this in turn would indicate that he was a new butcher unrelated to the previous one, since there would be a gap of some fifty years between the abandonment of Building 10 and the reappearance of a butcher in Building 25. Alternatively, the butcher's business may just have been conducted nearby but without leaving any trace on the site.

Table 21 Cattle and 'cattle-sized' body part representation from Open Area 24

Skeletal part	No. of frags
Head	67
Limb	38
Feet (from tarsals/carpals and below)	41
Ribs and vertebrae	285

Table 22 Cattle and 'cattle-sized' skeletal representation from Open Area 24

Skeletal part	No. of frags
Head	139
Limb	35
Feet (from tarsals/carpals and below)	32
Ribs and vertebrae	155

Building 25

Building 25 was a masonry building of rather peculiar plan
(Fig 76). The north wall, constructed of flint and tile courses,
was recorded for a length of 6.5m. The tile courses consisted
of Hadrianic period bricks (Reigate fabrics 3050 and 3061),
and roof tiles in the same fabrics were found in a structural
cut. Small fragments of unworked ragstone were also present
(Fig 82). The west frontage was truncated by the Battlebridge
sewer but the east wall was recorded during piling works and
was traced for 3.0m. A north–south wall butting up against the
north wall marked an internal partition and measured 1.7m.
However, this wall did not continue to the south, on the other
side of the modern truncation. Instead there was a north–south
wall 1.75m long offset to the east by c 1.0m. This nearly lined
up with another wall fragment 2.3m further south, which
returned to the west for c 1.0m and presumably linked up
with the western frontage of the building. The building does
not appear to be symmetrical with a wing extending to the
east. However, the occupation on either side of the surviving
stretch of wall seems to have been internal, suggesting another
wall for which no evidence survives.

The only way to make sense of the misalignment of the
internal walls is to have an east–west wall running down the
line of the modern truncation, but there is no direct evidence
for such a wall. The floors in this building were all of brickearth
or low quality mortar, and in some areas there was a series of
such floors one on top of another, indicating a reasonable
length of occupation. The most westerly room had evidence
for a hearth in it.

Associated with this building was a ceramic oil lamp
<R128>, one of the finest from the site, with a well-known
scene on the discus – one especially popular in the provinces –
showing entertainers, perhaps dwarves, who are performing
a dance and accompanying themselves with hand clappers
(Fig 83). The lamp was made at Lyon in southern Gaul in
the mid to late 1st century, and its survival intact until the
mid 2nd century raises the question of the length of use of such
objects and whether it had been preserved as an exotic import,
or perhaps an heirloom. The dump produced other domestic
items, including a mount or stud in the form of a lion's head
<R190>, a motif commonly used to adorn lock plates.

In situ destruction deposits from the building contained a
large quantity of roof tile as well as brick in Reigate fabrics 3050
and 3061, which presumably was used to roof this building; a
fragment of roof tile in late local fabric 2459b was also present.
Overfired and vitrified brick appears in several contexts, although
it should be noted that the Reigate bricks are generally highly
fired and may look burnt even when they are not.

Ceramic tesserae are associated with the use and disuse of
the building, and those from a brickearth dump occur in both
fabrics 2815 and 3050. Some of them are poorly made, being

Fig 82 Detail of walls of Building 25

Fig 83 Oil lamp with dancers
<R128> from Building 25 (2:3)

little more than tile chips. These fragments were not recorded
in situ and there is no evidence for a tessellated floor inside the
building, although there were suggestions – albeit inconclusive
– of a tiled area immediately to the north.

Some fragments of white-skimmed and red-painted wall
plaster came from an internal occupation layer, and may have
been from the internal walls of the building. A Radlett 'gridded'
combed flue occurred in occupation deposits, and a late Roman
combed box-flue in Reigate fabric 3061 in destruction levels.

The animal bone from contexts associated with this building,
both internal and external, comprised a total of 1228 fragments
(19.64kg).

An occupation layer in a room at the south of the building
contained few species. Again cattle dominate the assemblage,
constituting 70% (n=155) of the total. Limb elements are
present but only in low frequencies, with vertebrae and rib
fragments being most common. Butchery on the bones represents
mostly the initial processing of the carcass, including decapitation
through the occipital condyles of the skull, sub-division of the
carcass, and the removal of the lower limb/foot area. Seven
metapodials are clear examples of working waste; they had
been sawn through the distal end of the shaft by a fine saw
in order to prepare the shaft for further working. As a fragment
of bone pin was recovered from this context it is possible that
this was the intended end product. Two cattle first phalanges
had numerous knife marks on the proximal end of the shaft
consistent with waste from skinning. Fusion information was
very restricted, but what is present indicates that the majority
of animals were older than three years, while there are two
examples of juvenile metapodials. The tooth wear information
is even more limited, relating to only one young adult and one
old adult/senile beast.

Sheep/goat and pig bones were restricted to 'dressing'
waste. Grazing knife marks were evident on a single sheep/goat
metatarsal, and are likely to be skinning cuts. Two pig pelvises
had been chopped through the pubic region, possibly with the
aim of halving the carcass or at least the posterior part of it.
Further butchery to the bones included filleting marks on the
ischium, representing the removal of rump meat.

Two chicken bones (both lower leg) were recovered from
this context and probably represent the preparation of the bird
for the table.

Another occupation layer within the same room had a
species representation that was almost identical to the previous
one, only with a noticeable increase in the dominance of cattle
at 86% (n=577). The skeletal representation from this context
is also more distinctive (Table 23), being totally dominated
by vertebrae, ribs, head and metapodials. The butchery is very
similar to that described above. A single metacarpal had very
clear evidence of the removal of the feet with a single clean
transverse chop through the distal condyles. Two pathologies
were recorded, both on metatarsals: one had fused completely
with the tarsals above and the other had extensive pitting and
extra bone growth on the proximal epiphysis. These afflictions
are associated with spavin, a disease which (amongst others)
affects draught cattle (Baker and Brothwell 1980, 117).

The tooth wear information is very interesting, despite the
number of ageable individuals being limited (n=5). Of these,
four were aged to old adult/senile and the other to adult.
Discovered among the loose teeth was a single worn deciduous
premolar (dp4). There are two possible explanations for its
presence: either animals younger than 36 months (veal) were
being brought for butchery, or animals were being bred on the
site and this is a shed tooth. Unfortunately, there is no further
evidence to support either hypothesis.

A small number of the other contexts within this group
reproduced a pattern very similar to those described above,
with a dominance of cattle represented primarily by head,
vertebrae and rib fragments.

A single horse bone was recovered. The greatest lateral
length of the radius (all measurements following von den
Driesch 1976) was 300mm from which was calculated a
withers height of 12.8 hands (130.2cm) (following von den
Driesch and Boessneck 1974). This fits well into the range of
typical horse/pony statures for the Roman period (Rackham
1995, 170).

To the south of the building was an open area, Open Area
25, which contained a small linear feature, possibly a drip
gully formed by rain running off the roof of the building,
with a more substantial ditch further south which may
represent a formal property boundary. Alternatively it may
be related to Alley 5; although no trace of the alley itself
was recorded, according to its alignment it should have
crossed the site here.

Table 23 Cattle and 'cattle-sized' skeletal representation from Building 25

Skeletal part	No. of frags	Weight (g)	% of frags
Head	223	2550.1	49.12
Limb	8	132.0	1.76
Feet (tarsals/carpals and below)	63	2268.7	13.88
Vertebrae and ribs	160	1425.6	35.24

A colonnade alongside the road

The area between the building frontages and the road now became more formalised. A series of free-standing pier bases, rather irregularly spaced, suggests the construction of an arcade or colonnade, Structure 8, between the main road and the range of buildings (Fig 76). To the east of the arcade was a series of fine gravel surfaces, Open Area 15. The pier bases were finely made with well-finished tile courses, though the bases were not all constructed of the same material (Fig 84). There were five in all, though only two survived at foundation level. However, the tiles were generally of a different variety from those in Structure 7 to the east. It is possible to impose a regular pattern on the spacing if the bases were in fact low broken walls with intervening gaps of 3 Roman feet.

Fig 84 Detail of pier base from Structure 8

This group consisted of five masonry blocks:

Pier base 1 (S): Flint rubble in mortar; not dated.

Pier base 1 (N): Wall of brick in 3050/3061; dated to the late Hadrianic/Antonine period; the whole measured 1.9m north–south by 0.5m wide by c 0.75m high.

Pier base 2: Flint rubble; not dated; 0.85m x 0.55m x 0.3m.

Pier base 3: Flint rubble; not dated; 0.6m x 0.5m x 0.2m.

Pier base 4: Brick and roof tile, including Reigate fabrics 3050, 3061; dated to the late Hadrianic/Antonine period; 1.4m x 0.86m x 0.3m.

Pier base 5: Tegula mammata (fabric 2815/2452); not closely datable, but usually 1st- to early 2nd-century type; probably not reused; 1.1m x 0.8m x 0.8m.

Pier base 1 consisted of two parts, divided by a decayed vertical timber post, indicating that there was a timber superstructure over the masonry; this is interpreted as a timber-built roof over a pedestrian walkway, the roof joining Buildings 13 and 25.

Pier base 2 consisted of flint rubble in mortar, which is not datable; only the foundation and not the superstructure of this base survived. Pier base 3 was similar to 2.

Pier bases 4 and 5 were brick-built, but of different materials. Those in pier base 5 are tegulae mammatae and lydion (including complete examples). The tegula mammata is usually an early Roman form but they do not seem to have been reused. The type may be associated with public buildings. Their date of production, based on fabric type, is likely to be between AD 55 and 160, but they cannot be more closely dated. Pier base 4 was built of brick and roof tile, some in the Hadrianic/early Antonine Reigate fabrics, of which the roof tile was reused, and does not occur earlier than c AD 120–40.

It should be noted that the materials used in pier bases 4 and 5 are dissimilar, and do not suggest exact contemporaneity, though neither do they rule it out. Pier base 1, on the other hand, is closer in composition to base 4, which might imply contemporaneity. The Reigate brick in pier bases 1 and 4 is similar to that used in Structure 7, but complete dimensions for the bricks used in Structure 8 are not available, so it is not possible to say whether they belong to the smaller or larger size group.

No material in Structure 8 is necessarily later than AD 120–40. The lengths of pier bases 1 and 5, the best preserved, are more reminiscent of a low wall than a free-standing base, and it is possible that there was an interrupted wall frontage supporting the timber roof.

The southernmost of the bases is level with the south end of Building 25 and the line continues 25m to the north, to the northern limit of the excavation. It is presumed that the arcade starts north of Alley 5 and runs northwards towards the bridge. No bases were recorded on JSS92 but similar fine gravel surfaces were present and, coupled with the presence of a masonry building, the arcade may well have continued at least this far, giving a total length of at least 40m. The different forms of the pier bases indicate that this was not intended as a high-status arcade but as a more functional covered walkway constructed of whatever was to hand.

Structure 9, a north–south linear feature with large numbers of stakes and postholes similar to Structure 6, though slightly further to the east, was robbed out at this period (Fig 85). It was traced intermittently for c 16m and averaged 0.5m wide and 0.3m deep. This indicates a replacement of the roadside drain on the eastern side of the road. Again it appears that any wooden structure was completely removed at the time when the drain went out of use c AD 160. As with the previous drain it is presumed to have been in use for some time before its abandonment, so its use phase was probably in the previous period, though only evidence of its disuse survived.

Structures 10 and 11

To the east of Building 25, in Open Area 26, there was a large external feature, Structure 10, which was either a kiln or an oven (Fig 86). The feature was semicircular in shape and c 1.0m in diameter, though truncated to the east by a Victorian cellar. A set of raised mortar plinths formed part of the internal furniture of the structure. There were also a series of postholes at the western edge of the feature which represent part of the superstructure.

A substantial north–south ditch to the east of the structure may have marked a property boundary at the rear of the

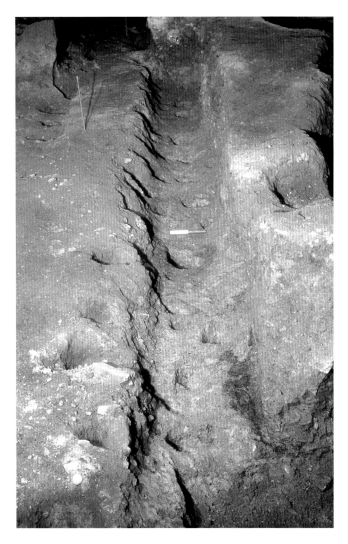

Fig 85 View of Structure 9

Fig 86 View of Structure 10

building. This was a re-cut of the ditch first dug in the latter part of the 1st century (see Chapter 6). The ditch was traced for 4.5m and was at least 2.35m wide (though truncated by a Victorian cellar to the west) and 0.4m deep.

On the far side of the ditch was another structure, Structure 11, consisting of a beamslot and assorted stakes and posts which may represent a building, but the evidence was ephemeral. The

possible beamslot was recorded at the very eastern limit of the site and no internal activity was present within the site boundaries. However, one find of note consisted of two joining fragments of a pipeclay figurine <R234> (one fragment came from the ditch to the west) imported from central Gaul (Fig 87). The subject is an animal but too little remains to judge whether it is a horse, a cult symbol of the goddess Epona and a symbol of fertility and healing, or a bull, symbolising strength and virility (Green 1989, 149). The early 2nd century saw the importation of such figurines reach its height.

Discussion

All these different elements, the masonry buildings, open area between and covered walkway, point to an expanded market hall for Southwark alongside the main road. The overall plan bears comparison with those at Wroxeter and Verulamium, with a central courtyard being surrounded by small shop units. The Southwark market hall, with a street frontage of up to 40m, is slightly larger than those of the other two, but it does not appear to extend as far back from the road.

The central open area, some 10m wide between two masonry buildings with an arcade or colonnade to the west, may have been some sort of communal open space or meeting place. There were a very large number of small stakeholes which were impossible to resolve into any coherent patterns but do suggest some prolonged activity. Perhaps this was a periodic market area, much like today's weekly markets, where light collapsible stalls are erected and taken down frequently. This could have supplemented the suggested permanent *macellum* in Building 13 to the north and indeed may have formed a large market complex with Building 25 to the south. A similar pattern of occupation has been suggested previously at Dorchester, among other places (Burnham and Wacher 1990, 120). Here the authors noted that there was a large, almost central open space 'bounded by a major second or third-century building containing a range of rooms flanked by verandas. As with other towns, this space probably served as a market place; whether the building, which is not unlike the range of a *macellum*, can be linked to it, is not certain'. However, our open area is on a much smaller scale.

Nonetheless, the presence of a *macellum* on the south bank, designed to serve the needs of the local community, seems plausible and would reflect the growing size and importance of the settlement. However, the Southwark building does not match the usual form of a *macellum* and this may reflect the more organic growth of the settlement, with a domestic building adapted over time and changing its function.

Timber-framed buildings at the south end of BGH95

At the south end of the excavation area it is difficult to discern any changes in the construction of buildings. The occupation continued largely unaltered, although this included repairs and some modifications to the clay and timber buildings. However, the appearance of the southern end of the site may not have been particularly different by this period. The vulnerability of these building to fire damage was either ignored or not considered significant when set beside the cheap and easily maintained construction of the buildings. Fire damage and total destruction of these buildings did happen on several subsequent occasions. The later stage of the development of the settlement included several buildings and structures, which were still being occupied in the late 2nd and 3rd centuries AD. Fragmentary elements of occupation and later structures are less well represented on the site, and it is difficult to establish the number and density of these structures.

Close to the St Thomas Street junction and at the eastern limit of the excavation area was an area of gravel surface. Gravel filled a slight hollow to a depth of 0.24m and this may form part of an east–west alley – a continuation in use of Alley 5. A damaged mortar from a cosmetic grinding set <R118> (Fig 87) was found in the gravels. It belongs to a class of objects which were apparently made only in Britain (Jackson 1985) and have been recognised with increasing frequency in London in recent years. There is evidence for the manufacture of cosmetic mortars at Skipton Street in Southwark (Jackson 1993). This is the second example to be found in Southwark, with another from 179 Borough High Street (Wardle in prep), and is unusual for London in having enamelled decoration, which would place its date in the 2nd century.

The site produced no military items of 2nd-century date, a time when London is known to have been garrisoned, although a fine carnelian intaglio <R60> (Fig 87), found in a post-Roman context at Borough High Street, is the type of object that may well have been worn by a soldier. Martin Henig has dated this gem, which bears the image of a heroic military figure, perhaps Achilles or Alexander the Great, to the Hadrianic period (see Chapter 11.3).

At the southern edge of the alley was a 1.6m wide drainage ditch that ran parallel with the alley. Immediately south of the alley were internal clay floor surfaces of Building 26 and Building 27. No building foundations were found at the northern or western limits of the floors associated with Building 26, but it is possible that the southern edge of the ditch by Alley 5 included an ill-defined and slumped construction slot. The southern edge of the possible construction cut indicated the northern extent of the building. The building was constructed over the earlier ditch and the northern element of Open Area 21. The resulting levelling and construction deposits included a seal box <R168> (Fig 87), a typical 2nd-century form, diamond-shaped, with coloured enamelling set within a grid. This is the only object from BGH95 that has any direct association with written communication. Quern fragments and a millstone also came from the construction deposits of the building, as well as a fragmentary buckle and buckle plate, probably from armour, but certainly residual by this stage.

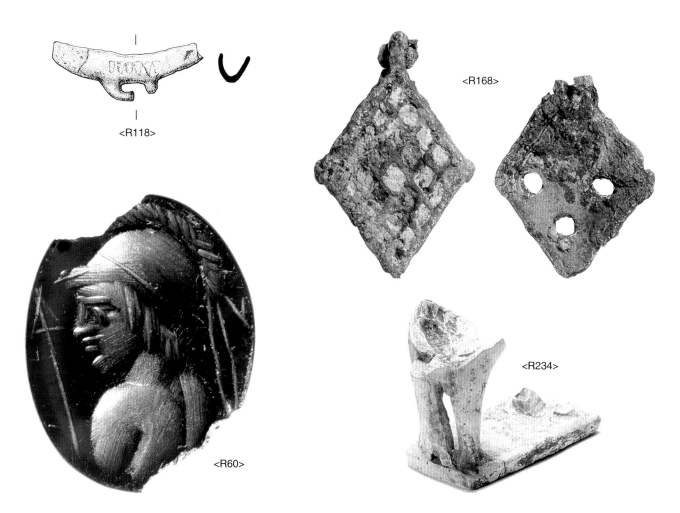

Fig 87 Finds group from period 6: cosmetic mortar <R118> (1:1); ceramic figurine <R234> (1:2); seal box <R168> (2:1); carnelian intaglio <R60> (4:1)

109

An oval-shaped hearth 1.0m long and 0.66m wide was located close to the line of the southern wall of the building. This bowl-like hearth had fragments of a clay lining and tegula and brick fragments used in its construction. No evidence for the function of the hearth was recovered.

Adjacent to the south of Building 26 was a further compacted clay floor laid on an extensive levelling deposit. The floor was very patchy, perhaps as a result of wear. A tiled hearth, consisting of broken or reused roof tile, was set into this floor. The flat hearth included an inner and outer setting of tiles, but only a 0.7m x 0.46m part of the hearth survived, the western half having been removed or disturbed. A stakehole was located with the hearth and may have been part of a structure associated with its use. The floor slumped partly into the backfilled, square-lined well. The well was finally backfilled during the construction of Building 26, which extended across the southern end of the earlier Open Area 21.

During the early 2nd century new make-up layers and floors were laid and Building 28 was constructed. It is possible that some elements of the previous Building 23 were reused. The ground plans of the buildings were very similar, though there may have been an extension further eastwards. Clay floor and internal wall foundation fragments indicate some areas of internal occupation, but the overall plan of the building was not revealed. The floor and occupation deposits included stem fragments and clover (*Trifolium* sp) seeds. These may have been derived from a floor covering such as hay.

The building may have departed from a simple strip form and may well have undergone some changes during another episode of floor replacement. This resulted from areas of localised slumping in the floors. Make-up dumps were used to fill in hollows and create a level area for the new floors. A fragment of a Venus figurine <R235>, the type of votive or cult object that could well have had a place in a domestic shrine, was recovered from the make-up. A large pit may have been dug during this period of refurbishment. This roughly square pit with rounded corners was 1.4m wide and 0.36m deep. Domestic rubbish, including animal bone and oyster shell, was dumped into it and this may have been its original function.

The building probably continued in use well into the 2nd century with further floors and occupation evident. The last of the sequence of floors contained a mixture of charred edible fruit seeds, including mulberry (*Morus* sp), blackberry/raspberry (*Rubus fruticosus/idaeus*), fig (*Ficus carica* L) and cherry (*Prunus cerasus/avium*). These may represent domestic debris derived from foodstuffs. Other seeds preserved by waterlogging from plants of semi-aquatic habitats suggest that the building was left exposed for a while after abandonment.

Immediately south of Building 28 an additional fragment of compacted clay floor may form part of Building 29, with a single foundation slot for a timber baseplate possibly marking the northern end of the building. The fragmentary remains of Buildings 28 and 29 at the southern end of the excavated area may also represent a single multi-roomed building of a more complex nature than a strip building.

Use and disuse of four 1st- to 2nd-century wells

Four wells were found in the south-east part of the site. These were broadly similar in construction and date and had characteristics in common with other Roman wells recorded in Southwark (Yule 1982). They appear to have gone out of use soon after AD 120 and were subsequently used as rubbish pits.

The wells were all dug through the top of natural sands down into lower gravels usually at or below OD. A large construction pit was dug for each of the wells and a timber frame inserted. The survival of the wooden elements was fragmentary and generally poor. Two of the wells did, however, have fragments of planks and posts surviving, but preservation conditions were not consistently good and no extensive internal framework was found. The surviving timber was not suitable for yielding dendrochronological dates. There was little other dating evidence available to indicate a time of construction, but what little there is suggests that the wells were all dug towards the end of the 1st century AD.

Well A had a circular shaft, possibly reusing a barrel, although no timber survived. The circular well shaft 1.2m in diameter was set in an approximately square, 1.8m wide construction pit. The pit was dug into the earlier floors of Building 18 and was backfilled with redeposited sand immediately after the central frame was inserted. There was some slumping and collapse of the well, possibly soon after construction. As there does not appear to have been an identifiable open phase between the two buildings, the well may have been in use for only a short period of time within an adapted room of Building 18, as indicated by a sequence of mortar floors, and which may have been open to the east.

After the well had gone out of use it was used as a rubbish pit. The timber frame or barrel and any clay lining may have been removed, but the survival of a vertical face of the well shaft suggests that the frame remained intact.

The remaining three wells were square and timber-framed. Well B was dug on the edge of Alley 4 adjacent to Building 20. The preservation of four vertical faces of the 0.6m square shaft suggests that there was a timber lining down to the base of the well at 0.3m OD. The primary silts did not provide dating for the exact period of use of the well, but this could have been relatively short.

Further east at the rear of the buildings were wells C and D, the latter situated 11m to the east within Open Area 19. Both wells had large construction pits, the large size of well pit C suggesting that it may have functioned originally as a quarry pit. These wells had a square shaft set centrally, and contained fragments of timber which must have formed elements of an internal frame. Two plank fragments and an upright post were found inside the wells. The fragment of post from well D had a vertical groove in two faces, probably to hold planks in position. Hence the frameworks for the square wells most probably included a plank lining supported by four corner posts.

Dating of wells and Open Area 19 disuse

WELLS C AND D

The wells appear to have gone out of use by the mid 2nd century and began to be backfilled with domestic rubbish. This secondary use as rubbish pits was apparent and in well D appears to continue after AD 250. The disuse and backfilling of the well clearly dates within period 6, and therefore the assemblage is discussed in this chapter. A second well, well C, was constructed in period 4, Open Area 19.

WELL C: [4123] (USE AND DISUSE) AND [4136] (DISUSE)

This very large assemblage is from two fills in well C and consists mostly of large joining sherds. The completeness of the vessels, the lack of residuality and the abundance of sherd links between the two layers in the well indicates that they were possibly deposited as a single event or within a very short time of each other. The combined total sherd count is 427 sherds, representing 13.53 EVEs and weighing 18,422g.

The assemblage includes a high number of vessels which exhibit typological variations characteristic of the early 2nd century, and where possible the forms have been aligned with the subdivisions within classes of vessel in the Southwark typology. These subdivisions are based on typological differences, some of which have chronological significance (Marsh and Tyers 1978, 546). For example, the large VRW reeded-rim bowl <P143> (Fig 88) is type 4A5 which is dated c AD 115–50; all three HWC everted-rimmed beakers <P144>–<P146> (Fig 88) are type 3F4 dated c AD 100–60; the AHSU flat-rimmed jar <P147> (Fig 88) starts being produced in c AD 90 (Lyne and Jefferies 1979, 25–7, fig 12, no. 3A.1–15); an HWC flat-rimmed bowl <P148> (not illustrated) is type 4F6 which is dated AD 100–60; and the VRW ring-necked flagon <P149> (Fig 88) is type 1B4 dated c AD 100–50. The HWC+ Black-Burnished type everted-rimmed jar <P150> (Fig 88) is type 2F10 which is dated c AD 120–60. Although the latter form has only been found at the kiln site in Highgate in phase IV, c AD 140–60 (Brown and Sheldon 1974), examples have been found in deposits sealed by the Hadrianic fire horizon in the City (Davies et al 1994, 83). Additionally there are a large number of lids particularly in the oxidised fabric LOXI <P151>–<P152>, which are characteristic of this period in the City (ibid, 213). There are also two SAMMV Drag. 37 bowls (for example <P154>, Fig 88) present in the assemblage, both dated c AD 100–25. Overall the assemblage is dated c AD 120–40.

None of the forms are particularly unusual, except for the OXID bowl <P155> (Fig 88) which is possibly an imported vessel, the GROG jar with applied decoration <P156> (Fig 88) and a LOMA ?strainer <P157> (not illustrated) (Marsh 1978, fig 6.20, no. 45.1). Piece <P155> does not fit into the Southwark typology but is possibly a variant of the reeded-rim bowl form (4A). It has a lightly reeded rim with unevenly spaced grooves occurring towards the outer edge. The rim slopes upwards at an unusual angle for this type of bowl. It is round-bodied, in contrast to the carinated bodies usually found on reeded-rim bowls which tend to be more common in the Flavian/Trajanic period (Marsh

and Tyers 1978, 571–2). The fabric has some similarities to the Rhineland fabrics (RHWW) but no parallel has been found for the form in this fabric. The GROG jar is only represented by two body sherds and is decorated with applied elongated oblique strips.

It was not possible to reconstruct a profile of the LOMA ?strainer from the sherds present. The identification of this vessel as a strainer of Marsh type 45 (Marsh 1978, 181, fig 6.20, no. 45) is on the basis of its unslipped interior, indicating that the vessel is closed, and the similarity of its base to the illustrated example in Marsh (ibid, no. 45.2). On the other hand, there are no drops of slip on the interior of these sherds, such as Marsh does note on vessel 45.2, indicating that the base comes from a strainer. The vessel differs from the more complete example illustrated by Marsh (ibid, no. 45.1) in that the body sherds have two cordons with a vertical wall in between, possibly indicating two carinations as opposed to one. However, the similarity of this form to the Marsh type 44.4 bowl has been noted, and as these bowls vary considerably in their decorative elements (ibid, 178–80, fig 6.20, no. 44.1–10; fig 6.20, no. 44.11–24), there may also be variety within the strainer version of the form.

The AHSU large necked jar <P158> (Fig 88) is round-bodied with a high shoulder but no carination. The rim has similarities to a 'figure 7' rim typical of the industry's early necked jars but is slightly more curved and not as angular. The form has no exact parallel among those illustrated from the kiln site, and although it displays similarities to the necked round-shoulder jars (2D2) it lacks the distinct zone of decoration on the shoulder which is diagnostic of this type. Furthermore, the burnished wavy line occurs on the mid to lower body, which tends to be a later tradition in the Alice Holt industry (for example, Lyne and Jefferies 1979, 37, fig 22, no. 32), although there are examples in the City and Southwark from Hadrianic groups (Davies et al 1994, fig 174, no. 1064; Bird et al 1978, 447, fig 197, no. 1476).

The reuse of the wells as rubbish pits may indeed have been a single opportunistic episode that included the depositing of large quantities of pottery. This process may also have involved the clearance of domestic dumps, including animal bone, from their primary positions and redeposition down the wells. The final backfilling of the wells may have included a gradual infilling continuing into the 3rd century AD.

Animal bone from Open Area 19 and wells

A total of 2648 fragments of animal bone (approximately 21kg) were recovered from Open Area 19. The bulk of the faunal remains were recovered from two well deposits, with only a single fragment of bone from the quarry pit (Table 24).

Well D produced a moderate species diversity. The only fragment of dog (a fused ulna) is probably from a complete skeleton that had been redeposited, which unfortunately has implications for the entire assemblage and must be borne in mind when considering the origin of the rest of the assemblage. A single juvenile chicken tibio-tarsus was also present, which despite the absence of butchery marks is presumed to be food waste.

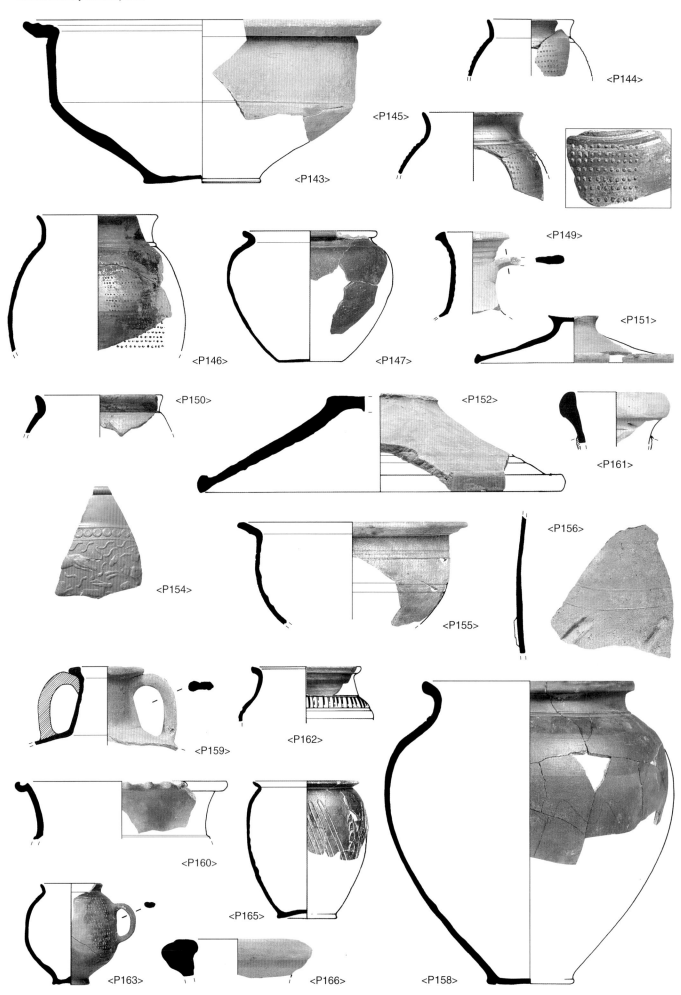

<P143>

<P144>

<P145>

<P146>

<P147>

<P149>

<P151>

<P150>

<P152>

<P161>

<P154>

<P155>

<P156>

<P159>

<P162>

<P160>

<P165>

<P163>

<P166>

<P158>

Species	Well subgroup 1006		Well subgroup 1009		Quarry pit subgroup 1048	
	No. of frags	Weight (g)	No. of frags	Weight (g)	No. of frags	Weight (g)
Cattle	51	2270.26	132	12767.24	0	0
'Cattle-sized'	60	1032.1	205	2843.55	1	53.15
Sheep/goat	11	66.07	25	184.26	0	0
Sheep	0	0	6	89.9	0	0
'Sheep-sized'	31	52.39	154	451.1	0	0
Pig	8	99.46	28	387.56	0	0
Dog	1	8.03	0	0	0	0
Roe deer	0	0	11	238.84	0	0
House mouse	0	0	1	0.01	0	0
Mouse/vole	4	0.11	11	0.55	0	0
Rat sp	0	0	2	0.2	0	0
Chicken	7	2.61	15	24.37	0	0
Small passerines	4	1.6	0	0	0	0
Frog/toad	1	0.05	2044	16.39	0	0
Unidentifiable	0	0	269	293	0	0
Unidentified birds	0	0	29	486.93	0	0
Unidentified fish	8	0.85	2	8.23	0	0

Table 24 Species representation in Open Area 19, wells and quarry pit

The cattle and 'cattle-sized' bone representation shows a dominance of food waste, particularly vertebrae and ribs.

This well deposit appears to consist of a mixture of material, largely comprising butchery waste although with a small volume from other sources. It seems probable that once the well had gone out of use it was backfilled with various waste materials. The small quantity of dog-gnawed bones may suggest a limited degree of redeposition. Most of the bones are, however, clearly in situ.

Well C contained almost 3000 fragments of bone, of which 69% were identified as amphibian bones. As expected, the majority of these frog/toad bones were recovered from samples removed from the lowest layers of the well, and this has implications for its hygiene. For this volume of amphibians to be present the well must have been uncovered for most, if not all, of the time, thus acting in a similar way to a 'pit-fall' trap. The frog and toad bones were not differentiated as this is notoriously difficult and time-consuming, relying largely on identifications based on slight variations of the pelvis. A minimum of 101 individuals (based on counts of left and right pelvises) and ranging in both size and age (both juveniles and adults) were present.

Roe deer was represented by a whole skull, but only one mandible and two metatarsals. The metatarsals from both left and right sides suggest that all the bones originate from a single adult. No butchery marks were observed, but these elements are among those removed during the initial stages of dressing the carcass, so it can be assumed that the animal was eaten. The roe deer is considered to be a high-status animal due to the time required for hunting it compared to the actual meat return.

A small quantity of chicken bones were also recovered; knife marks were identified on a femur and a tibio-tarsus, both of which were consistent with the dismemberment of the bird.

A substantial number of cattle and 'cattle-sized' bones were present (n=342), comprising a large proportion of vertebrae and ribs, with the remainder equally divided between the other major parts of the body (including feet). The knife marks on some of the phalanges are consistent with the cattle being skinned as well as butchered in the near vicinity. Almost all of the fusion information indicates that the cattle were fully mature, except one juvenile (a proximal unfused femur from an individual less than 36 months old). The dental evidence is very scant, with only three ageable mandibles: two are adult (including one 'senile'), and the other is very young (less than eight months old). The presence of the very old individuals suggests that they had had a previous use as dairy or draught animals before they were culled for their meat. The young mandible may be from a natural death or it may represent veal consumption.

Butchery on the sheep/goat and 'sheep-sized' elements is concentrated on the rib and vertebrae fragments. The former had been chopped transversely in order to subdivide the carcass into small units. The chops through the vertebrae are along the central plane, or just to either side, thus halving the carcass. There is a paucity of butchery marks on the other sheep/goat bones. A possible explanation for this is the small size of the animal in comparison to cattle and its greater ease of handling, this generally resulting in more use of the knife rather than the cleaver. Unfortunately, knife butchery is less likely to leave marks on the bone, unlike the heavy cleaver employed in cattle butchery. The few butchery marks present are a transverse chop through the ilium to remove the rear leg from the spinal column and grazing chops along the spine of a scapula to remove the meat from the bone. A single humerus had extra bone growth on the lateral edge of the distal epiphysis, which is commonly referred to as 'penning elbow'. Baker and Brothwell (1980, 127)

Fig 88 Pottery <P143>–<P147>, <P149>–<P152> (1:4), <P154> (1:2), <P155>–<P156>, <P158>–<P163>, <P165>–<P166> (1:4) from well C

suggest that a possible cause of such a pathology is repeated trauma to this relatively exposed area when the animal has been in a pen or put through races. The ageing information for the sheep/goats shows a range being slaughtered, with some younger than ten months old (three unfused pelvises) but most being fully adult.

Only a few pig bones were recovered (n=28). A femur and a humerus had both been butchered, with chops through the joints of the 'shoulder' and the 'hip'. A single mandible had two chops on the lateral edge just below the second molar to remove the cheek meat. Also, a fragment of skull had been chopped along the sagittal line to allow access to the brain.

One possible explanation for the high level of unidentifiable material is that it consists of heavily smashed fragments of bone which had been placed on top of the rotting piles in order to minimise the putrid smell.

The assemblage contained within well C is clearly composed of both domestic and butchery primary waste. It can be surmised that the waste was taken from a range of households: one 'high class', with the roe deer, possible consumption of veal and very young lambs, and the other 'lower class', represented by grazing chops on the low-value meat-bearing bones, exploitation of the very old cattle and the pig cheek meat.

Discussion of the wells

The well group does coincide with the largest available width within the excavated area of BGH95, some 23m west to east. This provided an opportunity to investigate an area likely to include yard areas to the rear of buildings. Two of the wells do occur in this open area, although medieval activity and post-medieval cellars at 31–37 Borough High Street have caused the truncation

of much earlier stratigraphy. The deeper-cut wells survive, but associated with only limited contemporary evidence.

Two wells occur amongst the buildings at the south end of BGH95, either in close proximity or in one case apparently within the footprint of the building. This arrangement may have been connected to a particular function such as dyeing, but no supporting evidence for this was found within the building. The wells may also have been relatively short lived, possibly in use for only 10–20 years.

The creation of the wells in this period may reflect the success of reclamation and drainage schemes on the northern eyot, which would mean that readily available water was now more distant than before. However, the location of wells close to buildings may also indicate a requirement for a nearby, manageable supply of water. This may have been associated with the function of the buildings either as domestic dwellings and/or as workshops. This might have included the need for a supply of clean water linked to dyeing, or even beer making, if the sprouted barley present elsewhere (see Chapter 9) was indicative of such a use. As a ready supply of water, the wells may have been poorly maintained if the quantity of frogs in well D is indicative of the well being open for much of its lifetime.

It could also be suggested that the past history of the settlement might also have persuaded shop and house owners of the virtue of having a water supply available close by in order to reduce the threat from fire.

The position of the wells might also reflect property and ownership status. This may be particularly the case for those wells which apparently occupied positions in very close proximity to the buildings. The two wells in the open areas may also have been linked to particular properties.

Land use	Feature	Grp/sgrp/context	Material	Date
Building 13	floor	65/298/[1542]	Rpot	120–160
	occupation	65/298/[1546]	Rpot	120–160
Building 25	wall	70/348/[1129]	BM	120–225
	wall	68/325/[1501]	BM	140–225
	make-up	68/331/[1659]	Rpot	120–160
	make-up	70/345/[1793]	Rpot	120–160
	occupation	70/346/[1671]	Rpot	140–160
	occupation	70/347/[1152]	Rpot	120–160
Building 26	make-up	161/910/[3570]	Rpot	120–250
Building 27	pit fill	209/956/[3085]	Rpot	140–160
	well fill	147/752/[3906]	Rpot	120–150
	drain	136/585/[3720]	Rpot	140–150
	demolition	147/880/[3675]	Rpot	140–160
	make-up	147/882/[3611]	Rpot	120–160
	make-up	157/938/[3333]	Rpot	150–160
Building 28	well fill	164/631/[3931]	Rpot	140–150
Open Area 24	posthole	69/343/[1269]	Rpot	120–140
	occupation	67/316/[1265]	Rpot	140–160
	dump	67/321/[1449]	Rpot	120–160
Structure 2	occupation	66/256/[1556]	Rpot	140–200
Smithy	make-up	66/307/[1450]	coin	117–161
	hearth	66/309/[1450]	coin	117–138
	make-up	66/308/[1553]	Rpot	120–160
Structure 10	oven	87/432/[2060]	Rpot	120–160

Table 25 Dating table for period 6

If the wells were no longer providing water by the mid 2nd century, it is possible that the nature of the water supply is indicated by a fragment of water pipe junction collar <R169>. This was one of the few identifiable iron objects from Open Area 19 and is a comparatively rare find in Southwark, although some fine examples of both water pipes and collars have been discovered elsewhere in the City, generally in more favourable, waterlogged deposits (Wheeler 1930, 39, pl 12). Each length of squared oak had a central bored hole and the circular iron collars were used to join the sections, being driven into the solid wood to enclose the channel. A median ridge on the collar, visible on this example, ensured that equal sections of collar entered each pipe, thus securing the joint (Manning 1985, 128). Outside London the presence of water pipes can frequently be inferred only from the iron junction collars, and the discovery of one at BGH95, an area where the preservation of ironwork is generally poor, is significant. This may demonstrate the advanced development of the infrastructure during the 2nd century.

Open areas to the east of the road

To the east of the road several areas appear to have remained undeveloped. The excavation areas of LBA95 and LBB95 may lie behind roadside buildings which have not yet been identified. Certainly the two areas continued to show evidence of having remained open, possibly as rough ground used for extensive dumping. At LBA95 Open Areas 3 and 5 continued to be used for dumping domestic debris into the mid 2nd century. Open Area 5 was crossed by a 1.5m wide and 0.3m deep ditch or gully which was backfilled with large amounts of pottery. The assemblage is very large and has a sherd count of 503, a total weight of 16,644g and constitutes 12.15 EVEs. The dating of this group corresponds to the latest Roman Ceramic Phase, RCP5, the early Antonine phase (c AD 140–60).

The overall trends in this assemblage are similar to those in RCP5 except for the low figures for fine wares and the high percentage of amphorae. Amphorae account for 12.5% of the assemblage by sherd count, 9.7% by EVEs and 45.1% by weight. This can be compared to the total percentages for amphorae in RCP5 where they represent 3% by EVEs and 25% by weight. Additionally, there is an unusually high percentage of Dressel 2-4 amphorae (8DR2-4) in this assemblage which is not seen in RCP5. As a percentage of the total amphorae from this group, Dressel 2-4s represent 17.9% by sherd count, 60.7% by EVEs and 30.5% by weight, while in RCP5 Dressel 2-4s represent just 3% by weight. At least three separate vessels are present in this assemblage and all are in different fabrics, <P167>–<P169> (Fig 89). The only sourced fabric is CAMP2 (not illustrated). The double rod handles, rounded bead rim and peg base are typical characteristics of this form. Also present in the group are Cam. 186 amphorae such as <P170> (Fig 89) from Cadiz in southern Spain. The rim present is Cam. 186C, a type which persists well into the 2nd century (Davies et al 1994, 14). Other amphorae present, but not illustrated, include Dressel 20, Cam. 189 and Gauloise type 4.

The VRW reeded-rim bowls are of Southwark type 4A5 (for example <P171>, Fig 89), dated to c AD 115–50 (Marsh and Tyers 1978, 573). The VRW cupped-mouth ring-necked flagon type (1B7) <P172> (Fig 89) is dated c AD 140–60. HWC is present but in the latest forms manufactured: everted-rim jars with acute lattice decoration <P173> (Fig 89) and flat-rimmed bowls <P174> (Fig 89). The HWC everted-rim jar is similar to the sub-type 2F10 in the Southwark typology and is dated from c AD 120 to the later 2nd century (Marsh and Tyers 1978, 562, fig 236, no. 2F.10). D-shaped rim bowls <P175>–<P176> and everted-rim jars <P177> (Fig 89) are present in Black-Burnished fabrics. Of particular interest is the SAND pinched-mouth flagon (1C) <P178> (Fig 89), as flagons in reduced wares are uncommon in London.

The dating of this group is especially important as pottery assemblages from the mid 2nd century are poorly understood, and few well stratified groups from this period in London have been identified and analysed. During this period the main industries that had supplied London in the 1st and early 2nd centuries, such as the Verulamium and Highgate industries, were in decline.

The pottery was originally dated to AD 160 on the presence of a possible AHBB bowl with a D-shaped rim (4H) <P179> (Fig 89); otherwise the group is dated from AD 140 based on the VRW cup-mouthed ring-necked flagon, a BB2F 4H1 AL and a BB2F plain-rimmed 'dog dish' (5J). The dating of the AHBB rounded-rimmed bowl is, therefore, important for this assemblage. Lyne and Jefferies in their report on material from the kiln sites date this form to c AD 150–220 (Lyne and Jefferies 1979, 49, fig 37, no. 6B1–3). However, at the kiln site this form occurs in dumps AH55 and well 2 which date respectively to AD 150–80 and AD 180–220, while the only dump pre-dating these is dated AD 90–100, a date which is earlier than the generally accepted date of AD 120 when this form first occurs in London in Black-Burnished type fabrics. As there are no published dumps from the kiln site dating to the period AD 100–50, which is the crucial period for the emergence of this bowl form, it is difficult to define exactly when the Alice Holt kilns start producing this form. The form is numbered 3 in Millett's study of the dating of the industry and is given a date range of c AD 100–240 (Millett 1979, fig 2, no. 3). Additional evidence supporting a late Hadrianic to early Antonine date is provided by the decorated samian, with the latest sherds dated c AD 125–50 and the mortarium stamps <P180>–<P182> (Fig 89) dated to c AD 110–40 (see Chapter 11.2). The pottery assemblage from Open Area 2, which is directly below Open Area 5, can be generally dated to c AD 120–60. Although most of the groups in Open Area 2 are small, so that this dating cannot be refined further, many of the dates for individual contexts are dated to the 1st century and it is conceivable that this group does not date beyond AD 140. The stamps include one <P182> (Fig 89) which is from another context but has sherd links to a vessel in this gully, so is illustrated here as dating evidence.

The group also contained a jar with a post-firing graffito <P183> (Fig 89). Mark Hassall (pers comm) reports that the reading is VIRI, with VIRILIS or perhaps VIRIUS being the most likely expansions.

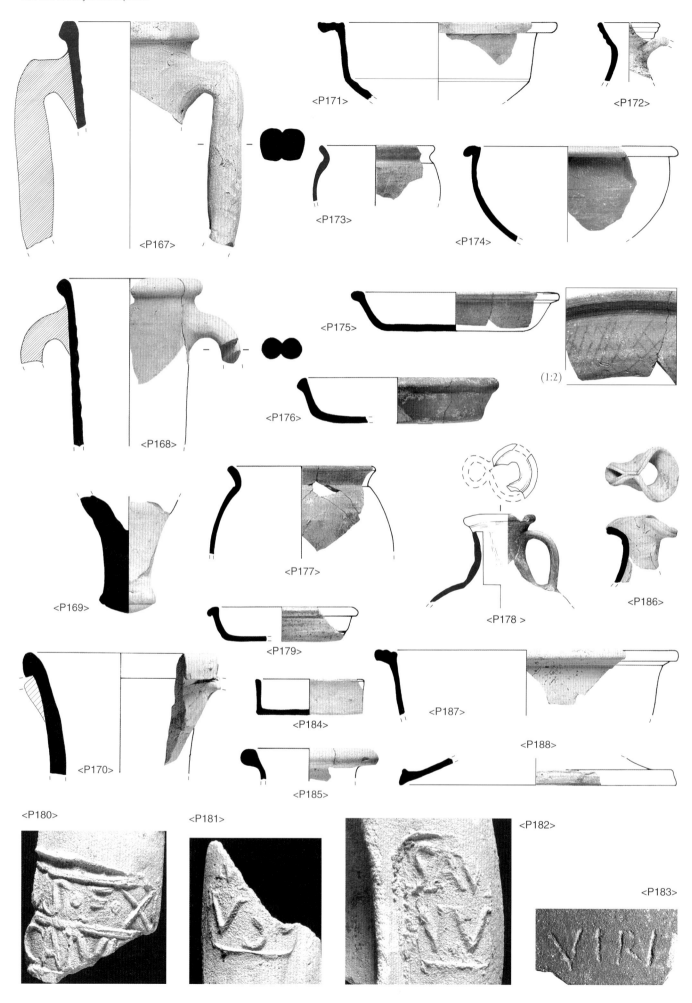

<P167>

<P171>

<P172>

<P173>

<P174>

<P168>

<P175>

<P176>

(1:2)

<P169>

<P177>

<P178 >

<P186>

<P179>

<P170>

<P184>

<P187>

<P188>

<P185>

<P180>

<P181>

<P182>

<P183>

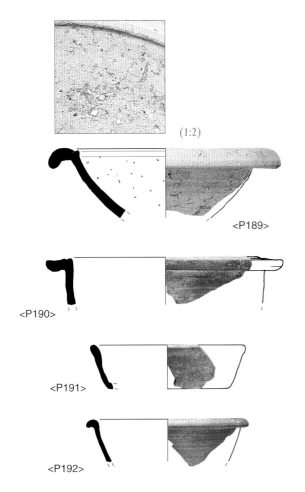

(1:2)

<P189>

<P190>

<P191>

<P192>

Fig 89 Pottery <P167>–<P179> (1:4), <P180>–<P183> (1:1), <P184>–<P192> (1:4) from LBA95 Open Area 5

Hadrianic and later activity to the east of the main road

Around AD 120 the whole area of the LBI95 excavation was cleared, with Buildings 2, 4 and 5 (which may in fact have formed one large building complex) being demolished and going out of use. There does not appear to have been any obvious reason for this, such as fire or flood, and it may reflect changes in ownership or simply general dilapidation of the clay and timber structures. Sunken room C contained large quantities of good quality painted wall plaster, though not necessarily originating from Building 2. A robber trench delineated the extent of room D but was quite shallow and not as substantial as other walls in Building 2, indicating either an internal wall or that the function of room C required larger walls. Building 4 had part of a collapsed painted plaster wall *in situ*, though it was heavily grouted and impossible to recover, and further quantities of painted wall plaster were found in its general demolition layers.

Painted wall plaster from Building 2

Most of the plaster came from destruction deposits filling room C, a sunken chamber with a drain leading off from the south-east corner. The plaster may well have come from the walls of rooms A and B which were demolished to make way

for a timber structure (B4) sometime in the mid Flavian period, or perhaps even from the walls of room C itself. The plaster dumped in room C is highly decorated and of good quality (Fig 90); it forms a reasonably coherent group, which indicates that it derived from a single room, or rooms in the same building. Only a number of dado fragments with thick plaster backing, and perhaps two small fragments with dark red paint, may derive from a separate room or building.

PAINTED WALL PLASTER FROM ROOM C

Most of the plaster found in room C seems to derive from the middle area of the walls, although there are a few large thick fragments from the lower dado area. The decoration comprises plain red panels decorated near the edge with a thin white line, and bordered by a thin white band followed by green. The green in turn seems to have been followed by another thin white band and then an area of black (Fig 90, no. 1). There are also a number of curved fragments from around door or window openings, two of which, from different areas, are shown in Fig 90, no. 3.

There are a number of highly decorated fragments painted in a wide variety of colours on a black background (Fig 90, no. 2). Whether these are from the area of black bordering the white and green bands mentioned above is not certain, although the border fragments seem to have slightly more green glauconite scattered through the backing layer. Elaborate decoration on a black background situated in between panels is a feature of early Flavian wall plaster at Winchester Palace in Southwark (Goffin in prep). Buildings in Cologne, Germany, were decorated in similar fashion (Thomas 1989, 2–10).

It is unfortunate that the LBI95 plaster is so abraded and fragmentary. There is very little indication as to the decorative motifs employed, although a number of pieces have green stem-like decoration. It is just possible that one fragment shows a yellow coloured fish (Fig 90, no. 2) suggesting an aquatic scheme, but this is by no means certain.

A number of black decorative fragments show two backing layers, the lower one 8mm beneath the top surface. The lower layer has an unpainted top coat which would suggest that a decision to add a further backing layer was taken before painting commenced.

One area of plain black borders a slightly curved area of white plaster, presumably marking the position of a doorway or window opening. Another similar fragment has white bordered by a curved area of green. The black and white curved fragment lies above a layer of yellow plaster, with a backing layer 3–6mm thick separating the two schemes. It is possible that this represents a localised repair rather than a wholesale replastering, bearing in mind that the area around doorways and window openings would have been particularly vulnerable to damage.

There are a number of fragments of plain yellow plaster, probably from either a wide border or a panel area. Some may have been attached to keyed daub walls as clear keying impressions are present on the back of one fragment. The yellow is bordered by black which may it turn have been bordered by bands of white and yellow (Fig 90, no. 4). One black fragment from the same area of wall is from a curved doorway or window

3a

4

5

1

2

3b

6

7

Fig 90 Painted wall plaster from LBI95 Building 2 (1:2)

opening (Fig 90, no. 3a). Another, much larger, curved fragment was recovered from room C; it is plain red apart from a small corner area in green and possibly white (Fig 90, no. 3b).

A number of thick dado fragments from the lower part of a wall were recovered from context [440]. The decoration comprises a yellow dado with large red and white splash decoration, bordered on the top edge by a broad red horizontal band with green above (Fig 90, no. 5). Two distinct backing layers are present. The initial layer, which is around 30–35mm thick, is cream in colour and was made using sand and white calcareous inclusions. The second, upper, layer is pink in colour and only 10–11mm thick. The pink colour derives from the addition of crushed red ceramic, probably tile, and has a similar appearance to *opus signinum*, although the crushed ceramic inclusions are somewhat smaller. The much thicker backing plaster of the lower dado area may have been an attempt to combat damp, which would have been much worse at the base of the wall.

The only other plaster with the same twin pink and white backing layers, and therefore almost certainly part of the same area of wall, is light greenish-blue in colour with a small area of dark red, possibly decoration (Fig 90, no. 6). How these fragments relate to other wall plaster found dumped in room C is uncertain. The other plaster from room C has more white-coloured backing layers.

There are two fragments painted in a darker red than any of the other plaster from room C. These may have come from a different room, as the backing layer contains slightly more white calcareous inclusions. They show a border area in yellow, white and dark red with additional decoration in white (Fig 90, no. 7). A small area of dark red dado with black and yellow splashes may perhaps come from the same wall area.

PAINTED WALL PLASTER FROM ROOM D

This room was also decorated with a high quality wall plaster of elaborate design. There are decorative fragments in maroon, yellow, green, pink, red and black. The black is probably the background colour, which would suggest a decorative colour scheme similar to that employed in room C. Associated with the decorative fragments is a small area of border in red, white and maroon. Regrettably, the plaster is even more fragmented than that from room C, so there is no indication as to the decorative motifs employed.

Found associated with Building 2, although not associated with any particular room, is a decorative fragment in three shades of green, black and red. This does not seem to relate in any way to the plaster recovered from rooms C and D. Other fragments found in the same deposit include a sharply curved corner piece in plain red with a single (accidental?) green splash. There is also a green and yellowish-brown border area with a similar green splash, which suggests that the painter may have been rather careless when it came to the application of the green painted surface.

There are also small border areas in green and white, and green, white and red, along with a small red fragment with a thin green band and another small red fragment with decoration in either yellow or cream.

Animal bone from Building 2 demolition

A total of 268 fragments of animal bone were recovered from the demolition layers of Building 2. Unfortunately, 70% of contexts (n=20) were very small (less than 10 fragments of bone). Yet despite this the species range from this layer was particularly diverse (Table 26).

The seven adult dog bones were three femurs, a radius, a tibia, a pelvis and a juvenile ulna. Results from the calculation of the stature of the adult dogs are shown in Table 27.

At least three individual dogs were present, two adults (one approximately 39–40cm to the shoulder and the other smaller at between 26–30cm) and one juvenile. All the skeletons are incomplete, suggesting that they originate from animals possibly buried together but which had then been disturbed and redeposited. This has implications for the rest of the assemblage.

Only a very limited quantity of the three main domesticates was present. Despite this there appear to be some discernible patterns. The cattle remains were dominated by mandible and metapodial fragments, indicating that the majority of the bones originated from the initial processing of the carcass and represent the 'dressing' waste. The sheep/goat remains are of particular interest. Only one bone could be positively identified as adult. The rest were categorised as juvenile or infant. Butchery was

Table 26 Species representation from LBI95 Building 2 demolition

Species	Context [429]		Context [435]	
	No. of frags	Weight (g)	No. of frags	Weight (g)
Cattle	2	51	3	280
Dog	0	0	7	60
Chicken	2	0.8	18	32
Roe deer	1	34	1	20
Pigeon sp	0	0	1	1.5
'Cattle-sized'	0	0	19	289
Duck	0	0	2	2.7
Cat	0	0	2	2.5
Goose	1	3	0	0
Hare	0	0	1	0.8
Sheep/goat	3	10	3	18
Sheep	0	0	1	18
'Sheep-sized'	5	3.5	33	87.5
Unidentified birds	0	0	7	4.1
Unidentified fish	0	0	4	0.8
Total	16	115.3	109	975.9

Table 27 Stature of two adult dogs from LBI95 Building 2 demolition

Element	Greatest length (mm)	Stature (mm)
Femur	129.8	394.612
Femur	97.8	294.132
Femur	100.4	302.296
Radius	78.6	269.458
Tibia	86.6	262.282

evident on a range of elements including an infant femur, and showed a preference for the use of heavy knife over cleaver to dismember the animals.

A total of six deer bones were present. A roe deer metatarsal and a radius came from destruction layers. The latter had three grazing chops on the shaft resulting from meat being filleted from the bone. From another dump mandibles and metatarsals of both roe deer and red deer were recovered. Despite no butchery marks being present it seems likely that these elements were waste from the dressing of the carcasses.

An extensive range of bird remains was recovered from these layers, many of them for the first time on the sites. At least three chicken skeletons were contained within one particular dump; the range of elements and the butchery is consistent with them being table waste. One tibio-tarsus displayed a slight irregular expansion of the shaft, as a symptom of the osteopetrosis that is a viral disease specifically of chicken (Baker and Brothwell 1980, 77). Also from this context came a butchered juvenile pigeon (sp) humerus and two adult duck metatarsals. Bird remains from the other contexts included examples of geese and teal. An exciting discovery was a single adult swan humerus, since swans are both rare and indicative of high status; no butchery was discernible on it.

The majority of this assemblage clearly represents high-status waste, possibly the remains from a single feast. The three main domesticates are present but only in minimal quantities. Furthermore, the majority of the sheep were very young, thus presumably very tender and probably expensive. Other costly animals present included roe deer, red deer and swan. The latter species was normally only consumed at feasts (Maltby 1979, 71). The three partial dog skeletons are of concern and strongly suggest the reworking of the deposit.

Rebuilding in the Antonine period

LBI95 Buildings 6 and 7, Open Areas 10 and 11

The arch in which Building 4 lay was truncated at this point by layers associated with the construction of London Bridge Station in the middle of the 19th century. However, Roman occupation layers continued in the other two arches (Table 29). The remains of a heavily truncated timber-framed building, Building 6, were represented by a series of postholes and a refuse pit (Fig 91). There were two parallel lines of posts running north–south c 5.0m apart with an east–west return at the south end, giving a minimum length of the building of 5.5m. The north end of the building was not recorded and there were no surviving occupation levels. To the west and east of the building were Open Areas 10 and 11, which contained quantities of domestic refuse. There were fragmentary remains of what may have been another building, Building 7 (not shown) to the east of Building 6 in Open Area 11. They consisted of a brickearth surface that may have been a floor, but no associated walls were found.

Approximately 860 fragments of animal bones were recovered from one particular pit fill. The species present (Table 28) were cattle, sheep/goat, cat, mouse/vole species, chicken and frog/toad species. Cattle and sheep/goat were represented by less than four bones in each case.

Frog/toad bones dominated the context (96%), with all elements of the skeletons being present. Through using counts of left and right pelvises it was possible to determine the presence of at least 19 individuals of varying sizes. Also recovered from this pit were two partial kitten skeletons, including a humerus, radius, scapula, ulna and four tibias. Three chicken bones were present (two tibio-tarsuses and one pelvis). A tibio-tarsus had been chopped transversely across the distal end to remove the feet and dress the bird for the table. A single hare tibia was also recovered, and despite the absence of butchery marks it is assumed to be food waste.

Along with the large quantity of amphibian bones another background species was recovered, a partial mouse/vole species skeleton.

The large volume of amphibian bones in the base shows that the pit was often, if not always, left uncovered. The presence of the partial skeletons of the kittens and a mouse/vole (sp) suggests that many of the bones had been reworked and the skeletons had become disarticulated. Clearly the refuse within this pit represents opportunistic dumping of small-scale waste.

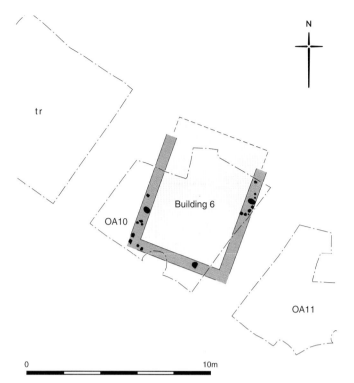

Table 28 *Species representation from LBI95 Building 6, Open Areas 10 and 11*

Species	Open Area 10	Building 6	Open Area 11
Cattle	1	2	0
'Cattle-sized'	4	8	5
Sheep/goat	1	1	1
'Sheep-sized'	0	3	49
Pig	0	1	5
Cat	8	0	0
Roe deer	0	2	0
Hare	1	0	0
House mouse	0	0	1
Mouse/vole	11	0	1
Rat	0	0	1
Chicken	3	1	75
Blackbird	0	0	6
Small passerines	0	0	68
Sturgeon	0	0	2
Frog/toad	829	0	2
Unidentified bird	5	0	25
Unidentified fish	0	0	4

Fig 91 *Plan of LBI95 Building 6*

Table 29 *Dating table for LBI95 Buildings 6 and 7*

Land use	Feature	Context	Material	Date
LBI95 B6	occupation	[88]	Rpot	120–160
LBI95 B7	construction	[304]	Rpot	120–160

Building 6 included animal remains recovered from three contexts: a make-up layer, a structural pit and another pit of indeterminate function. Only 18 bones were recovered from all these features. The majority of the remains are cattle or 'cattle-sized'. A single roe deer mandible was also present.

Only one pit within Open Area 11 contained faunal remains. This proved to be a very unusual assemblage with a complete dominance of bird remains, while the quantity of cattle, sheep and pig was negligible. The main bird species was chicken, with all parts of the skeleton represented. Adult and juvenile bones were equally represented, with one infant tarso-metatarsal also present. At least three individuals were represented. The other types of bird commonly encountered in this assemblage were the small passerine species, which could be any among many different bird species from thrush to swallow and the like. These smaller birds may have been caught with the use of a net, as was common practice in other Roman provinces (Wilson 1991, 115) or by one of a range of other techniques, for example liming. The majority of the small passerine bones were caudal vertebrae and tracheal rings (supporting the neck), with only a few limb bones present. The most notable recovery from this area were two dermal denticals of sturgeon, which during Roman times, as today, was considered to be a luxury foodstuff and a status symbol.

An analysis of the botanical remains from the pit shows that this is clearly a domestic and kitchen waste refuse pit. Its contents are full of remains of edible fruits, including sloe/cherry (*Prunus avium/cerasus/spinosa*), plum (*Prunus domestica* L), fig and blackberry/raspberry, available either as imports or growing locally. The mineralised remains show that cess or another mineralising agent (possibly lime) was also thrown into the pit.

A residential quarter?

In the 2nd century this area of the settlement appears to have been functioning more as a high-status residential quarter. If the first phase of Building 2 was a warehouse, this seems unlikely for the later phases. There are many indications of high status from the range of buildings centred around the second phase of LBI95 Building 2 and the later Building 6: the painted wall plaster, the age of the animals when they were slaughtered as compared to Borough High Street, the rarity of some of the animal species – swan, sturgeon, deer – and possible ritual activity, although the lack of a full range of high quality domestic objects might suggest otherwise. However, the presence of a melon bead <R65>, a copper alloy bracelet fragment, a fragmentary bone pin and a spoon <R126> does point to some degree of domestic status.

So far no definite residential quarters have been identified in Southwark, but the distance from the main road here suggests a quieter area, perhaps more suited for private homes. The LBI95 excavation was too small-scale for the north-east corner of the north island to be definitely designated as such, but it should certainly be borne in mind for purposes of future work in the area.

9

Evidence for later Roman activity

Augusta, formerly known as London...
Ammianus Marcellinus, 4th century AD

9.1 Late 2nd- to 3rd-century activity

Alongside the main road

Evidence for the later Roman settlement and activity on BGH95 had largely been removed. The northern end of the site was heavily truncated by the cellars of the post-medieval buildings on the west frontage of Borough High Street and by modern services. The evidence for 3rd-century activity is therefore limited to pits and possible 'dark earth' deposits, with the exception of one small area where the stratigraphy survived higher than elsewhere. Here Alley 5 continued in use and just to the north of it was another series of free-standing masonry blocks, Structure 12 (not illustrated). Their alignment was slightly askew to the edge of the excavation, with the result that only three were present within the limits of the site. This suggests that the road itself may have changed alignment very slightly. Whilst the general alignment is unlikely to have altered very much, hemmed in as it was between buildings on either side, it would not be surprising if there had been minor deviations in its course over the years.

These new blocks were of a different construction from Structure 8. It is not at all clear whether there was any relationship between the two sets of masonry blocks. There was no conclusive dating evidence for Structure 12, although eventually Alley 5 extended northwards over the most southerly of the blocks. It is possible that these blocks were contemporary with Structure 8 but, from their different construction and alignment, it is more likely that they were a later replacement. The materials used for the structure suggest a late 2nd- to early 3rd-century date (see below).

Structure 12 consisted of three masonry blocks. The first [27] was of brick and rubble construction and at least Trajanic in date (brick in fabric 3018). The presence of fabric 3055 and ferruginous sandstone suggests dates for the build or rebuild of AD 190–200+. Ferruginous sandstone is usually associated with the late 2nd-century City wall but can occur earlier (see Chapter 3.1). The bricks in sample 42, fabric 3018, appear to be small lydion of a similar size to those in Reigate fabric incorporated in Structure 7.

The second block [257] was of roof tile, brick and rubble construction. It included early Roman roof tile (probably reused) as well as ferruginous sandstone blocks, so it was probably built or rebuilt in AD 190–200+.

The third block [386] also contained early Roman roof tiles, again reused. There was no building material diagnostic of a later period.

Pier [27] was built almost completely of lydion bricks. The occurrence of fabric 3055 dates construction to the later 2nd or 3rd century. Both [257] and [386] contained reused 1st-century material, although the ferruginous sandstone rubble in [257] suggests that it was built or rebuilt in *c* AD 190–200.

Further to the east there was a small area of a destruction deposit, Open Area 28, sealing the north-east corner of the site. From this came two ring buckles, possibly of military origin. The first <R228> (Fig 92) has a circular, triangular-sectioned frame with a decorative extension on one side incorporating one of the belt studs; there is no tongue. Such buckles, both decorated and plain, are often shown on 3rd-century gravestone reliefs of infantry and cavalry (Bishop and Coulston 1993, 152). The reliefs show that the tapering belt ends passed through the ring from behind, then back along the front, and were held in place by two studs. Such buckles could also consist of plain rings, with or without a tongue, as in the second example, <R229> (Fig 92).

A third buckle from the same area, which could be a military type, is of a more familiar D-shaped form <R102> (Fig 92).

Later 2nd- and 3rd-century buildings

At the south end of the site, the latest surviving sequence of buildings included timber elements with fragmentary carbonised remains. However, little evidence of the nature and form of these buildings survived, restricted as it was to small islands of stratigraphy (Fig 93).

A later sequence of timber-framed buildings was also subject to increasing amounts of post-medieval and modern disturbance. There is little evidence, however, to suggest that the nature or style of the buildings occupying the southern end of the site during this period had changed significantly from those in earlier phases of occupation. Rather, there seems to have been a continuous sequence of replacement and renewal.

Building 30

At the eastern edge of the excavated area fragmentary remains of clay floors of Building 30 survived at a maximum level of 2.6m OD. It is likely that the remains represent a single room with additional parts of the building further west. Two 1.8m long segments of a tile and clay wall foundation may represent the foundations of an internal wall. This clay foundation with uneven tile courses may have formed the base for timber studs. Three flat and worn Reigate stones formed a small level area 1.15m long and 0.4m wide immediately adjacent to the foundation. This feature may have been the fragmentary survival of an internal doorway threshold or, alternatively, the surviving element of a stone floor.

The building was constructed on the demolition deposits of the earlier Building 27. The most diagnostic dating evidence is derived from the construction make-up layers, and includes a sherd of Cam. 306 bowl, dated in Southwark to c AD 200–400

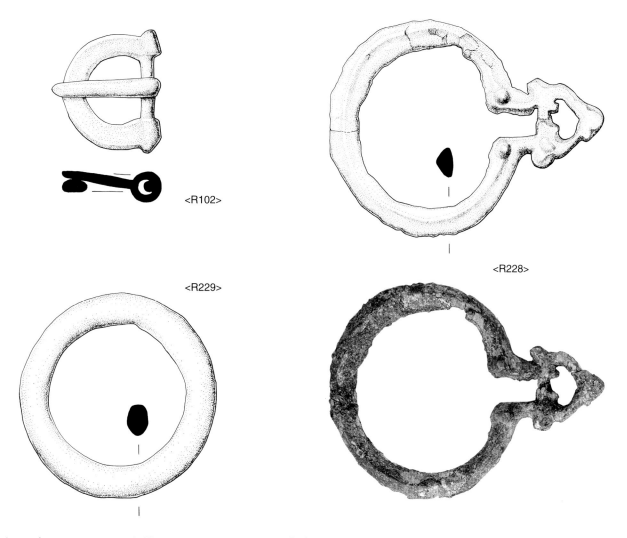

<R102>

<R229>

<R228>

Fig 92 Finds group from Open Area 28: ring buckles <R102>, <R228>, <R229> (1:1)

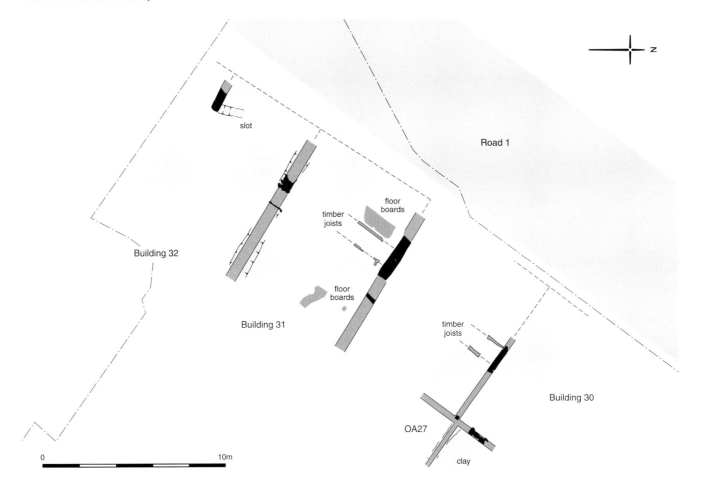

Fig 93 Plan of period 7 (south)

and, from the fill of stakeholes, the presence of AHFA and NVCC. The material incorporated within the occupation and floor levels includes considerable quantities of Black-Burnished wares, which were probably redeposited from the earlier building on this plot (B26/27). The disuse and demolition of Building 26/27 probably took place during the mid or late 2nd century, and the construction of Building 30 may have followed soon afterwards, towards the end of the 2nd century AD (Table 31).

The western room featured a timber plank floor constructed on top of collapsed debris from the previous building. The planking included traces of three or four floorboards which survived as soil staining and fragmentary carbonised remains. It is likely that this floor formed part of a complete rebuilding on this plot, although no clear reconstruction of the full extent of the building is possible. Six or seven postholes occurred, several within a 1.5m long and 0.2m wide slot, which might have been an internal sillbeam with uprights. It was not particularly substantial, but could have served as a base for a partition or, alternatively, might have been a beam for the wooden floor. The wooden floor was replaced by a clay version covering an area 2.0m long by 1.6m wide.

A second phase of timber planked floor was constructed, possibly as a result of earlier fire damage. This included an area of charred wood and charcoal fragments 1.15m wide and 1.8m long. The fragments of five discernible carbonised planks did

not survive intact, but ran from west to east. Small, carbonised fragments of oak (Quercus sp) and some stained areas represented more ephemeral remains. Beneath the planks were fragments of at least two carbonised beams or joists. Other joists were suggested by soil staining or as slight impressions in lower deposits.

The planks survived in a room south of an internal division where the original joists were probably supported on the wall foundation. It comprised reused rough opus signinum blocks, which incorporated at least two post-pad positions. The wall foundation might then have incorporated further clay bricks, but the evidence for upright post positions indicates that this building was primarily of timber construction.

The timber remains suggested a construction of oak floorboards supported on a series of joists (Fig 94). The joists were presumably set on larger sillbeams which acted as foundations for internal and external walls. These wooden floors replaced earlier clay floors and may originally have been constructed as suspended floors above the contemporary ground surface.

The burnt remains indicate that the building was destroyed by fire which caused the collapse of the internal wall. This demolition debris, which covered the charred planks as well as occupation debris, contained burnt clay, daub and opus signinum. The wall collapse, wall foundation and floorboard remains

Fig 94 Detail of floor of Building 30

included the latest material recovered from Building 30. The levelling of the building, probably in the later part of the 3rd century, caused the mixing of burnt and unburnt elements of foundations, walls and earlier occupation. Thus, although some of the assemblage is undoubtedly redeposited, residual material from earlier periods, with the presence of Alice Holt/Farnham grey ware (AHFA), east Gaulish samian (SAMEG) and the proportion of Black-Burnished ware 2 (BB2) and Black-Burnished type wares (BBS), which combined account for 51 of 174 sherds (29.3%), suggests a date in the later 2nd to early 3rd century. In the City the appearance of AHFA is generally dated to c AD 250, with some forms possibly being introduced slightly earlier. Also of interest in terms of dating is the presence of an oxidised dish form. The dish is in an unsourced fine oxidised fabric and has a slightly incurved flat rim, similar in shape to Hayes form 61 (Hayes 1972, 100–7, figs 16–17). A similar example has been found at Colchester, also in a fine oxidised fabric, from a group assigned to the period ending c AD 275 (Symonds and Wade 1999, 263, fig 5.29).

Building 31

Several small pits were dug in a small open area (OA27) to the south of Building 30. An east–west gulley 0.5m wide and a minimum of 2.4m long was also excavated. The gully had a V-shaped profile for part of its length, but was irregular in

dimensions and shape, suggesting that it may have functioned as an informal drainage gully. It may also have formed the boundary of the narrow gap between properties.

The yard area adjacent to Building 30 expanded after the destruction of the building. A pit was dug into the levelled remains of the building and two further pits were dug to the south. These rubbish pits were utilised and backfilled during the later 2nd and early 3rd centuries AD. The pits and stakeholes represent the latest undisturbed activity in this part of the site.

The northern limit of Building 31 was formed of a large baseplate or ground-beam. The 3.5m long slot contained very large quantities of charred wood from the beam, and the size of the slot suggests that the beam could have been at least 0.4m wide and 0.3m deep. Immediately below the beam and at right angles to it were two short slots approximately 1.0m long and 0.6m wide. The two short slots also contained dense charcoal remains and appear to represent evidence of wooden blocks beneath the larger beam. The two timbers could possibly be associated with an earlier construction phase, but with no obvious function. Alternatively, the blocks may have served to support the larger beam, thus preventing slumping, or to raise the beam to a required height or level.

An area measuring 2.2m x 3.2m immediately south of the beam was covered with charcoal fragments, including the discernible remains of four planks. These rested on the carbonised fragments of at least four smaller joists. The joists may then have rested on or been fixed to the baseplate. The resultant wooden floor replaced an earlier clay surface on which the remains of the timber beams rested. Two small postholes and a 1.2m long slot were probably further elements of support for the floor, which may originally have been raised above the contemporary ground surface.

A large quantity of charred cereal remains were found within the building (Table 30). They included over 2000 wheat grains within the foundation slot and floor levels. These abundant charred botanical remains also incorporated a small proportion of large weed seeds, including seeds of corncockle (*Agrostemma githago* L), cleavers (*Galium aparine* L) and vetch/tare/vetchling (*Vicia/Lathyrus* sp). These are seeds from plants which could have grown as weeds among the cereal crop. Ethnographic research among non-industrialised farming communities has shown that weeds are gathered in along with the cereal crop. In these communities the subsequent processing of the cereals prior to storage or milling involves the removal of weed seeds along with

Species		Building 31 % grains 1/64ss {317}	Rear of B31 % grains 1/64ss {314}	Floor of B31 % grains 1/64ss {311}	Total %
Spelt	*Triticum spelta* L	46.38	30.7	0	**38.78**
Emmer/spelt	*Triticum dicoccum* L *spelta*	21.09	32.3	85.45	**27.82**
Emmer	*Triticum dicoccum* L	14.58	5.34	0	**9.89**
Bread wheat/spelt	*Triticum aestivum spelta*	13.18	12.9	0	**13.04**
Rye	*Secale cereale* L	0.16	0.08	0	**0.12**
Barley	*Hordeum* sp	4.45	0.17	0	**2.34**
Oat	*Avena* sp	0.16	0.27	0	**0.21**
Barley (sprouted)	*Hordeum* sp	0	18.24	14.55	**8.90**

Table 30 Cereal remains within the grain store in Building 31

the separation of the chaff (the plant tissue enclosing the grains). These seeds could have remained behind after sieving and the processing of the grain.

The processed grain may have been stored in a part of the building with a raised wooden floor. The granary may have been used to store the grain prior to sale or further preparation, such as drying or milling.

The size of the building or room associated with the grain store could not be established due to truncation. It is possible that the structural elements form a room within a larger building. The presence of processed grain and a raised floor does suggest that the building was being used to store grain, and given its roadside position may have functioned as a shop or bakery.

The grain assemblage also contained 205 sprouted barley grains. This may suggest that brewing was taking place at this time, or that this was part of an assemblage deliberately burned because the grain had begun to germinate, which would have been possible in damp conditions.

A hairpin <R83> (Fig 95) found in Building 31 is a form which appears after AD 150.

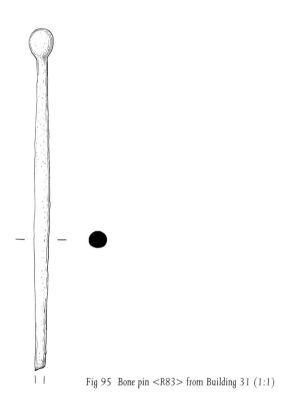

Fig 95 Bone pin <R83> from Building 31 (1:1)

This building, like Building 30, was also destroyed by fire. The degree of burning of the timbers, particularly of the baseplate, may indicate that this was a severe blaze. The walls collapsed and covered the floors and occupation debris. The pottery assemblage from these deposits included 46 sherds and is similar in composition to that of Building 30, suggesting a date of around the mid 3rd century for the destruction and burning of Building 31. Quantities by sherd count of each fabric type are low. Although 23 fabrics were identified, only four fabrics are represented by more than

three sherds. However, both AHFA and SAMEG are again recorded, alongside one sherd of Thameside, Kent (TSK) (Table 31).

Table 31 Dating table for period 7

Land use	Feature	Grp/sgrp/context	Material	Date
Building 30	wall	169/987/[3069]	BM	140–230
	wall	162/921/[3365]	Rpot	150–300
	occupation	169/989/[3135]	Rpot	180–250
	make-up	169/989/[3206]	Rpot	200–300
Building 31	structural cut	166/961/[3213]	Rpot	150–250
	floor	166/966/[3138]	Rpot	180–250
Building 32	structural cut	155/798/[3120]	Rpot	120–250
	structural cut	167/983/[3014]	BM	140–300
Open Area 27	ditch	170/946/[3421]	Rpot	150–250
	dump	170/949/[3431]	Rpot	140–200

Summary of Buildings 30 and 31

Both these buildings had internal planked floors supported on joists and beams. These floors may have originally been suspended above the ground surface, only subsequent slumping and settling causing them to rest on lower and earlier deposits. Alternatively, the presence of earlier clay floors directly beneath the planks might suggest that the planks simply represent a replacement floor covering. Other contemporary levels did not contain evidence for timber floors. This may have been due to areas of truncation or localised variations in preservation conditions. The timber floors may represent individual rooms with a specific function, within a larger building, one of which was a grain store.

The quantity of carbonised grain found in the beamslot of Building 31 was probably present as a result both of falling between the planks and being preserved during the destruction of the building by fire.

The construction of the two buildings may have varied slightly. Building 31 appears to have been formed largely of timber constructed on baseplates probably with upright studs, while Building 30 during the same phase included a reused *opus signinum* foundation possibly within a clay foundation. This may have served as an internal wall, other walls possibly having had timber baseplates and wattle and daub superstructure.

The buildings and construction techniques are similar to those from the reconstruction of waterlogged building timbers from Cannon Street (Goodburn 1991). Evidence from other sites indicates these structural features from baseplate upwards. The later Borough High Street buildings included a timber floor and were probably similar to the timber warehouse on the Courage's Brewery site (Brigham et al 1995). The presence of grain may suggest a raised floor or, alternatively, timbers may have been laid at ground level on inset baseplates.

Hearths

Within the roadside settlement on BGH95 a total of 28 hearths were present and were distributed among many of the buildings and associated open areas. Two of the hearths had metalworking evidence directly associated with them. The examples in Structure 2 were associated with large quantities of hammerscale and slag; these were used for smithing and are discussed above (see Chapter 8).

The vast majority of the hearths occur on the eastern side of the excavated area. This may reflect the functional areas and uses of the buildings and settlement. Those hearths located internally would have been housed in rooms to the rear of the buildings and external examples would have been in yards behind or adjacent to buildings. This might fit an accepted model of the functional areas within strip buildings, with the rear being used for workshop or domestic purposes and the front for commercial or retail activities.

Many of the hearths, ovens or fire pits have little or no evidence of a specific industrial activity. However, the surviving identified hearths must certainly include domestic versions used solely for cooking and/or heating. These have been located within many of the buildings, including Buildings 14, 20, 22 and 23, and may represent the residential function of many of the roadside buildings. These domestic hearths were often formed of reused roof tiles, as in Building 20 where they formed an approximately 0.8m square, flat base for an open fire. The tile base and adjoining areas were scorched, and there was charcoal present.

Other hearths outside the buildings in adjoining structures or yards were not particularly large. These were generally sunken hearths averaging 1.3m in length and 0.8m in width. Oval or circular forms are common (Hammer in prep) and were frequently lined with clay, tile or amphora sherds, but there is little distinct in situ evidence to suggest what form the superstructures might have taken, although they may have incorporated hearth bricks and been bowl-shaped. Hearth bricks and isolated stakeholes present in Open Area 9 may, however, indicate a superstructure for one or more hearths in that area.

There was no definite evidence for the processes taking place at many of these hearths, as the samples taken from hearth fills or from adjacent areas provided evidence for charcoal, but no specific uses. The external hearths produced plenty of burnt debris. In Open Area 9 there was evidence of four hearths, including two complete ones and the fragmentary lining or pit cut for two others. There were also large quantities of ashy debris and rake-out material cleared during the lifetime of the hearths. The ash and debris were presumably regularly cleared out of the fire pits and distributed around the working area to form make-up deposits for subsequent working surfaces. The quantity of debris may point to some intensive use and probable industrial function, but there was no evidence of glass production or metalworking.

Elsewhere on the site there were dumps of burnt debris, ash and scorched clay rake-out, some of which was derived from the various smithing areas and domestic hearths. Further variations were also recorded, forming more substantial structures including one circular oven and the fragmentary remains of a tile-built structure with a tile base and wall. This was extensively burnt and may have formed part of an oven or stokehole.

Baking

The presence of large quantities of processed wheat grain in the remains of adjacent buildings, including Buildings 36 and 28, might suggest that some of the hearths functioned as baking ovens, either as part of businesses or as shared communal ovens. The sizes of the hearths identified were not particularly great and may not correspond to examples of larger bread ovens recorded elsewhere.

Other activities

Other non-metallurgical activities are possible for various hearths, including their use as drying ovens; although once again the size and form of these fire pits do not match known forms of comparative drying ovens, as they were generally too small. Nevertheless, corn or grain drying remains a possible function in light of the indirect evidence.

The destruction by fire of timber-framed buildings may have been a constant and significant risk, but one that was taken, given that they provided cheap and rapidly built structures. The evidence for destruction of buildings by fire occurs frequently, but in most cases the lost building was replaced very swiftly.

Building 27 went out of use, possibly due to a change of function during the early 2nd century, if the abandonment of the hearths is indicative of an earlier industrial process. There follows a further rebuilding with the construction of Building 30.

Following their destruction by fire, Buildings 30 and 31 underwent a phase of rebuilding represented by clay floor surfaces. There is no evidence of new replacement timber floors, although this may be due to preservation conditions. These buildings may have continued in use, as indicated by the new phase of floor laying. It is not clear what structural elements accompany these floors, but this later use may be linked with other later 3rd-century building.

West of the main road

RWT93 Open Area 1

A small stretch of a robbed out wall was visible which was on the same alignment as the subsequent buildings (see below). It was not excavated as it was below the founding depth of the proposed works, but it appeared to contain a fill of burnt brickearth and daub, and probably represents the demolition phase of an earlier brickearth building.

This can probably be equated with Building 5 which was excavated to the north at 15–23 Southwark Street (site code 15SKS80) (Cowan 1992, fig 11). Open Area 1 contained concentrations of crushed daub, which can be compared to room 3 of 15SKS80 Building 5 which had a surface of crushed daub and clay. Layers of unused broken tile mixed with charcoal served as floor make-up to deliberately level the area at 15SKS80 Building 5 (ibid, pl 4), but although a large number of tegulae were collected from RWT93 Open Area 1 there was no indication of whether they were unused or not.

Over the robbed out wall were spread dumped deposits which levelled the area. One of these layers contained demolition material with flints and worked stone blocks. These possibly could have derived from 15SKS80 Building 4 which contained flint and Kentish rag in its foundations (Cowan 1992, 25). Several stakeholes were scattered around the area but no discernible pattern could be observed.

DATING

Pottery dated AD 140–60 and AD 150–200 came from the levelling dumps over the robbed out wall. The demolition of 15SKS80 Building 5 was dated to AD 90–120, which may need revising in the light of the dates from RWT93.

RWT93 Building 1

A series of postholes and remnants of a slot indicated a large building with at least three rooms. A north–south row of small double postholes formed a wall line separating rooms A and B. Two 0.15m deep slots formed a T-junction separating room B to the west from room C to the east.

Three large postholes 0.3m deep aligned east–west probably formed the south wall of the building as no floors were seen to the south. A few posts indicate further divisions or rooms to the north, although no floor surfaces were found here, which indicates that this area may have been external. A sandy dump and two small pits filled with debris support this interpretation, and the area to the north was dubbed Open Area 2. Similarly there was no further activity to the south of the south post line, and this too may have been an open area.

Brickearth layers formed thick make-up deposits for the floors. Over these deposits were laid floor surfaces. Room A had a mortar floor surface with an occupation layer over it (1.97m OD). A fine painted wall plaster may have decorated one of the walls of this room, as a demolition dump of wall plaster was found over the floor (MacKenna 1993).

The painted plaster reveals a high standard of workmanship, with two fragments in particular showing painting of the very highest quality. Regrettably, much of the plaster is so badly fragmented that it is only possible to reconstruct small fragments of the decorative schemes which would have been present (Fig 96).

There were a number of different dado schemes present, ranging from simple background with splashed paint to colours imitating various exotic marbles and other stones used as wall veneers. It seems likely that these schemes derived from either the same room or a suite of adjoining rooms. One of these schemes was a black and green decoration which was painted in an almost exact imitation of green porphyry from Marathonisi in Laconia, southern Greece. Certain dado patterns, although imitating stone, are not actually mimicking any known marble

types used in London. Other dado schemes were painted with more care, the colours being carefully selected to match actual decorative stone types. Fragments of a dark red dado with pink splashes, for example, represent an imitation of Egyptian 'imperial' red porphyry from Gebel Dokhan in the eastern desert (Pritchard 1986, 174–5). Other plaster present had yellow painting separated by thin, rounded red lines (replicating veining) and was imitating Chemtou marble (giallo antico) from Chemtou, Tunisia (S Pringle pers comm). It is perhaps significant that all three types of wall veneer were imported into London for decorative use in high-status masonry buildings.

Imitation marble was also used to decorate the main, middle zone above the dado, as evident in Building 1 where an imitation marble scheme of wavy red and yellow lines lay above a dark red dado with white splashes. In most north Southwark buildings, however, the middle zone usually comprised a series of panels in one colour, often red or plain white, surrounded by vertical and horizontal borders of various colours. The wall upper zone, the frieze, rarely survives in London buildings.

Associated with at least one of the dado or imitation marble schemes described above was one large area of red with floral decoration in cream, white, dark red and green, and bordered on one side by a yellow band. The most spectacular plaster decoration from RWT93, a scene from the labours of Hercules, may have been part of this decorative area. Hercules spent 12 years under the orders of Eurystheus, who imposed upon him the most arduous labours. One of these was to slay the Nemean lion and bring back the skin to Eurystheus (Henig 2000, 73). The piece of plaster shows Hercules wrestling with the Nemean lion (back cover). He removed the skin and from it made a garment which rendered him invulnerable.

A number of fragments from the same dump belonged to a different room from those above, which had, at some stage in its life, been repainted with green and white plaster of exceptionally poor quality. This paint overlies a white decorated scheme of better quality comprising white panels bordered by yellow and separated by a decorative black border. The decoration on the panels is of floral type with candelabra painted in black, green and red. The overlying white plaster displays the remains of a crude floral scheme in green and black. The crudity of the overpainting would suggest either that the building underwent a rapid decline in its socio-economic status, or that the function of the room from which the plaster came was altered. Whatever the reason, the social status of the repainted room had clearly gone into decline.

In room B was a very worn crushed plaster which may have been a floor surface as it respected a remnant of in situ wall plaster which would have decorated the east wall of the room. Unfortunately, this could not be conserved as it was in poor condition. In room C was a gravel layer compact enough to be a surface but with a more plausible brickearth floor over it.

Another brickearth slab sealed the occupation in room B. While this could be a floor, it seems more likely that it is a demolition layer or possibly a collapsed wall. It was cut by two narrow slots which contained a large number of robbed out stakeholes. The slot on the west side of room B was slightly

1 Imitation marble decoration of wavy red and yellow lines bordered on lower edge by wavy black line (5–6mm) above white globular shapes; below is dark red dado with white or sometimes yellow splashes. Both dado and marble decoration bordered on right side by vertical band of white (6mm) and dark maroon. Possibly border for opening (?doorway).

2a Marble panel bordered with very wavy black line below rounded white spots; this area borders dark red, probably part of a horizontal border.

2b White spotted border pattern as 2a but from different part of wall.

3 Imitation marble-brecca decoration with large and small roughly circular or oval yellow shapes separated by reddish-brown with occasional brown lines; bordered by horizontal white band (4mm) followed by dark red dado with pink splashes and at least one vertical band of white (9mm) and dark red. Dark red and pink dado is imitation of red (imperial) porphyry from Egypt.

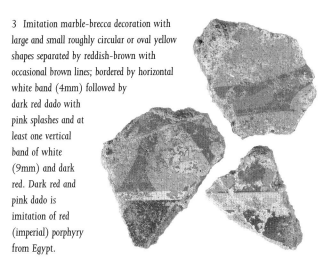

Fig 96 Painted wall plaster from RWT93 (1:2)

4 Imitation marble decoration with roughly round or semicircular yellow shapes, separated by much narrower red lines. Imitation of marble known as Chemtou (or giallo antico) from Tunisia.

5 Imitation marble decoration in same style as no. 4, but with white not yellow shapes; accurate imitation of green porphyry from southern Greece. Marble pattern bordered by cream and maroon, latter with ?pink splashes suggesting part of dado.

6 Imitation marble decoration of green oval shapes on a black background; bordered by horizontal white line (7mm) and dark red dado with pink splashes.

7 Dado design of dark red decorated with pink splashes with white border (6–7mm), bordering plain green panel; dado borders both base and sides of green area.

8 Dark red and pink dado design but with continuous white band replaced by series of individual white spots; further fragment shows green panel and white band bordered by plain dark red.

129

10a Probable imitation marble design in yellow on reddish-brown bordered by white band (5–7mm). Decorative scheme bordered by maroon band, green and area of white with remains of red decoration. Relationship of fragments is uncertain.

9 Lozenge-shaped imitation marble in pink and red on white bordered by black and white bands (5mm and 6mm respectively); one fragment shows red border after white band.

10b Yellow dado with fairly large white and dark red splashes.

11 Light grey-coloured dado with fairly large white and black splashes; on one fragment dado is split by vertical white band 8mm wide.

12 Triangular-shaped red area bordered by yellow; remains of white band between red and yellow area on two sides.

14 Fragment of red ?floral decoration on cream background.

15 Decorative scheme in red, cream and green on grey (originally black?) background.

13 Fragment with area of white with wavy red line, bordering area of yellow with decoration in brown or maroon. Colours are faded as in no. 12, so both may derive from same area of wall.

16 Yellow with remains of white band and decoration in white.

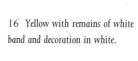

(Fig 96 cont)

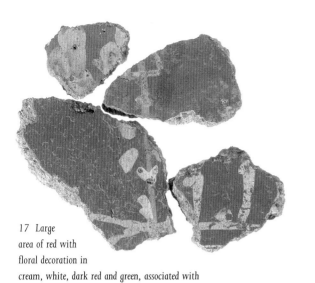

17 Large area of red with floral decoration in cream, white, dark red and green, associated with at least one of dado or imitation marble schemes.

18 Moulded fragment from wall junction at 90° angle.

19 Moulded fragment from around doorway or window opening.

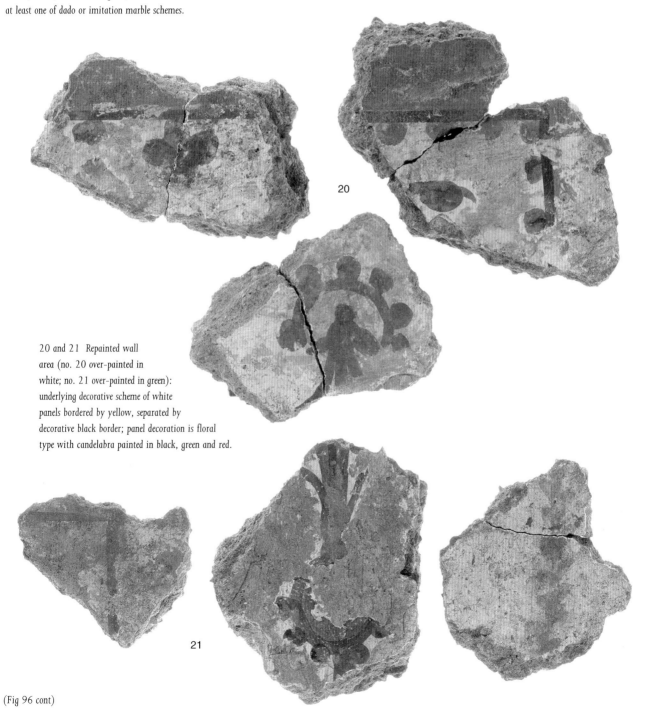

20

20 and 21 Repainted wall area (no. 20 over-painted in white; no. 21 over-painted in green): underlying decorative scheme of white panels bordered by yellow, separated by decorative black border; panel decoration is floral type with candelabra painted in black, green and red.

21

(Fig 96 cont)

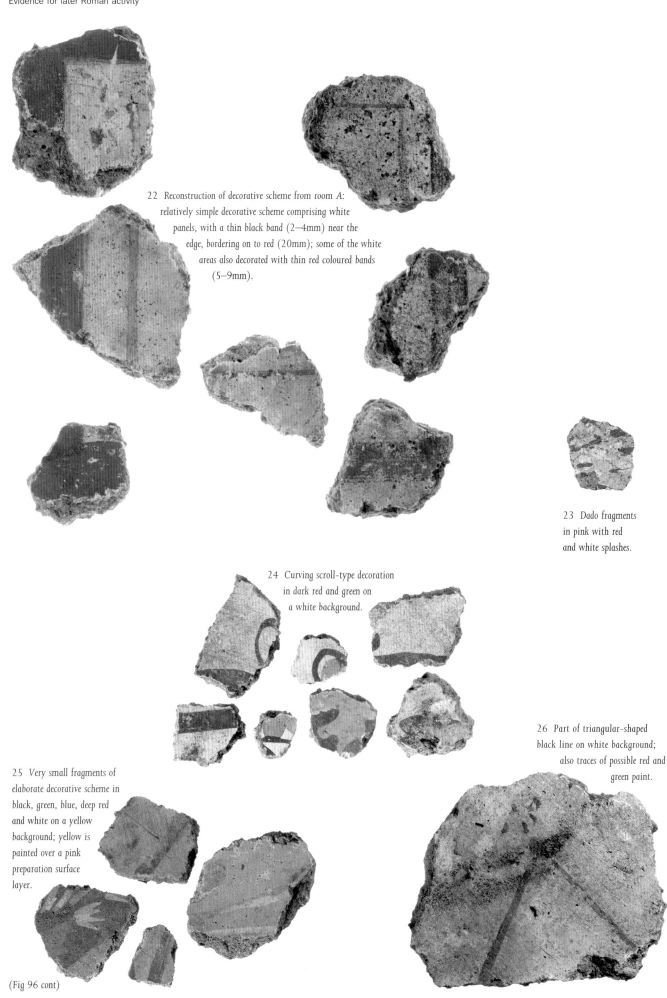

22 Reconstruction of decorative scheme from room A:
relatively simple decorative scheme comprising white
panels, with a thin black band (2–4mm) near the
edge, bordering on to red (20mm); some of the white
areas also decorated with thin red coloured bands
(5–9mm).

23 Dado fragments
in pink with red
and white splashes.

24 Curving scroll-type decoration
in dark red and green on
a white background.

26 Part of triangular-shaped
black line on white background;
also traces of possible red and
green paint.

25 Very small fragments of
elaborate decorative scheme in
black, green, blue, deep red
and white on a yellow
background; yellow is
painted over a pink
preparation surface
layer.

(Fig 96 cont)

to the east of the original wall and may have been an internal timber partition. This phase of activity might form part of room B or a secondary resurfacing.

In summary, Building 1 was represented by large posts indicating major load-bearing walls separating two rooms, A and B, and two external areas to the north and south. Additionally, two small slots presumably once containing clay walls separated rooms B and C. It is possible that these walls were internal, being of smaller and flimsier build. However, the area to the north of the wall slot was interpreted as an external area, Open Area 2. Although the floors appear to have been relatively modest, of mortar and brickearth, small areas of tesserae from the demolition deposits of Building 1 indicate that the building may have had a tessellated floor with red grouting similar to the one in room 10 at 15SKS80 Building 6. This would have been more in keeping with a wall plaster which was highly decorated and consisted of types normally reserved for high-status buildings. The plaster may have been from adjoining rooms or a suite of rooms. The overpainting of the candelabra-decorated wall plaster with crude floral green and white wall plaster is hard to interpret. It may be contemporary with the reflooring and addition of an internal partition in room B, which might indicate that room B had changed its function. If the wall plaster does come from room B, then this might indicate that the socio-economic status of the room had declined.

DATING
Only residual pottery came from Building 1; a date of AD 150–200 is derived from the preceding groups of Open Area 1.

DEMOLITION OF BUILDING 1
The painted wall plaster in room A had not collapsed *in situ* but had been levelled as make-up for the subsequent building. However, the similarity of much of the decoration suggests one source and it is probable that the plaster derived from Building 1 and had been reused as make-up for subsequent occupation. Brickearth dumps over the wall plaster probably also derived from Building 1 and were being reused as make-up for Building 2. Burnt demolition deposits were found in room C.

Discussion

Both RWT93 Building 1 and RWT93/RWG94 Building 2 may have been part of the large building complex on the adjacent site of 15–23 Southwark Street (15SKS80), the so-called *mansio* (Cowan 1992) represented by Buildings (phases) 4–7. RWT93 Building 1 was found to have similarities to 15SKS80 Building 6, while RWT93 Building 2 and RWG94 Building 2 were found to show similarities to 15SKS80 Building 7.

RWT93 BUILDING 1 AND 15SKS80 BUILDING 6
It is likely that RWT93 Building 1 was part of Building 6 at 15SKS80 (Cowan 1992, fig 12). Fig 97 shows the additions to the plan reconstruction of Building 6 including internal and external areas.

The major load-bearing walls between rooms A and B of RWT93 Building 1 may have been masonry-founded like those of 15SKS80 Building 6 and may be projected to the north to join the masonry-founded wall between room 1 and Open Area 9. It seems likely that the external walls of the building were masonry or masonry-founded and that the internal walls were less substantial and constructed of clay and timber.

The wall between rooms B and C of RWT93 Building 1, if projected northwards, would not align with the wall between rooms 6 and 8 of 15SKS80 Building 6. There were a few postholes in the path of the wall in RWT93 here but much of this area is thought to have been an external area, Open Area 2, as a sandy dump and two pits were situated here. It is likely that such a large building would have had open areas or atriums within it to make the roofing possible.

The corner wall between 15SKS80 Building 6's rooms 8 and 10 was not originally projected to create small rooms as no extensions of the corner could be seen during excavation in 15SKS80. Thus it is not clear how RWT93 Open Area 2 fits with 15SKS80 Building 6's rooms 8 and 10. However, there must have been some kind of division between them and walls must have existed if they were to accommodate RWT93 Open Area 2.

The wall between rooms A and B of RWT93 Building 1 can also be projected northwards and perhaps formed the west wall of 15SKS80 Building 6's room 6. It is not clear what existed to the west of 15SKS80 Building 6's room 6 at this date since there was no evidence of any activity in the RWG94 excavation. Between RWG94 Building 1 in the 1st century and RWG94 Building 2 in AD 150+ there was no evidence for occupation associated with buildings. The RWG94 area was presumed to have been an external area, just as it was to be later with the addition of a metalled area, Open Area 2, in the 2nd century.

Tessellated floors thought to be contemporary with Building 6 in rooms 6 and 10 (Cowan 1992, 36–7) now appear to have been added later (see RWT93 Building 2), and so rooms 6 and 10 may have had mortar floors like rooms 8 and 9.

DATING
Building 6 at 15SKS80 was dated to AD 120–60, and therefore should perhaps be revised to a little later, perhaps like RWT93 Building 1 to AD 150+.

The demolition of RWT93 Building 1 and subsequent construction of Building 7 and RWT93 Building 2 was also dated AD 150+, although the infilling of a small pit in Open Area 2 contained pottery dated AD 180+, a date which broadly accords with that of the late 2nd to early 3rd century proposed for 15SKS80 Building 7. Unfortunately, the pit could not be firmly placed in the stratigraphic sequence, so that this dating must be viewed with caution.

RWT93 Building 2

Piercing the plaster demolition layer of Building 1 was a construction cut which contained a remnant of masonry wall foundation aligned east–west. It was very truncated and was constructed of loosely mortared flint, chalk and greensand surviving to a depth of 0.14m; its base was at 2.06m OD. It was in almost the same position as the south wall of the previous

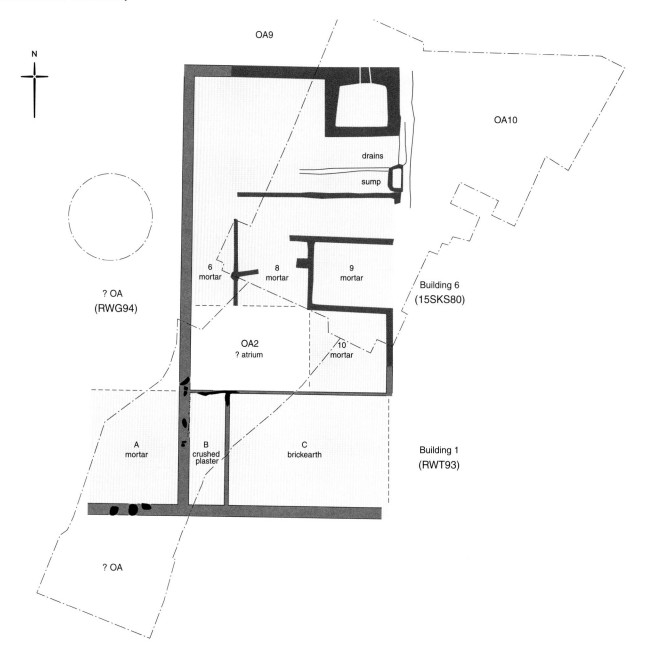

N

OA9

OA10

drains

sump

? OA
(RWG94)

6
mortar

8
mortar

9
mortar

Building 6
(15SKS80)

OA2
? atrium

10
mortar

A
mortar

B
crushed
plaster

C
brickearth

Building 1
(RWT93)

? OA

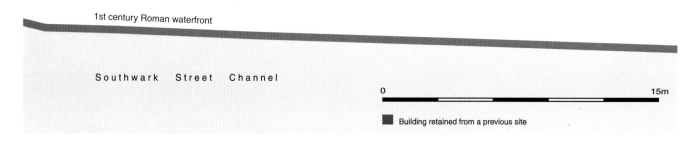

1st century Roman waterfront

Southwark Street Channel

0   15m

■ Building retained from a previous site

Fig 97 Plan of RWT93 Building 1 and 15SKS80 Building 6

Building 1. To the north of it were two robber trenches which divided the building into two separate rooms, A and B, with open areas to the north and south.

Room A had a mortar floor (2.23m OD) and room B had mortar bedding layers for tessellated floors above (2.45m OD). They probably represent the same floor but there were anomalies. There appeared to be two distinct areas of flooring with a clear join between them; the alignment of the tesserae was different; and one area of flooring was at a slightly higher level than the other. Furthermore, the easternmost area of flooring contained red and white tesserae, whilst the larger area to the west contained only red tesserae. There was no evidence either that one had been laid secondary to the other or that any partition had been left between the two areas of flooring, but it would appear that some of the tesserae were reused, perhaps from Building 1.

From the robbing fills came more tesserae which were smaller, not mosaic-sized, but probably from a finer than usual tessellated floor. This may indicate that Building 2 had a further tessellated floor, perhaps as a border to a mosaic in another room.

Demolition dumps contained large quantities of painted wall plaster within, and therefore probably derived from, room A. It was not as high-quality as that associated with Building 1. This room had a relatively simple decorative scheme comprising white panels, with a thin black band near the edge, bordering onto red. There are a number of curved fragments in red bordering on white which would have come from around doorways and window openings, together with fragments of dado in pink with red and white splashes (MacKenna 1993). Layers of compacted sand cut by a very large number of stakeholes of unknown function appear to represent an external surface to the north of the building, Open Area 3, corresponding to the previous Open Area 2. However, this area could merely have been make-ups for another, now removed, floor.

An external gravel surface, Open Area 4, was seen to the south of Building 2. Within this open area was an alignment of stakeholes situated at right angles to the south wall of Building 2; it represents either a fence line or part of another structure against the wall of the building, perhaps a portico or entrance from the channel frontage.

In summary, Building 2 was constructed of masonry with main load-bearing walls in the same position as in Building 1; the southern wall had shifted slightly to the south encroaching on the open area. Rooms B and C of Building 1 now appear to have been combined to make one room. The floor of this room was tessellated, but was constructed as two distinct areas on slightly different levels with a join between them. Perhaps a partition had been removed. Room A had a mortar floor but this may have been bedding for a tessellated floor over it, as seen in room B where the tessellated floor overlay a layer of mortar. The possible tessellated floor of room A may have had a red border to a mosaic. The quantities of Roman roof tiles present in the robbing dumps suggest that Building 2 had a ceramic tiled roof. The marble is probably from a wall veneer or other internal decoration. However, there were insufficient fragments of marble inlay and laminated sandstone for stone roofing to be sure that Building 2 possessed these features.

Fragments of combed and roller-stamped flue tile might indicate that the building had hypocausted rooms but there was no in situ evidence for this.

DATING

There was no dating evidence for the construction of Building 2, but a date of AD 150+ was derived from the previous groups of Building 1.

RWG94 wells

At RWG94, cut into the natural, but having no relationship to RWG94 Building 1, were two wells.

The first well, Structure 1, was probably constructed by excavating the shaft from within a box-frame set on a timber cradle at its base. Successive frames, one plank wide, were stacked onto the top as the shaft deepened. Brickearth was pushed in behind the shaft to act as a lining and was mixed with the natural sand that slumped in. After four timber frames had been dropped into the shaft, the cut was backfilled with chalk blocks, flint, sandstone and tile. The timber was oak and the box measured 0.9m x 0.9m. The planks were about 0.28m wide and 0.035m thick and had dovetail joints nailed through. The top of the timbers was at 0.44m and the base at −0.95m OD. Structure 1 had a construction date of AD 120+ derived from pottery in its construction backfill. A second well, Structure 2, was apparently constructed in the same way. It was slightly larger, measuring 1.0m x 1.0m with planks 0.4m wide and 0.05m thick. The top was at 0.5m and the base at −0.9m OD. Here too the planks were nailed and mortised.

The two wells were aligned with each other and their construction backfills appear to have been sealed beneath a gravel surface, Open Area 2 (1.61–1.98m OD). This did not extend up to the timber boxes of the wells as later robbing had taken place to obscure their relationships.

There were primary or usage fills within the wells. From the usage fill of well Structure 1 were many frog/toad bones representing a minimum of 28 individuals. The presence of such a considerable quantity strongly suggests that the well was left uncovered for much of the time it was in use. From within the usage fills of Structure 2 came fragments of leather shoes <R106>.

Also recovered from within the backfill of Structure 2 was a complete skeleton of a dog and three other partial dog skeletons. One of the dogs was very elderly and had evidently been cared for into old age. It may have been a favourite hunting dog and, if so, it would seem surprising that it was dumped into the well rather than being carefully buried. There was no evidence of ritual burial, however.

DATING

Structure 2 had a construction date of AD 150+ derived from pottery in its construction backfill and a dendrochronological date of AD 131+ (Tyers 1994). (Due to missing heartwood rings, Tyers suggests that it was probably constructed nearer the middle of the 2nd century.) Pottery from the metalling of Open Area 2 was dated to AD 150–250.

Pottery from the usage (or perhaps backfill) of Structure 2 was dated to AD 250+ and from Structure 1 it was also dated to AD 250+.

A large pottery assemblage came from the primary fill of well Structure 2 in Open Area 2. It consists of 105 sherds, 0.25 EVEs and weighs 6429g. Most of the assemblage (70.5% by sherd count) is comprised of three smashed vessels which are almost complete except for their rims. Over half of the assemblage (49.5% by sherd count, 54.5% by weight) is in the fabric AHFA, including at least three jars. There are three beakers in NVCC, which is the second most commonly occurring fabric (36.2% by sherd count, 10.0% by weight). Other fabrics include BB1, BBS and the late Dressel 20 amphora fabric, BAETL. There is a marked absence of rims despite the number of complete bases and lower halves of vessels.

There is no independent dating evidence such as coins for this layer. The difficulty in dating the ceramic assemblage is that for the number of sherds there is a relatively limited range of vessels present. Therefore it is difficult to refine the dating on the negative evidence of the absence of late fabrics such as OXRC since the number of vessels represented is so small. The NVCC necked globular beaker with white barbotine scroll decoration <P193> (Fig 98) is dated to the 3rd century (Howe et al 1980, 20, fig 5, no. 49). The NVCC pentice beaker <P194> (Fig 98) is generally dated to the 4th century (ibid, 20–2). However, there is evidence from Southwark that these already occur earlier there, in the late 3rd century. A very large assemblage from a well at 107 Borough High Street (107BHS81) dated to c AD 270–300 contains an NVCC pentice beaker. The dating evidence is provided by three coins, one coin of Severus Alexander (AD 222–35) and two irregular radiates of Tetricus (AD 270/80s). In addition there is the notable absence of OXRC, which starts to appear in London in c AD 270, and a very low percentage of AHFA, a fabric which becomes increasingly

common towards the end of the 3rd century (Yule 1982, 244; Rayner and Seeley in prep).

The large AHFA jar <P195> (Fig 98) has three panels of burnished curvilinear and wavy decoration separated by bands of solid burnishing. Burnished bands of curvilinear decoration on the lower bodies of jars do occur on earlier Alice Holt products in London (Davies et al 1994, fig 86, no. 545) although they tend to be more common on later vessels, a view supported by the evidence from the kiln site (Lyne and Jefferies 1979, fig 22, no. 1.32; fig 25, nos 1C.4 and 1C.6; fig 30, no. 4.44–5; Millett 1979, fig 6).

Structure 1 contained pottery dating to AD 250+ in its backfill and Structure 2 contained pottery dating to AD 270+, suggesting that they both lasted into the mid to late 3rd century. They also contained fragments of laminated sandstone roof tile which probably dates to the 3rd/4th century. A large group of building material including a tegula dated AD 250–350 was found in the backfill of Structure 2.

A bucket handle mount <R125> was found in the 'dark earth' deposits above and may have been associated with the wells.

Later robbing truncated the wells and removed the relationship between them, so it was not possible to ascertain if one was built before the other; but the gravel surface (OA2) over both of them alike points to their being contemporary. However, the dating evidence for the construction of Structure 1 gave AD 120+ and for Structure 2 gave AD 150+, suggesting that Structure 2 was a little later. It appears that they were both in use until AD 250+.

RWG94 Building 2

Overlying the robber pits, wells and gravel surface were dumped deposits. A coin found in them dated them to AD 335–41. It was not clear if they had been dumped against

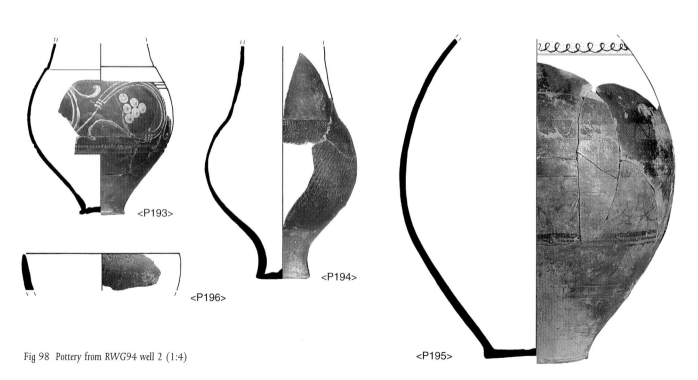

<P193>

<P196>

<P194>

<P195>

Fig 98 Pottery from RWG94 well 2 (1:4)

a now vanished wall (represented by robber trench RWG94), the wall probably being constructed from the level of the gravel surface of Open Area 2 and therefore contemporary with it.

Building 2 was represented only by a robber trench in the form of a three-sided trench 0.9m wide and 2.0m deep, and stepped down on its west side to make the base 0.56m wide. The large size and depth of this trench would suggest that Building 2 was a masonry building, and pieces of ragstone found within the robber backfills would appear to support this hypothesis. Fragments of sandstone roof tile, ceramic roof tiles, painted wall plaster, *opus signinum*, flue tile and tesserae conjure an appearance of the building as having decorated walls and a tessellated floor.

The wall plaster recovered from the robber trench shows what appears to be a dark red panel area decorated in yellow. The dark red was bordered by a white band (5–7mm thick) followed by an area of green on one fragment and black on another. Further plaster believed to come from Building 2 was recovered from the backfill of a well. This comprised small areas of plain white and red plaster and a larger border area in red followed by a white band (2mm thick) and what may have been a yellow dado area with red splashes.

Also found was a stone inlay of imported *fior di pesco* marble. The building materials from the robber trench are consistent with use in a good quality building equipped with a hypocaust. There is a piece of thick brick which probably came from one of the large bricks used for capping *pilae* in the hypocaust, and one fragment of cross-combed flue tile in Radlett fabric.

DATING

The coin dated AD 335–41 represents the date of the dumping which was probably contemporary with the robbing of RWG94 Building 2. There was no evidence to date the construction of Building 2.

Discussion

RWT93 BUILDING 2, RWG94 BUILDING 2 AND 15SKS80 BUILDING 7

RWT93 Building 2 was most likely part of 15SKS80 Building 7, although it is not clear how they fit together. The foundation described for RWT93 was not very similar to any of the other foundations in Building 7. However, Building 7 is made up of many different elements, for example tile and rubble foundations, brickearth walls, mortar and rammed chalk foundations (Cowan 1992, fig 14) for which it was not possible to distinguish phases. Fig 99 shows the additions to the plan reconstruction of Building 7 including internal and external areas.

Only two rooms were present in the area of excavation of RWT93 Building 2, rooms A and B. The wall of RWT93 Building 2 which divides rooms A and B can be projected northwards to meet up with the RWG94 Building 2 wall represented by the three-sided or apsidal robber trench. This would be in the same or a similar position to that of RWT93 Building 1, projected as having been the western wall of 15SKS80 Building 6, room 6. The flint and chalk foundation of RWT93 Building 2 was

comparable to that of 15SKS80 Building 7, while the robber trench of RWT93 Building 2 was 2.0m deep and therefore comparable to the deep foundations of Building 7 (Cowan 1992, fig 14). The masonry wall forming the southern limit of the building was slightly to the north of the wall posts that marked the southern limit of RWT93 Building 1.

It is possible that RWT93 Open Area 2 (now Open Area 3) could have been a courtyard or atrium. The interpretation of part of 15SKS80 Building 7 as Open Area 12 (Cowan 1992, fig 13) would now seem unlikely in the light of the new evidence, namely the presence of an apsidal section of wall from RWG94, and it is possible that Open Area 12 was in fact an internal area.

From the robbing of RWT93 Building 2 came a brick in fabric 3006 with part of a procuratorial stamp [P....], possibly die ?2A. This is significant, as an imbrex with a (different) procuratorial stamp was found at 15SKS80, residual in a medieval context. The robbing of RWT93 Building 2 also includes a roller-stamped flue tile in die 11. Tiles with the same die were found at 15SKS80, the earliest being associated with Building 7.

The western limit of RWT93 Building 2 would appear to be represented by the robber trench of RWG94 Building 2 and the metalled area, RWG94 Open Area 2, and the wells, Structures 1 and 2. The large robber trench of RWG94 was of curious alignment. Little of it remained in the area of excavation of RWG94 but it did appear to have a three-sided shape. It was similar in width and depth to the 15SKS80 large robber trenches (see additions to Building 7: Cowan 1992, fig 14) and could therefore have been contemporary. However, RWG94 Building 2 cannot be projected from RWG94 eastwards into the excavation area of 15SKS80 as no large robber trenches were seen here. It is possible that the three-sided robber trench represents an apsidal end to 15SKS80 Building 7 if it joined up with the west wall of RWT93 Building 2. The addition of hypocausts to 15SKS80 Building 7 would be compatible with the addition of the three-sided wall of RWG94 Building 2 as an indicator of increasing wealth and status. A feature originally interpreted as a pit may in fact have been a buttress or similar support (see pit [216]: Cowan 1992, 48) within the building (Fig 99).

The building material assemblage from RWG94 Building 2 is similar in character to that from the robber trenches of Building 7 at 15SKS80, but the quantity of material is too small to allow a definite connection to be made. Five imported white marble inlay fragments came from 15SKS80, as well as some pieces of Purbeck marble inlay and paving, most of which were associated with the construction and disuse of Buildings 6 and 7, but with some from later contexts. Given the quantity of imported marble at 15SKS80 and its general rarity in London, it is likely that the *fior di pesco* marble from RWG94 came from the same building. From the well construction backfill of RWG94 Structure 2 came a stamped flue tile in die 3; tiles from this die were also found at 15SKS80 associated with robber trenches from Building 7.

To the south of RWT93/RWG94 Building 2 was Open Area 4 which represented the southern limit of the building. Open Area 4 could have been a yard area alongside the Southwark Street Channel, and the post line in it could represent a portico or other entrance structure.

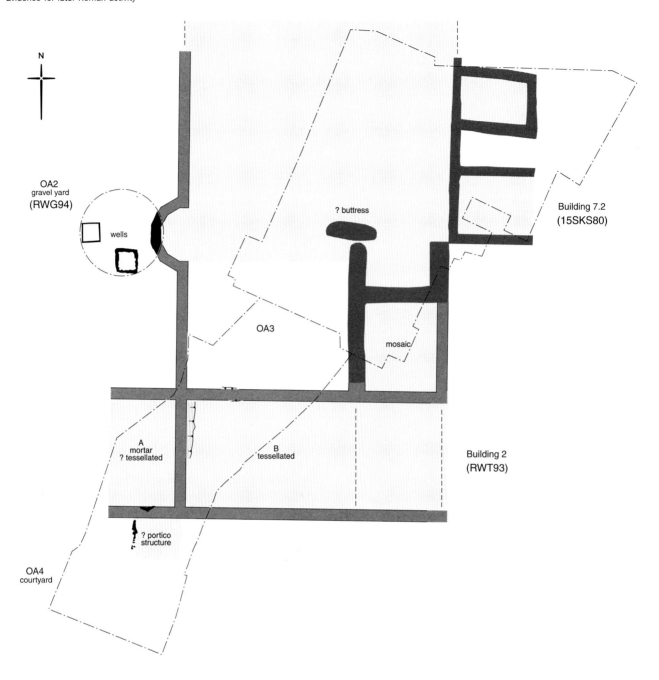

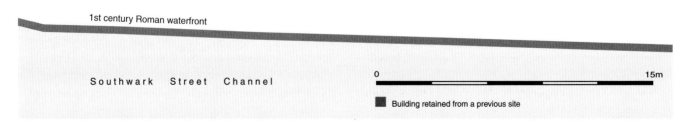

Fig 99 Plan of RWT93 Building 2

DATING

The demolition date of RWT93 Building 1 in AD 150/80+ and the construction date for RWT93 Building 2 broadly agrees with that proposed for 15SKS80 Building 7 of the late 2nd to early 3rd century, although Building 7 consisted of many phases and had a long life-span. This date is slightly later than that of AD 150+ for the construction of the wells and metalled Open Area 2 in RWG94, and it may be that these were previously in use with Building 6. It was thought that RWG94 Building 2 was constructed from and contemporary with the metalled Open Area 2, even though there was no dating evidence for this building. It may have been furnished with sandstone roof tile dating to the 3rd/4th century, and tiles dating to AD 250+ were indeed associated with this building. However, it is likely that the building was re-roofed and refurnished throughout the later Roman period, just like 15SKS80 Building 7. As mentioned above, it is possible that RWG94 Building 2 was contemporary with additions to 15SKS80 Building 7 (Cowan 1992, fig 14).

The wells of RWG94 appear to have still been in use in AD 250–70+. The disuse and demolition of the RWG94 wells and Open Area 2 was dated by a coin to AD 335–41, and the backfill of a robber trench at 15SKS80 contained a coin of AD 347–8. The dating evidence for the burials here was minimal, but a coin of the AD 340s from the burials at Courage's Brewery might indicate that all the Southwark Street area burials are from the mid 4th century. However, two coins from the 'dark earth' at RWT93 were dated AD 330 and 380+, suggesting Roman activity into the late 4th century. The demise of the building could thus be dated to the mid to late 4th century.

Conclusions

The phasing and interpretation of the building complex at 15–23 Southwark Street still remains unclear, even with the additions from RWT93 and RWG94, but it is clear that it was a high-status building complete with tessellated floors, imported marble and highly decorated wall plaster (Goffin 1992).

At the inn or *mansio* in Silchester there was a clear division of the accommodation in each wing into suites (Boon 1974, 138–40), and there were likewise indications of a suite of adjoining rooms in RWT93 Building 1. There is still no evidence for a bathhouse as at Silchester and other *mansiones*, although the *fior di pesco* marble from RWT93 may have come from something like a bathhouse.

At Silchester there was an apsidal, probably vaulted room in the west wing measuring nearly 6.0m x 5.0m which was interpreted as an audience chamber or a grand dining room. There is a similar chamber in the Caerwent *mansio* and the Bignor villa. This would seem a plausible use for the apsidal room of RWG94 Building 2, but in the absence of more archaeological data it is not possible to attribute functions to rooms with any certainty.

The building alignments do not match either of the roads that can be projected into the area. Road 3 can be projected from the north-east (Winchester Palace: Yule in prep) and may have formed a junction with Road 5 (Courage's Brewery study

area: Cowan in prep) in the north-west corner of 15SKS80 Open Area 9. The roads as projected must have ended here as they did not continue across the excavated area of 15SKS80. Open Area 9 remained an external area throughout the history of the 15SKS80 building.

It is possible that RWG94 Open Area 2 formed part of a yard alongside the road junction and indicates a western limit to room A of RWT93 Buildings 1 and 2. It may also be the case that the building complex was aligned with the channel to the south, perhaps with a courtyard area along the water's edge.

East of the road

LBA95 and LBB95

Across LBA95 Open Area 3 were a series of pits and ditches. These appear to have been primarily or subsequently used for domestic refuse, in particular a 1.0m wide, sub-circular pit at the northern limit of excavation. This contained a dumped fill which appears to have been deposited in a single event. The dump contained large quantities of domestic debris including a large amount of pottery. The assemblage included virtually no residual material, the exception being the rim of a necked jar from Alice Holt/Surrey dating from the mid 1st to mid 2nd century. The rest of the assemblage provides a closely dated, homogeneous and well preserved example of a 3rd-century ceramic group in Southwark, dated *c* AD 230–60 (Fig 100).

The assemblage contains a total of 102 sherds weighing 2612g and representing 3.68 EVEs. The group as a whole is dominated by Romano-British colour-coated wares which make up 42.2% of the assemblage by sherd count, 26% by weight and 44.6% by EVEs. Accordingly, beakers are the most dominant form, comprising 42.2% by sherd count and 44.6% by EVEs.

The composition of the group may be regarded as unusual, with the general lack of reduced wares present (20% by sherd count, 16.7% by weight, 22% by EVEs) and little apparent residuality. However, the dating of the group is significant because few 3rd-century groups have thus far been identified in Southwark. It may be that the mid 3rd century marks a peak in the use of beakers or that this deposit is a collection of favourite vessels which had rarely been used. The latter would account for the presence of the slightly earlier hunt cups and scroll beakers, which may have been used and retained as valued vessels, due to their highly decorative nature.

NVCC is the most common fabric by sherd count and EVEs. There are several different beakers represented in the assemblage, including bag-shaped beakers with cornice rims and hunt cups. The Nene Valley hunt cups (for example <P197>, Fig 100) are dated to the later 2nd to early 3rd centuries (Howe et al 1980, 8) and form part of the early repertoire of the industry's colour-coated vessels. The elongated animal figures form part of a typical hunt scene consisting of a dog chasing a deer. Other forms of decoration present include the barbotine scroll decoration. The scroll-decorated beaker is one of the most common types produced in NVCC, but it has been suggested that they may have had a relatively short floruit in production.

This vessel <P198> (Fig 100) has the 'tight scrollwork' which is only known as an under-slip decoration (Howe et al 1980, 16, fig 3, nos 29–30). The type is dated to the late 2nd to early 3rd centuries. The necked beaker with rouletted decoration <P199> (Fig 100) is unusual in that it is similar in style to the indented type, but there is no evidence of it being indented. At present no parallels have been found for this vessel among published material. The shift from bag-shaped beakers to the taller, narrower-necked type probably occurred in the second quarter of the 3rd century (ibid, 18). Another unusual vessel is the small undecorated beaker <P200> (Fig 100) which is 67–68mm in height and has a bead rim.

SAMEG represents 12.7% of the total assemblage by sherd count, 38.6% by weight and 33.4% by EVEs. Two vessels are present, both of which are illustrated. The Drag. 31 rouletted bowl <P201> (Fig 100) is a good example of its type, with the junction of the wall and floor marked by an internal ridge. The form Drag. 31R usually tends to date later than c AD 160 and east Gaulish examples were imported into Britain up to the mid 3rd century (Webster 1996, 35). The other SAMEG form present is a Ludowici plate Tf <P202> (Fig 100) which is complete except for a small section missing from the rim. This form is defined as a 'shallow dish with outwardly projecting ridge or reduced flange', and this example has a 'continuously rounded contour', a type which is regarded as a flanged variant of Drag. 32 (Oswald and Davies Pryce 1920, 207–8, pl 65, nos 6–7). The form is generally thought to date to the later 2nd to mid 3rd centuries.

The BB1 cooking pots <P203> and <P204> (Fig 100) in this group both have curved, everted rims that are of a similar diameter to the girth of the vessel and do not extend beyond it. The most complete example <P203> has a finely moulded rim with no thickening or beading and there is a relatively wide band of obtuse lattice that is well executed. A feint burnished line is present above the band of lattice, but this is not as deeply scored as the examples from New Fresh Wharf (Richardson 1986, 124–5, fig 1.172).

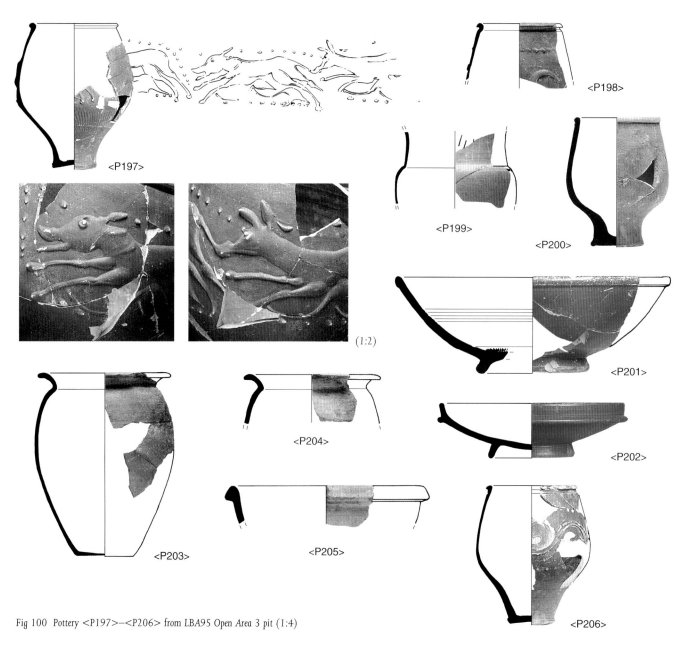

(1:2)

Fig 100 Pottery <P197>–<P206> from LBA95 Open Area 3 pit (1:4)

The dating of this vessel is somewhat problematic, but important for the dating of the context as a whole. The date for the introduction of obtuse lattice is now widely regarded as being in the early 3rd century, for instance the Vindolanda group dated c AD 223–5 (Holbrook and Bidwell 1991, 96). The vessel shape itself is most similar to Gillam type 8 dated c AD 235–65 (Gillam 1976, 63, fig 1, no. 8; Farrar 1981, 421, table 11). Although this dating scheme has been questioned, the style of the lattice decoration and the lack of a deeply scored line demarcating the lattice band, coupled with the dimensions of the vessel, does support a date in the early to mid 3rd century rather than later. The vessel has a coating of limescale residue internally, evidence of its use for cooking and boiling. Also present in this context is a body sherd with right-angle lattice decoration, which first appears on BB1 in the late 2nd century (Holbrook and Bidwell 1991, 96).

There are at least two BB2 D-shaped rimmed bowls with acute lattice decoration in the assemblage, one of which is illustrated <P205> (Fig 100). Colchester BB2 first appears in the City in RCP3 (c AD 100–20) but only as rare sherds. By RCP5 (c AD 140–60) Colchester BB2 accounts for over one quarter of all reduced wares and D-shaped rim bowls are the dominant form. This form is still present in the Leadenhall Court group 53 dated c AD 230–50/60, although it is noted that by this period quantities of BB2 are in decline (Symonds and Tomber 1991, 71–3).

The lack of any independent dating is a handicap, but the consistent dates for the Nene Valley colour-coated wares and the east Gaulish samian forms support the early end date given to the assemblage. The Black-Burnished ware cooking jar is probably the latest element in the group, and the combined features of form and decoration probably date at the earliest to c AD 235–40.

The absence of products from the Verulamium and Highgate kilns in the group continues to confirm the decline of these industries by the late 2nd to early 3rd centuries. Also of note, although bearing in mind the relatively small size of the group and numbers of vessels involved, is the absence of AHFA which is normally present only in small quantities in London by c AD 250 (Symonds and Tomber 1991, 71).

A series of intermittent dumps covered parts of Open Area 3. However, these were truncated by modern piles or late medieval foundations and may originally have been spread over much of the excavated area. These dumps included redeposited brickearth, possibly derived from a building, and domestic debris. One such dump included a virtually complete GAUL1 Gauloise 4 amphora <P207> which was found broken into 125 sherds (Fig 101). The sherds were found as a discrete scatter identifiable within the dump and it is possible that the vessel was broken in situ. No other pottery was found in the same context. This vessel is particularly interesting as it is a late example of its type. The Gauloise 4 amphora has been shown to exhibit a typological development of the neck and foot which has a chronological significance (Dangréaux and Desbat 1988, 128–9, fig 8, c–d). As the form develops the foot becomes narrower and the neck becomes shorter, resulting in the top of the handles becoming

raised parallel to the level of the rim by the late 2nd to early 3rd centuries. This vessel exhibits both these characteristics.

At the adjacent LBB95 there was a continuation of land use represented by Open Area 3, which included several partially revealed pits. Two features included timber linings, one containing a fragment of a barrel, and hence possibly a well, and the second a plank, possibly lining a pit. Pottery was recovered from pits and dumps and dated to c AD 150–250 on the presence of a SAMEG Drag. 37 bowl.

There was no apparent change in land use into the 3rd century as LBB95 Open Area 4 was also used for pits and domestic dumps. It is likely that the pits were associated with nearby buildings and that the domestic debris was derived from buildings possibly fronting onto Road 1.

The pottery date-range indicates that this activity was continuing in the period c AD 200–300. A single coin from an external dump is dated to AD 270–3. The pottery date-range is supported by the presence of Cam. 306 bowls which first occur in London in the 3rd century (Symonds and Tomber 1991, 70) and the late Roman colour-coated ware, NVCC, which predominates and occurs in a range of forms including a pinch-mouthed flagon and a Castor box lid.

Fig 101 Gaulish amphora <P207> from Open Area 3 (height 600mm)

Land reclamation

North-east of the island and Guy's Channel

The likely result of the combination of drainage and land reclamation processes, in conjunction with settlement growth, was an expansion of the settlement eastwards over previous marginal and unoccupied areas. The raising of the ground level by dumping domestic debris and levelling material must represent a successful programme of water management and land reclamation, which may have been fuelled by population or economic expansion in Southwark. As a result, by the middle of the 2nd century buildings were being constructed towards the eastern margin of the eyot.

To the south and east of LBI95, extensive reclamation of marginal land starts to take place in the late 2nd century. Pressure on building land alongside the main road meant that the settlement had to push eastwards into the more low-lying areas of the island in order to expand. The preliminary to any construction work was to raise the ground level above that of high tide and preferably above that of periodic floods.

At 20–26 London Bridge Street, LBJ95, the earliest dated activity was dumping in the mid to late 2nd century, cut by pits and drainage ditches. The dumping raised the ground level from 0.8m to at least 1.2m OD. This was sealed by a layer of waterlain sand, probably representing an inundation, indicating that the ground level needed to be raised further to avoid flooding. Further dumping ensued in the 3rd century with further ditches and pits. The fills of the ditches were initially waterlain, suggesting that they were dug for drainage. The dumps and pits had little in the way of occupation debris in them, pointing to the absence of domestic occupation in the immediate area generating any rubbish for disposal.

At TOM95, between St Thomas Street and London Bridge Street, a grouting shaft revealed dump layers accumulating from the middle of the 2nd century onwards (TOM95 OA1). No substantial occupation was revealed, but there were a series of pits and ditches dating to the 2nd and 3rd centuries. One of the pits contained a fragment of mosaic, which may have come from a bathhouse (D Neal pers comm), but there is no clue as to where such a structure might have been located. The mosaic, which is plain white with a single red tessera, is of good quality; the materials are hard chalk and tile. Most of the pot groups are small except for one medium sized group from the ditch. The latest date of AD 250 is provided by the BB1 later everted-rim jars with obtuse lattice decoration (BB1 2FX OL) which are present in the ditch fills. There is an absence of OXRC, which starts to appear in London assemblages in the last quarter of the 3rd century, and this indicates that these assemblages possibly pre-date the 4th century. Additionally, all these groups contain some earlier residual material dating to the 1st and early 2nd centuries.

A sample from one of the pit fills produced a rich environmental assemblage. Botanical remains consisted of charcoal fragments and charred remains of over 50 cereal grains of mainly free-threshing bread/club wheat (*Triticum aestivum* L) and barley. Free-threshing wheat tends to be less well represented than barley in Roman deposits in London although both have been found at other sites in Southwark, for example at the waterfront site of Fennings Wharf (Giorgi 1997). Roman deposits at Borough High Street also produced large numbers of wheat and barley grains (Gray-Rees 1996), while a large quantity of hulled barley was found at the Courage's Brewery site (COSE84) (Davis 1995). The cereal grains were probably accidentally burnt while being dried before storage or hardened for milling into flour. The cereals may have been used for bread, porridge, gruel and cakes (Wilson 1991, 234) and barley additionally for brewing and/or animal fodder. The burnt residues of crop-processing activities were also present in the sample in the form of cereal chaff and arable weeds, which include corncockle.

A range of fruit species were preserved by waterlogging and mineralisation, and included fruit stones of plum/bullace (*Prunus domestica* L), sloe/blackthorn (*Prunus spinosa* L) and seeds of grape (*Vitis vinifera*), fig (*Ficus carica*), apple/pear (*Malus/Pyrus* spp), elderberries (*Sambucus nigra*) and blackberry/raspberry (*Rubus fruticosus/idaeus*). All these fruits are common finds in Roman deposits in the City and Southwark – for example, from waterfront sites at Calverts Buildings (Pearson and Giorgi 1992), Winchester Palace (Giorgi in prep) and Fennings Wharf (Giorgi 1997) – and may have been used as food, either fresh or dried, for the preparation of drinks, and in cooking. The grape and fig seeds may represent imports of dried fruit although grapes may have been cultivated in Roman Britain (Wilson 1991, 325). Figs could also have been grown in sheltered areas in southern Britain although it is unlikely that the fruits would have produced fertile seeds. Elder and blackberry/raspberry seeds are particularly frequent finds in Roman deposits, but may represent weeds of waste ground rather than the residues of cultivated fruit.

The sample residues also produced other biological remains, with a small number of cattle, sheep/goat and fish bones, and artefactual evidence with occasional metal and pot fragments. The assemblage suggests that the pit had a dual function not only for the disposal of food refuse (from both preparation and consumption) but also occasionally for the residues from other domestic, commercial or industrial activities.

There was another major dumping phase in the 4th century, raising ground level to *c* 1.2m OD (TOM95 OA2), which was cut by a well. The sample from the backfill of the well contents also produced rich biological remains. The botanical remains included charred cereal remains with bread/club wheat, barley, rye (*Secale cereale*) and oat grains. The last two cereals, however, are infrequent finds on Romano-British sites and may simply represent weeds of the other cereals. A small number of charred pulses were represented but again it was not possible to establish whether these were cultivated or wild species. The waterlogged botanical component of the sample produced few definite foodstuffs other than fig seeds, but mainly weeds of disturbed (including arable) and waste ground, such as elder and blackberry or raspberry. Other biological remains included occasional sheep/goat and pig bones, fish bones and oyster shell, while a few pot fragments and building material fragments were also found in the sample residue.

The assemblage suggests that the well was backfilled with the residues from food preparation (cereals, fruit, bone, shell) and possibly consumption (fruit seeds) plus weed seeds from plants either growing in the vicinity of the well and/or imported onto the site with the cereals. There is also some evidence (charcoal, pot, building materials) for other domestic, commercial or industrial activities.

LBC95, on the western side of Joiner Street, included late Roman dump deposits. There was little other surviving evidence of Roman activity. Alluvial deposits had been forming on the site from the 2nd century AD and domestic debris was thrown into or on top of the alluvium.

LBD95, the escape shaft in Joiner Street, was located on the very edge of the island, with Guy's Channel a short distance to the east. The only Roman activity of note was a linear feature that may have been a robbed out box-drain linking the activity on LBE95 in the west to Guy's Channel in the east (LBD95 OA2). The fills dated from the late 2nd into the 3rd century and contained large quantities of amphorae. The latest date is provided by an OXWW Young type M17 mortarium, which is dated c AD 240–300 (Young 1977, 72, fig 21, M17). This context also contained several different types of amphorae including Dressel 20, Dressel 2-4, Cam. type 186, Gauloise and 'hollow foot'. The latter type of amphora is dated from c AD 180. The fills also contained some earlier residual material from the mid 1st to 2nd centuries. One fill was dated significantly earlier, to c AD 120–60, and may relate to the construction of the drain rather than its disuse. This feature was sealed by another layer of waterlain sand, indicating the continuing marginal nature of the area.

To the east of LBI95, in Mayor Sworder's Arches, extensive reclamation dumps covered the foreshore and early quarrying activity, dating from no earlier than the middle of the 3rd century (MSA92 OA2, OA4 and OA5). Open Area 5 covered the fragmentary remains of a clay and timber building (MSA92 B1) dating to the turn of the 3rd century. However, so little of the building survived that it is not possible to say anything about it, apart from the indication that this area was now occupied by buildings. The ground level had been raised by the dumping to c 1.5m OD, which would have been well above the level of all except the worst floods.

At LBE95 the eastern side of a large masonry building was revealed. This consisted of an eastern wall and a short, 2.2m length of the northern return wall located on the western limit of the excavated area. Thus the greater part of LBE Building 1 lay beyond the accessible excavation area. The foundations for the eastern wall extended for a minimum of 8.5m with the south-eastern corner lost due to later post-medieval truncation.

LBE95 Building 1 was constructed at the end of the 2nd century AD. This involved the construction of a foundation raft of rough cut, but closely set, chalk blocks in a 1.1m wide construction trench. This foundation probably formed the base for a masonry wall, from which the stone was subsequently robbed at a later date. Very little of the internal appearance of the building was revealed, with a strip less than 1.0m wide occurring within the excavated area. The construction levels for

the building may have begun at 0.9m OD, suggesting some raising of the ground level. In the construction deposits of the building was a circular barrel padlock case, made from copper alloy, with the remains of the iron locking mechanism inside. It is too fragmentary for reconstruction, but is of a type well known in Roman Britain.

No in situ floors or occupation deposits were identified inside the building. Demolition debris was present over the internal area and in the robber trench. During the 4th century (dated by coins of AD 364–78), the building was demolished and levelled. The resultant debris contained flue and roof tile and numerous tesserae. The quantities of tesserae included very small, fine examples, some of which were made from tile, including Reigate fabric. Tesserae also occur in late fabrics, indicating that tessellated or mosaic floors were in use after the middle of the 2nd century. Flue tile fragments were also found, all in the local red fabric. Most had combed keying and may have been part of voussoirs, suggesting that they may originally have been used in a high quality underheated building.

If this debris came directly from the building it indicates rooms originally forming part of a high-status building. However, the limited extent of the building plan revealed does leave much uncertainty as to the exact size and layout of the building and therefore doubts as to its exact nature and function. No evidence of internal walls or partitions survived on the site. There was little occupation debris available to investigate the dates of usage of the building, but the building material in the destruction debris suggests that it was constructed at the end of the 2nd century.

No timber piling was present (or none survived) beneath the chalk foundation. This may be indicative of a successful reclamation process that had recovered a significant area of land on the eastern side of the northern island adjacent to Guy's Channel. Its absence might also suggest that, although potentially extensive, the building construction was not particularly massive.

The building may have been partly situated within a ditched enclosure or adjacent to an enclosure. A north–south ditch runs close to the side of the building and this connects with an east–west ditch to form the possible enclosure. However, the ditch and building lie on two different alignments.

9.2 Activity in the 4th century

Alongside the road

There were two 4th-century features of note alongside the main road in BGH95. The first was a third robbed out roadside drain, Structure 13. This was the largest and best surviving stretch of robbing, being nearly 45m in length from north to south. The robbing cut was generally c 1.0m wide and nearly 1.0m deep where it was least truncated. This was backfilled with a 'dark earth' type deposit which contained a large number of mid to late 4th-century coins. Again there were large numbers of postholes associated with this feature, far more than would be needed for a drain; some were deep and quite massive, and were located to the west of the robbing cut and therefore separate from the drain itself. They may well represent a fence alongside the road. The large number of coins in itself indicates that there must still have been a considerable amount of traffic using the road. A total of 159 coins dating to AD 340–78 were recovered from the site, the majority from this feature.

The other feature of note was a roadside pit (OA29) which produced an important pottery group. A total assemblage of 104 sherds, 4747g in weight and forming 4.02 EVEs, was recovered from the backfill of the pit. This context was selected for quantification and illustration because of the presence of 4th-century vessels and very little earlier residual material. The sherds are large and many of the vessels can be reconstructed to profiles. The minimum number of vessels identified totals 70. Percentages are by weight and EVEs of the assemblage as a whole unless otherwise stated.

The dominant fabrics in this context are AHFA (18.6/15.9) and OXRC (13.8/5.0). Imported wares are relatively scarce and do not form an important component of the assemblage (39.4/38.1). Amphorae are only represented by BAETE (4.3/0), BAETL (20.8/5.7) and GAUL2 (2.1/0). One sherd of residual KOLN colour-coated ware (0.4/5.0) is the only imported non-samian fine ware present. MAYEN is the only imported coarse ware (5.3/24.9), its EVE value being inflated by the presence of a complete flagon rim. Both SAMCG (4.1/2.5) and SAMEG (1.9/0) are recorded, but are likely to be residual in this context.

Oxfordshire region wares form an important component of this assemblage, with a minimum number of 16 vessels recorded. OXRC is the most common fabric and is present in a range of forms including (all forms and dates are according to Young 1977 unless otherwise stated): C97 mortaria imitation of samian form Drag. 45 <P208> (Fig 102), dated AD 240–400+; three examples of form C51 bowl, imitating samian form Drag. 38, for example <P209> (Fig 102), dated AD 240–400+; a cordoned bowl with impressed rosette decoration, probably form C84 <P210> (Fig 102), dated AD 350–400+; form C53 bowl with short stubby flange; form C100 mortaria with upright rim and rouletted angular flange, and fragments from dishes with concentric rouletted decoration, imitating samian forms.

OXWW is represented by one M22 mortarium <P211> (Fig 102), dated AD 240–400+, and other mortaria base sherds. Sherd <P212> (Fig 102) may also be an OXWW product; only the rim of a large flagon or narrow-necked jar survives, but the fabric has strong similarities to OXWW. Of the flagons in Young's corpus, only W7.1 bears any resemblance to <P212> (Young 1977, 100–1, fig 30).

Oxfordshire White-Slipped ware (OXWS) is also recorded in form WC3 <P213> (Fig 102), a copy of the Oxfordshire Parchment ware (OXPA) form P24, dated AD 240–400+. This wall-sided carinated bowl has clear red painted decoration against the white slipped background and is less common than the OXPA versions.

The latest fabric type recorded is PORD (4.6/19.2) in the form of a necked jar with square profile rim <P214> (Fig 102). Also present are rilled body sherds from a second vessel. PORD is dated AD 350–400+ in the City and is present in the published Dowgate Hill and Billingsgate bathhouse groups (Symonds and Tomber 1991).

The MAYEN flagon <P215> (Fig 102) belongs to the group of fabrics termed Eifelkeramik, imported from the Rhineland. This flagon is thought to originate from the Mayen region, due to the presence of sedimentary rock inclusions in the fabric. The form is a trefoil-mouthed flagon, for which there is a parallel dated to the mid 3rd century (Gose 1976, pl 50, no. 513). Also present is a handle from a second Mayen flagon.

The fabric BB2F (1.3/4.0) does not appear in quantity until the early Antonine period in the City, but evidence from New Fresh Wharf suggests that by the late 2nd to early 3rd centuries it is one of the main BB2 fabrics in circulation. The undecorated rounded-rim bowls <P216> and <P217> (Fig 102) are the typical form in this fabric. This form is still present in Leadenhall Court group 51 dated AD 230–50/60, although it is noted that by this period quantities of BB2 are in decline (Symonds and Tomber 1991). Therefore it seems likely that the BB2F dishes are residual in this context.

Alice Holt/Farnham grey wares are an important component in this context (18.6/15.9). Included among them are a number of forms that appear to be particularly diagnostic of the 4th century. The large storage jar with cabled rim and incised decoration on the shoulder (class 10) <P218> (Fig 102) is dated from after AD 180 until the end of the industry (Lyne and Jefferies 1979, 51). In London the form appears to occur mainly in 4th-century groups, commonly alongside CALC and PORD, as for example in the Billingsgate bathhouse group (Symonds and Tomber 1991, 77).

The flat-bottomed, straight-sided dish <P219> (Fig 102) has grooves on the exterior below the rim and a band of incised wavy decoration between the grooves. It is very similar to class 6A.12, dated AD 270–420 (Lyne and Jefferies 1979, 48). There are burnished lines on both the underside and interior of the base and on the external surface of the wall, and the interior is also slipped.

The Alice Holt/Farnham grey ware bead and flanged bowls <P220> and <P221> (Fig 102) also confirm another trend identified in the Billingsgate bathhouse group, where it was suggested that small flanges are distinctive of this later period in the City (Symonds and Tomber 1991, 77). The flange on <P221> in particular is short and stubby and, despite being unslipped internally, is very similar to class 5B.8, which is dated AD 270–420 (Lyne and Jefferies 1979, 46).

Although amphorae are poorly represented in this context, there is the rim of a Dressel 20 olive oil container in the later fabric variant BAETL <P222> (Fig 102). The rim is dated AD 200–70 (Peacock and Williams 1986, 138, fig 66).

The decorated samian is residual in this context but the sherds have been identified as a central Gaulish (Lezoux) Drag. 37 decorated bowl, dated to the Hadrianic to early Antonine period.

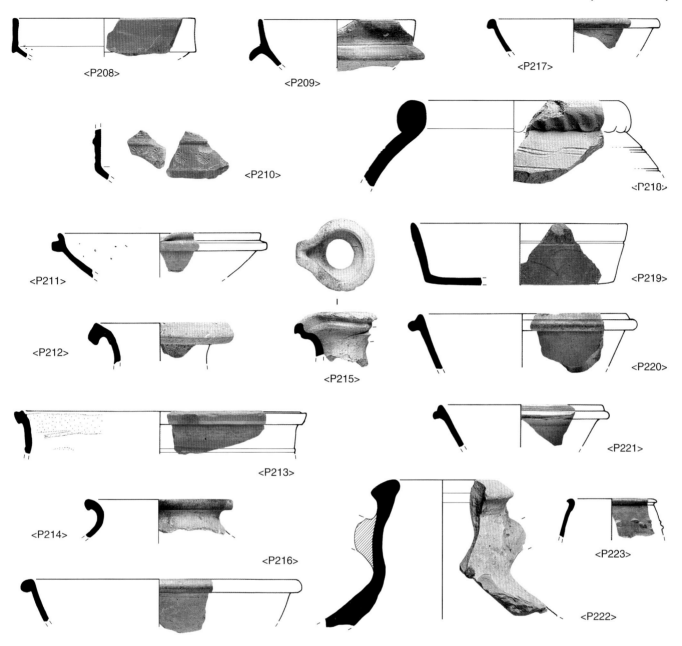

Fig 102 Pottery <P208>–<P223> from Open Area 29 late Roman pit (1:4)

As alluded to above, the pit also produced 12 coins: <17> AD 270–85; <21> AD 330–55; <27> AD 330; <28> AD 340–65; <29> ?4th century; <30> AD 379–402; <31> probably 4th century; <33> AD 355–65; <34> AD 355–65; <35> probably 4th century; <36> AD 355–65; <37> probably mid 4th century.

Dating

The latest element in this context is PORD, which is dated AD 350+ in the City. The importance of the Oxfordshire products, and the presence of CALC and MAYEN *Eifelkeramik*, is comparable to the published group from Billingsgate bathhouse which is dated *c* AD 350–400. The range of forms and fabrics from the Oxfordshire region kilns is also a feature of the Billingsgate group, reflecting the dependence of London

on regional wares after the collapse of more local industries. The low quantity of Black-Burnished types, especially BB1, supports a date in the 4th century (Symonds and Tomber 1991, 77). The similarity of the composition of this assemblage to the Billingsgate bathhouse group reinforces the late 4th-century date ascribed, and the coin finds – the latest of which dates to AD 379–402 – provide further supporting evidence.

The recovery of this assemblage from the backfill of a pit suggests that activity was continuing into the late 4th century in this area of Southwark. This should not be surprising as the main road would be the last part of this, or any, settlement to be abandoned. This assemblage is also important for the dating of late Roman pottery groups from Southwark. Comparison with groups from the City suggests that similar patterns of supply continued to serve both the City and Southwark during the latest phases of activity in London, and with the supporting coin evidence it seems that these patterns are contemporaneous on both sides of the river. In particular it appears that similar wares, especially PORD, CALC, AHFA and OXRC, are diagnostic of 4th-century groups in both the City and Southwark.

East of the road

In a pile cap as part of the Mayor Sworder's Arches programme of works (MSA92), a fragment of polychrome mosaic was uncovered (Fig 103). The mosaic consisted of a red tessellated border, with an inner rope-twist design in red, white and grey. To the north of the mosaic a robber trench for a masonry wall was recorded, with some chalk foundation blocks remaining in situ (MSA92 B2). A coin from the backfill of the robber trench was dated to AD 330–41. No part of the central design of the mosaic was present within the limited area of the pile cap (4.0m x 4.0m) and the surviving fragment was heavily truncated by later features. No other part of the building from which the mosaic came was recorded in this or any adjacent trench.

Clearly, however, this must have been a building of some status. It would have been located in the north-eastern corner of the settlement, about 40m west of the channel defining the eastern edge of the island and within the residential quarter suggested in the previous chapter, lending further weight to

this theory. This is only one of several substantial buildings on the northern sand island dating to the 4th century, others having been found at the Winchester Palace site and the 1–7 St Thomas Street site. In addition there is the note by Roach Smith about the masonry building under the south wing of St Thomas's Hospital. However, there has been little evidence for clay and timber buildings in this period. The settlement appears to have undergone a period of contraction, as witnessed by the presence of burials cut through what had previously been occupation zones, for example at Courage's Brewery and 15–23 Southwark Street. This contraction is not unique to Southwark but has been noted generally in south-east Britain from the 3rd century onwards. However, what persists is generally high-status or at least masonry buildings. There is no evidence for clay and timber buildings, and the activity recorded is clustered more closely around the main road and bridgehead. Of course, by the start of the 3rd century the City north of the river was walled and this may have contributed to a drift of occupation to the safer, better defended side of the river, especially in periods when the political and military situation was more uncertain. The construction of the riverside wall in the late 3rd century may have hastened this process, particularly if the City north of the river was also experiencing a decline, leaving vacant building plots for the citizens of Southwark to move into.

Fig 103 MSA92 mosaic

West of the road

Demolition and robbing of RWT93 Building 2

The south wall of Building 2 was robbed of its stone and dumps were spread around the former Open Area 4. A series of interconnecting cuts had removed virtually all evidence for the walls of Building 2 and appears to have followed its demolition. There was further activity within Open Area 3, where an area of burning was associated with another small gravel surface sealed by dump layers. Pottery from the robbing was dated AD 300+ and a 3rd- to 4th-century coin also came from the robbing phase, indicating that Building 2 survived into the 4th century.

Robbing of RWG94 Building 2 and wells

Both wells were robbed of some of their upper timber planks. Two circular pits cut through the gravel surface appear to have been robbing cuts to remove the timbers from the wells, as their bases were at the uppermost surviving levels of the timber planks (0.44–0.5m OD). Pottery from their backfills was dated AD 250–70+ and two coins were dated to the late 3rd to 4th century.

RWG94 Building 2

Overlying the robber pits, wells and gravel surface were dumped deposits. A coin found within these dated them to AD 335–41. It was not clear if they were dumped against a now vanished wall (represented by the robber trench), the wall probably being constructed from the level of the gravel surface and therefore contemporary with it.

The Southwark Street Channel

By the middle of the 4th century, the north and south islands would have been joined together by the backfilling of the Southwark Street Channel, though a canalised ditch may have survived.

Part of a small creek was excavated at USG94 (OA1). Only the eastern edge of the creek was visible but it was aligned north–south and was at least 0.36m deep (although truncated). It was filled with sand but also contained some pottery dated AD 180+. The base was sloping down to the north and presumably this creek eventually fed into the Southwark Street Channel. It is not clear if this was a natural feature or if it had been dug for drainage.

Dumping as reclamation continued from the 1st century at REW92 (OA2). The pottery dates of AD 140–200 from these deposits suggest that this dumping was being carried out throughout the 2nd century, and it thus appears to have taken place over a long period of time rather than representing rapid make-up for building construction as at OMS94.

The date is comparable to those for 52SOS89 (Cowan in prep) and 64–70 Borough High Street (Graham 1988b). At 52SOS89 dumps of sand were laid over the channel fills and sealed the waterfronts. Sand and gravel layers also infilled part

of the same channel to the east at 64–70 Borough High Street in the early 2nd century (ibid, 65). Only residual pottery was recovered from the dumps at 52SOS89, but as they superseded Waterfronts 4–6 a 2nd-century date seems more likely. It was unclear whether this represented a complete infilling or a narrowing of the channel to gain access to deeper water as it silted up and to acquire more land.

The land reclaimed at REW92 appeared not to have been used for occupation, at least not in the area of excavation; this is surprising and unlike the other sites in the vicinity, which appear to have been reclaimed and immediately used for building construction.

Structure 1 at USG94

A cut interpreted as a robbing trench from a masonry building, Structure 1, was excavated at USG94; it had been cut into the earlier creek. The cut was 0.84m deep and very irregular with sloping sides, and was backfilled with sands, silts, mortar, ragstone and chalk rubble. It seems probable that this is a robbing cut, although it appeared to be isolated and did not continue to the south within the limits of excavation, and despite the fact that no other structural remains were seen. Pottery from the backfill was dated to AD 120+ but Structure 1 cut through the fill of the earlier creek dated to AD 180+.

Structure 1 was situated close to the projected alignment of Road 2, which may have passed some 50m to the north, but did not appear to share this alignment.

9.3 Burials

West of the road

A few human burials were recorded in the area around Redcross Way. Such inhumations were not uncommon in the later Roman period in Southwark and indeed burials had previously been recorded on the 15–23 Southwark Street site (Cowan 1992). These graves are taken as an indication of the contraction of the settlement in this period, as areas that previously were designated for housing were now turned over to cemeteries.

REW92

Five definite and one possible burial were cut into the top of the dump layers at REW92 (OA3).

Burial 1 consisted of a grave cut in which was a coffin indicated by the presence of coffin nails. Within the coffin was the supine, extended skeleton of a mature, but not elderly, adult male, truncated from the right shoulder to the left elbow. What remained of the arm was extended and by the side of the body. The burial was aligned east–west with the head at the western end.

Burial 1 was truncated by burial 2. The grave cut enclosed a coffin, which was indicated by the presence of coffin nails. The skeleton was in a supine, extended position, truncated from below the left shoulder to the right wrist, and was that of an adult male, fully mature and not elderly. It was aligned east–west, whereby the head would have been at the western end. The left arm was flexed at the elbow with the hand in the groin region, while the right hand lay on top of the right leg. The legs were extended with the knees and feet close together.

To the north of these burials was burial 3. The grave cut enclosed a coffin again indicated by the presence of coffin nails. The skeleton was in a supine, extended position, aligned east–west with the head at the western end. The deceased individual may have been between 7 and 10 years of age. The burial was truncated to the north and the skull had been removed by burial 4. The right arm was extended and by the side of the body, with the hand beside the right leg. The left arm appeared to be flexed at the elbow, with the radius and ulna partially across the torso, although some post-mortem disturbance had occurred. A coin dated AD 270–365 came from the groin area, but it was not clear if it was from the burial itself or the backfill.

Lying above burial 3 was burial 4. There was no evidence of a coffin. The cut contained a supine, extended inhumation, aligned east–west with the head at the western end. The male individual was not fully mature and was aged approximately 16–20 years. The burial was truncated slightly to the south, with the right arm missing. The left arm was flexed at the elbow with the lower arm and hand resting on top of the pelvis. The legs were extended with the knees and feet together, the latter turned outwards. The individual was approximately 1.69m in height.

The other two burials were much less complete. Burial 5, in the north-east corner of the site, consisted of a few fragments of skull within a grave cut. So little of the skeleton was recovered that it was not possible to assign an age or sex to the individual.

Burial 6 consisted of a few, partially disarticulated, infant (neonate) bones which had been disturbed. They may have been placed on a Roman tegula of 1st- to mid 2nd-century date, which bore an incomplete and unidentifiable signature mark.

DISCUSSION

The dating of these burials is problematical. The ground surface had been removed down to the top of the grave cuts, leaving no overlying stratigraphy. All the pottery recovered from the backfilled graves was Roman, ranging in date from the 1st to 3rd centuries. A coin from within the grave fill of burial 3 was dated AD 270–365.

However, these burials are within the footprint of the Cross Bones burial ground, used from the 17th to the 19th century (Brickley and Miles 1999). While they do not conform to the 19th-century burial pattern observed within the cemetery, there must remain a possibility that they could be post-medieval in date. Nevertheless, given the presence of well dated Roman burials not far to the north at 15SKS80, it would not be surprising to find Roman burials here as well. Little pottery was recovered from the original cemetery excavations but much of what was found was Roman in date.

RWG94

Within 'dark earth' deposits at RWG94 (OA3) to the west were two inhumation burials, 7 and 8. Both had been disturbed in the 18th century and were not complete. No grave cuts or coffins were visible.

Half of the skeleton of burial 7 was present. Both femurs had been broken in recent times above the knees. The individual was a fully mature male adult about 1.71m tall.

About 20% of the skeleton of burial 8 remained and no grave cut or coffin was observed. The age of the male individual was around 17–18 years. Both burials were aligned north–south with their heads to the south.

A flat pennanular brooch <R57> (Fig 111) was found in burial 8 and could have been a grave good. A fragment of copper bracelet <R63> found near the skull of burial 7 could also have been a grave furnishing.

USG94

Burial 9 from USG94 Open Area 2 had a grave cut aligned north–south. Two large iron nails represented a coffin which contained the disarticulated bones of an incomplete skeleton. The backfill of this grave contained pottery dated to AD 180+ and a late 3rd- to 4th-century sandstone roof tile.

East of the road

On the other side of the island two inhumations were recorded on the eastern margins at LBE95, but the condition of the bones was too poor for any worthwhile analysis to be done. However, their presence should be noted as evidence that the eastern margins were abandoned as far as occupation was concerned and also turned over to burials. A fuller discussion of Roman burials in Southwark will form part of another forthcoming MoLAS volume.

10

Conclusion

A new account of the early development of Roman Southwark can be written in the light of the Jubilee Line excavations which comprise 30 interventions in north Southwark (Table 32). A refined picture of the natural topography of the sand islands has been drawn as, for the first time, a reasonable body of data from beneath London Bridge Station can be programmed in. This shows a previously unknown creek or inlet on the eastern side of the island which discouraged early settlement here until pressure for land saw it infilled in the 2nd century AD.

The main advance has been in the elucidation of the settlement in the decade after the founding of Londinium in AD 50. Before this only a very fragmentary picture had emerged from previous keyhole excavations alongside the main road. The Borough High Street Ticket Hall excavation allowed a 60m stretch of the buildings fronting onto the eastern side of Southwark Road 1 to be excavated for the first time. This has revealed intensive and well dated occupation, with at least two phases of use of some of the buildings, by c AD 60. It is safe to assume that occupation on the western side of the road would mirror this level of activity. A firm plan can now be drawn up of a reasonably sized ribbon development south of the Thames in the years preceding the uprising of the Iceni and Trinovantes.

The evidence from the Ticket Hall site now tips the balance of probabilities towards suggesting that this first period of occupation was ended by the Boudican revolt, though of course it must still remain a possibility that it was an accidental fire that swept through the combustible clay and timber buildings at some time around AD 60/1. This has implications for the size of the community and the date of the building of the bridge.

The post-Boudican reconstruction of the roadside settlement can now be documented and, in various different periods and with varying degrees of certainty, a butcher's shop, a blacksmith's workshop, a bakery, a market hall (*macellum*) and an open market can all be postulated. The expansion of Roman Southwark to the east in the last quarter of the 1st century can now be traced, where a different range of activities seems to take place. Here a possible warehouse or redistribution centre was replaced by a series of middling to high-status buildings. These appear to be primarily residential although some industrial activity might have been taking place as well.

In the mid 2nd century more masonry buildings were constructed alongside the main road and a colonnade erected to create a covered walkway between the road and the buildings. This is a functional construction, rather than ornamental, and may be linked to the open market and *macellum*.

Little could be added to the debate concerning the 3rd- and 4th-century contraction of the settlement in Southwark because of extensive truncation, but 'dark earth' type deposits did survive in places. The use of a metal detector enabled a large number of coins from this period to be recovered, which may have implications for considering the 'decline' of Southwark in the later period of the Roman occupation.

Table 32 MoLAS archaeological excavations for JLEP in north Southwark 1991–98

	Site address	MoLAS site code	JLE site name	Fieldwork date
1	Joan Street	JOA91	Southwark Station, Joan Street	Sep–Oct 1991
2	206 Union Street	UNI91	Union Street vent shaft	Oct 1991
3	Borough High Street	JSS92	Battlebridge sewer diversions	Jan–Feb 1992
4	St Thomas Street	STU92	Thames Water utilities	Mar–Apr 1992
5	Mayor Sworder's Arches	MSA92	Jubilee Line main ticket hall	Feb 1992–Jun 1994
6	Major Road, Bermondsey	MAJ92	Bermondsey station	Mar–Apr 1992
7	Old Jamaica Road	OJR92	Old Jamaica Road	Jul 1992
8	Redcross Way	REW92	Traction power substation	Nov 1992–Mar 1993/Jan–Feb 1996
9	Joiner Street/Telephone Ho.	JNS93	Engineers' test pits	Dec 1992–Jan 1993
10	Redcross Way	RWT93	Redcross Way cable trench	Jan–Feb 1993
11	Borough High Street	BTJ93	BT junction box	Mar–Apr 1993
12	Culling Road	CUG93	Vent shaft	Dec 1993
13	Druid Street	DRD94	Vent shaft	Apr 1994
14	Borough High Street	BUG94	29–39 underpinning	Jan–Dec 1994
15	Borough High Street	BSE94	Sewer diversion shafts	Dec 1995–Feb 1996
16	Redcross Way	RWG94	Redcross Way grout shaft	May–Jun 1994
17	Union Street	USG94	Union Street grout shaft	Aug–Sep 1994
18	O'Meara Street	OMS94	O'Meara Street grout shaft	Oct 1994
19	Warden's Grove	WGR95	Warden's Grove	Jun 1995–Jan 1996
20	Tooley Street	LBH94	3-way escalator	Dec 1994–Jul 1995
21	Station Approach	LBI95	Escalator shaft/ticket hall	Jan 1995–Apr 1996
22	London Bridge Street	LBJ95	20–26 underpinning	Jan–Mar 1995
23	Joiner Street	LBG95	4-way escalator	Watching brief 1995
24	MEPC Car Park	LBE95	Ticket hall/escalator shaft	Mar–Dec 1995
25	Joiner Street	LBD95	East escape shaft	Apr 1995
26	Borough High Street	BGH95	Borough High Street ticket hall	May–Nov 1995
27	Joiner Street	LBC95	East vent shaft	Aug–Sep 1995
28	London Bridge Street	LBA95	West escape shaft	Sep–Oct 1995
29	London Bridge Street	LBB95	West vent shaft	Oct 1995
30	St Thomas Street	TOM95	Grout shaft SN	Jan–Feb 1996

11

Specialist appendices

11.1 The building materials

Susan Pringle

Methodology

The excavations produced over 3477kg of Roman fired ceramic tile building material as well as building stone and wall plaster. (Ian Betts's report on the wall plaster has been integrated into the main text above.) The building material has been quantified by fabric, form and context using the standard Museum of London recording sheet and fabric codes. Samples of these fabrics are held at the Museum and are described in the Research Archive. The data was entered in a database to enable it to be analysed in conjunction with phased stratified sequence, and it has been used in the interpretation of the archaeological features on the site.

The ceramic building materials

Bricks

Roman bricks were produced to standard sizes, based on the Roman foot (*pes*) of approximately 296mm and its subdivisions, although their size was often reduced slightly by shrinkage of the clay during the drying and firing stages of manufacture. The types which were made specifically for use in hypocaust structures are square; these comprise the *bessalis, pedalis, sesquipedalis* and *bipedalis*. The lydion, used for wall bonding courses, is rectangular, as is its variant, the tegula mammata (Brodribb 1987, 34–43). Also rectangular are the small paving bricks used for *opus spicatum* flooring (ibid, 50–3). Identification of brick types is only possible when complete dimensions are present; on most sites the majority of the brick is in small fragments which cannot be securely identified. Each fabric or fabric group is thought to represent a different brick source. A brick with an official stamp was found on RWT93 and is discussed below.

LYDION

These bricks measure approximately one and a half by one Roman feet (443mm x 296mm), although their size may be less standardised than those of other brick types. Nineteen complete lydion bricks were found, all on the Borough High Street sites. Identifiable lydion bricks occur on BGH95 in four different fabric groups; local (fabric group 2815), the Reigate group (fabrics 3050 and 3061), and fabrics 3018 and 3055. The dimensions of this type fall into two groups in both the local and the Reigate bricks: a) smaller lydions, with lengths in the range 357–360mm in the local group, and 355–380mm in the Reigate bricks; and b) larger lydions, with lengths in the range 412–440mm and 426–470mm respectively. It thus appears that lydion bricks were being made to standards of both one and a half and one and a quarter Roman feet in the 2nd century; both sizes were used together in the carefully laid bonding courses in an *in situ* wall, BGH95 Structure 7.

All the complete lydions were from BGH95 period 6 structures. Table 33 shows how the sizes and fabrics of the complete lydion bricks vary between Structures 7 and 8 in period 6, and suggests that new bricks were entering Southwark for use in Borough High Street from at least two, and probably three, sources at this time, although firm conclusions cannot be drawn from such a small sample.

An interesting brick, probably rectangular and of lydion size, in a coarse, sandy fabric (3070) was recorded from BGH95 Open Area 22, on the southern part of the site. The brick was very thick at 80mm, with a breadth of 265mm, had holes 10–15mm in diameter in two corners, and was sooted and reduced. A thick brick in the same sandy fabric, but lacking the holes, has been found at Silvester Buildings, also from the southern part of Roman Southwark (Cowan et al in prep). This, too, has a burnt and reduced upper surface, suggesting that these bricks were of a type produced specifically for use in hearths or ovens, possibly with a superstructure. Both examples are likely to be of 1st-century date, and the BGH95 example is from pre-Boudican levels.

TEGULA MAMMATA

Tegula mammata is the name given to a brick, usually a lydion, which has clay lumps or bosses attached to its upper surface (Brodribb 1987, 60–2). The purpose of the bosses is uncertain, but they may have helped to key the brick to a mortared surface, as they were often used as bonding courses in walls, or as flooring. Most of the examples of this tile type, 29 fragments, came from BGH95, where all but one were in local fabrics (group 2815), the exception being in the north-west Kent

fabric, probably from the tile kilns at the Eccles villa. A single instance was noted from LBB95, also in a local fabric. Tegulae mammatae from sites in Southwark commonly have either a single central boss or two positioned at diagonally opposite corners. All but one of the examples from BGH95 are of the former type; only the earliest stratified example, which was associated with Boudican destruction deposits (period 3, OA5), had a corner boss. They appear in situ only once, in period 6, in what is thought to be the foundation pier for a portico, Structure 8.

PEDALIS

These bricks, which were approximately one Roman foot (296mm) square, were often used as bases and caps for *pilae* constructed from *bessales*. No definite examples were recorded, but fragmentary examples can be confused with lydion, which have the same approximate breadth.

BESSALIS

The *bessalis* was a small brick, usually approximately two-thirds of a Roman foot square, although evidence from BGH95 indicates that they may occasionally have been produced to a standard of half a foot. They were primarily used to form the pillars (*pilae*) which supported a hypocaust roof and the floor above. Seven complete or almost complete *bessales*, in three fabrics, were noted, of which five were in local fabrics, and one each in the north-west Kent and Radlett fabrics. The dimensions of most of the bricks fall within the range 190–220mm, although two smaller bricks, 146–158mm square, were recorded from BGH95. Table 34 shows the distribution of *bessales* types across the sites.

Building	Fabric	Range of dimensions (mm)	No. of examples
Structure 7 (brick wall)	Reigate (3050)	355 × 270 × 38	4
		364 × 264 × 39	
		374 × 274 × 40	
		380 × 290 × 45	
		437 × 288 × 36	
		455 × 300 × 33	3
		470 × 305 × 37	
Structure 7 (brick wall)	Reigate (3061)	368 × 269 × 40	2
		368 × 280 × 38	
		458 × 304 × 35	
		472 × 295 × 40	2
Structure 8 (pier base?)	local group (2815)	412 × 280 × 43	1
Structure 8 (pier base?)	Local group (2815)	357 × 260 × 32	2
		360 × 270 × 39	
Structure 8 (pier base?)	3018	365 × 275 × 40	2
		370 × 275 × 38	
Building 25	Reigate (3050)	440 × 285 × 37	2
		457 × 300 × 38	
Building 25	Reigate (3061)	426 × 288 × 40	1

Table 33 *The complete lydion bricks used in period 6 on BGH95*

Table 34 Bessalis bricks: fabrics and dimensions

Fabric	Site	Range of dimensions (mm square)	No. of examples
2815 group	BGH95, LBI95	190–220	3
2815 group	BGH95	146–158	2
3023	BGH95	191 × 187	1
2454	RWG94	191	1

BIPEDALIS AND SESQUIPEDALIS

Sesquipedales (one and a half Roman feet square) and *bipedales* (two Roman feet square), the two largest Roman bricks, rarely survive intact in London. Both were primarily used for capping and bridging the *pilae* in hypocaust systems, thus forming a floor surface in the heated room which was often finished with *opus signinum* or mosaic. There are no certain examples of a *bipedalis* from the excavations, but a large fragment of a *sesquipedalis* in fabric 3050, 458mm broad and 75mm thick, was found, probably reused, mortared into a period 6 wall on BGH95 (Structure 7)(Fig 104, <T7>). A number of brick fragments 60–75mm thick, in fabrics 2815, 3050 and 2454, are also likely to have come from either *sesquipedales* or *bipedales*.

OPUS SPICATUM

These distinctive small paving bricks, the lengths of which vary from about one-half to one-third of a Roman foot, were laid on edge in a herringbone pattern and bedded in mortar to form a substantial and hard-wearing surface. *Opus spicatum* floors are rarely found *in situ*, but buildings in the City known to have had areas of *opus spicatum* include a building at Watling Court (c AD 85/90–120), Cheapside baths (late 1st to early 2nd century) and the 2nd-century portico on the eastern side of the Basilica at Leadenhall (Milne 1992, 136).

At least four groups can be distinguished, as set out in Table 35. The bricks may be residual or reused, as there was no *in situ* evidence of properly laid *opus spicatum* flooring on the site. The earliest appearance on any of the sites was the fragment from Boudican destruction debris on BGH95, but most of the tiles were deposited on the site between c AD 61 and 100. Since none was associated with a masonry structure, it is probable that they had either been reused or were residual. *Opus spicatum* tiles have been found on several sites in Southwark, although bricks in Reigate fabrics have not so far been found on other Southwark sites.

Roof tile

Flanged tegulae and curved imbrices were used together to form a covering for a pitched roof which was both waterproof and more fire-resistant than alternatives such as wooden shingles or thatch. Large quantities of ceramic roofing tile were recovered in a variety of fabric types.

Tegulae appear in the earliest levels of Roman London; although mainly used for roofing, they were also utilised to make hearths, to construct and cover drains, and for paving.

Table 35 Opus spicatum brick groups

Fabric	Site	Dimensions (mm)	Period	Land use
2454	BGH95	100 × 53 × 20	4	OA12
2454	BGH95	92 × 58 × 22	4	OA14
2454	BGH95	? × 55 × 24	4	B20
2454	BGH95	94 × 58 × 22	7	OA27
2454	BSE94	? × 59 × 22	4	B2
2815 group	BGH95	? × ? × 25	3	OA10
2815 group	BGH95	? × 62 × ?	4	B18
2815 group	BGH95	? × 50 × 33	7?	OA27
2815 group	LBE95	? × 48 × 32	3	OA2
2815 group	LBI95	126 × 55 × 30	5	OA8
2815 group	RWT93	? × 62 × 30	3	OA2
3028	BGH95	103 × 71 × 25	4	OA15
3028	BGH95	100 × 69 × 24	4	OA12
3028	BGH95	? × 70 × 23	6	OA17
3050	BGH95	97 × 72 × 22	4	OA18

They were also used as bonding bricks, either with or without their flanges.

Only one complete tegula was found (local fabric group 2815), with complete dimensions of 475mm x 320mm. This is probably of fairly early production, being associated with BGH95 Building 9, period 4. Several tegulae were found which had been manufactured with nail holes, to allow firmer attachment to the roof. Most were in local fabrics (group 2815), but two examples, from BGH95 and MSA92, were in the Radlett fabrics (3023 and 3060). Only two of the tiles with nail holes, both in local fabrics, were associated with buildings, MSA92 Building 2 and LBE95 Building 1. Nail holes were not common before the mid 2nd century, and all the examples occur in deposits of AD 120–60 or later. Two examples of nail holes which had been bored or chipped through the tile after firing were found, one in a tile in north-west Kent fabric; this may be an indication of reuse.

One fragment of tegula is of interest as the top right corner had been removed with a diagonal knife cut, at approximately 180mm from the bottom of the tile (Fig 104, <T1>). This example, in a local fabric, is from *in situ* destruction debris from clay and timber Building 1 in Open Area 5, on BGH95 period 3. Such tiles, which are very rare in London, may have been specially made to fit the junction between two sections of roof, where one joins another at a 45° angle. Two examples of similar shaping were noted from the Courage's Brewery site in Southwark, and one from a late Flavian or Trajanic context at 24–25 Ironmonger Lane in the City. A very unusual tegula, if indeed it is a tegula, came from MSA92, where it was used in the make-up for period 5 Building 2. In a late local fabric (2459B), its upper face is heavily decorated, or keyed, with an assortment of wavy and straight bands of combing, executed with a 2.5mm wide, six-toothed, comb (Fig 104, <T2>).

An imbrex with part of an official stamp came from LBI95; this is discussed below.

153

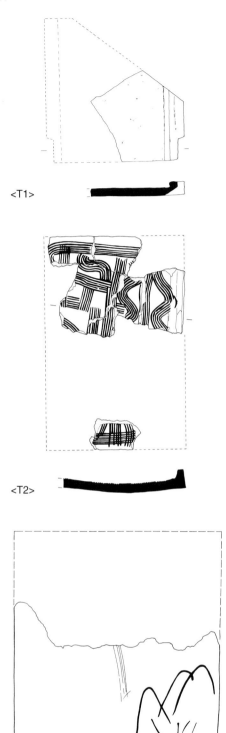

<T1>

<T2>

<T7>

Fig 104 Brick and tile: <T1> BGH95, shaped tegula; <T2> MSA92, heavily combed ?tegula (both 1:4); <T7> BGH95, graffiti on sesquipedalis (1:8)

Roof furniture

The precise function of Roman 'chimney pots' or louvers is not known; they may have been used in conjunction with some type of cavity walling to vent the hot air and gases produced by hypocaust furnaces, or positioned to allow removal of smoke from an open roof, or they may have been used as roof finials, their purpose purely decorative. They appear to have been made on a potter's wheel, the vents then being cut out with a knife, and are usually not in tile fabrics known from London. Only one chimney fragment was securely identified; with 'piecrust' decoration and triangular and curved knife cut vents, it came from a period 7 open area on BGH95 (<1807>).

Cavity walling

Included under this heading are wall tiles, half-box flue tiles, box-flue tiles and hollow voussoirs. All were made for use in buildings of masonry construction, their purpose being to create a cavity through which heated air from a hypocaust could circulate up through the building.

SCORED WALL TILES

Wall tiles, also known as *parietales*, are thin, rectangular tiles with lattice-scored keying on one face, the long edges notched near the corners. Complete examples found on sites north of the Thames have an average size of 403 x 261 x 31mm. The tiles were set vertically parallel to the wall surface, but separated from the wall by circular clay spacer bobbins. The cavity created by this technique allowed heated air to warm the entire wall surface as it passed upward towards the vents, unlike the box-flue system more widely used in London in which the hollow tiles were set into the wall at intervals. The wall tile heating system would have required both more fuel and more manpower than the box-flue system, and it seems likely that they would have been installed in important masonry buildings. In the City they are closely linked with public buildings, with examples coming from the complex of buildings known as Governor's House and the public baths at Huggin Hill.

The four definite and five probable examples of scored wall tile found, all in local fabrics, were fragmentary, and almost certainly residual or reused; only two, from BGH95 and LBI95, were found in association with masonry buildings, Building 13 and Building 2 respectively. The earliest stratified examples were from BGH95 period 4, associated with Building 13, and clay and timber Buildings 20, 21 and 30. Three of the examples, from BGH95, LBI95, and RWG94, were lattice-scored on the sanded base; four, all from BGH95, were scored on the top surface, while information was not recorded for the remaining two examples. Betts has suggested that wall tiles may have been made exclusively for use in London's public buildings during the late 1st and early 2nd centuries (Betts 1995, 214), and their presence in Southwark would in that case provide evidence for the existence of an early masonry public building south of the river.

HALF-BOX FLUE TILES

These are rather similar to tegulae, with tall flanges running down each side. Vents are cut in the centre of the flanged sides, and the sanded bases have lattice-scored keying. They were set against the wall with the scored base facing into the room to allow the attachment of wall plaster. Hot air passed up the flanged face of the tile, and the vents cut in the flanges allowed for lateral circulation. All the half-box flue tiles so far found in London have been too fragmentary to provide data on their original size, although complete examples found at York measure 525mm x 435mm with a flange depth of 77mm (Betts 1985, 181).

Very little securely identified half-box flue tile was recorded. One definite fragment came from LBE95 and one ambiguous fragment from BGH, which could also be from a scored box-flue; both were in fabric 2454. The LBE95 fragment is from Open Area 2, period 2. The significance of these fragments is that they are further evidence of the existence in Southwark of what must have been an important masonry building containing a hypocaust heating system, probably before AD 70–80.

BOX-FLUE TILES

Hollow rectangular box-shaped flues were the commonest type of tile for conducting hot air up through the walls of buildings. The wider front and back faces of the tile were normally keyed, with the two narrower side faces left plain. Most tiles have vents cut out of the plain sides to allow for lateral circulation of heat between adjacent tiles. There are three different kinds of keying on box-flue tiles; scored, combed and relief-patterned.

All the tile with knife-scored keying in a lattice pattern was in local fabrics (group 2815). Fabric 2452 seems to have been particularly common, the earliest stratified example coming from Boudican destruction deposits on BGH95. Examples with both rectangular and circular vents were noted. The fact that no imported fabrics were noted suggests that supplies of this tile type came from kilns near London.

The combed box-flue assemblage was fairly small, most of it coming from BGH95 and RWT93. First-century types were represented by tiles in Radlett (3023, 3060) and 'Sussex' (3054, 3059) fabrics, and fabric 3227 (source unknown). The Radlett tilery in Hertfordshire produced mostly combed flue-tiles with a variety of unusual combing patterns consisting of vertical lines, often with horizontal cross-combing, or diagonal lines, sometimes with diagonal cross-combing. The earliest well stratified combed box-flue from Radlett came from period 4 masonry Building 13 on BGH95. It was also present, together with similar material in related Radlett fabric 3023, on the Redcross Way sites. Box-flue tiles from the same source with the same distinctive keying patterns were found at 15–23 Southwark Street (Crowley 1992, 149, fig 45, nos 7a–c), as well as other sites in north Southwark. The tile from Borough High Street and Redcross Way was too fragmentary to provide dimensions, but curved or circular vent cuts were present, which accords with the evidence from 15–23 Southwark Street of two circular vent holes in each plain side.

Typical of the Flavian period in London are fragments of thick tile with wide, shallow combed keying brought into London from kilns in Sussex (fabrics 3054 and 3059); these are likely to have come from the box-flue tiles in this fabric which often had both coarsely combed and roller-keyed faces. Combed fragments first occur in period 4 on BGH95. Of interest are the two fragments of thin-walled box-flue from BGH95 in fabric 3227, one of which was associated with Building 24, period 5. This is a rare type, often decorated with very fine combed patterns, which is particularly associated with the Winchester Palace site in north Southwark (Crowley in prep) and the adjacent Hibernia Wharf.

In the course of the 2nd century, two new types appear: one in related fabrics from Reigate (3050 and 3061) is likely to have been manufactured after c AD 120–40, and the other in the later version of the local fabric (2459B) dates to post-AD 140. Almost all the Reigate tile, seven fragments, occurs on BGH95, where it is associated with period 6 masonry Building 16 and Structure 8, with a single fragment from LBE95. The local type appears in very small quantities on LBB95 and RWG94, Open Area 2, but is a little more common on BGH95, where it is associated with clay and timber Building 31 and Structure 7. A large quantity of this flue type was excavated at Winchester Palace from a building which was probably in use between AD 120 and 387.

Small quantities of two types of 3rd-century production were noted. Combed flue in fabric 3077, source unknown, was found in a late drain on BGH95, and in Open Area 2 on RWG94, and a single fragment of combed flue in the distinctive shelly fabric similar to that from kilns at Harrold in Bedfordshire (2456) came from RWT93, Open Area 5.

The third type of keying on flue tiles is known as relief-patterning, and was applied, usually to two faces of the tile, with a carved wooden roller. There were 31 fragments of roller-stamped tile from the excavations, 20 of which have identifiable designs (Table 36), which have been allocated die numbers assigned by Lowther (1948) and the Relief-Patterned Tiles Research Group (Betts et al 1994). It may be of interest that dies 3 and 11, both of which were found at 15–23 Southwark Street, occurred mainly on Redcross Way sites. Of particular interest are two new die types, both from BGH95: die 125 <1328>, the only roller-stamped design known on a box-flue tile in Radlett fabric, was found in a hearth in clay and timber Building 12, period 4, and die 126 <1451> came from a period 7 deposit in Open Area 15. The example of die 44 from TOM95 is of interest as it shows part of the pattern which had not hitherto been recorded; this die also occurs on LBB95 and LBE95.

On the whole the dating evidence for the roller-stamped fragments was not particularly good, as most were found in late Roman contexts where they were either residual or reused. However, dies 3 and 40 were found in Open Area 2, period 4, at RWG94, with pottery dated AD 120–250 and 250–350 respectively; the earliest occurrence of die 11 was also at RWG94 in period 4, but associated with the destruction of masonry Building 2. Dies 41 and 44 are here associated with the London Bridge sites, but as late deposits in open areas.

The Sussex group of tiles (fabric 3054), so called because their distribution suggests that they originate from a tilery in Sussex, is mainly associated with the sites in the Borough High Street area. The earliest stratified occurrence is an example of die 24 from Open Area 7, period 6. Roller-keyed flue tiles in this fabric first appear in early Flavian buildings (Betts et al 1994), which is about the same time that the distinctive fabric appears in London north of the Thames.

An example of rare die 51, not previously identified in London but occurring in Oxfordshire and Berkshire, comes from a period 7 ditch fill in BGH95 Open Area 42, associated with pottery dated AD 120–40; the fabric type is uncertain as the tile is overfired. Die 85 was associated with pottery of AD 90–100 in make-up for period 5 clay and timber Building 27 on BGH95.

There is no other evidence for hypocausts from any of the buildings on the site, so all the flue tile is likely to have been either reused or residual.

Table 36 Relief-patterned flue tiles

Die	Fabric	Site	Accession no.	Land use	Period
3	3006	BGH95	<253>	OA	?
3	3006	RWG94	<55>	OA2	4
11	3006	BGH95	<788>	ditch	7
11	2452	RWG94	<52>	OA2	4
11	3006	RWT93	<78>	B2	5
11	3006	RWT93	<64>	OA5	?
23	3054	BGH95	<1306>	ditch	7
24	3054	BGH95	<1247>	OA15	6
40	3054	BGH95	<766>	ditch	7
40	3054	RWG94	<54>	OA2	4
41	2459A	TOM95	<13>	OA1	1
44	2452	LBB95	<68>	?	?
44	3006	LBE95	<167>	OA7	6
44	3006	TOM95	<187>	OA2	2
51	?	BGH95	<1452>	OA27	7
65	3006	BGH95	<1462>	OA27	7
85	3006	BGH95	<1857>	B27	5
85	3006	BGH95	<1558>	B??	6
125	3060	BGH95	<1328>	B14	4
126	3006	BGH95	<1451>	OA27	7

Ceramic tesserae

An in situ mosaic floor set in a coarse, red, tessellated surround was excavated at MSA92 (see below, 11.10), and a substantial fragment of flooring in white chalk tesserae was recovered from TOM95. Frequent loose tesserae were also recorded. Their fabrics reflect those used on the site, and the vast majority were in the early local fabrics (group 2815). Other early tiles reused as tesserae were in the north-west Kent fabric (2454), the Radlett fabrics (3023 and 3060) and fabric 3028. Late fabric types noted were local (2459B), Reigate (3050), and the non-local calcareous fabric (2453).

Tile markings

Included under this heading are marks, such as stamps, tally marks and signature marks, which were added at the tilery during the manufacture of the tiles and have the potential to provide information about the organisation of the tile-making industry.

Procuratorial stamps

Two tiles, both in local fabric (3006), were found with fragmentary stamped inscriptions. An imbrex with [....]LON (<168>), came from LBE95 Open Area 8, and a brick with P[....] from RWT93, masonry Building 2. Both stamps

belong to the PPBRILON group, and the lettering is interpreted as standing for p(rocuratores) p(rovinciae) Bri(tanniae) Lon(dini), which translates as 'The procurators of the province of Britain at London'. Tiles stamped with these letters were made at an official local government-run tilery which is believed to have been situated at Brockley Hill in Hertfordshire (Betts 1995). Recent work in the City has confirmed that procuratorial stamped tiles were used in the construction of London's major public buildings during the period AD 70/80–120/5. Stamped tiles do occur in what may have been private residences, but these are clearly reused and must have come from the demolition of earlier public buildings (ibid).

The stamp on the imbrex is die type 2A, as is probably that on the brick. Several tiles stamped with this lettering, all either die type 2 or die type 3, have been found on sites in Southwark, namely Courage's Brewery, 15–23 Southwark Street, 11–15 St Thomas Street, Fennings Wharf and Winchester Palace, although none can at present be related to any specific building. The presence of these procuratorial stamped tiles in Southwark is evidence of a late 1st- to early 2nd-century public building which would have incorporated both procuratorial stamped roofing tile (imbrices) and brick, and may have been contemporary with the construction of the Basilica, where tiles marked with the same two procuratorial stamp dies were also used (Betts 1995, 223–4).

Signature marks

These marks were made with the tips of the fingers on the upper surface of bricks, tegulae and occasionally other types of tile and, being impressed in very wet clay, were probably added by the tile-makers themselves (Table 37). Signature marks were recorded on bricks and tegulae in local, north-west Kent and Radlett fabrics, and fabric 3028. Previously unrecorded signature marks were noted in fabric 3006, types 74 and 77; fabric 3050, type 8; and fabric 3061, type 1. As on other sites, the commonest marks were the single, double or triple hoops. Their exact significance is open to speculation, but they may have provided a way of identifying the output of different tile-makers.

Tally marks

These knife-cut marks on the edges of bricks and tegulae, and occasionally cut into the top edge of tegula flanges, are believed to represent Roman numerals. They were made at a later stage in the production process than the signature marks, being cut into leather-hard clay. The purpose of the marks is not known, but they are likely to have been made as some kind of stock control to identify a particular batch of tile; their rarity suggests that very few tiles were marked. They may have contained dating information to ensure that batches of tiles were fired in the correct sequence, or they may have been the numbers by which tiles made for specific orders were identified. The example from REW92 is unusual in that it is scratched into the clay instead of being knife-cut; the 'V' shown here in Table 38 represents a tick-shaped mark.

Signature type	No. of signatures
Fabric 2452	
1	11
2	6
3	3
24	1
38	1
59	1
Fabric 2454	
1	9
2	17
4	1
5	1
6	1
8	1
Fabric 2459a	
3	3
Fabric 2459b	
1	1
9	1
13	1
Fabric 3004	
1	1
3	1
19	1
Fabric 3006	
1	20
2	16
3	8
5	1
18	4
33	1
54	1
58	1
59	1
63	1
74	1
77	1
79	1
Fabric 3023	
3	2
6	2
Fabric 3028	
1	2
Fabric 3050	
8	1
Fabric 3060	
1	1
2	1
Fabric 3061	
1	1

Table 37 Building materials: signature marks

Table 38 Building materials: tally marks

Site	Fabric	Tile type	Tally mark
LBA95	3060	tegula	type 1: /
TOM95	2815 (3006)	tegula	type 2: X
REW92	2815 (3006)	brick	possible mark: V /

Graffiti

A fragmentary *sesquipedalis* from BGH95 (<1308>) in Reigate fabric (3050) was found to have cursive graffiti, made before the brick was fired, on its upper surface (partially obscured by mortar) (Fig 104, <T7>). This is as yet undeciphered. The brick was incorporated into Structure 7, a brick wall.

The tile fabrics

The majority of the ceramic building material found in London is made with clays containing varying amounts of quartz, which fire to a range of shades of red. Most tile from Southwark is in the same fabric types as those used in other areas of London, which means that it came from the same kilns. In the early Roman period, large quantities of tile are produced from local sources, but from the mid 2nd century there appears to be increasing reuse of tile from earlier buildings, accompanied by the appearance of new types of non-local tiles. By the 4th century it seems probable that most of the tile and brick used in building construction in London was reused material, supplemented by small amounts of non-local products. A list of the fabrics present is appended. Fabric descriptions have been described with the aid of a binocular microscope (x10 magnification). The following conventions are used in the descriptions. The terminology for the frequency of inclusions is as follows: occasional; few; moderate; common; frequent. Where grain sizes are not specified, average sizes of sand-sized inclusions (up to 2mm) are defined as follows: very fine, up to 0.1mm; fine, 0.1–0.25mm; medium 0.25–0.5mm; coarse, 0.5–1mm; very coarse, larger than 1mm.

Fabrics 2452, 2459A, 3004 and 3006 were probably not made after *c* AD 160, being replaced by tiles in related fabrics 2459B and 2459C from *c* AD 140 on. The early fabrics occur in abundance on all the sites in the area; the later ones appear in lesser quantities on most of the sites in all three areas.

Fabric group 2815 (2452, 2459, 3004, 3006)

These tiles, which all have red fabrics, come from a number of kilns situated along Watling Street between London and St Albans, within 30km of London (Betts 1987, 27–8). As the tileries used very similar clays, it is not usually possible to attribute the tiles which comprise fabric group 2815 to specific kiln sites.

FABRIC 2452
A fine fabric with few to moderate quartz (up to 0.5mm). Usually with few calcium carbonate and iron oxide (up to 2mm).

FABRIC 2459
A fine, sandy fabric with a scatter of quartz grains above 0.2mm in size. Few calcium carbonate and iron oxide (up to 1mm). Tiles in this fabric with very fine moulding sand (2459B) are later in date than those with normal moulding sand (2459A). A rarer late version has straw moulding (2459C).

FABRIC 3004
A sandy fabric with common to frequent, coarse to very coarse quartz grains (up to 0.7mm) and few iron oxide and calcium carbonate (up to 0.7mm).

FABRIC 3006
A fine, slightly sandy fabric with moderate to common coarse quartz (up to 0.3mm), with occasional iron oxide and calcium carbonate.

Fabric group 2454, 2455, 3022

The second important source of tile in the earliest period was north-west Kent, on the Medway. The distinctive yellow and white tiles (fabrics 2454, 3022), which are found on all sites in Southwark, and are particularly plentiful in the pre-Boudican deposits on the Borough High Street sites, closely resemble those from a late Roman kiln at the Eccles villa in that area, and the early production is thought to come from the same source. Their use in London seems to have ceased during the early Flavian period, c AD 70–80.

FABRIC 2454
A distinctive yellow, pink or yellowish-white fabric, usually well fired, with moderate to common colourless or 'rose' quartz (most up to 0.5mm), and few to medium iron oxide and calcium carbonate inclusions (up to 2mm). Some examples have red moulding sand.

FABRIC 2455
As fabric 2454, but with clean matrix with few quartz and calcium carbonate inclusions.

FABRIC 3022
As fabric 2454, with frequent quartz.

Fabric group 3023, 3060

These fabrics, the products from the tile kiln at Radlett in Hertfordshire, are made from a distinctive clay. They are present, usually in smaller quantities than the 2815 group and the north-west Kent products, in the pre-Boudican period, and seem to go out of production in the early to mid 2nd century.

FABRIC 3060
Red, orange or brown fabric with frequent fine quartz (up to 0.3mm), with common very fine black iron oxides (up to 0.1mm), and scatter of very coarse red iron oxides (up to 2mm).

FABRIC 3023
Similar to fabric 3060, but with

cream silty inclusions (up to 6mm).

Fabric group 3054, 3059

Tiles in these distinctive fabrics were probably made in Sussex, where villa sites contain relatively large quantities of the thick-walled roller-stamped and combed flues. They appear in London between c AD 70 and 140.

FABRIC 3054
Red, orange or light brown fabric with frequent coarse quartz (up to 1mm) and common red iron oxide. Occasional cream silty bands. Some tiles have coarse inclusions of red and cream tile fragments (grog) (up to 6mm).

FABRIC 3059
Fine orange to red fabric with common coarse quartz (up to 1mm), and a scatter of red iron oxide inclusions (up to 1mm). Characterised by varying amounts of chaff temper and distinctively curved voids.

Fabric group 3050, 3061

One of the distinctive groups of tiles occurring in the late Roman period in Southwark is that of tiles with varying amounts of dark coloured quartz, manufactured in kilns at Reigate in Surrey. The distribution of this group is centred on Borough High Street, where it occurs in some quantities in mid to late 2nd-century structures. Small amounts are present on the London Bridge sites, on LBE95 in periods 3 and 4, associated with Building 1, and TOM95. None was recorded from the Redcross Way sites. The date-range is c AD 120/40 to the early 3rd century or a little later.

FABRIC 3050
Usually highly fired with varying amounts (from few to common) of fine to medium, dark red 'rose' quartz (up to 0.3mm), with varying amounts of coarse colourless quartz (up to 0.8mm), few iron oxides and calcium carbonate. The clay matrix may have silty streaks and bands, or cream mottling.

FABRIC 3061
Similar to fabric 3050, with common, very coarse inclusions of red iron oxide or ferruginous sandstone. Few fine to medium dark red 'rose' quartz (up to 3mm).

Fabric group 2453 (fabrics 2453, 2457, 3013, 3026, 3229)

These distinctive calcareous tiles are widely distributed along the coast of southern and south-east England, but the location of the tilery or tileries supplying Southwark has still to be established. Tiles in these fabrics appear on most of the sites in all three areas, and the BGH95 drainage ditch, Structure 7. They date from the mid/late 2nd century to the end of the 3rd century. Tiles in this group of fabrics often have dark red moulding sand.

FABRIC 2453
Usually pink in colour, but cream, yellow or brown examples occur. Common very coarse inclusions of yellowish-white clay (up to 6mm) in often mottled clay matrix. Few iron oxide (up to 1mm). Some have common coarse quartz (up to 0.8mm).

FABRIC 2457
Light grey or greyish-brown fabric with frequent calcium carbonate and fine grey shell fragments with scatter of fine quartz (up to 0.2mm) in background clay matrix. Moderate coarse grey or white shell fragments (up to 6mm), coarse quartz (up to 0.8mm) and iron oxide inclusions (up to 0.8mm).

FABRIC 3013
Various shades of brown, sometimes with grey margins. Clay matrix contains common inclusions of quartz (up to 0.5mm) and calcium carbonate, with common very coarse grey silty (up to 0.5mm) and red iron oxide (up to 4mm) inclusions.

FABRIC 3026
Light brown or cream matrix with common quartz (up to 1mm) with scatter of large quartz grains (up to 3mm), occasional iron oxide and rounded silty inclusions.

FABRIC 3029
Pink, light orange. Frequent calcium carbonate including white shell (up to 0.5mm) with scatter of quartz (up to 0.3mm) and occasional iron oxide. Recorded on BGH95 and LBE95 in late contexts, both spot-dated to AD 350–400.

FABRIC 3229
Cream or white matrix with moderate rounded yellow clay inclusions (up to 5mm). Occasional iron oxide (up to 2mm) and white silty bands.

Fabric group 3018, 3028, 3238

These fabrics are characterised by the presence of cream, yellow or white silty inclusions in an orange or light orange clay matrix. Their most likely source is the Weald area south of London (see fabric 3018), although they may come from more than one kiln site. Fabric 3018 is present in small quantities in all areas, and is associated with Building 1 on LBE95.

FABRIC 3018
Light orange or orange fine clay matrix. Common orange clay and/or blocky siltstone inclusions (most up to 2mm). Few medium to coarse quartz (up to 1mm). Silty bands and inclusions in certain examples. Source: possibly Hartfield, East Sussex. Date: AD 100–20.

FABRIC 3028
Orange with common, well sorted, medium quartz (up to 0.4mm), few to common rounded silty inclusions (up to 6mm) and red iron oxide (up to 1mm). Some examples have bands of light coloured silty clay. Source unknown. Date: AD 70–100/20.

FABRIC 3238
Light orange fabric with few to common silty bands and rounded silty inclusions (up to 3mm). Common to frequent medium quartz and common coarse red iron oxide (up to 1.5mm). Often has fine moulding sand. Source: unknown. Date: AD 71–100.

Individual fabrics

FABRIC 2456
Grey core with light brown margins. Common shell inclusions (up to 4mm). This soft, shelly fabric matches samples from the tile kilns at Harrold in Bedfordshire which appear in Southwark in small amounts in the late 3rd and 4th centuries. Only two fragments were recorded, from BGH95 and RWT93.

FABRIC 3005
Pink, light orange or cream matrix, usually mottled and containing bands or lenses of clay, with very fine background quartz. Few to common inclusions of medium, colourless or rose, quartz and coarse red and yellowish-white fragments of clay or silt (up to 5mm). The only occurrence was as an imbrex on LBE95, associated with Building 1, period 4. The deposit is not, however, well dated; spot dates are AD 250–400.

FABRIC 3011
Orange matrix with varying amounts of medium quartz (up to 0.5mm), common red iron oxide and clay inclusions (up to 4mm). The source is unknown. Dating for this fabric is not well defined, ranging from AD 70/100 to 140–200 or later. The two occurrences on BGH95 are both in period 7.

FABRIC 3012
Hard, well fired matrix with occasional cream silty streaks, common blackish-brown ?rock fragments (up to 3mm), common quartz (up to 1mm), and few calcium carbonate (up to 2mm). Fabric 3012 resembles the fabrics in the Reigate group (3050, 3061). It is rare, with a single occurrence on BGH95 in period 7.

FABRIC 3016
Pink or brownish-pink matrix with distinctive fine yellow speckling, and few coarse iron oxide (up to 1mm). Little or no quartz. The source is unknown. Normally found in 3rd-century or later contexts in London, a date supported by the evidence from BGH95, LBE95 and RWG94. A fragment associated with LBE95 Building 1, period 4, in the 2nd century, comes from a context with spot-dates of AD 200–300.

FABRIC 3019
Light brownish-orange, sometimes with light grey core. Common blocky siltstone inclusions (up to 7mm) and red iron oxide (up to 4mm); moderate quartz (up to 0.3mm), and occasional calcium carbonate. Commonly a brick fabric, but roof tile in this fabric occurs in association with Buildings 9 and 12 on BGH95, and Building 1 on RWT93. The source is probably in Hampshire, possibly the kilns at Braxells Farm, near Southampton. This fabric is dated to AD 100–20+ in the City, but appears in period 1 (pre-Boudican) and period 4 (Flavian) contexts at BGH95 and period 2 (Building 4, Neronian to Flavian) on MSA92. Earliest spot dates are AD 50–70 and AD 55–85 on BGH95. It is possible that this early roof tile may not be from the same kilns as the 2nd-century brick production.

FABRIC 3020
Light orange-brown matrix with prominent yellowish-white silty streaks and bands and frequent fine quartz (up to 0.2mm). Occasional iron oxide. Source unknown. Rare. A brick in this fabric was recorded from a period 6 context at BGH95, spot-dated to AD 200–400.

FABRIC 3021
Orange, light brown margins. Sandy clay matrix with frequent fine quartz (up to 0.2mm), common coarse or very coarse sandstone, siltstone and calcium carbonate inclusions (up to 4mm), few iron oxide grains (up to 2mm). Source unknown. A single brick in this rare fabric, the date range of which has not yet been defined, was noted on LBA95, from a context which contained medieval pottery.

FABRIC 3051
Pink, orange or yellow mottled matrix with cream lensing. Common, poorly sorted, colourless or rose quartz (up to 0.4mm), moderate rounded iron oxide (up to 1.2mm), occasional calcium carbonate inclusions (up to 1.4mm) and larger rock fragments (up to 5mm). Commonly a brick fabric. Source unknown. Date: AD 50/70–80/120. Its earliest appearance on BGH95 was in Road 1, period 2 and Building 12, period 4, both in contexts spot-dated to AD 50–100.

FABRIC 3055
Pale orange matrix with light brown margins. Common fine to medium quartz (up to 0.5mm) with common orange or red iron oxide and clay inclusions (most up to 1mm, with some larger inclusions up to 5mm). Prominent greyish-white streaks and bands throughout clay matrix. Usually a brick fabric. Source unknown. Date: AD 200/50+. Brick and tegulae in this fabric appear relatively early on BGH95; there are instances from Open Area 5, period 3 (spot-dates AD 50–100), and Building 9, period 4 (spot-dates AD 70–100).

FABRIC 3068
Smooth orange to light brown matrix with common, poorly sorted quartz (up to 0.8mm) and fairly common cream silty bands (up to 7mm). Scatter of red iron oxide (up to 1mm). Source unknown. Date: AD 50/70–120/5. Occurs on BGH95, LBE95 and LBH94; its earliest appearance is in period 4 Building 9 on BGH95, in a context spot-dated to AD 50–100.

FABRIC 3069
Red, orange or light brown. Fine fabric with frequent fine to medium quartz (up to 0.3mm), common red iron oxide (up to 2.5mm), moderate silty pellets and bands (up to 3mm) and occasional calcium carbonate and flint fragments. The source may be kilns in Hertfordshire or Buckinghamshire. The date range is approximately AD 70/85–100. The only securely identified instance, a reused tegula, came from BGH95 period 7.

FABRIC 3070
Orange fabric with frequent inclusions of very coarse quartz (up to 1mm) and common very fine (less than 0.05mm) black iron oxides. Few, very coarse calcium carbonate inclusions of dark red iron oxide (up to 0.8mm). Coarser sandy texture than 3004. Rare. Source uncertain, but possibly from one of the kilns making tiles in fabric group 2815. Date: AD 55–80. Three of the four occurrences, all on BGH95, are in period 2. However, two of the fragments are probably part of a louver or chimney-pot and may be in a coarse pot fabric made from similar clays.

FABRIC 3074
Pink or light brown matrix with frequent very fine quartz (up to 0.1mm). Common rounded white calcium carbonate pellets (up to 4mm) and thin silty lenses. Occasional red iron oxide (up to 1mm). Fine moulding sand. An imbrex was found on LBB95 in a 4th-century context, spot-dated to AD 250–400.

FABRIC 3077
Fine orange matrix largely devoid of quartz, with numerous thin creamy silty lenses. Frequent iron oxide and clay inclusions (up to 3mm). Source unknown. Date: 3rd century or later. This fabric appears as combed box-flue on BGH95 in period 7, and on RWG94 from Open Area 2, in contexts spot-dated to AD 250–400.

FABRIC 3095
Pink or orange matrix with common inclusions of poorly sorted, rounded and blocky calcium carbonate (up to 5mm), occasional quartz (up to 0.3mm) and iron oxide/clay inclusions (up to 3mm). Source unknown. Found on BGH95 in period 2 deposits associated with Building 25, spot-dated to AD 50–160, and in period 4, associated with Building 20.

FABRIC 3227
Pinkish-orange or cream with a pinkish-orange core. Common quartz (0.2–1mm), moderate red to black iron oxide (0.6–4mm), fine black speckling and silty streaks. Thin-walled combed box-flue tile fabric. Source unknown. Date: probably AD 50–75/80, but the earliest appearance on BGH95 was in period 5 deposits associated with Building 28, spot-dated to AD 120–30.

FABRIC 3230

Fine, hard, orange to red background matrix (similar to fabric 2452), with moderate to common, very coarse, rounded, mottled pinkish-white calcareous inclusions (up to 7mm). Occasional dark 'rose' quartz crystals (up to 0.05mm). Tile in this new fabric is found on BGH95, where it is associated with period 4 Buildings 9, 12, 21, 26, 27 and 30, and on two London Bridge sites. On BGH95 it appears after the Boudican fire destruction, possibly c AD 70. It is certainly present in Building 21 by AD 80. On LBI95 it appears in deposits of periods 3 (spot-dated to AD 50–100) and 4 (earliest spot-date is AD 50–70). Bricks and roof tile in this fabric are certainly present in Southwark by c AD 70, the beginning of the Flavian period, and may even have reached the site earlier, soon after the Boudican destruction. There is no evidence for tile in this fabric in pre-Boudican deposits.

Stone inlay, paving and roofing

A quantity of stone slabs was recovered from the excavations. Slabs could be produced by two methods, either by splitting naturally foliated or laminated rocks, or by sawing slices of stone from larger blocks. Both methods of manufacture were seen in the stone assemblage. Sawing had two advantages over splitting: it allowed rocks which had no natural cleavage plane to be worked, and the resultant smooth, flat surface would take a polish which enhanced the natural markings and coloration of the stones. Split slabs were easier and quicker to produce, but were less regular in shape and were generally used as flagstones or for roofing. Stone tesserae were also produced by the splitting technique.

Sources of stone

The majority of the fissile stones which were split for use as paving and roofing tiles are the medium- and fine-grained sandstones. Their source is not known, but is likely to be in south-east England; they are similar, though not identical, to Horsham stone from the Wealden Beds in Sussex. There are also smaller amounts of a fine-grained, light grey laminated limestone, which is likewise from an unknown source.

The sawn and polished slabs are made from rocks with more diverse origins. The commonest British stone represented, particularly on BGH95, is Purbeck marble, from the Purbeck Beds of the Upper Jurassic, quarried on the Isle of Purbeck in Dorset. This is a blue-grey limestone, sometimes tinged with red or green, which is hard enough to take a high polish. It is composed of frequent small rounded shells of the freshwater snail, *Paludina carinifera* (Davey 1961). The other British stone commonly used for tiles is Wealden shale, a fine-grained, greyish-black mudstone of the Lower Cretaceous which is thought to have been quarried in Kent.

As well as exploiting the native British rock types, the Romans imported decorative stones from the Mediterranean into Southwark. Most of the pieces of imported marble were white, some of them veined or banded with grey. The sourcing of white marbles by eye is always unreliable, and it is particularly difficult when they have been buried in the iron rich conditions of urban London deposits, but at least one example from BGH95 is likely to be Carrara marble from the quarries at Luna in Italy. The coarser-grained white stones are probably from Aegean island quarries or Asia Minor. Only one coloured marble tile was recorded; this is the fine-grained, purple, white and red type known as *fior di pesco*, which was quarried at Chalcis in Euboea, Greece (Dodge and Ward-Perkins 1992, 156). The only other coloured imported stone was a single fragment of deep pink, shelly mudstone from a Mediterranean source from BGH95. There is no evidence for large-scale importation of marble from Mediterranean quarries to Britain, and it is likely that the Mediterranean marbles found in London were brought here, probably from Rome, for use in certain high-status buildings.

Decorative stone: veneers and inlays

Decorative stone inlays were found on the Borough High Street and the Redcross Way sites. Six pieces of Mediterranean marble were found, four of which were white or white and grey, including some from the Luna quarries (Carrara), and one of which was purple, red and white *fior di pesco* from Euboea in Greece. The sixth fragment (BGH95 <1490>) is currently missing. Also recorded was a very abraded piece of deep pink, shelly, mudstone with no surviving original surfaces; the occurrence of a triangular *opus sectile* tile in the same dull pinkish-red stone on a nearby site in St Thomas Street suggests that both may have come from the same building. A similar red mudstone was used in the Neronian 'palace' at Fishbourne (Cunliffe 1971, 16–17).

All the imported decorative stone on BGH95 came from period 4 Building 18 and period 5 Building 24. The white marble slabs had been sawn to between 13mm and 24mm thick, and were probably originally wall veneer. The fragment from BGH95 Building 18 showed clear signs of reuse, having been re-cut at least twice. The greyish-white marble, possibly Proconnesian, from RWG94 Building 2 had a nosed moulding. The *fior di pesco* slab from RWT93 was 29mm thick, and differed from the other marbles in having one roughly worked face; it was probably also a veneer, although it may have been used for internal paving, perhaps in a bathhouse.

Five contexts contained slabs of Purbeck marble, ranging in thickness from 20mm to 36mm. Most of the findspots were on BGH95, where it was associated with Buildings 15, 26 and 38. Its earliest appearance was the 29mm thick slab from Building 26, period 4. This was decayed and appeared to have been used as paving, but may originally have been wall veneer. A single fragment 25mm thick came from Open Area 3 at LBE95, period 3.

Wealden shale slabs were noted from three contexts, two of which were on BGH95. The most interesting piece was a fragmentary slab <1506> from BGH95 Open Area 2 with several saw cuts on its surface; this is almost certainly an offcut from the manufacture of *opus sectile* tiles, which were small, geometrically-shaped tiles laid to form patterned floor surfaces (Fig 29, <T8>). This fragment, from a pre-Boudican context, could be evidence that the stone was being worked in the vicinity, and at an early date. With its two sawn faces, this piece differs from the early *opus sectile* tiles from the City which have roughly chiselled under-surfaces (Pritchard 1986).

Stone tesserae

Loose tesserae were noted in Wealden shale from BGH95, MSA92 and RWT93, and in hard white chalk from BGH95, MSA92, RWT93 and TOM95; the section of white chalk tessellated floor from the last site is discussed elsewhere. Examples were recorded of single tesserae in grey limestone (BGH95), fine, soft, light brown sandstone (LBE95) and fine-grained sandstone (LBI95).

Flagstones

The two main types of stone used for paving were fine-grained and medium-grained laminated sandstones. Fragments of paving in fine-grained sandstone were found in all three areas of excavation. The earliest occurrence in the BGH95 area is on Open Area 18 in period 4, with pottery dates of AD 50–100. The majority of the material, however, occurs in BGH95 period 7, including several fragments in the fills of the late drainage ditch. On the Redcross Way sites, this stone appears on RWG94 period 4, where it is likely to have been used in the building on 15–23 Southwark Street, and on the London Bridge sites it is first seen in association with LBE95 Building 1, period 4. A fragment from LBB95 Open Area 4 had traces of *opus signinum* mortar on its base. Paving slabs in medium-grained laminated sandstone are mostly confined to BGH95, where their first appearance is in Building 22, room B in period 5 (pottery dates AD 70–100); other occurrences are in periods 6 and 7. However, a single flagstone in this stone was also noted from RWT93 Building 2, period 5.

Other stones occasionally used for paving are Kentish ragstone, and a fine-grained light grey limestone, source unknown. A soft, fine-grained, laminated brown sandstone flag, also from an unknown source, was recorded from LBE95 Building 1, period 4, and a loose tessera in a similar stone was noted from the same building.

Stone roof tiles

A number of fragments of laminated stone, thinner than those typically used for flagstones, are thought to have been used as roof tiles. Almost all were of fine-grained laminated sandstone, similar to that used for paving, and most occurred on either the Borough High Street or Redcross Way sites. None of this stone from the Borough High Street area, which all came from period 7, was directly associated with a building. All the RWG94 material came from period 4, and, like the paving stone from this area, may have come from the destruction of the building on 15–23 Southwark Street.

Building material in the early 2nd century

The tile used in London in the early 2nd century is not very different from that used in the Flavian period. The kilns which produced large quantities of tile in the local London fabrics in the 1st century seem to carry on until *c* AD 160, and they will have supplied the bulk of the roof tile and brick to the area of the site during the early part of the 2nd century. The Radlett kilns are thought to have continued in production until at least AD 120. The Eccles kilns were no longer producing tile for London, but their bricks and characteristically thick tegulae continued to be used and there is still a lot of it in deposits. Of the fabrics which occur in very small quantities, 3227 (used for thin-walled flue tiles in the 1st century), 3226 and 3069 seem to go out of production. The only new non-local fabrics found north of the Thames in this period are 3018, possibly from Hartfield, East Sussex, and 3019, which is thought to have been produced at kilns at Braxells Farm, and possibly Little London, Hampshire. No new tile types appear in this period, and the picture is one of continuity rather than change.

The only distinctively Trajanic fabric noted was fabric 3019. Although this appeared in some BGH95 deposits at the end of period 4 (Buildings 9 and 12), there are no occurrences in this period on BGH95. However, it appears in both MSA92 Building 4 and RWT93 Building 1.

As regards building stone, Kentish ragstone rubble was recorded, and a slab from LBI95 that could have been used for roofing. Small flakes of slate, probably roof tile, were noted from BGH95 Building 8, though these may have been intrusive. Flagstones were noted in fine-grained laminated sandstone. The only decorative stone recorded was a fragment of Wealden shale, probably inlay, and tesserae, one in hard chalk, the other in fine-grained laminated sandstone from LBI95 Building 7.

Summary of building materials

There is little sign of change in tile types or their sources in the early 2nd century. The situation in period 4, when much tile from earlier building seems to be reused, carries on. There is evidence of the use of tiles in new fabric 3019, which is thought to start in London *c* AD 100. However, this fabric was present in small quantities in period 4 in BGH95 Buildings 9, 12, 21 and Open Area 7. Possible explanations are that the fabric is earlier in Southwark than in the City, or that the material is intrusive in period 4 deposits.

There is no obvious change in the function or status of the buildings on the site. There is an increase in the quantity and types of flue tile, but much of this may be residual or reused. However, even as 'background noise' it does indicate that hypocaust material is being spread around from a high-status building or buildings somewhere in the vicinity.

11.2 The Roman pottery

Louise Rayner and Fiona Seeley

Introduction

For the Jubilee Line (Southwark) excavations approximately 370 boxes of Roman pottery were examined. The assemblages were assessed for potential in relation to the thematic research aims of the project and a programme for publication was then devised (Symonds 1997). Concurrently, backlog excavations from 60 sites in Southwark were being assessed as part of an English Heritage funded project which led to a further set of ceramic-specific research aims being defined (Rayner and Seeley 1996; 1998).

Methodology

The 21 site assemblages covered in this volume were dated over a five-year period from 1991 to 1996. For all assemblages the database includes a basic record by context of each type present as a unique record combining fabric, form and decoration codes, for example HWC 2E BUD. These represent a single type and constitute a 'record' or 'row'. The size of assemblage (small (S) = less than 30 sherds; medium (M) = 30–100 sherds; large (L) = 100+ sherds; very large (VL) = three+ boxes) and condition of pottery (burnt (B), abraded (A), laminated (L), residue (R), worn (W)) are both noted and for each context, an early date (edate) and late date (ldate) are assigned which constitutes the 'spot date'. The status of the assemblage was then ascribed as residual, contemporary or intrusive and general comments made for the assemblage as a whole. In autumn 1995 sherd count was introduced as a method of quantification at the spot-dating level, which coincided with the implementation of a new relational database system at MoLAS.

Spot-dating and 'rows'

Only those Roman assemblages spot-dated after this date (BGH95, LBA95, TOM95, REW92, half of LBI95 and the majority of STU92) include sherd counts and most of these assemblages have been analysed by both quantified sherd count data and qualitative 'rows' data. Sherd count as a method of quantification can be criticised as being a biased method for measuring the proportions of types, because of the variation of 'brokenness' that can occur between types and within the size range of one type (Orton et al 1993, 169). The spot-date process, however, records sherd count as a basic record of quantity and therefore remains the only quantitative data available for contexts that are not analysed in more detail. Here the sherd count quantification is used alongside figures derived from number of records or 'rows'. The percentages are mainly used to compare the quantities of one type between periods and within types of similar manufacture and size.

The remaining assemblages were analysed using the spot-date record as qualitative 'rows' data. This method utilises the vast body of detailed ceramic data generated during spot-dating, and although it is not as desirable as using fully quantified data, it does provide a broad picture of the assemblage composition. This method of analysis is discussed more fully by Davies (1992; 1993). The data from the Jubilee Line sites has been dealt with in a similar manner to the assemblage from Leadenhall Court (Davies 1993, 137). Only ceramic data from contexts fully phased and assigned to a period has been used in this study.

For the larger sites, the ceramic data has been examined by stratigraphic period to give percentages of fabrics and forms present. This enabled the identification of chronological trends in the assemblage and allowed comparison with the Roman Ceramic Phases (RCP) identified from City sites, published in the Early Roman Corpus (ERC) (Davies et al 1994). A key to the pottery codes used is provided in Tables 39–41.

Quantified groups

For selected contexts or groups of contexts the pottery has been fully quantified using weight and estimated vessel equivalents (EVEs). These groups are illustrated as diagnostic or key groups from the site sequence and were selected to address the research aims. They are discussed within the site narrative and tables of quantified data are presented in the relevant site period overview. The combined use of photography and traditional line drawings to present the assemblages results in a visual appreciation of the composition of Roman assemblages, not obtained from line drawings alone; amongst them are vessel types previously unpublished from London.

Intrusive material

The truncation of the later sequence on parts of the sites, the disturbance caused by the construction of the Battlebridge sewer at BGH95 and construction work carried out in advance of the excavation, has undoubtedly led to a certain amount of intrusive material. Some of this has, particularly in the early sequence, been relatively easy to isolate, but inevitably as the site sequence progresses throughout the periods it becomes harder to identify what is genuinely intrusive and what is contemporary with the phase of activity. The sherds or contexts deemed to be intrusive have been extracted from the data sets used for the period overviews; a list of the types for the BGH95 assemblage can be found in Table 42.

Main Ticket Hall, Borough High Street (BGH95)

Period 1

INTRODUCTION

For period 1 all percentages are given by EVEs followed by weight and are of the whole assemblage unless stated otherwise.

The earliest assemblage from BGH95 was recovered from the quarry pits and ditches in Open Area 2. These were later sealed by dumped layers prior to the construction of the first buildings.

Fabric code	Expansion	Earliest date AD	Latest date AD
AHBB	Alice Holt Black-Burnished type ware	160	250
AHFA	Alice Holt/Farnham ware	250	400
AHSU	Alice Holt/Surrey ware	50	160
AMPBS	Amphora with black sand inclusions	50	400
AMPH	Miscellaneous amphora type	50	400
BAET	Baetican Dressel 20	50	300
BAETE	Baetican Dressel 20/Haltern 70 fabric, early	50	170
BAETL	Baetican Dressel 20 fabric, late	170	300
BB1	Black-Burnished 1 ware	120	400
BB2	Black-Burnished 2 ware	120	250
BB2F	Black-Burnished 2 ware with fine fabric	140	250
BBS	Black-Burnished-style ware	120	400
BHWS	Brockley Hill white slip	50	160
C186	Camulodunum type 186 amphora	50	140
C189	Camulodunum type 189 amphora	50	150
CADIZ	Cam. type 186 amphora fabric (Peacock & Williams, 17–18)	50	140
CADIZ1	C186 variant	50	140
CALC	Late Roman 'calcite-tempered' wares	300	400
CAMP1	Campanian black sand fabric	50	100
CAMP2	Campanian volcanic fabric	50	150
CAT	Catalan Dressel 2-4 fabric	50	150
CC	Miscellaneous colour-coated wares	50	400
CCGW	Copthall close grey ware	70	150
CCIMP	Miscellaneous imported colour-coated wares	50	400
CGBL	Central Gaulish/Lezoux black colour-coated ware	150	250
CGGW	Central Gaulish glazed ware	50	100
CGOF	Central Gaulish colour-coated ware, other fabrics	50	130
CGWH	Central Gaulish colour-coated ware, white fabric	50	130
COAR	Miscellaneous coarse wares	40	400
COLEC	Colchester early colour-coated ware	50	100
COLWW	Colchester white ware	50	250
DR20	Dressel 20 amphora	50	300
DR28	Dressel 28 amphora	50	200
ECCW	Eccles ware	50	100
EIFL	'Eifelkeramik'	200	400
ERMS	Early Roman micaceous sandy	50	100
ERSA	Early Roman sandy a	50	70
ERSA/B	Early Roman sandy a/b	50	120
ERSB	Early Roman sandy b	50	120
ERSI	Early Roman sandy/iron-rich ware	50	70
ERSS	Early Roman sandy shell	50	120
FINE	Miscellaneous fine wares	50	400
FLIN	Miscellaneous flint-tempered wares	50	200
FMIC	Fine micaceous black/grey ware	50	120
G238	Gillam 238 mortaria and allied types	60	160
GAUL	Miscellaneous Gaulish amphora	50	250
GAUL1	Pélichet 47/Dressel 30 amphora fabric (Peacock & Williams 27/30)	50	250
GAUL2	London-type 555/Haltern 70 type amphora fabric	50	120
GAUL3	Gaulish Dressel 2-4 amphora fabric	50	150
GBWW	Gallo-Belgic white wares	40	70
GROG	Grog-tempered ware	40	400
GROGSH	Grog/shell-tempered ware	40	400
HOFA	Hollow foot amphora	180	400
HOO	Hoo ware	50	100
HWB	Highgate Wood 'b' grog-tempered wares	40	100
HWB/C	Highgate Wood 'b'/'c' ware	65	85
HWBR	Highgate Wood 'b' red-slipped	40	100
HWC	Highgate Wood 'c' sand-tempered wares	70	160
HWC+	Highgate Wood 'c' wares with added coarse sand	120	160
IMPT	Unidentifiable but probable imported Roman fabric	50	400
ITFEL	Italian felspathic Dressel 2-4 amphora fabric	50	150
ITMO	Italian mortaria	50	100
KOLN	Cologne colour-coated ware	100	140
L555	London type 555 amphorae	50	120
LIPR	Lipari (Richborough 527) amphora fabric (Peacock & Williams, 13)	50	150
LOMI	Local/?London mica-dusted ware	70	120
LOXI	Local oxidised ware	90	160

Table 39 Roman pottery fabric codes

Fabric code	Expansion	Earliest date AD	Latest date AD
LONW	London ware	70	120
LOEG	Local/?London eggshell ware	70	120
LOMA	London marbled ware	70	120
LOMI	Local/?London mica-dusted ware	70	120
LONW	London ware	70	120
LOXI	Local oxidised ware	90	160
LRMA	Late Roman marbled ware	200	400
LRRA	Late Roman rilled amphora	200	400
LYON	Lyon colour-coated ware	50	70
MAYEN	Mayen ware	200	400
MHAD	Much Hadham ware	200	400
MICA	Miscellaneous mica-dusted ware	50	400
MLEZ	Micaceous Lezoux ware	50	100
MORT	Miscellaneous mortaria types	50	400
MOSL	'Moselkeramik'	200	275
NAFRI	North African lime-rich amphora fabric	140	200
NARS	North African red-slipped ware	70	400
NFCC	New Forest colour-coated ware	250	400
NFSE	North French/south-east English oxidised ware	50	160
NKGW	North Kent grey ware	100	150
NKSH	?North Kent shell-tempered ware	50	150
NVCC	Nene valley colour-coated ware	150	400
OXID	Miscellaneous oxidised wares	50	400
OXIDF	Fine oxidised fabric	50	400
OXMOB	Oxfordshire burnt white ware	240	400
OXPA	Oxfordshire parchment ware	240	400
OXRC	Oxfordshire red/brown colour-coated ware	270	400
OXWS	Oxfordshire white-slipped red ware	240	400
OXWW	Oxfordshire white ware	180	400
PORD	Portchester 'd' ware	350	400
PRW	Pompeian red ware	50	150
PRW1	Pompeian red ware 1	50	100
PRW3	Pompeian red ware 3	50	150
RDBK	?Verulamium region 'ring & dot' beaker fabric	50	100
RHMO	Rhineland mortaria (other than Soller)	50	300
RHOD	Rhodian fabric	50	150
RHOD1	Rhodian style amphora fabric (pink) (Peacock & Williams, 9)	50	150
RHOD2	Rhodian style amphora fabric (yellow) (Peacock & Williams, 9)	50	150
RHWW	Rhineland white ware (other than Soller)	50	300
RVMO	Rhône Valley mortaria	50	120
RVOX	Rhone Valley oxidised ware	50	120
RWS	Roman miscellaneous red- & white-slipped wares	50	300
SAM	Samian ware	50	250
SAMCG	Central Gaulish samian ware	120	250
SAMEG	East Gaulish samian ware	150	300
SAMLG	La Graufesenque samian ware	50	100
SAMMT	Montans samian ware	50	100
SAMMV	Les Martres-de-Veyre samian ware	100	120
SAMMV2	Les Martres-de-Veyre samian ware 2	100	120
SAND	Miscellaneous sand-tempered wares	50	400
SEAL	Amphora seal	50	300
SESH	South Essex shell-tempered ware	50	150
SGCC	South Gaulish colour-coated ware	50	70
SHEL	Miscellaneous shell-tempered wares	40	400
SLOW	Sugar Loaf Court ware	50	80
SOLL	Soller-type mortaria	150	200
SPAN	Spanish colour-coated ware	50	70
SUG	Sussex grog-tempered ware	50	250
TN	Terra nigra	40	80
TNIM	Terra nigra imitations	40	100
TNMIC	Micaceous terra nigra variant	50	100
TSK	Thameside Kent ware	180	300
VCWS	?Verulamium region coarse white-slipped wares	70	200
VRG	Verulamium region grey wares	50	200
VRMI	?Verulamium region mica-dusted ware	70	120
VRR	Verulamium region red ware	50	160
VRW	Verulamium region white ware	50	160

(Table 39 cont)

Form code	Expansion	Earliest date AD	Latest date AD
-	Unidentified	0	0
I	Miscellaneous or otherwise unidentifiable flagon	50	400
IA	Collared (or Hofheim-type) flagon	50	100
IB	Ring-necked flagon	50	200
IBI	Ring-necked flagon with wide mouth	50	100
IB2	Ring-necked flagon with flaring mouth	70	120
IB3	Ring-necked flagon with vertical neck	70	100
IB4	Ring-necked flagon with everted neck; prominent rim	100	150
IB5	Ring-necked flagon with very prominent rounded rim	120	140
IB6	Ring necked flagon with slightly flaring short neck	120	140
IB7	Cupped-mouthed ring-necked flagon	140	200
IB7-9	Cupped-mouthed ring-necked flagon	140	200
IC	Pinch-mouthed flagon	60	160
ID	Disc-mouthed flagon	50	100
IE	Two-handled flagon with squat bulbous body	50	160
IH	Flagon with continuous body	120	200
IJ	Two-handled amphora-type flagon	50	160
IK	Pulley-rim flagon	50	250
2	Miscellaneous or otherwise unidentifiable jar	40	400
2/3	Jar or beaker; enclosed vessel	40	400
2A	Bead-rimmed jar	40	100
2A1-4	Bead rim jar: simple thickening, triangular section	40	120
2A12-13	Bead rim jar: high round shoulder, well formed bead	50	160
2A14	Bead rim jar: high shoulder and cordon	40	80
2A15	Finely-moulded bead-rimmed jar with grooves beneath rim	50	100
2A16	Lid-seated bead-rimmed jar	50	100
2A17	Black-Burnished-type bead-rimmed jar	120	200
2A7-8	Bead rim jar: square bead section with external & girth groove	40	80
2B	Short-necked jar (often with vl)	50	100
2C	Necked jar with carinated shoulder; 'figure 7' rim	50	150
2D	Round-bodied necked jar with 'figure 7' rim	60	160
2E	Round-bodied necked jar with burnished shoulder	100	160
2F	Black-Burnished-type everted-rimmed jar	120	250
2F10	Black-Burnished-type everted-rimmed jar	120	200
2F13	Everted 'cavetto'-rim jar	180	400
2F8	Black-Burnished-type everted-rimmed jar	160	200
2FX	Late version of 2F	250	400
2G	Necked jar; usually with cordon at shoulder	50	160
2G4	As 2G but with groove on outer edge of rim	140	200
2H	Large neckless jar with near-horizontal rim	100	200
2J	Neckless 'unguent' jar	60	160
2K	Two-handled 'honey pot' jar	50	150
2M	Rolled-rimmed storage jar	60	160
2N	Necked jar with high rounded shoulder	50	80
2R	Narrow-necked jar/flask	60	160
2T	Otherwise indistinguishable necked jar	50	400
2U	Narrow-necked globular jar	50	400
2V	Storage jar (other than 2M)	50	400
2Z	Alice Holt/Surrey flat-rimmed jar	50	270
3	Miscellaneous or otherwise unidentifiable beaker	50	400
3A	Butt beaker	50	80
3B	Ovoid beaker	55	100
3C	Everted-rimmed beaker	50	100
3DE67	Dechelette 67	70	130
3E	Beaker with short everted rim	70	160
3F	'Poppyhead' beaker	70	160
3F1	Variant of 3F with short rim/neck	70	120
3F2	Variant of 3F with very short rim/neck	70	100
3F4	'Poppyhead' beaker with short rim & low shoulder; usually has cordon below rim	100	160
3G	Carinated beaker with tall upright plain rim	50	100
3J	Bag-shaped beaker	100	200
3K	Necked globular beaker	180	400
4	Miscellaneous or otherwise unidentifiable bowl	40	400
4/5	Bowl/dish	50	400
4A	Reeded-rimmed bowl	50	160
4A3	Horizontal rim with thickened outer edge, forming wedge; little or no moulding	80	110
4A5	Reeded-rim bowl with rim which is thickened on outer edge but not folded back	115	150

Table 40 Roman pottery form codes

Form code	Expansion	Earliest date AD	Latest date AD
4B	Bowl with long Aoste mortarium-like flange	70	120
4CU11	Curle 11	70	150
4D	Wide bowl with carination & mouldings. Imitation Drag. 29	50	100
4DR29	Dragendorff 29	50	120
4DR30	Dragendorff 30	50	250
4DR30/37	Dragendorff 30/37	50	400
4DR37	Dragendorff 37	70	400
4DR38	Dragendorff 38	150	400
4E	Imitation Drag. 37 in FMIC	90	160
4F	Bowl with flat, hooked or folded-over rims	60	160
4F1	Bowl with constriction	70	120
4F2	Bowl less constricted than 4F1	60	160
4F4	Folded down rim; constriction below rim	70	140
4F6	Bowl with flat, square profile rim	100	160
4G	Flat-rimmed bowl with vertical wall	120	160
4H	Rounded-rimmed Black-Burnished-type bowl	120	300
4H1	Rounded-rimmed Black-Burnished-type bowl	120	300
4K	'Surrey bowl'	50	140
4M	Black-Burnished-type flanged bowl	250	400
4M34	Bowl with curved flanged rim	70	150
4M35	Bowl with slight carination & unreeded flanged rim	70	150
4MX	Other flanged bowl	50	400
4P	Carinated bowl	50	400
4Q	Tripod bowl	50	400
4RT12	Ritterling 12	50	80
5	Miscellaneous or otherwise unidentifiable plate	50	400
5A	Plate with plain exterior profile	50	100
5B	Plate with exterior moulding	50	100
5C	Plate with wide flat rim	90	130
5CU23	Curle 23	90	250
5DR15/17	Dragendorff 15/17	50	100
5DR18	Dragendorff 18	50	100
5DR18/31	Dragendorff 18/31	90	150
5DR18R	Dragendorff 18r	50	100
5DR22	Dragendorff 22	50	100
5DR22/23	Dragendorff 22/23	50	100
5DR31	Dragendorff 31	150	300
5DR35/36	Dragendorff 35/36	50	250
5DR36	Dragendorff 36	50	250
5DR42	Dish or cup Drag. 42	70	140
5J	Dish with simple rim	50	400
5J1	Plain-rimmed dish	120	250
5J2	Plain-rimmed dish	120	250
5J3	Dish with simple inturned rim	50	140
5RT1	Ritterling 1	50	70
5WA79	Walters 79	160	250
6	Miscellaneous or otherwise unidentifiable cup	50	400
6A	Copy of Drag. 27	50	120
6B	Conical cup with short vertical upper wall	50	100
6DR24/25	Drag. form 24/25	50	70
6DR27	Drag. form 27	50	160
6DR33	Drag. form 33	70	200
6DR33A	Drag. form 33a	70	120
6DR35	Drag. form 35	50	250
6DR40	Drag. form 40	160	250
6DR46	Drag. form 46	70	250
6H	Hemispherical cup	50	100
6KN78	Knorr 78	70	150
6RT8	Ritterling 8	50	70
6RT9	Ritterling 9	50	60
7	Miscellaneous or otherwise unidentifiable mortarium	50	400
7BEF	Bead and flange mortarium	140	200
7DR45	Dragendorff 45	150	300
7EWAL	Early wall-sided mortarium	50	70
7G236	Hartley group i	55	85
7G238	Hartley group ii	50	100
7HAM	Hammerhead mortarium	200	300

(Table 40 cont)

Form code	Expansion	Earliest date AD	Latest date AD
7HOF	Hooked flange mortarium	50	140
7WAL	Wall-sided mortarium	50	250
8	Miscellaneous amphora	50	400
8IJ	Romano-British flat-bottomed amphora	50	100
8C139	Camulodunum 139	50	100
8C184	Rhodian-type	50	150
8C186	Camulodunum 186	50	150
8C189	Camulodunum 189	50	150
8DR2-4	Dressel 2-4	50	150
8DR20	Dressel 20	50	300
8DR20PW10	Peacock & Williams, fig 65.10	50	400
8DR20PW11	Peacock & Williams, fig 65.11	50	400
8DR20PW12	Peacock & Williams, fig 65.12	40	400
8DR20PW13	Peacock & Williams, fig 65.13	55	400
8DR20PW15	Peacock & Williams, fig 65.15	55	400
8DR20PW16	Peacock & Williams, fig 65.16	55	400
8DR20PW17	Peacock & Williams, fig 65.17	70	400
8DR20PW18	Peacock & Williams, fig 65.18	70	400
8DR20PW20	Peacock & Williams, fig 65.20	80	400
8DR20PW22	Peacock & Williams, fig 65.22	80	400
8DR20PW23	Peacock & Williams, fig 65.23	80	400
8DR20PW24	Peacock & Williams, fig 65.24	100	400
8DR20PW28	Peacock & Williams, fig 66.28	110	400
8DR20PW8	Peacock & Williams, fig 65.8	40	400
8DR20PW9	Peacock & Williams, fig 65.9	40	400
8DR21-22	Dressel 21-22 (Peacock & Williams type 7)	50	100
8DR28	Dressel 28	50	200
8G	Pélichet 47/Dressel 30/Gauloise-type	50	250
8G12	Gauloise type 12	50	250
8G4	Gauloise type 4	50	250
8G5	Gauloise type 5	50	250
8H70	Haltern 70	50	100
8K117	Kingsholm 117	50	150
8KOAN	Dressel 2-4	50	100
8L555	London 555	50	120
8NACA	North African cylindrical amphora	200	400
8PW65	Peacock & Williams type 65. Callender amphora	50	400
8R527	Richborough 527 (Lipari)	50	150
8RHOD	Rhodian type (general)	50	150
8V1908	Verulamium 1908	50	150
9A	Lid	50	400
9B	Amphora seal	50	400
9C	Tazza	50	250
9D	Serium/dolium	50	400
9H	Colander	50	400
9J	Patera	50	400
9LA	Lamp	50	400
9N	Unguentarium; small 2j type.	50	400
9NP	Unguentarium with pedestal base/amphora stopper	50	400
9RT13	Inkwell (Ritterling 13)	50	250
9U	Bucket	40	400

(*Table 40 cont*)

The 'spot-dates' given to contexts during assessment suggested that this activity was pre-Flavian. The total assemblage from Open Area 2 was quantified by weight and EVEs because of the well-defined stratigraphic sequence, the presence of relatively complete vessels and the lack of residual material, due to the position in the sequence. The Open Area 2 data is compared with the quantified data for RCP1A from the City and the unquantified pre-Flavian assemblage from 201BHS89. The quantified assemblage totalled 848 sherds from 251 rows, 33,112g and 14.74 EVEs (Table 43). Table 44 and Table 45 summarise the period 1 assemblage by fabric and form respectively.

AMPHORAE
BAETE Dressel 20 olive oil amphorae are the dominant type and account for 73.4% of all amphorae. Otherwise there is a limited range of other amphorae types and these are present in only small quantities. Gaulish amphorae are represented by GAUL1 flat-bottomed wine amphorae (Gauloise 4) and are the second most abundant type. Five sherds are recorded of CADIZ

Table 41 *Roman pottery decoration codes*

Decoration code	Expansion	Earliest date AD	Latest date AD
AL	Black-Burnished-type acute lattice	120	250
ALX	Other acute lattice	50	400
ARCX	Arcs on later Black-Burnished forms	250	400
BAD	Barbotine	50	400
BDD	Barbotine dot	50	400
BFD	Barbotine figure	50	400
BR	Bead rim	40	400
BRD	Ring & dot barbortine decoration	50	400
BUD	Burnished	50	400
CL	Curvilinear decoration	120	250
CLX	Later curvilinear decoration	250	400
COMB	Combed	50	400
CR	Cornice rim	50	400
DEC	Decorated	50	400
EMD	Embossed	50	400
FCD	Fingered cabling decoration	50	400
FRLD	Frilled decoration on tazza	50	400
HPD	Hair-pin barbotine	50	400
HPOF	Post-firing hole(s)	50	400
MOD	Moulded	50	400
NCD	Incised	50	400
OL	Obtuse lattice	250	400
RCD1	Sand/quartz roughcast decoration	50	120
RCD2	Clay pellet/grog roughcast decoration	50	300
RLD	Rilled decoration	50	400
ROD	Rouletted	50	400
RPD	Red painted decoration	50	400
SCD	Barbotine scale	50	400
SPT	Spout	50	400
STAB	Stabbed	50	400
STD	Stamped	50	400
VL	Ungrouped vertical lines	50	400
WBAD	White barbotine decoration	180	300
WL	Wavy line decoration	50	250
WLX	Later wavy line decoration	250	400
WPD	White painted decoration	270	400

Table 42 *Details of sherds deemed intrusive and not included in the analysis*

Period	Context	Fabric	Form	Dec	Sherd count	Rows
1	[2223]	SAMLG	4DR37	DEC	1	1
1	[4125]	SAMLG	4DR29	DEC	1	1
1	[6039]	SAMCG	6DR33		1	1
1	[7084]	SAMLG	4DR37	DEC	1	1
2	[184]	HWC	9A	-	1	1
2	[522]	SAMMV	4DR37	DEC	1	1
2	[695]	HWC	2	-	1	1
2	[702]	MHAD	-	-	1	1
2	[797]	NVCC	3	-	1	1
2	[880]	HWC	4F	-	1	1
2	[4064]	HWC	-	-	1	1
2	[4069]	HWC	3	BDD	2	1
2	[4192]	FINE	3F	-	2	1
2	[4195]	HWC	3F	BDD	9	1
2	[7090]	SAMCG	6DR33	-	1	1
2	[7097]	HWC	2	-	1	1
3	[1874]	SAMLG	4DR29	ROD	3	1
3	[1874]	SAMLG	4DR29	DEC	18	1
3	[1874]	SAMLG	4DR37	DEC	6	1
4	[1726]	BB2	4/5	AL	1	1
4	[1889]	BBS	2	AL	1	1
4	[3950]	BB2	4/5	AL	1	1
4	[1826]	BB1	2		1	1
4	[738]	AHFA	4	BUD	1	1
4	[1781]	MHAD			1	1
4	[505]	OXRC	4/5		1	1
4	[595]	OXRC	4		1	1
4	[746]	SAMCG	5DR18/31		1	1
4	[849]	SAMCG	6DR35		1	1
4	[1861]	SAMCG	6DR33		1	1
5	[3372]	BB2	2F		1	1
5	[3528]	BBS?			1	1
6	[1211]	AHFA	2	COMB	1	1
6	[3317]	MHAD			1	1
6	[3317]	NVCC	3K		1	1
6	[3352]	OXRC	4	WPD	1	1
6	[4089]	PORD			1	1
6	[4089]	AHFA	4/5		1	1
6	[691]	CALC	2		1	1
6	[691]	EIFL	4/5		1	1
6	[691]	MHAD			1	1
6	[608]	AHFA	4M		1	1
6	[1556]	AHFA	4/5		1	1
6	[3439]	OXWW	7BEF		4	1

Cam. form 186, an amphora type used to transport fish products, and only one sherd each is present of CAMP1 Dressel 2-4, RHOD2 Cam. form 184 and GAUL2 London 555.

REDUCED WARES

Within the assemblage as a whole reduced wares predominate and these are mostly from unknown sources. HWB (11.9/2.3) forms an important component of this ware group, but is not as abundant in this assemblage as it appears to be in the City at this period. In the Open Area 2 assemblage HWB accounts for 11.9% (by weight) of all reduced wares, whereas in RCP1A it accounts for 37% (Davies et al 1994, 74). This is possibly due to a slight difference in the suggested chronological ranges of RCP1A and period 1. The data used for RCP1A covered the period up to and including the Boudican fire, whereas Open Area 2 only relates to the earliest part of that period.

The presence of ERSA/B is of note in Southwark. This fabric is one of the Early Roman Sandy wares, presumed to be of local production and present in minimal quantities in the City from RCP1A. Its identification confirms the circulation of these wares, in similar quantities, in Southwark. ERSI is also recorded in

small quantities, which supports the evidence from the City, that this is a sparse ware occurring in pre-Boudican levels (Davies et al 1994, 168). AHSU is present in small quantities, but is not yet amongst the dominant fabrics. VRG is present (only one sherd), which is also a rare fabric in RCP1A.

OXIDISED WARES

Unsourced oxidised fabrics (OXID) (8.1/3.5) are abundant in the assemblage, where they account for 32.5% (by weight) of all oxidised wares. This figure is similar to RCP1A, where they account for c 30% (Davies et al 1998, 168). Sourced oxidised wares are recorded in small quantities compared to unsourced, but include products from Kent such as ECCW and HOO, which is a pattern previously noted from Southwark (Bird et al 1978, figs 102–4) and in the City. BHWS is also present in this earliest

Ware	BGH95 OA2		RCP1A		BGH95 OA2		RCP1A	
	Wt	% wt	Wt	% wt	EVEs	%EVEs	EVEs	%EVEs
AMPH	20532	62.0	41054	40.1	2.3	15.6	2.58	4.7
OXID	5285	16.0	24915	24.4	3.65	24.8	4.85	34.2
REDU	6345	19.2	32069	31.3	5.89	40.0	22.08	40.0
FINE	102	0.3	1003	0.9	0.57	3.9	2.35	4.2
SAM	848	2.6	3296	3.2	2.33	15.8	9.41	17.0
Total	33112	100.0	102337	100.0	14.74	100.0	55.39	100.0

Table 43 Pottery data from Open Area 2 by ware with comparative data from RCP1A

Fabric	Sherd count	% sherd count	Rows	% rows	Wt	% wt	EVEs	%EVEs
AHSU	19	2.2	9	3.6	371	1.1	0.59	4.0
AMPH	26	3.1	8	3.2	2470	7.5	1	6.8
BAETE	143	16.9	21	8.4	15063	45.5	1.15	7.8
BHWS	11	1.3	2	0.8	154	0.5	0.5	3.4
CADIZ	5	0.6	4	1.6	394	1.2	0.15	1.0
CAMPI	1	0.1	1	0.4	49	0.1	0	0.0
COLEC	2	0.2	1	0.4	14	0.0		0.0
COLWW	4	0.5	2	0.8	418	1.3	0.24	1.6
ECCW	11	1.3	6	2.4	243	0.7	0	0.0
ERMS	14	1.7	2	0.8	139	0.4	0.22	1.5
ERSA/B	38	4.5	3	1.2	349	1.1	0.63	4.3
ERSB	10	1.2	3	1.2	134	0.4	0.1	0.7
ERSI	7	0.8	4	1.6	149	0.4	0.36	2.4
FINE	4	0.5	2	0.8	56	0.2	0.5	3.4
FMIC	4	0.5	3	1.2	16	0.0	0.07	0.5
GAUL	26	3.1	6	2.4	1206	3.6		0.0
GAUL1	30	3.5	4	1.6	1219	3.7		0.0
GAUL2	1	0.1	1	0.4	90	0.3		0.0
GROG	77	9.1	21	8.4	1970	5.9	0.55	3.7
HOO	9	1.1	4	1.6	50	0.2		0.0
HWB	27	3.2	10	4.0	755	2.3	1.76	11.9
LYON	8	0.9	2	0.8	7	0.0		0.0
NFSE	5	0.6	4	1.6	1382	4.2	1.32	9.0
NKSH	13	1.5	3	1.2	512	1.5		0.0
OXID	60	7.1	28	11.2	1171	3.5	1.2	8.1
OXIDF	44	5.2	3	1.2	546	1.6		0.0
PRW3	1	0.1	1	0.4	9	0.0		0.0
RHOD2	1	0.1	1	0.4	41	0.1		0.0
RWS	49	5.8	5	2.0	250	0.8	0.17	1.2
SAMLG	90	10.6	50	19.9	848	2.6	2.33	15.8
SAND	55	6.5	16	6.4	802	2.4	0.71	4.8
SEAL	2	0.2	1	0.4	19	0.1	0.12	0.8
SESH	1	0.1	1	0.4	13	0.0	0.11	0.7
SHEL	31	3.7	11	4.4	1142	3.4	0.86	5.8
VRG	1	0.1	1	0.4	9	0.0		0.0
VRW	18	2.1	7	2.8	1052	3.2	0.1	0.7
Total	848	100.0	251	100.0	33112		14.74	100.0

Table 44 Period 1 pottery assemblage by fabric

period. VRW is recorded in relatively small quantites (0.7/3.2), but already accounts for 19.9% (by weight) of all oxidised wares.

FINE WARES

South Gaulish samian (15.8/2.6) is virtually the only imported fine ware present in this period. At 2.33 EVEs, this is the highest value for this period, although it must be borne in mind that fine wares are frequently over-represented by EVEs. Other imported fine wares are scarce, consisting of only one sherd from a PRW3 dish and eight sherds from two LYON lamps. No other imported colour-coated or Gallo-Belgic wares are present, although Romano-British colour-coated wares are recorded, such as a COLEC beaker with rough-cast decoration. Romano-British reduced fine wares are present in only small quantities, and this is reflected in the forms, with only the everted-rim beaker (3C) identified.

The absence of other pre-Flavian fine wares, particularly LYON vessels, is noteworthy. In the City it is generally the most abundant imported fine ware after samian and is seen as diagnostic of the pre-Flavian period. The absence may again be a reflection of chronology rather than an indication of low status and lack of access to imported goods.

Form	Sherd count	% sherd count	Rows	% rows	Wt	% wt	EVEs	%EVEs
-	163	19.2	47	18.7	1547	4.7	0.17	1.2
I	11	1.3	6	2.4	400	1.2	0	0.0
IA	11	1.3	2	0.8	686	2.1	1.5	10.2
2	175	20.6	41	16.3	3676	11.1	0	0.0
2/3	1	0.1	1	0.4	4	0.0	0.07	0.5
2A	38	4.5	16	6.4	1215	3.7	2.25	15.3
2A1-4	1	0.1	1	0.4	9	0.0	0.04	0.3
2A15	31	3.7	1	0.4	315	1.0	0.63	4.3
2A7-8	4	0.5	2	0.8	91	0.3	0.22	1.5
2B	11	1.3	1	0.4	98	0.3	0.22	1.5
2T	14	1.7	7	2.8	270	0.8	1.06	7.2
2U	1	0.1	1	0.4	109	0.3	0.17	1.2
2V	2	0.2	2	0.8	154	0.5	0.05	0.3
3	3	0.4	2	0.8	21	0.1	0.26	1.8
3A	5	0.6	3	1.2	55	0.2	0.28	1.9
3C	1	0.1	1	0.4	7	0.0	0.2	1.4
4	4	0.5	4	1.6	45	0.1	0.63	4.3
4/5	7	0.8	4	1.6	136	0.4	0	0.0
4A	4	0.5	1	0.4	95	0.3	0.13	0.9
4DR29	8	0.9	6	2.4	101	0.3	0.08	0.5
4F	3	0.4	1	0.4	132	0.4	0.16	1.1
4F2	1	0.1	1	0.4	81	0.2	0.11	0.7
4RT12	1	0.1	1	0.4	15	0.0	0.06	0.4
5	18	2.1	12	4.8	174	0.5	0.17	1.2
5A	8	0.9	3	1.2	342	1.0	0.83	5.6
5DR15/17	7	0.8	4	1.6	30	0.1	0.43	2.9
5DR18	26	3.1	11	4.4	265	0.8	0.44	3.0
5RT1	2	0.2	1	0.4	27	0.1	0.13	0.9
6	2	0.2	2	0.8	7	0.0	0.07	0.5
6DR24/25	7	0.8	4	1.6	41	0.1	0.88	6.0
6DR27	8	0.9	3	1.2	46	0.1	0.24	1.6
6RT9	2	0.2	1	0.4	6	0.0	0	0.0
7	6	0.7	3	1.2	898	2.7	0.1	0.7
7EWAL	3	0.4	2	0.8	404	1.2	0.24	1.6
7G238	1	0.1	1	0.4	759	2.3	0.32	2.2
8	34	4.0	11	4.4	1001	3.0	0	0.0
8C186	5	0.6	4	1.6	394	1.2	0.15	1.0
8DR2-4	14	1.7	2	0.8	2070	6.3	1	6.8
8DR20	142	16.7	20	8.0	14948	45.1	1.15	7.8
8G	46	5.4	9	3.6	2285	6.9	0	0.0
8RHOD	1	0.1	1	0.4	41	0.1		0.0
9A	6	0.7	2	0.8	86	0.3	0.18	1.2
9B	2	0.2	1	0.4	19	0.1	0.12	0.8
9LA	8	0.9	2	0.8	7	0.0	0	0.0
Total	848	100.0	251	100.0	33112	100.0	14.74	100.0

Table 45 Period 1 pottery assemblage by form

FORMS

Jars are overwhelmingly the dominant form type (32.0/17.9).
Native-style, bead-rimmed jars are the most common type
comprising 66.9% (EVEs) and 27.4% (weight) of all jars.
Beakers are poorly represented, a reflection of the low
quantity of fine wares present, both imported and Romano-
British. Dishes account for 13.6% (EVEs) and of these 50%
(EVEs) are samian forms. Cups account for 8.1% (EVEs),
of which 94.1% (EVEs) are samian, again emphasising the
paucity of other fine wares.

COMPARISON WITH RCP1A

The period 1 assemblage was directly compared with the
quantified data from RCP1A, although the difference in
overall quantities must be noted. The period 1 assemblage

totalled 14.74 EVEs and 33,112g, whereas the total dataset
used for RCP1A was 55.39 EVEs and 102,337g. RCP1A also
covers a longer time span than the dates assigned to period 1.
Despite this, however, the general pattern of assemblage
composition is comparable, with the wares falling into the
same order of importance. This suggests that the early pattern
of ceramic supply to Southwark was the same as in the City,
and that broadly the same range of wares were in circulation
on both sides of the Thames from the outset of occupation.

Comparison of the EVEs data shows that the relative
quantities of each major form type are also very similar in
Open Area 2 and RCP1A. The comparison of Fig 105 with
that published in the ERC (Davies et al 1994, 175, fig 148)
shows that jars are overwhelmingly the dominant form type
in this period. The higher proportion of amphorae from Open

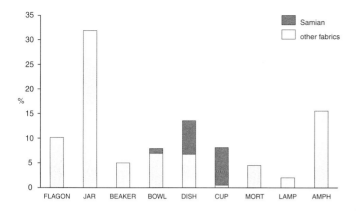

Fig 105 Quantified EVEs data from Open Area 2 by form type

Table 46 Quantified assemblage from Open Area 2 quarry pits

Context	Fabric	Form	Decor	Sherd count	EVEs	Wt
[940]	BAETE	8DR20	-	1		370
[940]	SHEL	2	-	1		48
[940]	SHEL	2A	RLD	12	0.41	506
[5100]	BAETE	8DR20	-	1		2
[5100]	OXID	2	BUD	6		77
[5102]	AHSU	2U	BUD	1	0.17	109
[5102]	BAETE	8DR20	-	8		1369
[5102]	GROG?	2	-	2		91
[5102]	GROG	2T	-	2	0.19	126
[5102]	RHOD2	8RHOD	-	1		41
[5102]	SAND	2	-	1		40
[5102]	SAND	5A	-	2	0.16	160
[5102]	SHEL	2A	-	5	0.28	347
[5152]	GROG	2	-	2		34
[5036]	ECCW	-	-	1		15
[5036]	OXID	-	-	2		32
[5036]	SAND	-	-	1		5
[5038]	BAETE	8DR20	-	1		96
[5038]	GAUL?	8G	-	1		50
[5038]	OXID	2A	-	1	0.18	52
[5038]	RWS	-	-	1		12
[5038]	SAMLG	5DR18	-	3		40
[5038]	SAMLG	6DR27	-	1		12
[6051]	GROG	2T	-	1	0.12	23
Total				58	1.51	3657

Area 2 is probably a reflection of the problems associated with quantifying amphorae and, given the overall smaller dataset, the presence of a complete amphora rim in [873] gives amphorae an inflated value.

Within RCP1A the overall quantities of bowls, dishes and cups are similar, but from Open Area 2 dishes record a higher value than both bowls and cups, and are slightly more abundant than in RCP1A.

The assemblage from Open Area 2 was also compared with the assemblage from 201–211 Borough High Street (Bird et al 1978, 53–176). Although published there is no quantified data available for the 201BHS89 assemblage, but the catalogued vessels include a range comparable to that recorded from Open Area 2. At 201BHS89 the pre-Flavian activity relates to construction of the road with associated channels and ditches. The assemblages recovered from these features (groups 1–8) are represented in the publication by 173 illustrated vessels. Jars are clearly the dominant form, particularly bead-rimmed examples, which form c 40% of the published group (Tyers 1996, 143). The fabrics are commonly unsourced sand, grog or shell-tempered fabrics and few vessels have been sourced to the Romano-British industries, such as Verulamium, Highgate Wood or Alice Holt, Surrey. Some published forms are very closely paralleled by examples from Open Area 2, including the rilled jar with a diamond-shaped rim discussed in Chapter 3. The presence of early wall-sided mortaria, large collared flagons and several dishes with smooth profiles must also be noted as appearing frequently in both assemblages.

The recovery of both assemblages from features associated with the construction of Road 1 and the similarity in composition suggests that the assemblages are broadly contemporary, both dating to within a few years of c AD 50.

QUANTIFIED GROUPS

Quarry pits

(Group 4, subgroups 10 and 12; group 5, subgroup 1100; group 6, subgroup 17; group 42, subgroup 183)
A total assemblage of 58 sherds (3657g/1.51 EVEs) was recovered from the quarry pits in Open Area 2 (Table 46). A relatively limited range of fabrics is represented with only 11 identified, including unsourced SAND, OXID, SHEL and GROG. BAETE, GAUL and RHOD1 are the only amphorae fabrics present and with the addition of four sherds of SAMLG are the only imported wares identified. The pottery from three of the quarry pits is discussed in more detail in Chapter 3 (Fig 16, <P1>–<P6>).

Ditches

(Group 42, subgroup 181; group 42, subgroup 182; group 80, subgroup 395 and 397)
An assemblage of 156 sherds (43 rows), totalling 3629g and 1.82 EVEs, was recovered from ditches in Open Area 2 (Table 47). This assemblage is discussed in more detail in Chapter 3 (Fig 17, <P7>–<P11>).

Dumped deposits

(Group 125, subgroup 544; group 5, subgroup 14; group 6, subgroup 18; group 7, subgroups 19 and 21; group 8, subgroup 22; group 43, subgroups 184, 186, 188 and 189; group 80, subgroup 398; group 116, subgroup 534)
The dumped deposits above the ditches and quarry pits produced a large assemblage of 457 sherds (126 rows) totalling 16,450g and 8.33 EVEs (Table 48). The largest assemblage is from context [873] (group 8, subgroup 22) which is discussed in Chapter 3 (Fig 20, <P12>–<P38>).

Period 2

INTRODUCTION

Percentages for fabrics are given by sherd count; within the brackets this is followed by percentages by 'rows'. Table 49 and Table 50 summarise the period 2 assemblage by fabric and form respectively.

Table 47 *Quantified assemblage from Open Area 2 ditches*

Context	Fabric	Form	Decor	Sherd count	EVEs	Wt
[2210]	SAMLG	4DR29	-	1	0.08	34
[2222]	AMPH	8		3		81
[2222]	BAETE	8DR20	-	1		146
[2222]	OXIDF	-		5		82
[2222]	RWS	-		1	0.17	11
[2222]	SAMLG	6		1	0.07	0
[2223]	AMPH	8		1		106
[2223]	BHWS	1A	-	10	0.5	146
[2223]	CADIZ	8C186	-	2		133
[2223]	ECCW	1	-	4		62
[2223]	FINE	5A	-	3	0.24	49
[2223]	GAUL1	8	-	10		140
[2223]	GROG	2	-	14		649
[2223]	GROG	2	VL	1		9
[2223]	GROG	5	-	1	0.07	9
[2223]	OXID	-	-	7		51
[2223]	OXID	3A	-	1	0.17	18
[2223]	OXIDF	8?	-	9		207
[2223]	RWS	-	-	45		193
[2223]	SAMLG	4	DEC	1		3
[2223]	SAMLG	4DR29	DEC	2		27
[2223]	SAMLG	4DR29	ROD	1		4
[2223]	SAMLG	4DR30/37	DEC	1		14
[2223]	SAMLG	4RT12	-	1	0.06	15
[2223]	SAMLG	5DR18	-	4		41
[2223]	SAND	2T	-	2	0.2	45
[6039]	GAUL	8G	-	3		104
[6039]	GAUL1	8G	-	1		105
[6039]	SAMCG	6DR33	-	1	0.1	5
[6039]	SAMLG	5	-	1		2
[6039]	SAMLG	6DR24/25	ROD	1	0.16	19
[6040]	AMPH	8	-	1		12
[6040]	BAETE	8DR20	-	3		687
[6040]	ECCW	-	-	1		36
[6040]	GROG	2	-	1		128
[6040]	HOO	-	-	1		5
[6040]	OXID	-	-	3		38
[6040]	OXID	1?	-	1		35
[6040]	RWS	-	-	1		20
[6040]	SAND	-	-	1		9
[6040]	SHEL	2	-	2		88
[6046]	HWB	2	-	1		26
[6046]	VRW	-	-	1		35
Total				156	1.82	3629

Table 48 *Quantified assemblage from Open Area 2 dumped deposits*

Context	Fabric	Form	Decor	Sherd count	EVEs	Wt
[873]	AHSU	2	-	10		139
[873]	AHSU	2	BUD	1		18
[873]	AHSU?	2A	-	1	0.16	17
[873]	AHSU	2A?	ALX	1		13
[873]	AHSU	2T	-	2	0.16	33
[873]	AHSU	5	-	1	0.1	13
[873]	AMPH	8	-	5		153
[873]	AMPH	8DR2-4?	-	1		137
[873]	BAETE	8DR20	-	9	1	2880
[873]	BAETE	8DR20	<1850>	1		391
[873]	CADIZ?	8C186	-	1		60
[873]	COLEC	3	RCD1	2		14
[873]	COLWW	7	-	2		70
[873]	COLWW?	7EWAL	-	2	0.24	348
[873]	ECCW	1	-	2		90
[873]	ERSB	2	-	6		92
[873]	ERSB	2	BUD	1		31
[873]	ERSB	2T	-	3	0.1	11
[873]	ERSI	2A	-	2	0.14	39
[873]	ERSI	2A7-8	-	2	0.16	62
[873]	GAUL1	8G	-	18		954
[873]	GAUL2?	8	-	1		90
[873]	GROG	2	-	32		377
[873]	GROG	2A	-	1	0.07	18
[873]	GROG	2V	-	1	0.05	58
[873]	HOO	-	-	6		33
[873]	HOO	3A?	ROD	1		3
[873]	HWB	2	-	13		311
[873]	HWB	2A	-	1	0.15	26
[873]	HWB	2A1-4	-	1	0.04	9
[873]	HWB	2T	-	2	0.24	16
[873]	HWB	5	-	1		8
[873]	HWB	5A	-	3	0.43	133
[873]	LYON	9LA	<1152>	5		0
[873]	NFSE	1A		1	1	540
[873]	NKSH?	2	-	1		36
[873]	OXID		--	4		59
[873]	OXID	1	-	2		129
[873]	OXID	2	-	1		9
[873]	OXID	2A	-	2	0.08	58
[873]	OXID	3C	-	1	0.2	7
[873]	OXID	4A	-	4	0.13	95
[873]	OXID	7	SPT	1		43
[873]	OXID	7EWAL	-	1		56
[873]	OXID	9A	-	4	0.18	53
[873]	OXIDF	-	-	30		257
[873]	PRW3	5	-	1		9
[873]	SAMLG	-	-	2		8
[873]	SAMLG	4	<1791>	1		29
[873]	SAMLG	4DR29	DEC	2		18
[873]	SAMLG	5	-	4		36
[873]	SAMLG	5	<1793>	1		2
[873]	SAMLG	5	ROD	1		6
[873]	SAMLG	5DR15/17	-	1		3
[873]	SAMLG	5DR18	-	3	0.13	21
[873]	SAMLG	5DR18	<1792>	1		26
[873]	SAMLG	5DR18	<1794>	1		33
[873]	SAMLG	6	-	1		7
[873]	SAMLG	6DR24/25	ROD	4	0.72	15
[873]	SAMLG		-	6	0.24	32
[873]	SAND	2	-	27		263
[873]	SAND	2	BUD	2		28
[873]	SAND	2	VL	1		32
[873]	SEAL	9B	-	2	0.12	19

AMPHORAE

BAETE remains the dominant amphorae type, accounting for 67.2% of all amphorae, and amongst the assemblage as a whole is one of the most abundant types (19.6/9.2). GAUL1 (4.8/3.7) is also an important component, accounting for 16.4% of all amphorae. One sherd of Cam. 189, commonly known as the 'carrot' amphora, and 15 sherds of GAUL3 Dressel 2-4 are recorded from this period, but otherwise the range of amphorae is unchanged from period 1.

(Table 48 cont)

Context	Fabric	Form	Decor	Sherd count	EVEs	Wt
[873]	SESH	2A	-	I	0.11	13
[873]	SHEL	2	-	5		82
[873]	SHEL	2A	-	I	0.08	15
[873]	VRG	-	-	I		9
[873]	VRW	-	-	9		87
[873]	VRW?	7	-	3	0.1	785
[877]	BAETE	8DR20	-	I		14
[877]	CADIZ	8C186	-	I		89
[877]	GROG	-	-	2		12
[877]	GROG	2T	-	2	0.05	16
[918]	AMPH	8	-	I		37
[918]	LYON	9LA	-	3		7
[918]	OXID	-		-2		9
[918]	OXID	2		-I		11
[918]	OXID	2A		-I	0.15	30
[918]	SHEL	2A		-I	0.09	13
[2232]	AHSU	2		-I		9
[2232]	AMPH	8		-I		11
[2232]	BAETE	8		-I		115
[2232]	GROG	2		-2		36
[2232]	OXID	-		-4		31
[2232]	OXID	-	RCD I	I		9
[2232]	OXID	9A		-2		33
[2232]	SAMLG	-	-	I		3
[2232]	SAND	-	-	I		11
[2232]	SHEL	2	-	I		9
[5014]	HOO	-	-	I		9
[5066]	ECCW	-	-	I		16
[5066]	NFSE?	-	-	I		66
[5084]	OXID	-	-	I		138
[5095]	GAUL	8G	-	2		27
[5095]	SAMLG	5DR15/17	-	2	0.12	6
[5098]	BAETE	8DR20	-	10	0.15	1771
[5098]	GAUL	8G	-	I		15
[5098]	OXID	3A	RPD	3	0.11	34
[5098]	SAMLG	5RT I	-	2	0.13	27
[6036]	SAMLG	5DR18	-	I	0.08	14
[6038]	GAUL	8G	-	16		812
[6041]	BAETE	8DR20	-	3		534
[6041]	CADIZ	8C186	-	I	0.15	112
[6041]	FINE	3	-	I	0.26	7
[6041]	FMIC	-	-	I		0
[6041]	GAUL	8G	-	3		198
[6041]	GROG	2	-	I		37
[6041]	NFSE	7G238	-	I	0.32	759
[6041]	OXID	-	-	I		0
[6041]	RWS	-	-	I		14
[6041]	SAMLG	5DR15/17	-	3	0.21	12
[6053]	BAETE	8DR20	-	I		291
[6053]	GROG	2	-	I		75
[6053]	SAMLG	4DR29	DEC	I		4
[6053]	VRW	-	-	I		45
[6061]	SAMLG	4	DEC	I		
[6061]	SAMLG	5DR18	-	2	0.04	16
[6061]	SAMLG	6DR27	-	I		2
[6061]	SAND	2	-	3		34
[6061]	SAND	2A	-	2	0.2	42
[6061]	VRW	I	-	I		61
[6079]	SAMLG	5DR18	-	7	0.04	46
[7096]	BAETE	8DR20	-	2		220
[7096]	OXID	-	-	I		12
[7096]	SAMLG	5DR18	-	2	0.1	23
[7146]	BAETE	8DR20	-	70		899
Total				457	8.33	16450

Table 49 Period 2 pottery assemblage by fabric

Fabric	Sherd count	% sherds	Rows	% rows
AHSU	84	5.4	31	5.8
AMPH	15	1.0	11	2.1
AMPH1	6	0.4	3	0.6
AMPH2	1	0.1	1	0.2
BAETE	303	19.6	49	9.2
BHWS	3	0.2	3	0.6
CADIZ	24	1.5	11	2.1
COAR	28	1.8	7	1.3
COLWW	13	0.8	5	0.9
ECCW	1	0.1	1	0.2
ERMS	42	2.7	18	3.4
ERSB	7	0.5	6	1.1
FINE	4	0.3	2	0.4
FMIC	10	0.6	6	1.1
GAUL	5	0.3	5	0.9
GAUL1	74	4.8	20	3.7
GAUL2	6	0.4	4	0.7
GAUL3	15	1.0	3	0.6
GROG	111	7.2	43	8.0
HOO	8	0.5	8	1.5
HWB	160	10.3	25	4.7
LYON	14	0.9	2	0.4
MORT	5	0.3	1	0.2
NFSE	27	1.7	10	1.9
NKSH	20	1.3	2	0.4
OXID	70	4.5	33	6.2
OXIDF	4	0.3	2	0.4
PRW	1	0.1	1	0.2
PRW1	2	0.1	2	0.4
RDBK	16	1.0	5	0.9
RHOD2	2	0.1	1	0.2
RVOX	4	0.3	2	0.4
RWS	13	0.8	8	1.5
SAMLG	178	11.5	90	16.8
SAND	109	7.0	44	8.2
SHEL	12	0.8	10	1.9
SLOW	4	0.3	4	0.7
SPAN	2	0.1	2	0.4
SUG	12	0.8	2	0.4
TN	2	0.1	2	0.4
TNIM	5	0.3	3	0.6
TNMIC	2	0.1	1	0.2
VCWS	3	0.2	2	0.4
VRG	2	0.1	1	0.2
VRW	120	7.7	43	8.0
Total	1549	100.0	535	100.0

REDUCED WARES

The slight increase in AHSU (5.4/5.8) conforms with the general pattern in the City. HWB, however, is still dominant (10.3/4.7), accounting for 27.3% of all reduced wares, with other unsourced GROG (7.2/8.0) also well represented at 18.9%. ERMS has slightly increased in quantity from period 1, confirming that it has a similar date of circulation as in the City. ERSB is also first recorded in this period.

OXIDISED WARES

Unsourced OXID and OXIDF fabrics (4.5/6.2; 0.3/0.4) are still a considerable component of the assemblage and account for 26.9% of all oxidised wares. However, VRW

Table 50 Period 2 pottery assemblage by form

Form	Sherd count	% sherd count	Rows	% rows
-	236	15.2	123	23.0
I	41	2.6	16	3.0
IA	14	0.9	3	0.6
IJ	24	1.5	4	0.7
2	181	11.7	82	15.3
2/3	2	0.1	2	0.4
2A	32	2.1	19	3.6
2A1-4	100	6.5	1	0.2
2A16	1	0.1	1	0.2
2B	9	0.6	7	1.3
2C	2	0.1	1	0.2
2K	15	1.0	1	0.2
2M	2	0.1	1	0.2
2N	25	1.6	1	0.2
2T	27	1.7	10	1.9
2V	67	4.3	10	1.9
3	14	0.9	5	0.9
3A	13	0.8	4	0.7
3B	13	0.8	1	0.2
4	7	0.5	6	1.1
4/5	9	0.6	5	0.9
4A	2	0.1	1	0.2
4DR29	72	4.6	24	4.5
4DR30	1	0.1	1	0.2
4F	4	0.3	3	0.6
4K	3	0.2	2	0.4
4P	3	0.2	2	0.4
4RT12	5	0.3	3	0.6
5	20	1.3	9	1.7
5A	3	0.2	2	0.4
5B	4	0.3	2	0.4
5DR15/17	18	1.2	10	1.9
5DR18	34	2.2	18	3.4
5DR18R	4	0.3	2	0.4
5J	1	0.1	1	0.2
5RT1	1	0.1	1	0.2
6	3	0.2	3	0.6
6DR24/25	1	0.1	1	0.2
6DR27	11	0.7	9	1.7
6RT8	1	0.1	1	0.2
7	5	0.3	5	0.9
7EWAL	1	0.1	1	0.2
7G238	1	0.1	1	0.2
7HOF	38	2.5	8	1.5
8	53	3.4	23	4.3
8IJ	1	0.1	1	0.2
8C186	24	1.5	11	2.1
8DR2-4	18	1.2	6	1.1
8DR20	261	16.8	40	7.5
8DR20PW15	7	0.5	1	0.2
8DR20PW8	2	0.1	2	0.4
8DR20PW9	19	1.2	1	0.2
8G	70	4.5	19	3.6
8G4	2	0.1	2	0.4
8H70	3	0.2	1	0.2
8L555	6	0.4	4	0.7
8RHOD	2	0.1	1	0.2
9A	3	0.2	3	0.6
9B	1	0.1	1	0.2
9C	2	0.1	1	0.2
9D	2	0.1	2	0.4
9LA	2	0.1	2	0.4
9NP	1	0.1	1	0.2
Total	1549	100.0	535	100.0

has substantially increased (7.7/8.0) and in this period accounts for 43.6% of all oxidised wares.

SLOW appears in this period, but only in very small quantities (0.3/0.7). In the City SLOW occurs in most Neronian assemblages and is considered a diagnostic ware for the pre-Boudican period. It has a variable distribution, being abundant only at the type site, Sugar Loaf Court (SLO82) and at 5–12 Fenchurch Street (FEN83). From Southwark SLOW has also been found at the Courage's Brewery sites (COSE84), 52 Southwark Street (52SOS89), Park Street (PRK90) (Cowan in prep) and 51–53 Southwark Street (Precious 1997) but again only in small quantities. At 52SOS89 the quantified data records SLOW at 1.2% by weight and 3.2% by EVEs of the total assemblage.

In RCP1A SLOW accounts for almost half of all oxidised wares, which even when considered to be an inflated figure due to the inclusion of data from SLO82 and FEN83, is a figure nowhere near matched by any assemblage from Southwark to date. However, it must also be noted that few other excavations in Southwark have produced extensive pre-Boudican activity.

FINE WARES

SAMLG (11.5/16.8) remains the dominant imported fine ware, although a LYON beaker and PRW1 are also present. SPAN is represented by fragments from a lamp. Gallo-Belgic wares are present in this period with small quantities of TN, TNMIC and TNIM.

FORMS

The range and proportions of forms recorded is very similar to period 1. Tazze are recorded for the first time in this period and highly Romanised vessel types, such as mortaria and flagons, have increased in proportion. Flagons are represented by collared rim (1A) and small double-handled types (1J). Mortaria with hooked flanges appear in this period alongside the early wall-sided type.

QUANTIFIED GROUPS

Destruction of Building 5
(Group 102)
The destruction horizon of Building 5 produced an assemblage of 235 sherds (9562g/1.9 EVEs) (Table 51), which is discussed in Chapter 4 (Fig 27, <P40>–<P42>).

Open Area 8 pits
(Group 184, subgroups 1020, 1021, 1022 and 1023)
The assemblages from the four pits in Open Area 8 were quantified and are discussed in Chapter 4 (Fig 30, <P44>–<P52>).

A total number of 278 sherds (53 rows) were recovered from these pits (20,122g/2.95 EVEs) (Table 52). The assemblage is dominated by tempered wares, which account for 59.7% by sherd count (7881g; 2.12 EVEs); reduced wares and amphorae are the next most common types. The high figure for tempered wares is made up of: HWB 102 sherds (2095g; 0.64 EVEs), GROG 44 sherds (3236g; 0.48 EVEs), NKSH 18 sherds (2529g; 1.0 EVEs) and SHEL 2 sherds (21g; 0.0 EVEs). A small range of amphorae is present with BAETE Dressel 20, CADIZ Cam. form 186 and GAUL2 London 555. The only imported fine ware recorded is SAMLG.

Table 51 Quantified assemblage from destruction of Building 5

Context	Fabric	Form	Decor	Sherd count	EVEs	Wt
[5047]	BAETE	8DR20	-	6		1664
[5047]	SAMLG	-	-	1		1
[5047]	SAMLG	4DR29DEC		1		6
[5047]	SAMLG	4DR29ROD		1		4
[5047]	SAMLG	5DR18	-	7	0.17	38
[5048]	AHSU	2	-	3		7
[5048]	BAETE	8DR20	-	1		394
[5048]	SAMLG	-	-	3		9
[5048]	SAMLG	5DR18	-	1		3
[5048]	SAND	4	-	1		27
[5048]	VRW	-	-	3		9
[5068]	AHSU	2	-	2		9
[5068]	AMPH?	8	-	1		395
[5068]	BAETE	8DR20	-	84		4525
[5068]	BAETE	8DR20	-	1		295
[5068]	ECCW	-	-	2		23
[5068]	ERMS	2	VL	1		6
[5068]	ERSI	2	-	5		69
[5068]	FMIC	-	-	1		9
[5068]	GAUL	8G	-	7		270
[5068]	GROG	-	-	5		49
[5068]	GROG	2A1-4	-	1	0.15	40
[5068]	GROG	2V	STAB	34	0.3	652
[5068]	OXID	-	-	3		24
[5068]	RWS	3	ROD	2	0.1	14
[5068]	SAMLG	3?	ROD	1		1
[5068]	SAMLG	5DR18	-	2		39
[5068]	SAMLG	6DR27	-	1	0.1	2
[5068]	SAND	2		2		14
[5068]	SAND	4M35	-	38	0.77	527
[5068]	VRR	-	-	1		73
[5068]	VRW	-	-	9		159
[5068]	VRW	1	-	1		42
[5028]	BAETE	8DR20	-	1		113
[5028]	SAMLG	5DR18	-	1	0.05	2
[5028]	VRW	1B1	-	1	0.26	48
Total				235	1.9	9562

Table 52 Quantified assemblage from Open Area 8 pits

Context	Fabric	Form	Decor	Sherd count	EVEs	Wt
[4137]	VRW	-	-	2	0	11
[4142]	OXID	-	-	1	0	10
[4144]	AHSU	2	-	1	0	10
[4144]	BAETE	8DR20	-	30	0	9645
[4144]	CADIZ	8C186	-	1	0	211
[4144]	FMIC	-	-	1	0	25
[4144]	GROG	-	-	3	0	36
[4144]	HWB	2A	-	1	0.11	62
[4144]	HWB	2A1-4	-	100	0.28	1382
[4144]	NKSH	7HOF	SPT	18	1	2529
[4144]	OXIDF	-	-	3	0	27
[4144]	SAND	-	-	1	0	4
[4144]	SAND	2/3	-	1	0.05	9
[4144]	SHEL	-	-	2	0	21
[4144]	VRW	7HOF	-	3	0	205
[4146]	AHSU	-	-	5	0	12
[4146]	BAETE	8DR20	-	1	0	428
[4146]	SAMLG	6	-	1	0	2
[4147]	SAMLG	4	DEC	1	0	4
[4147]	SAMLG	4DR29	DEC	2	0.11	29
[4147]	SAMLG	5	-	1	0.05	2
[4148]	BAETE	8DR20	-	1	0	231
[4148]	ERMS	2	-	2	0	42
[4148]	ERMS	2	VL	1	0	9
[4148]	ERMS	2B	-	1	0.11	20
[4148]	GROG	-	-	1	0	14
[4148]	RDBK	3	BDD	1	0	14
[4148]	VRW	-	-	1	0	21
[4150]	ERMS	2	-	1	0	11
[4150]	HWB	2	-	1	0.25	93
[4150]	OXID	7	SPT	1	0	54
[4151]	GAUL2	8L555	-	1	0	287
[4151]	NFSE	7G238	-	1	0	104
[4151]	OXID	-	-	1	0	8
[4151]	SAMLG	-	-	1	0	2
[4151]	SAMLG	5DR18	-	1	0	4
[4151]	SAND	3A	BUD	4	0	116
[4152]	GROG	4F?	-	1	0	19
[4153]	SAMLG	4	DEC	1	0	6
[4154]	AHSU	5	-	8	0.15	87
[4155]	ERMS	2	VL	8	0	42
[4155]	GROG	2V	COMB	9	0.15	634
[4155]	SAMLG	5DR18	-	1	0.1	9
[4155]	TN	5J	-	1	0.11	16
[4155]	VRW	-	-	1	0	4
[4156]	AHSU	2	-	1	0	74
[4156]	AHSU	2A	-	1	0.15	73
[4156]	ERMS	2B	VL	3	0	46
[4156]	GROG	2V	COMB	30	0.33	2533
[4156]	SAMLG	4DR30	DEC	1	0	11
[4160]	ERMS	-	-	10	0	13
[4161]	SAMLG	4DR29	DEC	1	0	4
[4161]	SAND	3A	BUD	2	0	38
Total				278	2.95	19303

Period 3

INTRODUCTION

As the majority of the period 3 assemblage is derived from the destruction of buildings and open areas in use in the previous period it is not surprising that the assemblage is very similar to that of period 2. The fire horizon encapsulates a short-lived event and provides a 'snapshot' of wares in circulation at the time of the fire, but also undoubtedly includes redeposited material from the earlier period. Consequently, there are no new fabrics or forms introduced in this period and the assemblage has an overall date-range of AD 55–60.

The RCP1A includes assemblages from the Boudican fire horizon and uses it as a dividing point between RCP1A and RCP1B (Davies et al 1994, 166). As RCP1A covers a date-range equal to BGH95 periods 1, 2 and 3, the assemblages from these periods have been amalgamated for comparison (Table 53). Table 54 and Table 55 summarise the period 3 assemblage by fabric and form respectively.

Our current fabric codes are assigned to one of eight ware categories, but the ERC uses five, combining reduced and tempered wares together under REDU and imported (FNMP), Romano-British (FNRB) and reduced fine wares (FNRD) under one grouping of FINE (Davies et al 1994, 168, table 2). Table 53 shows the combined data for periods 1–3 amalgamated and

Ware	Periods 1–3 combined Sherd count	% sherd count	Rows	% rows	RCP1A Weight	% weight	EVEs	%EVEs
AMPH	763	25.8	177	18.2	41054	40.1	2.58	4.7
OXID	582	19.7	223	23.0	24915	24.4	4.85	34.2
REDU	1073	36.3	341	35.1	32069	31.3	22.08	40.0
FINE	163	5.5	49	5.0	1003	0.9	2.35	4.2
SAM	372	12.6	181	18.6	3296	3.2	9.41	17.0
Total	2953	100.0	971	100.0	102337	100.0	41.27	100.0

Table 53 Combined pottery data for periods 1, 2 and 3 with comparative data from RCP1A

Table 54 Period 3 pottery assemblage by fabric

Fabric	Sherd count	% sherd count	Rows	% rows
AHSU	9	1.6	5	2.7
AMPH	6	1.1	4	2.2
BAETE	35	6.3	12	6.5
BHWS	6	1.1	1	0.5
CADIZ	4	0.7	3	1.6
COLWW	4	0.7	3	1.6
ECCW	2	0.4	2	1.1
ERMS	28	5.0	8	4.3
ERSA	1	0.2	1	0.5
ERSB	4	0.7	2	1.1
FINE	14	2.5	7	3.8
FMIC	55	9.9	2	1.1
GAUL	2	0.4	1	0.5
GAUL1	23	4.1	2	1.1
GAUL2	9	1.6	1	0.5
GROG	61	11.0	16	8.6
GROGSH	7	1.3	2	1.1
HOO	9	1.6	3	1.6
HWB	34	6.1	12	6.5
HWBR	2	0.4	1	0.5
LYON	2	0.4	1	0.5
NKSH	2	0.4	1	0.5
OXID	25	4.5	11	5.9
OXIDF	1	0.2	1	0.5
RDBK	8	1.4	2	1.1
RWS	16	2.9	5	2.7
SAMLG	104	18.7	41	22.2
SAND	45	8.1	20	10.8
SLOW	4	0.7	2	1.1
TN	6	1.1	1	0.5
TNIM	1	0.2	1	0.5
VRW	27	4.9	11	5.9
Total	556	100.0	185	100.0

Table 55 Period 3 pottery assemblage by form

Form	Sherd count	% sherd count	Rows	% rows
-	138	24.8	53	28.6
1	12	2.2	5	2.7
1A	2	0.4	1	0.5
2	68	12.2	23	12.4
2/3	6	1.1	1	0.5
2A	17	3.1	6	3.2
2A1-4	6	1.1	3	1.6
2A7-8	1	0.2	1	0.5
2B	18	3.2	3	1.6
2T	11	2.0	5	2.7
2V	8	1.4	3	1.6
3	3	0.5	2	1.1
3A	4	0.7	1	0.5
3B	6	1.1	1	0.5
3C	4	0.7	3	1.6
4	3	0.5	3	1.6
4/5	1	0.2	1	0.5
4A	2	0.4	2	1.1
4DR29	35	6.3	8	4.3
4DR30	1	0.2	1	0.5
4MX	53	9.5	1	0.5
4RT12	3	0.5	3	1.6
5	7	1.3	3	1.6
5A	2	0.4	2	1.1
5DR15/17	17	3.1	6	3.2
5DR18	11	2.0	2	1.1
5J	6	1.1	1	0.5
6DR24/25	2	0.4	1	0.5
6DR27	11	2.0	4	2.2
6DR35	1	0.2	1	0.5
6RT8	1	0.2	1	0.5
7	2	0.4	2	1.1
7HOF	4	0.7	2	1.1
8	12	2.2	7	3.8
8IJ	2	0.4	1	0.5
8C186	4	0.7	3	1.6
8DR20	32	5.8	10	5.4
8DR20PW8	1	0.2	1	0.5
8G	23	4.1	2	1.1
8L555	9	1.6	1	0.5
9A	3	0.5	2	1.1
9B	1	0.2	1	0.5
9LA	2	0.4	1	0.5
9RT13	1	0.2	1	0.5
Total	556	100.0	185	100.0

grouped in the same way to allow comparisons to be made. The data for RCP1A is available as quantified weight and EVEs values, but for periods 1–3 combined only sherd count and 'rows' are available.

The study using the ceramic records from Leadenhall Court and other City sites found that the quantified data used for RCP1B and RCP2 compared well with the presence or 'rows' data. Although not as preferable as directly comparable data, the use of the presence or 'rows' data does increase the scope for analysis using the database created during spot-dating. Within the Leadenhall Court study the qualitative data proved valuable when used within contemporary chronological periods (for further discussion of this methodology see Davies 1993, 137).

As Table 53 shows, this would appear to be the case when comparing the pre-Boudican assemblages from BGH95 with the quantified data from RCP1A. The figure for amphorae is the most inconsistent between the four types of data, which probably

Table 56 *Quantified assemblage from Open Area 10 (Building 4 destruction)*

Context	Fabric	Form	Decor	Sherd count	EVEs	Wt
[999]	BAETE	8DR20	-	6	0	848
[999]	ERMS	2T	BUD	4	0.18	83
[999]	FINE	2/3	COMB	6	0	47
[999]	GROG	-	-	16	0	196
[999]	GROG	-	BUD	4	0	27
[999]	GROG	2	BUD	4	0	67
[999]	GROG	2A	-	1	0.14	23
[999]	GROGSH	-	-	5	0	54
[999]	GROGSH	2	BUD	2	0	7
[999]	HWB	2	-	8	0	445
[999]	HWB	2A1-4	-	2	0.2	152
[999]	HWB	2V	-	5	0.3	295
[999]	SAMLG	5DR18	-	1	0.05	5
[999]	VRW	-	-	1	0	7
Total				**65**	**0.87**	**2256**

Table 57 *Period 4 pottery assemblage by fabric*

Fabric	Sherd count	% sherd count	Rows	% rows
AHSU	389	8.5	141	8.5
AMPBS	11	0.2	2	0.1
AMPH	78	1.7	47	2.8
AMPH1	6	0.1	4	0.2
AMPH2	1	0.0	1	0.1
BAET	2	0.0	2	0.1
BAETE	633	13.9	110	6.6
BB1	2	0.0	1	0.1
BHWS	29	0.6	9	0.5
C186	9	0.2	1	0.1
C189	9	0.2	3	0.2
CADIZ	26	0.6	20	1.2
CAMP1	2	0.0	2	0.1
CC	2	0.0	2	0.1
CCGW	3	0.1	1	0.1
CGGW	1	0.0	1	0.1
CGWH	3	0.1	1	0.1
COAR	17	0.4	4	0.2
COLWW	3	0.1	3	0.2
ECCW	25	0.5	5	0.3
ERMS	272	6.0	53	3.2
ERSA/B	17	0.4	4	0.2
ERSB	56	1.2	25	1.5
ERSI	6	0.1	2	0.1
FINE	30	0.7	20	1.2
FLIN	1	0.0	1	0.1
FMIC	121	2.7	61	3.7
G238	1	0.0	1	0.1
GAUL	29	0.6	14	0.8
GAUL1	77	1.7	35	2.1
GAUL2	85	1.9	4	0.2
GAUL3	5	0.1	2	0.1
GROG	161	3.5	68	4.1
HOO	45	1.0	19	1.1
HWB	146	3.2	59	3.6
HWBR	1	0.0	1	0.1
HWC	71	1.6	44	2.7
ITMO	1	0.0	1	0.1
LIPR	2	0.0	1	0.1
LOEG	2	0.0	1	0.1
LOMI	7	0.2	4	0.2
LOXI	2	0.0	2	0.1
LYON	8	0.2	3	0.2
MICA	3	0.1	2	0.1
MLEZ	2	0.0	2	0.1
NFSE	23	0.5	15	0.9
NKGW	1	0.0	1	0.1
NKSH	76	1.7	24	1.4
OXID	110	2.4	58	3.5
OXIDF	28	0.6	11	0.7
PRW3	3	0.1	1	0.1
RDBK	22	0.5	14	0.8
RHOD1	1	0.0	1	0.1
RHOD2	31	0.7	10	0.6
RVOX	3	0.1	3	0.2
RWS	36	0.8	23	1.4
SAM	4	0.1	3	0.2
SAMLG	709	15.6	340	20.5
SAND	489	10.7	156	9.4
SESH	1	0.0	1	0.1
SHEL	28	0.6	12	0.7
SLOW	3	0.1	2	0.1
TN	4	0.1	1	0.1
TNIM	3	0.1	2	0.1
VCWS	14	0.3	11	0.7
VRG	15	0.3	11	0.7
VRR	1	0.0	1	0.1
VRW	551	12.1	166	10.0
Total	**4558**	**100.0**	**1656**	**100.0**

reflects the problems associated with quantifying amphorae more than any significant difference in the assemblages. Amphorae as a type, because of their shape and size, are frequently over-represented by weight and underestimated by EVEs.

Aside from amphorae, the wares fall into the same order, with reduced wares dominant, followed by oxidised, samian and finally fine wares. The direct comparison between the quantified data from period 1 and RCP1A showed the assemblages to be very similar and this is still the case when the qualitative data from all three pre-Boudican periods are compared.

QUANTIFIED GROUPS

Open Area 10
(Context [999])
The assemblage from the
in situ destruction of Building 4 was quantified by weight and EVEs (Table 56). This assemblage is discussed in Chapter 4 (Fig 41, <P64>– <P67>).

Period 4

INTRODUCTION
Period 4 at BGH95 is dated AD 60/1–100 and stratigraphically post-dates the fire horizon. Table 57 and Table 58 summarise the period 4 assemblage by fabric and form respectively.

AMPHORAE
The range of amphorae is similar to the pre-Boudican assemblage, although the Lipari Richborough 527 amphora appears for the first time in this period; in the City it is also first identified in RCP1B (Davies et al 1994, 186). BAETE still accounts for 61.2% of all amphorae.

REDUCED WARES
HWB is still a dominant fabric amongst the assemblage as a whole, but by this period it accounts for only 8.0% of all reduced wares. The variant HWBR is recorded in this period,

Table 58 Period 4 pottery assemblage by form   (Table 58 cont)

Form	Sherd count	% sherd count	Rows	% rows
-	1241	27.2	464	28.0
1	90	2.0	28	1.7
1A	9	0.2	5	0.3
1B	8	0.2	7	0.4
1B1	1	0.0	1	0.1
1B2	6	0.1	4	0.2
1B3	2	0.0	2	0.1
1B6	1	0.0	1	0.1
1E	9	0.2	3	0.2
1J	4	0.1	2	0.1
2	456	10.0	195	11.8
2/3	15	0.3	6	0.4
2A	141	3.1	31	1.9
2A1-4	2	0.0	2	0.1
2A15	23	0.5	4	0.2
2A16	4	0.1	1	0.1
2B	116	2.5	21	1.3
2C	8	0.2	6	0.4
2D	32	0.7	4	0.2
2E	3	0.1	1	0.1
2F	2	0.0	1	0.1
2G	1	0.0	1	0.1
2M	16	0.4	3	0.2
2R	7	0.2	2	0.1
2T	157	3.4	48	2.9
2V	106	2.3	18	1.1
3	37	0.8	24	1.4
3A	13	0.3	8	0.5
3B	15	0.3	7	0.4
3C	5	0.1	3	0.2
3DE67	12	0.3	4	0.2
3E	1	0.0	1	0.1
3F	16	0.4	8	0.5
3G	4	0.1	4	0.2
4	56	1.2	37	2.2
4/5	30	0.7	18	1.1
4A	13	0.3	8	0.5
4B	1	0.0	1	0.1
4D	4	0.1	1	0.1
4DR29	176	3.9	55	3.3
4DR30/37	1	0.0	1	0.1
4DR37	15	0.3	9	0.5
4F	28	0.6	18	1.1
4FI	3	0.1	1	0.1
4K	25	0.5	5	0.3
4M34	2	0.0	1	0.1
4M35	38	0.8	1	0.1
4MX	2	0.0	2	0.1
4P	3	0.1	2	0.1
4RT12	16	0.4	7	0.4
5	52	1.1	35	2.1
5A	9	0.2	4	0.2
5B	8	0.2	5	0.3
5DR15/17	45	1.0	25	1.5
5DR18	129	2.8	53	3.2
5DR18R	4	0.1	4	0.2
5DR35/36	7	0.2	5	0.3
5DR42	4	0.1	1	0.1
5J	6	0.1	4	0.2
5J3	5	0.1	2	0.1
5RT1	1	0.0	1	0.1
6	24	0.5	18	1.1
6B	1	0.0	1	0.1
6DR24/25	4	0.1	3	0.2
6DR27	93	2.0	39	2.4
6DR33	2	0.0	2	0.1
6DR33A	1	0.0	1	0.1
6DR35	6	0.1	3	0.2
6RT8	1	0.0	1	0.1
7	28	0.6	23	1.4
7EWAL	1	0.0	1	0.1
7G236	3	0.1	2	0.1
7G238	2	0.0	2	0.1
7HOF	32	0.7	28	1.7
8	127	2.8	76	4.6
8IJ	26	0.6	6	0.4
8C139	1	0.0	1	0.1
8C184	4	0.1	2	0.1
8C186	29	0.6	16	1.0
8C189	6	0.1	2	0.1
8DR2-4	27	0.6	11	0.7
8DR20	576	12.6	91	5.5
8DR20PW12	3	0.1	2	0.1
8DR20PW17	2	0.0	2	0.1
8DR20PW9	1	0.0	1	0.1
8G	76	1.7	32	1.9
8G5	1	0.0	1	0.1
8H70	41	0.9	9	0.5
8KOAN	1	0.0	1	0.1
8L555	85	1.9	4	0.2
8R527	2	0.0	1	0.1
8RHOD	26	0.6	8	0.5
9A	68	1.5	35	2.1
9B	1	0.0	1	0.1
9C	4	0.1	1	0.1
9RT13	3	0.1	2	0.1
9NP	4	0.1	1	0.1
Total	4558	100.0	1656	100.0

which again is the same as in the City, when it first occurs in RCP1B. HWC comprises 1.5% of the assemblage as a whole and 3.5% of all reduced wares, whilst AHSU now accounts for 22.3% of all reduced wares. ERMS has also increased to 15.7% of all reduced wares. Of the Early Roman Sandy wares, ERSA/B comprises 0.4% of the assemblage as a whole, but the more Romanised variant ERSB is more abundant, comprising 1.2% of the assemblage and accounting for 3.2% of all reduced wares. Most significantly, unsourced GROG has now fallen to 3.6% of the assemblage as a whole, compared to 8.4% of the pre-Boudican assemblage (periods 1–3 combined).

BB1 is also present in this period and has not been deemed intrusive on the basis that the two sherds were recovered from the backfill of Structure 2 and may date to the early Trajanic period and thus the latest phase of period 4. Rare sherds of BB1 have been found in the City from layers sealed by Hadrianic fire deposits, assigned to RCP3. The quantity is so small that if the sherds are intrusive the figures are not substantially altered.

OXIDISED WARES

VRW is now dominant, accounting for 63.1% of all oxidised wares. The white-slipped ware from the same region, BHWS, accounts for 3.4% of all oxidised wares by this period. LOXI is also present in this period although it was recovered from the disuse of Building 16 and certainly dates to the latest phase.

FINE WARES

The fine wares are still dominated by SAMLG, but MLEZ is also present. A wider range of Romano-British fine wares are present in this period, and evidence from the City shows that these become increasingly important from this period and throughout the 2nd century. Mica-dusted wares LOMI and MICA are present, as is LOEG, although all are in relatively small quantities. RDBK accounts for 11.5% of all Romano-British fine wares and 10.7% of all non-samian fine wares. Non-samian imported fine wares are still scarce, but the range has increased with the appearance of wares from central Gaul (CGGW and CGWH).

FORMS

A number of new forms appear in period 4 and in general a wider variety of forms are present; this is particularly true of the more 'Romanised' types such as flagons and mortaria. Flagons now include a range of ring-necked types alongside the collared-rimmed examples found in periods 1–3. Also present in period 4 is the squat two-handled type with a beaded rim (1E) which was not present in periods 1–3.

A number of more 'Romanised' jar forms are present, including the round-shouldered jars with burnished decoration on the shoulder (2D and 2E), which are standard forms of the Alice Holt and Highgate Wood industries. Also present is the necked jar (2G), which is commonly produced in VRW and is one of the few oxidised jars recorded in London.

The increased range of vessel types can also be seen in the beakers. The samian beaker Dech. 67 is present, which is usually dated from AD 70. 'Poppy-head' beakers (3F) and neckless everted-rim beakers (3E) also first appear in this period.

The most obvious change among the types as a whole is the increase in lids. This type records 0.4% in periods 1–3 combined, but in period 4 has increased to 1.5%. In the City this trend was noted in conjunction with an increase in bowls, which can also been seen when comparing periods 1, 2 and 3 individually, but is much less clear when looking at the pre-Boudican assemblage as a whole. Only a very small increase is noted in period 4, and in period 5 the percentage of bowls has fallen.

COMPARISON WITH THE PRE-BOUDICAN ASSEMBLAGE

The pre- and post-Boudican fire assemblages were compared to examine changes in composition and proportion. Despite the inevitable inclusion of redeposited material relating to the pre-Boudican phase, in the City RCP1B assemblages did show a decrease in the number of imports present, including a near absence of LYON and SGCC. The decline of SLOW and the increase of VRW and AHSU in particular are seen as diagnostic features of the post-Boudican assemblage (Davies et al 1994, 186).

It is difficult to identify these traits in the BGH95 assemblage primarily because of the small quantities of imported fine wares present in the assemblage as a whole. However, it must be noted that in period 4 LYON has fallen to 0.2% by sherd count from 0.8% in periods 1–3. Other imported non-samian fine wares such as SGCC and SPAN are either not recorded at all from BGH or are represented only by lamps. Similarly SLOW is present in such small quantities that it is difficult to detect reliable patterns.

However, the Romano-British wares compare much better with the overall trends in the reduced and tempered wares, reflecting the pattern identified in the City. RCP1B shows a consolidation of wares from the Romano-British industries, particularly from Alice Holt, Surrey and the Verulamium region, and the decline of unsourced, 'native' type GROG fabrics, which is a pattern mirrored in the BGH95 assemblage.

Table 59 Quantified assemblage from Open Area 14 external dump

Context	Fabric	Form	Decor	Sherd count	EVEs	Wt
[2220]	AHSU	2	-	1	0	13
[2220]	AHSU	5A	-	1	0.17	40
[2220]	AMPH	8	-	1	0	9
[2220]	BAETE	8DR20	-	4	0	658
[2220]	BAETE	8H70?	-	9	0.35	452
[2220]	COAR	2V	-	14	0.24	2294
[2220]	COLWW	7	-	1	0	298
[2220]	ECCW	1A	-	3	0.65	62
[2220]	ERMS	2B	VL	10	0.2	111
[2220]	ERSB	2	-	2	0	51
[2220]	FMIC	2/3	-	2	0	19
[2220]	GROG	2	-	5	0	35
[2220]	GROG	2M	-	2	0.08	68
[2220]	GROG	2T	-	1	0.06	91
[2220]	GROG	2V	-	4	0	243
[2220]	HOO	3A?	ROD	3	0	24
[2220]	HWB	2	-	10	0	329
[2220]	NKSH	2	-	5	0	130
[2220]	OXIDF	-	-	2	0	21
[2220]	RDBK	3	-	1	0	13
[2220]	RDBK	3	BDD	1	0	13
[2220]	SAMLG	-	-	1	0	0
[2220]	SAMLG	-	BR	2	0.12	5
[2220]	SAMLG	4DR29	DEC	1	0.05	6
[2220]	SAMLG	5	-	1	0	44
[2220]	SAMLG	5	<*>	2	0	13
[2220]	SAMLG	5DR15/17	-	1	0	5
[2220]	SAMLG	6DR27	-	1	0.2	11
[2220]	SAND	2	-	8	0	159
[2220]	SAND	2A	BUD	5	0.08	165
[2220]	SAND	3A	ROD	3	0.15	30
[2220]	SHEL	2A	-	1	0.16	63
[2220]	VRW	-	-	2	0	33
[2220]	VRW	1	-	3	0	78
Total				113	2.51	5586

QUANTIFIED GROUPS

Open Area 14 external dump
(Group 84, subgroup 412,
context [2220])
The assemblage from a dump
in Open Area 14 (Table 59) is
discussed in detail in Chapter 6
(Fig 48, <P69>–<P77>).

Building 15 demolition
(Group 62, subgroup 277,
context [1751])

Building 15 was sealed by a
dump which contained a large
quantity of pottery (Table 60).
The quantified assemblage
from the dump totalled 266
sherds, 10,426g and 4.64 EVEs.
The assemblage is dated to
AD 70–80 and is associated
with a coin dated AD 64–5.
The assemblage is discussed
in detail in Chapter 6 (Fig 54,
<P78>–<P96>).

Period 5

INTRODUCTION

Table 61 and Table 62 summarise the period 5 assemblage by
fabric and form respectively.

AMPHORAE

Amphorae as a type now account for 16.2% of the assemblage as
a whole, which is a slight decline from the pre- and immediately
post-Boudican assemblages. BAETE is still the dominant type and
accounts for 59.7% of all amphorae. The range of other amphorae
types recorded has not altered from the previous phase and the
only types present in any quantity are GAUL1 (7.3% of all
amphorae) and CADIZ (3.9% of all amphorae).

REDUCED WARES

The shift in dominance between HWB and HWC is very visible
by period 5. HWB now accounts for only 4.8% of all reduced
and tempered wares, whereas HWC has increased to 16.5%.
AHSU is the dominant reduced ware in this period, accounting
for 38.3% of all reduced and tempered wares. ERMS has fallen
to a level similar to that recorded in RCP3, and now accounts
for less than 5% of all reduced wares. ERSB accounts for 6.4%,
which is a slight increase on period 4.

BB1 and BBS both record one sherd each in this period,
reflecting (as in period 4) the very rare presence of this ware
in pre-Hadrianic levels.

OXIDISED WARES

VRW is clearly the dominant ware, accounting for 75.5% of all
oxidised wares. The decline in oxidised products from Kent is
evidenced, with ECCW now absent and HOO reduced to 2.6%
of all oxidised wares. LOXI increases slightly in this period.

FINE WARES

The dominant imported fine ware is still SAMLG, which accounts
for 9.5% of the assemblage as a whole and 84.3% of all samian.
Both MLEZ and SAMMV are also present, with SAMMV accounting
for 13.8% of all samian. Samian as a whole comprises 44.4% of
all fine wares. Central Gaulish wares continue to be represented
and CGOF is also recorded, although all are in very small
quantities. KOLN colour-coated ware is also present in this period,
although it only accounts for 2.6% of all non-samian fine wares.

Table 60 Quantified assemblage from Building 15 demolition

Context	Fabric	Form	Decor	Sherd count	EVEs	Wt
[1751]	AHSU	-	-	21		330
[1751]	AHSU	2	<1473>	1	0	10
[1751]	AHSU	2	BUD	1	0	27
[1751]	AHSU	2A	-	1	0.1	27
[1751]	AHSU	2T	-	2	0.17	42
[1751]	AHSU	3A?	-		1	0.1949
[1751]	AHSU	4F?	-	1	0.11	23
[1751]	AHSU	5	-	1	0.1	33
[1751]	AMPH	8	-	5		200
[1751]	BAETE	8DR20	-	36	0.15	5260
[1751]	BAETE	8H70?	-	1	0.27	82
[1751]	BHWS?	-	-	1		5
[1751]	CADIZ	8	-	1		63
[1751]	CC	9A	-	1	0.08	28
[1751]	ERMS	2	-	2		17
[1751]	ERSB?	2	-	4		47
[1751]	ERSB?	2	VL	1		21
[1751]	FMIC	-	-	4		10
[1751]	FMIC	-	ROD	17		72
[1751]	FMIC	6B	-	1	0.05	8
[1751]	GAUL1	8G	-	2		76
[1751]	GROG	9A	-	1	0.05	6
[1751]	HOO	-	-	4		45
[1751]	HWB	2	-	10		438
[1751]	HWB	2T	-	2	0.22	162
[1751]	HWB	2V	NCD	3	0.09	98
[1751]	HWB	4F1	-	3	0.18	75
[1751]	LOEG	4M34	-	2	0.3	92
[1751]	NKSH	-	-	3		111
[1751]	OXID	-	-	1		5
[1751]	OXID	7HOF	-	1	0.11	134
[1751]	RDBK	3	BRD	1		22
[1751]	RDBK	3B	-	1	0.1	4
[1751]	RHOD2	8	-	2		175
[1751]	RWS	-	-	2		58
[1751]	SAMLG	-	-	7		46
[1751]	SAMLG	4/5	-	2		21
[1751]	SAMLG	4RT12	-	4	0.34	15
[1751]	SAMLG	5	-	1		6
[1751]	SAMLG	5	<1472>	1	0	40
[1751]	SAMLG	5	<1475>	1	0	27
[1751]	SAMLG	5DR18	-	3	0.19	23
[1751]	SAMLG	5DR35/36	BAD	3	0.12	19
[1751]	SAMLG	6	-	6		17
[1751]	SAMLG	6	<1476>	1	0	41
[1751]	SAMLG	6?	<1477>	1	0	34
[1751]	SAMLG	6	<1478>	1	0	32
[1751]	SAMLG	6DR27	-	7	0.22	67
[1751]	SAND	-	-	16		170
[1751]	SAND	2	<1797>	2		9
[1751]	SAND	2	BUD	2		22
[1751]	SAND	2	NCD	1		55
[1751]	SAND	2	ROD	3		69
[1751]	SAND	2T	-	1	0.2	79
[1751]	SAND	4A	-	1	0.19	32
[1751]	SAND	4D	VL	4	0.32	143
[1751]	SAND	5A	-	5	0.22	73
[1751]	SAND	9A	-	1	0.13	33
[1751]	SESH	9A	-	1	0.13	59
[1751]	VRG	4/5	<1771>	1		26
[1751]	VRW	-	-	49	0	929
[1751]	VRW	1B?	-	2	0.2	25
[1751]	VRW	7	-	3		499
[1751]	VRW	7HOF	-	1	0.1	179
Total				**272**		**4.63**

Table 61 *Period 5 pottery assemblage by fabric*

Fabric	Sherd count	% sherd count	Rows	% rows
AHSU	545	16.6	141	11.6
AMPBS	5	0.2	1	0.1
AMPH	61	1.9	25	2.1
AMPH1	5	0.2	4	0.3
AMPH2	8	0.2	2	0.2
AMPH3	4	0.1	1	0.1
BAET	3	0.1	2	0.2
BAETE	319	9.7	72	5.9
BB1	1	0.0	1	0.1
BBS	1	0.0	1	0.1
C186	1	0.0	1	0.1
C189	6	0.2	2	0.2
CADIZ	21	0.6	9	0.7
CADIZ1	1	0.0	1	0.1
CAMP1	4	0.1	4	0.3
CC	1	0.0	1	0.1
CCIMP	2	0.1	2	0.2
CGGW	11	0.3	4	0.3
CGOF	2	0.1	2	0.2
CGWH	1	0.0	1	0.1
COAR	2	0.1	2	0.2
COLWW	1	0.0	1	0.1
ERMS	61	1.9	26	2.1
ERSA/B	2	0.1	2	0.2
ERSB	92	2.8	24	2.0
FINE	94	2.9	31	2.6
FMIC	263	8.0	78	6.4
GAUL	8	0.2	7	0.6
GAUL1	39	1.2	19	1.6
GAUL3	1	0.0	1	0.1
GBWW	1	0.0	1	0.1
GROG	49	1.5	28	2.3
HOO	13	0.4	5	0.4
HWB	63	1.9	30	2.5
HWC	235	7.2	88	7.2
IMPT	3	0.1	1	0.1
KOLN	12	0.4	4	0.3
LIPR	1	0.0	1	0.1
LOMI	14	0.4	8	0.7
LOXI	10	0.3	3	0.2
LYON	3	0.1	3	0.2
MICA	8	0.2	4	0.3
MLEZ	5	0.2	4	0.3
NFSE	10	0.3	7	0.6
NKGW	5	0.2	5	0.4
NKSH	21	0.6	9	0.7
OXID	54	1.6	32	2.6
OXIDF	2	0.1	2	0.2
PRW3	20	0.6	3	0.2
RDBK	21	0.6	11	0.9
RHOD1	4	0.1	3	0.2
RHOD2	43	1.3	7	0.6
RVOX	4	0.1	4	0.3
RWS	21	0.6	7	0.6
SAM	2	0.1	2	0.2
SAMLG	303	9.3	178	14.7
SAMMV	50	1.5	21	1.7
SAMMV2	1	0.0	1	0.1
SAND	299	9.1	122	10.0
SHEL	17	0.5	7	0.6
TN	3	0.1	2	0.2
VCWS	5	0.2	5	0.4
VRG	29	0.9	13	1.1
VRMI	2	0.1	2	0.2
VRW	376	11.5	123	10.1
Total	3274	100.0	1214	100.0

Table 62 *Period 5 pottery assemblage by form*

Form	Sherd count	% sherd count	Rows	% rows
-	826	25.2	313	25.8
1	55	1.7	29	2.4
1A	1	0.0	1	0.1
1B	22	0.7	8	0.7
1B2	15	0.5	7	0.6
1D	2	0.1	1	0.1
1E	3	0.1	2	0.2
1J	1	0.0	1	0.1
2	451	13.8	111	9.1
2/3	107	3.3	17	1.4
2A	24	0.7	22	1.8
2A15	4	0.1	4	0.3
2B	52	1.6	9	0.7
2C	95	2.9	13	1.1
2D	65	2.0	4	0.3
2E	25	0.8	4	0.3
2F	2	0.1	2	0.2
2G	1	0.0	1	0.1
2K	6	0.2	3	0.2
2M	2	0.1	2	0.2
2N	3	0.1	3	0.2
2T	142	4.3	62	5.1
2V	17	0.5	9	0.7
3	94	2.9	39	3.2
3A	3	0.1	3	0.2
3B	33	1.0	8	0.7
3C	5	0.2	4	0.3
3E	4	0.1	3	0.2
3F	61	1.9	19	1.6
3F1	2	0.1	2	0.2
3F2	11	0.3	4	0.3
3G	2	0.1	1	0.1
3J	1	0.0	1	0.1
4	33	1.0	21	1.7
4/5	19	0.6	13	1.1
4A	32	1.0	19	1.6
4CU11	1	0.0	1	0.1
4D	3	0.1	2	0.2
4DR29	39	1.2	28	2.3
4DR30	11	0.3	4	0.3
4DR30/37	2	0.1	1	0.1
4DR37	23	0.7	12	1.0
4E	2	0.1	2	0.2
4F	41	1.3	27	2.2
4F4	3	0.1	1	0.1
4K	1	0.0	1	0.1
4MX	5	0.2	2	0.2
4P	18	0.5	3	0.2
5	38	1.2	21	1.7
5A	1	0.0	1	0.1
5B	2	0.1	1	0.1
5C	7	0.2	2	0.2
5DR15/17	13	0.4	11	0.9
5DR18	67	2.0	30	2.5
5DR18/31	5	0.2	3	0.2
5DR18R	5	0.2	2	0.2
5DR35/36	1	0.0	2	0.2
5DR36	2	0.1	1	0.1
5J	3	0.1	1	0.1
5J3	1	0.0	1	0.1
6	6	0.2	6	0.5
6A	2	0.1	1	0.1
6DR24/25	3	0.1	2	0.2
6DR27	58	1.8	24	2.0
6DR35	2	0.1	2	0.2
6KN78	4	0.1	2	0.2
6RT9	2	0.1	2	0.2

(Table 62 cont)

Form	Sherd count	% sherd count	Rows	% rows
7	25	0.8	17	1.4
7EWAL	2	0.1	1	0.1
7G238	1	0.0	1	0.1
7HOF	19	0.6	15	1.2
8	108	3.3	49	4.0
8IJ	3	0.1	1	0.1
8C184	8	0.2	1	0.1
8C186	20	0.6	8	0.7
8C189	1	0.0	1	0.1
8DR2-4	5	0.2	5	0.4
8DR20	277	8.5	61	5.0
8DR20PW13	2	0.1	2	0.2
8DR20PW16	1	0.0	1	0.1
8DR20PW17	2	0.1	1	0.1
8DR20PW20	1	0.0	1	0.1
8DR20PW22	22	0.7	1	0.1
8DR20PW24	1	0.0	1	0.1
8G	35	1.1	17	1.4
8G4	1	0.0	1	0.1
8K117	5	0.2	1	0.1
8KOAN	6	0.2	2	0.2
8R527	1	0.0	1	0.1
8RHOD	38	1.2	8	0.7
9A	85	2.6	45	3.7
9C	7	0.2	4	0.3
9D	4	0.1	2	0.2
9N	1	0.0	1	0.1
9RT13	1	0.0	1	0.1
Total	**3274**	**100.0**	**1214**	**100.0**

Romano-British fine wares are dominated by FMIC and FINE, which account for a combined 87.1% of all Romano-British fine wares. RDBK accounts for 5.1% of all Romano-British fine wares, which is a decrease from the previous period.

FORMS

Lids continue to increase in quantity throughout this period. Otherwise the composition of the types remains similar to period 4. Some forms not previously recorded are present, including the disc-mouthed flagon (1D) and the double-handled jar or 'honey-pot' (2K). Also recorded is the bag-shaped beaker (3J) which mirrors the appearance of KOLN. Two forms in the London ware or FMIC repertoire, the hemispherical decorated bowl (4E) imitating Drag. 37 and a shallow dish with a broad flat rim, commonly rouletted (5C), are both recorded in this period. Although the decorated bowls are recorded in RCP2, both forms are present in RCP3 and the dish first appears in this phase in the City.

QUANTIFIED GROUPS

Building 23

(Group 160, context [3136])
An assemblage from the construction of Building 23 is discussed in detail in Chapter 7 (Fig 73, <P121>–<P142>). A total of 446 sherds were recovered from a make-up layer for the building, with a total weight of 13,540g and 15.83 EVEs (Table 63).

Table 63 Quantified assemblage from Building 23 construction

Context	Fabric	Form	Decor	Sherd count	EVEs	Wt
[3136]	AHSU	2	-	30		276
[3136]	AHSU	2	BUD	1	0	13
[3136]	AHSU	2C	-	54	0.66	763
[3136]	AHSU	2C	BUD	22	0.82	486
[3136]	AHSU	2T	-	8	0.89	170
[3136]	AHSU	4	-	1	0	7
[3136]	AHSU	4F	-	1	0.21	62
[3136]	AMPH	8	-	1		22
[3136]	BAETE	8DR20	-	6		1214
[3136]	BAETE	8DR20PW17	-	2	0.7	424
[3136]	BAETE	8DR20PW22	-	22	1	1730
[3136]	CADIZ	8C186	-	1	0.29	234
[3136]	ERMS	2	-	1		26
[3136]	ERSB	2	-	1		28
[3136]	FINE	2/3	-	3	0	50
[3136]	FMIC	-	-	3		22
[3136]	FMIC	2/3	-	66	0.99	583
[3136]	FMIC	2/3	ROD	1		6
[3136]	FMIC	2B	-	2	0.2	16
[3136]	FMIC	3F	BDD	14	0.52	101
[3136]	FMIC	4E	NCD	1		43
[3136]	FMIC	6A	-	2	0.27	25
[3136]	FMIC	9A	-	2	0.22	14
[3136]	GAUL?	8	-	1	0	123
[3136]	GAUL1	8G	-	1		15
[3136]	GROG	2V	-	1		41
[3136]	HWC	2	-	7		190
[3136]	HWC	4F	-	6	0.64	192
[3136]	HWC	4F4	-	3	0.27	83
[3136]	HWC	9A	-	9	0.19	230
[3136]	LOMI	4	-	1	0.26	47
[3136]	LOXI	5?	-	5	0.24	169
[3136]	NFSE	1D	-	2	1	116
[3136]	NFSE	7	-	1		170
[3136]	NKSH	2V	-	5		362
[3136]	OXID	-	-	3		44
[3136]	OXID	1B	-	5	0.8	101
[3136]	OXID	1B2	-	2	0.35	26
[3136]	PRW3	9A	-	17	0.88	340
[3136]	RVOX	7	-	1	0	23
[3136]	SAMLG	4DR29	ROD	1	0.05	4
[3136]	SAMLG	4DR30	DEC	2		57
[3136]	SAMLG	4DR37	DEC	11	0.44	296
[3136]	SAMLG	5DR18	-	5		35
[3136]	SAMLG	5DR18	<1749>	15	0.89	255
[3136]	SAMLG	5DR18	<1753>	5	0.45	116
[3136]	SAMLG	6DR27	-	8	0.85	82
[3136]	SAMLG	6DR27	<1748>	1		87
[3136]	SAMLG	6KN78	DEC	2		15
[3136]	SAND	2	-	19		407
[3136]	SAND	2T	-	1	0.11	16
[3136]	SAND	3	-	6		38
[3136]	SAND	4F	-	1	0.15	56
[3136]	SAND	9A	-	4	0.1	328
[3136]	SHEL	2	-	7		84
[3136]	VRG	4A	-	3	0.25	86
[3136]	VRW	-	-	30		808
[3136]	VRW	1	-	3		214
[3136]	VRW	1B2	-	1	1	141
[3136]	VRW	7	-	4		687
[3136]	VRW	7	-	1	0	107
[3136]	VRW	7HOF	-	1		72
[3136]	VRW	7HOF	<1756>	2	0.26	832
[3136]	VRW	9D	-	3	0.37	166
Total				**451**	**16.32**	**13576**

Period 6

INTRODUCTION

Table 65 and Table 66 summarise the period 6 assemblage by fabric and form respectively.

AMPHORAE

Amphorae as a type now account for 11.2% of the assemblage as a whole and the types present remain unchanged from the preceding period. BAETE remains the dominant type and accounts for 56.8% of all amphorae. NAFR1 appears for the first time in this period, which accords with evidence from the City that the type appears in the mid 2nd century AD.

REDUCED WARES

The most diagnostic wares of the Hadrianic period are Black-Burnished wares (BB1, BB2, BB2F, BBS) and the increase in circulation of these fabrics is clearly seen in period 6. Black-Burnished wares now account for 23.5% of all reduced wares and BB2 is the largest group present. AHSU still accounts for 28.1% of all reduced wares, but increased residuality may be a factor here. However, in RCP4, AHSU has decreased by almost half to 11% of all reduced wares by EVEs (Davies et al 1994, 209), so the quantity of AHSU in this period may be significant. HWC now accounts for 32.2% of all reduced wares and the later variant HWC+ is present in this period. These proportions are now more in line with the composition of RCP4, where HWC comprises just under 25% of all reduced wares by EVEs. Of the smaller industries that form an important component of the earlier periods only ERMS and ERSB are still represented in any quantity, but have substantially decreased in importance. ERSB now accounts for 3.2% of all reduced wares and ERMS for 2.5%, both of which are slightly higher than the values in RCP4 by weight. However, it seems likely that this difference is due to residuality and the comparison of qualitative with quantified data.

OXIDISED WARES

VRW remains the most important ware and still accounts for 64.5% of all oxidised wares, although the slight decline noted in RCP4 is also seen here. VCWS now accounts for 7.1% of all oxidised wares, which is a substantial increase from period 5. Of importance is the increase of LOXI which now accounts for 6.9% of all oxidised wares.

FINE WARES

The range of fine wares present has increased in this period. Central Gaulish products are still present and now account for 5.8% of all non-samian fine wares. KOLN colour-coated ware has also increased and now accounts for 5.5% of all non-samian fine wares. SAMCG and SAMEG are both present in more substantial quantities, but SAMLG is still the most abundant type and accounts for 48.8% of all samian wares, although residuality is again a factor. SAMCG is the next most abundant type and now accounts for 30% of all samian wares. SAMMV is at the height of its circulation in the earlier part of this period and overall accounts for 17.7% of all samian.

Amongst the Romano-British fine wares, NVCC appears for the first time, although it is only present in small quantities. LOMA and LOMI are important components of the non-samian fine wares and with other MICA wares account for 18.9% of all non-samian fine wares. FMIC still accounts for 34.9% of all non-samian fine wares, but again this figure is susceptible to residuality.

FORMS

The majority of the forms are consistent from period 4 but also present are a few new types that are diagnostic of the Hadrianic period. For flagons the most important introduction are ring-necked flagons with prominent upper ring (1B4 and 1B5); also present in this period are the later ringed-necked forms, 1B7–9. These emerge in RCP5 in the City and are generally accepted as having an early Antonine date; here they clearly relate to the lower end of period 6. The flagon type 1H also first appears in this period. This form is common in the LOXI and LOMI repertoire and its appearance is contemporaneous with the rise in importance of these fabrics.

The other group of forms that increase and are diagnostic of this period are the everted-rim cooking pots (2F, 2F8, 2F10) that constitute the major component of Black-Burnished vessels. This type now account for 11.2% of all jars.

Later samian forms associated with products from central and east Gaulish production areas also appear in this period and become increasingly important in the later 2nd and 3rd centuries. The flanged bowl Drag. 38, spouted mortaria Drag. 45, and dish Walters 79 are all recorded for the first time in this period.

COMPARISON WITH RCP4 AND RCP5

Period 6 at BGH95 spans the same date-range as RCP4 (AD 120–40) and RCP5 (AD 140–60). Table 64 shows the comparison by ware using the qualitative data from period 6 and the quantified data for RCP4 and RCP5 (Davies et al 1994, 168). The table shows the clear dominance of reduced wares in all three datasets. Also of interest are the fine wares and samian, which in the RCPs are at similar levels, while at BGH95 samian is slightly more abundant. This may be because of the large amounts of residual SAMLG in this assemblage.

QUANTIFIED GROUPS
Open Area 9
(Group 181, contexts [4123], [4136])
An assemblage from Open Area 9 is discussed in detail in Chapter 8

(Fig 88, <P143>–<P166>).
A total of 427 sherds were recovered from the fills of a well, with a total weight of 18,442g and 13.53 EVEs (Table 67).

Table 64 Comparison by ware of pottery from period 6, RCP4 and RCP5

	Period 6		RCP4		RCP5	
Ware	% sherd count	% rows	% EVEs	% weight	% EVEs	% weight
AMPH	11.1	10.2	16	43	3	25
OXID	24.1	20.6	28	23	34	28
REDU	46.9	45.3	40	29	51	42
FINE	5.9	8.1	8	3	6	2
SAM	11.8	15.6	8	2	6	3

Table 65 Period 6 pottery assemblage by fabric

Fabric	Sherd count	% sherd count	Rows	% rows
AHSU	550	10.7	151	6.8
AMPH	66	1.3	34	1.5
BAET	1	0.0	1	0.0
BAETE	329	6.4	97	4.4
BAETL	6	0.1	3	0.1
BB1	93	1.8	51	2.3
BB2	241	4.7	132	5.9
BB2F	19	0.4	13	0.6
BBS	107	2.1	60	2.7
BHWS	7	0.1	3	0.1
C189	2	0.0	2	0.1
CADIZ	13	0.3	10	0.4
CAMP1	2	0.0	1	0.0
CAT	2	0.0	2	0.1
CC	4	0.1	4	0.2
CCIMP	3	0.1	3	0.1
CGOF	17	0.3	3	0.1
CGWH	1	0.0	1	0.0
COAR	7	0.1	5	0.2
COLWW	21	0.4	12	0.5
DR28	1	0.0	1	0.0
ERMS	49	1.0	34	1.5
ERSA	1	0.0	1	0.0
ERSB	62	1.2	29	1.3
ERSI	2	0.0	1	0.0
FINE	70	1.4	50	2.2
FMIC	107	2.1	61	2.7
GAUL	12	0.2	11	0.5
GAUL1	127	2.5	57	2.6
GAUL2	3	0.1	2	0.1
GROG	40	0.8	25	1.1
HOO	19	0.4	13	0.6
HWB	62	1.2	27	1.2
HWBR	1	0.0	1	0.0
HWC	631	12.2	231	10.4
HWC+	14	0.3	10	0.4
ITFEL	1	0.0	1	0.0
KOLN	17	0.3	10	0.4
LOMA	10	0.2	3	0.1
LOMI	38	0.7	24	1.1
LOXI	86	1.7	25	1.1
LYON	2	0.0	1	0.0
MICA	10	0.2	4	0.2
MLEZ	1	0.0	1	0.0
NAFRI	1	0.0	1	0.0
NFSE	15	0.3	9	0.4
NKGW	8	0.2	3	0.1
NKSH	75	1.5	29	1.3
NVCC	6	0.1	6	0.3
OXID	115	2.2	61	2.7
OXIDF	20	0.4	10	0.4
PRW	1	0.0	1	0.0
PRW3	2	0.0	2	0.1
RDBK	12	0.2	6	0.3
RHMO	8	0.2	2	0.1
RHOD	1	0.0	1	0.0
RHOD2	6	0.1	3	0.1
RVOX	3	0.1	2	0.1
RWS	51	1.0	38	1.7
SAM	5	0.1	2	0.1
SAMCG	183	3.6	77	3.5
SAMEG	13	0.3	11	0.5
SAMLG	297	5.8	197	8.9
SAMMT	2	0.0	2	0.1
SAMMV	103	2.0	52	2.3
SAMMV2	5	0.1	5	0.2
SAND	417	8.1	178	8.0

(Table 65 cont)

Fabric	Sherd count	% sherd count	Rows	% rows
SESH	4	0.1	2	0.1
SHEL	33	0.6	16	0.7
SLOW	4	0.1	4	0.2
SOLL	1	0.0	1	0.0
VCWS	89	1.7	51	2.3
VRG	11	0.2	10	0.4
VRMI	2	0.0	2	0.1
VRR	1	0.0	1	0.0
VRW	801	15.5	227	10.2
Total	5152	100.0	2223	100.0

Table 66 Period 6 pottery assemblage by form

Form	Sherd count	% sherd count	Rows	% rows
-	1476	28.6	569	25.6
1	70	1.4	43	1.9
1A	2	0.0	2	0.1
1B	18	0.3	3	0.1
1B1	3	0.1	3	0.1
1B2	14	0.3	7	0.3
1B4	1	0.0	1	0.0
1B5	5	0.1	3	0.1
1B7-9	7	0.1	4	0.2
1C	6	0.1	4	0.2
1D	3	0.1	3	0.1
1E	4	0.1	1	0.0
1H	11	0.2	5	0.2
1J	6	0.1	4	0.2
2	648	12.6	264	11.9
2/3	45	0.9	22	1.0
2A	42	0.8	26	1.2
2A12-13	28	0.5	1	0.0
2A16	2	0.0	1	0.0
2B	12	0.2	8	0.4
2C	4	0.1	3	0.1
2D	56	1.1	9	0.4
2E	30	0.6	14	0.6
2F	147	2.9	53	2.4
2F10	1	0.0	1	0.0
2F8	1	0.0	1	0.0
2G	36	0.7	5	0.2
2G4	3	0.1	3	0.1
2H	1	0.0	1	0.0
2K	4	0.1	1	0.0
2M	8	0.2	5	0.2
2R	27	0.5	1	0.0
2T	176	3.4	88	4.0
2V	36	0.7	12	0.5
2Z	25	0.5	2	0.1
3	165	3.2	73	3.3
3B	20	0.4	5	0.2
3C	3	0.1	1	0.0
3D	6	0.1	1	0.0
3DE67	1	0.0	1	0.0
3E	6	0.1	2	0.1
3F	45	0.9	25	1.1
3F2	3	0.1	2	0.1
3F4	19	0.4	2	0.1
3G	3	0.1	3	0.1
4	90	1.7	53	2.4
4/5	144	2.8	90	4.0
4A	28	0.5	16	0.7

(Table 66 cont)

Form	Sherd count	% sherd count	Rows	% rows
4A5	24	0.5	1	0.0
4CU11	3	0.1	3	0.1
4DR29	37	0.7	23	1.0
4DR30	12	0.2	8	0.4
4DR37	48	0.9	37	1.7
4DR38	3	0.1	2	0.1
4F	75	1.5	41	1.8
4F4	1	0.0	1	0.0
4F6	7	0.0	1	0.0
4G	6	0.1	7	0.3
4H	84	1.6	47	2.1
4K	3	0.1	3	0.1
4MX	11	0.2	4	0.2
4RT12	2	0.0	2	0.1
5	60	1.2	39	1.8
5B	1	0.0	1	0.0
5CU23	1	0.0	1	0.0
5DR15/17	8	0.2	7	0.3
5DR18	68	1.3	33	1.5
5DR18/31	120	2.3	14	0.6
5DR18/31R	1	0.0	1	0.0
5DR18R	3	0.1	3	0.1
5DR35/36	7	0.1	3	0.1
5DR36	2	0.0	2	0.1
5J	21	0.4	14	0.6
5J1	1	0.0	1	0.0
5J2	4	0.1	2	0.1
5WA79	2	0.0	1	0.0
6	17	0.3	13	0.6
6DR24/25	3	0.1	3	0.1
6DR27	55	1.1	37	1.7
6DR33	18	0.3	18	0.8
6DR35	13	0.3	6	0.3
6DR46	1	0.0	1	0.0
7	32	0.6	27	1.2
7BEF	4	0.1	4	0.2
7DR45	1	0.0	1	0.0
7G238	2	0.0	2	0.1
7HAM	1	0.0	1	0.0
7HOF	86	1.7	35	1.6
8	116	2.3	54	2.4
8J	5	0.1	4	0.2
8C186	10	0.2	7	0.3
8C189	1	0.0	1	0.0
8DR2-4	9	0.2	7	0.3
8DR20	294	5.7	85	3.8
8DR20PW12	1	0.0	1	0.0
8DR20PW18	1	0.0	1	0.0
8DR20PW22	1	0.0	1	0.0
8DR20PW23	3	0.1	2	0.1
8DR20PW28	1	0.0	1	0.0
8DR20PW9	1	0.0	1	0.0
8DR28	1	0.0	1	0.0
8G	98	1.9	50	2.2
8G12	1	0.0	1	0.0
8G4	24	0.5	7	0.3
8H70	2	0.0	2	0.1
8L555	3	0.1	2	0.1
8NACA	1	0.0	1	0.0
8PW65	1	0.0	1	0.0
8RHOD	5	0.1	2	0.1
9A	191	3.7	75	3.4
9B	1	0.0	1	0.0
9C	26	0.5	9	0.4
9H	9	0.2	2	0.1
9LA	1	0.0	1	0.0
9N	6	0.1	3	0.1
9NP	1	0.0	1	0.0
9RT13	2	0.0	1	0.0
9U	2	0.0	1	0.0
Total	**5152**	**100.0**	**2223**	**100.0**

Table 67 Quantified assemblage from Open Area 9 well C

Context	Fabric	Form	Decor	Sherd count	EVEs	Wt
[4123]	AHSU	-	-	1	0	11
[4123]	AHSU	2T	WL	36	0.76	1391
[4123]	AHSU?	2Z	-	17	0.38	155
[4123]	BAETE	8DR20	-	17	0	2735
[4123]	CGOF	3	-	1	0	10
[4123]	CGOF	3B	HPD	15	0.9	155
[4123]	FINE	2/3	-	2	0.1	26
[4123]	FINE	3	BDD	4	0	71
[4123]	FMIC	3	BDD	2	0	31
[4123]	GAUL1	8G4	-	1	0.45	144
[4123]	GROG	-	-	1	0	5
[4123]	GROG	2	MOD	1	0	165
[4123]	HWC	-	-	8	0	13
[4123]	HWC	2/3	-	1	0.09	6
[4123]	HWC	2E	BUD	3	0.24	32
[4123]	HWC	3	BDD	35	0	287
[4123]	HWC	3E	BDD	5	0.12	123
[4123]	HWC	3F	-	1	0.15	9
[4123]	HWC	3F4	BDD	5	0.37	66
[4123]	HWC	4	-	1	0	60
[4123]	HWC	4F	-	2	0.3	117
[4123]	HWC	4F6	-	2	0.09	39
[4123]	HWC	9A	-	9	0.45	190
[4123]	HWC+	2	AL	5	0	218
[4123]	HWC+	2F10	-	1	0.2	34
[4123]	KOLN	-	RCD2	1	0	2
[4123]	LOMA	9H?	-	6	0	32
[4123]	LOMI	1?	-	1	0	35
[4123]	LOXI?	-	-	3	0	15
[4123]	LOXI	9A	-	40	2	2764
[4123]	NFSE	-	-	1	0	12
[4123]	OXID	4	-	14	0.68	558
[4123]	SAMCG	4DR37	-	1	0.05	7
[4123]	SAMLG	5	-	3	0.12	16
[4123]	SAMLG	5DR18	<1852>	1	0	70
[4123]	SAMMV	4	DEC	1	0	5
[4123]	SAND	-	-	7	0	68
[4123]	SAND	2T	-	2	0	17
[4123]	SAND	4F	-	1	0	15
[4123]	SAND	9A	-	4	0.19	72
[4123]	VRW	-	-	46	0	977
[4123]	VRW	1	-	1	0	26
[4123]	VRW	1E	-	4	1	246
[4123]	VRW	2?	-	1	0.05	2
[4123]	VRW	4A5	-	24	0.77	3775
[4123]	VRW	7	-	1	0	7
[4123]	VRW	7	<1853>	1	0	125
[4123]	VRW	9C	FRLD	8	0.33	206
[4136]	AHSU	2	-	2	0	57
[4136]	AHSU	2T	WL	12	0	635
[4136]	AHSU?	2Z	-	8	0	121
[4136]	AMPH?	8DR2-4	-	1	0	122
[4136]	BAETE	8DR20	-	2	0	329
[4136]	BAETE	8DR20PW18?	-	1	0.48	373
[4136]	CGOF	-	-	1	0	3
[4136]	GROG	2	-	1	0	27
[4136]	HWC	3	BDD	4	0	38
[4136]	HWC	3F4	BDD	14	1.2	267
[4136]	HWC	4	-	3	0	161
[4136]	HWC	9A	-	1	0.05	9
[4136]	HWC+?	2	AL	1	0	12
[4136]	LOMA	9H?	-	3	0	8
[4136]	LOMI?	4/5	-	1	0	107
[4136]	LOXI	9A	-	11	0.58	283
[4136]	SAMMV	4DR37	DEC	1	0.05	91
[4136]	SAND	4F	-	3	0.11	68
[4136]	SAND	9A	-	2	0.27	32
[4136]	VRW	-	-	3	0	158
[4136]	VRW	1?	-	3	0	221
[4136]	VRW	1B4	-	1	1	172
Total				**427**	**13.53**	**18442**

Fourth-century activity

A 4th-century assemblage from a roadside pit is discussed in detail in Chapter 9.2 (Fig 102, <P208>–<P223>). A total assemblage of 104 sherds, 4747g and 4.02 EVEs was recovered (Table 68).

St Thomas Street, Thames Water utilities (STU92)

Introduction

The assemblage from STU92 produced a total of 906 sherds (137 rows). During assessment the assemblage was only scanned to provide initial dating and identifications. During analysis the contexts relating to the early Roman sequence were spot-dated and [98] was fully quantified by weight and EVEs. Many of the groups are early in date, the activity at Open Area 2 probably dating to the first few years of settlement at Southwark. The assemblage from Open Area 2 is discussed in Chapter 4 (Fig 32, <P53>–<P63>).

The earliest stratigraphic features in Open Area 2 did not produce much pottery; the V-shaped gully (context [99]) had only one handmade sherd of GROG (22g) and the pit (context [93]) had one sherd of BAETE (63g) and two handmade sherds of reduced grey wares (10g).

The pairs of Table 70 and Table 71, and Table 72 and Table 73, respectively summarise the period 2 and period 4 assemblages by fabric and form.

Context [98] external dump in Open Area 2

Context [98] forms an external dump, part of a sequence of layers upon which Building 1 was constructed; it contained a total of 108 sherds (3215g/ 2.24EVEs/ 22 rows) (Table 69). The assemblage composition is similar to the general pattern outlined for Open Area 2 (see Chapter 4). A tripod bowl is present which has a complete profile. This form is not common in the London area but probably dates from the 1st into the early 2nd century (Marsh 1978, 160).

Building 1

The assemblage associated with STU92 Building 1 is discussed in Chapter 4 (Fig 32, <P53>–<P63>).

Building 2

Building 2 was constructed after the fire horizon and continued to have floors laid with large quantities of BAETE amphorae, especially surface context [27]. Very little other pottery is associated with Building 2, with a total of only 60 sherds recovered. The fabrics present date from the late Neronian to the early Flavian period, and the continued practice of laying amphorae sherds as flooring might suggest that the building continued under the same ownership and retained the same function as before the fire.

Table 68 Quantified assemblage from roadside pit

Context	Fabric	Form	Decor	Sherd count	EVEs	Wt
[32]	AHFA	2	-	I		23
[32]	AHFA	2	BUD	2		49
[32]	AHFA	2FX	-	3	0.2	70
[32]	AHFA	2V	-	5	0	426
[32]	AHFA	2V	BUD	I		26
[32]	AHFA	2V	FCD	2	0.07	247
[32]	AHFA	4/5	-	I		20
[32]	AHFA	4/5	CLX	I		122
[32]	AHFA	4M	-	4	0.37	198
[32]	AHFA	5J	-	I		19
[32]	AHFA	5J	BUD	I		107
[32]	AHSU	2	-	I		20
[32]	AMPH?	8?	-	I		23
[32]	BAETE	8DR20	-	I		205
[32]	BAETL	8DR20	-	3	0.23	986
[32]	BBI	2F	-	I		22
[32]	BBI	4/5	CL	2		34
[32]	BB2	2F	-	I	0.11	18
[32]	BB2	4/5?	-	I		39
[32]	BB2F	4H	-	2	0.16	64
[32]	BBS?	2	-	2		29
[32]	BBS	2	AL	I	0	12
[32]	CALC	2	-	I		101
[32]	COAR	2T	-	I	0.14	36
[32]	FINE	2?	-	2		30
[32]	GAUL2	8L555	-	I		101
[32]	GROG	2	-	3		83
[32]	HWC	-	-	2		12
[32]	HWC	2	BUD	I		5
[32]	KOLN	3J	BAD	I	0.2	17
[32]	LOXI	-	-	I		14
[32]	MAYEN	I	-	2	I	253
[32]	NVCCP	3	-	2		44
[32]	NVCCP	3	ROD	2		15
[32]	NVCCP	3	WBAD	I		14
[32]	OXID	-	-	3		53
[32]	OXID	I	-	I	0.17	81
[32]	OXID	2	-	2		25
[32]	OXID	3	-	I	0	31
[32]	OXRC	-	-	I	0	4
[32]	OXRC	3	-	I		37
[32]	OXRC	4	-	I		62
[32]	OXRC	4	STD	2		36
[32]	OXRC	4/5	-	3		205
[32]	OXRC	4/5	ROD	2		11
[32]	OXRC	4DR38	-	3	0.07	212
[32]	OXRC	7	-	I		50
[32]	OXRC	7C100	ROD	I		9
[32]	OXRC	7DR45	-	I	0.13	35
[32]	OXWS	4	RPD	I	0.1	59
[32]	OXWW	7	-	2		178
[32]	OXWW	7M22	-	I	0.06	28
[32]	PORD	2	RLD	5		61
[32]	PORD	2T	-	3	0.77	158
[32]	SAMCG	4DR37	DEC	3		43
[32]	SAMCG	5	-	2	0.1	8
[32]	SAMCG	6DR33	<128>	I	0	42
[32]	SAMCG	7	-	I		85
[32]	SAMCG	7DR45	-	I	0	16
[32]	SAMEG	5	ROD	I		27
[32]	SAMEG	7	-	I	0	27
[32]	SAMEG	7DR45	-	I		36
[32]	SAND	2	-	4		47
[32]	SAND	2	BUD	I	0	9
[32]	SAND	2T	-	2	0.14	35
[32]	TSK	2	AL	I		4
Total				112	4.02	5198

Table 69 Quantified assemblage from STU92 Open Area 2 external dump

Context	Fabric	Form	Decor	Sherd count	EVEs	Wt
[98]	AMPH	8	-	I	0	31
[98]	BAETE	8DR20PWII	-	8	0.2	1565
[98]	ECCW	-	-	I	0	13
[98]	ECCW	IA	-	20	I	120
[98]	ERSI	2A	-	4	0.2	35
[98]	FINE	-	-	4	0	8
[98]	GROG	-	-	16	0	191
[98]	GROG	2	COMB	I	0	23
[98]	GROG	2A	-	I	0.1	15
[98]	GROG	2A1-4	-	I	0.17	28
[98]	GROG	4?	-	3	0.2	60
[98]	NFSE	I	-	9	0	305
[98]	OXID	-	-	10	0	122
[98]	OXID	I	-	2	0	89
[98]	OXID	4Q	-	7	0.15	157
[98]	RWS	-	-	5	0	220
[98]	SAMLG	4	DEC	I	0	I
[98]	SAMLG	5	-	I	0	65
[98]	SAND	-	-	2	0	43
[98]	SAND	2A	-	I	0.11	20
[98]	SAND	5	-	4	0.11	48
[98]	SHEL	-	-	6	0	56
Total				108	2.24	3215

Table 71 STU92 period 2 pottery assemblage by form

Form	Rows	% rows	Sherd count	% sherd count
-	35	32.4	129	15.7
I	6	5.6	23	2.8
IA	3	2.8	26	3.2
IB	2	1.9	2	0.2
2	12	11.1	24	2.9
2/3	I	0.9	11	1.3
2A	5	4.6	9	1.1
2A1-4	I	0.9	I	0.1
2T	I	0.9	I	0.1
2V	2	1.9	4	0.5
4	2	1.9	4	0.5
4DR29	2	1.9	5	0.6
4DR30	2	1.9	12	1.5
4Q	I	0.9	7	0.9
5	3	2.8	6	0.7
5A	I	0.9	4	0.5
5B	I	0.9	I	0.1
5DR15/17	I	0.9	2	0.2
6	I	0.9	I	0.1
6DR24/25	I	0.9	I	0.1
6DR27	2	1.9	5	0.6
6H	2	1.9	2	0.2
6RT8	I	0.9	3	0.4
7	2	1.9	2	0.2
8	10	9.3	12	1.5
8DR20	7	6.5	515	62.8
8DR20PWII	I	0.9	8	1.0
Total	108	100.0	820	100.0

Table 70 STU92 period 2 pottery assemblage by fabric

Fabric	Rows	% rows	Sherd count	% sherd count
AHSU	4	3.7	13	1.6
AMPH	5	4.6	5	0.6
BAETE	12	11.1	529	64.5
ECCW	10	9.3	46	5.6
ERMS	I	0.9	4	0.5
ERSI	I	0.9	4	0.5
FINE	I	0.9	4	0.5
GAUL	I	0.9	I	0.1
GBWW	I	0.9	3	0.4
GROG	13	12.0	40	4.9
HOO	I	0.9	I	0.1
HWB	I	0.9	I	0.1
LYON	2	1.9	2	0.2
NFSE	2	1.9	14	1.7
NKSH	I	0.9	I	0.1
OXID	10	9.3	34	4.1
OXIDF	I	0.9	4	0.5
RWS	3	2.8	17	2.1
SAMLG	16	14.8	37	4.5
SAND	13	12.0	22	2.7
SHEL	I	0.9	6	0.7
VRW	8	7.4	32	3.9
Total	108	100.0	820	100.0

Table 72 STU92 period 4 pottery assemblage by fabric

Fabric	Rows	% rows	Sherd count	% sherd count
AHSU	I	3.4	I	1.2
BAETE	8	27.6	58	67.4
ECCW	I	3.4	I	1.2
ERMS	I	3.4	I	1.2
HWB	I	3.4	I	1.2
NFSE	I	3.4	I	1.2
OXID	3	10.3	4	4.7
OXIDF	I	3.4	2	2.3
RHOD2	I	3.4	I	1.2
RWS	2	6.9	2	2.3
SAMLG	2	6.9	2	2.3
SHEL	I	3.4	I	1.2
VRW	6	20.7	11	12.8
Total	29	100.0	86	100.0

Table 73 STU92 period 4 pottery assemblage by form

Form	Rows	% rows	Sherd count	% sherd count
-	7	24.1	10	11.6
I	2	6.9	3	3.5
IA	3	10.3	4	4.7
2	2	6.9	2	2.3
3A	1	3.4	1	1.2
4	1	3.4	1	1.2
5	1	3.4	1	1.2
5A	1	3.4	1	1.2
7HOF	1	3.4	3	3.5
8	2	6.9	2	2.3
8DR20	7	24.1	57	66.3
9B	1	3.4	1	1.2
Total	29	100.0	86	100.0

Table 74 BSE94 pottery assemblage by fabric

Fabric	Rows	% rows
AHSU	18	11.2
AMPH	8	5.0
BAET	1	0.6
BAETE	4	2.5
BB2	3	1.9
CADIZ	1	0.6
CC	1	0.6
ECCW	1	0.6
ERMS	2	1.2
ERSB	12	7.5
FMIC	7	4.3
GAUL1	4	2.5
GROG	1	0.6
HOO	3	1.9
HWB	7	4.3
HWBR	1	0.6
HWC	9	5.6
KOAN	1	0.6
KOLN	1	0.6
NFSE	1	0.6
NKGW	2	1.2
NKSH	2	1.2
OXID	7	4.3
RDBK	1	0.6
RWS	2	1.2
SAMCG	3	1.9
SAMLG	28	17.4
SAND	7	4.3
VCWS	4	2.5
VRG	1	0.6
VRR	2	1.2
VRW	16	9.9
Total	161	100.0

Table 75 BSE94 pottery assemblage by form

Form	Rows	% rows
-	50	31.1
I	1	0.6
IA	1	0.6
IJ	1	0.6
2	15	9.3
2A	3	1.9
2B	1	0.6
2C	4	2.5
2D	1	0.6
2F	2	1.2
2J	1	0.6
2R	1	0.6
2T	5	3.1
2V	1	0.6
3	4	2.5
3B	2	1.2
3BI	1	0.6
4	6	3.7
4/5	1	0.6
4A	1	0.6
4DR30	3	1.9
4DR37	1	0.6
4F	2	1.2
4K	1	0.6
5	3	1.9
5DR18	5	3.1
5DR36	1	0.6
5J	1	0.6
5RTI	1	0.6
6	1	0.6
6DR27	6	3.7
6DR33	1	0.6
7	3	1.9
7BEF	1	0.6
7HOF	3	1.9
8	9	5.6
8C186	1	0.6
8DR20	5	3.1
8G	4	2.5
9A	5	3.1
9C	1	0.6
9LA	1	0.6
Total	161	100.0

Borough High Street (BSE92)

Introduction

The Roman assemblage from BSE92 was spot-dated and assessed before the introduction of sherd count.

Roman pottery was recorded from a total of 19 contexts (161 rows). All of the contexts produced small-sized assemblages, but the range of types present results in relatively well dated groups. Building 2, Building 3 and Open Area 2 produced similar assemblages, dating to the early Flavian period, which could not be defined further in relation to the stratigraphic sequence. Building 3 is thought to form part of BGH95 Building 13, both elements of which have a construction date in the early Flavian period, c AD 70–5.

Four periods of activity have been identified:1, 2, 4 and 6 (Table 76). As contexts assigned to period 4 accounted for 120 of the 161 rows of pottery, the data from this site has not been broken down by period, and therefore Table 74 and Table 75 are breakdowns by fabric and form for the site assemblage as a whole.

Borough High Street, BT junction (BTJ93)

Introduction

The Roman assemblage from BTJ93 was spot-dated and assessed before the introduction of sherd count. Roman pottery was recorded from 30 contexts (89 rows). All of the contexts are small in size, but only ten contexts have less than five rows recorded. Four periods are recorded: 2, 4, 5 and 6 (Table 79). Building1, Building 2 and Open Area 3 are all assigned to period 4. The assemblages from these contain a similar range of types and are all dated to the early Flavian period. As a result of the small groups recovered from each land use it has not been possible to refine the dating within this period.

One record of LOMI and one of GAUL1 8G are residual in a post-Roman open area (OA6).

As a total of only 89 rows were recorded (87 from stratified Roman levels) the assemblage is not broken down by period and therefore Table 77 and Table 78 are breakdowns by fabric and form for the site assemblage as a whole.

Borough High Street (BUG94)

Introduction

The Roman assemblage from BUG94 was spot-dated and assessed before the introduction of sherd count. Roman pottery was recovered from 51 contexts and totalled 236 rows. All of the assemblages are small in size with the exception of one medium and one large group. Four periods are identified: 1, 2, 4 and 6, with most of the pottery recovered from period 4, which consisted of Open Area 4, Open Area 8 and Building 1. However, there is both later Roman and medieval pottery intrusive in these features due to robbing, truncation and modern pitting. For these reasons

Table 76 Dating table: BSE94 periods and land use interpretations

Period	Lu-int	Grp	Edate	Ldate	Rows	Dating types	Comments
I	OA1	2	50	70	14	BAETE 8DR20; ERSB 2, 9A; RDBK 3B; SAMLG 4DR30, 5DR18, 6DR27; VRW 1A; HWB? 2T	There are no types present that must date to the Flavian period, although both RDBK and ERSB are wares that increase in circulation in the Flavian period.
2	B1	3	50	100	3	HWB 2V	Small group; only two fabric types recorded.
4	B2	5	70	75	54	AHSU 2A, 2C, 2T; ERSB 2T; FMIC 3B, 2R; HWC 9A, 3 BDD; VCWS; SAMLG 4DR30, 5DR18, 6DR27; VRW 7HOF	The relative quantities of wares in the assemblage from this group suggest a construction date in the early Flavian period (AD 70–5). HWC is present alongside ERSB, AHSU and HWB.
4	B3	7	70	75	38	AHSU 2D?; ERMS; ERSB 2T; FMIC 3B; HWB 4F; HWC 9A; NKSH; SAMLG 6DR27	The range of types is similar to B2 giving the same date range for these two buildings.
4	OA2	4	70	75	28	HWC 3 BDD; AHSU 2C, 4K, 2C; ERSB; HWBR; VRW 4A, 1J, 7HOF	Again a similar range of types to B2 and B3.
6	B4	8	120	160	24	BB2 2F, 5J; RWS 7BEF; KOLN 3 RCD; SAMCG 5DR36, 6DR33; VCWS 2J?, 9C	

Table 77 BTJ93 pottery assemblage by fabric

Fabric	Rows	% rows
AHSU	7	7.9
AMPH	3	3.4
BAET	3	3.4
BAETE	2	2.2
CC	1	1.1
CCGW	3	3.4
ERMS	5	5.6
ERSA/B	1	1.1
ERSB	3	3.4
FINE	1	1.1
FMIC	4	4.5
GAUL1	2	2.2
GROG	1	1.1
HWB	2	2.2
HWB/C	1	1.1
HWC	2	2.2
KOAN	1	1.1
LOMI	1	1.1
NFSE	5	5.6
NKGW	1	1.1
OXID	8	9.0
RDBK	1	1.1
SAMLG	10	11.2
SAND	12	13.5
SHEL	2	2.2
VRG	1	1.1
VRW	6	6.7
Total	**89**	**100.0**

Table 78 BTJ93 pottery assemblage by form

Form	Rows	% rows
-	31	34.8
1	8	9.0
2	14	15.7
2A	1	1.1
2B	3	3.4
2T	4	4.5
3	2	2.2
3F	1	1.1
4	1	1.1
4D	1	1.1
4DR29	3	3.4
4DR37	1	1.1
4F	2	2.2
5DR36	1	1.1
6DR27	2	2.2
8	4	4.5
8DR20	5	5.6
8G	2	2.2
9A	3	3.4
Total	**89**	**100.0**

Table 79 Dating table: BTJ93 periods and land use interpretations

Period	Lu-int	Grp	Edate	Ldate	Rows	Dating types	Comments
2	OA2	2	50	100	1	SAMLG 4DR29	
4	B1	3	50	160	2	FINE 3 BDD; SAND	
4	B2	6	50	100	17	AHSU 2A; ERSB; GAUL1 8G; SAMLG 6DR27; VRW 9A	One record of HWC? 4F which may either be intrusive or an early example of this ware. MPOT is also from context [70] suggesting intrusion is possible.
4	OA3	5	60	100	10	HWB/C; ERMS 2B?; VRW; SHEL	Assemblage dates to late Neronian/early Flavian period. HWC is absent.
5	B3	8	70	100	30	CCGW; HWC; ERSB; SAMLG 5DR36, 4DR29, 6DR27; SAND 3F?; VRG 4F; ERMS 2B; FMIC 4D	Assemblage dates to early Flavian period.
5	OA4	7	70	100	18	SAMLG 4DR37, 4DR29; CCGW; ERSA/B 2T	Assemblage dates to early Flavian period.
6	OA5	9	50	100	5	SAMLG?; FMIC; AHSU 2T; SHEL	Small assemblage; poorly dated.
6	OA5	11	50	300	4	BAETE	Small assemblage; poorly dated.

the assemblage is presented by fabric and form as a whole (Table 80; Table 81) and not broken down by period.

Battlebridge sewer diversion, Borough High Street (JSS92)

Introduction

The Roman assemblage from JSS92 was spot-dated and assessed before the introduction of sherd count.

Roman pottery was recorded from a total of 50 contexts (171 rows). Of the 50 contexts, 43 have five or less rows recorded, indicating that only small assemblages were recovered from the vast majority of contexts. Consequently, these groups are poorly dated with wide date-ranges, and the

ceramic dating evidence does not reflect the chronological development indicated by the stratigraphy. In fact, despite the presence of activity assigned to periods 1–6 and a total of 12 individual land uses, there are only four contexts with an early date later than AD 50. For these reasons the assemblage data is presented in Table 82 and Table 83 only on a site basis and is not broken down into periods or land use interpretations.

Of note from this assemblage are sherds from a marbled SAMLG Drag. 27 cup, a LOEG hemispherical bowl, and ECCW early walled mortaria which are a previously recorded but uncommon type in London.

JSS92 Open Area 3 has been equated with BGH95 Open Area 10 and there is nothing to suggest that the horizons are of different date. The assemblage from Open Area 3 is small (only 13 rows) and limited to the presence of ERMS, GROG, RVMO, SAMLG and SAND. There is nothing present with an obvious industrial function or usage from the contexts associated with the ceramic moulds.

Building 1 has the highest number of rows of ceramic data recorded, with a total of 61. The range of fabric and forms identified is limited but suggests domestic occupation. No indication of a more specialised function for Building 1 can be gleaned from the assemblage.

Road 1 produced only a small assemblage with a total of only 15 rows recorded. The types present include AMPH, BAET, ERMS, GAUL1, SAMLG, SAND, SHEL and VRW, suggesting a date in the range AD 50–70.

Table 80 BUG94 pottery assemblage by fabric

Fabric	Rows	% rows
AHFA	1	0.4
AHSU	23	9.7
AMPH	6	2.5
BAETE	23	9.7
BAETL	1	0.4
BB1	2	0.8
BB2	3	1.3
CADIZ	1	0.4
CGGW	1	0.4
CGOF	1	0.4
COAR	5	2.1
ERMS	11	4.7
ERSB	5	2.1
ERSI	1	0.4
FINE	4	1.7
FMIC	4	1.7
GAUL1	3	1.3
GROG	7	3.0
HOO	2	0.8
HWB	17	7.2
HWB/C	1	0.4
HWC	9	3.8
KOAN	3	1.3
LYON	2	0.8
MHAD	1	0.4
NFSE	3	1.3
NKSH	2	0.8
NVCC	1	0.4
OXID	8	3.4
OXRC	2	0.8
PRW3	1	0.4
RDBK	7	3.0
RHOD	2	0.8
RWS	2	0.8
SAMCG	1	0.4
SAMEG	1	0.4
SAMLG	30	12.7
SAND	12	5.1
SHEL	4	1.7
SLOW	3	1.3
VRG	1	0.4
VRW	19	8.1
Total	236	100.0

Table 81 BUG94 pottery assemblage by form

Form	Rows	% rows
-	97	41.1
1	4	1.7
1J	1	0.4
2	27	11.4
2A	8	3.4
2B	4	1.7
2T	4	1.7
2V	3	1.3
3	6	2.5
3F	1	0.4
4	3	1.3
4/5	1	0.4
4DR29	5	2.1
4DR30	1	0.4
4DR37	1	0.4
4G	1	0.4
4H1	1	0.4
5	1	0.4
5A	1	0.4
5DR15/17	5	2.1
5DR18	4	1.7
5DR35/36	1	0.4
6	1	0.4
6DR27	4	1.7
6DR33	1	0.4
7	2	0.8
7DR45	1	0.4
7G238	2	0.8
7HOF	1	0.4
8	10	4.2
8C186	1	0.4
8DR2-4	1	0.4
8DR20	24	10.2
8G	3	1.3
9A	4	1.7
9LA	1	0.4
Total	236	100.0

Table 82 JSS92 pottery assemblage by fabric

Fabric	Rows	% rows
AHFA	1	0.6
AHSU	11	7.1
AMPH	6	3.9
BAET	17	11.0
BB1	1	0.6
BB2	1	0.6
CALC	1	0.6
COAR	1	0.6
ECCW	2	1.3
ERMS	9	5.8
FMIC	1	0.6
GAUL1	8	5.2
GROG	6	3.9
HOO	2	1.3
HWB	2	1.3
HWC	2	1.3
KOAN	2	1.3
LOEG	1	0.6
OXID	12	7.8
OXRC	1	0.6
RVOX	1	0.6
SAMLG	35	22.7
SAND	18	11.7
SHEL	2	1.3
VRG	2	1.3
VRW	9	5.8
Total	154	100.0

Table 83 JSS92 pottery assemblage by form

Form	Rows	% rows
-	60	39.0
1	2	1.3
1A	1	0.6
2	5	3.2
2A	2	1.3
2B	1	0.6
2F	1	0.6
2T	3	1.9
3	2	1.3
4	3	1.9
4DR29	10	6.5
4F	1	0.6
4RT12	3	1.9
5	1	0.6
5DR15/17	3	1.9
5DR18	7	4.5
6	1	0.6
6DR24/25	3	1.9
6DR27	3	1.9
6RT9	1	0.6
7	4	2.6
7WAL	2	1.3
8	8	5.2
8DR20	17	11.0
8G	8	5.2
9A	2	1.3
Total	154	100.0

West escape shaft, London Bridge Street (LBA95)

Introduction

The assemblage from LBA95 consists of 1448 sherds (449 rows). Pottery was recovered from 52 contexts. The latest dated pottery on site is an OXRC bowl which is a copy of the samian form Drag. 38. This is dated from AD 270 and was recovered from a post-Roman context.

Period 2 (c AD 50–160; ceramic dates c AD 120–60)

In all 151 sherds of pottery (81 rows) were recovered from features in this period, mostly from pits and external dumps in Open Area 2. The group is dated post-AD 120 on the presence of Black-Burnished type wares and forms, which account for 5.3% of the total assemblage by sherd count and 8.6% by rows (BB2 accounting for 4.6% by sherd count and 7.4% by rows). The dominant reduced ware is HWC which accounts for 15.2% by sherd count and 14.8% by rows. Only a small amount of tempered wares are present (2% by sherd count, 3.5% by rows) but these do include two sherds of SUG which occurs rarely in London assemblages (Davies et al 1994, 117). Fabrics which

are common in 1st-century assemblages such as HWB and the Early Roman Sandy fabrics (ERSA, ERSB, ERSA/B, ERSS, ERMS) are absent from period 2. The most commonly occurring type of samian is SAMLG (13.9% by sherd count, 11.1% by rows) although SAMCG is also present (3.3% by sherd count, 4.9% by rows). The most common samian form is the Drag. 37 bowl. Due to the small size of the assemblage it is difficult to further refine the dating, although the proportion of HWC to BB2 most resembles the trends seen in RCP4 dated c AD 120–40 (Davies et al 1994, 209).

Period 3 (c AD 160–300)

A total of 1192 sherds (277 rows) were recovered from pits, ditches and external dumps in Open Areas 3 and 5. The assemblages from each land use are dealt with separately.

OPEN AREA 5 (CERAMIC DATES C AD 140–60)

The only feature in Open Area 5 is a gully which contained a large assemblage of pottery. This group has been quantified by EVEs and weight (503 sherds/ 12.15 EVEs/ 16,644g) (Table 84). Discussion of the dating and composition of this assemblage (context [62]) can be found in Chapter 8 (Fig 89, <P167>–<P192>).

Context	Fabric	Form	Decor	Sherd count	EVEs	Wt
[62]	AHBB	4H	-	2	0.08	49
[62]	AHSU	2	-	1	0	8
[62]	AHSU	2T	-	1	0.08	27
[62]	AMPH	8	-	3	0	67
[62]	AMPH1	8DR2-4	-	1	0.38	917
[62]	AMPH2	8DR2-4	-	7	0.5	664
[62]	AMPH3	8DR2-4	-	3	0	687
[62]	AMPH4	8	-	3	0	331
[62]	AMPH5	8	-	1	0	105
[62]	BAETE	8DR20	-	5	0	379
[62]	BB1	2	BUD	2	0	23
[62]	BB2	2	-	4	0	40
[62]	BB2	2	AL	2	0	11
[62]	BB2?	2	HPOF	3	0	87
[62]	BB2?	4	-	1	0	29
[62]	BB2	4/5	-	6	0	259
[62]	BB2	4/5	AL	3	0	101
[62]	BB2	4H	AL	6	0.38	131
[62]	BB2?	5J?	-	1	0.06	4
[62]	BB2F	4HI	AL	6	0.41	254
[62]	BBS	2	-	2	0	6
[62]	BBS	2	<36>	2	0	26
[62]	BBS	2	AL	20	0	247
[62]	BBS	2F	-	1	0.07	14
[62]	BBS	2F	AL	33	0.47	504
[62]	BBS	4/5	-	2	0	92
[62]	BBS	4H	AL	12	0.48	224
[62]	C189	8C189	-	1	0	82
[62]	CADIZ	8C186	-	18	0.3	3146
[62]	CAMP2?	8DR2-4	-	1	0	54
[62]	COLWW	-	-	17	0	120
[62]	COLWW	7	-	1	0	93
[62]	ERSB?	5	-	1	0.08	25
[62]	FINE	-	-	2	0	48

Table 84 Quantified assemblage from LBA95 period 3 Open Area 5

Context	Fabric	Form	Decor	Sherd count	EVEs	Wt
[62]	FMIC	-	-	I	0	8
[62]	GAUL1?	8	-	7	0	234
[62]	GAUL1	8G	-	I3	0	845
[62]	HWBR	5	-	I	0	8
[62]	HWC	2	AL	7	0	65
[62]	HWC	2/3	-	21	0	232
[62]	HWC	2F	-	2	0.29	32
[62]	HWC	2F	BUD	I	0.33	352
[62]	HWC	2T	-	3	0.34	39
[62]	HWC	3	BDD	I	0.16	2
[62]	HWC	3F	-	I	0	3
[62]	HWC	4F	-	I	0.07	20
[62]	HWC	4F2	BUD	II	0.77	439
[62]	HWC	9A	-	3	0.21	31
[62]	LOMI	-	-	4	0	33
[62]	LOMI	I?	-	I	0	12
[62]	LOMI	3	EMD	I	0	2
[62]	LOXI	9A?	-	24	0.94	562
[62]	LOXI	9C	FRLD	2	0	92
[62]	NKSH	-	-	2	0	44
[62]	OXID	-	-	I2	0	I08
[62]	OXID	4/5	-	I	0.09	9
[62]	RHMO	7	-	2	0	I5I
[62]	RWS	-	-	8	0	78
[62]	RWS	4/5	-	I	0	I2
[62]	SAMCG	4DR37	DEC	2	0	23
[62]	SAMCG	6DR33	-	4	0.I6	38
[62]	SAMLG	-	-	2	0	9
[62]	SAMLG	4DR37	DEC	3	0	21
[62]	SAMLG	5	-	I	0	22
[62]	SAMLG	5DR36	BAD	I	0.17	I6
[62]	SAMLG	6DR33	-	I	0.I	20
[62]	SAMLG	6DR42	-	I	0.08	8
[62]	SAMMV	5	-	4	0	34
[62]	SAMMV	6DR33	-	2	0.08	26
[62]	SAND	-	-	44	0	507
[62]	SAND	-	ALX	I	0	8
[62]	SAND	IC	-	6	0.7	153
[62]	SAND	4F	-	3	0.41	56
[62]	SAND	9A	-	I	0.06	II
[62]	VCWS	-	-	6	0	49
[62]	VCWS	4A4	-	I	0.18	109
[62]	VRG	-	-	I	0	5
[62]	VRW	-	-	66	0	848
[62]	VRW	I	-	4	0	97
[62]	VRW	IB7	-	I	0.55	78
[62]	VRW	IC	-	3	I	102
[62]	VRW	4A	-	I	0.15	109
[62]	VRW	4A5	-	I7	0.45	652
[62]	VRW	5J	-	7	0.36	I77
[62]	VRW	7	-	I	0	55
[62]	VRW	7HOF	-	4	0.31	453
[62]	VRW	7HOF	<40>	I	0.27	301
[62]	VRW	7HOF	<34>	I	0.08	63
[62]	VRW	7HOF	-	I	0.05	94
[62]	VRW	8IJ	-	4	0.27	105
[62]	VRW	9A	-	3	0.23	128
Total				503	I2.I5	I6644

(Table 84 cont)

OPEN AREA 3 (CERAMIC DATES *C* AD 230–60)

Open Area 3 consists of a number of pits and external dumps. There is a total sherd count of 658 (190 rows) (Table 85). The ceramic dates of c AD 230–60 are provided by the fill of one pit (context [57]) which contains a high percentage of NVCC. This group has been quantified by EVEs and weight and is discussed in Chapter 9.1 (Fig 100, <P197>–<P206>). The remaining assemblages are generally dated from AD 120 or AD 150 and none of these groups contain any of the later colour-coated wares such as NVCC, but are composed mostly of fabrics which dominate 2nd-century assemblages such as BB2 and HWC. The high percentage of GAUL1 by sherd count

Context	Fabric	Form	Decor	Sherd count	EVEs	Wt
[57]	AHSU	2T	-	1	0.16	30
[57]	BB1	2	BUD	1	0	14
[57]	BB1	2F	-	1	0.09	30
[57]	BB1	2FX	OL	12	0.49	228
[57]	BB1	4	BUD	1	0	12
[57]	BB2	4	-	1	0	33
[57]	BB2	4	AL	1	0	34
[57]	BB2	4H	AL	1	0.07	28
[57]	CCRB	3	ROD	1	0	6
[57]	GAUL1	8	-	8	0	255
[57]	NVCC	3J	BAD	8	0.17	226
[57]	NVCC	3J	BFD	17	0.53	340
[57]	NVCC	3J	CR	1	0.15	19
[57]	NVCC	3K	BR	12	0.79	52
[57]	NVCC	3K	ROD	4	0	37
[57]	OXID	-	-	13	0	196
[57]	OXIDF	-	-	1	0	6
[57]	SAMCG	6DR33	-	1	0	11
[57]	SAMEG	5DR31R	ROD	10	0.32	430
[57]	SAMEG	5LUDTG/TF	-	3	0.91	577
[57]	SAND	-	-	2	0	27
[57]	VCWS	-	-	2	0	21
Total				102	3.68	2612

Table 85 Quantified assemblage from LBA95 period 3 Open Area 3 pit

(153 sherds/23.3%) is due to the presence of a single smashed Gauloise 4 amphora (context [13]) which is also discussed in Chapter 9.1 (Fig 101, <P207>).

West vent shaft, London Bridge Street (LBB95)

Introduction

Roman pottery was recovered from 15 contexts, four of which date to the post-Roman period. The pottery was assessed before the introduction of sherd count. A total of 123 rows were inputted, 93 being from Roman contexts.

Period 3 (c AD 60–200; ceramic dates c AD 150–250)

Pottery was recovered from pits and an external dump in Open Area 3 (14 rows). The pottery from period 3 is dated c AD 150–250 on the presence of a SAMEG Drag. 37 bowl. However, within one of the pits is a coin dated AD 365–75 (context [123]) which has not been deemed to be intrusive.

Period 4 (c AD 200–300; ceramic dates c AD 200–300)

The pottery (79 rows) was recovered from the fills of pits and an external dump in Open Area 4. The overall pottery date-range for this period is c AD 200–300. There is also one coin from this period dated AD 270–3 (context [111]). The pottery date-range is supported by the presence of Cam. 306 bowls which first occur in London in the 3rd century (Symonds and Tomber 1991, 70) and the late Roman colour-coated ware, NVCC, which dominates the assemblage. This fabric occurs in a range of forms including a pinch-mouthed flagon and a Castor box

lid. Late Roman imported colour-coated wares include MOSL and CGBL which are each represented by one row. All the main regions of samian production are represented, with a slightly higher row count for SAMEG. Additionally there is an absence of fabrics which characterise the later 3rd and 4th centuries, such as OXRC, OXWW, OXPA, CALC and PORD, and there is only one row of AHFA. Forms which first occur in the mid 3rd century such as the BB-type flanged bowls are also absent.

East vent shaft, Joiner Street (LBC95)

Introduction

Roman pottery was recovered from 14 contexts, six of which date to the post-Roman period. The pottery was assessed before the introduction of sherd count. A total of 132 rows were inputted, 118 of them from Roman contexts.

Period 2 (c AD 300–400; ceramic dates c AD 300–400)

All the Roman contexts belong to one period and land use, period 2, Open Area 2, and are mostly fills from external dumps. There is a high level of residuality within the assemblage, with fabrics that have an end date of before or equivalent to c AD 160 accounting for 26 rows. Overall, fabrics that start appearing in London c AD 150 or after are only represented by 20 rows in this period. The latest fabric dating the assemblage is PORD (dated c AD 350–400) which is represented by one row. Additionally there are six rows of OXRC, a fabric which, although it occurs in London and Southwark during the later 3rd century, tends to be more common during the 4th century (Symonds and Tomber 1991, 73).

East escape shaft, Joiner Street (LBD95)

Introduction

Roman pottery was recovered from a total of six contexts, two of which were post-Roman in date. The pottery was not sherd-counted. A total of 81 rows were inputted, ten of which are residual in post-Roman contexts.

Period 2 (*c* AD 50–400; ceramic dates *c* AD 240–300)

The assemblage (71 rows) is mixed in date, with the majority of the forms and sourced fabrics dating to or before the end of the 2nd century. There is a high number of fabrics and forms that pre-date AD 160; of the 55 identified form rows, 31 have an end date before or equal to AD 160 and 25 fabric rows have an end date before or equal to AD 160. The most commonly occurring type of samian is central Gaulish. The only fabric that exclusively dates to the 1st century is SAMLG. The latest dated vessel is an OXWW Young type 17 mortarium. Other fabrics present that first occur in the late 2nd century are NVCC, TSK and the 'hollow foot' amphora fabric, HOFA. Black-Burnished type fabrics including TSK account for seven rows.

Ticket hall and escalator shaft, MEPC car park (LBE95)

Introduction

Roman pottery was recovered from 118 contexts, 84 of which dated to the post-Roman period. The assemblage was only partially sherd-counted and therefore only rows are used in this overview. A total of 1056 rows were inputted from Roman contexts. The periods for this site cover relatively long spans of time and do not correspond to any Roman Ceramic Phases. Therefore only brief comments are made on the nature and dating of the assemblage.

Period 2 (*c* AD 60–120; ceramic dates *c* AD 70–100)

There are a total of 60 rows of data recorded for this period. The pottery was retrieved from pits and ditches in Open Area 2. There is nothing to date the pottery assemblage later than AD 70–100, except for one sherd of SAMCG which is dated from AD 120; however, this sherd is possibly intrusive. Otherwise the assemblage is dated post-AD 70 by the presence of HWC (2 rows). There are no diagnostic pre-Flavian fabrics or forms such as SLOW, LYON or Drag. 24/25 cups. The most common fabric from this period is SAMLG (11 rows).

Period 3 (*c* AD 120–200; ceramic dates *c* AD 150–250)

This period has a total of 570 rows, of which nine are dated post-AD 200. These sherds come from the construction levels of Building 1 and are possibly intrusive. Other land uses assigned to this period are Open Areas 3 and 4. Black-Burnished wares account for 13.7% of the total assemblage (78 rows). Samian is present in almost equal amounts (76 rows/13.3%). Overall the most common reduced ware is HWC (9.3%). NVCC, a fabric which first appears in London assemblages in the latter half of the 2nd century, is present in small quantities (13 rows/2.3%).

Period 4 (*c* AD 200–300; ceramic dates *c* AD 270–300)

There are a total of 274 rows of data for this period. This material was retrieved from disuse levels of Building 1 and Open Area 5. BB1 (22 rows/8%) is present in almost equal quantities to HWC (24 rows/8.8%). These are the most commonly occurring reduced wares in the assemblage. HWC, like VRW (22 rows/8%), is probably residual by the beginning of this period as the industries which produced these wares (Highgate and the Verulamium region) declined in the mid to late 2nd century. The assemblage as a whole contains a large percentage of residual fabrics and forms.

There is a single entry for the late 'indicator' fabric PORD, which is dated post-AD 350, but this may be intrusive. Apart from this, the latest dated pottery in this period is from the Oxfordshire industries, in particular OXRC (6 rows/2.2%). Oxfordshire mortaria include the Young forms M17 and M22 (1 row each). Other late forms and fabrics include late 'cavetto' everted-rimmed jars (2F13) (2 rows), AHFA (8 rows/2.9%), MOSL (3 rows) and EIFL (1 row). Late amphora types include hollow-foot (2 rows), late Roman rilled (4 rows) and Biv (3 rows). NVCC is the most common Romano-British fine ware (9 rows/3.3%).

Period 5 (*c* AD 300–400; ceramic dates *c* AD 350–400)

Only one land use belongs to this period, Open Area 6, which contains pits and external dumps. There are a total of 152 rows of data. The assemblage has a high percentage of residual material, for example HWC represents 8.6% (13 rows) of the assemblage, SAMLG 7.9% (12 rows) and VRW 8.6% (13 rows). There is a range of late Romano-British and imported fabrics which are possibly all 4th-century in date, but these are only present in small quantities. They include PORD (2 rows), OXRC (4 rows), AHFA (8 rows), NVCC (6 rows), MHAD (1 row) and LRRA (1 row).

Lower machine chamber, Tooley Street (LBH94)

Introduction

Roman pottery was recovered from seven contexts, four of which date to the post-Roman period. The pottery was not sherd-counted. A total of 17 rows were inputted, ten of which represent intrusive pottery from the post-Roman contexts. No pottery is present that can be dated exclusively to the 1st century, and all the sourced samian is central Gaulish and dated from *c* AD 120.

Period 2 (c AD 120–250; ceramic dates c AD 150–250)

There are seven rows of Roman pottery from period 2, Open Area 2. The latest vessel for this period is a SAMCG mortarium from the ditch, which is dated c AD 150–250.

Escalator shaft and ticket hall, Station Approach (LBI95)

Introduction

A total of 2122 rows of Roman pottery were inputted from 184 Roman contexts. The assemblage was only partially sherd-counted and therefore only rows are used in this overview.

Period 1 (pre-AD 70; ceramic dates c AD 60–100)

This period is represented by 70 rows of data. Overall the pottery is dated c AD 60–100. There are no 'definitive' pre-Flavian fabrics such as SLOW, LYON or forms such as Drag. 24/25 cups or Ritterling 1 dishes. The fabric HWC which is usually indicative of post-AD 70 assemblages does appear but, as discussed earlier, it can occur in pre-Flavian assemblages. The most notable feature of the assemblage is the high percentage of imported wares at 35.7%. These include SAMLG which is the most common fabric for this period. The high percentage of amphorae (22.9%) is discussed in the chronological narrative as there is a concentration of amphorae in Open Area 3.

Period 2 (c AD 70–80; ceramic dates c AD 60–100)

INTRODUCTION

There are a total of 423 rows of data for this period. Table 86 and Table 87 summarise the period 2 assemblage by fabric and form respectively.

WARES

The percentage of amphorae is down from the previous period to 16.8% but the small size of the period 1 assemblage should be taken into account. Samian is still high at 12.8%. Reduced wares increase (31.4%) as tempered wares decrease to half of their figure in period 1. Another notable increase is the higher percentage of fine reduced wares from 6.4% compared to 1.4% in the preceding period. Oxidised wares are still high at 18.9%; in the preceding period they were at 20%.

TYPES

The biggest increase in this period from the preceding phase is in those vessels used for serving and drinking liquids. Cups are up from 2.9% to 4.2%, beakers from 1.4% to 6.4% and flagons from 1.4% to 5.0%. Overall the functional category for drinking is up from 4.3% to 10.9%. The amphorae assemblage is characterised by a wide range of different forms such as: Cam. types 184, 186, 189; Haltern 70; Dressel types 2-4 and 20; Gauloise types 4 and 5. Although none of these amphorae are unusual for this period the range of different types is

Table 86 LBI95 period 2 pottery assemblage by fabric

Fabric	Rows	% rows
AHSU	32	7.6
AMPH	7	1.7
AMPH1	2	0.5
AMPH2	1	0.2
BAETE	21	5.0
BHWS	3	0.7
C189	2	0.5
CADIZ	10	2.4
CAMP1	1	0.2
CCIMP	1	0.2
CGGW	1	0.2
CGWH	2	0.5
COLWW	1	0.2
ERMS	7	1.7
ERSB	15	3.5
FINE	11	2.6
FMIC	15	3.5
GAUL	5	1.2
GAUL1	12	2.8
GAUL2	6	1.4
GROG	16	3.8
HOO	10	2.4
HWB	17	4.0
HWBR	1	0.2
HWC	21	5.0
LOMI	1	0.2
MICA	2	0.5
MLEZ	2	0.5
NFSE	1	0.2
NKSH	1	0.2
OXID	20	4.7
OXIDF	3	0.7
PRW3	1	0.2
RDBK	12	2.8
RHOD1	2	0.5
RHOD2	2	0.5
RVOX	1	0.2
RWS	4	0.9
SAMLG	52	12.3
SAND	51	12.1
SHEL	3	0.7
TN	1	0.2
VRG	7	1.7
VRW	37	8.7
Total	**423**	**100.0**

Intrusive sherds

BB1	2	
BBS	1	
HWC+	2	
SAMMV	2	

Table 87 LBI95 period 2 pottery assemblage by form

Form	Rows	% rows
-	92	21.7
1	12	2.8
1B	5	1.2
1B2	1	0.2
1C	1	0.2
1E	2	0.5
2	63	14.9
2/3	6	1.4
2A	12	2.8
2A1-4	2	0.5
2A12-13	2	0.5
2A15	1	0.2
2C	3	0.7
2D	1	0.2
2K	1	0.2
2T	17	4.0
2V	1	0.2
3	19	4.5
3B	4	0.9
3B1	1	0.2
3C	1	0.2
3F	1	0.2
3G	1	0.2
4	11	2.6
4/5	3	0.7
4A	4	0.9
4A1	1	0.2
4DR29	5	1.2
4DR37	2	0.5
4E	1	0.2
4F	3	0.7
4F2	2	0.5
4K	1	0.2
4MX	1	0.2
5	8	1.9
5DR18	7	1.7
5DR22	1	0.2
5DR22/23	1	0.2
5J	3	0.7
5J3	1	0.2
6	4	0.9
6DR27	13	3.1
6DR33	1	0.2
6DR35	1	0.2
7	3	0.7
7G238	1	0.2
7HOF	2	0.5
8	20	4.7
8C184	1	0.2
8C186	9	2.1
8C189	1	0.2
8DR2-4	2	0.5
8DR20	15	3.5
8DR20PW10	1	0.2
8DR20PW15	1	0.2
8G	10	2.4
8G4	1	0.2
8G5	2	0.5
8H70	2	0.5
8L555	6	1.4
9A	17	4.0
9B	1	0.2
9C	2	0.5
9J	2	0.5
9RT13	1	0.2
Total	**423**	**100.0**

distinctive. The majority of these vessels are from the floor levels of Building 2, rooms A and B.

FABRICS

The most common reduced ware is AHSU (7.6%), exceeding HWC (5%) and HWB (4%). The trends seen here are more indicative of middle to late Flavian assemblages than early Flavian ones as seen at Leadenhall Court (Groves 1993, 123, figs 76–7). BAETE remains the dominant amphora fabric (5%). Unlike the assemblage from period 1 there is a range of imported fine wares including terra nigra (TN), central Gaulish glazed (CGGW) and colour-coated wares (CGWH) and Pompeian red ware 3 (PRW3).

FORMS

The most common samian dish form is the Drag. 18. The bowl form Drag. 29 (1.2%) is more common than the Drag. 37 (0.5%) and the figure for the Drag. 27 cup form is higher (3.1%) than for the Drag. 33 cup (0.2%). These trends are similar to those seen in RCP2 (Davies et al 1994, 199, fig 153). Forms which are seen as key indicators of Flavian assemblages appear in small quantities, such as 'poppy-head' beakers (0.2%), imitation Drag. 37 bowls (0.2%) and ring-necked flagons with flaring mouths (0.2%).

Period 3 (c AD 80–100; ceramic dates c AD 70–100)

INTRODUCTION

There are a total of 428 rows for this period. A coin in context [195] is dated AD 54–68. Table 88 and Table 89 summarise the period 3 assemblage by fabric and form respectively.

WARES

Most of the wares are present in the same proportions as in the preceding period. Amphorae are virtually the same at 15.9%. The biggest increase is in the percentage of oxidised wares from 18.9% to 30.6%. Reduced wares are down from 31.4% to 22.7%.

TYPES

Jars are down from 25.8% in the preceding phase to 16.6%, which is reflected in the percentage of reduced wares. Forms which tend to occur in oxidised wares are all more prominent, including mortaria (3%).

FABRICS

The trends in proportions of fabrics in period 3, especially reduced wares, are different from those seen in the corresponding period at Leadenhall Court (LCT84 periods 4–5) (Groves 1993, fig 77). At LBI95, AHSU is the most common sourced reduced ware (9.8%); however, the figure for HWC is lower (2.1%) than in period 2 and below that of HWB (2.8%). The proportions of AHSU to HWB are similar to those at LCT84 periods 4–5, although the relationship between HWB and HWC is the opposite of that at LCT84 where the percentage of HWC is slightly higher than HWB. The assemblage also differs in that ERMS increases to 2.3%, unlike in the corresponding phase at LCT84, where it is

Table 88 LBI95 period 3 pottery assemblage by fabric

Fabric	Rows	% rows
AHSU	42	9.8
AMPH	17	4.0
BAETE	17	4.0
C186	6	1.4
C189	2	0.5
CADIZ	1	0.2
CAT	2	0.5
COAR	1	0.2
ECCW	1	0.2
ERMS	10	2.3
ERSB	7	1.6
FINE	4	0.9
FMIC	11	2.6
GAUL	21	4.9
GAUL2	2	0.5
GROG	16	3.7
HOO	21	4.9
HWB	12	2.8
HWC	9	2.1
NFSE	9	2.1
NKSH	6	1.4
OXID	30	7.0
RDBK	10	2.3
RWS	8	1.9
SAMLG	72	16.8
SAND	26	6.1
SLOW	6	1.4
VRG	3	0.7
VRW	56	13.1
Total	**428**	**100.0**

Intrusive sherds

BB2	1
HWC+	1
SAMCG	1

Table 89 LBI95 period 3 pottery assemblage by form

Form	Rows	% rows
-	135	31.5
1	17	4.0
1B	2	0.5
1B1	2	0.5
1B2	2	0.2
1B3	1	0.2
1E	1	0.2
1J	8	1.9
2	50	11.7
2A	3	0.7
2A15	2	0.5
2B	4	0.9
2C	1	0.2
2T	8	1.9
2V	3	0.7
3	7	1.6
3B	3	0.7
3F	3	0.7
4	3	0.7
4/5	2	0.5
4CU11	1	0.2
4DR29	15	3.5
4DR30	1	0.2
4DR37	4	0.9
4F	6	1.4
4K	2	0.5
4RT12	3	0.7
5	4	0.9
5DR15/17	3	0.7
5DR18	15	3.5
5DR18R	2	0.5
6	2	0.5
6DR24/25	1	0.2
6DR27	12	2.8
6DR33A	1	0.2
7	5	1.2
7G238	3	0.7
7HOF	5	1.2
8	15	3.5
8C186	7	1.6
8C189	2	0.5
8DR2-4	11	2.6
8DR20	17	4.0
8G	19	4.4
8G4	2	0.5
8K117	1	0.2
8L555	2	0.5
9A	5	1.2
9B	1	0.2
9C	2	0.5
9N	1	0.2
9NP	1	0.2
Total	**428**	**100.0**

Intrusive sherds -

2	
4H	1

decreasing as a percentage of the assemblage. The percentage of VRW is higher than that of period 2 (8.7%) at 13.1%. NFSE also increases to represent 2.1% of the assemblage. The Romano-British reduced fine ware FMIC is down from 3.5% in period 2 to 2.3%, which is the opposite of the trends seen at LCT84, where it increases slightly in the later Flavian period (ibid, 123). There is still a notable variety in the range of amphorae occurring on the site, just as there was in the preceding phase. Gaulish amphorae are more common than Dressel 20 amphorae.

FORMS

One of the most marked changes is in the number of bead-rimmed jars (2A) which is down considerably from period 2 (4%) to 1.2%. The percentage of ring-necked flagons (IB) (1.6%) is similar to that in period 2 (1.2%). The changes between periods 2 and 3 at LBI95 do not reflect some of the key trends within forms seen at Leadenhall Court (Groves 1993, 125–7). In period 3 the percentage of lids (1.2%) is lower than the figure for period 2 (4%), unlike at LCT84 where the rise in the number of lids is the most marked trend in the late Flavian period.

The trends within samian forms are also unlike those seen at LCT84. Drag. 29 bowls (3.5%), Drag. 15/17 (0.7%) and

Drag. 18 (3.5%) dishes are all more common in period 3 than they were in period 2 (1.2%, 0%, 1.7%). At LCT84 all these forms decrease in number towards the end of the 1st century (Groves 1993, 126). Drag. 37 bowls are slightly more common in period 2 (0.9% from 0.5%) and Drag. 27 cups are present in similar numbers to period 2.

Period 4 (*c* AD 100–40; ceramic dates *c* AD 120–60)

INTRODUCTION

There are a total of 537 rows of data for this period. One group of pottery from Open Area 7 (Table 90) is discussed in the main text (group 11 [412]). This period covers two of the Roman Ceramic Phases, RCP3 and RCP4 (Davies et al 1994). The ceramic dates reflect the latest date of the entire assemblage; however, a large proportion of the material is earlier than AD 120. Table 91 and Table 92 summarise the period 4 assemblage by fabric and form respectively.

Context	Fabric	Form	Decor	Sherd count	EVEs	Wt
[412]	AHSU	-	-	10	0	160
[412]	AHSU	2	-	1	0.16	34
[412]	AHSU	2A12-13	-	2	0.26	66
[412]	AHSU	2T	-	7	0.82	189
[412]	AMPH1	8DR2-4	-	5	0	564
[412]	AMPH2	8	-	13	0.16	633
[412]	AMPH3	8	-	23	0.29	1524
[412]	BAETE	8DR20	-	14	0	3497
[412]	C189	8?	RLD	3	0	4
[412]	C189	8K117	-	3	0	222
[412]	COLWW	7	-	1	0	64
[412]	FMIC	4	NCD	1	0	6
[412]	GAUL1	8G	-	3	0	292
[412]	HOO	-	-	1	0	15
[412]	HWB	-	-	2	0	6
[412]	HWB	4/5?	-	1	0	18
[412]	HWC	-	-	7	0	157
[412]	HWC	2A	-	4	0.48	163
[412]	LOXI	9A	-	3	0.16	161
[412]	MICA	-	-	1	0	8
[412]	NKSH	-	-	1	0	40
[412]	OXID	4A	-	1	0.17	72
[412]	SAMLG	4/5?	BR	1	0.05	8
[412]	SAMLG	4DR37	DEC	5	0	128
[412]	SAMLG	5DR36	BAD	1	0.15	13
[412]	SAMLG	6DR27	-	1	0.11	10
[412]	SAMLG	6DR33	-	3	0.14	23
[412]	SAMLG	6DR35	-	2	0.4	39
[412]	SAMLG	6KN78	DEC	1	0.16	13
[412]	SAND	-	-	14	0	196
[412]	SAND	2T	-	3	0.2	12
[412]	SAND	9A	-	2	0	73
[412]	SHEL	-	-	1	0	111
[412]	VRW	-	-	16	0	297
[412]	VRW	1	-	1	0	122
[412]	VRW	1B?	-	1	0.24	14
[412]	VRW	4	-	4	0	112
[412]	VRW	4A3	-	2	0.08	130
[412]	VRW	7	-	2	0	100
[412]	VRW	7	SPT	4	0	339
[412]	VRW	9A	-	1	0.07	20
[412]	VRW	9C	FRLD	1	0	19
Total				173	4.1	9674

Table 90 Quantified assemblage from LBI95 period 4 Open Area 7 external support

Table 91 LBI95 period 4 pottery assemblage by fabric

Fabric	Rows	% rows
AHSU	52	9.7
AMPH	15	2.8
AMPH1	1	0.2
AMPH2	1	0.2
AMPH3	1	0.2
BAETE	15	2.8
BB1	9	1.7
BB2	5	0.9
BB2F	1	0.2
BBS	5	0.9
C186	3	0.6
C189	6	1.1
CADIZ	3	0.6
CAMP	1	0.2
CAMP1	1	0.2
CAT	3	0.6
COAR	3	0.6
COLWW	1	0.2
ERMS	6	1.1
ERSB	10	1.9
FINE	18	3.4
FMIC	18	3.4
GAUL	12	2.2
GAUL1	4	0.7
GAUL3	1	0.2
GROG	12	2.2
HOO	8	1.5
HWB	12	2.2
HWC	41	7.6
HWC+	2	0.4
ITMO	1	0.2
LOMI	1	0.2
LOXI	6	1.1
LYON	2	0.4
MICA	1	0.2
NARS	1	0.2
NFSE	5	0.9
NKGW	1	0.2
NKSH	10	1.9
OXID	20	3.7
PRW3	1	0.2
RDBK	11	2.0
RWS	10	1.9
SAMCG	4	0.7
SAMLG	52	9.7
SAMMV	1	0.2
SAMMV2	1	0.2
SAND	55	10.2
SHEL	5	0.9
SLOW	1	0.2
VCWS	5	0.9
VRG	1	0.2
VRW	72	13.4
Total	537	100.0

Table 92 LBI95 period 4 pottery assemblage by form

Form	Rows	% rows
-	148	27.6
1	11	2.0
1B	2	0.4
1B2	1	0.2
1J	4	0.7
2	56	10.4
2/3	3	0.6
2A	14	2.6
2A12-13	1	0.2
2B	5	0.9
2C	5	0.9
2D	3	0.6
2F	10	1.9
2G	1	0.2
2K	4	0.7
2N	1	0.2
2T	26	4.8
2V	8	1.5
3	23	4.3
3A	1	0.2
3B	1	0.2
3C	1	0.2
3E	3	0.6
3F	7	1.3
4	12	2.2
4/5	5	0.9
4A	6	1.1
4A3	1	0.2
4B	1	0.2
4DR29	8	1.5
4DR37	4	0.7
4F	7	1.3
4G	1	0.2
4H	2	0.4
4K	1	0.2
4RT12	3	0.6
5	3	0.6
5DR15/17	1	0.2
5DR18	9	1.7
5DR18/31	1	0.2
5DR22/23	1	0.2
5DR36	1	0.2
5J3	2	0.4
6DR27	12	2.2
6DR33	5	0.9
6DR35	1	0.2
6DR40	1	0.2
6KN78	1	0.2
6RT9	1	0.2
7	8	1.5
7G238	1	0.2
7HOF	8	1.5
8	18	3.4
8C186	6	1.1
8C189	4	0.7
8DR2-4	8	1.5
8DR20	13	2.4
8G	15	2.8
8G4	1	0.2
8H70	2	0.4
8K117	1	0.2
9A	16	3.0
9C	2	0.4
9D	1	0.2
9LA	2	0.4
9NP	2	0.4
Total	537	100.0

WARES

Amphorae (12.5%) are reduced in comparison with period 3 (15.9%). Not unsurprisingly Black-Burnished type wares start to appear on the site (3.7%). The figure for other reduced wares is also increased from period 3 (22.7%) to 31.1%. Reduced fine wares increase from 3.5% in period 3 to 6.9%. A similar trend is seen in RCP3 where the Romano-British reduced fine wares, FINE, LONW and FMIC, all occur in their greatest numbers during this phase (Davies et al 1994, fig 147). Other Romano-British fine wares at LBI95 period 4 are present in equal quantities to period 3. Oxidised wares are reduced to 24% from 30.6%. Samian is also lower at 10.8% compared to period 3's 16.8%.

TYPES

Apart from amphorae the other main vessel types that are reduced considerably in number from period 3 are dishes (3.4% from 5.6%) and flagons (5.8% to 2.6%). Beakers (6.7%) and jars (25.5%) have increased from period 3. None of these trends is discernible in the corresponding phases of RCP3 and RCP4.

FABRICS

HWC is the single most commonly occurring sourced reduced ware (7.6%), as also seen in both RCP3 and RCP4 (Davies et al 1994, fig 146). VRW is the most common oxidised ware (13.4%). The majority of samian is from southern Gaul (9.7%) although smaller amounts from Les Martres-de-Veyre (0.4%) and central Gaul (0.7%) are also present.

FORMS

This period differs from the preceding phase in that it contains a wider variety of forms, especially of jars. To some extent this is a result of the emergence of the new Black-Burnished ware forms such as everted-rimmed jars (2F) and flat-rimmed bowls (4G). One interesting point is that there is a higher percentage of Gaulish amphorae (3%) than Dressel 20 (2.4%). This is not reflected in the Roman Ceramic Phases where Dressel 20 is the most common type of amphora throughout the early Roman period.

Period 5 (*c* AD 140+)

There are a total of 664 rows of data for this period. The majority of the pottery is attributable to the late 1st and 2nd centuries. There are eight rows of fabrics that post-date AD 150 including NVCC, TSK, SAMEG and BAETL. The latest dated sherd is AHFA. Due to the mixed nature of the assemblage and the length of the period there is no overview of the period 5 assemblage.

20–26 London Bridge Street (LBJ95)

Introduction

Roman pottery was recovered from four contexts, all of which belong to period 2, Open Area 2. The pottery was not sherd-counted. A total of 30 rows were inputted.

Period 2 (Roman; ceramic dates *c* AD 120–60/200)

The pottery date-range for this period is *c* AD 120–60/200. The majority of the samian is central Gaulish which is dated in London from *c* AD 120. There are no fabrics or forms present that date exclusively from the 1st century. The identified SAMCG forms include Drag. 18/31 and 18/31R dishes which are dated to *c* AD 150 (Webster 1996, 35) and a Drag. 33 cup. Black-Burnished wares dominate the reduced wares and there is one row of the later Highgate fabric, HWC+, all of which are dated in the City from *c* AD 120 (Davies et al 1994, 107). Additionally, there is an absence of the later colour-coated ware NVCC, which first appears in London during the late 2nd century.

Traction substation, Redcross Way (REW92)

Introduction

A total of 555 sherds (236 rows) of Roman pottery were recovered from 17 contexts.

Period 2 (*c* AD 70–100/20; ceramic dates *c* AD 70–90)

In all 210 sherds (65 rows) of Roman pottery were recovered from external dumps (group 3) in Open Area 2. The majority of pottery from this period comes from a single pit group (context [231] 183 sherds/ 5.13EVEs/ 3881g/ 49 rows) which has been quantified (Table 93) and is discussed in Chapter 6 (Fig 66, <P107>–<P120>).

Period 3 (*c* AD 120–60; ceramic dates *c* AD 120–60)

A total of 266 sherds (115 rows) of Roman pottery were recovered mostly from external dumps in Open Area 2 (groups 4 and 5). The latest dated form in the assemblage is a ring-neck flagon with a cupped mouth (1B7-9), a type which generally occurs in substantial quantities from *c* AD 140 (Davies et al 1994, 42, fig 33). The reduced wares are dominated by almost equal amounts of HWC (16.9% by sherd count; 13.9% by rows) and Black-Burnished wares (18.4% by sherd count; 13.9% by rows). Black-Burnished type forms are prominent in the assemblage, everted-rimmed jars being the most common single type of jar (6.4% by sherd count, 7% by rows). Although VRW is by far the most common oxidised ware (18% by sherd count; 11.3% by rows), VCWS is also present in substantial amounts (10.5% by sherd count; 3.5% by rows). Equal amounts of SAMCG and SAMLG are present. There is a Drag. 18/31 dish in SAMCG which is the predominant plate form during the Roman Ceramic Phases covered by this period, RCP4 and RCP5 (Davies et al 1994, 213; 217) and is generally dated up to *c* AD 150 (Webster 1996, 35). No later Black-Burnished ware forms are present, such as Gilliam type 226 bowls or jars with open acute lattice which occur more frequently in the mid to late 2nd century. There is also an absence of later fine wares such as NVCC,

which start occurring in assemblages in the second half of the 2nd century. Therefore this assemblage has been given an end date of *c* AD 160.

Period 5 (*c* AD 300–400; ceramic dates *c* AD 150–250)

A total of 79 sherds (56 rows) were recovered from grave cuts in Open Area 3. The majority of the fabrics (52 sherds) have an end date before or equal to AD 250. The latest dated vessel is a SAMEG mortarium which dates from *c* AD 150. There is an absence of any fabrics and/or forms which would indicate a 3rd- or 4th-century date.

Grouting shaft, Redcross Way (RWG94)

Introduction

Roman pottery was recovered from a total of 19 contexts. A total of 285 rows were inputted, 254 for period 4 and 31 for period 5. The pottery was not sherd-counted.

Period 4 (*c* AD 160–300; ceramic dates *c* AD 250/70–300)

The majority of the pottery from the site was recovered from the disuse fills of pits and wells in Open Area 2 (Table 94). The dates of these fills are mainly *c* AD 250–300/400. Black-Burnished fabrics dominate the reduced wares, accounting for 24% of the total assemblage with BB2 and BB1 being the most commonly represented fabrics. AHFA accounts for 6.3% of the assemblage and occurs in forms typical of the later Alice Holt industry such as flanged bowls, later everted-rimmed jars and large storage jars. Other late Roman fabrics which are present but in small quantities are OXRC (1 row), LRRA (2 rows), MHAD (1 row) and OXWW (3 rows). NVCC is the most commonly occurring fine ware accounting for 12 rows (4.7%). The majority of the samian is central Gaulish. Two types of Black-Burnished bowl are the most common on site, the rounded-rimmed (8 rows) and the flanged bowls (7 rows). The latter type appears in London assemblages in substantial quantities from *c* AD 250. Other late forms include pentice and necked beakers, everted-rimmed jars with obtuse lattice and late mortarium forms, including one example with a hammerhead rim, a Young type 17 (Young 1977, 72, fig 21, M17-11) and a Drag. type 45. The assemblage from one well (group 3) is discussed in Chapter 9.1 (Fig 98, <P193>–<P196>).

Period 5 (*c* AD 300–400; ceramic dates *c* AD 250–400)

Only a small amount of the pottery (31 rows) was recovered from Open Area 3 and it comes from the backfill of graves and an external dump. The latest date is from an external dump (subgroup 42) which contains AHFA. Late Roman colour-coats include MHAD, NVCC and NFCC. NFCC is a very rare occurrence in London or Southwark. It is present in a late Roman group from Billingsgate bathhouse dated *c* AD 350–400+ (Symonds and Tomber 1991, 77).

Context	Fabric	Form	Decor	Sherd count	EVEs	Wt
[231]	AHSU	2	-	25	0	346
[231]	AHSU	2T	-	3	0.15	29
[231]	AMPH	8	-	3	0	302
[231]	BAETE	8DR20	-	1	0	151
[231]	ERMS	2	-	2	0	16
[231]	ERMS	2B	-	3	0.45	44
[231]	ERSB	2	-	1	0	41
[231]	ERSB	2A	-	1	0.11	19
[231]	FINE	2/3	-	1	0.09	8
[231]	FINE	3	-	1	0	10
[231]	FINE	3	BDD	4	0	10
[231]	FMIC	-	-	7	0	22
[231]	FMIC	3B	-	1	0.11	9
[231]	GAULI	8	-	7	0	598
[231]	GROG	-	-	7	0	50
[231]	GROG	9A	-	1	0.06	4
[231]	GROG	9LB?	-	2	0	48
[231]	HWB	-	-	8	0	100
[231]	HWB	2A	-	1	0.05	9
[231]	HWB	4F	-	2	0.18	41
[231]	HWB	4FI	-	2	0.25	76
[231]	HWB	9A	-	1	0.21	41
[231]	HWC	4	-	1	0	19
[231]	HWC	4F	-	1	0.1	18
[231]	LYON	6H	SCD	30	0.67	56
[231]	OXID	-	-	1	0	45
[231]	RDBK?	-	-	1	0	0
[231]	RDBK	3B	BDD	1	0	3
[231]	RDBK?	6DR27	-	1	0.1	9
[231]	RHOD2	8RHOD	-	1	0	80
[231]	RWS	-	-	2	0	3
[231]	SAMLG	-	-	3	0	5
[231]	SAMLG	4	-	1	0	55
[231]	SAMLG	5DR18	-	4	0.37	71
[231]	SAMLG	5DR18	<14>	1	0	
[231]	SAMLG	5DR36	-	1	0	37
[231]	SAMLG	6DR27	-	4	0.31	20
[231]	SAMLG	6DR33	-	1	0	3
[231]	SAND	-	-	8	0	109
[231]	SAND	2T	-	2	0.24	53
[231]	SHEL	2A	-	1	0.05	42
[231]	TNIM	5J3	-	4	0.23	100
[231]	VRG	-	-	1	0	34
[231]	VRW	-	-	20	0	465
[231]	VRW	IB	-	1	0.2	6
[231]	VRW	IB2	-	3	1	227
[231]	VRW	7	-	2	0	311
[231]	VRW	7HOF	-	2	0	125
[231]	VRW	9LB?	-	1	0.2	11
Total				183	5.13	3881

Table 93 Quantified assemblage from REW92 period 2 Open Area 2 pit

Context	Fabric	Form	Decor	Sherd count	EVEs	Wt
[54]	AHFA	-	-	4	0	37
[54]	AHFA	2	-	4	0	782
[54]	AHFA	2	BUD	40	0	2572
[54]	AHFA?	2T	WLX	4	0	114
[54]	BAETL	8DR20	-	1		1321
[54]	BBI	5J	ARCX	1	0.09	35
[54]	BBS	2	-	1	0	94
[54]	BBS	2	AL	4	0	59
[54]	BBS	4/5	-	1	0	3
[54]	GAUL	8	-	3	0	34
[54]	NVCC	3K	WBAD	19	0.16	320
[54]	NVCC	3L	ROD	19		324
[54]	SAND	-	-	1		2
[54]	SAND	2	-	2		673
[54]	VRW	-	-	1		59
Total				105	0.25	6429

Table 94 Quantified assemblage from RWG94 period 4 Open Area 2 Structure 2 well

Cable trench, Redcross Way (RWT93)

Introduction

Pottery was retrieved from 69 contexts. A total of 607 rows were inputted. All are within periods 3–6, except for one row which was in the post-Roman sequence. The assemblage was not sherd-counted.

Period 3 (c AD 120–60; ceramic dates c AD 140–200)

A total of 320 rows were inputted for period 3. This period covers two Roman Ceramic Phases, RCP4 and RCP5, with which the general trends within fabrics and forms can be compared (Table 95; Table 96). The main difference between these two ceramic phases is not the types of forms and fabrics present, which tend to be similar, but the proportions in which they occur (Davies et al 1994, 213). There are three land uses belonging to period 3: Building 1, Open Area 1 and Open Area 2. Fabrics and forms which are dated post-AD 120 are NVCC (2 rows), BB2F (1 row), SAMEG (1 row), 1B7 (5 rows) and 7BEF (1 row). These latest fabrics and forms occur in the first land use of this period, Open Area 1 (NVCC, 1B7, SAMEG). The dominant reduced ware is HWC (57 rows/17.8%), while AHSU (30 rows/9.4%) and Black-Burnished wares (33 rows/10.3%) are present in almost equal quantities. The Early Roman Sandy fabrics are absent from the assemblage. The predominance of HWC as opposed to Black-Burnished type wares is more indicative of RCP4 than RCP5 (Davies et al 1994, fig 146). The only fabric present which dates exclusively to the 1st century is SAMLG, which is the most frequently occurring type of samian. VRW is the most common oxidised ware (41 rows/12.8%). The predominant type of flagon is the late cupped-mouthed ring-necked flagon (1B7), the most common jar is the everted-rimmed jar (24 rows/7.5%) and the 'poppy-head' beaker (11 rows/3.4%) is the dominant type of beaker; these figures reflect trends seen in RCP5 (ibid, 214–17). The types of bowls present also reflect general trends within RCP5: Black-Burnished type bowls with triangular rims are the most common type of form (6 rows/1.9%), and reed-rimmed bowls and flat-rimmed bowls are present in equal amounts (4 rows/1.3%).

Overall the trends within proportions of vessel types and fabrics from this period indicate a later start date of c AD 140 rather than AD 120. The presence of NVCC, which tends to be indicative of late 2nd- and 3rd-century assemblages, would also support a later date for this assemblage, and therefore an end date of c AD 200 is suggested.

Period 4 (c AD 160–300; ceramic dates c AD 160–250)

Period 4 covers two land uses, Open Area 3 and Open Area 4. Only 33 rows were inputted for this period. The sparsity of pottery and the difficulty in defining assemblages from the late 2nd to early 3rd centuries has meant that this assemblage is given a wide date-range. The latest dating evidence is provided

Table 95 RWT93 period 3 pottery assemblage by fabric

Fabric	Rows	% rows
AHSU	30	9.4
AMPH	1	0.3
BAET	14	4.4
BB1	14	4.4
BB2	8	2.5
BB2F	1	0.3
BBS	10	3.1
C189	1	0.3
CADIZ	6	1.9
CC	1	0.3
COLWW	3	0.9
FMIC	4	1.3
GAUL1	10	3.1
GROG	3	0.9
HWB	10	3.1
HWB/C	1	0.3
HWC	57	17.8
KOAN	4	1.3
KOLN	2	0.6
LOMI	8	2.5
LOXI	5	1.6
MLEZ	1	0.3
MORT	1	0.3
NKSH	4	1.3
NVCC	2	0.6
OXID	11	3.4
RDBK	1	0.3
RHOD	1	0.3
RWS	5	1.6
SAMCG	3	0.9
SAMEG	1	0.3
SAMLG	14	4.4
SAND	27	8.4
SEAL	1	0.3
SHEL	2	0.6
VCWS	10	3.1
VRG	2	0.6
VRW	41	12.8
Total	**320**	**100.0**

Table 96 RWT93 period 3 pottery assemblage by form

Form	Rows	% rows
-	60	18.8
1	3	0.9
1B	1	0.3
1B5	2	0.6
1B7	5	1.6
1E	1	0.3
1F	3	0.9
1J	2	0.6
1K	1	0.3
2	67	20.9
2A	1	0.3
2A1-4	1	0.3
2A17	2	0.6
2D	3	0.9
2E	3	0.9
2F	24	7.5
2T	8	2.5
2V	4	1.3
3	14	4.4
3B	1	0.3
3F	11	3.4
4	10	3.1
4/5	1	0.3
4A	4	1.3
4DR30	1	0.3
4DR37	3	0.9
4F	4	1.3
4H	4	1.3
4HI	2	0.6
5DR18	5	1.6
5DR18/31	2	0.6
5J	2	0.6
6DR27	4	1.3
6DR33	1	0.3
7	4	1.3
7BEF	1	0.3
7HOF	1	0.3
8	6	1.9
8C186	6	1.9
8DR2-4	1	0.3
8DR20	13	4.1
8G	10	3.1
8H70	1	0.3
9A	17	5.3
Total	**320**	**100.0**

by a COLWW mortarium which is similar in rim form to those thought to be produced by the potter Cunopectus from c AD 160 into the 3rd century (Hartley 1999, fig 4.14, nos 259 and 261; fig 4.15, no. 273). There is a notable absence of the late Roman fine wares such as NVCC which are usually present in 3rd-century assemblages.

Period 5 (c AD 300–400; ceramic dates c AD 300–400)

Period 5 has one land use, Building 2, from which 195 rows were inputted. The date of c AD 300 is based on the presence of CALC (1 row). Other late fabrics include OXRC (2 rows), MHAD (1 row), HOFA (1 row) and AHFA (13 rows). The assemblage features a high degree of residuality, with over

50% (101 rows) of it having an end date equal to or before AD 250, and 54 of these rows having an end date equal to or before AD 160. The Black-Burnished type wares dominate the assemblage, accounting for 25% of the total number of rows (49 rows/25.1%), with BB2 as the most common reduced fabric overall (17 rows/8.7%). The amount of residuality is also apparent in the sparsity of late forms in the assemblage, with the predominant form being the everted-rimmed jar with acute lattice (26 rows/13.3%) as opposed to the later version of this form (1 row/0.5%).

Period 6 ('dark earth'; ceramic dates *c* AD 270–400)

Period 6 has one land use, Open Area 5 (58 rows). No fabrics are present that date any earlier than AD 270.

Grouting shaft, St Thomas Street (TOM95)

Introduction

Roman pottery was recovered from a total of 18 contexts, six of which date to the post-Roman period. The total sherd count was 239 and a total of 129 rows were inputted. The site has material dating from the 1st to 4th centuries, but apart from SAMLG those fabrics dated exclusively to the 1st century are missing from the assemblage as a whole.

Period 1 (*c* AD 50–300; ceramic dates *c* AD 200–300)

All the pottery from this period comes from the fills of pits and ditches in Open Area 1 (84 sherds/52 rows). The pottery ranges in date from the 1st to 3rd centuries although the majority of it dates from *c* AD 120. There is very little pottery that dates exclusively to the 1st century except for one sherd of SAMLG. The most commonly occurring samian fabric is SAMCG, which is represented by five sherds (5 rows). The main industries producing reduced wares for the London region in the period *c* AD 50–160 are only represented by single sherds (AHSU, HWC). In contrast Black-Burnished wares, which start coming into London *c* AD 120 (BB1, BB2, BBS, TSK) account for 27 sherds (11 rows, 32% of the total assemblage by sherd count). Although there are eight sherds of VRW (3 rows), no forms are identified. Forms that are normally indicative of the later 2nd century are present including a Drag. 45 mortarium and a Gilliam 226 bowl. Diagnostic 3rd-century forms include a Cam. 306 bowl, a hammerhead mortarium and a later everted-rimmed jar with obtuse lattice decoration. The later colour-coated ware NVCC is present, although other fine wares which tend to appear in London slightly later like MHAD, and products from the Oxford industry, are absent.

Period 2 (*c* AD 300–400; ceramic dates *c* AD 300–400)

All the pottery is from the fills of a well, a pit and an external dump in Open Area 2 (139 sherds/64 rows). The majority of the pottery is from the large external dump (group 5, subgroup 11) that seals the earlier features in Open Area 1. The latest fabric in this period is one sherd of PORD, which is usually dated post-AD 350 in London. The assemblage is quite mixed in date with a large quantity of residual material. There are seven sherds of the later Alice Holt fabric, AHFA (3 rows), but there are also nine sherds of the earlier ware, AHSU (3 rows). There are only seven sherds of Black-Burnished wares (5 rows), which represents 5% of the total assemblage by sherd count compared to almost 30% in period 1. Early oxidised wares include VRW and NFSE. SAMLG, SAMMV, SAMCG and SAMEG are all present, with equivalent sherd counts for both south (6 sherds/3 rows) and east Gaulish samian (6 sherds/6 rows). There are ten sherds of NVCC representing 7.2% by sherd count (2 rows), while other late fine wares include LRMA, MOSL and MHAD. No OXRC was identified, although there is an OXWW Young type 17 mortarium which is dated in London from *c* AD 240. Several early amphora fabrics and/or forms are in evidence which pre-date AD 150, such as RHOD, CAT, Dressel 2-4 and Cam. 189 amphorae. The latest dated amphora is a BAETE 8DR20 rim similar to rim type 36 illustrated by Peacock and Williams (1986, fig 66, no. 36) which is dated *c* AD 150–220.

Grouting shaft, O'Meara Street (OMS94)

Introduction

Pottery was recovered from seven contexts, all of which belong to period 2. The pottery was not sherd-counted.

Period 2 (*c* AD 70–100; ceramic dates *c* AD 50–70)

The pottery from this period is pre-Flavian in character and therefore earlier than the date of AD 70–100 given for this phase. This is due to much of the material being recovered from features relating to the consolidation of the ground surface prior to the construction of Building 1.

This assemblage is characterised by an unusually large amount of imported wares, comprising 25 rows out of a total of 57. SAMLG is the most common fabric by number of rows. Tempered wares account for eight rows while sand-tempered reduced wares are represented by seven rows. These characteristics are also noticeable in early assemblages from the City, where quantities of imported wares tend to be higher in the pre-Boudican period than any subsequent period (Davies et al 1994, 167) and grog-tempered fabrics, particularly HWB, are most common (ibid, 168; 186). Early forms include a butt beaker, a collared flagon and a Drag. type 24/25 cup, and diagnostically early fabrics include RVOX and ECCW. There is an absence of HWC, which tends to start occurring in substantial quantities in the Flavian period. Rare or unusual forms include a Kingsholm 117 amphora and a GROG dolium.

Grouting shaft, Union Street (USG94)

Introduction

Pottery was retrieved from a total of five contexts (30 rows), all belonging to period 4, Open Area 2. The pottery was not sherd-counted.

Period 4 (*c* AD 160–300; ceramic dates *c* AD 170/240–250/300)

The dating of the pottery from this period is problematical as it is dated from AD 240 on one example of the rare Oxfordshire industry fabric, OXMOB (Young 1977, 116). Otherwise, the early date for this assemblage is AD 170 based on the presence of the late amphora fabric, BAETL. However, the difference between the early and late Baetican amphora fabrics lies primarily in the amounts of the main inclusions, which change over time. This transition from the earlier to the later fabric is gradual, and therefore the presence of BAETL on its own is not usually used to date an assemblage. In addition, there is an absence of any of the late Roman fine wares or reduced fabrics that normally indicate 3rd-century assemblages such as NVCC, MHAD, OXRC or AHFA. Black-Burnished wares are the most common type of reduced ware in the assemblage but none of the forms, fabrics or types of decoration indicate a starting date any later than *c* AD 120.

Stamped mortaria

Kay Hartley

Introduction

This report concerns four mortarium stamps from the Jubilee Line excavations. Two stamps, LBA95 <34> and <40>, are from the quantified assemblage in Open Area 5, context [62]. Discussion of the dating and composition of this assemblage can be found in Chapter 8 (Fig 89, <P167>–<P192>). A third stamp, LBA95 <35> [58], which has sherd links to the LBA95 assemblage, is also discussed. A fourth stamp is from LBI95 <85> [144] <P224> (Fig 106) and has been selected for publication due to its rarity in London.

Only those fabrics that are uncommon in London have been published in this report. Fabric descriptions of each individual sherd are held in the archive. 'Right-facing' and 'left-facing' when applied to stamps indicate the relation of the stamp to the spout looking at the mortarium from the outside.

LBA95 <34> [62] period 3 Open Area 5 gully/ditch

(See Chapter 8, Fig 89, <P180>)

KENT OR VERULAMIUM REGION WHITE WARE (VRW)
A flange fragment in light brown fabric (Munsell 5YR 7/6), perhaps with self-coloured slip. The matrix is very fine-textured, but the frequent tiny to small inclusions (transparent and pinkish quartz, opaque red-brown and black) are sufficient to give a slightly granular feel to the surface. The matrix is more visible than in the finer type of fabric produced in the Verulamium region, which this fabric resembles in some ways. There is a drab cream core in the thicker parts of the flange, which was probably also present near the base.

A broken, left-facing, two-line stamp survives, reading from the inside of the vessel outwards, VS.F.X / CATV[...]; unusually, the name is on the lower line. When complete this stamp reads VS.F.X / CATVLL for *Catullus fecit*, X being used as a space-filler. Other mortaria stamped with the same die have been recorded from near Gravesend and London (Walters 1908, M2776); mortaria stamped with a second, single-line die of his have been recorded from Canterbury and Westgate Court, Thanet. Many of his mortaria, including this example, can be attributed to an unknown source in Kent, probably in the Canterbury area where most of the mortarium production occurred. His two other mortaria from London are, however, probably in Verulamium fabric, and any activity in the Verulamium region would probably pre-date that in Kent. His rim-profiles indicate a date within the period AD 100–40, with an optimum date of AD 110–30. He was a contemporary of the Valentinus who produced similar fabrics, indicating a similar move to Kent.

LBA95 <35> [58] period 3 Open Area 3 external dump

(See Chapter 8, Fig 89, <P182>)

VERULAMIUM REGION WHITE WARE (VRW)
The incompletely impressed stamp on the left-facing side reads SATV[...]/NV[...] for SATVRNI/NVS followed by a leaf stop, TV ligatured. The fragmentary right-facing stamp probably preserves the bottom of the first stroke of the N on the lower line. These stamps are from the larger of two dies with identical reading. The larger die had a counterstamp reading FEC (Walters 1908, M2825), but it was rarely used and most of his mortaria had, like this one, a name-stamp on each side.

Saturninus i is not to be confused with potters of the same name who worked at Colchester, in the Catterick area and at Corbridge. Most of his mortaria are found in the south and south-east of England, but one recorded from High House milecastle (50TW) on Hadrian's Wall provides the earliest firm dating of about AD 125 (Gillam 1953, 36, fig 7, no. 38), while a stamp at Verulamium was found in a deposit dated AD 130–40 (Hartley 1972, 378, no. 36, B II 28C). The rim-profiles and spouts used by Saturninus i all point to activity within the period AD 110–40. The spout on this example is identical to that on the sherd from Hadrian's Wall. This spout-type was in common use at the potteries in the Verulamium region in the early 2nd century, having lost features typical of the Flavian period there. Diam 270mm.

LBA95 <40> [62] period 3 Open Area 5 gully/ditch

(See Chapter 8, Fig 89, <P181>)

VERULAMIUM REGION WHITE WARE (VRW)
Flange fragment with the left-facing part of the spout surviving. This is a second mortarium of Saturninus i, but the stamp [......]/[....]VS is too fragmentary to allow the die to be identified. The spout is of a different type from the preceding example.

LBI95 <85> [144] period 3 Building 4 occupation debris

(Fig 106, <P224>)

BAVAY (NORTH FRENCH/SOUTH-EAST ENGLAND (NFSE))
A flange and right-facing fragment from the spout of a mortarium in quite hard, self-coloured, fine-textured, cream fabric. Few inclusions are visible at x20 magnification (opaque black [?slag], quartz and probably flint), with rare larger, but still small fragments. A line along the section, near to the surface, shows where additional clay was added to form the spout. The row of larger grits (including flint) visible along this line marks the surface of the flange, the whole of which was already gritted and scored before any clay was added.

The stamp, impressed across the flange, reads PRASSO OF retrograde from the inner edge of the bowl. OF is an abbreviation for *officina*, and PRASSO is an abbreviation for the genitive form *Prassonis*, the whole phrase meaning 'the workshop of Prasso'. Decorative space-fillers were used at the beginning and end of the letters and the two words are separated by an X. Only three other mortaria of Prasso are known, all stamped with the same die, from Cirencester, London (Walters 1908, M2796) and Minnis Bay, Birchington, Kent. The mortaria examined all have the deeply hooked rims indicative of Hartley group I mortaria, which are attributable to northern France and dated within the period AD 50–85 (Hartley 1998, 206). It is worth noting that there are only two other certain examples of the use of the word *officina* in mortarium stamps, both in stamps of potters who worked in northern France, but who made Hartley group II mortaria.

Fig 106 Stamped mortarium <P224> from LBI95 (1:2)

Decorated samian ware

Joanna Bird

(See Table 97)

Samian potters' stamps

Brenda Dickinson

See Table 98. Each entry gives: excavation number, potter, (i, ii where homonyms are involved), die, form, reading, published example (if any), pottery of origin, date. Superscript (a), (b) and (c) indicate:
(a) A stamp attested at the pottery in question;
(b) Not attested at the pottery in question, but other stamps of the potter known from there;
(c) Assigned to the pottery on the evidence of fabric, distribution, etc. Ligatured letters are underlined.

Amphorae from the JLE sites

Robin Symonds

Introduction

Looking first of all at the entire body of amphorae from the JLE sites, it is clear from Tables 99–101 that there are no substantial differences between JLE as a whole and other sites in Southwark and the City of London. It is true that, compared to sites in the City other than Regis House (KWS94) or No. 1 Poultry (ONE94), the JLE sites have a somewhat high percentage of (early) Dressel 20 amphorae (BAETE) by sherd count (56% versus 41.7%), but this difference is not reflected in the percentages by rows (see below), and may therefore have been adversely affected by the high proportion of JLE sites (or contexts) which have not been quantified by sherd count. (The sites included in the grouping entitled 'EH S'wark' are: 107BHS81, 11STS77, 120BHS89, 170BHS79, 175BHS76, 179BHS89, 213BHS77, 2SSBS85, 4STS82, AB78, CH75, CW83, GDV96, GHL89, HIB79, SB76, SCC77, SKS88, STE95, STS88, USA88 and USB88; the site codes for the City sites included are: BAX95, ETA89, FCC95, IRL95, NST94, OBL97 and SUF94.)

Quantification

Rows can be defined as the number of records in the MoLAS Oracle database, each of which contains all examples of each unique fabric, form and decoration combination. The percentages at the bottom of Table 99 show clearly that a much higher percentage of the JLE sites or contexts have not been quantified by sherd count than is the case for other sites recorded in the MoLAS Oracle database. Interestingly, systematic differences between rows and sherd count are only really noticeable with Dressel 20 amphorae, and to a slightly lesser extent with non-specific amphorae (AMPHs); this is clearly caused by the fact that Dressel 20 amphorae break disproportionately into many small fragments, while non-specific amphorae are represented by single sherds more often than any other type.

Table 97 Decorated samian from the JLE excavations

BGH95 Period	Lu	Grp	Sgrp	Context	Comment
I	OA2	8	22	[873]	Drag. 29, SG (2 sherds). The lower zone has a band of arrowheads above corded medallions: the medallions contain hares and a rosette, and there are birds perched on the vertical beads between them. A closely similar medallion is on Knorr 1952, pl 30, B. The rosette is very fragmentary but may be the one on a mould-signed bowl of Masclus (pl 36, C), which has a similar row of (larger) arrowheads. The hares are Hermet pl 26, no. 55 and possibly no. 74, the bird a pair to pl 28, no. 57. c AD 50–65.
I	OA2	80	395	[2210]	Drag. 29, SG. Upper zone panels with corded medallions alternating with massed leaf-tips; the fragmentary lower zone is probably a scroll with corded buds. Several of the motifs in the upper zone occur on mould-stamped bowls of Murranus: the medallion and leaf-tips are on Knorr 1952, pl 45, F and G, and similar small rings on pl 45, D. A similar corded motif to that in the lower zone is on pl 45, E. One medallion contains a hare, cf Hermet pl 26, no. 54. c AD 50–70; the panel design suggests a date late in this range.
I	OA2	80	397	[2223]	Drag. 29, SG. Lower zone scroll with small frilled leaf and palmate leaf. c AD 50–70.
I	OA2	80	397	[2223]	Drag. 29, SG. Lower zone scroll with palmette leaves and small geese, over grouped arrowheads. Similar palmettes and arrowheads occur, for example, on stamped bowls of Labio (Knorr 1952, pl 32, B and C). The goose is Hermet pl 28, no. 68 left. c AD 50–70.
I	OA2	80	397	[2223]	Drag. 37, SG. The ovolo is rather blurred but the position of the trident tip suggests it is one used by M Crestio – here above a wreath of bifid leaves. c AD 75–95.
I	OA2	116	539	[3976]	Drag. 29, SG. The upper zone scroll has a palmette found on stamped bowls of Celadus (Knorr 1919, pl 21, B) and Crestio (Glasbergen 1944, fig 56, no. 3) and mould-stamped bowls of Murranus (Knorr 1952, pl 44, B). c AD 50–70.
I	OA2	179	1001	[4125]	Drag. 29, SG. The upper zone includes a wreath medallion containing a bird. c AD 70–85.
I	OA2	43	184	[6053]	Drag. 29, SG. Part of scroll in the upper zone, but no terminals survive. c AD 50–65.
2	OA8	184	1020	[4147]	Drag. 29, SG. Upper zone scroll with lyre-shaped leaves. For the leaf, cf Knorr 1952, pl 78, B, stamped by Scottius, with a rather more spacious scroll. c AD 50–65.
2	OA8	184	1020	[4147]	Drag. 29, SG (2 sherds). Upper panel of massed leaf-tips alternating with hunting scenes, including a hound and hares. The lower zone has a scroll, probably over a spiral motif. Similar hunting panels were produced by several Neronian to early Flavian potters, with alternating boxes of leaf-tips or arrowheads. The two hares are probably those on Knorr 1952, pl 23, A, stamped by Felix, and pl 44, C, signed and stamped by Murranus; the crouched hound is Hermet pl 26, no. 22. c AD 55–75.
2	OA8	184	1023	[4156]	Drag. 30, SG, in the style of Masclus. The ovolo with rosette-tipped tongue and the berry cluster are on a signed bowl, Knorr 1952, pl 36, B. Similar large palmate leaves occur on a number of Drag. 30s of Neronian date. c AD 50–65.
2	OA8	184	1020	[4161]	Drag. 29, SG. Upper zone fragment with scroll and possibly trifid leaves. c AD 55–75.
2	B5	102	479	[5047]	Drag. 29, SG. Tip of small corded medallion and vertical corded lines in the upper zone, gadroons in the lower. c AD 50–65.
3	OA5	48	207	[1874]	Drag. 29, SG (15 sherds). The treatment of the central cordon indicates that the upper and lower zones belong together. For the general arrangement of the lower zone, with its alternating vertical ornaments and narrow wreath festoons, cf Knorr 1952, pl 42, C, stamped by Modestus, though it has different individual motifs. A similar arrangement of poppyheads on a stem composed of an astragalus and a narrow wreath, with the pinnate leaves on tendrils, is on pl 44, A, mould-stamped by Murranus. However, the arrangement of the upper zone, wreath festoons alternating with panels incorporating diagonal wavy lines, suggests a somewhat later date than the lower, so probably c AD 65–85.
3	OA10	48	207	[1874]	Drag. 29, SG (2 sherds). Upper zone wreath festoons with spirals, and trifid pendants between them. This arrangement is found among the Pompeii Hoard material: for the pendant, cf Atkinson 1914, pl 5, no. 29, stamped by Vitalis, while a similar festoon is on pl 5, no. 19, stamped by Mommo. c AD 70–85.
3	OA10	48	207	[1874]	Drag. 37, SG (5 sherds). An early example of the form with an ovolo that was probably used by Calvus i (Dannell et al 1998, type CF); the decoration of narrow friezes is carefully and delicately modelled. A trifid wreath sits above panels with paired hares and hounds, probably alternating with a lattice of wavy lines and small rings; below is a chevron wreath, then a further broken frieze. The general style is close to a number of the Pompeii Hoard bowls, especially those of the 'Large Rosette Potter' (Atkinson 1914). The hare is probably Hermet pl 26, no. 60; the hound is broken but cf Hermet pl 26, no. 12. Traces of a fingerprint are visible in the slip. c AD 65–80.
3	OA10	48	207	[1874]	Drag. 37, SG. The ovolo (Dannell et al 1998, type KK) was used by the 'Large Rosette Potter' (Calus i) of the Pompeii Hoard; below is a scroll with a frilled leaf (cf Atkinson 1914, pl 8, nos 43 and 45) and, probably, a small bird. c AD 70–85.
5	B23	160	907	[3136]	Drag. 30, SG (2 sherds). The design consists of paired panels with a robed figure below arcades with a hound, alternating with a saltire of lyre-shaped and corded buds and grouped arrowheads below a fragmentary panel with tendrils. Hermet pl 74, no. 4, is from a closely similar mould; the ovolo on it is type CH (Dannell et al 1998), an uncommon type also recorded on form 37. The robed figure is Hermet pl 20, no. 131, the hound no. 26, no. 21. c AD 70–85.
5	B23	160	907	[3136]	Drag. 37, SG. Basal wreath of bifid leaves below a band of triple festoons separated by trifid pendants. Similar wreaths are found among the Pompeii Hoard material (eg Atkinson 1914, pl 11, nos 54–5 and, with this type of festoon, pl 13, no. 63), while the triple festoon is typically Flavian. c AD 75–95.

Table 97 cont

Period	Lu	Grp	Sgrp	Context	Comment
5	B23	160	907	[3136]	Knorr 78, SG (2 sherds). Chevron wreath at base. *c* AD 75–100.
5	S10	206	416	[2192]	Drag. 29, SG, stamped in the base. Lower zone scroll of small frilled leaves and berries, winding over medallions with alternating facing birds (cf Hermet pl 28, nos 39–40). Brenda Dickinson comments: 'The stamp reads OF.C[E]LSI, from Die 7a of L. C-Celsus of Le Rozier (Thuault & Vernhet 1986, 112), where it was used on bowls of form 29 and rouletted dishes. L. C-Celsus is the only potter from Le Rozier whose stamp occurs with any frequency in Britain, and, given his overall distribution, it seems likely that he started his career at La Graufesenque, where some of his dies may have originated. A pre-Flavian date seems certain, since stamps from dies recording *tria nomina* occur on forms such as 16 and 24 and others with the *cognomen* only have been noted on forms Ritt. 8 and 9. Site evidence includes Hofheim I, Usk and the group of samian from the Oberwinterthur *Keramiklager* (Christa Ebnöther, pers comm).' *c* AD 55–70.
6	OA9	181	1009	[4123]	Drag. 37, in the style of Drusus I (X-3) of Les Martres-de-Veyre. The frieze of paired dolphins, the beads and the arcades are on Stanfield & Simpson 1958, pl 12, no. 142, the rosette and arcades on pl 12, no. 144. *c* AD 100–25.
6	OA9	181	1009	[4136]	Drag. 37 in the style of X-12 (Ioenalis) of Les Martres-de-Veyre. He regularly used the beaded ring in place of an ovolo (eg Stanfield & Simpson 1958, pl 40, no. 468). The lion and probably the same leopard are on pl 40, no. 462, while the smaller lion is not clearly identifiable; the twig motif is on pl 40, no. 469. The stag was used by an associated potter, X-11 (pl 37, no. 432). The horseman is Oswald 263. *c* AD 100–25.
7	Pit	38	159	[32]	Drag. 37 in the style of Sacer of Lezoux. Stanfield & Simpson 1958, pl 82, no. 1, shows the ovolo and beads. *c* AD 125–50.
7	Pit	38	159	[32]	Drag. 37, Lezoux. The pointed leaves are Rogers 1974, types J49 and J67: the vine leaf is too incomplete to identify certainly. The wavy-line border, the general style, and what survives of the ovolo tip suggest X-6 or the Quintilianus group (rather than Advcisus, who is also recorded for the pointed leaves): cf Stanfield & Simpson 1958, pl 73, no. 46 and pl 76, no. 30. Hadrianic/early Antonine.
7	Pit	38	159	[32]	Drag. 37, Lezoux. The figure is Neptune, Oswald 13, here in a panel with crisp wavy-line borders. Hadrianic/early Antonine.
LBA95				[62]	Drag. 37 in the style of the Quintilianus group at Lezoux. The leaf ornament, Rogers 1974, L12, is recorded on their work, and they frequently used the basal wreath (eg Stanfield & Simpson 1958, pl 68, no. 5). The lozenge motif is not the one shown in Stanfield & Simpson, and is not identifiable: perhaps cf the leaf, Rogers J94. *c* AD 125–50.
				[62]	Drag. 37 in the style of the Quintilianus group at Lezoux. For the festoons, cf Stanfield & Simpson 1958, pl 69, nos 12–13; the circles (in pairs) are on pl 70, no. 19. *c* AD 125–50.
				[62]	Drag. 37, Lezoux. The figure is Mars (a smaller version of Oswald 150), here in a panel with wavy-line borders. Hadrianic/early Antonine.
LBI95				[412]	Drag. 37, SG (5 sherds). Late trident-tongued ovolo above a panel design: the panels apparently consist of saltires alternating with other motifs, including a faun (Hermet pl 19, no. 93) above a goose (Hermet pl 28, no. 68 left), and a composite tree after the style of Germanus. There is a chevron wreath at the base. The details of the saltire, with its doubled wavy lines, the coarse modelling and poor moulding, suggest a date *c* AD 90–110.
				[412]	Knorr 78, SG. Boar (cf Hermet pl 27, no. 49) on grass-tufts beside a composite tree with acorns. *c* AD 90–110.
MSA92				[107]	Drag. 29, SG. Upper zone scroll with trifid leaves and rosettes, winding over massed leaftips. The leaf-tips occur on bowls stamped by such Neronian potters as Albus (Knorr 1919, pl 5, A) and Modestus (Knorr 1952, pl 42, B). *c* AD 55–70.
				[107]	Drag. 29, SG. Upper zone of grouped vertical wavy lines alternating with groups of at least three vertical rows of large arrowheads. For the arrowhead panels, cf Hermet pl 52, no. 30, which has the same large motif. The lower zone has a wreath of ringed bifid leaves (as Hermet pl 44, no. 57) over panels of arrowheads alternating with small medallions, one of which has a bird (cf Hermet pl 28, no. 58). The central wreath was badly smudged during finishing. *c* AD 55–70.
				[107]	Drag. 30, SG. Scroll with beaded bindings and palmate leaves, between wreaths of palmettes. Traces of fingerprints are present in the slip. *c* AD 60–75.

It is self-evident that interpretation of the data in Table 99 must be extremely subjective. All of the major amphora types are present in the JLE assemblage in roughly the expected proportions, and there are no unusual quantities of rare types. Some variations in the table are almost certainly due to the chronological specificity of certain sites: looking at the percentages for late Dressel 20 amphorae (BAETL), for example, these are better represented in the EH Southwark sites and at No. 1 Poultry than at Regis House (KWS94) or the other City sites, probably because the former sites have more significant late Roman occupation, and it is therefore much more likely that the low figures (1.9% by rows; 1.1% by sherds) for the JLE sites are

Table 98 Samian potters' stamps from the JLE excavations at BGH95

No.	Period	Lu	Grp	Sgrp	Context	Acc.	Comment
1	1	OA2	8	22	[873]	<1793>	Albinus iii 4a Drag. 15/17 or 18 [O]F.ALBINI (Hermet 1934, pl 110, 3) La Graufesenque[a]. c AD 45–65.
2	1	OA2	8	22	[873]	<1792>	Fortis Ia Drag. 15/17 or 18 FORTIS (Durand-Lefebvre 1963, 101, 310) La Graufesenque[a]. c AD 45–65.
3	1	OA2	116	539	[3976]	<1784>	Modestus i 4e Drag. 15/17 or 18 [OFM]OES La Graufesenque[a]. c AD 50–65.
4	4	B15	59	277	[1751]	<1472>	Primus iii 12f Drag. 15/17 or 18 OFPR[IMI] (Durand-Lefebvre 1963, 192, 599) La Graufesenque[b]. c AD 50–65.
5	4	B15	59	277	[1751]	<1475>	Rosette on Drag. 42. Stamped twice, in the centre of the base and nearer the wall. South Gaulish and late Neronian or early Flavian. c AD 65–80?
6	4	B15	59	277	[1751]	<1476>	Niger ii 5a Drag. 27g OFNIGR La Graufesenque[a]. c AD 50–65.
7	4	B15	59	277	[1751]	<1477>	Patricius i 4d Drag. 27g OFPATRIC La Graufesenque[a]. c AD 60–75.
8	5	B23	160	907	[3136]	<1748>	Illiterate on Drag. 27 South Gaulish. Flavian.
9	5	B23	160	907	[3136]	<1749>	M—O in frame with swallow-tail ends, on Drag. 18 South Gaulish. Flavian.
10	5	B23	160	907	[3136]	<1753>	Censor i 3a Drag. 18 OF.C[EN] (Durand-Lefebvre 1963, 67, 204) La Graufesenque[a]. c AD 70–90.
11	6	OA9	181	1009	[4123]	<1852>	Pass(i)enus 24a Drag. 18 PASSENI.-. La Graufesenque[a]. Only the tops of the letters survive. c AD 65–85.
12		Pit	38	159	[32]	<128>	Miccius Ia Drag. 33 MICCI.VSF (Dannell 1971, 310, 65) Lezoux[a]. c AD 140–70.

a reflection of a chronological bias than of low distribution of this particular amphora type. In fact it is hard to detect any similar phenomenon reflected in the percentages of the more exotic late amphora types, such as those from the eastern Mediterranean or North Africa, but all of these types are so generally rare throughout all the sites – none achieves as much as 1% by any measure – that statistical analysis is of little relevance. This is almost certainly due to a radical change in the late Roman period in the nature of amphora distribution: whereas the arrival of amphorae from distant origins in the 1st and 2nd centuries is clearly a phenomenon of both the Romanisation of the empire and its commercialisation, late Roman amphorae seem to reach a remarkably wide range of destinations in remarkably small numbers (Vilvorder et al in prep).

Amphorae and their contents

One of the most interesting developments of amphora studies in recent decades has been the identification and analysis of the contents which amphorae were used to transport. It has been known for a long time that the main commodities shipped in amphorae were olive oil, wine and fish sauce (sometimes referred to as garum and/or muria), and these arrived in Britain in amphora types which clearly announced by their shape alone both their contents and their region of origin. Globular Dressel 20 amphorae have a distinct shape which automatically indicates that they contain olive oil from Baetica; flat-bottomed conical

'Gauloise' amphorae announce that they contain wine from Gallia Narbonensis, while the long thin Dressel 2-4 types with bifid handles announce that they contain wine from other origins in Italy, Baetica or Tarraconensis – in the latter instance the general shape clearly indicates wine, while the fabric and colour and some subtleties of shape indicate the region of origin.

While at present on average some 95% of all amphora sherds for which a type of contents can be identified come from amphorae which contained either olive oil, wine or fish sauce, other commodities are known to have been transported, and the number of types whose contents remain unknown is slowly declining. The discovery in 1983 of an amphora which contained black olives in syrup (de frutum) seems to have clarified the role of both Haltern 70 amphorae and that of the type known in Britain as London 555 (Sealey and Tyers 1989). Recent work on the type known as Richborough 527 has indicated both a region of origin (the Aeolian island of Lipari) and a commodity, alum (a product used in fixing dyes to textiles) for this amphora type (Borgard 1994). Useful summaries of the other possible commodities transported in amphorae can be found in Callender (1965, 37–41) and in Peacock and Williams (1986, 17–18).

By associating sherds of identifiable amphora types with their respective known contents, it is possible to quantify, at least in general terms, the commodities represented in each assemblage. Table 102 shows the percentages of the various identifiable commodities present at the major London sites

Fabric code	% rows						% sherds					
	JLE	EH	S'wark	KWS94	ONE94	City	JLE	EH	S'wark	KWS94	ONE94	City
Common types												
BAET	3.7	3.5	0.1	1.9	0.9		0.3	2.4			0.7	0.4
BAETE	32.2	31.7	29.4	37.6	32.8		56.0	46.4	46.4	58.2	41.7	
BAETL	1.9	4.4	0.5	4.3	1.6		1.1	5.3	0.5	2.2	0.8	
C189	1.8	1.3	1.6	0.4	1.4		1.1	0.8	0.7	0.4	1.2	
CADIZ	6.0	4.6	10.6	5.0	8.0		3.2	2.3	13.8	4.6	6.8	
CAMP1	1.0	1.0	1.8	1.0	1.3		0.6	0.6	0.7	0.5	0.5	
GAUL	6.1	3.8	3.2	4.6	5.8		2.4	1.9	2.0	2.7	4.3	
GAUL1	18.1	20.2	18.7	17.0	18.6		15.4	19.9	16.2	14.8	17.6	
GAUL2	1.5	1.7	3.0	0.9	1.2		3.3	0.8	2.8	0.8	0.6	
RHOD2	1.5	0.5	3.3	2.4	1.5		1.9	0.3	1.9	3.2	2.0	
R-B amphs	1.8	3.0	4.0	1.3	2.4		1.2	4.4	2.4	1.4	1.9	
Rare types (normally less than 1%)												
AMPBS	0.3	1.0		0.1	0.4		0.4	0.5		0.1	0.1	
BAET3	0.0	0.4	0.3	0.2	0.1		0.0	0.3	0.1	0.1	0.0	
BIV	0.1	0.3	0.1	0.1	0.5		0.0	0.1	0.0	0.0	0.2	
CAMP	0.2	0.0	0.1	0.0	0.1		0.0	0.0	0.0	0.0	0.0	
CAMP2	0.2	0.2	1.1	0.1	0.6		0.5	0.0	0.6	0.1	0.4	
CAT	0.5	0.1	0.7		0.3		0.1	0.1	0.4		0.1	
CHALK	0.0	0.1					0.0	0.0				
CRET			0.1						0.0			
DR28	0.1	0.0			0.1		0.0	0.0			0.0	
F148		0.0			0.3			0.0			8.8	
GAUL3	0.4	0.3	0.5	0.2	0.2		0.4	0.2	0.7	0.2	0.1	
GAUL4		0.2			0.1				0.1		0.0	
GAZA			0.1	0.0	0.1				0.0	0.0	0.0	
HOFA	0.4	0.4	0.1	0.1	0.1		0.1	0.2	0.0	0.0	0.0	
ITCAL	0.1						0.8					
ITFEL	0.0	0.3	0.2	0.0			0.0	0.1	0.1	0.0		
LIPR	0.1	0.4	0.3	0.2	0.3		0.1	0.3	0.3	0.0	0.1	
LRRA	0.7	0.4		0.1	0.1		0.3	0.4		0.0	0.0	
NAFR	0.1				0.1		0.0				0.0	
NAFR1	0.5	0.4	0.2	0.5	0.3		0.3	0.1	0.2	0.2	0.1	
NAFR2	0.1	0.3	0.1	0.2	0.1		0.1	0.1	0.1	0.1	0.0	
PALS				0.1	0.1					0.0	0.0	
RHOD	0.2	0.6	0.3	0.5	0.3		0.1	0.2	0.1	0.2	0.2	
RHOD1	0.3	0.1	0.4	0.1	0.3		0.1	0.0	0.2	0.0	0.1	
RHOD3		0.1	0.1		0.3			0.1	0.1		0.2	
AMPHs	19.8	18.9	18.9	20.6	19.8		10.0	12.0	9.7	9.3	11.6	
Total %	100.0	100.0	100.0	100.0	100.0		100.0	100.0	100.0	100.0	100.0	
Total	2139	2761	1484	2038	1475		5626	8471	5079	6272	4455	

Sherds per row (*):						2.63	3.07	3.42	3.08	3.02

Rows without sherd count					% rows without sherd count (*)				
543	156	54	119	5	25.4	5.7	3.6	5.8	0.3

* Not all sites involved were recorded with sherd count, and some sites were only partially recorded with sherd count, but sherd count is included here, along with the ratio of sherds per row at the bottom, because in each column the majority of records do have sherd count, and the percentages seem relatively consistent. The numbers and percentages of rows without sherd count are shown at the bottom for each group of sites.

Table 99 *Percentages of amphora types in the City and Southwark, by rows and sherds*

Fabric	% rows						% sherds					
	JLE	EH	S'wark	KWS94	ONE94	City	JLE	EH	S'wark	KWS94	ONE94	City
Baetica	43.9	44.6	40.8	49.1	43.5		60.9	56.7	60.8	65.8	49.8	
Tarraconensis	0.5	0.1	0.7	0.0	0.3		0.1	0.1	0.4	0.0	0.1	
Rhône Valley	26.3	26.0	25.7	22.7	26.1		21.5	22.8	21.7	18.6	22.5	
Italy	2.0	2.9	3.5	1.5	2.7		2.3	1.6	1.6	0.7	1.2	
North Africa	0.7	0.7	0.3	0.8	0.5		0.4	0.2	0.3	0.3	0.2	
Eastern Med.	5.1	3.7	6.1	4.0	4.8		3.6	2.2	3.1	4.0	12.7	
R-B amphs	1.8	3.0	4.0	1.3	2.4		1.2	4.4	2.4	1.4	1.9	
Other amphs	19.8	18.9	18.9	20.6	19.8		10.0	12.0	9.7	9.3	11.6	
Total	100.0	100.0	100.0	100.0	100.0		100.0	100.0	100.0	100.0	100.0	

Table 100 *The origins of amphora types in the City and Southwark, by percentages of rows and sherds*

Fabric	LBI95 amphorae from the earliest & Flavian occupation						Regis House (KWS94) amphorae from Roman period I					
	Rows	rows %	Sherds	sherds %	rows %	sherds %	Rows	rows %	Sherds	sherds %	rows %	sherds %
BAET3							1	0.4	1	0.1		
BAETE	14	7.7	101	16.2			26	9.3	145	18.4		
CADIZ	6	3.3	17	2.7			9	3.2	52	6.6		
Southern Spain					11.0	19.0					12.8	25.1
CAT							1	0.4	1	0.1		
Eastern Spain					0.0	0.0					0.4	0.1
CAMP1	2	1.1	11	1.8			2	0.7	2	0.3		
ITFEL							1	0.4	1	0.1		
Italy					1.1	1.8					1.1	0.4
GAUL	4	2.2	8	1.3			2	0.7	11	1.4		
GAUL1	7	3.8	25	4.0			12	4.3	33	4.2		
GAUL2	7	3.8	68	10.9			6	2.1	65	8.2		
GAUL3							1	0.4	19	2.4		
Rhône Valley					9.9	16.2					7.5	16.2
RHOD								0.4	2	0.3		
RHOD1							1	0.4	1	0.1		
RHOD2	2	1.1	15	2.4			5	1.8	12	1.5		
Rhodes					1.1	2.4					2.5	1.9
SLOW							1	0.4	1	0.1		
Romano-British					0.0	0.0					0.4	0.1
AMPHs	8	4.4	15	2.4	4.4	2.4	14	5.0	32	4.1	5.0	4.1
Total	50	27.5	260	41.8	27.5	41.8	83	29.5	378	47.9	29.5	47.9
All pottery	182	100.0	622	100.0			281	100.0	789	100.0		

Table 101 Comparison of amphorae from JLE Southwark site LBI95 and Regis House (KWS94)

Contents	% rows					% sherds				
	JLE	EH S'wark	KWS94	ONE94	City	JLE	EH S'wark	KWS94	ONE94	City
Olive oil	35.0	31.2	26.5	37.7	29.8	54.5	45.3	43.9	57.2	39.7
Wine	32.1	31.2	37.4	28.7	32.4	23.5	28.8	26.5	23.6	27.3
Fish sauce	6.0	4.7	10.8	5.0	8.3	3.4	2.3	13.8	4.6	6.8
De frutum	1.1	0.2	2.3	0.6	0.9	1.0	0.1	1.6	0.4	0.7
Olives	1.5	1.6	3.2	0.9	1.3	3.2	0.8	2.8	0.8	0.6
Alum	0.1	0.4	0.3	0.2	0.3	0.1	0.3	0.3	0.0	0.1
-	24.1	30.7	19.6	26.8	27.1	14.3	22.4	11.1	13.4	24.8
Total %	100.0	100.0	100.0	100.0	100.0	100.0	100.0	100.0	100.0	100.0
Total	2091	2681	1459	1902	1437	5685	8473	5079	6273	4455

Table 102 The contents of amphora types in the City and Southwark, and at Argenton-sur-Creuse, by percentages of rows and sherds, and of minimum numbers of individuals (NMI)

or groups of sites. It should be immediately apparent that these figures should be treated with the same degree of dispassion as that warranted by the figures in the preceding tables. The fact that at the JLE sites there is a higher percentage of olive oil than of wine, when measured by rows, and that this is also the case for No. 1 Poultry, while the reverse is true at Regis House and the other City sites, is very likely to be related as much to the overall chronology of these sites as to the proportions of consumption at a given moment.

Table 102 has been produced by assigning a 'content' to each fabric-form combination in the respective assemblages. Thus the unidentified fabrics, such as 'AMPH', may be assigned a content if the form is 8DR2-4, which is a wine amphora form. Equally, while pieces identified as BAETE but without a specified form cannot be associated with a content, because both Dressel 20 and Haltern 70 amphorae share that fabric but not the same content, pieces identified as BAETL, or late Baetican ware, must have contained olive oil, as there is only one form associated with that fabric. An overall average of some 25.7% of rows and 17.2% of sherds could not be associated with identifiable contents.

Discussion of Table 103

Table 103 is an attempt to put the amphorae found at the JLE Southwark sites in a northern European context, by comparing them quantitatively with the recently published amphorae from four sites in Gaul. This type of quantitative comparison has only recently become possible as a result of what might be called a teamwork approach ('projet collectif de recherche') to the study of Roman amphorae developed by a group of 20 to 30 researchers and their associates under the direction of Mme Fanette Laubenheimer, under the auspices of the Centre National de la Recherche Scientifique (CNRS; originally programme H13 of the CNRA, under the heading 'Les Ateliers antiques: organisation et diffusion', now programme H26, under the heading 'Culture matérielle de l'antiquité aux temps modernes'). Two volumes of papers on amphorae have so far been produced by the group, under the title Les Amphores en Gaule: Production et Circulation (Vol I, 1992 and Vol II, 1998), both edited by Mme Laubenheimer. The amphorae from the four sites referred to here are presented in four separate papers in Vol II (Bavay: Marlière 1998; Titelberg (Luxembourg): Laubenheimer and Hénon 1998; Strasbourg: Baudoux 1998; Mâlain-Mediolanum (Côte-d'Or): Olmer 1998). (Similar data is available for a few other sites, but none that would add significantly to what is presented here.) What is particularly advantageous about the teamwork approach is that all the participants have become increasingly consistent in methods of identification and quantification of their amphorae, and in the presentation of the results. This means that for each of the four

Table 103 Comparison of JLE amphorae with amphorae from four sites in Gaul

Origin	Form	JLE % sherds	Bavay * % sherds	Strasbourg % sherds	Luxembourg* % sherds	Mâlain * % sherds	JLE % rows	Bavay * %NMI opti	Strasbourg %NMI opti	Luxembourg* %NMI opti	Mâlain * %NMI opti
Italy	8C139	0.0					0.1				
	8DR2-4	0.9	0.1	1.0	2.6	1.2	1.1	0.2	1.0	4.3	3.2
	8DR21-22	0.8					0.1				
	8R527	0.1			0.6	0.1	0.1				2.2
	other/ind	0.2				0.5	0.6				3.2
Baetica	8C186	3.4	6.2	0.5	2.9	17.7	6.2	6.2	0.5	15.2	7.5
	8DR20	58.4	16.7	40.0	70.1	45.0	42.1	20.1	40.0	39.1	22.6
	8DR23		0.5			1.5		0.9			1.1
	8H70	1.1	1.5	0.5		0.3	1.4	1.7	0.5		2.2
	other/ind	2.8	0.3	3.6	0.3	0.2	4.5	0.5	3.6	2.2	1.1
Tarraconensis	8DR2-4	0.2	1.4			0.5	0.5	1.4			4.3
	8DR28	0.0	0.1			0.1	0.1	0.2			1.1
	other/ind	0.0				0.6	0.1				4.3
Rhône Valley	8DRI		0.2					0.2			
	8DR2-4	0.5	0.3			0.2	0.5	0.5			1.1
	8GI			0.5		0.1			0.5		1.1
	8G2		0.2					0.5			
	8G/8G4	15.0	19.9	29.1	13.0	15.1	19.3	9.4	29.1	13.2	17.0
	8G5	0.1		1.0	1.4		0.2		1.0	6.5	
	8L555	3.3					1.7				
	8DR9S		0.4		0.6	0.5		0.7		4.3	3.2
	8AUG21		0.2					0.5			
	other/ind	2.7	1.0		1.7	6.0	4.7	1.4		6.5	10.8
Northern Gaul	8G12	0.0					0.1				
Regional	8G13		23.0		4.6			26.8		2.2	
Britain	8IJ	0.8					0.9				
	8DR2-4	0.0					0.1				
Regional	other/ind	0.8	11.1	7.7			1.3	10.7	7.7		
Eastern Med.	8BIV	0.1					0.2				
	8C189	0.9				5.5	1.6				3.2
	8CHK	0.0					0.1				
	8DR2-4		0.1	1.5			0.1	0.2	1.5		1.1
	8HOFA	0.1					0.1	0.3			1.1
	8KI17	0.2					0.2				
	8LRRA	0.2					0.3				
	8RHOD	1.9	0.2	0.5	0.9		1.9	0.5	0.5	4.2	
	other/ind	0.7	0.1				1.4	0.2			
North Africa	8NACA	0.3	1.3	0.5			0.5	1.4	0.5		
	other/ind	0.1	1.0	0.5		0.1	0.3	1.4	0.5		1.1
Unknown	8DR2-4	1.5	0.2	1.0			2.4	0.5	1.0		
	other/ind	10.0	8.9			1.4	17.5	12.8			4.3
		100.0	100.0	100.0	100.0	100.0	100.0	100.0	100.0	100.0	100.0
Total		5557	1252	195	348	885	1724	422	195	46	93

*Indicates the sites from which Dressel 1 amphorae have been removed from the statistics.

sites referred to here, there is a table of amphora types from the site produced in an almost identical manner, and in most cases there is also a table comparing the proportions of the amphorae in terms of the commodities represented by different amphora types.

Unfortunately the mutual consistency of Continental amphora researchers (and of researchers of other types of archaeological pottery) has not aimed at consistency with the methods currently in use in Britain. The standard method of quantification in use throughout francophone countries and much of Continental Europe is the NMI ('nombre minimum d'individus', minimum number of vessels), nowadays frequently weighted or corrected (cf Protocol Beuvray 1998). Usually tables are presented which show the number of sherds present (described as NR, or 'nombre de restes'), in the case of amphorae divided into rims, handles, body sherds and bases/spikes, and 'NMI opti', or corrected NMIs. In Britain in the last two decades or so, since quantitative studies have begun to be published in earnest, the main methods of quantification in vogue are weight and estimated vessel equivalents, or EVEs. In London, while the latter two methods remain important for quantitative studies of important assemblages, we have also instituted sherd count for all pottery at the spot-dating phase. The Oracle system also allows us to quantify in terms of number of records, or rows, which often produce numbers of a similar magnitude to NMIs. This means that for direct comparisons with Continental pottery, we can compare sherd counts directly, and it is probably justifiable to compare the percentages of rows with NMIs, although there may be some problems with the latter comparisons.

A second problem with inter-site comparisons is chronology. All the data in Table 103 is derived from global tables pertaining to entire sites, or at least those parts of sites dated from roughly AD 40 to 400. Some of the Continental sites were occupied substantially before AD 40, however, and this can be reflected in later periods by the presence of considerable numbers of Dressel 1 amphorae, which must be residual. This is not the case with Strasbourg (Baudoux 1998, table 3), but in the case of the Titelberg (Laubenheimer and Hénon 1998, table 1) Italian Dressel 1 amphorae account for between 16.7% (sherd count) and 22% (NMIs) of the assemblage, and in the case of Mâlain (Olmer 1998, table 1) they account for between 57.1% (NMIs) and 75.7% (sherd count). Clearly in the latter case the numbers are so overwhelming that the assemblage is not comparable with the other sites if the Dressel 1s are included, but in fact the table in question presents the amphora data in six chronological phases (La Tène D2, 70–30 BC; pre-Augustan, 30–20 BC; Augustan, around the turn of the century (sic); Augustan–Claudian, first half of the 1st century; second half of the 1st century; and 2nd and 3rd centuries). It is very clear that the Italian Dressel 1 amphorae are residual in the last three phases of the site, and for the purposes of comparison here should therefore be removed from consideration. In order to be consistent the Dressel 1 amphorae were also therefore removed from the Titelberg figures, and from Bavay (Marlière 1998, fig 2), although in the latter case the small number of Dressel 1 amphorae are of Rhône Valley origin rather than Italian.

Inevitably this manipulation of the data may be seen as somewhat controversial, yet it seems essential if the various tables are to be compared at all. One further general comment on chronology is that of course it would be much more desirable to compare assemblages from much briefer phases. In London we may eventually be able to compare data from at least nine Roman phases between AD 50 and 400 (the first six being defined by Davies et al 1994, 8), but the bottom line of Table 103 here shows how dramatically larger London sites are compared with the Continental sites in question. Until comparable quantification is available for much larger sites in Gaul, broken down into chronological phases similar to those observed in Britain, there is little point in more detailed comparisons.

The figures presented in Table 103 do show an intriguing picture, but one which seems to confirm that London sites such as JLE Southwark were supplied in a broadly similar manner to the Continental sites. Dressel 20 olive-oil amphorae are the predominant amphora type everywhere except at Bavay, where regional types (both the specific Gauloise type 13 and other regional types) comprise more than one-third of the amphorae present. Bavay lies on a major Roman axis, the road from Bavay to Cologne, but what this evidence suggests – and this comment is also echoed by Marlière (1998, 61–2) without benefit of comparison with other sites – is that compared with London, Strasbourg and Luxembourg in particular Bavay was not especially wealthy in amphorae. Marlière suggests that this may be because of an unusually large supply of regional amphorae, or the supply of an unusually high proportion of goods in non-ceramic containers (barrels or skins), or a town occupied by a relatively low population. While all or some of these hypotheses may be true, it is also worth noting that the regional amphora types are mostly thought to be chronologically late, for example mid 3rd-century or later (cf also Baudoux et al 1998, 35–6). This is obviously not the case with regionally produced amphorae found in London, which are dominated by products from Verulamium dating to the second half of the 1st or the early part of the 2nd century (Symonds 1993).

In many respects the five sites are remarkably similar in terms of their amphorae, and this is the main conclusion to be drawn, although it is the differences in the details which provoke interest. Whereas Bavay is distinguished by its high number of regional amphorae and low numbers of Dressel 20s, Strasbourg is remarkable for its high number of Rhône Valley flat-bottomed amphorae (8G/8G4), and by its generally low numbers of many rarer types. The Titelberg has the highest number of Dressel 20s, and a very low number of rarer types. Mâlain, the southernmost site considered, undoubtedly was strongly influenced by the proximity of Lyon and Gallia Narbonensis from the 1st century BC until the end of the Augustan period, which explains the very high numbers of Dressel 1 amphorae (see above), but in the periods considered for this exercise, with Dressel 1s excluded, it becomes the site with perhaps the closest match with the JLE sites.

What distinguishes the JLE sites is the broad variety of amphora types present, coupled with the substantial numbers of Dressel 20s and Rhône Valley types. Perhaps this variety can be explained simply by the large size of the assemblage – almost all of the more rare types are present, rather than just a few. Yet the overall proportions of amphorae coming from different regions of the empire suggests that these London sites are not otherwise in any specific way abnormal by comparison with sites in northern Gaul. More London sites need to be included in this type of study, along with more Continental sites; data for both are likely to become available in the near future, and these new data are likely to clarify some of the questions which are bound to arise from Table 103 here.

BGH95 [1753]: A NOTE ON THE STAMPS

L.DOL... / LVP...

...RA (upside-down)

The vessel in question is a Dressel 2-4 of Italian origin with similar dimensions to those shown by a group of amphorae from Saint-Romain-en-Gal, published by Desbat and Savay-Guerraz (1990, fig 4). The size and placement of the stamps is similar, and the fact that one of the Saint-Romain-en-Gal vessels has been stamped upside-down as well as the right way up also seems significant. While the reading of our stamps does not correspond with any of the group published by Desbat and Savay-Guerraz, it seems at first view that they belong to the same or to a very similar production. The fabric of our vessel appears similar to that described generally by Desbat and Savay-Guerraz, which, according to the appendix (Picon and Desbat 1990) is convincingly Italian from the region of Vesuvius, although the Saint-Romain-en-Gal vessels belong to several groups, probably from different workshops in the region. However, in a recent comment on our vessel, Armand Desbat (pers comm) observes that while the fabric is indeed undoubtedly Italian, it is different from that of the Saint-Romain-en-Gal amphorae, and probably comes from another source.

The dating of BGH95 [1753] is AD 70–100. The vessels published by Desbat and Savay-Guerraz come from two substantial assemblages of Dressel 2-4s in rooms 28 and 25 of the 'Maisons des dieux Océans' dated from the first quarter of the 2nd to the first half of the 3rd century. Desbat and Savay-Guerraz discuss the dating of their vessels in some detail. Dressel 2-4 amphorae from the Pompeii region are usually rare after AD 79. Although there are similarities with 1st-century amphorae from the same source, the Saint-Romain-en-Gal examples are notably distinguished by the presence of stamps on the neck, which are absent on the earlier vessels. Also, earlier Italian Dressel 2-4s are fairly rare at Saint-Romain-en-Gal, whereas these two assemblages consist of, in the first instance, 400kg and c 52 vessels, and, in the second instance, 'a bed of broken amphorae'. Recent evidence begins to suggest that, contrary to previous views, production of Dressel 2-4s in the Pompeii region may have declined during the 2nd century, but it did not disappear. Desbat and Savay-Guerraz also consider the possibility that these amphorae may have been substantially residual, or else the wine in them may have been aged for some time before the vessels were distributed, but although this possiblity is considered less likely, the earliest possible date for the amphorae must be the first quarter of the

2nd century. There is some evidence of other imports to Saint-Romain-en-Gal from Italy during the 2nd and 3rd centuries, notably lead-glazed wares (Desbat 1986; Picon and Desbat 1986) and a large Italian mortarium with a stamp on two lines not dissimilar to these amphora stamps (Leblanc and Desbat 1992, 141, fig 10.6). Curiously, therefore, unless our vessel is in fact intrusive in the context (fairly unlikely in view of the fact that the sherd measures some 190mm long and 170mm in circumference), it would seem that despite the long distance from either central Italy or the Rhône Valley this is one of the earliest known examples of an Italian Dressel 2-4 amphora stamped on the neck.

11.3 The accessioned finds

Angela Wardle

Introduction

The excavations at BGH95 produced over 1500 accessioned finds, and the accessions from the other sites in the JLE project bring the total assemblage considered here to about 2000 objects, all of which have been recorded on the MoLAS relational database (Oracle). Extensive use was made of metal detectors on the site and this method of retrieval has undoubtedly contributed to the recovery of large numbers of copper alloy and lead objects. The number of such objects recovered, especially coins, contrasts favourably with the retrieval on other earlier excavations in the area. Many of the metal objects from Borough High Street are, however, in extremely poor condition. Radiography and selective investigative cleaning have permitted the identification of a large percentage of the finds but in many cases the heavy corrosion, even after remedial conservation, obscures many details. For example, few brooches can be recognised with certainty beyond a general type, and catalogue descriptions are of necessity not detailed. Although it is known that there was a smithy on the site, there are very few recognisable iron artefacts. Iron is highly perishable and was also regularly recycled in antiquity.

Despite these caveats, at least 1000 objects (including coins) were identified and some are of extreme interest. There is a well-stratified group of pre-Boudican material, and analysis of the material by period permits comparison of the different groups. In recent years it has been found useful to quantify and compare Roman finds by their function, an analysis which crosses the material boundaries. Clearly it is possible to interpret many items in more than one way and such analysis is to some extent subjective, but it remains a useful method of summarising an assemblage. The tables below give the total number of finds from each overall period that can be ascribed to the functional categories devised by Nina Crummy (1983), with some minor adjustments to suit the London assemblages. Some categories are not applicable to the Southwark assemblages, but have been retained for future comparison with London groups on a wider basis. The categories are:

1. Objects of personal adornment and dress
2. Toilet and pharmaceutical implements
3. Textile manufacture and working
4. Household utensils and furniture
5. Objects used for recreational purposes
6. Weights and measures
7. Objects associated with written communication
8. Objects associated with transport
9. Buildings and services
10. Tools
11. Fasteners and fittings
12. Agricultural implements
13. Military equipment
14. Objects associated with religious beliefs and practice
15. Metalworking waste
16. Leatherworking waste and tools
17. Objects of uncertain function

The pre-Boudican levels

Metalwork from the pre-Boudican phase is generally in very poor condition and the number of identified objects does not therefore adequately reflect the general level and intensity of occupation. There is a substantial number of copper alloy objects for which no identification is possible, beyond noting that they represent parts of objects rather than waste. Ironwork is always under-represented in the archaeological record in London, with the exception of major waterlogged deposits, partly due to its perishable nature and partly because of the practice of the recycling of the metal in antiquity. Nevertheless, it has been possible with the assistance of radiography and investigative conservation to identify a number of metal artefacts, while others are of less perishable materials. While the numbers from individual buildings and areas may be too small to ascribe functions to particular buildings, it is well worth examining the assemblage in its entirety and making comparisons with other early assemblages from Southwark and Londinium north of the river.

Table 104 shows the numbers of objects represented in each of the functional categories defined in the introduction. They have been broken down by period, period 3 representing Boudican destruction material that is presumed to have derived from the earlier levels. As the numbers that can be ascribed to each period are very small, the following discussion covers the finds from the entire pre-Boudican sequence.

Six of the items in the first category are brooches, two from Open Area 2 (which in most places underlies the earliest buildings), all types of the early to mid 1st century. The simple one-piece 'Nauheim derivative' brooch <R1> (Fig 18), a plain and functional design with a wire bow, developed from a Continental prototype, is one of the most common early types in Britain. A poorly preserved Aucissa brooch <R2> (Fig 18) also dates from the early to mid 1st century and a second example was found in a later context <R41> (Fig 107). Aucissas, so called after the name of a maker which is sometimes stamped on the head, are found on both pre- and post-Conquest sites in Britain and very frequently on military sites. The discovery of the type, particularly in association with other more obvious militaria, could therefore strengthen evidence for a military presence in the area. Excavated sites in the City of London between 1974 and 1989 produced only two Aucissa brooches but there are another 12 Aucissas or their derivatives in the Museum of London collection. Finds from more recent sites have increased this number, with examples from No. 1 Poultry, Bishopsgate and the Guildhall amphitheatre site. The first two sites are in areas which have produced other military material, but it is clear that Aucissas are comparatively rare in London as a whole. The remaining brooches are too fragmentary and corroded for precise identification, but all could be of mid 1st-century types with the exception of part of an enamelled headstud brooch <R5> from the area of Building 4. This is likely to date from the late 1st or 2nd century and it is intrusive in this context. There is a strong possibility of contamination caused by an underlying quarry pit in the immediate area into which later material had slumped.

Other items of jewellery and dress accessories from the pre-Boudican levels comprise a copper alloy hairpin <R7> from Open Area 9, a glass melon bead <R6> (Fig 107) and a buckle tongue <R9>. Items of personal grooming are poorly represented, with only one ligula <R10> (Fig 107). The larger number of domestic items of category 4 is chiefly due to the presence of four ceramic lamps, all imported and indicative of extensive trade or movement of such goods at an early period. Oil-burning lamps, which used imported olive oil, were a quintessential Roman artefact, and the group from the early levels contains two of particular interest. Lamps in the form of the human foot wearing a sandal were made in both ceramic and metal, and <R16> (Fig 28) is an exceedingly fine example. The motif might well have some symbolic significance not now apparent to us, and it is noticeable how many of the known ceramic lamps of this type have been found in the military areas of the north-west provinces, where this example apparently

Category	1	2	3	4	5	6	7	8	9	10	11	12	13	14	15	16	17	Total
Pre-Boudican																		
Period 1	3			2					1		1							7
Period 2	4			8	1	2			2		8		1		6			32
Period 3	2	1		2						1	2				10			18
Total	9	1	0	12	1	2	0	0	3	1	11	0	1	0	16	0	0	57

Table 104 Pre-Boudican registered finds by functional category

originated. The Eros with alabastron and shell on the lamp <R13> (Fig 19) made at Lyon in south Gaul from period 1, Open Area 2, is a typically Roman motif, common throughout the Roman Empire (Bailey 1988, 11, Q3047). The remaining lamps are fragmentary, but were imported from Spain, southern Gaul and northern Italy. The other domestic items are two fragments of ceramic 'chimney' and the handle of a copper alloy vessel <R11> (Fig 107), again a typical Roman form. A rare fragment of glass 'stand' or table <1203> is one of a very small number from Southwark, with other examples from Winchester Palace, Hibernia Wharf, and Calvert's Buildings (Shepherd 1992, 136, a). Two pieces of quernstone are of imported Niedermendig (Mayen) lava.

The sole artefact from this period in any way associated with leisure activity is a glass counter of standard type <R23> (Fig 22), while weights and measures, perhaps indicative of commercial activity, are represented by only two lead weights <R24> and <R25> (Fig 22). No recognisable iron tools survive and only one hone <R26>. As is usual on Roman urban sites, even at an early period, there are several locks and keys and other miscellaneous fittings, for example <R27> and <R28>. A robust mount from BUG94 could be a harness or cart fitting <R32>. Only one object is with certainty 'military', a chape from a dagger scabbard <R38> (Fig 107), but as has been noted above there are several other items frequently found in military contexts and the early groups also contain a number of irregular Claudian coins, again thought to be associated with military activity (Hammerson 1978).

In addition to the artefacts from the pre-Boudican groups, there are some items of mid 1st-century date from later contexts, some of which may have come originally from these areas and buildings. An Aucissa brooch was found at BGH95 in a period 6 context and a similarly early Hod Hill type brooch came from MSA92. This form is also frequently associated with military activity. The two bilobed harness pendants <R230> and <R231> (see below, period 4) could also be pre-Boudican in date. Many objects, for example hairpins, cannot be dated closely but are almost certainly residual in later levels.

Overall, although only a relatively small number of artefacts can be identified, these include a high proportion of imports which reflect considerable Roman influence, or at least the possession and use of the paraphernalia of a Roman way of life. Whether they were used by the foreign or the native settlers in this new town is another question.

Evidence for industrial activity

Apart from the evidence for ironworking (see below, 11.6), there is no evidence for other industrial activity at BGH95 in the pre-Boudican period. There is, however, substantial evidence from the nearby site at JSS92 (Joiner Street), where large quantities of ceramic mould <R39> (Fig 37), found in a restricted part of JSS92 Open Area 3, indicate the casting of copper alloy. The quantity of mould, which includes several joining fragments, would suggest that a large single item such as a statue or large vessel had been produced, presumably in a

furnace placed above the ground which would leave no archaeological trace. Fragments of copper alloy waste, apparently sweepings from a workshop floor, were found in the same period 2 and period 3 contexts as the ceramic mould.

The later 1st and 2nd centuries

The pre-Boudican finds are well sealed, and form a discrete group. It is more difficult to isolate the objects from the later periods, due to general disturbance by succeeding phases of occupation and the increasing volume of residual material. Table 105 summarises the finds from each period, with the number in each category expressed as a percentage of each period assemblage. Despite the varying numbers of identified objects for each period it can be seen that the overall balance is similar, with high percentages of fasteners and fittings at all times, comprising nearly a quarter of the assemblage in period 7. Personal ornament and dress accessories are usually the second largest component, and that is the case for two of the periods here. The high numbers in periods 6 and 7 are partly due to the presence of several residual items and partly to a large number of fragmentary hairpins, many undoubtedly also residual. The number of domestic artefacts found in period 4 contexts has been increased by the inclusion of numerous quern fragments. The overall picture is also distorted by the large quantities of non-ferrous metalworking waste from the pre-Boudican and period 4 groups at JSS92. The assemblages from each period are discussed in detail below and further comparisons made between the period 4 finds and a contemporary sealed group north of the river at Leadenhall Court, where the construction of the Basilica provided a secure *terminus ante quem* for the later 1st-century material (Milne and Wardle 1993).

Period 4 (AD 62–100)

The coins from the period 4 groups mostly fall within the second half of the 1st century, with Claudian copies from the immediate post-Conquest period. Metalwork is again poorly preserved and numbers of identifiable artefacts are comparable, although the total number recovered was greater. Few artefacts can be associated with specific buildings, although, as might be expected, many of the open areas have produced more substantial groups. The immediately noticeable difference between the pre- and post-Boudican groups lies in the quality and preservation of the non-metal finds and in the relatively small numbers of imported goods. In quantity the numbers of items of jewellery and dress accessories are not greatly different from the preceding periods, 12 as opposed to nine, but five of the seven brooches, four from Open Area 14, the other from Building 20, are fragmentary examples of native British types which superseded the Aucissas and Nauheims in the second half of the 1st century. The other identified brooch, an enamelled Dragonesque <R47>, found in Open Area 16, is also a British type, of slightly later date. This brooch form originated in northern Britain and occurs predominantly on military sites north of the Severn–Humber line. The only other items used for personal adornment or as dress accessories are a fragment of melon bead <R64>, parts of shafts from hairpins and a buckle tongue, none closely datable. A poorly preserved buckle plate <R227> could be from armour. The only other military finds from this group are both bilobed harness pendants <R230> (Fig 112) and <R231> found at BUG94 (OA8) and at LBE95 (OA2); they are mid 1st-century types.

The few toilet implements are also incomplete, comprising a fragmentary stone cosmetic palette <R119> (Fig 52) from Building 15, a ligula <R112> from Open Area 16, part of a glass stirring rod <R120> and two fragments of copper alloy mirror <R108>. Domestic items include a small part of an imported ceramic lamp from deposits associated with Building 11, in Lyon ware, which is likely to be residual, and nine quern fragments, also imported but all broken. A fragment of an open lamp <R134> from BSE94, which forms part of the same area, could have been made in northern France or southern Britain.

One glass gaming counter <R160> was found, and weights came from Buildings 15 and 23, <R163> and <R164>. The latter is a heavy lead weight with an iron suspension loop, for use on a large steelyard, while <R163> is a much lighter copper alloy example, weighing only 3g. This would have been used in a scale pan, perhaps for weighing more expensive but relatively light commodities.

Again, with the exception of a bone handle which retains a fragment of iron blade in the socket <R170> (Fig 68), from Building 14, no other identifiable metal tools have survived, but hones provide indirect evidence for bladed tools. As always the groups produced miscellaneous fittings, nails, rings and studs for example, and it is likely that the large numbers of unidentified copper alloy fragments would include more. One mount <R189> (Fig 111), from Building 18, is of especial interest, being in the form of a lion modelled in the round. The exact function of this object is unclear but it may have been part of a pin or perhaps a badge rather than a finial, on analogy with others found on the Continent (Zadoks-Josephus Jitta et al 1973, 94). A lock bolt from JSS92 <R186> is the only example of security equipment found in this period. A bell <R238> (Fig 112) from Open Area 14 could have had any number of functions from a door chime to an animal bell,

but in view of the often apotropaic nature of such artefacts, and their perceived role in warding off evil spirits, it has been placed with cult or 'religious' objects in category 14. The other object in this category is an enigmatic fragment of cast copper alloy from Open Area 15, which could represent stylised drapery or feathers from a figurine <R236> (Fig 52).

Fragments of copper alloy waste from JSS92 are almost certainly residual, but a fired clay investment mould <R249> (Fig 65) from LBI95 Building 3 is of interest. X-ray fluorescence (XRF) analysis has confirmed that it contains copper alloy, and it would have been used for the production of a single copper alloy object, although too little survives for its identification.

Overall this appears to be a very utilitarian group, lacking the exotic goods of the earlier phase. The composition of the glass assemblage reinforces this view (see below, 11.4). When compared with a sealed Flavian group from the City, such as Leadenhall Court (Milne and Wardle 1993), this contrast is even more marked, but it would be premature to draw firm conclusions at this stage (Table 106). Although the assemblage at Leadenhall Court falls within the same broad date range, there appear to have been unique circumstances which have affected the survival of the finds, and the problem of residual material in later groups is virtually non-existent, as the area was completely sealed by the new Basilica. Comparison of the proportions of different types of object shows that as always items of personal adornment, fasteners and fittings, and 'domestic' items comprise the largest groups. It is noticeable that there are fewer gaming pieces and other leisure items and objects associated with written communication at Borough High Street than at Leadenhall Court, but the one category that occurs only in Southwark is metalworking waste. Valid conclusions, however, should be based on a far larger body of evidence, and it is hoped that future analytical work in Southwark and the City on the great number of sites which have now been excavated will provide secure data on which to base future research.

Period 5 (AD 100–20)

The most important item of jewellery dating from this period is the fine carnelian intaglio <R60> (Fig 87) which is unstratified. Martin Henig considers that the piece, which

Category	1	2	3	4	5	6	7	8	9	10	11	12	13	14	15	16	17
Pre-Boudican	15.8	1.8	0	21.1	1.8	3.5	0	0	0	7	19.3	0	1.8	0	28.1	0	0
Period 4	17.9	7.5	0	14.9	1.5	2.9	0	0	0	7.5	20.9	0	4.5	1.5	19.4	0	1.5
Period 5	14.7	11.8	5.9	20.6	2.9	2.9	0	0	2.9	8.8	20.6	0	0	2.9	5.9	0	0
Period 6	34.7	6.1	2	16.3	2	2	2	0	2	2	20.4	0	0	2	4.1	4.1	1.6
Period 7	35.4	3.1	0	10.8	3.1	4.6	0	0	0	4.6	21.5	0	3.1	1.5	7.7	3.1	1.5

Table 105 Comparison of percentage of registered finds in each functional category for the main periods at BGH95 and related sites

Category	1	2	3	4	5	6	7	8	9	10	11	12	13	14	15	16	17
LCT84	23.7	9.2	2.7	21.6	9.2	2.2	2.2	0.5	0	4.9	21.6	0	1.1	1.1	0	0	0
BGH95 period 4	17.9	7.5	0	14.9	1.5	2.9	0	0	0	7.5	20.9	0	4.5	1.5	19.4	0	1.5

Table 106 Comparison of percentage of registered finds in each functional category for Leadenhall Court (LCT84) and BGH95 period 4

depicts a military figure, perhaps Mars or Alexander the Great, may well have been owned by a soldier, and it dates from around the time of Hadrian's visit to Britain. The only other piece of jewellery from BGH95, actually from a period 5 context, is a fragment of strip bracelet <R61> from Building 22, which may be intrusive as the type is usually dated after AD 200. A second strip bracelet of similar date came from Open Area 1 at RWT93, ascribed to the same or the succeeding period. Other personal items included beads <R65> and <R66> from LBI95 and a bone hairpin <R78> from MSA92. A nail cleaner <R114> (Fig 110) from BGH95 Building 23 and tweezers <R115> from the surface of Alley 5 are the types of object used for personal grooming which were often worn on a chatelaine and are sometimes found in sets. Construction/use deposits in Building 23 also produced two edge fragments from a circular hand mirror <R108> (Fig 72), a type which dates from the late 1st to early 2nd centuries, but which may have had a long period of use. Mirror fragments were also found at RWT93, Open Area 1. Another find in this general category, from BGH95 Open Area 20, is a chain link handle <R117> (Fig 69) which would have been attached to a glass oil flask containing oil for use in the baths. It is a quintessentially 'Roman' artefact, typical of the urban Roman way of life, which included frequent visits to the baths. No large bath complex has yet been found in Southwark, but there is evidence for heated rooms in the form of hypocaust *pilae* and flue tiles at several sites.

Three of the domestic objects in this group are fragments of quern, but in addition there is a part of an open lamp <R133>. A Lyon ware lamp <R130> from Building 4 at LBI95 is residual. The only evidence for tools is again in the form of the hones used to sharpen them. Two joining fragments of pipeclay figurine <R234> (Fig 87), imported from central Gaul, were found in Open Area 20 and Open Area 26 (period 7). The subject is an animal but insufficient remains to judge whether it is a horse, a cult symbol of the goddess Epona and a symbol of fertility and healing, or a bull, symbolising strength and virility (Green 1989, 149). The early 2nd century was the heyday of the importation of such figurines. Two needles from RWT93, <R122> and <R123>, both forms consistent with a 2nd-century date, were found in period 3 contexts at RWT93, equivalent to periods 5 and 6 at BGH95.

To summarise, the small group of objects associated with the buildings and features of period 5, which covers a span of only 20 years, are quite varied. The group contains some residual artefacts, but also several that are contemporary with the date of the deposits. The presence of the figurines, which may have had significance as cult or votive objects in a domestic environment, should be noted. It appears to be primarily a 'domestic' group of material with no clear evidence of industrial or commercial activity from the finds alone.

Period 6 (AD 120–60)

Three of the six bone hairpins found in Buildings 13, 22 and 29 are types which are consistent with a mid 2nd-century dating. The remainder, all from Structure 2, are fragments of

shaft and two could be needles rather than hairpins. An Aucissa brooch <R41> (Fig 107) from Open Area 15, comparable to those found in the pre-Boudican deposits, is residual, as are four fragments, a catchplate, a spring head and pins from unidentified types. Open Areas 3 and 4 at LBE95 produced several brooches, a Nauheim derivative <R40> and a Colchester <R43>, both residual, but also a broadly contemporary enamelled umbonate plate brooch <R55> (Fig 108) with a 2nd-century date. A bone pin <R84> (Fig 108) is a later Roman type.

Two personal items from BGH95 are of particular interest. A damaged mortar from a cosmetic grinding set <R118> (Fig 87) from the surface of Alley 5 belongs to a class of objects which were apparently made only in Britain (Jackson 1985) and have been recognised with increasing frequency in London in recent years. There is evidence for the manufacture of cosmetic mortars at Skipton Street (Jackson 1993). This is the second example to be found in Southwark, with another from 179BHS89 (Wardle in prep), and is unusual for London in having enamelled decoration, which would place its date in the 2nd century. The other personal item of quality is a cylindrical lathe-turned bone box <R107> (Fig 109) from Structure 6. This is a well-made object, and could have had a variety of uses, as a trinket-box for example, or for keeping cosmetics or powders.

A fragmentary buckle and buckle plate (probably from armour) from Building 27 are, by this stage, certainly residual. Leather has not survived from Roman contexts and there are very few hobnails, which now constitute the only evidence for footwear. Part of a nailed shoe, represented by a scatter of hobnails, came from Open Area 24.

There are few domestic items, but among them is one of the finest lamps from the site, found in a dump outside Building 25. The imported lamp <R128> (Fig 83), which is made of Lyon ware, dates from the mid 1st century, and is obviously residual, but its remarkable state of preservation raises the question of the length of use of such objects, and whether it had been preserved as an antique or heirloom. Unlike the attractive foot lamp from a much earlier context, the nozzle shows no obvious trace of sooting, although the exterior surface is very abraded. The scene on the discus is a popular one widely encountered in the provinces, depicting entertainers, possibly dwarves, who are performing a dance with hand clappers. The wooden staves were, on analogy with ones known from Egypt, fitted with small bronze cymbals (Wardle 1982). The only other lamp found in this group (OA24) is a factory-made example from central Gaul, but in a more expected, incomplete condition.

The remaining domestic items are quern fragments and a millstone from the construction deposits of Building 27, and Structures 9 and 2, while a copper alloy handle from Structure 7 could be part of a spoon.

There are surprisingly few gaming pieces or counters from the entire series of excavations, and period 6 contexts produced only one counter cut down from a ceramic vessel <R162>, from Open Area 19. There are also only single examples of needles (B22, destruction) and weights (also B22). Object <R166> (Fig 81) is a large triangular weight, made from a local aluminium-rich clay known as septarian nodule, and although of a shape conventionally ascribed to loom weights, may have functioned as a general-purpose or even a steelyard weight.

A seal box <R168> (Fig 87) from the make-up layers of Building 27 is a typical 2nd-century form, diamond-shaped, with coloured enamelling set within a grid. This is the only object from the entire assemblage that has any direct association with written communication.

One of the few identifiable iron objects from Open Area 19 demonstrates the advanced development of the infrastructure during the 2nd century. A fragment of water pipe junction collar <R169> is a comparatively rare find in Southwark, although some fine examples of both water pipes and collars have been discovered elsewhere in the City, generally in more favourable, waterlogged deposits (Wheeler 1930, 39, pl 12). Each length of squared oak had a central bored hole and the circular iron collars were used to join the sections, being driven into the solid wood to enclose the channel. A median ridge on the collar, visible on the present example, ensured that equal sections of collar entered each pipe, thus securing the joint (Manning 1985, 128). Outside London the presence of water pipes can frequently be inferred only from the iron junction collars, and the discovery of one at BGH95, an area where the preservation of ironwork is generally poor, is significant. The general dearth of ironwork is again emphasised by the fact that the only item in the tools category is a hone from Open Area 24.

Fixtures and fittings include a number of basic nails and studs and rings, and a copper alloy lock bolt <R183> from Open Area 25. A copper alloy mount <R195> from Structure 2 may be a reinforcing strip from a box, and a fine mount in the shape of a stylised lion's head is of a type often used to decorate the lock plates of caskets, although it could also have been used on furniture (Liversidge 1969). A bell-shaped stud from LBE95 <R203> (Fig 111) is a type of object often found in military groups (Allason-Jones 1985) and a notable discovery from the same site, found in the construction levels of Building 1, is a circular barrel padlock case <R187> made from copper alloy, with the remains of the iron locking mechanism inside. It is, unfortunately, too fragmentary for reconstruction, but is of a type well known in Roman Britain.

A fragment of Venus figurine <R235>, the type of votive or cult object that could well have had a place in a domestic shrine, came from the construction levels of Building 28 at BGH95.

The later Roman period

Period 7 (AD 160–400)

The later levels at BGH95 had been severely truncated and the sequence is less well defined, making the final phase, period 7, extremely long. Many objects are from dumps and spreads in open areas and there is increasing evidence of residuality. The only brooch found in contexts of this period at BGH95 is a damaged Colchester form of the mid to late 1st century <R53> from a well. A penannular brooch of 4th-century date <R57>

(Fig 108), contemporary with its date of deposition, came from burial 8 in Open Area 3 at Redcross Way (RWG94). A bracelet from the same area is contemporary. A fragmentary jet finger ring <R59> found at BGH95 in Open Area 29 would date from after AD 200.

Several glass necklace beads came from open areas, but again there are more hairpins than any other type of object in this category. Most of the 13 pins are fragments of shaft but types such as <R83> (Fig 95) from Building 31, with a swelling shaft, were made from the mid 2nd century onwards. Earlier forms are also represented from Open Area 15, Structure 7 and Building 31.

The only item from a manicure set is a pair of tweezers <R116> from Structure 13, but a more substantial copper alloy object that might have been part of a surgical or medical implement <R113> (Fig 110), from Open Area 30, is of interest. Although its precise function remains uncertain, the decorative details on the robust handle are similar to those on surgical tools, and it is possible that it held a needle or blade.

As in earlier phases, the domestic material is limited and much is residual, for example a fragment of firmalampe from Structure 19 deposits. Most quern fragments, all from different areas, are small, although one <R149> from Open Area 9 is a worn upper stone. Bone counters <R155> and <R156> from Open Areas 28 and 30 represent leisure pursuits and three lead weights, from different areas, may represent commercial activity. A knife blade <R171> from a dump in Open Area 29 is one of the few iron tools to have survived; otherwise the only tools are again hones.

There are a larger number of fasteners and fittings, including a hasp from a lock <R188> from Open Area 30, and from Open Area 19 a ring key from a rotary lock <R180> (Fig 111) used for securing small boxes or chests. A lock bolt used with a tumbler-lock slide key came from a post structure. An iron swivel from a well <R224> would have been attached to a chain. Such objects had many possible functions, including the suspension of cooking pots over a fire. A lead strip with a projecting hook <R256>, from Building 30, could have been used as an identification tag, although there is no sign of any inscription.

Another fragment of the animal figurine <R234> came from Open Area 28 and a circular-bodied bell <R237> was found in Open Area 27. Two of the few items that are certain to be of later Roman date are a pair of copper alloy ring buckles <R228> and <R229> (Fig 92), a military accessory seen on 3rd-century cavalry and infantry gravestone reliefs.

Many of the artefacts from period 7 contexts are residual but the latest material from the site also came from these groups, which with the coin evidence suggests continuity of occupation into the 4th century. The most securely dated material comprises the 3rd-century ring buckles from Open Area 45 at BGH95, a fragmentary jet finger ring from Open Area 29 at BGH95, late Roman glassware from STU92, which is unstratified, and several 4th-century objects from the Redcross Way sites further to the east. It is significant that the complete penannular brooch and bracelet fragment from RWG94 were found in burials – in themselves an indication that urban occupation in the immediate area had ceased.

Catalogue of the registered finds from the pre-Boudican levels

Note: where no site code is given the finds are from BGH95. The following conventions are used:

<Rn>: catalogue number

<n>: accession number

[n]: context within which the object was found

Pn: Period. For sites other than BGH95 the period number is followed by the equivalent period number at BGH95

B: Building

S: Structure

OA: Open Area

Personal ornament

BROOCHES
Copper alloy
<R1>, <798>, [873]; P1, OA2, group 8,22, Fig 18
Almost complete; L 38mm. One-piece Nauheim derivative with plain wire bow; spring of four turns; catchplate and pin broken. AD 10–60.

<R2>, <1416>, [5098]; P1, OA2, group 7,21, Fig 18
L 38mm. Aucissa, in two fragments; complete apart from the missing pin, but very corroded, with much detail lost. The head has a single cross band below the axial bar and the bow has two ribs; cross mouldings at the junction of bow and foot. There are traces of white metal plating (tinning) on the bow and knobbed foot. AD 10–60.

<R3>, <697>, [183]; P2, Alley 2, group 18,70 (not illustrated)
Incomplete; surviving L 30mm. Rosette brooch, fragment of plate and foot. 1st-century type.

<R4>, <751>, [934]; P2, OA4, group 12,38 (not illustrated)
Catchplate.

<R5>, <886>, [934]; P2, OA4, group 12,38 (not illustrated)
Incomplete; surviving L 33mm; W 25mm. Headstud brooch, head and part of bow remaining. The oval button on the back below the head is enamelled; part of the chain loop survives

and the full width of one arm. Although this comes from a group connected with pre-Boudican Building 1, it is likely to date from the late 1st century at the earliest, and might reflect possible contamination of this context by an overlying quarry pit.

NECKLACE
Glass frit
<R6>, <1219>, [3960]; P3, OA10, group 129,597, Fig 107
Complete; Diam 20mm. Melon bead; good turquoise colour.

HAIRPINS
Copper alloy
<R7>, <1037>, [3436]; P2, OA9, group 120,553 (not illustrated)
Incomplete; W of head 11mm. Biconical head and slender shaft (incomplete). Encrusted but appears to belong to Cool group 10 or 23; no decoration visible. Possibly 2nd century and intrusive.

Bone
<R8>, <1110>, [4093]; P1, OA2, group 180,1003 (not illustrated)
Incomplete; L 69mm. Point and fragment of regularly expanding shaft.

BUCKLE
Copper alloy
<R9>, <900>, [999]; P3, OA10, group 20,77 (not illustrated)
L 45mm; buckle pin.

Toilet and medical implements

LIGULA OR SPATULA
Copper alloy
<R10>, <833>, [989]; P3, OA10, group 20,76, Fig 107
Surviving L 100mm; W of blade 5mm. Rod handle of uniform circular section, broken at one end. The other end is flattened and terminates in a lozenge-shaped spoon or blade.

Household utensils

VESSEL
Copper alloy
<R11>, <909>, [5166]; P2, OA6, group 20,76, Fig 107
L 160mm. Handle from skillet or colander; flat waisted handle, with residual lobes above the junction with the bowl (now broken) and a splayed terminal. Examples of such vessels are relatively common in Roman Britain, see for example South Shields (Allason-Jones and Miket 1984, 152, 3.373), Colchester (Crummy 1983, 73, no. 2043, fig 76), Verulamium (Goodburn 1984, fig 19, nos 173–4). For the form of the complete vessel see Boersted 1956, no. 53.

SPOONS
Bone
<R12>, <1517>, [3954]; P2, B6, group 124,568, Fig 107
Incomplete; surviving L 90mm; Diam of bowl 23.5mm. Round bowl; circular-sectioned handle of uniform thickness, incomplete. Standard cochleare form, common in the 1st and 2nd centuries.

LAMPS
Ceramic
<R13>, <1152>, [873]; P1, OA2, group 8,22, Fig 19
Incomplete; W 68mm; H 24.5mm. Volute lamp, type uncertain as nozzle is missing, with discus scene of Eros with scallop-shell and alabastron, part of which can be seen in the right hand, above a break. The figure type is common throughout the Roman Empire (Bailey 1988, 11, Q3047) and may be a libation scene. Most of the discus is complete, but the nozzle is lost and only the spring of a volute can be seen. Lyon ware; mid 1st century.

<R14>, <1851>, [918]; P1, OA2, group 5,14 (not illustrated)
Fragment, type uncertain. Lyon ware.

<R15>, <1770>, [3915]; P3, OA10, group 129,600 (not illustrated)
Incomplete; small fragment of side-wall; Lyon ware.

<R16>, <426>, [522]; P2, OA6, group 98,466, Fig 28
Complete; L 100mm; W 38mm; H 42mm. Plastic lamp in the shape of a right foot wearing a thonged sandal. The wick hole is in the big toe, where there are traces of sooting, and the filling hole is at the ankle, which is closed with a palmette design. Part of a ring handle remains at the rear, and on analogy with other examples, it is likely that there was also a leaf-shaped handle ornament, which is now lost. The whole object is very well moulded and very detailed. The toes are depicted in a naturalistic style and the thonging of the sandal is complete and realistic. The sandal appears to have straps cut from a single piece of leather which support the heel and ankle; the ankle strap has a slot at the terminals which meet on top of the foot, through which pass five straps which bind the front of the shoe. These straps are knotted through the ankle strap terminals and decorative medallions are shown on the central strap and two side straps; the shoe is heavily hob-nailed on the underside in a regular pattern. The lamp is very similar in style to a left foot lamp in the British Museum (Bailey 1988, 457, Q1138bis), which is probably Italian; but apart from being a right foot, the London lamp differs in detail, particularly in the thonging where there is a lozenge-shaped medallion on the central strap. Apparently made in the Netherlands (north-west provinces), perhaps in an army workshop (D Bailey pers comm). Other ceramic footlamps have been found in this area, for example two from Nijmegen (Evelein 1928, pl 16, nos 10–11), respectively a left and a right foot, the latter

stamped 'VITALIS'. These are less well modelled than the BGH95 example, with simpler strapping, although they also show hobnails.

Bailey (1988, 457) cites several close parallels for the British Museum foot lamp, most of which are from the north-west provinces, for example from Cologne, Vindonissa, Cannstatt and Xanten, all military bases.

<R17>, <1773>, [1875]; P2, Alley 2, group 44,1103 (not illustrated)
Fragment of side-wall, form uncertain. ?Spanish fabric.

<R18>, BUG94 <22>, [270]; P2, OA2, group 2,4 (not illustrated)
Small edge fragment of discus, type uncertain. Central Gaulish fabric.

<R19>, LBI95 <17>, [226]; P1=P1/2, OA3, group 3,3 (not illustrated)
Fragment of side-wall, oxidised fabric, very abraded; type uncertain.

QUERNS
All Niedermendig (Mayen) lava; all incomplete

<R20>, <1046>, [690]; P2, OA8, group 17,64 (not illustrated)
Lava; hole for handle, but no original surface survives.

<R21>, <1519>, [3436]; P2, OA 9, group 120,553 (not illustrated)
Lava; striations on edge, worn surface; possibly a lower stone.

<R22>, <1274>, [686]; P3, OA10, group 20,78 (not illustrated)
Lava; upper stone; radial grooves on grinding surface, worn. Six fragments, no definite sign of rim.

Recreational activity

GAMING PIECE
Glass
<R23>, <571>, [707]; P2, Alley 2, group 18,71, Fig 22
Complete; Diam 16.5mm. Plano-convex counter in natural blue glass, now opaque.

Weights and measures

WEIGHTS
Lead
<R24>, <824>, [5026]; P2, B4, group 9,25, Fig 22
Diam 24mm; H 18mm; Weight 64g. Cylindrical pan weight, with slightly domed head. Lead is an unstable metal and it is possible that the object weighed three Roman ounces originally (at 24 scruples to the ounce).

<R25>, <678>, [880]; P2, OA3, group 200,52, Fig 22
Diam 11mm; present H 8mm; Weight 6g. Small weight, originally conical, but with the upper part cut away or broken as the top is irregular in contrast to the neatly made lower half.

Tools

HONE
Stone
<R26>, <1496>, [3960]; P3, OA10, group 81,401 (not illustrated)
Surviving L 50mm; W 35mm; H 20mm. Rectangular fragment, very sharply cut; burnt on the underside and broken at both ends.

Fasteners and fittings

KEY
Copper alloy
<R27>, <1058>, [2174]; P3, OA10, group 81,401 (not illustrated)
Complete; L 45mm. Tumbler-lock slide-key with six teeth on a rectangular bit; now in two pieces and very corroded.

LOCKS
Copper alloy
<R28>, <1417>, [7049]; P3, OA10, group 129,597 (not illustrated)
L 83mm. Heavy lock bolt with eight triangular perforations, arranged in two groups. Drawn from X-ray 5189.

<R29>, <1257>, [7054]; P2, B6, group 126,257 (not illustrated)
L 80mm. Hasp from lock of box or chest. The hinge remains at the wider end, with the hasp

loop towards the tapering foot. There are two groups of decorative mouldings on the upper surface. This is a well-known form, with many examples known from Britain; very similar to one from Courage's Brewery (Wardle in prep).

MOUNTS
Copper alloy
<R30>, <783>, [818]; P2, OA4, group 17,57, Fig 107
L 58mm; max W 19mm. Triangular plate, incomplete at the wider end; with a perforated circular terminal at the other. There is a single rivet hole at the centre of the wider part. Possibly a casket mount or reinforcement.

<R31>, <1337>, [7071]; P2, OA7, group 127,594 (not illustrated)
L 29mm; W 19mm. Rectangular mount, with circular aperture at the centre, set at the end of a slot and a single circular projection or terminal on the opposite end.

<R32>, BUG94 <16>, [199]; P2, OA2, group 19,27 (not illustrated)
L 70mm; L of plate 45mm. Robust mount. Square sectioned shank on which is set a stout ring, with a projecting moulding at the junction of shank and ring. A square plate is set on the top of the ring. This could be a cart fitting, or similar, perhaps a guide for the attachment of awning; alternatively a form of terret or some other type of harness equipment.

STUDS
Copper alloy
<R33>, <1421>, [873]; P1, OA2, group 8,22 (not illustrated)
Flat circular head-fragment.

<R34>, <819>, [5016]; P2, B4, group 9,25 (not illustrated)
Diam c 30mm. Heavy flat circular head, very corroded; shank missing.

<R35>, STU92 <13>, [70]; P2, B4, group 64,13 (not illustrated)
Incomplete; fragment.

JOINERS DOG
Iron
<R36>, <1323>, [7097]; P2,

OA7, group 127,593 (not illustrated)
Incomplete; approx. L of arm 100mm. Joiner's dogs were used for securing the joint between two pieces of wood.

FERRULE
Copper alloy
<R37>, <1160>, [1896]; P2, B2, group 45,195 (not illustrated)
Diam 15mm; H 12mm. Circular ferrule, open at both ends, but severely corroded.

Military equipment

WEAPONS
Copper alloy/iron
<R38>, <1320>, [7126]; P2, B7, group 123,562, Fig 107
Incomplete; surviving L 44mm. Chape from sword or dagger. Biconical copper alloy terminal surmounted by two cordons, above which is the iron chape socket, which consists of two U-shaped bindings joined at the lower end. There are traces of mineral-replaced organics, likely to be wood and/or leather, both inside and outside the socket. This piece is typical of the terminals of such chapes used in the 1st century and would have been fastened to the wood and leather casing of the scabbard. In form it appears to belong to the 'Pompeii' type (Ulbert 1969, 97) although it differs from an example from Verulamium, which also comes from a context that pre-dates the Boudican revolt (Goodburn 1984, 32, fig 11, no. 71), in having side bindings of iron instead of copper alloy. The present chape appears, with the Verulamium piece, to be one of the earliest excavated examples of the type (Bishop and Coulston 1993, 70).

Metalworking waste

FIRED CLAY
<R39>, JSS92 <73>, [41]; <75>, [42]; <74>, [67]; <76>, [72]; <77>, [79]
P3, OA3, Fig 37
Five contexts produced large quantities (7kg) of fired clay mould. Stratigraphic evidence

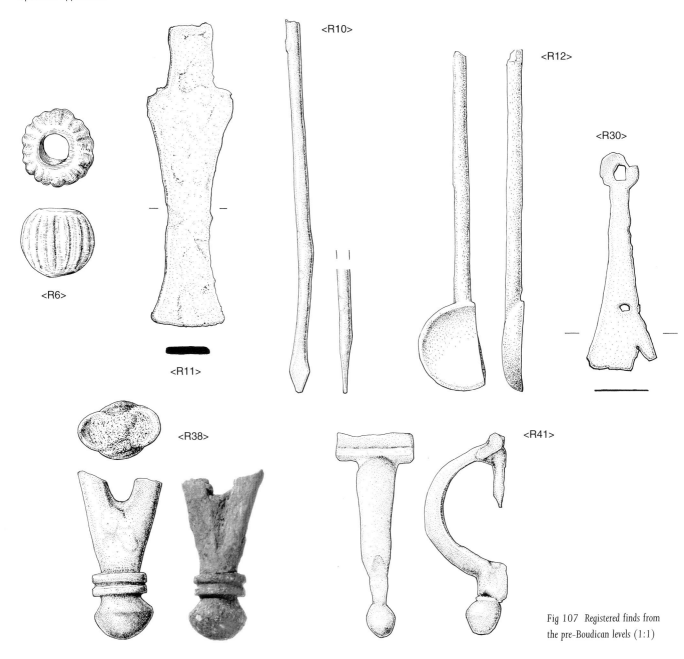

<R10>

<R12>

<R30>

<R6>

<R11>

<R38>

<R41>

Fig 107 Registered finds from
the pre-Boudican levels (1:1)

suggests that the deposit is well
sealed and it is confined to a
small area. There are occasional
traces of copper alloy residues
on the inner surfaces of the
fragments, most of which are
flat and heavily burnt. On
several pieces the interior is
rounded or curved and there
are a very few fragments with
a curved outer surface. It
is possible that the mould
represents some sort of
structural hearth lining, but it
is also a reasonable supposition
that it is an investment mould
used for the production of a
large copper alloy object, such
as a large vessel, or even a
statue. Insufficient remains for
this question to be resolved.

COPPER ALLOY

The site also produced several
small fragments of copper alloy
waste, which could be casting
residue, but there are no diagnostic
fragments, such as sprues, dribbles,
sheet metal or part-formed objects.
Most fragments are irregular
vesicular lumps, containing
charcoal, copper alloy fragments
and small pebbles, and seem likely
to represent sweepings from a
workshop floor, or perhaps from
the edge of a furnace. Unlike the
ceramic mould, the copper alloy
waste is distributed throughout the
sequence, although the most
substantial fragments come from
Open Area 3, in the same area as
the mould, from contexts [42],
[60], [69] and [83].

Catalogue of the registered finds from post-Boudican periods

Note: where no site code is given the finds are from BGH95.
The following conventions are used:
<Rn>: catalogue number
<n>: accession number
[n]: context within which the object was found
Pn: Period. For sites other than BGH95 the period number
is followed by the equivalent period number at BGH95.
B: Building
S: Structure
OA: Open Area

Personal ornament and dress

BROOCHES
Copper alloy
<R40>, LBE95 <17>, [166];
P3=P6, OA4, group 6,34 (not

illustrated)
Surviving L 32.5mm. One-
piece Nauheim derivative,
with flat bow; distorted,
catchplate missing. Residual,
AD 10–60.

<R41>, <169>, [282]; P6, OA15, group 32,132, Fig 107 Complete; L 50mm. Aucissa with knobbed foot and deeply arched bow, but even after conservation few details are visible. Residual, AD 10–60.

<R42>, MSA92 <34>, [228]; unphased (not illustrated) Incomplete; surviving L 22mm. Hod Hill, poorly preserved. Fragment of bow with horizontal mouldings and trace of a thin hinged pin. Mid 1st century.

<R43>, LBE95 <77>, [265]; P3=P6, OA4, group 4,26, Fig 108 L 42mm. Colchester two-piece; ribbed decoration on the bow; spring of six turns, plain catchplate; pin missing, otherwise complete. Mid 1st century.

<R44>, <175>, [312]; P6, S8, group 29,122 (not illustrated) Fragmentary head of sprung brooch; W 16mm.

<R45>, <1125>, [422]; P4, OA15, group 28,116 (not illustrated) Incomplete; W of head 12.5mm; head and upper part of bow. A hinged pin is concealed by a turned-back head. There is a single moulding at the top of the bow, below which is a deeply cut saltire with circles within the angles of the cross; possibly enamelled originally.

<R46>, <880>, [1322]; P6, OA25, group 205,352 (not illustrated) Catchplate only.

<R47>, <1050>, [1729]; P4, OA16, group 85,418, Fig 108 Complete; L 57mm. Dragonesque brooch. The radiograph shows an enamelled lozenge with an internal circle at the centre and enamelled 'eyes' at the terminals. Severe corrosion precludes the identification of further details after corrosion; pin missing. The general type originated in north Britain and occurs predominantly on military sites north of the Severn–Humber line (Allason-Jones and Miket 1984).

<R48>, <1135>, [2147]; P4, OA14, group 85,418 (not illustrated) Incomplete; surviving L 49mm. Two very corroded fragments of a sprung bow brooch (spring of eight turns), probably a Colchester type.

<R49>, <1347>, [2147]; P4, OA14, group 84,418 (not illustrated) Incomplete; W of head 34mm. Head, spring of twelve turns, probably a Colchester type.

<R50>, <1042>, [2158]; P4, OA14, group 82,406 (not illustrated) Incomplete; W of head 24mm. Probably a dolphin, from general profile. Head, with hinge and part of bow, active corrosion precludes recovery of detail.

<R51>, <1230>, [2220]; P4, OA14, group 84,412 (not illustrated) Incomplete; W of head 24mm. Head only; spring of eight turns; very corroded but probably a Colchester form.

<R52>, <1492>, [3855]; P4, B18, group 139,633 (not illustrated) Incomplete; W of head 29mm. Two-piece Colchester; head and upper part of bow; very corroded.

<R53>, <968>, [4070]; P7, OA27, group 212,1006 (not illustrated) Incomplete; surviving L 34mm; W of head 20mm. Bow brooch with ?sprung head, possibly a Colchester, small. Trace of pin, but foot and catchplate missing.

<R54>, BSE94 <8>, [119]; P4, OA2, group 4,6 (not illustrated) Incomplete; L 41.5mm. Bow brooch; four corroded fragments among which only part of the bow and catch plate can be distinguished. Type unidentifiable.

<R55>, LBE95 <75>, [234]; P3=P6, OA3, group 4,26, Fig 108 Almost complete; W 31.5mm. Umbonate disc brooch. The centre is well preserved with two concentric zones of triangular cells containing alternately red and blue enamel, surrounding a small central circular zone; the copper

alloy surface retained traces of tinning (confirmed by XRF). The boss is surrounded by a deep groove and the outer rim of the brooch is damaged. It is probable that it originally had four lugs; the two surviving lugs concealed the hinge and catch plate. 2nd century.

<R56>, MSA92 <7>, [+]; unstratified (not illustrated) L 34mm. Oval plate brooch with series of lugs around the edge, originally 10, and a projecting bar or loop in the centre; hinged pin. Probably 2nd century.

<R57>, RWG94 <8>, [13]; P5=P7, OA3, group 4,43, Fig 108 Complete; inner Diam 20mm. Penannular brooch. The flat ring has V-shaped notches around the outer edge; the turned-back terminals are also carved in a stylised zoomorphic design; the pin has a slight inward curve. Found in an inhumation, burial 8, probably a grave good and possibly worn. Late Roman, 4th century.

<R58>, <1266>, [3961]; P6, B27, group 136,810 (not illustrated) Fragment of loop in loop chain, probably from a brooch.

FINGER RINGS
Jet
<R59>, <1599>, [445]; P7, OA29, group 33,136 (not illustrated) Fragment of hoop; H 4mm.

INTAGLIO
Martin Henig

<R60>, <1423>, [4065]; unphased, OA38, group 189,1039, Fig 87 Carnelian intaglio; 16mm x13mm. The device is the head and shoulders of a youth who is viewed partly from behind, so that the line of his spine is apparent, although his face is in profile to the left (to the right in an impression). He is nude, apart from his plumed Corinthian helmet from which emerge luxuriant locks of hair which cascade down his neck. In front of him is an upright spear, rather crudely engraved as though as an afterthought and perhaps by a local jeweller. The modelling is assured and classicising, but the

patterned hair is suggestive of 2nd-century work (Henig 1988, 149–51). The gem was most plausibly cut in the reign of Hadrian (AD 117–38) who certainly admired such ephebic beauty; the locks, indeed, somewhat recall those of his favourite, Antinoos.

The subject is the same as that depicted on two red jasper intaglios respectively from the amphitheatre at Caerleon in Monmouthshire and from Italica in Spain, which incidentally was Hadrian's birthplace (Henig 1979). In addition an earlier (1st-century) sardonyx intaglio from Arthur's Seat, Edinburgh, showing the half-length figure of a helmeted youth may be noted (Henig 1974/ 1978, no. 467). The exact identity of the subject remains uncertain. While it cannot be ruled out that the type was interpreted as a youthful Mars like the bronze figurine from the Foss Dyke, Lincolnshire (Toynbee 1962, 131, no. 16, pl 19), it is much more likely that it is Achilles, who is often shown on intaglios holding a spear. Statues of youths holding spears often stood in gymnasia and were called Achilleae (Pliny, *Naturalis Historia* XXXIV.18). Alternatively, the subject might well be that of Alexander the Great, who attempted to emulate and assimilate himself to that hero (Henig 1970, 252–5; 264–5); it will be recalled that the emperor Augustus at one time employed a seal cut with an image of Alexander (Suetonius, *Divus Augustus* L; Pliny, *Naturalis Historia* XXXVII.10).

The heroic subject of the Borough High Street gem would have been highly suitable for a soldier or an official, possibly serving in Britain at the time of Hadrian's visit in AD 122, and is the most attractive gem yet recorded from Southwark.

BRACELETS
Copper alloy
<R61>, <1136>, [1677]; P5, B22, group 62,278 (not illustrated) W 8mm. Fragment of strip bracelet with tapering terminal, its hook missing; grooved decoration on edge. Corroded and distorted.

<R62>, RWT93 <8>, [343]; P3=P5, OA1, group 2,3 (not illustrated)
Incomplete; surviving L 55.5mm; W 6mm. Fragment of strip bracelet, which tapers towards the terminal, now lost; continuous vertical line decoration along the strip; flat back and slightly convex outer surface. A 3rd- to 4th-century type.

<R63>, RWG94 <9>, [24]; P5=P7, OA3, group 4,41 (not illustrated)
Incomplete; W 4.2mm. Fragment of strip bracelet, broken at both ends and now bent, decorated with a series of punched dots, irregularly placed, on one side. From fill of burial 7. Date: 3rd/4th century.

NECKLACES/BEADS
Glass
<R64>, <1063>, [1815]; P4, B14, group 58,260 (not illustrated)
Melon bead, fragment.

<R65>, LBI95 <133>, [392]; P5=P6/7, OA13, group 29,103 (not illustrated)
Complete; Diam 13mm; pale turquoise.

<R66>, LBI95 <134>, [335]; P=P6/7, B5, group 22,119 (not illustrated)
Incomplete; Diam c 12mm.

<R67>, <1707>, [1055]; P7, OA30, group 72,319 (not illustrated)
Diam 3.5mm. Biconical, blue glass (Guido 1978, 97, fig 37).

<R68>, <1597>, [1034]; P7, OA30, group 72,364 (not illustrated)
D 4.5mm. Annular, opaque white glass.

<R69>, <592>, [1082]; P7, OA31, group 73,375 (not illustrated)
Diam 15mm. Globular, natural green glass (Guido 1978, 134, group 5c).

<R70>, <1709>, [1125]; P7, OA31, group 73,374 (not illustrated)
Diam 4.5mm. Biconical, blue glass (Guido 1978, 97, fig 37).

<R71>, [3011] <1579>; P7, OA27, group 174,994 (not illustrated)
Two beads from a necklace:
Diam 6mm. Lentoid section; dark purple glass.
Diam 5mm. Annular; green glass.

<R72>, LBI95 <31>, [18]; P3=P5, B7, group 20,36 (not illustrated)
L 10.5mm; W 7.3mm. Green glass bead, faceted, five-sided, perhaps in imitation of an emerald crystal (as on a gold necklace from Cottons Wharf, CW83). Typical of the form of beads popular in the Roman period, where precious, semi-precious and paste beads were sometimes strung on the same necklace.

HAIRPINS
(typology after Crummy 1983)

Bone
Type 1: Plain conical head
<R73>, <874>, [1597]; P6, OA24, group 64,295, Fig 81
Almost complete; L 80mm; W of head 3mm. Slender with fine conical head; well fashioned.

<R75>, <1627>, [1074]; P7, OA30, group 72,31 (not illustrated)
Surviving L 26mm; head only.

<R74>, <740>, [1290]; P6, B13, group 65,303 (not illustrated)
Surviving L 62.5mm. Wide conical head, roughly finished; shank broken.

<R76>, RWT93 <27>, [150]; P5=P7, B2, group 12,28 (not illustrated)
Incomplete; surviving L 44.5mm. Very slender shaft with slight swelling and small conical head.

<R77>, REW92 <7>, [214]; P3=P5/6, OA2, group 5,5 (not illustrated)
Incomplete; surviving L 60mm. The plain head is roughly squared; broken at about the mid point of the shaft.

Type 2: Transverse grooves beneath a conical head
<R78>, MSA92 <54>, [105]; P3=P5, B4, group 15,26 (not illustrated)

L 80mm. Three grooves and two cordons below a conical knob head; tip missing.

<R79>, <764>, [3242]; P6, B29, group 138,787 (not illustrated)
Complete; L 111mm. Single groove below a conical head; slender shaft, regularly tapering.

<R80>, BUG94 <1>, [17]; P6, B2, group 22,32 (not illustrated)
Incomplete; L 55mm. Two grooves and cordon below conical head; shank fractured.

<R81>, <837>, [3171]; P7, B28, group 211,711, Fig 108
Surviving L 77mm; W of shaft 3.5mm. Two grooves beneath conical head; point missing. Slender and quite well made.

<R82>, <1602>, [42]; P7, S13, group 37,156 (not illustrated)
Fragment of head, recovered in sieving.

Type 3: Spherical head
<R83>, <1626>, [3213]; P7, B31, group 166,961, Fig 95
Incomplete; surviving L 92.5mm. Head type A, globular; swelling shaft, broken above the point.

Type 5: One or more reels beneath a conical or ovoid head
<R84>, LBE95 <68>, [158]; P3=P6, OA4, group 6,28, Fig 108
L 59.5mm. Conical head over a wide baluster-shaped cordon which has lattice decoration; tapering shaft, incomplete. This appears to be a variant of type 5, which usually has plain reels below the head and is generally dated to the 4th century (Crummy 1983, 23–4).

Miscellaneous and fragments (none illustrated)
<R85>, <729>, [3160]; P7, OA27, group 210,754
L of head 7mm. Small flame-shaped head, similar to Crummy 1983, 25, no. 437, fig 23; shank of uniform width broken.

<R86>, <1598>, [798]; P4, B12, group 22,90
Fragment of shaft.

<R87>, <1582>, [1266]; P6, S2, group 66,309
Fragment of shaft, possibly needle.

<R88>, <1633>, [1337]; P6, S2, group 66,309
Shaft and point, abraded; ?needle.

<R89>, <1634>, [1337]; P6, S2, group 66,309
Fragment of shaft.

<R90>, <52>, [43]; P7, S13, group 37,153
Shaft with swelling at mid point, as types 3, 5 and 6.

<R91>, <332>, [475]; P7, S13, group 109,507
Fragment of shaft; slight swelling.

<R92>, <466>, [1045]; P7, OA31, group 73,373
Fragment of shaft; slight swelling.

<R93>, <717>, [3120]; P7, B32, group 155,798
Fragment of shaft and point; regular taper.

<R94>, <816>, [3167]; P7, OA27, group 151,754
Shaft fragment.

<R95>, <1612>, [3441]; P7, OA32, group 170,947
Shaft fragment; uniform section.

<R96>, <966>, [4070]; P7, well, group 212,1006
Fragment of slender shaft, tapering regularly to the point.

<R97>, <1653>, [4072]; P7, well, group 181,1006
Point and fragment of shaft.

<R98>, LBI95 <133>, [392]; P5=P6/7, OA13
Fragment of shaft, lower end.

Jet
<R99>, RWT93 <23>, [6]; P6 (post-Roman), OA5, group 13,33 (not illustrated)
Incomplete; surviving L 27mm. Fragment of pin shaft, apparently tapering towards the lower end, but the point has been smoothed off, perhaps reworked.

Glass
<R100>, <1740>, [7056]; P4, B20, group 134,609 (not illustrated)
Incomplete; L 76mm. Plain shaft in natural green blue glass, tapering at one end, with a slight

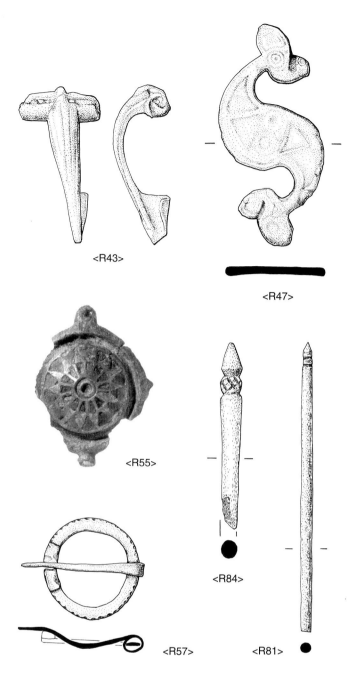

<R43>

<R47>

<R55>

<R57>   <R84>   <R81>

Fig 108 *Registered finds from periods 4–7 (1:1)*

<R103>, LBE95 <54>, [82];
P4=P6, B1, destruction, group
8,47 (not illustrated)
Incomplete; W 28mm.
Fragmentary buckle plate with
trace of attachments for pin.

FOOTWEAR
The only evidence for shoes at
BGH95 comes from the corroded
fragments of iron hobnails (none
illustrated); no Roman leatherwork
survives on the site.

<R104>, <715>, [1265]; P6,
OA24, group 67,316

<R105>, <685>, [1231]; P7,
OA28, group 71,355

<R106>, RWG94 <45>, [54];
P4, OA2, group 3,36

Fragments of ?two shoes:
a) Part of the sole at the heel
end; triple construction with
stitching around the edge; only
a very small fragment of the sole
survives (c 10mm), with larger
pieces of the interlining and
inner sole. Dimensions 73mm x
48mm
b) Irregular fragment of sole,
double layer of leather with nail
holes; no nails have survived.
No nail pattern is recoverable.
Max. surviving L 81mm.

Toilet, surgical and pharmaceutical implements

BOX
Bone
<R107>, <420>, [608]; P6, S6,
group 108,505, Fig 109
H 50mm; Diam 33mm. Lathe-
turned cylindrical box, shaped
externally with grooves and
mouldings at the lower end.
The base is plugged with a
separate bone disc, which has
a turning mark in the centre,
decorative grooves on the
underside and a bevelled edge
on the upper face which is
inside the box. There is seating
for a (missing) lid at the top of
the box.
　　Such boxes had many possible
functions, for example for

holding cosmetics, powders
or unguents (Beal and Feugère
1983), but there are no traces
of residue. The true pyxis is a
classical form rarely found in
Britain, although there are a
few very early examples, such
as the box found in a pre-
Conquest grave at King Harry
Lane, Verulamium (Greep 1983,
261; Stead and Rigby 1989,
108, fig 109,8), which certainly
at an early period are likely
to have been imported. The
present example is of a simple
cylindrical form and may well
have been made in Britain by
this period. The shape is
paralleled in turned wooden
boxes from 179 Borough High
Street, also in Southwark
(Wardle in prep).

Fig 109 *Bone box <R107> (1:1)*

MIRRORS
Copper alloy
<R108>, <720>, [3136]; P5,
B27, group 160,907, Fig 72
L 48mm; W 32mm; approx
Diam 130mm. Two edge
fragments from a circular hand-
mirror with dot and circle
decoration around the edge of
the reflecting surface; one
illustrated.

<R109>, LBE95 <60>, [160];
P3=P6, B1, group 7,45 (not
illustrated)

shaping which could be the start
of a swelling head. Possibly a
stirring rod, but the tapering shaft
makes it more likely to be a hairpin.
Such objects are rare, perhaps partly
due to the fragility of the material,
but are known from burial contexts,
as at Colchester (Crummy 1983,
28) where their position makes
identification as hairpins almost
certain.

BUCKLES
Copper alloy
<R101>, <4346>, [508]; P4,

OA15, group 25,102 (not
illustrated)
Incomplete; L 36mm. Buckle
tongue fragment, flat tapering
strip.

<R102>, <567>, [1134]; P7,
OA28, group 71,360, Fig 92
H 31.5mm; inner H (W of
strap) 17mm; W 29mm.
D-shaped loop with decorative
terminals at each end of axle
bar; circular eye at end of
tongue for attachment to bar.
Possibly military.

Max L 19mm; Th 1.5mm. Three small fragments, all with irregular fracture, reflecting surface visible.

<R110>, RWT93 <10>, [266]; P3=P5, OA1, group 2,5 (not illustrated)
Surviving L 38mm; Th 2.5mm (corroded). Mirror fragment; very corroded irregular fragment, with the distinctive sharp breaks seen in the alloy used for mirrors; no original surface remains.

LIGULAE
Copper alloy
<R111>, <997>, [1707]; P6, S7, group 61,275 (not illustrated)
Incomplete; surviving L 62mm. Flat, narrow strip, tapering at one end, where it is broken, and expanding into a spoon or blade at the other. Possibly a handle for a form of ligula, spatula or small spoon.

<R112>, <1049>, [1729]; P4, OA16, group 63,290 (not illustrated)
Fragment of circular-sectioned handle and part of a flat spoon.

SOCKETED HANDLE
Copper alloy
<R113>, <1073>, [1668]; P7, OA30, group 72,365, Fig 110
L 90mm; W of squared end 9mm. Robust, solid octagonal-sectioned handle (incomplete) at the upper end of which is a square-sectioned terminal with above it a small decorative finial with a knob and baluster mouldings. The handle is broken at the lower, functional end but there is a trace of a narrow circular socket (Diam c 1.5mm). Mouldings on the terminal and at the junction of the squared end with the handle are reminiscent of ligulae and related medical tools, and the octagonal handle is typical of those dating after AD 300 (R Jackson pers comm). Ralph Jackson also comments that, although the finial is unusual, the overall size of the object makes it probable that it is related to the range of 'handled needles' used in Roman medicine (Jackson 1994, 176, fig 3, 1–4) and served as a needle grip. Iron needles, which rarely survive, were inserted into a narrow tubular socket in the copper alloy handle and were

used, according to Celsus in *De medicina*, for puncturing the skin, lancing pustules and in various other operations (ibid, 177).

NAIL CLEANER
Copper alloy
<R114>, <691>, [3057]; P5, B27, group 160,907, Fig 110
L 44mm. Leaf-shaped, with head positioned at right angles to the blade. Type 2a (Crummy 1983, 58); mid to late 1st century.

TWEEZERS
Copper alloy
<R115>, <664>, [698]; P5, Alley 5, group 23,1102 (not illustrated)
Incomplete; L c 49mm. Plain arms, small looped head; very corroded and in three fragments.

<R116>, [43]<51>; P7, S13, group 37,152 (not illustrated)
Complete; L 54mm. Plain arms, standard form, with slightly inturned terminals.

BATH FLASK HANDLE
Copper alloy
<R117>, <975>, [2011]; P5, OA20, group 89,438, Fig 69
Two rings, Diam 25mm, to which are joined lengths of square-sectioned loop-in-loop chain. The whole is very encrusted but there is a trace of a third ring or junction loop. Although corroded, this appears to be the carrying handle of a glass oil flask or *aryballos* (Isings 1957, 78, form 61). The rings fitted through the dolphin-shaped handles set on either side of the neck and the chain allowed the flask to be attached to the owner's wrist. It was usual also for a length of chain to secure the stopper, as found on an example from Pompeii (Ward-Perkins and Claridge 1976, no. 231: Naples Museum 133293). A well-preserved flask with chain is now on display in the Museum of London (Guildhall Museum 1908, pl 8, no. 1). A similar fragment was found at 201–211 Borough High Street (Bird et al 1978, 156, no. 7).

COSMETIC GRINDER
Copper alloy
<R118>, <950>, [3308]; P6, Alley 5, group 156,942, Fig 87

<R113>

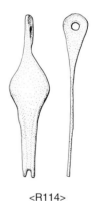

<R114>

Fig 110 Copper alloy nail cleaner <R114> and surgical implement <R113> (1:1)

Surviving L 40mm; W 10mm. Mortar, with central suspension loop; enamelled decoration in a series of triangular cells on the sides. These implements, which appear to be made only in Britain, have been identified as mortars used in the preparation of cosmetics or medicaments (Jackson 1985). They are now more frequently recognised on British excavations

and their distribution pattern is no longer confined to East Anglia and the south-east, although these areas have produced more examples than anywhere else. At least eight mortars or pestles have been found in London and there is evidence for their manufacture elsewhere in Southwark, with the discovery of a lead prototype at Skipton Street (Jackson 1993).

PALETTE
Stone
<R119>, <1833>, [1856]; P4, B15, group 59,1109, Fig 52
Incomplete; W 73.5mm; Th 9mm. Fine grained grey sandstone; one side, with bevelled edges, survives.

STIRRING ROD
Glass
<R120>, <854>, [3250]; P4, B20, group 133,622 (not illustrated)
Incomplete; Diam 9.5mm, L 24mm. Twisted rod in natural green blue glass.

Textile manufacture and working

NEEDLES
Bone
<R121>, <1453>, [1620]; P6, B22, group 64,293 (not illustrated)
Incomplete; L of shaft 54mm. Needle, broken above point and across ?round eye, as Crummy type 1.

<R122>, RWT93 <25>, [265]; P3=P5, B1, group 7,16 (not illustrated)
L 85mm; point missing. Type 1 with conical head and figure of eight eye, drilled.

<R123>, RWT93 <68>, [266]; P3=P5, OA1, group 2,5 (not illustrated)
L 55mm; fragment. Type uncertain, only a trace of the eye survives.

?NETTING NEEDLE
<R124>, LBI95 <134>, [334]; P4=P5, OA7, group 10,80 (not illustrated)
Incomplete; L 94.5mm. Copper alloy shaft with traces of a forked terminal at each end. This appears to be an incomplete example of the standard form of netting

needle which had a pair of forked prongs at each end (Crummy 1983, 67, no. 1996).

Domestic utensils and furniture

BUCKET

Iron

<R125>, RWG94 <26>, [22]; P5=P7, OA3, group 4,42 (not illustrated)
Surviving L 71mm. Bucket side mount. Strap with eye below rounded terminal; the other end broken.

SPOONS

Bone

<R126>, LBI95 <135>, [435]; P5=P7, OA13 (not illustrated)
Incomplete; L of bowl 67.5mm. Large oval bowl with part of a square-sectioned handle.

Copper alloy

<R127>, LBE95 <81>, [278]; P3=P6, OA3, group 4,21 (not illustrated)
Surviving L 54.5mm; Diam of bowl 26.5mm. Cochleare, standard form; the round bowl is fractured and the handle broken.

LAMPS

Ceramic

<R128>, <1151>, [1318]; P6, B25, group 70,350, Fig 83
L 93mm; W 65.5mm; H 23.5mm. Volute lamp with a scene of entertainers on the discus, Loeschcke type IV. The two dancers, possibly dwarves, are holding pairs of clappers (crotala), used as a form of castanet. The percussion instrument, of which these are stylised representations, had small bronze cymbals set on the long wooden handles. The discus scene belongs to a class depicting entertainers, widely encountered in the provinces and clearly popular. The lamp is residual in its context, but very well preserved, possibly as an heirloom. Lyon ware; mid to late 1st century.

<R129>, <1481>, [1840]; P4, B11, group 52,231 (not illustrated)
Incomplete; W 63mm; approx H 37mm. Lyon ware; small wheel-made closed circular lamp, the discus/filling hole missing; plain shoulders with plain nozzle, the end broken, in which there is a small air hole; trace of a ring handle.

<R130>, LBI95 <80>, [70]; P4=P5, B7, group 20,35 (not illustrated)
Incomplete; picture lamp, discus only. Very abraded, the scene on discus now unrecognisable. Lyon ware, residual.

<R131>, <1806>, [1522]; P6, OA24, group 67,320 (not illustrated)
Firmalampe; fragment of shoulder; Central Gaulish White ware.

<R132>, <1849>, [4072]; P5, OA19, group 181,1006 (not illustrated)
Firmalampe; fragment of base, with concentric rings. North Italian fabric.

Open forms

<R133>, <1545>, [3529]; P5, B23, group 158,851 (not illustrated)
Fragment. Open lamp, fine micaceous oxidised ware.

<R134>, BSE94 <15>, [121]; P4, OA2, group 4,6 (not illustrated)
Fragment of side-wall and base. North France/South-East ware, AD 60–150.

<R135>, LBD95 <4>, [8]; P2=P7, OA2, group 3,5 (not illustrated)
Fragment of open lamp. Local fabric: ?local oxidised ware, late 1st/2nd century.

QUERNS

Most are small fragments; dimensions are given only for the more substantial examples. All are Niedermendig lava, except where stated otherwise. Only the first example illustrated.

<R136>, <1435>, [3887]; P4, B20, group 139,643, Fig 55
Upper stone; about one-third remaining with collar and characteristic bi-directional grooving. Part of the central hopper also survives and the grinding surface is very worn.

Diam c 420mm; Th at rim 72mm; Th at centre 25mm.

<R137>, <1502>, [3795]; P4, B20, group 139,639
One side retains traces of a grinding surface, but no original edges or other surfaces survive.

<R138>, <1603>, [734]; P4, B9, group 27,112
Fragment.

<R139>, <1538>, [879]; P4, B18, group 106,496
Fragment, no surfaces remaining. Max L 140mm.

<R140>, <1834>, [1931]; P4, B11, group 52, 234
Fragment.

<R141>, <1215>, [726]; P4, OA15, group 28,114
Millstone grit. ?Upper stone, worn surface. Diam c 490mm; Th 55mm.

<R142>, <1571>, [2220]; P4, OA14, group 84,412
Lower stone; edge very worn. Diam c 360mm; Th at rim 65mm.

<R143>, <1604>, [3250]; P4, B20, group 133,622
Fragment with central hole.

<R144>, <1547>, [3596]; P5, B23, group 146,831
Fragment of upper stone, with striations.

<R145>, <1434>, [3596]; P5, B23, group 146,831
Upper stone, about 25% present. Diam 430mm; Diam of hopper at top 40mm; at centre 25mm; Th at edge 50mm. Striations on outer edge.

<R146>, <1436>, [3961]; P6, B27, group 136,810
Coarse-grained sandstone, upper stone. Diam 330mm; domed profile, with central hole, Diam 30mm; max Th 75mm; at centre 20mm.

<R147>, <1437>, [1556]; P6, S2, group 57,256
Diam uncertain but c 800mm; Th at edge 70mm; very worn. In view of its large diameter this is likely to be a fragment of millstone.

<R148>, <1153>, [326]; P6, S6, group 30,124
Fragment of upper stone.

<R149>, <690>, [442]; P7, OA29, group 35,142
Upper stone, with collar, grooves worn; edge present. Diam c 450mm; Th at edge 55mm.

<R150>, <1065>, [475], P7, S13, group 109,57
Fragment.

<R151>, <1487>, [3028]; P7, OA27, group 174,993
Fragment.

<R152>, <1515>, [3478]; P7, OA27, group 170,949
Fragment with part of grinding surface.

<R153>, LBE95 <64>, [94]; P4=P6, B1, group 8,55
Four abraded fragments.

<R154>, MSA92 <56>, [310]; P3=P5, OA3, group 5,7
Fragment, possibly part of an upper stone, but no original surfaces survive.

Recreational activity

GAMING EQUIPMENT/COUNTERS

Bone

<R155>, <1637>, [1062]; P7, OA28, group 71,362, Fig 111
Complete; Diam 21mm. Plain with countersunk upper surface, Crummy (1983) type 1. Abraded.

<R156>, <593>, [1082]; P7, OA30, group 73,373 (not illustrated)
Complete; Diam 19.3mm. As above, central lathe-mark.

<R157>, LBE95 <98>, [266]; P5=P7, OA6, group 8,72 (not illustrated)
Complete; Diam 19.6mm. As above, plain disc with flat surfaces and central lathe-mark on one face. Abraded.

<R158>, LBI95 <135>, [422]; P2=P4, B2, group 6,65 (not illustrated)
Complete; Diam 20mm. Crummy type 1, with flat sides, lathe-mark on face.

<R159>, LBI95 <36>, [132]; P4=P5, OA 9, group 19,28 (not illustrated)
Complete; Diam 19mm. Crummy type 1 with flat sides, lathe-mark on one face. Well finished, bevelled outside edge.

Glass
<R160>, <1568>, [1769]; P4, B14, group 58,260 (not illustrated)
Complete; Diam 15mm. Plano-convex, blue glass.

Ceramic
<R161>, MSA92 <44>, [341]; P5=P7, OA5, group 10,18 (not illustrated)
Diam 34mm. Counter, cut from a potsherd; Alice Holt/Farnham ware (AHFA).

<R162>, <1768>, [3676]; P6, OA19, group 150,628 (not illustrated)
Diam 50mm. Counter, cut from a potsherd with lattice decoration, Black-Burnished ware.

Weights and measures

WEIGHTS
Copper alloy
<R163>, <1624>, [7021]; P4, B23, group 145,819 (not illustrated)
Circular pan weight; Diam 16mm; Th 3mm; Weight 3g, perhaps for three scruples. This is an almost identical weight to an example from Colchester (Crummy 1983, 101, no. 2512).

Lead
<R164>, <1454>, [1906]; P4, B15, group 59,264 (not illustrated)
Diam 60mm; H 41mm; Weight 1054g. Steelyard weight; irregular cylindrical weight with slightly convex sides; iron suspension loop, very corroded.

<R165>, STU92 <9>, [6]; unphased, OA5, group 7,31 (not illustrated)
Diam 34.5mm; H 29mm; Weight 139g. Cylindrical pan weight, surfaces now abraded.

Stone
<R166>, <970>, [1596]; P6, B22, group 64,293, Fig 81

H 122mm; W 90mm; Weight 676g. Almost complete, but fractured weight; roughly triangular in form, with a slightly rounded base. A single suspension hole (Diam 13mm) has been made through the upper part. This has been drilled from both sides and there is a step in the hole where the two holes have failed to meet precisely at the mid-point; turning marks are visible on one side. The material is a septarian nodule, an aluminium-rich clay found in the Thames estuary and often used as building rubble in the Roman period (S Pringle pers comm). Grooves radiating from the outer edges of the hole, which may have been caused by wear from a cord in the soft material. Although the object is undoubtedly a weight, and is of generally similar form to ceramic weights conventionally described as loom weights, it is possible that it functioned with a general purpose, or even as a steelyard weight, and may have no connection with the working of textiles.

?STEELYARD
Copper alloy
<R167>, <692>, [3068]; unphased, group 175,970, Fig 111
L 71.5mm; W of hook 26mm. U-shaped hook formed by a square- changing to circular-sectioned rod with a conical terminal. At the other end the rod is attached to a wider rectangular bar from which projects a flat circular plate with a central suspension hole. A split ring is inserted into the hole and around this is looped a small fragment of square-sectioned chain. This is probably from a steelyard, although it is larger and more elaborate than others from London.

Objects associated with written communication

SEAL BOX
Copper alloy
<R168>, <1124>, [3611]; P6, B27, group 147,882, Fig 87
L 32mm; W 21mm. Diamond-shaped, with enamelling set within a grid. The inner diamond

consists of red and yellow cells around a central cell which now appears white; all cells in the outer zone appear white. There are remains of lugs on the corners, one concealing the hinge, and the box has four holes in the base. This is a standard form, found widely in Roman Britain, and dates from the 2nd century.

Buildings and services

WATER PIPE JUNCTION COLLAR
Iron
<R169>, <1197>, [4069]; P6, OA16, group 182,1018 (not illustrated)
L 70mm; Diam not recoverable but likely to be c 85mm. Fragment of collar, showing stop ridge; traces of mineral-replaced wood (oak) on surfaces. The collar joined two sections of oak water pipe; for discussion of the type see Manning 1985, 128.

Tools

KNIVES
Bone/iron
<R170>, <1400>, [1753]; P4, B14, group 58,261, Fig 68
Surviving L 63mm; L of handle 47mm; W of handle 6mm. Knife, with trace of an iron blade, the tang set into a handle which has been carved from a single length of bone and appears to be complete. Each side is decorated with a pair of carved Xs, separated by groups of three lines, which continue around the edge. The short length of the handle suggests that the blade was also short, so that this may be a razor.

Iron
<R171>, <320>, [471]; P7, OA29, group 35,141 (not illustrated)
Incomplete; L 38mm. Fragment of knife blade.

HONES
Stone
<R172>, <1535>, [1983]; P4, B11, group 52,233, Fig 47
L 75mm; W 29mm; Th 19mm. Rectangular, worn in the middle and possibly complete, although very short. The wear is concentrated on the sides and the upper surface. Fine-grained grey sandstone.

<R173>, <790>, [870]; P4, OA12, group 21,84 (not illustrated)
W 34mm; Th 31mm. Rectangular hone, made from a fine-grained grey sandstone, broken at both ends. One side shows considerable wear.

<R174>, <1276>, [698]; P5, Alley 2, group 23,1102 (not illustrated)
W 61mm; Th 9mm. Flat fragment of fine-grained stone, with one rounded edge, probably from a hone.

<R175>, <684>, [3141]; P5, B23, group 149,952 (not illustrated)
L 180mm; W 30mm. Complete; rectangular in form with slightly bevelled edges and tapering ends, the surfaces now irregular and worn through use.

<R176>, <931>, [2011]; P5, OA20, group 89,438 (not illustrated)
Surviving L 83mm; W 32mm; Th 15mm. Fragment of rectangular hone; fine-grained grey stone, broken at both ends. The upper surface and the sides are worn.

<R177>, MSA92 <20>, [105]; P3=P5 (not illustrated)
Surviving L 88mm. Fragment of hone, split, with one worn surface. Fine-grained sandstone.

<R178>, <897>, [1522]; P6, OA24, group 67,320 (not illustrated)
Incomplete; W 33mm; Th 22mm. Rectangular cross-section; fine-grained grey stone.

<R179>, <1516>, [3497]; P7, B30, group 162,919 (not illustrated)
Surviving L 120mm; W 32mm. Part of a hone with rectangular cross-section. Well-shaped; broken at both ends; the upper surface is worn.

Fasteners and fittings

KEYS
Copper alloy
<R180>, <205>, [3008]; P7, OA27, group 174,993, Fig 111
Diam 21mm. Ring key; rotary

key with flat front panel set on a D-sectioned ring.

<R181>, <1270>, [3961]; P6, B27, group 136,810 (not illustrated)
L 65mm. Key. Ring loop handle on a wide shank; the bit is set at right angles as if for a tumbler lock lift key, but no details are recoverable.

<R182>, <744>, [1258]; P7, OA28, group 71,355 (not illustrated)
Surviving L 32mm. ?Key handle. Rectangular shank with two sets of linear mouldings, surmounted by a loop made from a rectangular-sectioned strip, with a small terminal projecting from its top. At the lower end there are traces of metal projecting from the handle, which may be the bit of a key.

LOCKS
Copper alloy
<R183>, <1051>, [1511]; P6, OA25, group 70,351 (not illustrated)
L 39mm. Lock bolt with four triangular perforations; tang incomplete.

<R184>, <402>, [3054]; P7, S18, group 173,768 (not illustrated)
L 73mm. Lock bolt, complete, with four square and one D-shaped cut-outs; for use with a tumbler-lock slide-key.

<R185>, <719>, [3136]; P5, B27, group 160,907 (not illustrated)
L 78mm. Lock bolt, complete, with six rectangular perforations.

<R186>, JSS92 <16>, [51]; P4, B1, group 7,11, Fig 111
L 58mm. Lock bolt. Small example with, unusually, circular perforations arranged in two rather irregular rows of ?three; the upper row is incomplete.

Iron and copper alloy
<R187>, LBE95 <142>, [177]; P3=P6, B1, group 7,6 (not illustrated)
Incomplete; L c 110mm; Diam 45mm. Lock, circular copper alloy case, with iron locking mechanism. This appears to be a barb-spring padlock, although

the hasp has not survived. The case would have had a rectangular hole at one end into which the bolt, which had a central spine, with one or more barb-like springs riveted to its tip, was inserted. Once inside the case the springs were released, thus trapping the bolt. The lock was opened by means of an L-shaped key, which was pushed through a hole in the opposite end. A square hole in the bit compressed the springs, thus allowing the bolt to be withdrawn. Traces of at least two iron spines can be seen inside this case, but the metal is too corroded to permit reconstruction. The barb-spring padlock was known in Britain from the end of the Iron Age (Manning 1985, 95).

HASP
Copper alloy
<R188>, <512>, [1067]; P7, OA30, group 72,318 (not illustrated)
Incomplete; surviving L 28mm; W 11.5mm; Depth of loop 13.5mm. Hasp from small lock, such as used on a box or chest; rectangular plate with projecting loop. One end of the plate is rounded, the other incomplete; the method of attachment no longer visible.

MOUNTS
Copper alloy
<R189>, <774>, [735]; P4, B18, group 106,495, Fig 111
Overall W 85mm. Zoomorphic mount. Standing lion, modelled in the round; details of the mane and head are now obscured by corrosion but appear originally to have been well depicted. The creature is attached by its paws and tail to a plate which narrows to a central socket. The object appears to have been set on a shank, and may be part of a pin or badge, rather than a knife handle mount. A similar object from Nijmegen, a lion standing on a capital with a ring in its base, is described as the head of a pin (Zadoks-Josephus Jitta et al 973, 94, no. 167).

<R190>, <1464>, [1208]; P6, B25, group 70,347 (not illustrated)

Diam 22.5mm. Lion-head mount, with the muzzle in high relief surrounded by the stylised ears and well-formed mane. Such mounts were frequently used to adorn the lock plates of caskets and were, in view of the symbolic power of the lion, particularly suitable for those placed in burials. There is no suggestion here that this stud came from a funerary context, and this common motif could well have adorned a chest or other item of furniture (Liversidge 1969). Method of attachment lost, but on analogy with other mounts it probably had a lead infill.

<R191>, <1147>, [3704]; P6, B27, group 147,888 (not illustrated)
L 15.5mm; Diam 20mm. Heavy mount with moulding below the circular knobbed head; trace of a shank, probably iron. Possibly from a piece of furniture.

<R192>, <30>, [227]; P7, S13, group 37,148 (not illustrated)
Diam 20.5mm. Dome-headed mount or stud with central perforation, probably for a shank, which may have had a decorative terminal on the outer side of the object.

<R193>, <511>, [1067]; P7, OA30, group 72,318 (not illustrated)
L 43mm. Narrow strip, plano-convex cross-section, bent at right angles about 10mm above one broken end. The other end terminates in a closed ring. Possibly a box or casket fitting.

<R194>, <1131>, [2133]; P5, OA20, group 89,422 (not illustrated)
L 15mm. Knob or finial. Spherical knob with conical attachment, separated from the knob by a short shank.

<R195>, <178>, [326]; P6, S6, group 30,124 (not illustrated)
Surviving L 65mm; W 10mm. Narrow strip with three rivets, placed at intervals of 30mm. Probably a reinforcing strip from a box.

STUDS
Copper alloy
Flat circular heads; no decoration. None illustrated.
<R196>, <105>, [198]; P7, S13, group 37,148
Diam of head 20mm; surviving L 17mm.

<R197>, <1294>, [1000]; P7, OA31, group 73,370
Head only; incomplete.

<R198>, RWT93 <9>, [35]; P4=P7
Diam 34.5mm. Flat circular head, very highly patinated and thin, with broken slender shank on the reverse. Probably mounted on wood, to decorate item of furniture or box.

Domed heads. None illustrated.
<R199>, <546>, [693]; P7, OA29, group 35,139
Diam c 16mm. Head only.

<R200>, <1411>, [1828]; P4, B16, group 60,273
Diam 17mm. Head.

<R201>, <206>, [3008]; P7, OA27, group 174,993
L 32.5mm; Diam of head 20.5mm. Plain domed head, large; tapering square-sectioned shank.

<R202>, <570>, [698]; P5, Alley 5, group 23,1102
Diam of head 21mm; Th 6mm; overall L 39mm. Heavy, thick, circular head set on a square-sectioned tapering shank. Possibly a furniture stud.

<R203>, LBE95 <46>, [114]; P3=P6, OA3, group 4,37, Fig 111
Complete; L 38.5mm; Diam of head 20mm. Bell-shaped stud; cast circular head with a countersunk face with central dimpled boss, set on a collar below which is a tapering rectangular-sectioned shank, cast in one piece with the head. This belongs to a class of objects discussed by Allason-Jones (1985) and falls into her type 1 form, although with a copper alloy, not an iron, shank. The shank appears to be complete and there is no sign of any perforation. Allason-Jones (ibid, 102) concludes that studs of type 1, with unperforated (iron) shanks, were

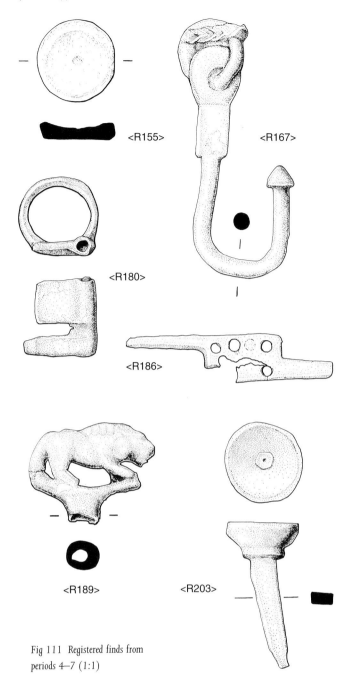

<R155>

<R167>

<R180>

<R186>

<R189>

<R203>

Fig 111 Registered finds from periods 4–7 (1:1)

used for a variety of purposes, including use on some military fittings, and they tend to be found on military sites, although not exclusively so (ibid, 100). Type 2 studs with perforated shanks were used as box fittings.) As Allason-Jones notes, further evidence is required to test this hypothesis, but the presence of a probable type 1 stud in London could be regarded as further evidence of military activity in the town, a not unsurprising circumstance at this period.

CLAMPS/JOINERS DOGS
Copper alloy
<R204>, REW92 <4>, [231]; P2=P1, OA2, group 3,3 (not illustrated)
Overall L 67mm; L of arm 30mm. L-shaped clamp or joiner's dog, probably with three arms originally, two of which remain. For similar in iron form, see Neal et al 1990, 148, fig 136, nos 687–8 (from Gorhambury).

NAILS
Copper alloy
Globular, biconical or bun-shaped heads; probably used

in furniture upholstery. None illustrated.
<R205>, <77>, [58]; P7, S13, group 37,156
L c 18mm; globular head.

<R206>, <801>, [963]; P4, OA12, group 21,83
L 18mm; globular head.

<R207>, <1126>, [1746]; P4, B14, group 58,1107
Spherical head, incomplete.

<R208>, <1348>, [2147]; P4, OA14, group 85,418
Globular head; fractured shank; corroded.

<R209>, <1646>, [7112]; P6, B?, group 165,709
Almost complete; L 25mm. Well formed biconical head, with rounded top and polygonal-sectioned shaft; pinched at join of head and shaft.

<R210>, <1113>, [1160]; P6, S2, group 66,310
L 55mm; W of head 3mm. Very small nail with conical head; appears to be complete.

Flat heads. None illustrated.
<R211>, <701>, [824]; P5, Alley 5, group 23,92
Diam 8mm; circular head; fractured shank.

<R212>, <489>, [1052]; P7, OA24, group 71,358
Flat head, fractured shank; possibly post-Roman.

<R213>, <1591>, [1161]; P6, B13, group 65,306
Diam of head 5.5mm; L 12mm. Slightly domed head; very small.

RINGS
Copper alloy (external and internal diameters are given)
None illustrated.
<R214>, <812>, [1316]; P6, B25, group 70,346
Diam 20mm; 13.5mm.

<R215>, <948>, [2011]; P5, OA20, group 89,438
Diam c 39mm; 25mm; half remaining; encrusted; worn on one side.

<R216>, <845>, [3171]; P7, B28, group 211,711
Complete; Diam c 27mm. Plain

with D-shaped cross-section; encrusted.

<R217>, <830>, [3012]; P7, B30, group 169,940
Diam 28mm; 21mm; slightly worn on one side.

<R218>, LBE95 <153>, [114]; P3=P6, OA3, group 4,37
Diam c 32.5mm. Incomplete; circular cross-section.

<R219>, LBI95 <40>, [38]; P4=P5, B7, group 20,38
Diam c 37mm. Incomplete; circular cross-section; corroded, but appears to be worn on one side.

<R220>, LBI95 <12>, [192]
Diam 19mm. Incomplete; circular cross-section.

<R221>, REW92 <6>, [212]; P5=P7, OA3, group 6,9
Diam 26.5mm; 19mm. Decorative ring fitting; incomplete. The heavy oval-sectioned ring has a double moulding running around the outer surface.

Iron
<R222>, <586>, [608]; P6, S6, group 108,505 (not illustrated)
Diam c 70mm; corroded.

<R223>, <1338>, [3877]; P7, OA27, group 168,720 (not illustrated)
Diam c 65mm.

SWIVEL
Iron
<R224>, <1184>, [4072]; P7, well, group 212,1006 (not illustrated)
Surviving L 60mm. Part of an oval loop with curved ends, one of which is flattened and is pierced with an eye, through which passes a swivel. This is incomplete and is now pulled upwards into the loop where it has a flat circular head. On analogy with other examples (Manning 1985, 138, S4) the swivel may have terminated in a loop. Such pieces were often attached to chains and could have had many functions, including the hanging of cooking pots over the fire. Manning cites numerous examples from Britain and Germany.

Military equipment

WEAPON
Iron
<R225>, <714>, [1265]; P6,
OA24, group 67,316, Fig 112
Overall L 70mm; L of head
33mm; W 11mm. Bolt or small
spearhead. Plain circular socket
with an elongated oval head.

ARMOUR
Copper alloy
<R226>, <1299>, [3947]; P6,
B27, group 136,585 (not
illustrated)
L of plate c 29mm. Fragment of
buckle and buckle plate, from a
lorica segmenta; very corroded,
identified from X-ray 5054.

<R227>, <826>, [5027]; P4,
B20, group 102,481 (not
illustrated)
Surviving L 28mm. Buckle plate,
rectangular and very corroded,
identified from X-ray 5001.

<R228>, <598>, [1093]; P7,
OA28, group 17,313, Fig 92
L 75mm; Diam of ring 56mm.
Ring-buckle. Circular frame,
triangular in section, with
decorative extension on one
side, which enclosed one of
the belt studs. There is no
tongue. Such buckles, both
decorated and plain, are often
shown on 3rd-century
gravestone reliefs of infantry
and cavalry (Bishop and
Coulston 1993, 152). The
reliefs show that the tapering
belt end passed through the
ring from behind, back along
the front and was held in place
by two studs. Bishop (ibid, fig
108, no. 6) illustrates an exact
parallel from the Saalburg
(Oldenstein 1976, nos
1058–60). Such buckles could
also consist of plain rings, with
or without a tongue, as in
<R229>. Date: 3rd century.

<R229>, <1861>, [1093]; P7,
OA28, group 17,313, Fig 92
Internal Diam 37mm; external
Diam 54mm. Ring-buckle. Plain
circular frame with flattened oval
section. Date: 3rd century.

CAVALRY HARNESS MOUNTS
Copper alloy
<R230>, BUG94 <7>, [155];
P4, OA8, group 9,17, Fig 112

W 62mm; H 47.5mm. Bilobed
harness pendant, with central
round terminal below a
rectangular moulding;
suspension loop missing.

<R231>, LBE95 <89>, [276];
P2=P4, OA2, group 2,88 (not
illustrated)
Surviving L 48mm. Harness
pendant; lozenge-shaped terminal
set on a thin plate, now triangular,
but probably bilobed originally.
Date:1st century.

<R232>, RWT93 <18>, [0];
unstratified (not illustrated)
Complete; L 21.5mm. Pelta-
shaped mount; single stud with
footring on reverse for
attachment to a leather strap.
Military in style, typical of 3rd-
century equestrian equipment
(eg Bishop and Coulston 1993,
156, no. 9 from the Saalburg).

Objects associated with ritual and religion

ALTAR
Stone
<R233>, <1893>, [2153]; P5,
S5, group 208,430, Fig 70
Part of a small altar; surviving
W 127mm; H 123mm. The
upper corner survives, with part
of one scroll moulding and faint
trace of a second to its left,
defining the focus. Below this
is a triple stepped moulding
surmounting the narrower
body of the altar, which is
broken. There is no trace of
any inscription. This is part
of a miniature altar, suitable
for use in a household or small
shrine. Fine-grained oolitic
limestone, probably from
northern France (S Pringle,
T Blagg pers comm).

FIGURINES
Ceramic
<R234>, <1406>, [2010]; P7,
OA28, group 92,450, Fig 87
L of base 70mm; W of base
40mm. Part of a quadruped;
pipeclay, the base and hind parts
of the animal preserved in two
joining fragments. It could be
either a horse, an animal linked –
among other associations – to the
cult of the goddess Epona, and a
symbol of fertility and healing
(Green 1989, 149), or more

probably a bull, symbolising
strength, virility and fertility
(ibid). The rounded hind
quarters appear more bovine
compared to examples from
France (cf Rouvier Jeanlin 1972,
337, no. 1019 for a similar base,
no. 1028 for similar animals).

<R235>, [3427]; P6, B28,
group 164,854 (not illustrated)
Surviving L 120mm. Venus
figurine. Classic pose, the right
arm raised to the head, which
is missing, the left hand holding
drapery. The lower part of the
legs and the base are also lost.
Venus figurines were mass-
produced in the Allier region
of France (Rouvier Jeanlin 1972)
and may have been placed in
domestic shrines.

Copper alloy
<R236>, <583>, [517]; P4,
OA15, group 28,114, Fig 52
Surviving dimensions 58mm x
24mm. ?Figurine. Cast fragment;
thick sheet copper alloy, slightly
curved in profile, plain on one
side, the back, the other heavily
ridged; it is not clear if any
original edge remains. The ridges
are heavy and almost straight, but
this could be very stylised drapery
or, less probably, feathers of a
bird figurine.

BELLS
Copper alloy
<R237>, <1148>, [3672]; P7,
OA27, group 170,495 (not
illustrated)
H 29.5mm; Diam 27mm.
Circular base and rounded body
with part of circular suspension
loop; the clapper would probably
have been of iron, and there is a
trace of iron corrosion inside the
body of the object. A small bell
of this type could well have been
used in a set of *tintinnabula* or door
chimes, as on a phallic example
from Pompeii (Ward-Perkins and
Claridge 1976, no. 216), which
frequently appear to have had an
apotropaic as well as a practical
function. Webster (1996, 55)
cites numerous examples of the
use of *tintinnabula* to ward off evil
spirits in both ritual and everyday
contexts. In a domestic context
bells could have been used in a
private shrine. Use as an animal
bell cannot be excluded, but
here too the practical function

and some element of ritual
significance could have been
combined.

<R238>, <1166>, [2220]; P4,
OA14, group 84,142, Fig 112
W at base 30mm; surviving
H 47mm. Bell. Square body with
feet projecting at each corner;
almost complete. The object is
badly corroded and is broken at
the base of the handle, which on
analogy with other examples
would have been polygonal.

Metalworking waste

COPPER ALLOY
BGH95
In X-ray the majority of these
fragments are clearly not objects,
but have the appearance of
sweepings from the floor of a
workshop, scraps of copper alloy
mixed with charcoal and
corrosion products; they could
indeed be fire residues rather
than industrial waste. An
occasional fragment, eg <R239>,
is more certainly metalworking
waste. None are illustrated.

<R239>, <1413>, [3164]; P6,
OA14, group 141,802
Sprue

<R240>, <582>, [517]; P4,
OA15, group 28,114

<R241>, <1134>, [2147]; P4,
OA14, group 85,418

<R242>, <1174>, [3599]; P5,
B23, group 146, 831

<R243>, <69>, [107]; P7, S13,
group 37,151

<R244>, <322>, [475]; P7,
S13, group 109,507

<R245>, <362>, [1010]; P7,
OA32, group 74,379

JSS92
The copper alloy from JSS is
particularly poorly preserved
(see below, 11.10) but this
site also produced similar
'sweepings', most from period
4 contexts, some of which may
have been associated with the
metalworking known to have
been carried out in the mid
1st century.

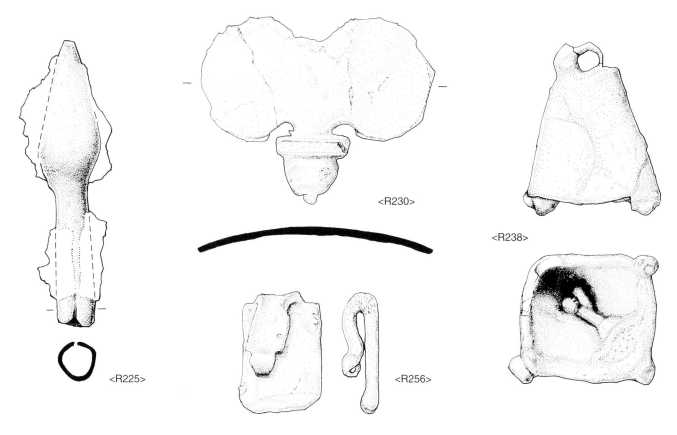

Fig 112 *Registered finds from periods 4–7 (1:1)*

<R246>, <1343>, [7002]; P6, B25, group 135,604 (not illustrated)
L 60mm. Very heavy, round-sectioned tapering cast fragment incomplete at the upper end, where knife marks suggest that it had been cut from the rest of the object. The casting is poor, with air holes, and the whole piece is very roughly fashioned. It was at first thought to be a medieval vessel foot from a tripod vessel, although the workmanship would be unusually poor, but it is from a secure Roman context. It is possible that this represents waste intended for recycling.

CERAMIC
<R247>, <787>, [475]; P7, S13, group 109,507 (not illustrated)
Crucible; small body sherd with thin outer layer. Residual. Verulamium Region White ware (VRW).

<R248>, MSA92 <45>, [282]; P5=P7, OA4, group 6,10 (not illustrated)
Crucible; rim fragment; VRW.

<R249>, LBI95 <25>, [131]; P4, B4, group 18,25, Fig 65
L 65mm. Incomplete fired clay investment mould, used for the production of a single copper alloy object. Justine Bayley of the Ancient Monuments Laboratory has confirmed that the mould was used for casting copper alloy, but it has not been possible to identify the product (J Bayley pers comm). It is probable that the surviving part is the channel into which the molten metal was poured and not the main body of the mould. A funnel-shaped hole is plugged by a detachable central core, which shows signs of burning. Investment moulds, which are more typical of Iron Age technology, are not common in the Roman period, and this is therefore an unusual, although possibly residual find.

Boneworking waste

<R250>, <355>, [480]; P7, OA29, group 35,140 (not illustrated)
L 32mm. Fragment of ?bos longbone with sawn ends; possibly a stage in hinge-making.

<R251>, <445>, [608]; P6, S6, group 108,505 (not illustrated)
W 11mm. Sawn fragment of long-bone.

<R252>, <1459>, [4123]; P6, OA19, group 181,1009 (not illustrated)
Antler, the tines sawn off; knife or saw cuts visible above one sawn edge.

<R253>, LBI95 <71>, [386]; P5=P6/7, OA13, group 29,110 (not illustrated)
Sawn long bone (cow metatarsal, distal end, adult), with knife cuts. Apparently from a Roman context, but the bone looks more recent, possibly intrusive (A Pipe pers comm).

Miscellaneous or uncertain function

COPPER ALLOY
<R254>, <2>, [181]; P4, OA12, group 26,111 (not illustrated)
Surviving L 46mm. Fragment of sheet copper alloy, with thickened edge, inlaid with a running scroll design in tin (AML, XRD). The metal is very corroded and powdery, and the inlay only appears on X-ray, even after remedial conservation and cleaning. The function of the object is uncertain; it could be part of an inlaid vessel or possibly of armour.

<R255>, <1207>, [1931]; P4, B11, group 52,234, Fig 47
L 49mm. ?Pin. Round-sectioned shank, tapering to the lower end, which appears to be almost complete; flattened at the upper end and rolled into a crozier-like terminal. The terminal is too elaborate to function as a buckle or brooch pin.

LEAD
<R256>, <393>, [3012]; P7, B30, group 169,940, Fig 112
L 30mm; W 21.5mm; Th 3mm. Tag or label. Rectangular tag with projecting hooked tang for attachment, now bent. The lower edge is thickened and turned upwards. No trace of any mark or inscription. Such objects are thought to have been used as identification tags and sometimes record the name of the owner.

11.4 The glass

Angela Wardle (discussion) and John Shepherd (identifications)

Pre-Boudican

Period 1

Open Area 2 at BGH95 yielded eight fragments, comprising three of bottle glass and five of unidentified vessels. Two of the latter are in strongly coloured glass, typical of the 1st century, but nothing is diagnostic of dating. There were two fragments of similar vessel and bottle glass at LBB95 Open Area 1.

Period 2

The Period 2 buildings produced very small groups, the largest, consisting of three fragments, from Building 2. Tablewares included two 1st-century pillar-moulded bowls, one in amber glass <1429>, dated to the middle part of the 1st century, and two other bowls, one in blue glass and the other <1261> in a colourless metal. Six vessel fragments are in naturally coloured glass or the strong blue of the mid 1st century.

The open areas contain a similar mix of material, broadly dated to the 1st century (although the conventional date of some forms is L1–E2). Identified vessels comprise a pillar-moulded bowl, a jar or flagon, a phial and standard bottles. The most unusual item is a fragment of stand or tray <1203> in dark green glass from Road 1. Glass stands, used as centrepieces at table or under serving dishes, were imported items, more frequently found in Italy than in Britain, but there are now four known from Southwark (Shepherd 1992, 136). Miscellaneous vessel glass includes blue and naturally coloured fragments and there are two fragments of window glass, both from Road 1.

Period 3

There is very little glass from Open Area 10 at BGH95, which represents Boudican destruction material: only three bottle and three vessel fragments.

Summary of the glass from the pre-Boudican levels

The assemblage is small, with a total of 41 fragments, and most of it comes, unsurprisingly, from period 2, in association with the use of the buildings and open areas, rather than in the overlying Boudican destruction material. A limited range of tablewares and containers is present. Pillar-moulded bowls, the common vessel of the mid to late 1st century, are represented, both in strongly coloured (amber) and in naturally coloured glass. These bowls were made by a casting process, with the interior being ground and polished.

Two other bowls were recognised, one in colourless glass <1261>, but there is only one drinking vessel, a naturally coloured beaker from Open Area 6 <475> (?L1–E2), and little

appears to be of high quality, although there are a few fragments of strongly coloured glass among the miscellaneous vessel fragments. An exception is a fragment of stand <1203> in dark green glass, of a type used as a table centrepiece, but this is very abraded. There is only one quality container, a flagon or jar, and one phial, but there are several utilitarian bottles in which liquids were transported.

Post-Boudican

Vessel fragments and identified vessels are made from naturally coloured glass unless otherwise stated.

Summary of period 4 (AD 61–100)

This group, comprising 73 accessions, produced a limited range of vessels, all common forms seen in the second half of the 1st century AD. The greatest number of identified fragments are bottles, vessels used for the transportation and storage of liquids. Other containers are represented by one jar and two fragments of jars or flagons. There are small numbers of tablewares, chiefly the cast, ground and polished pillar-moulded bowls in natural green blue glass. These were among the last vessels to be made by the technique of casting and were in the heyday of their use during this period. The other bowl (Isings 42) was free blown (Isings 1957). The group includes fragments, but no identifiable forms, of strongly coloured monochrome vessels typical of the mid 1st century. A noticeable feature of this group is the complete absence of drinking vessels, and there are only two fragments of colourless glass, which was introduced for high quality vessels in the later 1st century. Several varieties of beaker were introduced during this period (Cool and Price 1995, 213) but all are missing here.

The picture is very different from that presented, for example, by Leadenhall Court (LCT84) north of the river (Shepherd 1993), where a great variety of vessel forms are represented, some of extremely high quality. At Leadenhall Court, however, the circumstances of deposition were extremely unusual, in that it appears that buildings were cleared in order to make way for construction work on the new Basilica at the end of the 1st century. Shepherd concludes that the large dumps of material may have been the result of indiscriminate dumping, perhaps at a time when recycling facilities were not available.

The period 4 assemblage at BGH95 is not sealed in this way and it would be reasonable to suppose that the missing forms may be represented in groups from the succeeding periods. There is certainly a quantity of residual non-ceramic finds in the construction deposits of overlying buildings, which it may be supposed came from earlier phases. The possibility that glass was collected for recycling should also be considered. The largest collection of glass from Southwark (at 179BHS89), dating from a slightly later period, although including many 1st-century forms, also appears to have unusual circumstances of deposition.

Summary of period 5 (AD 100–20)

This group of glass (74 accessions) comes from the shortest chronological period, apart from the pre-Boudican phases, so the relatively large quantity could represent the increased use (or loss) of glass at this time. Even so the group is not large, but a slightly wider range of vessel types is represented, again perhaps reflecting the general increase in the production and range of glassware available in the late 1st and early 2nd centuries, an increase which is represented by a diversification of existing forms (Cool and Price 1995, 215). The collection includes fewer of the pillar-moulded bowls of the earlier periods, although these could still have been in use at this time, and far less strongly coloured glass, which is increasingly likely to be residual. An increase in the number of colourless fragments is to be expected, but there is still only one identified vessel form in colourless glass, [2034] <1440>, a quality facet-cut bowl or cup from Open Area 20. The overall range includes a platter, an indented beaker, beakers or bowls, a jug with trail decoration [1807] <1721>, a flagon, jars, jars or flagons, and a phial, all in naturally coloured glass. The most numerous single type of vessel was again the bottle, in both prismatic and cylindrical form.

In this period most of the glass was found in contexts associated with the buildings rather than the open areas, but most individual buildings produced small groups, in many cases with only one identified vessel form. The largest group came from Building 24 where four vessels were recognised, together with bottles and vessel fragments.

Summary of period 6 (AD 120–60)

The assemblage (total number of accessions: 100) covers a similar range of vessel types to the preceding period, and in terms of glass production there is no change from period 5. In her analysis of the glass from Colchester, Cool's period 3 (Cool and Price 1995, 215) runs from AD 100 to 170, covering our stratigraphic periods 5 and 6.

There are more quality colourless vessels from mid 2nd-century contexts, notably beakers from Building 27 [3512] <1330>, Building 26 [3557] <1004>, Open Area 24 [1063] <1600>, and a beaker and a cup or bowl from Structure 8 [1256] <1665>, [1266] <1601>. A ribbed flagon in amber glass dating from the late 1st to early 2nd century from Building 28 also represents good quality tableware, and there are additional fragments of flagons and flasks. As in the preceding period there are few fragments of pillar-moulded bowl. Bottles again are the most numerous of the recognisable forms.

A surprising find is two fragments of waste, one certainly a moil from Building 27. Moils are distinctive by-products from glass production and would not have been introduced into the archaeological record in the normal course of trade. Their presence suggests the working of glass somewhere in the area, although not necessarily in any of the structures considered here. The waste was found in a make-up deposit, the source of which must remain uncertain.

Summary of period 7 (AD 160–400)

The total size of the group is 75 accessions, making it relatively smaller than the early 2nd-century groups, taking into account the greater length of the period. There are a small number of identified vessels, including good quality colourless beakers, bowls, flagons, jars and the ubiquitous bottles. Nothing at BGH95 is dated to the later Roman period and most of the glass in the later levels must be residual.

Full descriptions of the glass can be referred to in the archive.

11.5 The Roman coins

Michael Hammerson

Introduction

Although the exact number of Roman coins excavated in north Southwark over the past three decades has not been assessed, the last major published report on Southwark's Roman coinage (Hammerson 1992) gave a total of 962 coins. That paper noted that the 108 Roman coins from 15–23 Southwark Street were the largest group from a single site in the locality, representing 12% of the total.

Subsequent excavations up to the present had probably not increased this total significantly. However, BGH95 produced 443 Roman coins, a higher total than from any other Southwark site by a factor of over 400%, and increasing the total of coins so far excavated from Roman Southwark by 46%, thus making it, potentially, a highly significant group. Of these coins, some 70% were of the later 3rd and 4th centuries; many of these came from post-Roman levels and the 'dark earth', thanks to a policy of searching all spoil, according to context, with a metal-detector, to ensure maximum recovery of material.

Later Roman coins are smaller than the earlier issues, some significantly so. Further, they will only occur in late and post-Roman contexts, including the featureless 'dark earth', which have in many past excavations been excavated and searched less thoroughly than clearly stratified levels; as a result, small artefacts, such as late Roman coins, many only a few millimetres in diameter, are easily missed during rapid hand-excavation of spoil. While this was normally an inevitable result of the lack of time or resources to comprehensively excavate a site, and the enforced need to impose strict priorities in order to extract the essential stratigraphic detail from a site, it has long been a profound concern of the writer that the result has been a serious, if unquantifiable, distortion of the Roman coin patterns from Southwark (and other) sites in favour of the earlier periods. It is considered that the coin histogram from BGH95, studied in more detail in the following sections, demonstrates that these concerns have been justified, and that a careful re-examination of the evidence for the precise nature and date of late Roman Southwark's 'decline' may be necessary in the light of these results.

In the present case, it is unfortunate that the value of the BGH95 group has been diminished by the inability to allocate sufficient resources to conservation of the coins, with the result that only some 15% of them, from the most archaeologically critical contexts, were cleaned. Although, with the additional aid of X-ray photographs, it was possible to provide adequate identification for 328, or 74%, of the coins, the remaining 115 (24%) could not be included in that table as sufficiently close identification was not possible; but an unknown proportion of those may well have been so badly corroded as to preclude close identification in any case.

However, even in the case of coins which could be dated, lack of cleaning meant, in a high proportion of cases, that it was not possible to identify either obverse or reverse types or legends, or to assign standard RIC (Mattingly et al 1923ff) or LRB (Carson et al 1965) numbers to more than a small proportion. Particularly in the case of 1st- to 3rd-century coins, this also meant that it was often not possible to date individual coins as near to their year of issue as might otherwise have been achieved.

Coin summaries

Dates of individual emperors or coins are not given in the summary tables, but may be found in the detailed coin list available in the research archive of the Museum of London. Table 107 summarises, by numismatic period, the coins from BGH95. Table 107 is broken down into a more detailed summary, for closer analysis, in Table 108.

Table 107 Coins from BGH95 by numismatic period

Period	No.	Period	No.
(i) Closely identifiable			
Pre-Conquest	-	378–388	3
41–54	40	388–402	7
54–69	10	Subtotal	328
69–81	16		
81–96	3		
96–117	7	(ii) Less closely identifiable	
117–138	5	Claudius I or Nero	1
138–161	8	Uncertain Flavian	1
161–192	2	Uncertain 1st C	3
192–222	1	Uncertain 1st/early 2nd C	14
222–238	1	Uncertain 96–138	1
238–253	-	Uncertain 1st–2nd C	12
253–273	18	Uncertain 40–250	1
273–287	38	Uncertain mid/late 2nd C	1
287–296	6	Uncertain 2nd C	1
296–310	-	Uncertain 200–268	1
310–320	-	Uncertain Constantinian	2
320–330	2	Uncertain c 340–365	21
330–340	1	Uncertain later 3rd/4th C	51
340–350	36	Illegible/uncertain	5
364–378	24	Subtotal	115
		Total	443

Claudius I, regular	1
Claudius I, copies (including 2 Antonia)	33
Uncertain, possibly Claudius I copies	5
Nero	8
Uncertain, possibly Nero	4
Claudius I or Nero	1
Vespasian	15
Domitian	3
Uncertain Flavian–Trajanic	2
Uncertain c 60–100	1
Nerva	2
Trajan	5
Hadrian	5
Trajan or Hadrian	1
Antoninus Pius and Faustina I, II	7
Marcus Aurelius	1
Commodus	1
Uncertain Antonine	2
Uncertain c 140–220	1
Uncertain 1st/2nd C denarius	1
Uncertain AE, c 40–140	18
Probably 'lightweight' AE copies	4
Plated copies of 1st/2nd C denarii	4
Septimius Severus	2
Severus Alexander	1
Gallienus	4
Uncertain c 220–268	2
Claudius II	3
Gallic Empire, regular	4
Irregular copies, Claudius II	4
Irregular copies, Gallic Empire	30
Uncertain antoniniani or copies, c 259–285	7
Probus	1
Carausius	5
Allectus	2
Constantinian, 320–330	2
Constantinian, c 320–340	1
'Urbs Roma'	1
Irregular copies, c 340–350	
Irregular copies, Constantinopolis	7
Irregular copies, 'Urbs Roma'	3
Irregular copies, 'two standards'	1
Irregular copies, 'one standard'	13
Irregular copies, 'memorial' issue	1
Irregular copies, 'Virtus'	1
Irregular copies, Helena	1
Irregular copies, Theodora	1
Irregular copies, c 347–350, 'two Victories'	7
Uncertain Constantinian, c 330–350	1
Constantinian, 'phoenix' issue	1
Magnentius, irregular copy	4
Constantius II, 'fallen horseman', regular	2
Constantius II, 'fallen horseman', irregular	64
Probably Constantius II, 'fallen horseman', irregular	19
Possibly Constantius II, 'fallen horseman', irregular	6
Uncertain irregular, c 340–365	7
Probably uncertain irregular, c 340–365	13
Valens	4
Gratian	2
Valentinianic, probably cast copies	5
Uncertain Valentinianic	9
Possibly Valentinianic	4
Valentinian II	2
Arcadius	1
Honorius	1
Uncertain Theodosian	6
Uncertain, probably c 270–365	51

Table 108 Detailed summary list of coins for closer analysis

The BGH95 coin histogram

General

It should be noted that reference to 'Southwark' here means, unless otherwise stated, the Roman settlement or town in the area south of London Bridge, and not to the modern Borough.

In Hammerson 1996 (and also summarised in Hammerson 1992, 141–4) an attempt was made to analyse the distribution of Roman coins across Southwark. It was noted that coin patterns from individual towns and other settlements have, in the past, been studied mainly through amalgamating the totality of excavated coins and commenting on the resultant pattern by analogy with other settlements; fig 19.4 compared the coin totals from Southwark with those of four other small towns in the Greater London area.

The study cautioned that Roman coin histograms are, effectively, a grouping of artefactual evidence which displays such behavioural differences through time that comparisons of the same material, on different parts of the same histogram, were fraught with pitfalls. It drew attention to six key reservations to be made in analysing Southwark's Roman coinage, and then went on to break down the coin total from Southwark into individual histograms according to the nine most productive Southwark sites, in terms of coins.

This revealed six different coin patterns, according to location and function within Southwark, only one of which (15–23 Southwark Street) in any way resembled the overall pattern. It clearly suggested that caution is needed in interpreting the overall coin histogram for a Roman settlement, and that

differences in intensity of occupation across the settlement may in general terms be better discerned and understood by a parallel study and comparison of patterns from the individual sites making up that settlement.

From comparison of the BGH95 coin histogram (Fig 113) with that for the whole of Roman Southwark (Fig 114), (which is an amalgam of Hammerson 1996, 62, fig 19.5, top, and the BGH95 data), and by reference to Hammerson 1996, fig 19.5, it will be seen that the BGH95 histogram bears no close resemblance to any of the other sites studied, except to reflect the general pattern observed for 15–23 Southwark Street (Cowan 1992), a site also located in the core of the northern part of the settlement and similarly showing occupation from the pre-Flavian period to the mid 4th century, and use into the late 4th century.

It should be noted that the BGH95 pattern bears no resemblance to that from 4–26 St Thomas Street, physically the closest site to it; this may therefore lend support to the suggestion that similarities between site coin patterns may be based on function rather than proximity. However, even this evidence must be interpreted cautiously and with due regard to the full archaeological record from each site; the histories of occupation on each site will almost certainly be different in particular phases of the Roman era, and it would, indeed, be unreasonable to expect other than considerable variation in the nature and intensity of occupation at various periods between sites. Given this inevitability, however, the similarity of coin patterns between Southwark sites with a *prima facie* functional identity (ie roadside, riverfront, main settlement, beyond the settlement) may be significant and

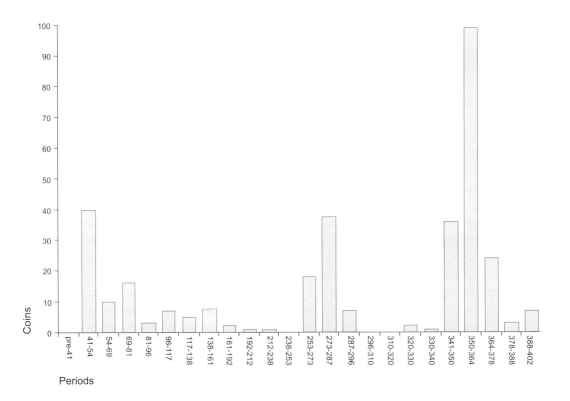

Fig 113 Coin histogram from BGH95

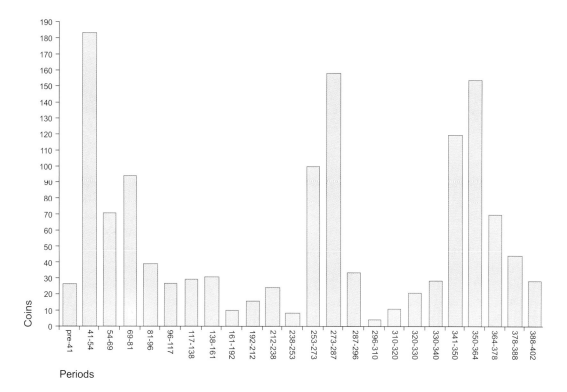

Fig 114 Coin histogram from Southwark

merit further study, both in Southwark and in other towns, particularly Londinium itself.

Since there may thus be a functional perspective to individual site coin patterns, what is noticeable, and perhaps somewhat contrary, about BGH95 is its close resemblance to the overall Southwark pattern. This may mean no more than that sites within the core of the Roman settlement and occupied for most of the Roman era will produce coins of all periods, in the proportions generally expected at the various times of the Roman occupation on most 'average' Romano-British sites, whereas other functionally more specialised or limited sites (eg waterfront, roadside) will lack, or have a concentration of, coins of particular periods. This is clearly evident from studying the histograms for coins from 1st- to 2nd-century levels, which tend to survive relatively intact on most sites. However, survival of later Roman levels is less consistent between sites, and differences in the numbers of 4th-century coins between sites may equally be a reflection of the removal of those levels in post-Roman disturbance and development. A further factor, already alluded to above, is the care with which late and post-Roman levels with minimal stratigraphy are searched for coins. Only when all these factors have been determined for each site can a more confident assessment of the site's coin histogram be reached.

In the case of BGH95, there was both substantial survival of late and post-Roman levels, and care was taken to maximise coin recovery from these. The BGH95 coin histogram may, therefore, be quite accurately representative of an intensively occupied core site in Southwark. Some detailed observations may also be made.

A few Iron Age coins have been found in Southwark, though the stratigraphic evidence for the period is scattered and limited, and their presence or absence on a particular site is hard to predict; therefore their absence from BGH95 is not remarkable. However, in view of the fact that the origin of Roman Southwark dates to *c* AD 50, the total absence of pre-Conquest Roman coins is an interesting phenomenon. These coins certainly came to Britain with the invading armies in some quantity, as the main coinage available at the time – the Conquest taking place not long after the beginning of Claudius' reign – and evidence suggests their use in varying quantities, throughout Britain, during the 1st century. A number have been found in Southwark, and their absence from coin losses of the period at BGH95 is puzzling. It may perhaps suggest that, whatever may have been the function of the pre-Boudican and immediately post-Boudican buildings found here, either the activity was not primarily of a commercial nature where coin exchange regularly took place – though the presence of adequate supplies of Claudian copies would appear to suggest otherwise – or it was an area with surfaces either regularly cleaned or of a nature where lost coins could be found relatively easily. It would not have been unreasonable to expect that a small number of pre-AD 43 coins might have been lost on BGH95 in the general course of circulation.

Coin losses of the later 1st century are generally not dissimilar to those for other Southwark sites, though closest to 15–23 Southwark Street. The slight rise in numbers from the Hadrianic to the early Antonine period, which occurs in several Southwark sites, may be noted; even though the numbers involved are, in all cases, quite small and, statistically, not overly helpful. However, of some interest is the extreme scarcity of coins from the Severan period to the mid 3rd century. This is a distinct departure from the general Southwark pattern which BGH95 otherwise displays. It is a feature shared mainly by roadside sites such as 199 and 201–211 Borough High Street, though not the extreme southern roadside site at Arcadia Buildings. Although, again, coin numbers involved for the period AD 192–253 are normally not large on many sites across Britain, their overall relative scarcity means that they probably have some significance in terms of activity on site when found, even in small numbers; though, of course, such an interpretation of negative evidence needs to be made cautiously. Their virtual absence from BGH95, where there does not appear to have been significant destruction of levels of this period, suggests an absence of 'normal' economic activity at the time; awkwardly worded, perhaps, but, in the absence of other empirical data on which to base the analysis, a means of at least flagging up, from the numismatic evidence, the possibility of an abnormal occupation pattern.

The coin losses for the period AD 253–96 mirror the overall Southwark pattern. It must again be emphasised here that the sudden significant jump in coin numbers in this period (and again in the mid 4th century) does not indicate a renewed increase in activity following a stagnant period. Both periods are in fact characterised by economic phenomena, still not yet satisfactorily identified, which trigger the appearance in circulation of large quantities of a coinage markedly inferior to that of the previous period, and with a purchasing power correspondingly low. Therefore, not only were there significantly more coins in circulation – making losses more likely – but the value of each coin was such that loss was probably not a serious matter and searching for it not always bothered with. It may indicate high inflation but, as some 20th-century inflationary periods have demonstrated, not necessarily an accompanying prosperity. It may be that the coinage of these Roman periods was so inferior that it may have circulated by weight, rather than individual value.

The pattern for the following period, AD 296–341, although in general not prolific of coins as site finds (except for the period AD 330–41), is atypically low for Southwark, where the overall histogram shows a steady and consistent increase in numbers. Interestingly, the other Southwark sites showing an absence or virtual absence of coins of this period are 15–23 Southwark Street and 4–26 St Thomas Street, both close to BGH95 and both core 'settlement' sites (though the marked difference from 4–26 St Thomas Street in other respects has been noted above). There is insufficient other archaeological evidence to enable it to be determined whether the mid Constantinian period in central Southwark saw any contraction or lessening of intensity of occupation.

However, it may be significant that numbers of official coins of AD 330–41 are low, relative to those of the copies of these issues which circulated in the following decade. Official coins of AD 330–41 are common in hoards and, presumably, as site finds in other Roman towns and sites, and should be expected in Southwark in greater numbers. (Unfortunately, the evidence for the City of London, in this and other aspects of its

Roman coinage, remains to be assessed and analysed.) It is regrettable that the extensive copying of these coins is a phenomenon which has not been generally recognised, and has received little study (Hammerson 1980; King 1987; Butcher 1992), and reassessment of finds across Britain will be necessary to establish whether, in fact, official coins are scarcer than previously recognised.

Though normally quite common, for the first time on a Southwark site the 'fallen horseman' copies of c 355–65 comprise the largest group of coins. Given the frequency of these coins in hoards and as site finds elsewhere in Britain, this is not surprising, and it is likely that the careful searching techniques used during the excavation are responsible for the high recovery rate of these coins, many of which are so small as to constitute the smallest coins from Roman Britain, often less than 10mm in diameter, sometimes significantly so. In actual numbers, this part of the BGH95 histogram shows a significant increase over numbers of other Roman coins relative to the overall Southwark pattern, and the fact that recovery with metal-detectors was not previously used on other major Southwark sites (except, to a limited extent, at Bermondsey Abbey, in itself an atypical site well away from the main settlement) gives rise to the writer's concern that the histograms for other Southwark sites of this period, and where late and post-Roman levels survive, may be depressed by an unquantifiable, but possibly significant, amount.

For the last three numismatic periods of the Roman era, the BGH95 pattern again generally follows the overall Southwark one. The paucity of coins of AD 378–88 and the increase in numbers during AD 388–402 is not significant; coins of Valentinian II are normally scarce, and Theodosian coins are in any case not common on Southwark sites, though in some towns and other settlements they can be very common. This may, therefore, be some confirmation of a 'decline' in the Southwark settlement after the mid 4th century, to be read in conjunction with other evidence such as the scarcity of pottery closely datable to that period, and the appearance of cemeteries on sites formerly occupied by buildings (eg 15–23 Southwark Street, 4–26 St Thomas Street).

In summary, then, the Roman coinage from BGH95 both bears a significant resemblance to the overall coin pattern from Southwark, and yet displays differences and anomalies which suggest that the pattern is a specific 'local' phenomenon within the settlement and contains information indicating differences in occupation from other sites at various stages of the Roman period.

Coin circulation and loss on BGH95

A coin histogram can be misleading if taken uncritically as an indicator of the periods at which occupation of a site was at its most intensive. While coins of the later 3rd and 4th centuries did not, in general terms, see lengthy circulation beyond the period during which they were minted, those of the 1st and 2nd centuries did experience long circulation. (An exception to this is the high quality silver of the 1st century, which appears to have been withdrawn from circulation – though not from use in savings hoards – with the appearance of gradually more debased silver during the 2nd century.)

Therefore, to simply interpret the BGH95 histogram as suggesting an 'intensity' of occupation during the Claudian period, and a 'decline' thereafter until the later 3rd century, is to seriously misinterpret coin evidence. The date of the individual coins recovered should not be taken to signify the date of their arrival, or loss, without more detailed analysis of their stratigraphic contexts and their state of wear. For example, it is likely that the Claudian copies saw circulation until at least the middle Flavian period, so their state of wear also needs careful study before making any assertion that they are evidence of Claudian-period occupation. Similarly, a heavily worn coin of Hadrian need not have been lost on site until the late 2nd century, or even later; indeed, worn 1st- and 2nd-century bronze has been found in hoards of the mid 3rd century. Finally, it must be understood that Roman coin production, and its distribution to the various provinces, was periodic and not regular, and that the 1st- to 2nd-century pattern of the Southwark histogram reflects countrywide characteristics. All these, and other, problems of coin interpretation have been considered by us elsewhere (Hammerson 1996).

An analysis of the 1st- and 2nd-century coins follows, along these lines, as in Hammerson 1992 (143–4) and Hammerson 1996 (157–8).

BGH95 1st- to 2nd-century coins

The majority of the 19% illegible examples were from pre-Flavian levels; the virtual absence of identifiable Neronian coins from the three earliest phases (which, interestingly, include the Neronian period) suggests that most of them may have been the Claudian copies so common on Southwark sites and studied in detail elsewhere (Hammerson 1978, 588–93; 1988, 419–20). The manufacture of these coins seems securely placed within the Claudian, and perhaps early Neronian period, before the better coinage of Nero and, by AD 69, Vespasian became available to replace what was a decidedly inferior coinage. However, it will be seen that 62% of the Claudian copies come from Flavian or later levels, with the majority of those being

lost in the Flavian era to the early 2nd century, suggesting clearly that these coins circulated well beyond the period of their manufacture, and into at least the earlier 2nd century.

It is also of interest to note that some 36% of the Claudian coins were recovered from pre-Flavian levels; this is in contrast to between 19% and 26% seen in Hammerson 1978. Perhaps this is an indication that the coins were in use in some quantity, within the bridgehead area, from the earliest phases of occupation in Southwark; certainly, finds on this and other sites confirm their continuation in use into the later part of the century, but this is clearer evidence of their circulation in some numbers in the earliest phases of occupation in Southwark.

At what rate these copies circulated is not known; however, given the extreme scarcity in Britain of the fractional bronze *semisses* and *quadrantes* found on the Continent throughout the 1st and 2nd centuries, it may be possible that the Claudian copies fulfilled that role, at least after the Flavian period.

The remainder of the 1st- and 2nd-century coins from BGH95 show little else which is not obvious from a superficial study of Table 109 and, particularly in the case of the 2nd- and 3rd-century contexts, there are too few to determine with any great confidence to what extent the coin finds are the result of loss in use, or residuality, as in the case of those from the later and post-Roman levels.

Coin wear and date of deposition

However, the period of coin loss on site may, as indicated above, also be studied from the viewpoint of coin wear. This may give a useful indication, however subjective, of the likely length of time a coin had been in circulation before loss. In the following two tables, the criteria used are:

A = unworn;

B = light wear;

C = 'average' wear;

D = fairly heavy wear;

E = heavy wear.

The first (Table 110) summarises state of wear, in those examples where it was ascertainable, according to reign. The second, more detailed, Table 111 breaks down the above information according to period.

Ruler	B	Bd	IPB	LI	LI–E2	2C	L2–E3	3+	LR	DE	PR
Claudius I (copies)	9	2	3	16	2	I	I	I	I	-	2
Nero	I	-	-	3	2	I	I	-	-	-	3
Vespasian	-	-	-	2	2	3	-	-	2	-	5
Domitian	-	-	-	-	I	-	I	-	-	-	I
Nerva/Trajan	-	-	-	2	-	2	-	-	3	-	-
Hadrian	-	-	-	I	-	I	-	-	I	-	I
Antoninus Pius etc	-	-	-	-	-	2	-	I	-	I	-
Marcus Aurelius etc	-	-	-	-	-	-	I	-	2	-	-
Commodus	-	-	-	-	-	-	-	-	-	-	-
'Lightweight' copies	-	-	-	-	-	-	Ia	-	I	Ia	I
Uncertain	Ib	-	Ic	-	-	-	-	-	-	Id	-
Illegible	5	4	3	2	2	I	I	-	-	I	3

Table 109 Coins from the 1st and 2nd centuries

	A	B	C	D	E	Uncrt
Claudius I	-	145	4	-	15	-
Nero	2	2	-	-	-	7
Vespasian	1	2	2	-	1	7
Domitian	-	1	-	-	-	2
Nerva/Trajan	-	2	-	1	1	3
Hadrian	1	-	-	-	1	2
Antoninus Pius etc	-	-	1	2	1	-
Marcus Aurelius etc	-	-	1	1	1	-
Commodus	-	-	-	-	1	-
Illegible	-	-	-	-	2	23
Totals	4	21.9	8	7	59	

Table 110 Coin wear according to reign

Ruler	B	Bd	IP	LI	LI–E2	2C	L2–E3	3+	LR	DE	PR
Claudius I (copies)	B-4	B-1	B-1	B-4	B-1	B-1	B-1	B-1			
	C-1		C-1	C-3							
	D-1	D-1		D-1	D-1						
	?-3		?-1	?-8					?-1		?-2
Nero				A-2							
				B-1	B-1						
	?-1				?-1	?-1	?-1				?-3
Vespasian											A-1
											B-2
					C-1				C-1		
									E-1		
				?-2	?-1	?-3					?-2
Domitian					B-1						
							?-1				?-1
Nerva/Trajan						B-1			B-1		
						D-1					
									E-1		
				?-2					?-1		
Hadrian				A-1							
									E-1		
						?-1					
Antoninus Pius etc							C-1				
						D-1				D-1	
						E-1					
Marcus Aurelius etc							C-1				
						D-1					
										E-1	
Commodus										E-1	
'Lightweight' copies						?-1			?-1	?-1	?-1
Uncrt/illegible	E-1				E-1						
	?-4	?-4	?-3	?-2	?-2	?-1				?-1	?-3

Table 111 Detailed coin wear

It was, unfortunately, not possible to determine the state of wear of 59 of the 108 1st- to 2nd-century coins, some 54% of the total. However, several interesting trends are visible.

Firstly, all Claudian coinage showed some degree of wear, though much of it only light, suggesting intensive use, and loss, quite early on in its period of circulation, followed by a lesser volume of circulation – perhaps, as suggested by Table 111, throughout the 1st century, but lessening in intensity towards its end. This may further indicate that the loss was probably from use on site rather than redeposition in Flavian construction activity. However, the coins from late 1st- to early 2nd-century levels do not show significantly heavy wear, suggesting that they may have fallen out of circulation, perhaps by gradual withdrawal as new supplies arrived, as the Flavian period progressed. It should also, however, be noted that three coins from Boudican and earlier levels showed average to fairly heavy wear.

Following on from this, light wear shown by all identifiable coins of Nero, the succeeding coin series, certainly suggests that these saw circulation at the same time as the Claudian coins, but possibly not beyond; it is, therefore, unfortunate that more comprehensive cleaning could not have been undertaken, in order that this clearly useful supplement to an assessment of the site's history might be better understood.

The three coins of Domitian do not enable any useful conclusions to be drawn about them. However, the remaining

1st- to 2nd-century coinage is of interest in that, with the exception of two lightly worn coins of Trajan and one of Hadrian (from a context dated late 1st century and perhaps therefore intrusive), it all appears to show average to heavy wear and thus presumably circulated well into the 2nd century or even beyond, particularly in the case of the latest coins. One exception is an unidentifiable but heavily worn coin from a pre-Boudican context. It is unlikely that any newly-minted coin would have experienced such heavy wear in such a short time, unless deliberately, and it may well be a pre-Claudian coin (or else intrusive).

Except for the last-mentioned coin, all the coins in D and E condition come, not unexpectedly, from 2nd-century or later contexts, but in the case of those from later Roman levels and 'dark earth' it is, of course, not possible to establish when they were lost as their contexts are almost certainly residual. However, it is most likely that they saw circulation well into the late 2nd or 3rd century – in the case of the worn coin of Commodus, probably until at least the mid 3rd century – and even if they derive from late Roman dumping brought onto the site, they still probably indicate late circulation for these coins somewhere in the vicinity.

Stratigraphic analysis of the later coins

Although the later Roman stratigraphy from this site, in common with most other Southwark sites, is in less of a complex sequence, the contexts from which the 3rd- and 4th-century coins were recovered are set out in Table 112. The dates are of generally used numismatic periods, rather than specific reigns, although each period normally begins or ends either with a reign, a dynasty or a change of coinage.

There is little of archaeological note that can be discerned from this table other than the clear occurrence of a small number of intrusive 3rd- to 4th-century coins in 1st- to 3rd-century contexts. Otherwise the bulk of the later Roman coins come from the backfill of a 4th-century drain, and from miscellaneous 4th-century and post-Roman levels, precluding any stratigraphic interpretation of their significance. Approximately 45% of the coinage of AD 350–64 (mainly the 'fallen horseman' imitations, some of which are very small) are from 'dark earth' and post-Roman levels. It may therefore be conceivable that a hoard of this period was disturbed in the post-Roman period, but, in view of the low value of the coinage of this period, a hoard of these coins might be expected to be considerably larger, and the likelihood is not high.

Other coins

Antoninus Pius, *dupondius*, rev type BRITANNIA (<655>): An uncommon reverse type, found predominantly in Britain and possibly minted in the province, although there is no evidence for the production of 'official' coinage in Britain before the reign of Carausius. Nevertheless, it is likely that the bulk of 'irregular' coinage produced at various periods during the Roman occupation had official sanction.

'Lightweight' copies of 1st- to 2nd-century bronze coins (<82>, <460>, <635>, <667>): These are undersized and often badly cast examples of the official coinage. They are, however, too infrequent to be likely to have constituted an official supplementary coinage, and may be true contemporary forgeries. Their date of manufacture is not known; most 2nd-century types are copied, and the examples recovered are often heavily worn (or were made from worn specimens themselves), suggesting that they are a phenomenon of the later period of currency of the 1st- to 2nd-century bronze, namely from the later 2nd to mid 3rd centuries.

Date	1–2C	L2–3	Misc 3rd C	4th C drain fill	Other 4th C	Late Roman +	Dark earth	Post-Roman
192–222			1					
222–238		1						
Uncertain 220–268								1
238–253								
253–273	2		2	2	3	3	8	3
273–287		1	1	5	8	1	11	11
287–296	2				2		2	1
296–310								
310–320								
320–330					1		1	
330–340							1	
340–350				12	8	1	9	6
350–364	2		1	33	15	2	18	28
Uncertain 340–364				11	4	1	3	4
364–378	2			7	6	1	3	5
378–388				2	1			
388–402				4				3
Uncertain late 3rd/4th C	4	1	1	10	7	1	5	14

Table 112 Coins from the later Roman stratification

Plated copies of *denarii* (<636>, <967>, <1061>, <1409>): Occasional imitations of *denarii* are found, which consist of a bronze alloy core (presumably cast from an official silver coin) covered with a thin silver wash to give the appearance of a good coin. Though *denarii* of most reigns were copied, the frequency of Severan examples suggests that this is a phenomenon accompanying the debasement of the silver coinage under Septimius Severus (AD 193–212), with the forgers producing plausible copies for everyday use while keeping the better silver as savings hoards, which become quite common in this period.

The remainder of the coins from BGH95 reflect the normal coinage to be encountered in varying proportions on a Southwark site, and have been commented on as appropriate in the preceding sections.

11.6 Iron smithing

Lynne Keys

Introduction

Iron smithing slag is found on Roman sites all over the country but it is unusual for a smithy to be recognised as such while excavations are still in progress, allowing specific questions to be asked and excavation techniques to be tailored to answer those questions; it is even more unusual to locate two different types of smithy during one excavation. In the case of the Borough High Street Ticket Hall excavation this did not happen by accident: the results owe much to foresight, the training of the excavators, and the very close cooperation between the on-site field, finds and environmental staff during excavation.

Previous work had shown that iron smithing was an important activity in Southwark during the Roman period, and it was hoped that work on the Borough High Street Ticket Hall site might add to the evidence. Smithing slag had been located at the Courage's Brewery site, at 210–211 Borough High Street and at St Thomas Street (Dennis 1978), the latter very near the Borough High Street site, but none had specifically looked for evidence of a smithy. Preliminary work (BUG94) on the site before the larger excavation began also produced smithing slag, and it was on the basis of this that recommendations were made as to methods which might be used to locate hammerscale and the site of any building used for smithing. It was decided that every attempt should be made to locate any building which had served as a smithy (if one were present).

Methodology and explanation of terms

At the start of excavations, during an on-site finds induction, the excavation team were introduced to hammerscale and shown its reaction to a magnet. The metal-detector user was also familiarised with the sound produced when his machine was passed over a quantity of hammerscale, so that he was then able to detect it around hearths and surfaces and in sections. Magnets were made available to site staff to use around hearths and on floor surfaces; information on ironworking was available on site and field staff referred to it more and more often as work went on. Soil samples were taken whenever micro-slags were detected or expected, and environmental samples were frequently sub-sampled for hammerscale, the environmental processor allowing extra time to sieve these. The finds staff gently washed all slag over a 1mm mesh, facilitating identification of the types found without sacrificing smaller evidence such as charcoal and hammerscale. This also made the later quantification and assessment of the slag cleaner and easier than for most sites.

The presence of extensive electrical wiring and large metal pipes immediately above and between areas of excavation made magnetic susceptibility surveying impracticable, but the team attempted to plot areas of hammerscale and took samples. They recorded all features – even if ephemeral or not completely understood – within buildings which appeared to have been used as smithies.

Over 146kg of iron slag and related debris were recovered (Table 113). Almost all the slag was found in areas A and B and was related to two, possibly three, buildings and the dumps or pits immediately adjacent to them. The absence of any large amount of slag, including hammerscale, from the rest of the site throws attention back upon the buildings that were recognised as potential smithies during excavation.

The slag was visually examined and categorised on the basis of morphology, density, vesicularity and colour.

Metalworking activity involving iron can take two forms:

1) The manufacture of iron from ore and a flux in a smelting furnace, usually (but not always) near the iron ore source. The resulting products are slag and a spongy mass called an unconsolidated bloom consisting of iron with a considerable amount of slag still trapped inside.

2a) Primary smithing (hot working) of the bloom on a stringhearth, usually near the smelting furnace, to remove excess slag.

2b) Secondary smithing (hot working) of an iron shape by a smith to turn it into a utilitarian object.

The two activities – smelting and smithing – generate slags, some of which are diagnostic of the process being carried out and others not. Only certain types of slags are diagnostic of a particular ironworking process (eg iron smithing), while other slags (undiagnostic) may derive from either smelting or smithing, and the process can only be determined in the light of any diagnostic evidence recovered. Other types of debris such as vitrified hearth lining or fired clay may be the result of various kinds of high temperature activity – including domestic fires – and cannot automatically be taken to indicate ironworking taking place. However, if diagnostic ironworking slags are present, the association of the other debris with these can provide more information about the activity.

Type of waste	Wt (g)
Cinder	5287
Dense ironworking slag	775
Fayalitic runs	25
Fuel ash slag	225
Fired clay	538
Ferruginous concretion	90
Hammerscale	60330
Hearth bricks	740
Iron objects with slag	1182
Smithing hearth bottoms	48280
Smithing slag	22555
Undiagnostic	1350
Vitrified clay	5

Table 113 Weight of slag and other categories of ironworking waste

Measurement	Range	Mean	Standard deviation
Weight (g)	60–1900	307	235
Length (mm)	55–140	94	21
Width (mm)	40–135	72	17
Depth (mm)	20–85	43	13

Table 114 Smithing hearth bottoms from BGH95

BGH95 ironworking evidence

Diagnostic iron slag

Tap slag is a dense, low porosity, fayalitic (iron silicate: $FeO.SiO_2$) smelting slag with a ropey, flowed structure. It is formed as the liquid slag is allowed to flow out through a hole at the bottom of a smelting furnace, a feature introduced into Britain by the Romans. There was no tap slag amongst the BGH95 material, but a small quantity of dense slag was found. This is similar in consistency to tap slag but lacks the flowed surface. It usually represents smelting activity but is sometimes found in small amounts in smithing assemblages where no evidence for smelting exists. The small amount present here and the absence of any diagnostic smelting slags amongst the assemblage argue overwhelmingly for its also being produced by iron smithing.

The smithing hearth bottom is the most distinctive product of smithing activity. Both smithing hearth bottoms and smithing slag lumps were the result of high-temperature reactions between the iron, iron-scale and silica from either a clay furnace lining or the silica flux used by the smith to clean the surface of the iron and inhibit further oxidation of the iron during hot working. The predominantly fayalitic material produced by this reaction dripped down into the hearth base during smithing, forming smithing slag. If not cleared out this grew into the characteristic plano-convex-shaped smithing hearth bottom in front of and below the tuyère where the air from the bellows enters (the hottest part of the hearth). The hearth bottom would continue to grow and could eventually impede the air flow from the bellows or greatly reduce the area of working. At this stage, or whenever a hearth was cleared out, its hearth bottom was discarded.

Smithing hearth bottoms were frequent amongst the iron slag from BGH95, 157 examples being recovered. Each was weighed and measured; the ranges, means and standard deviations are given in Table 114. One example (from area D, context [7055]) had a large fragment of iron rod projecting from its upper surface and also included numerous tiny pieces of iron, square in section, in its makeup.

Iron smithing also produces micro-slags (hammerscale) of two types: flake and spheroidal. Flake resembles silvery fish scales and is the product of the ordinary hot working and hammering of a piece of iron where fragments of the oxide/silicate skin flake off from the iron and fall to the ground. Spheroidal are small solid droplets of liquid slag expelled from within the iron during the primary smithing of a bloom or the fire-welding of two pieces of iron. Hammerscale is not visible to the naked eye when in the soil but is highly diagnostic of smithing activity, often remaining in the area around the anvil and near the hearth when macro-slags have been cleared out of the smithy and dumped elsewhere. Since it is generally highly magnetic, its detection with a magnet while excavating can allow the spatial relationship of the anvil to the hearth to be recorded and can pinpoint the smithing activity more precisely (Mills and McDonnell 1992).

Large quantities of both types of hammerscale were recovered during excavation, almost all from occupation debris in Building 3 in area A and Structure 2 in area B, or contexts such as dumps or pits immediately surrounding these two. There was some evidence for hammerscale in occupation debris, in structural cuts and make-up levelling from Building 4 (area A) which might indicate that some smithing activity took place there also. It may, however, have found its way there from nearby Building 3 since Open Area 4 (which lies between B3 and B4) also produced hammerscale. The quantity produced by Building 3 may have been such that it found its way into most features cut or filled in within its vicinity.

Undiagnostic iron slag

This slag could have been produced by either iron smelting or smithing. The small amount present and the absence of any diagnostic smelting slags amongst the assemblage argue overwhelmingly for its being produced by iron smithing. A quantity of fayalitic runs are also undiagnostic but probably originated in the smithing process.

Other debris

Hearth lining can vary from highly vitrified hearth lining nearest the tuyère region (the region of highest temperature) to lightly fired clay. Cinder is formed at the interface between the alkali fuel ashes and siliceous materials, and is usually the lighter portion of vitrified hearth lining. Both these categories of material are not, by themselves, diagnostic of ironworking but may be attributed to the process by association.

Fragments of two possible hearth bricks were found in area A (contexts [595] and [880]). Both come from deposits which contained ironworking slag.

Fuel ash slag is a residue produced by the reaction between the ash from fuel used in a hearth and siliceous material such as a clay lining. It can be produced by any high-temperature activity where these two constituents are present, including accidental fires, domestic hearths and even cremations.

Ferruginous concretion is made up of a redeposition of iron hydroxides (rather like iron panning) but is enhanced by surrounding archaeological deposits, particularly if there is iron-rich waste present as a result of ironworking.

BUG94 and LBI95 slag

BUG94

This site yielded 3.5kg of weathered slag, mostly smithing slag; context [201] produced 2.5kg of this. No magnet test was made on site so it is not known whether hammerscale was present.

LBI95

From this site 1.9kg of slag was recovered, most of this weight represented by smithing hearth bottoms (1.8kg) (Table 115). Smithing slag lumps accounted for 93g.

Measurement	Range	Mean	Standard deviation
Weight (g)	110–469	259	154
Length (mm)	70–125	93	19
Breadth (mm)	45–105	77	20
Depth (mm)	25–60	43	13

Table 115 Smithing hearth bottoms from LBI95

11.7 The botanical remains

Lisa Gray

Introduction

This report describes the plant remains in environmental samples recovered during the excavations in Southwark during the Jubilee Line Extension excavations. The results are analysed and discussed with reference to the research questions defined in the Project Design (Drummond-Murray and Swain 1997). These samples were taken from prehistoric, Roman, medieval and post-medieval contexts from a range of features (eg ditches, pits, floors). Sample sizes were generally between 10 and 20 litres. Details of the samples are presented in Tables 116–24.

Sampling and processing methods

Most of the samples were processed in a Siraf type flotation tank with mesh sizes of 1mm for the residue and 0.25mm for the flot. These flots and residues were dried prior to

sorting. Samples from contexts with a high organic content were processed by taking a 250g subsample (ss) and wet-sieving the soil through a 0.25mm mesh. These samples were kept wet and stored in Industrial Methylated Spirit.

Sixty-three samples were selected for analysis on the basis of the assessment report (Giorgi 1996; Gray-Rees 1996). For the assessment each sample was scanned and its level of species richness was noted. Those samples with dates, archaeological information and plant remains which could give information about diet, economy or environment were recommended for further analysis. For this project only the samples from Roman contexts were selected. Efforts were made to ensure that this analysis covered a range of features and land-use entities.

Several samples were large and contained abundant cereal remains. These were sub-sampled using a riffle box. The results tables display the raw scores and give the proportion of sample examined.

Each selected sample was examined using a binocular microscope with magnifications of between x10 and x40. Charred remains were counted. Waterlogged and mineralised remains were given estimated levels of abundance as follows:

+ = 1–10,   ++ = 11–50,
+++ = 51–150,   ++++ = many 100s.

This information was stored in the MoLSS Botanical Oracle database which contains habitat and economic codes for each species. Details of the samples are presented in this appendix. Modern seed reference collections and reference manuals were used for the identification of the seeds (eg Anderberg 1994; Beijerinck 1947; Berggren 1969; 1981). Identifications were made to species wherever possible and genus and family where diagnostic features were less clear.

Wherever possible attempts have been made to identify the cereal grains to species but charring tends to cause grains to swell, which distorts many of the identification criteria, for example reducing the prominence of a dorsal ridge and increasing the curvature of the sides of the grains. The chaff was better preserved and it was possible to identify it to species. The grains were identified by comparison with modern reference material and the criteria for the identification of charred cereals designed by G Hillman (pers comm 1995; Hillman 1972). Trends in morphology were used to separate groups of grains. Categories of spelt (*Triticum spelta* L), emmer/spelt (*Triticum dicoccum* /*spelta*), emmer (*Triticum dicoccum* L), spelt/bread wheat (*Triticum spelta/ aestivum*) and bread wheat (*Triticum aestivum* L) were used.

Results

Preservation

Most of these remains were preserved by charring and waterlogging. Charring occurs when plant remains are exposed to high temperatures in fires with limited oxygen supply. This converts the organic material in the plant remains to carbon which is then immune to the decaying effects of bacteria or fungi (Zohary and Hopf 1993, 3–4). Waterlogged remains are preserved by anaerobic conditions in contexts such as waterlogged ditches, ponds, wells, pits and marshland which limit the decomposition of plant remains. Four analysed samples contained mineralised taxa. Mineralisation occurs when organic remains are exposed to urine or lime which replaces the organic compounds in the remains with calcium phosphate (Greig 1982, 49), calcium carbonate or silica (Zohary and Hopf 1993, 6).

Description of the results

Full details of the results are given in Tables 116–24. In this section areas and feature descriptions from the Oracle database are given.

LBI95

[308] {102} pit
This sample contained six charred taxa, five mineralised taxa and nine waterlogged taxa. The charred remains included between 11 and 50 fragments of stem and many hundreds of wood fragments. Also present were seven spelt/bread wheat (*Triticum spelta/aestivum*) grains, two oat (*Avena* sp) grains, two indeterminate cereal grains and one grape (*Vitis vinifera* L) seed. The mineralised remains included between 11 and 50 mallow (*Malva* sp) seeds, between one and ten hemlock (*Conium maculatum* L) seeds, 296 sloe/cherry (*Prunus spinosa/avium/cerasus*) kernels, 200 (*Prunus* sp) kernels and one oat grain. Waterlogged remains included abundant fig (*Ficus carica* L) and blackberry/raspberry (*Rubus fruticosus ideaus*) seeds, and seeds from plants from a mixture of habitats, for example stinging nettle (*Urtica dioica* L), campion/catchfly (*Silene* sp), hemlock (*Conium maculatum* L) and sedge (*Carex* spp).

[324] {105} cooking pit
Eleven taxa in this sample were charred, two were mineralised and none were preserved by waterlogging. The charred remains included abundant wood and stem fragments, one knotgrass (*Polygonum* sp) seed, one greater celandine (*Chelidonium majus* L) seed, one spike-rush (*Eleocharis* sp) seed, eight emmer (*Triticum dicoccum* sp) grains, 35 barley (*Hordeum sativum* L) grains, one lentil (*Lens culinaris* L) and one pea (*Pisum* sp) seed. The mineralised remains included five vetch/tare/vetchling (*Vicia/Lathyrus* spp) seeds and seven peas (*Pisum* sp).

LBH94

The only charred remains in these samples were wood fragments. The rest of the remains in the samples were preserved by waterlogging.

[86] {9} peat in channel
The most abundant taxon was wild cabbage/turnip/mustard (*Brassica* spp). It was possible to identify a small number of these seeds to species, white mustard (*Sinapis alba* L).

[87] {10} peat in channel
Abundant fragments of waterlogged plant tissue, possibly cereal bran fragments, were present along with 11 to 50 corncockle (*Agrostemma githago* L) seeds and other seeds from weeds of cultivated or disturbed ground, for example chickweed (*Stellaria* sp) and semi-aquatic habitats, for example sedge (*Carex* spp) and spike-rush (*Eleocharis* sp).

[88] {11>} peat in channel
One charred grass (Poaceae) seed was present along with abundant cereal bran fragments. Also present were 11 to 50 cabbage/mustard (*Brassica/Sinapis* spp) seeds and corncockle (*Agrostemma githago* L) seeds.

LBE95

No abundant economically useful taxa were present in either sample.

OA7 [245] {25} channel
Abundant charred wood fragments and one indeterminate cereal grain fragment were present in this sample. The rest of the plant remains in the sample were preserved by waterlogging and included a mixture of damp and disturbed ground plant seeds, for example duckweed (*Lemna* sp) and elder (*Sambucus nigra* L).

OA2 [299] {24} natural erosional feature
The only charred remains were wood fragments. The rest of the remains were preserved by waterlogging and included horned pond weed (*Zannichella palustris* L) and duckweed (*Lemna* sp).

BGH95
PERIOD 1: BUILDING OF THE ROAD AND ESTABLISHMENT OF THE SETTLEMENT AD 55
Open Area 2
D[3645] {365}
Few plant remains were present in this sample. It was dominated by waterlogged remains, for example tormentil (*Potentilla* cf *erecta*), elder (*Sambucus nigra* L), stinging nettle (*Urtica dioica* L) and spike-rush (*Eleocharis* sp). Economic plant remains were present in small amounts. These were waterlogged hazelnut (*Corylus avellana* L) shell fragments, fig (*Ficus carica* L) seeds and seven charred barley (*Hordeum sativum* L) grains.

Open Area 2 quarry pits
A[5038] {506}, A[5099] {517}, A[939] {97}
Three samples from the quarry pits were analysed. Each sample was dominated by waterlogged remains, for example buttercup (*Ranunculus acris/repens/bulbosus* spp), sedge (Cyperaceae), spike-rush and lesser stitchwort (*Stellaria graminaea* L). Charred remains were scarce and consisted of three poorly preserved barley grains, one indeterminate cereal grain and a fragment of hazelnut (*Corylus avellana* L) shell.

Open Area 2 ditches
B[6040] {673} (1/2 ss), {675} (1/2 ss)
{673} This subsample contained one charred remain, a charred indeterminate cereal (*Avena/Hordeum/Secale/Triticum*) grain. The rest of the remains in the subsample were preserved by waterlogging and were dominated by buttercup (*Ranunculus* spp) and spike-rush (*Eleocharis* sp) seeds, hazelnut (*Corylus avellana* L) shell fragments and indeterminate cereal glume fragments.

{675} This subsample was distinctively different from the previous one. Ten charred taxa types were preserved. Abundant charred wood and stem fragments were present. Also present were seeds of legume (Fabaceae), sedges (*Carex* spp), buttercup (*Ranunculus* sp), vetch/tare/vetchling (*Vicia/Lathyrus* sp), club-rush (cf *Scirpus* sp) and grains of barley (*Hordeum* sp) and wheat (*Triticum* sp).

C[2245] {231}
Small numbers of waterlogged taxa dominated this sample, with elder (*Sambucus nigra* L) seeds being the most abundant.

C[2223] {225} (1/16 ss)
Charred cereal grains were present in this subsample. Most of them were too badly preserved to be identified but 21 could be identified as spelt (*Triticum* cf *spelta*), two as emmer (*Triticum* cf *dicoccum*), five as wheat (*Triticum* sp), one as barley (*Hordeum sativum* L) and four as oat (*Avena* spp). Remains preserved by waterlogging were most abundant. These were dominated by persicaria (*Polygonum* cf *persicaria*), self-heal (*Prunella vulgaris* L) and cleavers (*Galium aparine* L).

External dumps
A[920] {96}
One charred barley (*Hordeum sativum* L) grain was present. That and moderate charred indeterminate wood fragments were the only charred remains in this sample. The rest of the remains were preserved by waterlogging and were low in number. The most abundant taxa were spike-rush (*Eleocharis* sp) and sedge (*Carex* sp).

D[7129] {700} (1/2 ss) natural marsh deposit
In this subsample nine indeterminate charred cereal grain fragments and seven barley (*Hordeum* sp) grains were recovered. Remains preserved by waterlogging were most abundant. These were dominated by hazelnut (*Corylus avellana* L) shell fragments, sedge (*Carex* sp), rush (*Juncus* sp) and buttercup (*Ranunculus* sp).

No chaff, apart from the possible waterlogged glume fragments in [6040] {673} were present in any samples in this area.

PERIOD 2: CONSTRUCTION OF THE FIRST SETTLEMENT AD 55–61

B2 A[822] {71} occupation debris, A[825] {73} floor

{71} All of these remains were charred except for two waterlogged self-heal (*Prunella vulgaris* L) seeds and two goosefoot (*Chenopodium* spp) seeds. The charred remains included abundant possible cereal stem fragments. Cereal remains were present. These consisted of 64 hulled barley (*Hordeum sativum* L) grains, 34 emmer/spelt (*Triticum dicoccum/spelta* sp) grains, two oat (*Avena* sp) grains and hundreds of indeterminate cereal grain fragments. Charred seeds were also present. These included brome (*Bromus* sp), red-veined dock (*Rumex sanguineus* L), curled-dock (*Rumex crispus* L) and water pepper (*Polygonum hydropiper* L).

{73} All of these remains were charred. Abundant possible straw fragments were present as were indeterminate cereal grain fragments. Also 23 emmer/spelt (*Triticum dicoccum/spelta* sp) grains, 39 spelt (*Triticum spelta* L) grains, four barley (*Hordeum* sp) grains and one twisted barley grain. Charred seeds were present and were dominated by 13 brome (*Bromus* spp) seeds and seven vetch/tare/vetchling (*Vicia/Lathyrus* spp) seeds.

B5 A[5108] {507} floor
This sample contained a small number of plant remains, all preserved by charring. The assemblage consisted of four wheat (*Triticum* spp) grains, one hulled barley (*Hordeum sativum* L) grain, ten indeterminate cereal grain fragments and 18 fragments of indeterminate plant tissue, probably cereal grain tissue. Also present were one stem fragment, one legume (Fabaceae) fragment and a small number of seeds from cultivated and waste ground plants, such as grass (Poaceae) and knotgrass (*Polygonum* sp) seeds.

B7 D[7083] {397} floor
All of the plant remains were charred. Many of the remains were poorly preserved, unidentifiable seeds. Those that were identifiable were identified to genus and included knotgrass (*Polygonum* sp),

dock (*Rumex* sp), sedge (*Carex* sp) and brome (*Bromus* sp). Three stem fragments were also present.

B7 D[3995] {394} (1/4 ss) occupation debris
Most of the plant remains in this subsample were charred. Cereal grains dominated. These included 104 indeterminate grains, 33 barley (*Hordeum* sp) grains, 133 wheat (*Triticum* sp) grains, 14 bread wheat (*Triticum aestivum* L) grains, 15 spelt (*Triticum spelta* L) grains, 24 emmer (*Triticum dicoccum* L) grains, 15 bread wheat/spelt (*Triticum aestivum/spelta* sp) grains, 34 spelt grains, 16 straight barley (*Hordeum sativum* L) grains, one twisted barley grain and one oat (*Avena* sp) grain. Chaff and seeds were also present, one spelt (*Triticum spelta* L) wheat glume, one wheat glume and one oat floret base. The seeds included one brome (*Bromus* sp) seed, one spike-rush (*Eleocharis* sp) seed, one vetch (*Vicia* sp) seed and one grass seed. Other charred remains included five hazelnut (*Corylus avellana* L) fragments and one stone pine (*Pinus pinaea* L) kernel. A small number of stem fragments were present. The waterlogged remains were few and included a possible blackberry/raspberry (*Rubus fruticosus/idaeus* L) fruit.

OA4 A[934] {98} occupation debris
All of these remains were charred and dominated by cereal remains. Most of these remains were too badly preserved to be identified but 11 grains were identified as emmer/spelt (*Triticum dicoccum/spelta* L) and ten as emmer (*Triticum dicoccum* L) grains. One charred spike-rush (*Eleocharis* sp) seed was part of this assemblage.

OA8 E[4067] {404} natural soil deposit
All the remains in this sample were preserved by charring and consisted of one spelt (*Triticum spelta* L) grain, one bread wheat/spelt (*Triticum aestivum/spelta* sp) grain, one fragment of rush (*Juncus* sp) stem and one dock (*Rumex* sp) seed.

PERIOD 3: DESTRUCTION OF THE FIRST SETTLEMENT AD 61/2

OA10 D[3960] {390} destruction surface

Similar amounts of remains were preserved by waterlogging and charring. Between 50 and 250 indeterminate cereal grain fragments and abundant charred wood fragments dominated the assemblage. Identifiable grains consisted of one spelt (*Triticum spelta* L) grain, two emmer/spelt (*Triticum dicoccum/spelta*) grains, one oat (*Avena* sp) grain, one bread wheat/spelt (*Triticum aestivum/spelta*) grain and six wheat (*Triticum* spp) grains. Other remains consisted of two lentil (*Lens culinaris*) seeds, abundant straw fragments, three grass (Poaceae) seeds, one knotgrass (*Polygonum* sp) seed and one legume (Fabaceae) seed. Waterlogged remains consisted of small numbers of seeds, for example fat hen (*Chenopodium album* L), medick (*Medicago* sp) and nipplewort (*Lapsana communis* L).

C[2166] {217} structural cut
Only charred remains were present in this sample. These consisted of charred wood fragments, one emmer (*Triticum dicoccum* L) glume fragment, a small number of indeterminate cereal grain fragments, one spike-rush (*Eleocharis* sp) seed, seven bread wheat/spelt (*Triticum aestivum/spelta*) grains, five spelt (*Triticum spelta* L) grains, one emmer/spelt (*Triticum dicoccum/spelta*) grain and one knotgrass (*Polygonum* sp) seed.

PERIOD 4: REBUILDING THE STREET AD 62–100

B9 A[734] {62} destruction debris
This sample only contained charred remains. These consisted of one barley (*Hordeum* sp) grain, nine emmer/spelt (*Triticum dicoccum/spelta*) grains, five stem fragments, one spike-rush (*Eleocharis* sp) seed testa, 11 to 50 indeterminate cereal fragments, one goosefoot (*Chenopodium* sp) seed testa, one spelt (*Triticum spelta* L) grain and one cherry/plum (*Prunus* sp) stone.

B5 A[779] {76} structural cut, posthole
Very little was recovered from this sample. The remains consisted of charred cereal stem fragments and a fragment of brome (*Bromus* sp) seed.

B18 D[3017] {345} structural cut

All of these remains were charred and consisted of wood fragments, grains and a small number of seeds and stem fragments. The cereal grains included nine emmer/spelt (*Triticum dictum/spelta*) grains, ten spelt (*Triticum spelta* L) grains and 16 probable spelt tail grains. One dock (*Rumex* sp) seed was present along with five stem fragments.

B13 B[1161] {136} pit, unspecified
All of the remains in this sample were preserved by charring and included indeterminate cereal grains, one bread wheat (*Triticum aestivum* L) grain, three emmer (*Triticum dicoccum* L) grains, one naked barley (*Hordeum sativum* L) grain and one oat (*Avena* sp) grain. Charred seeds were also present and included one brome (*Bromus* sp) seed, one dock (*Rumex* sp) seed, two grass (Poaceae) seeds, one knotgrass (*Polygonum* sp) seed and one clover (*Trifolium* sp) seed.

B10 B[1808] {654} pit, refuse
Almost all of the remains in this sample were preserved by charring. Between 50 and 250 indeterminate cereal grains were present along with five barley (*Hordeum* sp) grains, a fragment of lentil (*Lens culinaris* L) seed, one wheat (*Triticum* sp) grain, three indeterminate stem fragments and seeds of wild plants. The seeds consisted of a cluster of rush (*Juncus* sp) seeds preserved together in the fruit head, two vetch/tare/vetchling (*Vicia/Lathyrus* sp) seeds, one dock (*Rumex* sp) seed and two knotgrass (*Polygonum* sp) seeds. One seed of self-heal (*Prunella vulgaris* L) was preserved by waterlogging.

S1 A[734] {62} destruction surface
This sample contained purely charred remains. This small assemblage consisted of one barley (*Hordeum* sp) grain, nine emmer/spelt (*Triticum dicoccum/spelta*) grains, one spelt (*Triticum spelta* L) grain, five stem fragments, one spike-rush (*Eleocharis* sp) testa, indeterminate cereal grain fragments, one goosefoot (*Chenopodium* sp) testa and one cherry/plum (*Prunus* sp) stone.

OA14 C[2218] {222} cesspit
Mineralised remains were present in this sample. These consisted of

one apple/pear (*Malus/Pyrus* sp) seed and one mineralised or waterlogged stem fragment.

OA19 E[4041] {402} (1/16 ss) ditch
All of the remains in this sample were charred. It contained large numbers of charred cereal grains. These grains were dominated by spelt grains and also included grains of spelt/breadwheat (*Triticum spelta/aestivum*), emmer (*Triticum dicoccum* L), emmer/spelt (*Triticum dicoccum/spelta*), oat (*Avena* sp) and barley (*Hordeum* sp). Seeds of weeds of cultivation were present, also charred, including corncockle (*Agrostemma githago* L) and brome (*Bromus* sp).

PERIOD 5: DEVELOPMENT OF THE STREET AND ITS FUNCTIONS, EARLY 2ND CENTURY

B22 [1635] {611} hearth RA
All of these remains were preserved by charring. This assemblage consisted of six indeterminate cereal grains, six emmer (*Triticum dicoccum* L) grains, two spelt (*Triticum spelta* L) grains, one indeterminate chaff fragment, ten cherry/plum (*Prunus* sp) stone fragments, two brome (*Bromus* sp) seeds, one buttercup (*Ranunculus* sp) seed and one knotgrass (*Polygonum* sp) seed.

OA21 [7069] {398} (1/4 ss)
Most of these remains were preserved by waterlogging. These included seeds of buttercup (*Ranunculus* sp), spike-rush (*Eleocharis* sp) and lesser stitchwort (*Stellaria graminaea* L). Charred remains consisted of one charred barley (*Hordeum* sp) grain and one stem fragment.

B22 [1819] {651} occupation debris RB
Most of these remains are charred. The charred remains include three emmer/spelt (*Triticum dicoccum* L) grains, three spelt (*Triticum spelta* L) grains, six indeterminate cereal grains, eight hazelnut (*Corylus avellana* L) shell fragments, one curled dock (*Rumex crispus* L) seed and one buttercup (*Ranunculus* sp) seed head. Waterlogged remains consisted of one cinquefoil/tormentil (*Potentilla* sp) seed, two knotgrass (*Polygonum* sp) seeds and a small amount of bran fragments.

B23 [3388] {325} hearth
All of these remains are charred but the sample is small, dominated by wood fragments. One barley (*Hordeum* sp) grain was present.

B24 [3103] {702} floor
Charred and waterlogged remains were present here. The charred assemblage consisted of cereal grains, seeds and chaff. The seeds came from plants from semi-aquatic habitats, for example, bulrush (*Schoenoplectus lacustris* L) and cultivated/disturbed ground, for example brome (*Bromus* sp) and lesser stitchwort (cf *Stellaria graminaea* L). A small number of emmer (*Triticum dicoccum* L) and spelt (*Triticum spelta* L) grains were present along with three indeterminate cereal glume fragments. The remains preserved by waterlogging included seeds from plants of damp grassland such as gypsy-wort (*Lycopus europaeus* L) and crowfoot (*Ranunculus* subgen *Batrachium*).

S12 [2188] {227} pit, unspecified
This sample contained abundant charred wood fragments and a small amount of waterlogged seeds including blackberry/raspberry (*Rubus fruticosus/idaeus*), elder (*Sambucus nigra* L) and fig (*Ficus carica* L) along with one charred grass (Poaceae) seed and one mineralised stem fragment.

PERIOD 6: CHANGES TO THE STREET, MID 2ND CENTURY

B13 [1161] {136} pit, unspecified
All of the remains in this sample were preserved by charring and included indeterminate cereal grains, one bread wheat (*Triticum aestivum* L) grain, three emmer (*Triticum dicoccum* L) grains, one naked barley (*Hordeum sativum* L) grain and one oat (*Avena* sp) grain. Charred seeds were also present and included one brome (*Bromus* sp) seed, one dock (*Rumex* sp) seed, two grass (Poaceae) seeds, one knotgrass (*Polygonum* sp) seed and one clover (*Trifolium* sp) seed.

OA19 [4041] {402} (1/16 ss) ditch
All of the remains in this sample were charred and included large numbers of charred cereal grains. These grains were dominated by spelt grains and also included

grains of spelt/bread wheat (*Triticum spelta/aestivum*), emmer (*Triticum dicoccum* L), emmer/spelt (*Triticum dicoccum/spelta*), oat (*Avena* sp) and barley (*Hordeum* sp). Seeds of weeds of cultivation were present, also charred, and included corncockle (*Agrostemma githago* L) and brome (*Bromus* sp).

B27 [3176] {223} floor
Charred remains in this sample included clover (*Trifolium* sp), knotgrass (*Polygonum* sp), dock (*Rumex* sp) and sedge (*Carex* sp). Waterlogged remains included abundant stem fragments and stem/leaf fragments, and seeds of buttercup (*Ranunculus* sp), elder (*Sambucus nigra* L), nettle-leaved goosefoot (*Chenopodium murale* L), fine-leaved water-dropwort (*Oenanthe aquatica* L), blackberry/raspberry (*Rubus fruticosus/idaeus*), spike-rush (*Eleocharis* sp) and sedge (*Carex* sp).

B28 [3414] {337} (1/4 ss) structural cut
All of these remains were preserved by charring apart from one fig (*Ficus carica* L) seed. The charred remains consisted of seeds of sloe/cherry (*Prunus avium/cerasus*), blackberry/raspberry (*Rubus fruticosus/idaeus*), buttercup (*Ranunculus* sp), brome (*Bromus* sp), mulberry (*Morus* sp), knotgrass (*Polygonum* sp) and sedge (*Carex* sp).

OA19 [4067] {404} natural soil deposit
All the remains in this sample were preserved by charring and consisted of one spelt (*Triticum spelta* L) grain, one bread wheat/spelt (*Triticum aestivum/spelta* sp) grain, one fragment of rush (*Juncus* sp) stem and one dock (*Rumex* sp) seed.

PERIOD 7: AD 160+

B30 (?bakery) [3395] {342} (1/16 ss), {343} (1/6 ss) floor
These two samples contained abundant charred wood fragments, indeterminate plant tissue and fragments of daub with no clear plant impressions.

B31 [3191] {314} (1/64 ss) structural cut
This subsample contained abundant charred grains including 145 bread wheat/spelt (*Triticum*

aestivum/spelta) grains, 345 spelt (*Triticum spelta*) grains, 363 emmer/spelt (*Triticum dicoccum/spelta*) grains, 60 emmer (*Triticum dicoccum* L) grains, two barley (*Hordeum* sp) grains, 205 sprouted barley grains, one rye/oat (*Secale cereale/Avena* sp) grain and three oat grains. A relatively small amount of chaff was recovered. This consisted of one emmer/spelt spikelet fork base and one spelt glume. A small number of seeds were present, five pea (*Pisum* sp) seeds, one legume (Fabaceae) seed, two brome (*Bromus* sp) seeds and one grass (Poaceae) seed.

[3133] {312} (1/8 ss) floor
All of these remains were charred. Abundant indeterminate grain fragments were present along with one cleavers (*Galium aparine* sp) and one sedge (*Carex* sp) seed.

[3122] {311} (1/4 ss) make-up levelling
All of these remains were preserved by charring and included hundreds of indeterminate cereal grains, eight sprouted barley (*Hordeum* sp) grains, 47 emmer/spelt (*Triticum dicoccum/spelta*) grains, one dock (*Rumex* sp) seed and one legume (Fabaceae) seed.

[3213] {317} (1/64 ss) structural cut
All of the remains in this subsample were charred. These included abundant wood fragments and indeterminate cereal grain fragments. Identifiable remains consisted of 177 emmer (cf *Triticum dicoccum* L) grains, two barley (*Hordeum* sp) grains, 256 emmer/spelt (*Triticum dicoccum* L) grains, 563 spelt (*Triticum spelta* L) grains, 160 bread wheat/spelt (*Triticum aestivum/spelta*) grains, two oat (*Avena* sp) grains, 54 barley (*Hordeum* sp) grain fragments and two rye (*Secale cereale* L) grains. A small amount of chaff was present, one emmer glume base, four spelt glume bases, one spelt spikelet fork base and one indeterminate culm node. Also present were a small number of seeds, such as corncockle (*Agrostemma githago* L), rye-brome/lop-grass (*Bromus secalinus/mollis*), cleavers (*Galium aparine* L) and vetch/tare/vetchling (*Vicia/Lathyrus* sp).

S7 [42] {11} ditch
Charred remains dominated this sample and included spelt (*Triticum spelta* L) grains and charred oat (*Avena* sp) grains and seeds. Other charred economic remains were present, namely one lentil (*Lens culinaris* L) seed, a cherry/plum (*Prunus* sp) stone fragment and three Celtic bean (*Vicia faba* L) seeds. Mineralised remains included three possible peppercorns (*Piper nigrum* L). These seeds have previously been recorded among waterlogged remains in one sample from the Roman eastern London cemetery sites (Davis 2000) and in late Roman deposits from the

excavation at Lloyd's Register (Gray-Rees in prep). Waterlogged remains also included a fig (*Ficus carica* L) seed and a possibly mineralised grape seed.

S18 [3089] {306} structural pit
All of these remains were charred. They included abundant indeterminate cereal fragments, two spelt (*Triticum spelta* L) grains, 28 emmer/spelt (*Triticum dicoccum/spelta*) grains, four sprouted wheat (*Triticum* sp) grains, two spelt (*Triticum spelta* L) tail grains, 11 emmer (*Triticum dicoccum* L) grains, one oat (*Avena* sp) grain and one bread wheat (*Triticum aestivum* L) grain.

Discussion

The following themes are ones which it was hoped that this analysis could address:

'What were the characteristics and functions of the buildings through time?
What were the physical characteristics of the settlement's natural environment, including open areas and river channels?
How did the settlement and its means of communication develop?
How and when did the settlement contract and come to an end?
Which industries were carried on, where and when?
What distributive trades were there?
What was the extent of agriculture, horticulture, pasturage and fishing?' (Drummond-Murray and Swain 1997)

The nature of the evidence has opened the way for discussion of the functions of buildings, structures and open areas in the processing and storage of cereals and the possible role of this area as a distribution-point for cereals. Cereal remains dominated the charred remains in most samples. The presence of chaff and charred seeds in many of them permits the processing stage to be considered, and the identification of the seeds enables the ecology of the crop fields to be reconstructed. Abundant waterlogged seeds in features such as ditches has enabled the reconstruction of the possible flora growing in the area of the settlement throughout its existence.

The functions of the buildings and structures

BGH95
These assemblages have been interpreted by considering the 'context-related variation' in the composition of the charred remains in each sample (Hillman 1981, 124). In suggesting possible functions for these buildings the possible causes of the creation of the charred remains have been examined. Hillman's ethnographic interpretations of crop husbandry defined four ways in which plant material becomes charred. From his observations he was able to state that '... the bulk of charred remains on British

sites represent only those classes of plant products that were likely to end up in hearths, ovens or bonfires ...' (ibid, 139). He goes on to list the four types of product which are indicated here below and notes that '... fuels potentially provided the bulk of charred crop cereal remains ...' (ibid, 140):

a) Crop products: processing waste, dried or parched grains in kilns, ovens or over open fires;
b) Diseased crop products: weed-infested grain in need of sterilisation or destruction by intense heating or burning;
c) Crop processing waste used as fuel;
d) Food products rendered palatable by roasting or cooking.

The composition of charred remains used as fuel tends to consist of grains (tail grains removed with light chaff), glume bases and spikelet forks, shorter rachis fragments, awn fragments (especially oat), straw nodes, culm bases and weed seeds (Hillman 1981, 140).

The crop processing stage represented by the charred assemblage can be inferred by interpreting the remains using the ethnographic approaches of Hillman (1981) and Jones (1984). The effects of the processing stages for free-threshing and hulled grains are summarised by van der Veen (1992, 81):

Free-threshing cereals:
  Harvesting - to remove the crop from the field
  Threshing - to release the grain from the straw and chaff
  Winnowing - to remove the light chaff and straw fragments, and the light weed
  Coarse sieving - to remove the weed heads, large weed seeds, unthreshed ears and straw
  Fine sieving - to remove the small weeds from the grain
Glume wheats:
  Parching - to render the glumes brittle
  Pounding - to release the grains from the glumes
  Second winnowing - to remove the light chaff fragments and light weed seeds
  Second coarse sieving - to remove the remaining weed heads, large weeds, straw nodes etc
  Fine sieving - to remove the glume bases and small weed seeds

For this study the charred assemblage in each building or structure will be interpreted by using Hillman's observations to determine why they were charred and by using van der Veen's cereal processing stages to work out which type of waste they represent. In this way it is hoped that the botanical remains can provide some useful information about the function of these features.

Van der Veen's study also discussed the possible sources of semi-aquatic/aquatic plant seeds. At Borough High Street most of the charred assemblages include spike-rush (*Eleocharis* sp) or sedge (*Carex* sp) seeds. It is possible that these would have been growing in the drainage ditches near the buildings and were deliberately brought in as flooring. Van der Veen (1992, 76) suggested that this type of plant could have become charred during '... the cleaning out of settlement ditches ...' or have been gathered with a crop from areas of arable fields which were damp or adjacent to damp ground.

It is interesting to note here Hillman's observation that in countries with wet summers processing tended to take place indoors and on a small scale as clean grain was needed, but that in climates characterised by dry summers large-scale winnowing and sieving took place in the open and the semi-cleaned grain was then stored indoors; in wet climates grain would have been stored as whole spikelets (Hillman 1981, 138). No whole spikelets were recovered from the samples taken from this site, and it is possible that climatic conditions favoured outdoor processing or that this grain was imported from drier areas. The large semi-clean grain stores found at this site seem to suggest this.

PERIOD 2: CONSTRUCTION OF THE FIRST SETTLEMENT AD 55–61

Five of these samples contained botanical assemblages rich enough to merit further analysis. These were those from Building 3, Building 19, Building 22 and Building 23. The rest of the buildings produced samples containing only fragments of charred wood and very small amounts of grain.

B2 A[822] {71}, A[825] {73}

Charred grain and stem fragments were abundant in this feature, suggesting that cereals were stored or processed here. Barley (*Hordeum* sp) and wheat (*Triticum* sp) were both present. A small number of oat (*Avena* sp) grains were also recovered and could have been present as a weed of cultivation. The presence of straw and charred seeds means that some of this assemblage could have been coarse- or fine-sieving waste and used in this context as fuel. A smaller number of seeds from semi-aquatic habitats, for example spike-rush (*Eleocharis* sp), were present and could have entered these contexts as floor-covering or been brought in accidentally from outside the building.

B5 A[5108] {507}

This charred assemblage was very similar to that in Building 3 but was on a much smaller scale. From the poor condition of the grains and the small number of grains and seeds it is likely that these remains were sieving waste and charred while being used as fuel.

B7 D[7083] {397}

All of these remains were charred. The seeds were from plants that grow in cultivated and semi-aquatic ground. It is possible that this assemblage could have been coarse- or fine-sieving waste used as fuel and contained plant debris from the local environment.

B7 D[3995] {394}

Cereal remains dominated this sample. A mixture of emmer (*Triticum dicoccum* L) and spelt (*Triticum spelta* L) wheat and barley (*Hordeum* sp) grains were present. Grains vastly outnumbered the amount of chaff and weed seeds, so it is clear that these remains are a prime grain store charred accidentally during storage or while being roasted or parched. It is possible that this is a store not yet put through the fine-sieving stage, which would have removed the small weed seeds and chaff fragments.

OA4 A[934] {98}, OA21 D[7069] {398}, OA8 E[4067] {404}

Each of these open areas contained a small amount of charred grain and stem fragments. It is possible that this is debris from winnowing or coarse sieving or could have been trampled through from building to building.

PERIOD 3: DESTRUCTION OF THE FIRST SETTLEMENT AD 61/2

C[2166] {217}, C[3960] {390}

The samples from this area contained a range of remains of charred economic plants, including lentil (*Lens culinaris* L) and waterlogged seeds from plants in the locality. The charred assemblages in both samples, grains and seeds, are most likely to have come from a prime grain store.

PERIOD 4: REBUILDING THE STREET AD 62–100

B18 A[779] {76}, B24 D[3017] {345}

These were similar to those from the pre-Boudican fire contexts. The same mixture of barley (*Hordeum* spp) and wheat (*Triticum* spp) grains, very little chaff (just a few straw fragments) and charred remains of spike-rush (*Eleocharis* sp), goosefoot (*Chenopodium* sp) and dock (*Rumex* sp). These are probably fine-sieving residues used as fuel.

OA19 E[4041] {402}

The large number of grains deposited in this feature could be the remains of a dump of accidentally burnt stored grain. The presence of corncockle (*Agrostemma githago* L) among the charred seeds suggests that this assemblage could also be coarse-sieving waste. Corncockle is characteristic of stored grain deposits because its seeds are the same size as the grains and can get milled along with the grain.

B13 B[1161] {136}

This sample contained a small assemblage of charred grain and seeds and was probably present as fine-sieving residue used as fuel.

B10 B[1808] {654}

Sieving waste used as fuel is the most likely explanation for the charred assemblage, including charred lentil (*Lens culinaris* L) and vetch/tare/vetchling (*Vicia/Lathyrus* sp) in this building. Using van der Veen's criteria, the presence of a complete weed head places this waste at the coarse sieving stage for both free-threshing cereals and glume wheats.

S1 A[734] {62}

This sample's small assemblage is probably processing and domestic waste used as fuel. The presence of a charred cherry/plum (*Prunus* sp) stone reinforces this hypothesis.

OA14 C[2218] {222}

The mineralised remains present in this sample could have come from cess, floor-covering, manure or any other context in which mineralisation could occur. It needs to be stressed here that mineralised remains are rare in the Borough High Street samples. This could mean that cess (human or animal) was not generally dumped in this area or that the last use of these areas and buildings did not encourage the mineralisation of organic material.

PERIOD 5: DEVELOPMENT OF THE STREET AND ITS FUNCTIONS, EARLY 2ND CENTURY

B22 B[1635] {611} RA, B[1819] {651} RB

These samples also contained a small number of glume wheat grains and seeds. The sample from an occupation layer [1819] {651} included a weed head with a cluster of what appeared to be buttercup (*Ranunculus* sp) seeds. This type of waste would have been produced during coarse sieving. The other sample is from a hearth and contained ten cherry/plum (*Prunus* sp) stones and small amounts of spelt (*Triticum spelta* L) and emmer (*Triticum dicoccum* L) grains, and seeds including a buttercup (*Ranunculus* sp) seed. This could be clear evidence that sieving waste was being burnt as fuel.

B23 D[3388] {325} HE

This sample was taken from another hearth context and contained only charred wood and one barley (*Hordeum* sp) grain.

B[31] D[3176] {337} S

This sample contained an interesting mixture of charred disturbed/cultivated ground seeds and edible fruit seeds. Mulberry (*Morus* sp), blackberry/raspberry (*Rubus fruticosus/idaeus*), fig (*Ficus carica* L) and cherry (*Prunus cerasus/avium*) were represented. The fig seed was the only one of the remains preserved by waterlogging and may be intrusive. No clearly identifiable cereal remains were present. This could also just be domestic debris accidentally burnt as fuel.

B32 D[3176] {223} FL, D[3103] {702} FL

Waterlogged remains dominated these samples. No charred cereals were present, although a large number of charred stem fragments survived. These could be the remains of floor-covering or hay. Greig's work on the type of wild plants present in hay (Greig 1984) lists some of the plant types present in sample [3103] {702}. These are large numbers of rush (*Juncus* sp) and buttercup (*Ranunculus* sp) seeds. Although the interpretation of these features needs to consider the large number of seeds preserved by waterlogging from plants of semi-aquatic habitats, it is the waterlogged material that suggests that this feature was left exposed for a while after abandonment.

S5 C[2188] {221}

It is possible that this pit contained domestic refuse, possibly cess, at some stage, although this assertion is based on fragments of mineralised stem seeds of blackberry/raspberry (*Rubus fruticosus/idaeus*), fig (*Ficus carica* L) and elder (*Sambucus nigra* L). No cereal remains were present in this sample.

PERIOD 6: CHANGES TO THE STREET, MID 2ND CENTURY ONWARDS

B36 [3465] {347}

Few cereal remains or other remains were present with environmental or economic significance. The wheat grains and grass seed would probably have entered the archaeological record as fuel.

B37 D[3191] {314}, D[3213] {317}, D[3122] {311}, D[3133] {312}

Abundant cereal remains were present in this building. It appears to have been a prime grain store or a place where grain was being dried or parched. This assemblage also contained 205 sprouted barley (*Hordeum* sp) grains. This may show that brewing was taking place at this time or that this was part of an assemblage deliberately burnt because the grain had begun to germinate. Emmer/spelt (*Triticum dicoccum/spelta*) grains dominated. The sprouted grains could have germinated in damp conditions or been stored for use in brewing.

Samples [3191] {314} and [3213] {317} were the richest ones. The presence of large weed seeds, pea (*Pisum* sp), legume (Fabaceae), corncockle (*Agrostemma githago* L), cleavers (*Galium aparine* L) and vetch/tare/vetchling (*Vicia/Lathyrus* sp) means that this grain store could be in its pre-fine sieving state, although these large seeds would have been difficult to separate by sieving. The other samples [3133] {312} and [3122]

{311} contained smaller numbers of identified grains and seed. The grains may have been mixed when charring occurred or stored as a mixed crop.

S18 D[3089] {306}

This sample also appears to be from a prime grain store before fine sieving. Sprouted wheat (*Triticum* sp) grains were present which could mean that this assemblage was from a grain store contaminated by germinating wheat.

S7 A[42] {11}

The mixture of remains of cereals and other economic plants, such as lentil (*Lens culinaris* L) and vetch/tare/vetchling (*Vicia/Lathyrus* sp) suggests that this feature contained sieving waste and domestic refuse used as fuel. Lentil, an imported exotic, is likely to have been present as domestic refuse.

OA19 E[4041] {402}

This is an almost completed cleaned grains assemblage dominated by spelt (*Triticum spelta* L). Chaff and weed seeds were very low in number. This suggests that it is an assemblage of prime grain accidentally charred while being stored or dried. The presence of corncockle (*Agrostemma githago* L) seeds among the charred seeds suggests that this assemblage could also include coarse sieving waste.

LBI95

[308] {102} pit

This is clearly a domestic/kitchen waste refuse pit. Its contents are full of remains of edible fruits available either as imports or growing locally. The mineralised remains show that cess or another mineralising agent (possible lime) was also thrown into the pit.

[324] {105} cooking pit

This contained a charred assemblage reminiscent of those found in the buildings and structures of Borough High Street. The mixture of wheat (*Triticum* sp) grains and weed seeds, including a lentil (*Lens culinaris* L) and pea (*Pisum sativum* L) seed, suggest the use of sieving waste as fuel. But seven further, mineralised, peas are present, so it may be possible that peas were part of a dish cooked or disposed of in this pit. The lentil

seed (an exotic plant) could also have arrived in the samples as food waste rather than sieving waste.

The natural environment of the settlement: open areas and river channels

BGH95

PERIOD 1: BUILDING OF THE ROAD AND ESTABLISHMENT OF THE SETTLEMENT AD 55

OA2 D[3645] {365}

Disturbed ground, scrub/woodland and grassland species were present in small quantities in this sample.

OA2 quarry pits

A[5038] {506}

Apart from the many charred and waterlogged wood and stem/leaf fragments, the most abundant taxon in this sample was buttercup (*Ranunculus acris/repens/bulbosus*) and sedge (*Carex* sp) followed by knotgrass etc (*Polygonum* sp), lesser stitchwort (*Stellaria graminea* L) and spike-rush (*Eleocharis* sp). These plants grow in disturbed ground, scrub/woodland and semi-aquatic habitats. A small number of water plantain (*Alisma* sp) seeds means that temporary pools of water may have been present in this pit.

A[5099] {517}

Abundant waterlogged stem fragments dominated the sample. The next most abundant taxa were buttercup and sedge, plants of disturbed, scrub/woodland and semi-aquatic ground. The rest of the taxa were from these habitats.

A[939] {97}

Abundant waterlogged leaf and stem fragments dominated this sample. Next in abundance were seeds of cinquefoil/tormentil (*Potentilla* sp), found in a range of habitats. A small number of pondweed (*Potamogeton* sp) seeds may, like sample {506}, mean that pools of water were temporarily present in this feature.

OA2 ditches

A[920] {96}

Along with abundant waterlogged wood fragments there were between 11 and 50 sedge and spike-rush seeds. These were the most abundant seed taxa present

and grow in semi-aquatic habitats. The remaining taxa were from plants growing in scrub/woodland, grassland and damp ground.

B[6040] {673}

In general the plant remains in this sample came from a variety of habitats, cultivated/disturbed ground, grassland, damp ground and scrub/woodland. No taxon appeared to dominate. Equal numbers of buttercup and sedge seeds were present. A small amount of possible waterlogged cereal glume fragments were recovered. This may mean that this sample contains processing waste preserved by waterlogging, but the preservation of these possible glume fragments was poor, making it impossible to identify them clearly.

B[6040] {675}

Once again seeds from plants of disturbed/cultivated ground, grassland and scrub dominate. The presence of water-dropwort (*Oenanthe aquatica* L) and pondweed means that open water may have been present in the feature at this time.

C[2245] {231}

This sample was dominated by seeds from plants of cultivated/disturbed ground, grassland and woodland/scrub.

C[2223] {225}

The range of habitats represented by the abundant species in this sample seem to be evenly spread between disturbed/cultivated ground and semi-aquatic habitats.

D[7129] {700}

The most abundant taxa in this sample were sedge and rush (*Juncus* sp) seeds, reflecting the damp, marshy ground in the area. Smaller numbers of damp ground taxa were also present and included gypsy-wort (*Lycopus europaeus* L), lesser spearwort and yellow iris (cf *Iris pseudacorus*).

PERIOD 2: CONSTRUCTION OF THE FIRST SETTLEMENT AD 55–61

These features contained waterlogged remains which are more likely to reflect the local environment than the charred assemblages.

B2 [822] {71}

Of the charred seeds, grass (Poaceae) seeds were the most dominant and probably arrived in this context as weeds of cultivation in cereal waste. The waterlogged remains which may have come from the local environment were few and represented the same type of habitats (disturbed ground, scrub, damp grassland) as those in the ditch and quarry pit samples.

B2 [825] {73}

Charred brome (*Bromus* sp) seeds were the most abundant charred seed present. This is a weed of cultivation and likely to have been deposited as part of cereal waste. No waterlogged seeds were present.

B7 [3995] {394}

A waterlogged blackberry/raspberry (*Rubus fruticosus/idaeus*) fruit was recovered. This is likely to have been growing locally as a plant of scrub/woodland and would have provided an accessible wild food source.

OA21 D[7069] {398}

This sample was dominated by remains preserved by waterlogging. The habitats represented by the taxa included cultivated and disturbed ground, grassland, woodland/scrub and marsh/damp ground. The most abundant taxa were from semi-aquatic ground and included spike-rush (*Eleocharis* sp), lesser spearwort (*Ranunculus* cf *flammula*), sedge (*Carex* sp) and rush (*Juncus* sp).

PERIOD 3: DESTRUCTION OF THE FIRST SETTLEMENT AD 61/2

OA10 [3690] {390}

Most of the waterlogged and charred taxa from this feature came from disturbed ground, grassland and woodland/scrub habitats. The other sample from this feature C[2166] {217} contained only one charred seed which is most likely to have been brought in with cereals, straw or thatch.

PERIOD 4: REBUILDING THE STREET AD 62–100

B9, B13, B10, B18, B24

All of these remains were charred and associated with cereal remains, so they are probably sieving waste rather than from local habitats.

OA14 C[2218] {222}

The modes of preservation of the remains in this sample are most likely to have been anthropogenic, so the seeds do not reflect the local environment as much as a ditch feature would. But the weed seeds present are the familiar disturbed/cultivated ground and grassland/scrub types prevalent on this site.

OA19 E[4041] {402}

The only weeds seeds in this sample are corncockle (*Agrostemma githago* L) and brome (*Bromus* sp) which would most likely have arrived in this context as sieving waste.

PERIOD 5: DEVELOPMENT OF THE STREET AND ITS FUNCTIONS, EARLY 2ND CENTURY

No samples from ditches or open areas were analysed for this period. The wild plant seeds present in the charred assemblages are generally from disturbed/cultivated ground and the wet assemblages from semi-aquatic ground.

PERIODS 6: CHANGES TO THE STREET, MID 2ND CENTURY ONWARDS

As for the previous period no sample from natural features was rich enough to merit analysis, and most of the samples here are from grain stores or features where they are most likely to have been fuel. It is interesting to note the absence of purely aquatic plant remains in these samples, which may point to drier conditions in the locality.

Industries and distributive trades

The large prime grain assemblages seem to indicate that grain was being stored here. It is possible that the cereals were being dried prior to milling, so that the archaeological hypothesis of Buildings 30 and 31 being bakeries could be correct. The small number of lentils present in several samples would have been imported either as a crop in their own right or as a crop weed.

It is not possible to say whether this means that the grain had been imported because many native seeds were also present in the samples, and lentils could have been imported as a crop in their own right. What is clear is that the grain was in a state ready for consumption in or distribution from Southwark.

Agriculture

When this topic is considered, the question of whether the site is a producer or a consumer site arises. Hillman's archaeobotanical and ethno-archaeological work on cereal production and processing allowed him to observe that cereals would have been most commonly traded in the form of semi-cleaned grain for free-threshing wheat or semi-cleaned spikelets of glume wheat in wet areas (Hillman 1981, 142). The archaeobotanical record for a consumer/trading site would consist of prime grain with weed seeds too large to be sieved out, such as corncockle, and very few chaff fragments (ibid). This is the type of assemblage in many of the Borough High Street samples. Other samples analysed here contain a generally equal proportion of charred chaff, grain and seeds. This is to be expected on sites producing or consuming glume wheats such as emmer and spelt where glume wheat was brought in as spikelets (ibid).

These grain assemblages appear to be prime grain on a consumer site. The effects of charring on the preservation of lighter chaff found on producer sites may mean that the archaeobotanical record is skewed towards evidence for consumption rather than production (Boardman and Jones 1990, 9).

Similar assemblages have been found in other parts of the City of London and the Southwark area, for example the nearby sites of Regis House (Straker 1984; Gray-Rees 1997) and Courage's Brewery (Davis 1995).

Conclusions

The botanical evidence seems to point to the area of Borough High Street being a centre for storage and processing of animal and plant foods. This activity, as revealed by the archaeological record, seems to increase in the mid 2nd century. The surrounding sites (LBI95, LBH95 and LBE95) broaden the environmental and economic information through the modes of preservation of the remains: that is, more general domestic/kitchen waste.

Details of samples

Habitat and use codes:

A = weeds of cultivated land;

B = weeds of arable and disturbed ground;

C = woods, scrub, hedgerows;

D = grassland;

E = damp or marshy ground;

F = edible wild;

G = medicinal;

H = wild with economic uses;

I = cultivated

Table 116 Borough High Street period 1

Latin name	Common name	Plant part	Habitat/use codes	[5038] {506} Quarry pit	[5099] {517} Quarry pit	[939] {97} Quarry pit	[6040] {673} Ditch	[6040] {675} Ditch	[920] {96} External dump	[2245] {231} Ditch	[2223] {225} Ditch	[7129] {700} Peat	[3645] {365} Road 1
Charred remains													
Fabaceae indet	legume fragments	seed	-	-	-	-	-	1	-	-	-	-	-
cf Fabaceae	legume fragments	seed	-	-	-	-	-	-	-	-	2	-	-
Indet	-	stem fragments	-	-	-	-	-	++++	-	-	-	-	-
Indet	-	wood fragments	-	++++	++++	-	-	++++	+++	++	++++	++++	+++
Poaceae indet	grass	seed	ABCDEFGHI	-	-	-	1	4	-	-	-	-	-
Cyperaceae indet	sedge	seed	ABCDEFI	-	-	-	-	5	-	-	-	-	-
Ranunculus sp	buttercup	achene	ABCDEG	-	-	-	-	1	-	-	-	-	-
Vicia/Lathyrus sp	vetch/tare/vetchling	seed	ACDEFI	-	-	-	-	1	-	-	-	-	-
Avena sp	oat	grain	AFI	-	-	-	-	-	-	-	4	-	-
Hordeum sp	barley	grain	BDFI	-	3	-	-	13	1	-	-	-	-
Corylus avellana L	hazel	shell fragments	CF	-	1	-	-	-	-	-	-	-	-
cf *Scirpus* sp	club-rush	seed	EH	-	-	-	-	1	-	-	-	-	-
Triticum cf *dicoccum*	emmer	grain	FI	-	-	-	-	-	-	-	2	-	-
Triticum cf *spelta*	spelt	grain	FI	-	-	-	-	-	-	-	12	-	-
Triticum sp	wheat	grain	FI	-	-	-	-	5	-	-	5	-	-
Hordeum sativum L	barley	grain	FI	-	-	-	-	-	-	-	-	1	7
Avena/Hordeum/ Secale/Triticum	indet cereal	grain	FI	-	-	-	-	-	-	-	21	-	-
Fabaceae indet	legume fragments	seed	-	-	-	-	-	-	-	-	-	1	-
Waterlogged remains													
Indet	-	seed	-	-	-	+++	-	-	-	-	-	-	-
Indet	-	leaf fragments	-	-	-	++++	-	-	-	-	+	-	-
Indet	-	stem fragments	-	+	++++	++++	++++	++++	-	-	++	++++	-
Indet	-	wood fragments	-	++++	-	++++	++++	++++	+++	-	++++	++++	-
Indet	-	plant tissue fragments	-	-	++	-	-	+	-	-	-	-	-
Bryophyta indet	moss	-	-	+	++	++	++	++++	-	-	+	+++	-
Raphanus raphanistrum L	wild radish/charlock	seed	A	-	-	-	-	-	-	-	++	-	-
Agrostemma githago L	corncockle	seed	AB	-	-	-	-	+	-	-	-	-	-
Chenopodium cf *rubrum*	red goosefoot	seed	AB	-	-	+	-	-	-	-	-	++	-
Sonchus cf *asper*	spiny milk/sow-thistle	seed	AB	+	-	-	-	-	-	-	-	-	-
Fumaria sp	fumitory	seed	ABC	-	+	-	-	-	-	-	-	-	-
Rumex acetosa/ crispus/obtusifolius	dock	seed	ABCD	-	-	-	-	-	+	-	-	-	-
Galium sp	bedstraw	seed	ABCDE	-	+	-	-	-	-	-	++	-	-
Polygonum sp	knotgrass etc	seed	ABCDEFG	++	-	+	+	++	-	+	+++	-	-
Polygonum spp	knotgrass etc	seed	ABCDEFG	-	++	-	-	-	-	-	-	-	-
Rumex sp	dock	seed	ABCDEFG	-	-	-	-	+	-	-	+++	-	-
Cyperaceae indet	-	seed	ABCDEFI	-	-	++	-	-	-	-	-	-	-
Ranunculus acris/ repens/bulbosus	buttercups	achene	ABCDEG	-	-	++	-	-	+	-	+	-	-
Ranunculus cf *acris/ repens/bulbosus*	buttercups	achene	ABCDEG	+++	+++	-	-	-	-	-	-	-	-
cf *Ranunculus acris/ repens/bulbosus*	buttercups	achene	ABCDEG	-	-	-	++	+++	-	-	-	+++	-
Ranunculus sp	buttercups	achene	ABCDEG	-	-	-	-	+	-	-	-	-	-
cf *Ranunculus* sp	buttercups	achene	ABCDEG	-	-	+	-	-	-	-	-	-	-
Stellaria sp	chickweed/stitchwort	seed	ABCDEG	-	-	-	-	+	-	-	-	-	-
Silene sp	campion/catchfly	seed	ABCDF	+	-	-	+	-	-	-	-	+	-
Chenopodium sp	goosefoot etc	seed	ABCDFH	-	-	+	+	++	+	-	++	-	-
Chenopodium spp	goosefoot etc	seed	ABCDFH	-	+	-	-	-	-	-	-	-	-

(Table 116 cont)

Latin name	Common name	Plant part	Habitat/use codes	[5038] {506} Quarry pit	[5099] {517} Quarry pit	[939] {97} Quarry pit	[6040] {673} Ditch	[6040] {675} Ditch	[920] {96} External dump	[2245] {231} Ditch	[2223] {225} Ditch	[7129] {700} Peat	[3645] {365} Road I
Viola sp	violet	seed	ABCDG	-	+	+	-	+	-	-	-	+	-
Mentha sp	mint	seed	ABCEFGI	-	+	-	-	-	-	-	-	-	-
Carduus/Cirsium sp	thistles	seed	ABDEG	-	+	-	-	-	-	-	-	-	-
Polygonum cf lapathifolium	pale persicaria	seed	ABE	-	-	+	-	-	-	-	-	-	-
Polygonum persicaria L	persicaria	seed	ABEH	-	-	-	-	-	-	+	-	++	-
Polygonum cf persicaria	persicaria	seed	ABEH	+	-	-	-	-	-	-	++++	-	-
Chenopodium cf album	fat hen	seed	ABFH	+	-	-	-	-	-	-	-	-	-
Brassica/sinapis sp	cabbage/mustard	seed	ABFGHI	-	-	-	-	-	-	-	-	-	-
Polygonum aviculare L	knotgrass	seed	ABG	-	-	-	-	++	-	-	-	-	-
Stachys sp	woundwort	seed	ACEG	-	++	-	+	+	-	+	-	+	-
Juncus spp	rush	seed	ADEH	-	-	+	-	-	-	-	-	++++	-
Anagallis arvensis L	scarlet pimpernel	seed	AG	-	-	-	-	+	-	-	-	-	-
Chelidonium majus L	greater celandine	seed	BC	-	-	-	-	-	-	-	-	+	-
Rumex crispus L	curled dock	tepal	BC	-	-	-	-	-	-	-	-	-	-
Rumex sanguineus/ conglomeratus spp	dock	seed	BC	-	-	+	-	-	-	-	-	-	-
Galium verum/ mollugo spp	bedstraw	seed	BCD	-	-	-	-	+	-	-	-	+	-
Myosotis sp	forget-me-not	seed	BCDE	-	-	-	-	-	-	-	-	+	-
Potentilla sp	cinquefoil/tormentil	achene	BCDEFGH	-	++	+++	-	-	-	+	-	+++	+
Potentilla/Fragaria sp	cinquefoil/wild strawberry	achene	BCDEFGH	-	+	+	-	-	-	-	-	-	-
Urtica dioica L	stinging nettle	seed	BCDEFGH	+	-	-	+	+++	-	+	-	++	I
Prunella vulgaris L	self-heal	seed	BCDG	+	+	++	+	++	+	+	-	++	-
Sambucus nigra L	elder	seed	BCFGH	+	-	+	-	+	-	++	-	++	+
Galium aparine L	cleavers	seed	BCG	-	-	-	-	-	-	-	+++	-	-
Hypericum sp	cat's ear	seed	BD	-	+	-	-	-	-	-	-	-	-
Chenopodium murale L	nettle-leaved goosefoot	seed	BD	-	-	-	-	+	-	-	-	-	-
Chenopodium cf murale	nettle-leaved goosefoot	seed	BD	+	-	-	-	-	-	-	-	+	-
Leontodon sp	hawkbit	seed	BDF	+	+	+	+	+	-	-	-	++	-
Hyoscyamus niger L	henbane	seed	BDG	-	+	-	-	-	-	-	-	-	+
Solanum nigrum L	black nightshade	seed	BF	-	-	-	-	-	-	-	-	+	-
cf Crataegus monogyna	hawthorn	seed	C	-	-	-	-	-	-	-	-	+	-
Stellaria graminea L	lesser stitchwort	seed	CD	++	++	-	+	++	+	+	++	+++	-
Potentilla cf erecta	tormentil	seed	CDEGH	+	-	-	-	-	-	+++	+++	+++	+
Carex sp	sedge	seed	CDEH	+++	-	+	-	-	++	-	+++	-	-
Carex spp	sedge	seed	CDEH	-	+++	++	-	+	-	-	-	++++	-
Corylus avellana L	hazel	shell	CF	+	-	-	++	+++	+	+	-	+	+
Rubus fruticosus/idaeus	blackberry/ raspberry	seed	CFGH	+	-	-	-	+	+	-	-	+	-
Prunus avium L	cherry	seed	CFGI	-	-	-	-	+	-	-	-	-	-
cf Plantago lanceolata	ribwort	seed	D	-	-	-	-	-	-	-	++	-	-
Leontodon cf taraxacoides	hairy hawkbit	seed	D	-	-	-	-	-	-	-	+++	-	-
Oenanthe sp	dropwort	seed	DE	-	+	+	-	++	-	-	+++	++	-
Eleocharis sp	spike-rush	seed	DE	++	+	+	++	++	++	-	-	+	+
Eleocharis spp	spike-rush	seed	DE	-	-	-	-	-	-	-	+++	-	-
cf Eleocharis sp	spike-rush	seed	DE	-	++	-	-	-	-	-	-	-	-
Ranunculus sceleratus L	celery-leaved crowfoot	seed	E	-	+	-	-	-	-	-	-	-	-
Mentha cf aquatica	water mint	seed	E	-	-	-	-	-	-	+	-	-	-
Alisma sp	water-plantain	seed	E	+	-	-	-	-	-	-	-	-	-
Potamogeton sp	pondweed	seed	E	-	-	-	-	+	-	-	-	-	-
cf Potamogeton sp	pondweed	seed	E	-	-	+	-	-	-	-	-	-	-
cf Iris pseudacorus	yellow iris/ yellow flag	seed	E	-	-	-	-	-	-	-	-	+	-
Ranunculus flammula L	lesser spearwort	achene	EG	+	-	+	-	-	-	-	-	-	-
Ranunculus cf flammula	lesser spearwort	achene	EG	-	-	-	-	-	-	-	+++	+	-
Alisma cf plantago-aquatica L	water-plantain	seed	EG	-	-	-	-	-	-	-	-	+	-
Lycopus europaeus L	gypsy-wort	seed	EH	-	-	-	+	-	-	-	-	+	-
Morus sp	mulberry	seed	FHI	-	-	-	-	+	-	-	-	-	-
Avena/Hordeum/ Secale/Triticum	indet cereal	glume fragments	FI	-	-	-	++	-	-	-	-	-	-
Ficus carica L	fig	seed	FI	+	-	-	-	-	-	-	-	+	+

251

Table 117 Borough High Street period 2

Latin name	Common name	Plant part	Habitat/ use codes	[4067] {404} Open Area 8	[934] {98} Open Area 4	[5108] {509} Building 5	[7083] {397} Building 7	[822] {71} Building 3	[825] {73} Building 2	[3995] {394} Building 7	[7069] {398} Open Area 21
Charred remains											
cf Leguminosae	legume fragments	seed	-	-	-	1	-	-	-	-	-
Indet	-	seed	-	-	-	-	-	3	2	-	-
Indet	-	stem fragments	-	+	-	+++	-	++++	+	++++	
Indet	-	wood fragments	-	++++	++++	++++	++++	++++	++++	++++	++++
Indet	-	plant tissue	-	-	-	18	7	-	-	-	-
Rumex cf acetosa/ crispus/ obtusifolius spp	dock	seed	ABCD	-	-	-	-	-	1	-	-
Polygonum sp	knotgrass etc	seed	ABCDEFG	-	-	-	-	1	-	-	-
Polygonum spp	knotgrass etc	seed	ABCDEFG	-	-	-	5	-	-	-	-
Rumex sp	dock	seed	ABCDEFG	1	-	-	-	1	-	-	-
Poaceae	grass	seed	ABCDEFGHI	-	-	2	-	-	-	1	-
cf Poaceae indet	grass	stem fragments	ABCDEFHI	-	-	-	-	4	-	-	-
cf Poaceae indet	grass	seed	ABCDEFHI	-	-	-	-	5	-	-	-
Cyperaceae indet	sedge	seed	ABCDEFI	-	-	-	8	-	-	-	-
Ranunculus acris/ repens/bulbosus spp	buttercups	achene	ABCDEG	-	-	-	-	-	1	-	-
Bromus sp	brome	seed	ABD	-	-	-	2	2	13	1	-
Polygonum aviculare L	knotgrass	seed	ABG	-	-	1	-	-	-	-	-
Avena sp	oat	grain	AFI	-	-	-	-	2	-	4	-
Avena sp	oat	floret	AFI	-	-	-	-	-	-	1	-
Rumex crispus L	curled dock	tepal	BC	-	-	-	-	1	2	-	-
Rumex sanguineus L	red-veined dock	seed	BCD	-	-	-	-	-	1	-	-
Rumex cf sanguineus	red-veined dock	seed	BCD	-	-	-	-	1	-	-	-
Sambucus nigra L	elder	seed	BCFGH	-	-	-	1	-	-	-	-
Galium aparine L	cleavers	seed	BCG	-	-	-	-	-	1	-	-
Hordeum sp	barley	grain	BDFI	-	-	-	-	-	1	33	4
Centaurea cf nigra	lesser knapweed	seed	BDG	-	-	-	-	1	-	-	-
Vicia sp	vetch	seed	CD	-	-	-	-	-	-	1	-
Carex sp	sedge	seed	CDEH	-	-	-	-	1	-	-	-
cf Carex sp	sedge	seed	CDEH	-	-	-	-	1	-	-	-
Corylus avellana L	hazel	shell fragments	CF	-	-	-	-	1	-	5	-
cf Thalicrum flavum/minus spp	meadow rue	seed	DE	-	-	-	-	1	-	-	-
Eleocharis sp	spike-rush	seed	DE	-	1	1	-	-	-	1	-
cf Eleocharis sp	spike-rush	seed	DE	-	-	-	-	2	-	-	-
Polygonum cf hydropiper	water pepper	seed	E	-	-	-	-	1	-	-	-
Pinus pinea L	stone pine	nut	FHI	-	-	-	-	-	-	1	-
Triticum cf dicoccum	emmer	grain	FI	-	10	-	-	-	-	24	-
Triticum spelta L	spelt	grain	FI	1	-	-	-	-	-	34	-
Triticum cf spelta	spelt	grain	FI	-	8	-	-	7	39	-	-
Triticum cf spelta	spelt	glume base	FI	-	-	-	-	-	-	1	-
Triticum dicoccum/ spelta	emmer/spelt	grain	FI	-	11	-	-	34	-	15	-
Triticum cf dicoccum/spelta	emmer/spelt	grain	FI	-	-	-	-	-	23	-	-
Triticum spelta/ aestivum	spelt/bread wheat	grain	FI	1	-	-	-	-	-	15	-
Triticum sp	wheat	grain	FI	-	-	4	-	-	-	115	-
Hordeum sativum L	barley	grain	FI	-	-	1	-	63	-	16	-

(Table 117 cont)

Latin name	Common name	Plant part	Habitat/ use codes	[4067] {404} Open Area 8	[934] {98} Open Area 4	[5108] {509} Building 5	[7083] {397} Building 7	[822] {71} Building 3	[825] {73} Building 2	[3995] {394} Building 7	[7069] {398} Open Area 21
cf *Hordeum sativum*	barley	grain	Fl	-	-	-	-	-	4	-	-
Avena/Hordeum/ Secale/Triticum	indet cereal	grain	Fl	-	2	-	-	4	-	-	-
Avena/Hordeum/ Secale/Triticum	indet cereal	grain	H	-	-	-	-	-	4	-	-
Avena/Hordeum/ Secale/Triticum	indet cereal	grain	Fl	-	-	10	-	-	-	104	-
Vicia faba L	celtic bean/ horsebean	seed	Fl	-	-	-	-	1	-	-	-
Waterlogged remains											
Indet	-	stem fragments	-	-	-	-	-	-	-	-	++++
Indet	-	wood fragments	-	-	-	-	-	-	-	-	++++
Bryophyta indet	moss	-	-	-	-	-	-	-	-	-	++++
Chenopodium cf *rubrum*	red goosefoot	seed	AB	-	-	-	-	-	-	-	+
Galium sp	bedstraw	seed	ABCDE	-	-	-	-	-	-	-	++
Polygonum sp	knotgrass etc	seed	ABCDEFG	-	-	-	-	-	-	-	+++
cf *Ranunculus acris/ repens/bulbosus* sp	buttercups	achene	ABCDEG	-	-	-	-	-	-	-	++++
Silene sp	campion/ catchfly	seed	ABCDF	-	-	-	-	-	-	-	+
Chenopodium sp	goosefoot etc	seed	ABCDFH	-	-	-	-	-	-	-	+
Chenopodium spp	goosefoot etc	seed	ABCDFH	-	-	-	-	+	-	-	-
Carduus/ Cirsium spp	thistles	seed	ABDEG	-	-	-	-	-	-	-	++
Polygonum persicaria L	persicaria	seed	ABEH	-	-	-	-	-	-	-	++
Juncus spp	rush	seed	ADEH	-	-	-	-	-	-	-	+++
cf *Rumex crispus* L	curled dock	tepal	BC	-	-	-	-	-	-	-	++
Galium verum/ mollugo spp	bedstraw	seed	BCD	-	-	-	-	-	-	-	++
Potentilla sp	cinquefoil/ tormentil	achene	BCDEFGH	-	-	-	-	-	-	+	-
Potentilla/ Fragaria spp	cinquefoil/ wild strawberry	achene	BCDEFGH	-	-	-	-	-	-	-	+
Urtica dioica L	stinging nettle	seed	BCDEFGH	-	-	-	-	-	-	-	+
Prunella vulgaris L	self-heal	seed	BCDG	-	-	-	-	+	-	-	+++
Sambucus nigra L	elder	seed	BCFGH	-	-	-	-	+	-	-	-
Galium aparine L	cleavers	seed	BCG	-	-	-	-	-	-	-	+
Leontodon sp	hawkbit	seed	BDF	-	-	-	-	-	-	-	++
Stellaria graminea L	lesser stitchwort	seed	CD	-	-	-	-	-	-	-	+++
Hypochoeris cf *radicata*	cat's ear	seed	CD	-	-	-	-	-	-	-	+
Potentilla erecta (L) Rausch	tormentil	seed	CDEGH	-	-	-	-	-	-	-	++
Carex spp	sedge	seed	CDEH	-	-	-	-	-	-	-	+++
cf *Rubus fruticosus/ idaeus* spp	blackberry/ raspberry	head	CFGH	-	-	-	-	-	-	+	-
Plantago lanceolata L	ribwort	seed	D	-	-	-	-	-	-	-	++
Oenanthe sp	dropwort	seed	DE	-	-	-	-	-	-	-	++
Eleocharis sp	spike-rush	seed	DE	-	-	-	-	-	-	-	++++
Ranunculus cf *flammula*	lesser spearwort	seed	EG	-	-	-	-	-	-	-	+++
Vitis vinifera L	grape	seed	Fl	-	-	-	-	-	-	+	-

Table 118 Borough High Street period 3

Latin name	Common name	Plant part	Habitat/ use codes	[3960] {390} OA10
Charred remains				
Leguminosae indet	legume fragments	seed	-	I
Indet	-	stem fragments	-	4
Indet	-	wood fragments	-	++++
Polygonum sp	knotgrass etc	seed	ABCDEFG	I
Poaceae indet	grass	seed	ABCDEFHI	3
Mentha sp	mint	seed	ABCEFGI	I
Avena sp	oat	seed	AFI	I
Medicago sp	medick	seed	BD	I
cf Triticum dicoccum/spelta	emmer/spelt	grain	FI	I
Triticum cf spelta	spelt	grain	FI	I
Triticum spelta/aestivum	spelt/bread wheat	grain	FI	I
Triticum sp	wheat	grain	FI	6
Cerealia	indet cereal	grain	FI	3
Lens culinaris L	lentil	seed	FI	2
Waterlogged remains				
Lapsana communis L	nipplewort	seed		+
Polygonum sp	knotgrass	seed	ABCDEFG	+
Rumex sp	dock	seed	ABCDEFG	+
Chenopodium album L	fat hen	seed	ABFH	+
cf Chelidonium majus	greater celandine	seed	BC	+
Carex sp	sedge	seed	CDEH	+

Table 119 Borough High Street period 4a

Latin name	Common name	Plant part	Habitat/ use codes	SG112 [734] {62} B9	SG221 [1808] {654} B10	SG306 [1161] {136} B13	SG417 [2218] {222} OA14	SG491 [779] {76} B18	SG542 [7083] {397} B7	SG664 [3017] {345} B24
Charred remains										
Indet	-	seed	-	2	-	I	-	-	-	-
Indet	-	stem fragments	-	5	3	-	-	I	2	5
Indet	-	wood fragments	-	++++	-	++++	+	++++	++++	++++
Indet	-	plant tissue fragments	-	-	3	-	-	-	7	-
Polygonum sp	knotgrass etc	seed	ABCDEFG	-	2	I	-	-	-	-
Polygonum spp	knotgrass etc	seed	ABCDEFG	-	-	-	-	-	5	-
Rumex sp	dock	seed	ABCDEFG	-	I	I	-	-	-	I
Poaceae indet	grass	seed	ABCDEFHI	-	-	2	-	-	-	-
Cyperaceae indet	sedge	seed	ABCDEFI	-	-	-	-	-	8	-
Chenopodium sp	goosefoot etc	seed	ABCDFH	I	-	-	-	-	-	-
Bromus sp	bromes	seed	ABD	-	-	I	-	-	2	-
Trifolium sp	clover	seed	ABDI	-	-	I	-	-	-	-
Vicia/Lathyrus sp	vetch/tare/ vetchling	seed	ACDEFI	-	2	-	-	-	-	-
Avena sp	oat	grain	AFI	-	-	I	-	-	-	-
Sambucus nigra L	elder	seed	BCFGH	-	-	-	-	-	I	-
cf Prunus sp	cherry/plum	stone	CFGI	I	-	-	-	-	-	-
Eleocharis sp	spike-rush	seed	DE	I	-	-	-	-	-	-
Triticum cf dicoccum	emmer	grain	FI	-	-	3	-	-	-	-
Triticum spelta L	spelt	grain	FI	I	-	-	-	-	-	-
Triticum cf spelta	spelt	grain	FI	-	-	-	-	-	-	26
Triticum dicoccum/ spelta	emmer/spelt	grain	FI	9	-	-	-	-	-	9
Triticum spelta/ aestivum	spelt/bread wheat	grain	FI	-	-	I	-	-	-	-
Triticum sp	wheat	grain	FI	-	I	-	-	-	-	-
Hordeum sativum L	barley	grain	FI	I	-	I	-	-	-	-
cf Hordeum sativum	barley	grain	FI	-	5	-	-	-	-	-
Cerealia	indet cereal	grain	FI	2	-	4	-	-	-	-
Lens culinaris L	lentil	seed	FI	-	I	-	-	-	-	-
Mineralised remains										
Pyrus/Malus sp	pear/apple	seed	CFI	-	-	-	+	-	-	-
Waterlogged remains										
Ranunculus sp	buttercup	seed	ABCDEG	-	-	-	+	-	-	-
Prunella vulgaris L	self-heal	seed	BCDG	-	+	-	-	-	-	-
Indet	-	stem fragments	-	-	-	+	-	-	-	-

Table 120 Borough High Street period 4b

Latin name	Common name	Plant part	Habitat/ use codes	SG280 [1635] {611} B22	SG282 [1819] {651} B22	SG428 [2188] {221} S5	SG855 [3414] {337} B31	SG900 [3388] {325} B23	SG954 [3103] {702} B32	SG957 [3176] {223} B32
Charred remains										
Triticum cf dicoccum	emmer	grain	FI	6	3	0	-	-	3	-
Triticum cf spelta	spelt	grain	FI	2	3	-	-	-	I	-
Triticum cf spelta	spelt	glume base	FI	-	-	-	-	-	3	-
Triticum cf dicoccum/ spelta	emmer/spelt	grain	FI	-	3	-	-	-	-	-
Hordeum sativum	barley	grain	FI	-	-	-	-	I	-	-
Cerealia	indet cereal	grain	FI	6	6	-	-	-	5	-
Ranunculus acris/ repens/bulbosus	buttercups	seed	ABCDEG	I	-	-	I	-	-	-
Ranunculus sp	buttercups	seed	ABCDEG	-	I	-	-	-	-	-
cf Trifolium sp	clover	seed	ABDI	-	-	-	-	-	-	I
Rubus fruticosus/ idaeus	blackberry/ raspberry	seed	CFGH	-	-	-	I	-	-	-
Prunus avium/cerasus	sloe/cherry	seed	CFGI	-	-	-	2	-	-	-
Prunus sp	cherry/plum	seed	CFGI	10	-	-	-	-	-	-
cf Apium sp	marshwort	seed	EFI	-	-	-	-	-	I	-
Polygonum sp	knotgrass etc	seed	ABCDEFG	I	-	-	4	-	-	-
Rumex crispus L	curled dock	tepal	BC	-	I	-	-	-	-	-
Rumex sp	dock	seed	ABCDEFG	-	-	-	-	-	-	3
Morus sp	mulberry	seed	FHI	-	-	-	2	-	-	-
Corylus avellana L	hazel	shell	CF	-	8	-	-	-	-	-
cf Schoenoplectus lacus/tabernae	bulrush	seed	E	-	-	-	-	-	II	-
Carex sp	sedge	seed	CDEH	-	-	-	2	-	-	-
Bromus sp	bromes	seed	ABD	2	-	-	2	-	I	-
Poaceae indet	grass	seed	ABCDEFHI	-	-	I	-	-	-	-
Indet	-	seed	-	3	-	-	-	-	-	-
Indet	-	wood	-	++++	++++	++++	++++	++	++++	-
Indet	-	plant tissue	-	-	-	-	15	-	-	-
Mineralised remains										
cf Viola sp	violet	seed	ABCDG	-	-	-	-	-	++	-
Pyrus/Malus sp	pear/apple	seed	CFI	-	-	-	-	-	-	-
Indet	-	stem	-	-	-	+	-	-	-	-
Waterlogged remains										
Avena/Hordeum/ Secale/Triticum	indet cereal	bran	FI	-	+	-	-	-	-	-
Ranunculus acris/ repens/bulbosus	buttercups	seed	ABCDEG	-	-	-	-	-	-	++
cf Ranunculus flammula	lesser spearwort	seed	EG	-	-	-	-	-	+	-
Ranunculus subgen Batrachium (DC)A	crowfoots	seed	E	-	-	-	-	-	+	-
Ranunculus sp	buttercups	seed	ABCDEG	-	-	-	-	-	-	-
cf Stellaria graminea	lesser stitchwort	seed	CD	-	-	-	-	-	+	-
Chenopodium murale L	nettle-leaved goosefoot	seed	BD	-	-	-	-	-	-	++
Chenopodium cf rubrum	red goosefoot	seed	AB	-	-	-	-	-	+	-
Rubus fruticosus/ idaeus	blackberry/ raspberry	seed	CFGH	-	-	+	-	-	-	+
Potentilla sp	cinquefoil/ tormentil	seed	BCDEFGH	-	+	-	-	-	-	-
Potentilla spp	cinquefoil/ tormentil	seed	BCDEFGH	-	-	-	-	-	++	-
Oenanthe cf aquatica	fine-leaved waterdropwort	seed	E	-	-	-	-	-	-	++
Polygonum sp	knotgrass etc	seed	ABCDEFG	-	+	-	-	-	++	+
Rumex sp	dock	seed	ABCDEFG	-	-	-	-	-	+	-
Urtica dioica L	stinging nettle	seed	BCDEFGH	-	-	-	-	-	+	-
cf Ficus carica	fig	seed	FI	-	-	-	+	-	-	-
Mentha sp	mint	seed	ABCEFGI	-	-	-	-	-	+	-
Lycopus europaeus L	gypsy-wort	seed	EH	-	-	-	-	-	+	-
Sambucus nigra L	elder	seed	BCFGH	-	-	+	-	-	-	+
Leontodon sp	hawkbit	seed	BDF	-	-	-	-	-	+	-
Juncus spp	rush	seed	ADEH	-	-	-	-	-	+++	-
Eleocharis sp	spike-rush	seed	DE	-	-	-	-	-	-	+
Carex sp	sedge	seed	CDEH	-	-	+	-	-	+++	-
Carex spp	sedge	seed	CDEH	-	-	-	-	-	-	++
Cyperaceae indet	sedge	seed	ABCDEFI	-	-	-	-	-	-	+
Indet	-	leaf	-	-	-	-	-	-	-	++++
Indet	-	stem	-	-	-	-	-	-	-	++++
Bryophyta indet	moss	leaf	-	-	-	-	-	-	-	++

Table 121 Borough High Street periods 5 and 6

Latin name	Common name	Plant part	Habitat/ use codes	SG156 [42] {11}	SG765 [3089] {306}	SG922 [3395] {342}	SG922 [3395] {343}	SG961 [3191] {314}	SG961 [3213] {317}	SG966 [3133] {312}
Charred remains										
Triticum dicoccum	emmer	seed	FI	-	11	-	-	60	-	-
Triticum dicoccum	emmer	glume base	FI	-	-	-	-	-	I	-
Triticum cf dicoccum	emmer	seed	FI	-	-	-	-	-	177	-
Triticum spelta	spelt	seed	FI	-	-	-	-	345	563	-
Triticum spelta	spelt	glume base	FI	-	-	-	-	I	-	-
Triticum cf spelta	spelt	seed	FI	-	2	-	-	-	-	-
Triticum cf spelta	spelt	spiklelet fork	FI	-	-	-	-	-	I	-
Triticum cf spelta	spelt	glume base	FI	-	-	-	-	-	4	-
Triticum cf dicoccum/ spelta	emmer/spelt	seed	FI	-	28	-	-	-	256	-
Triticum cf dicoccum/ spelta	emmer/spelt	spikelet fork	FI	-	-	-	-	I	-	-
Triticum cf dicoccum/ spelta	emmer/spelt	glume base	FI	-	-	-	-	-	I	-
cf *Triticum dicoccum/ spelta*	emmer/spelt	seed	FI	-	-	-	-	523	-	-
Triticum cf aestivum s.l.	bread/club wheat	seed	FI	-	I	-	-	-	-	-
Triticum spelta/aestivum	spelt/bread wheat	seed	FI	29	-	-	-	145	160	-
Triticum sp	wheat	seed	FI	-	4	-	-	-	-	-
Secale cereale	rye	seed	FI	-	-	-	-	-	2	-
Triticum/Secale sp	wheat/rye	seed	FI	-	-	-	-	I	-	-
Hordeum sativum	barley	seed	FI	-	-	-	-	2	2	-
cf *Hordeum sativum*	barley	seed	FI	-	-	-	-	10	54	-
Hordeum sativum	barley	sprouted	FI	-	-	-	-	195	-	-
Avena sativa L	cultivated oat	seed	FI	-	-	-	-	3	-	-
Avena sp	oat	seed	AFI	-	I	-	-	-	2	-
cf *Avena sp*	oat	seed	AFI	5	-	-	-	-	-	-
Avena/Hordeum/Secale/ Triticum	indet cereal	seed	FI	3	4	-	-	-	4	-
Avena/Hordeum/Secale/ Triticum	indet cereal	culm node	FI	-	-	-	-	-	I	-
Avena/Hordeum/Secale/ Triticum	indet cereal	seed	FI	-	-	-	-	4	-	3
Ranunculus sp	buttercups	seed	ABCDEG	I	-	-	-	-	-	-
Agrostemma githago L	corn cockle	seed	AB	-	-	-	-	-	3	-
Stellaria sp	chickweed/ stitchwort	seed	ABCDEG	I	-	-	-	-	-	-
Trifolium sp	clover calyx	seed	ABDI	2	-	-	-	-	-	-
cf *Trifolium sp*	clover calyx	seed	ABDI	-	-	-	-	I	-	-
cf *Lens culinaris*	lentil	seed	FI	I	-	-	-	-	-	-
Vicia faba	celtic bean/ horsebean	seed	FI	3	-	-	-	-	-	-
Mineralised remains										
Vicia/Lathyrus sp	vetch/tare/ vetchling	seed	ACDEFI	2	-	-	-	-	2	-
Pisum sp	pea	seed	FI	-	-	-	-	5	-	-
Fabaceae indet	legume fragments	seed	-	-	-	-	-	I	I	-
cf Fabaceae	legume fragments	seed	-	I	-	-	-	-	-	-
Prunus avium/cerasus	sloe/cherry	seed	CFGI	-	I	-	-	-	-	-
Prunus sp	-	seed	CFGI	I	-	-	-	-	-	-
Galium aparine L	cleavers	seed	BCG	-	-	-	-	-	-	I
Galium cf aparine	cleavers	seed	BCG	-	-	-	-	-	2	-
cf *Anthemis cotula*	stinking mayweed	seed	ABGH	2	-	-	-	-	-	-
Carduus/Cirsium sp	thistles	seed	ABDEG	I	-	-	-	-	-	-
Carex sp	sedge	seed	CDEH	-	-	-	-	-	I	I
Poaceae	grass	seed	ABCDEFGHI	-	-	-	-	I	-	-
Bromus cf secalinus/ mollis	rye-brome/ lop-grass	seed	ABD	-	-	-	-	3	9	-
Bromus sp	bromes	seed	ABD	2	2	-	-	2	-	-
Indet	-	stem	-	+	-	-	-	-	-	-
Indet	-	wood	-	++++	++++	++++	++++	++++	++++	++++
Indet	-	plant tissue	-	-	-	4	-	-	4	-
Malva sp	mallow	seed	BCDF	I	-	-	-	-	-	-
cf *Piper nigrum*	pepper	seed	FGI	I	-	-	-	-	-	-

(Table 121 cont)

Latin name	Common name	Plant part	Habitat/use codes	SG156 [42] {11}	SG765 [3089] {306}	SG922 [3395] {342}	SG922 [3395] {343}	SG961 [3191] {314}	SG961 [3213] {317}	SG966 [3133] {312}
Waterlogged remains										
Fumaria sp	fumitory	seed	ABC	+	-	-	-	-	-	-
Agrostemma githago L	corncockle	seed	AB	+	-	-	-	-	-	-
Chenopodium sp	goosefoot etc	seed	ABCDFH	+	-	-	-	-	-	-
Vitis vinifera L	grape	seed	FI	+	-	-	-	-	-	-
Rubus fruticosus/idaeus	blackberry/raspberry	seed	CFGH	+	-	-	-	-	-	-
Pyrus/Malus sp	pear/apple	seed	CFI	+	-	-	-	-	-	-
Ficus carica L	fig	seed	FI	+	-	-	-	-	-	-
Galium sp	bedstraw	seed	ABCDE	+	-	-	-	-	-	-
Sambucus nigra L	elder	seed	BCFGH	+++	-	-	-	-	-	-
Carex sp	sedge	seed	CDEH	+	-	-	-	-	-	-

Latin name	Common name	Plant part	Habitat/use codes	SG5 [86] {9}	SG5 [87] {10}	SG5 [88] {11}
Charred remains						
Poaceae indet	grass	seed	ABCDEFHI	-	-	I
Indet	-	wood	-	++++	++++	++++
Waterlogged remains						
cf *Myrrhis odorata* (L)	sweet cecily	seed	-	+	+	+
Indet		bud	-	-	-	+
Indet	-	stem	-	++++	++++	+
Indet	-	wood	-	-	-	+++
Indet	-	plant tissue	-	-	+	++
Thlaspi arvense L	field penny-cress	seed	AB	-	+	-
Agrostemma githago L	corncockle	seed	AB	-	++	++
Sonchus cf *oleraceus*	milk-/sow-thistle	seed	AB	++	-	-
Onopordum acanthium L	scotch thistle	seed	ABC	-	-	+
Stellaria media (L) Vill.	chickweeds	seed	ABCDE	-	+	-
Polygonum sp	knotgrass etc	seed	ABCDEFG	+	+	+
Rumex sp	dock	seed	ABCDEFG	+	-	+
Poaceae indet	grass	seed	ABCDEFHI	-	+	-
Cyperaceae indet	sedge	seed	ABCDEFI	+	-	-
cf *Ranunculus acris/repens/bulbosus*	buttercups	seed	ABCDEG	+	+	+
Stellaria sp	chickweed/stitchwort	seed	ABCDEG	+	-	+
Silene sp	campion/catchfly	seed	ABCDF	+	+	-
Carduus/Cirsium sp	thistles	seed	ABDEG	+	-	-
Centaurea sp	knapweed/thistle	seed	ABDGH	-	+	-
Sonchus sp	milk-/sow-thistle	seed	ABE	-	-	+
Atriplex sp	orache	seed	ABFGH	-	+	-
Brassica/Sinapis sp	wild cabbage/mustard	seed	ABFGHI	-	+	++
Sinapis alba L	white mustard	seed	ABFGHI	+	-	-
cf *Sinapis alba*	white mustard	seed	ABFGHI	+	-	+
Chenopodium album L	fat hen	seed	ABFH	-	+	+
Chenopodium cf *album*	fat hen	seed	ABFH	+	-	-
Brassica sp	wild cabbage/turnip/mustard	seed	ABFI	++	-	-
Polygonum aviculare L	knotgrass	seed	ABG	-	-	+
Anthemis cotula L	stinking mayweed	seed	ABGH	+	+	+
Torilis japonica/nodosa	hedge-parsley	seed	ACD	-	+	-
Sonchus cf *arvensis*	field milk-thistle	seed	ADE	+	-	-
Chrysanthemum segetum L	corn marigold	seed	AHI	+	-	+
Rumex crispus L	curled dock	tepal	BC	-	+	-
cf *Rumex crispus* L	curled dock	tepal	BC	-	-	+
Urtica dioica L	stinging nettle	seed	BCDEFGH	-	+	-
Prunella vulgaris L	self-heal	seed	BCDG	-	+	+
Hyoscyamus niger L	henbane	seed	BDG	-	-	+
Centaurea nigra L	lesser knapweed	seed	BDG	-	-	+
Stellaria graminea L	lesser stitchwort	seed	CD	+	-	+
Carex sp	sedge	seed	CDEH	-	+	-
Carex spp	sedge	seed	CDEH	-	-	+
Leontodon cf *hispidus*	rough hawkbit	seed	D	+	-	-
Eleocharis sp	spike-rush	seed	DE	-	+	+
Alisma sp	water-plantain	seed	E	-	-	+
Avena/Hordeum/Secale/Triticum	indet cereal	bran	FI	-	++++	++++

Table 122 Samples from LBH94

Latin name	Common name	Plant part	Habitat/ use codes	SG128 [308] {102}	SG91 [324] {105}
Charred Remains					
Indet	-	stem	-	2	2
Indet	-	wood	-	++++	++++
Indet	-	plant tissue	-	-	3
Polygonum sp	knotgrass etc	seed	ABCDEFG	-	I
Chelidonium majus L	greater celandine	seed	BC	-	I
Eleocharis sp	spike-rush	seed	DE	-	I
Triticum dicoccum L	emmer	grain	FI	-	8
Triticum spelta/aestivum	spelt/bread wheat	grain	FI	7	-
Hordeum sativum L	barley	grain	FI	-	II
cf Hordeum sativum	barley	grain	FI	-	24
Avena cf sativa	cultivated oat	grain	FI	2	-
Avena/Hordeum/ Secale/Triticum	indet cereal	grain	FI	2	-
Vitis vinifera L	grape	seed	FI	I	-
cf Lens culinaris	lentil	seed	FI	-	I
Pisum sp	pea	seed	FI	-	I
Mineralised remains					
Vicia/Lathyrus sp	vetch/tare/ vetchling	seed	ACDEFI	-	+
Malva sp	mallow	seed	BCDF	++	-
Conium maculatum L	hemlock	seed	CEG	+	-
Prunus spinosa/avium/ cerasus	sloe/cherry	seed	CFGI	++++	-
Prunus cf domestica	plum/bullace	seed	CFI	++++	-
Avena cf sativa	cultivated oat	grain	FI	+	-
Pisum sativum L	pea	seed	FI	-	+
Waterlogged remains					
Lamium purpurem L	red dead nettle	seed	AB	++	-
Silene sp	campion/catchfly	seed	ABCDF	+	-
Urtica dioica .	stinging nettle	seed	BCDEFGH	++	-
Sambucus nigra L	elder	seed	BCFGH	+	-
Carex sp	sedge	seed	CDEH	+	-
Conium maculatum L	hemlock	seed	CEG	+	-
Rubus fruticosus/idaeus	blackberry/ raspberry	seed	CFGH	++++	-
Vitis vinifera L	grape	seed	FI	+	-
Ficus carica L	fig	seed	FI	++++	-

Table 123 Samples from LBI95

Latin name	Common name	Plant part	Habitat/ use codes	SG76 [299] {24}	SG78 [245] {25}
Charred remains					
Avena/Hordeum/Secale/ Triticum	indet cereal	grain	FI	-	I
Indet	-	wood	-	++++	++++
Waterlogged remains					
Raphanus raphanistrum L	wild radish/charlock	siliqua	A	+	-
Agrostemma githago L	corncockle	seed	AB	+	-
Polygonum sp	knotgrass etc	seed	ABCDEFG	+	-
Rumex sp	dock	seed	ABCDEFG	+	-
cf Ranunculus acris/ repens/bulbosus	buttercups	seed	ABCDEG	++	-
Silene sp	campion/catchfly	seed	ABCDF	+	-
Chenopodium sp	goosefoot etc	seed	ABCDFH	-	+
Polygonum persicaria L	persicaria	seed	ABEH	+	-
Chenopodium album L	fat hen	seed	ABFH	+	-
Chenopodium cf album	fat hen	seed	ABFH	++	-
Polygonum aviculare L	knotgrass	seed	ABG	+	-
Anthemis cotula L	stinking mayweed	seed	ABGH	+	-

Table 124 Samples from LBE95

Latin name	Common name	Plant part	Habitat/ use codes	SG76 [299] {24}	SG78 [245] {25}
Waterlogged remains					
cf *Vicia/Lathyrus* sp	vetch/tare/vetchling	seed	ACDEFI	-	+
Brassica cf *oleraceus*	cabbage	seed	ADFI	+	-
Chrysanthemum segetum L	corn marigold	seed	AHI	+	-
Coronopus squamatus (Fskl) Ascherson	swine-cress	seed	B	+	-
Chelidonium majus L	greater celandine	seed	BC	+	-
Rumex crispus L	curled dock	tepal	BC	+	-
Potentilla sp	cinquefoil/tormentil	seed	BCDEFGH	-	+
Urtica dioica L	stinging nettle	seed	BCDEFGH	+	+
Malva sp	mallow	seed	BCDF	+	-
Sambucus nigra L	elder	seed	BCFGH	+	+
Hyoscyamus niger	henbane	seed	BDG	+	+
Cannabis sativa L	hemp	seed	BGHI	+	-
Ranunculus cf *parviflorus*	small-flowered buttercup	seed	CD	-	++
Corylus avellana L	hazel	seed	CF	+	-
Rubus fruticosus/idaeus	blackberry/ raspberry	seed	CFGH	-	+
Ranunculus sceleratus L	celery-leaved crowfoot	seed	E	-	+
Ranunculus subgen. *Batrachium* (DC)A	crowfoots	seed	E	+	-
Menyanthes trifoliata L	bogbean	seed	EFG	+	-
Avena/Hordeum/Secale/ Triticum	indet cereal	bran	FI	-	+
cf *Carduus/Cirsium*	thistles	seed	ABDEG	+	-
Alisma sp	water-plantain	seed	E	+	+
Zannichellia palustris L	horned pond-weed	seed	E	+	-
Lemna sp	duckweed	seed	E	-	+
Eleocharis sp	spike-rush	seed	DE	++	+
Carex sp	sedge	seed	CDEH	+	+
Indet	-	stem	-	++++	-
Indet	-	wood	-	+	-
Bryophyta indet	moss	-	-	+	-

(Table 124 cont)

11.8 The animal bones

Charlotte Ainsley

Introduction

This report focuses on selected Roman contexts from the Jubilee Line Extension Project. This was a series of excavations which were undertaken in 1995 and 1996. The sites included in the remit of this report are Borough High Street (BGH95), London Bridge sites (LBA95, LBB95, LBE95, LBI95) and the Redcross Way sites (RWG94 and REW92). The remains were selected from a series of periods:

Period 1 AD 50–60, pre-Boudican fire
Period 2 AD 62–160. The bulk of the faunal remains fall into this period. It was easily divided into three subdivisions:
    2a AD 62–100

    2b AD 100–20
    2c AD 120–60
Period 3 AD 160–200
Period 4 AD 300–400

Some of the information has been integrated with the main text where it was particularly relevant, and has not been repeated here.

Methodology

Bones were collected by hand recovery and through the taking of bulk samples. The extent of sampling and the volume of soil processed varied from site to site. Generally the samples were between 1 and 20 litres. Each sample was wet-sieved through a mesh size of 1mm and the residue was then hand-sorted. The importance of the inclusion of faunal remains recovered from samples cannot be over-stressed. Hand-collected bone, by definition, is dominated by the remains from the larger animals, such as cattle, as these are more easily identified. Consideration of hand-collected material alone will lead to a bias of these animals over smaller ones such as sheep and pigs. Sampling, on the other hand, not only facilitates the full recovery of these smaller animals, thereby redressing the balance, but also allows the retrieval of much smaller constituents of the faunal assemblage including birds, amphibians and fish. From a closer study of the latter elements of the faunal list it is occasionally possible to determine the nature of the immediate ecology surrounding the sample area during the period in question.

The animal bones were recorded, on an individual basis, directly on to the MoLSS Environmental Archaeology Section Oracle database. Identifications of species and anatomy were aided by using the MoLSS Environmental Archaeology Section reference collections in conjunction with Schmid (1972) and Cohen and Serjeantson (1996). The anatomical identification for each fragment included which bone, the part present (eg shaft) and the proportion of the bone present. A zonal method was also used (following Rackham 1986), here recording non-repeatable characteristics of the majority of skeletal parts. Age of the bone was determined through analyses of tooth wear stages (following Grant 1982), epiphyseal fusion (following Silver 1969) and horncores (following Armitage 1982). Where identified, the position of butchery marks was accurately recorded and, if possible, the method and direction of the knife mark or chop. The location of any pathologies was similarly recorded, complete with a description and possible cause of such a pathology. The other modifications that were recorded on a systematic basis were gnawing and burning. The former was attributed to either rodent or carnivores wherever possible, and for both the location and degree of severity were also noted. Measurements were taken largely following von den Driesch (1976). Information referring to the height of the animals is generally an approximate shoulder height, unless otherwise stated. These were calculated by employing standard conversion factors taken from von den Driesch and Boessneck (1974). Where it was impossible to determine exact identifications to species, approximate classifications based on size were used, namely 'cattle-sized', 'sheep-sized' and 'chicken-sized'.

The quantification methods used include total fragment count, total weight and a weighted method involving non-repeatable zones (following Rackham 1986). With this method, a minimum count can be made for each of the skeletal parts, these being limited to those which can be identified to species (excluding ribs and most of the vertebral column). The calculation of species representation also takes into account the expected frequencies of various parts. Most of the bones should be divided by a factor of two, accounting for the left and right sides of the body, while others, such as pig metapodials, need to be divided by 16. In general, however, the calculations involve a doubling of those parts which are single, such as the atlas and axis, and then a division of all parts which occur more than twice. The purpose of the calculations is to avoid an over-representation of certain species, for example pig, which possess large numbers of certain skeletal parts.

Summary statistics

A total of 18,241 fragments (approximately 265.5kg) of animal bone was recorded from the study area. The species representation (hand-collected and sampled combined), with fragmentation counts and weight for all sites, is shown in Table 125.

It should be stressed that included within this report is only a small proportion of the excavated bone. This is due to the focused nature of the project, which is limited to the development of the area during the Roman period. However, the remaining bones have been assessed and an extensive report has been compiled (Rielly 1997).

Borough High Street AD 50–60

Open Area 8

Faunal remains were recovered from a series of pits and a single ditch. Both the quantity and the species diversity were exceptionally limited; cattle and 'cattle-sized' material dominated followed by sheep/goat, pig, and goose only. Pig and goose were each represented by a single fragment. The goose bone was a tarso-metatarsus that had been chopped transversely through the distal epiphysis to prepare the bird for the table. Knife marks located on the shaft of this bone indicate the removal of meat. It represents small-scale dumping of both domestic and initial butchery wastes.

Open Area 14

Located to the east of Open Area 13 was Open Area 14; it contained two external hearths, a number of post- and stakeholes and an associated cesspit.

The bone from the cesspit was very limited in both species range and actual fragment counts (Table 126). The only species recovered were cattle and 'cattle-sized' plus a single sheep/goat bone. It is noteworthy that this bone was a radius from a very young animal (infant); unfortunately no butchery was evident, which makes it impossible to determine whether this is evidence for the consumption of lamb on the site or whether it only represents a natural death.

All the subgroups are dominated by cattle and 'cattle-sized' bones. The non-cattle component of the assemblage was very small, consisting of only minimal quantities of sheep/goat and pig, while [2107] was slight more diverse. The only exception to this was subgroup 415 which contained only an adult sheep/goat mandible.

There is a wide distribution of cattle skeletal parts, with the exception of foot elements. These are represented by a single third phalange from [2137] and a first phalange from [2170]. This suggests that the feet had been removed prior to the carcass reaching the area, possibly remaining attached to the hide for transport to the tannery. Further support for this idea comes from the fact that the third phalange does have a transverse knife mark on the lateral edge of the proximal articulation which could be associated with skinning. Butchery

Table 125 Summary of animal bone species recovered from selected sites and periods from the Jubilee Line Extension Project

Species	Borough High Street		London Bridge (all sites)		Redcross Way		Total	
	No. of frags	Wt (g)	No. of frags	Wt (g)	No. of frags	Wt (g)	Frags	Wt (g)
Cattle (Bos sp domestic)	2967	116861	632	31049.8	40	5581	3639	153491.8
'Cattle-sized'	3286	47596.96	905	18402.4	29	587.5	4220	66586.86
Sheep/goat (Ovis/Capra sp)	182	1745.13	122	3010.5	5	51.5	309	4807.13
Sheep (Ovis aries)	33	523.34	33	2156.5	2	37	68	2716.84
Goat (Capra hircus)	0	0	2	7	0	0	2	7
'Sheep-sized'	828	3088.77	661	11432.05	52	136.1	1541	14656.92
Horse (Equus caballus)	7	738.73	20	1632	11	1610	38	3980.73
Pig (Sus scrofa)	375	5071.36	287	4992.5	13	120.5	675	10184.36
Cat (Felis domesticus)	0	0	34	338.5	0	0	34	338.5
Dog (Canis familiaris)	7	109.26	10	125	81	1752.5	98	1986.76
Red deer (Cervus elaphus)	2	88.38	11	316	0	0	13	404.38
Roe deer (Capreolus capreolus)	14	282.31	9	152	0	0	23	434.31
Hare (Lepus europeus)	0	0	14	52.45	2	8.5	16	60.95
Rat (Rattus sp)	7	0.8	5	1.05	0	0	12	1.85
Mouse sp/vole sp	64	3.3	95	698.45	34	1.78	193	703.53
House mouse (Mus musculus)	2	0.11	6	0.51	0	0	8	0.62
Wood mouse (Apodemus sylvaticus)	0	0	0	0	5	0.32	5	0.32
Field vole (Microtus agrestis)	0	0	0	0	5	0.05	5	0.05
Unidentified small mammal	1	0.1	0	0	0	0	1	0.1
Unidentified mammals	3653	3900.2	281	139.3	108	91.5	4042	4131
Chicken (Gallus gallus)	36	78.54	117	377.35	2	6	155	461.89
'Chicken-sized'	33	11.82	190	85.48	11	3.25	234	100.55
Duck (Anas sp)	3	4.7	13	8.5	2	2	18	15.2
Goose (Anser anser)	2	12	411	0	0	6	23	
Blackbird (Turclus merula)	1	2	6	0.12	0	0	7	2.12
Buzzard (Buteo buteo)	1	1.1	0	0	0	0	1	1.1
Pigeon sp (Columba sp)	0	0	1	1.5	0	0	1	1.5
Heron (Ardeidae sp)	0	0	1	3	0	0	1	3
Partridge (Perdix perdix)	1	0.2	0	0	0	0	1	0.2
Swan (Cygnus sp)	0	0	1	23	0	0	1	23
Teal (Anas crecca)	0	0	3	1	0	0	3	1
Woodcock (Scolopax rusticola)	0	0	1	0.2	2	0.1	3	0.3
Small passerines	16	2.66	84	32.06	4	0.25	104	34.97
Unidentified birds	65	29.59	161	112.26	18	0.6	244	142.45
Frog/toad (Rana sp/Bufo sp)	1591	17.87	863	48.24	12	0.7	2466	66.81
Cod (Gadus morhua)	5	0.2						
Whiting (Merlangius merlangius)	2	0.1						
Mackerel (Scomber scomber)	1	0.1						
Bass sp	5	0.4						
Salmonidae	1	0.5						
Cyprinidae	3	0.3						
Sturgeon (Acipenser sturio)	0	0	2	22	0	0	2	22
Unidentified fish	12	9.98	13	1.1	8	0.51		
Total	13207	180172.9	4588	75360.82	446	9991.66	18241	265525.4

Subgroup	No. of frags	Wt (g)
406	71	3402.07
412	111	7660.77
415	3	34.38
418	99	3372.17
420	23	660.73
422	47	819.65
424	92	448.39

Table 126 Fragment counts of animal bone remains from Open Area 14 (BGH95)

marks on the rest of the carcass are extensively located on the limb bones, the majority being grazing chops running along the shaft and showing that meat was removed before cooking. The elemental distribution suggests that both good and poor quality meat-bearing elements were exploited in the near vicinity. A small quantity of gnawing marks were identified; dog gnawing on one cattle tibia, and rodent gnawing on a cattle metacarpal and a sheep/goat metatarsal. It can perhaps be suggested that most of the bones in this assemblage had been quickly buried, with a small proportion redeposited from a surface or open occupation dump.

Seven fragments of bone recovered from [2107] showed evidence of having been burnt. They were blue/white in colour. This is only achieved when complete incineration of the bones has occurred. Conditions required to reduce bone to such a state are a combination of extreme high temperatures and exposure for prolonged periods of time. It seems likely that these bone fragments originate from the hearth and had become incorporated into the general waste.

One apparent non-food bone was a fragment of horse maxilla from [2147]. The teeth were severely worn and indicative of old age. Its presence is very odd, and possibly represents the reworking of a dismembered skeleton. If this supposition is correct it has implications for the rest of the assemblage. The remainder of the assemblage was composed of single fragments of chicken, mouse/vole and frog/toad.

In summary, this assemblage was clearly derived from a number of sources, with tough domestic waste of both high and low quality predominating.

Structure 3

A total of 33 fragments of bone were recovered from three contexts: [2182] and [2192], both make-up layers, and [2191], a floor layer. The quantity of bone is too minimal to offer any interpretation of the origins or usage of the bone prior to disposal. It is highly possible that they merely represent scattered debris.

Building 13 (phase 1)

The faunal remains were recovered from make-up layers of this large masonry building of post-Boudican fire construction. A total of 2282 fragments were recovered, almost all of which were removed from make-up layer subgroup 215. Only three fragments were present in subgroup 213. The species range from subgroup 215 shows moderate diversity (Table 127).

Roe deer is represented by the proximal end of a radius from a sub-adult individual. While there were no butchery cuts, it would seem likely to represent food waste. There were a small number of chicken lower limbs/feet, perhaps removed from the rest of the carcasses during preparation of these birds for the table.

Five pig bones were recovered, including fragments of femur, ulna, calcaneum and a second phalange (all adult) plus a juvenile radius. The calcaneum had been chopped transversely across the shaft, which is consistent with the removal of the lower rear leg (the trotters) through the ankle joint.

The sheep/goat and 'sheep-sized' material showed a mixed skeletal representation. Despite the majority being vertebrae, ribs and metapodials, the respective quantities are very minimal. Two of the vertebrae had been sagitally chopped (along the central line) and a further three had been transversely divided through the posterior aspect. The former results from the halving of the carcass and the latter from the division of the body into smaller, more manageable, portions. From [1841] in particular a number of burnt fragments were recovered. Identifiable remains included 'sheep-sized' carpals and sesamoides, both of which are expected waste from the dismemberment of the lower limb. There was very little ageing evidence due to the highly fragmentary nature of the material, but it was possible to determine that both adults and juvenile examples were present.

Species	No. of frags
Cattle	157
'Cattle-sized'	232
Sheep/goat	8
Roe deer	1
'Sheep-sized'	34
Pig	5
Mouse/vole	1
Chicken	4
Small passerines	1
Unidentified mammal	1836

Table 127 Species range from Building 13, subgroup 215 (BGH95)

The cattle and 'cattle-sized' remains originate from all areas of the skeleton. There was fairly even distribution of all aspects except that feet, vertebrae and ribs were severely under-represented. These are the elements that are discarded during the initial stages of butchery, suggesting that the majority of the bone was from carcasses which had already been 'dressed'.

The elemental representation of cattle and 'cattle-sized' shows a remarkably close correlation to that of Open Area 11 (Fig 115). Based on this, it appears that the two assemblages (Open Area 11 and Building 13 phase 1) originated from a single common source. It seems likely that the butcher would have disposed of waste in the area immediately surrounding his premises, as has already been discussed above. It also seems natural that, when levelling the area for the construction of the building, the builders would have used material that was convenient and close to hand, ie the accumulated butchery waste dumps. A large percentage of the bone would have been crushed so as to provide a level surface, thus explaining the high number of unidentifiable fragments.

Structure 2

Only one single fragment of animal bone was recorded from this structure, a fragment of 'sheep-sized' bone.

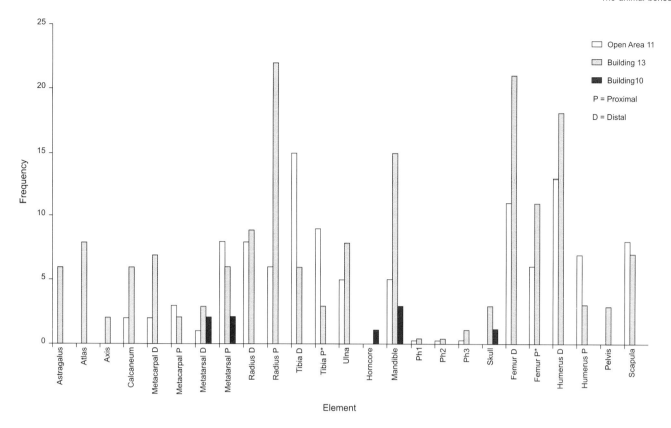

Fig 115 Cattle skeletal representation from Building 10, Building 13 and Open Area 11

Borough High Street AD 100–60

Open Area 25 (AD 120–60)

This open area was located to the south of Building 25. It contained a small linear feature and a substantial ditch. The majority of the animal bones were recovered from external layers, occupational and make-up layers.

Limited remains from the three main domesticates make up the bulk of the faunal assemblage. A small number of bones have evidence of dog gnawing, and as all are high meat-bearing bones it seems reasonable to assume that the animals were being fed from the table rather than scavenging waste.

A single chicken tibio-tarsus bears evidence of knife marks on the distal epiphysis which is consistent with the removal of the feet during preparation of the bird for the table.

This group probably represents a small mixed deposit of butchery and general domestic waste most likely originating from Building 25.

London Bridge sites AD 70

Construction of Building 2

GROUP 6, SUBGROUPS 58–61, 63–65
A total of 79 fragments of animal bone were recovered from contexts relating to the construction of Building 2. The majority (87%) of the animal bones were from a single make-up layer [444]. The other contexts each contained less than five fragments of animal bone. A single juvenile goat mandible was recovered from [459]. This is the earliest positive identification of this species on any of the sites within the Jubilee Line Extension Project. Unfortunately, no butchery was present, which raises the question of the origins of the bone.

Context [444] was a make-up layer delineated by the wall of room D. The anatomical representation for cattle shows a mixture of household and primary butchery waste with a slight dominance of the latter. Filleting marks were observed on two scapulae. A single radius had been dog-gnawed slightly towards one end, which suggests that the animals had been fed from the table rather than scavenging from uncovered pits. The only sheep bones identified belonged to a partial lamb skeleton and included a mandible, scapula, metapodials and a single vertebra. Despite no butchery being identified it seems probably that it was intended for consumption. Animals as small as lambs could be easily dismembered with a knife rather than using a heavy cleaver, with less chance of leaving marks on the bones. Pigs were limited to only a single juvenile femur and an adult mandible. Lateral knife marks on the distal epiphysis of the former indicate that meat was being removed from the bone. The only bird remains present were a number of chicken tibio-tarsuses (n=6). Each had knife marks across the distal end, indicating the removal of the feet during the preparation of the bird for the table. This assemblage probably represents a single dumping event of a small quantity of initial butchery and household waste.

London Bridge sites AD 70–100

Construction of Building 3

GROUP 17/18, SUBGROUPS 23–27

A series of seven small contexts was recovered from the layers associated with Building 3, make-up layers, occupational layers and floor surfaces. Unfortunately, only one context [131] contained in excess of ten fragments. The majority of the bones are only fragments, and identification is limited to only cattle and sheep-sized. Also present was a single unidentified frog/toad species scapula and a fragment of non-specific mouse/vole long bone. It seems likely that this assemblage represents waste left inside the building, which was missed when the floor was being swept; from this it can be inferred that it was not thoroughly cleaned, which has implications for the hygiene standard and use of the building.

London Bridge sites AD 100–20

Building 2, room D (continuation of usage)

GROUP 13, SUBGROUPS 84–86; GROUP 14, SUBGROUPS 97, 99 AND 100

Both the group 13 and 14 assemblages were very small, consisting of only 28 and 16 fragments respectively. Also very limited is the species range, comprising only cattle, chicken, duck and pig. There is a noticeable absence of any sheep/goat bones.

Context [411] is interesting in that it is described as a hearth. Six fragments of bone were recovered, including a cattle radius, a tibia and the shaft of a pig long bone. However, none bore any indications of being burnt. Therefore it seems reasonable to assume that these bones were deposited after the hearth had gone out of use.

A duck metatarsal was recovered from [394]; it was fully fused (adult) and had been scorched black.

The rest of the faunal material from both of these deposits appears to be waste from a variety of sources, but unfortunately there is insufficient information on which to base an interpretation. Not only was there a lack of sheep/goat but also an absence of any expected background mammals (eg mice or rats) or small passerines, which were present in earlier phases of this building. This implies that this small volume of material was both dumped and covered rapidly.

Redcross Way

RWG94 well Structures 1 and 2: dogs

Remains were recovered from four well contexts of RWG94 Structures 1 and 2. A substantial percentage (95%) of the bones were recovered from one context, the backfill of well Structure 2, and included bone that represented at least three dogs: one very old adult, one adult and one juvenile.

The skull of the old individual had teeth so extremely worn that it would have been difficult for the animal to eat properly.

It seems highly probable that this animal would have required special care in the later stages of its life. A maxillary second premolar was absent; this loss had occurred much earlier in the animal's life as the hole had healed. The presence of a number of complete long bones allowed calculations of the stature of the animal to be made (Table 128).

This dog is of a considerable size, the largest recovered from all the sites within the JLE project. Its height falls between 61cm and 64cm (to the shoulder) which is within the height range for an average German Shepherd breed. Its size means that the animal could have fulfilled a number of possible functions: as a pet, a guard dog, a hunting dog or a fighting dog. The first option seems unlikely given the considerable size of the dog, as does the last due to the lack of pathology on the bones. It is impossible to determine the dog's role with absolute certainty, but as it was looked after into old age it seems most likely that it was a favourite hunting dog. A number of elements are absent from the skeleton, including some of the metapodials and vertebrae and all the phalanges; it is possible that these were missed during excavation.

The partial juvenile dog skeleton included two radii, a tibia, two femurs, a humerus and an ulna. The proximal radius is one of the first elements to fuse in the canine skeleton; this had not yet occurred here, meaning that the animal was less than eight months old when it died.

The adult individual was represented by two femurs divided between two well fills. Stature calculations indicated that the animal was 49cm high to the shoulder. No more of the animal was recovered.

The fact that the older individual was clearly cared for makes it peculiar that it was dumped into a well rather than being placed in a sealed deposit. This, combined with the separation of the paired femurs of the other adult individual between two contexts, makes it likely that these skeletons had been redeposited in the wells (post-use) and the pit.

Table 128 Stature of an old adult dog from well Structure 2, RWG94

Element	Greatest length (mm)	Stature (mm)
Femur	200.5	616.61
Femur	204	627.6
Humerus	187	614.87
Humerus	186	611.44
Radius	193	633.25
Radius	194	636.43
Tibia	208	616.77
Tibia	208	616.77
Ulna	225	631.71
Ulna	227	637.27

Range: 616.61mm to 637.27mm
Mean: 624.272mm
Standard deviation: 9.93363
Number: 10

RWG94 well Structure 1: amphibians and small mammals

Amphibian remains were very abundant within the usage fill of Structure 1, with in excess of 780 fragments of frog/toad species. They represent a minimum of 28 individuals based on left and right pelvis counts. The preservation of the bone was exceptional, allowing two pathologies to be recorded, both on the tibio-fibulae; one had broken and healed at an angle and the other had a localised infection. The presence of such a considerable quantity of amphibians strongly suggests that the well was uncovered for a large majority (if not all) of the time it was in use, acting similarly to a pit-fall trap.

Also recovered from the well deposit were two positively identified rodent species, wood mouse and field vole. At least three individuals were present, two of which were adult and the other juvenile. The wood mouse is one of the most common small rodent species, mostly living in woodland but also inhabiting hedgerows, fields and gardens, and sometimes found in open grassland. The field vole prefers rough grassland where it can construct a network of tunnels just below the surface of the ground; however, it has been recorded in almost every type of habitat up to an altitude of 1000m.

Summary

The majority of the animal bone analysed in this report is directly related to food consumption, with all stages of preparation being represented. Despite a fairly diverse species range, cattle were by far the most common species recovered. This correlates with the pattern for other Roman sites in London. In comparison both sheep/goat and pig play only minor roles in the diet. The relative proportions of all three species do fluctuate both temporally and spatially (Fig 116).

The main domesticates

CATTLE: BOROUGH HIGH STREET

The sparse quantity of cattle bone for the pre-Boudican fire period (period 1) was too limited to allow any valid statistical discussion. Yet clearly cattle represent at least 60% of the three main domesticates. Ageing information was also limited, with only small quantities of fusion and sufficiently complete mandibular tooth rows recovered, but it does suggest that the cattle were more than 30 months old when they were culled (Table 133; Table 134ab).

The dominance of cattle in period 2 was pronounced. They maintain a high plateau throughout the whole of the period (Fig 116). In contrast to this were the fluctuating proportions of the sheep/goat and pigs. The ageing information revealed a pattern of culling which was repeated throughout all three sub-periods. The percentage of cattle that showed completed fusion in excess of 48 months (66.02%) was exceptionally high (Table 134ab). Additionally, there was a slight increase in the volume of unfused epiphyses, particularly within period 2b (Table 134b). Clearly there is a pattern of two-stage culling emerging: an initial minor culling at 24–36 months and a major culling stage of animals beyond 48 months. The fusion information relating to the vertebrae indicates that a high percentage of the cattle were considerably older than 48 months (Table 129). Schmid (1972) states that fusion of these elements occurs between seven and nine years.

The younger cattle represent animals that had been slaughtered in order to obtain good quality meat. The later and much more substantial slaughter represents secondary exploitation of older, in some cases 'senile', animals which met the bulk of the meat requirements. These animals would have outlived their primary usage, for example as dairy or draught beasts. Support for a mixture of primary uses (dairy with a

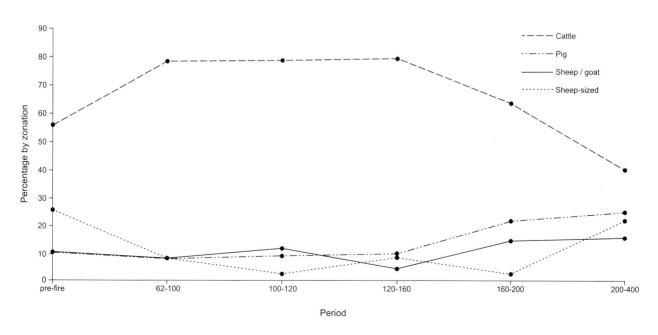

Fig 116 *The variation of the three main domesticates over selected periods (BGH95)*

Table 129 *Vertebral fusion states from Borough High Street (BGH95)*

Element	Age			Total
	Adult	Young	Juvenile	
Cervical	64	18	64	146
Lumbar	10	3	7	20
Thoracic	79	17	104	200
Total	153	38	175	366

Adult = fully fused
Young = fusion in progress (fusion line visible)
Juvenile = unfused

small draught component) comes from the fact that there are a number of examples of pathologies that are related to 'spavin', which afflicts draught animals, among others. However, due to a lack of sexing data it is difficult to comment further. The meat from these older cattle would have been of poor quality.

There were a number of infant and foetal/neonatal individuals present (Table 134ab). If all the cattle were being imported onto the site in order to satisfy the two age cullings, then very young deaths such as these should not be seen. There are two possible explanations for their occurrence: either cattle were being bred on site on a very limited scale during periods 2a and 2c, or veal was being imported and consumed on a very limited scale. Without more evidence it is impossible to comment further.

Cattle's dominance of the diet declines slightly during period 3 to just above 60%. This decline continues into period 4 when it falls to less than 40%. The culling pattern has also altered. There is no longer any indication of a first minor slaughter, and heavy reliance on very old animals had diminished.

OTHER SITES

The available data for the status of cattle at LBI95 was much less than at Borough High Street. The majority of the diet was contributed by cattle during period 2a, but this then underwent a rapid decline to less than 25% during period 2b. A slight recovery of beef's popularity occurred during the later stages of period 2c.

The ageing evidence was also limited. A total of 17 mandibles proved to be ageable through tooth wear analysis (Table 135). The majority of these were recovered from period 2a, where seven mandibles were defined as 'old adult/senile', five as adult and one as juvenile. The fusion data indicated one major culling stage as the cattle reached maturity (Table 136ab), but to supplement this slightly older cattle were also being slaughtered, albeit in much reduced numbers.

In contrast to the very old cattle that were being slaughtered at Borough High Street, LBI95 cattle were being deliberately bred for their meat and the majority were being slaughtered at their maximum weight return age.

The cattle information from the other sites within this report was too limited to allow a worthwhile interpretation.

However, at LBA95 27% of the cattle (n=11) were very young (less than ten months) but the majority were not killed until they were fully mature. At RWG94 cattle remains were only recovered from periods 3–4. The fusion information for these cattle shows that they all survived into full maturity.

METRIC INFORMATION

The cattle measurements discussed here (Table 132) were chosen on the basis of age (adult rather than juvenile) and comparability to other bone reports. The two greatest length measurements were taken from metacarpals: one from Borough High Street and one from LBI95, both from period 2. These converted into withers heights (following von den Driesch and Boessneck 1974) of 121.8cm and 107.3cm respectively. A further three greatest length measurements for metatarsals from Borough High Street and one from LBI95, both also period 2, gave withers calculations of 106.3cm to 136.3cm for Borough High Street and 111.2cm for LBI95. These results agree with metapodial measurements for the early Roman period at Winchester Palace (Rielly in prep b). The plentiful metatarsal distal width measurements from Borough High Street seemed to provide a good opportunity to examine any temporal variations at this site. At first appearances the mean of the distal width does increase with time from 43.6mm in period 1 to 53.3mm in period 4. However, this apparent increase in the robustness of the metatarsal may only be a reflection of the small data sets for all periods excluding period 2; additionally, the range of measurements for period 4 does fall within the period 2 range.

SHEEP/GOAT AND PIGS: BOROUGH HIGH STREET

The relative proportions which these animals contributed to the diet fluctuated within limits in all periods. Both maintained an equally low level of contribution (less than or equal to 15%) until period 3. From AD 160 onwards the level of contribution to the diet by pigs increases to over 20%. Sheep/goat also increased but by a smaller proportion. This increase continues into period 4, when over half of the diet was supplied by sheep/goat and pigs, replacing cattle as the staple meat source.

The tooth wear information for the pigs was very limited (Table 137). However, it did suggest that the majority of the pigs were slaughtered at approximately two years old, with a small older component. The fusion information illustrates this more clearly (Table 138ab). Within period 2 there are a small number of very young deaths. This is suggestive of pigs being bred on the site, and these unfused elements represent the expected background level of natural deaths, rather than representing an importation of piglets for consumption. A pig could easily have been maintained in a small household yard; being omnivores they could be fed on a variety of domestic waste and slaughtered at the maximum meat return point. The paucity of evidence for this occurring in other periods is probably more a reflection of inadequate numbers rather than the absence of this practise. The sex information was very limited, showing no preferred gender cullings, except possibly within period 2c, when there appears to be a slight bias towards killing males.

Due to the lack of positive evidence for goat it was assumed that the majority (if not all) of the sheep/goat were sheep. A constraining factor in the discussion of sheep is the lack of ageing information (Table 141; Table 142ab). Only in period 2 was there adequate fusion information to justify a discussion. Similarly to cattle, there appears to have been a two-stage culling occurring. The initial minor culling stage was prior to the sheep reaching 12 months, indicating a limited requirement for lamb meat, and the second when the animals had reached full maturity. The animals involved in this second stage would also have been available to provide wool during their lives and for breeding to maintain the herd numbers. They would only have been killed later in life once their initial usage became unproductive, and their meat would have been tough, poor quality and cheap.

OTHER SITES

The pattern for the relative proportion of sheep/goat at LBI95 mimics that of Borough High Street, maintaining a very low level up to AD 120 (less than 10%) and then a slight increase during the following period AD 120–40.

Two positive identifications of goat were recovered from LBI in the form of two juvenile mandibles. The tooth wear information (Table 143) was again very limited but indicates that a range of animals were being killed, from juvenile (less than six months, M1 unworn) to very old (M3 in heavy wear). The fusion information indicated a slightly clearer pattern (Table 144ab). The majority of the animals were culled at approximately two years old, with only a third of the individuals represented surviving beyond this age into full maturity. In addition, three infant bones were recovered from period 2a: a radius, a tibia and a scapula. No other ageable sheep/goat bones or mandibles were recovered from the other sites.

The proportional representation of pigs on LBI95 differs greatly from the pattern demonstrated at Borough High Street. They maintained a high level throughout periods 2a, 2b and 2c, at approximately 25%. During period 3 pigs declined to a very low level, but this may only be a result of the very small dataset for this period at LBI95. Both the fusion information and the tooth wear analysis indicate that pigs were being slaughtered at an earlier age than on Borough High Street. The tooth wear analysis (Table 139) showed that the majority of the pigs were culled prior to the M2 coming into wear (approximately between 6 and 12 months), with a small number of older animals also present. The fusion data (Table 140ab) agrees with this pattern, 32% of the pigs present being less than 12 months old (distal scapula, distal humerus and proximal radius all unfused). Two infant bones were recovered from period 2a, a femur and a humerus. A very limited number of pigs were culled beyond three years old. However, the sexual dimorphic data was very limited, making it impossible to draw any further conclusions.

LBA95 produced only two ageable pig bones, both sub-adult. No ageable pig bones were recovered from any other site.

METRIC INFORMATION

Selection for suitable sheep/goat and pig measurements was based on the same criteria as for cattle (Table 132). Only a small dataset of sheep/goat measurements was available for analysis. Calculations of withers heights (following conversion factors in Teichert 1975) were possible on three metatarsals from Borough High Street, period 2. These gave a range of 57.7cm to 64.7cm. Distal width measurements were available from Borough High Street, periods 2 and 4 only. The dataset was too small to be statistically viable, but if it is a true reflection of the stature of the sheep during these periods then a slight decrease in height did occur over time. The mean tibia distal width measurement during the early Roman phase at Winchester Palace (Rielly, in prep b) was 24.2mm (n=3), which is broader than at Borough High Street.

The dataset available for pigs was too limited to justify any discussion.

Other mammals

These can be easily divided into two groups, wild and domestic. Domestic animals were represented by dog, horse and cat, wild animals by hare, red deer and roe deer.

Only dog and horse were recovered from Borough High Street, both being best represented within period 2, with only one further horse bone from period 3. Red deer and roe deer followed a similar pattern, both being present in period 2, with only a limited number from period 3. Calculations based on the lateral length of the horse radius recovered from period 2 (following Kiesewalter 1888 cited in von den Driesch and Boessneck 1974, 333) gave a withers height of 12.8 hands. This falls within the size-range of horses given by Rackham (1995, 169) for the Romano-British period.

The quantity of 'other mammals' was slightly expanded at LBI95, with a small number of domestic animals being found. Two partial kitten skeletons were recovered from LBI95, and a further four bones from a juvenile individual at LBB95. A total of 91 dog bones were recovered from sites other than Borough High Street. The majority (91%) of these bones originated from three partial skeletons recovered from RWG94: one very old individual, one adult and one juvenile (see above). Seven dog bones were present at LBI95 and found to represent at least three individuals (two adult and one juvenile). Three further dog bones were from LBA95, all possibly originating from one individual. The withers heights of the dogs differ greatly. The smallest, recovered from LBI95 Open Area 13 [435], was 26–30cm, placing it at the small end of the Romano-British dog skeleton range (Harcourt 1974). This was probably a house- or lap-dog, a new type of breed introduced during the Roman period. The largest, from RWG94, had a shoulder height of 61–64cm, which places it at the opposite end of Harcourt's scale. The idea of it being a hunting dog has been discussed above.

A total of 12 fragments of deer were recovered from LBI95. Nine were from roe deer and the others from red deer. They were present in all periods from AD 70 to AD 140+, with AD 120–40 accounting for the majority.

Birds

There was relatively limited species diversity, with the majority of remains originating from domesticated species, especially chicken. It can be assumed that a large percentage of the chicken-sized and unidentified bird bones come from chickens, but they were just too fragmentary to allow positive identification.

From period 1 at Borough High Street (Table 130) only one fragment of goose was recovered, with a noticeable lack of chicken; this is possibly explained by these birds being less readily accepted as a source of food on un-Romanised sites (Maltby 1997). By period 2 chicken are the dominant bird on the site, perhaps reflecting their popularity as a domesticated bird during the Roman period (ibid), and demonstrating a rapid adjustment in dietary habits. At LBI95 chicken was prominent throughout (Table 131). It is interesting that chicken surpassed the fragment counts of the three main domesticates for the period AD 100–20 and was equally as well represented as them during the period AD 120–40. This closely mimics the pig representation pattern.

Chickens would not only have contributed meat to the diet, but their eggs would have been used as well.

Measurements of length of femur from both LBI95 and Borough High Street, period 2 were possible. The mean values for both of these sites are very similar. The mean was also larger than that recorded from the early Roman period at Winchester Palace (mean = 73.4, n=9) (Rielly in prep b).

At Borough High Street duck was present in periods 2 and 3 but only in very limited numbers (one and two fragments respectively), in keeping with the accepted pattern of them being uncommon on Roman sites (Maltby 1979). Ten of the 13 fragments of duck recovered from LBI95 were from the period AD 100–20. It is unknown whether these birds were domesticated or if they had been taken from the wild. If the former, then it would be reasonable to expect the quantities to be much larger, so by default the second option seems the more acceptable.

The London Bridge sites produced a number of other species which were not present at Borough High Street. From Open Area 13 (AD 120–40) a single pigeon (probably *Columba livia domestica*) humerus was recovered. As only one fragment was recovered it is likely that these birds were not domesticated. Six blackbird bones were recovered from Open Area 11 ([308] AD 140), all possibly originating from one individual. The blackbird was very much appreciated in Roman Italy and Switzerland, but the numbers recovered from British sites suggest that blackbird never caught on as a food source here. This individual may have been eaten but there are no butchery marks to support this suggestion.

The limited presence of woodcock (one fragment) and teal (three fragments) suggests that people were exploiting the woodland margins, polls and marshlands, especially in winter. It is also possible that these birds were purchased from a market.

The high numbers of small passerines present at Borough High Street and LBI95 (especially in the period AD 140+) may represent the usage of small birds by adding them to dishes of many ingredients, such as sausages, pieces of liver and brain from larger animals, pulses and herbs (Wilson 1973).

A fragment of swan humerus was also recovered from LBI95. This is a rare but not unknown species from Roman London sites; six swan bones were recovered from a similar period at Regis House (Rielly in prep a).

Fish

These were very poorly represented. A lack of fish remains from Roman sites is common (K Rielly pers comm). It is possible that the Roman preference for *garum*, imported from the Mediterranean, meant that fish were not widely consumed. The majority of the fish remains were highly fragmentary and/or poorly preserved, which limited identification. The Salmonidae species could have been caught or trapped during migration up the Thames. Marine species such as whiting, cod, bass and mackerel are present, in low numbers, indicating the exploitation of the Thames estuary and the surrounding coast.

Period	No. of frags	% frags for period
I	I	2.08
2	133	1.10
3	17	2.36
4	12	1.93

Table 130 Percentage of birds recovered from each period of Borough High Street (BGH95)

Period	Cattle	Sheep/goat	Pig	Chicken	Total
AD 50–70	0	0	0	I	I
AD 70–100	244	40	99	37	420
AD 100–120	75	31	81	134	321
AD 120–140	30	19	26	30	105
AD 140+	3	3	6	79	91

Table 131 Fragment counts of the three main domesticates and chicken from LBI95

Species	Site	Bone	Dimension	Phase	Number	Range	Mean
Cattle	BGH95	MTC	distal width	2	40	45.1–65.5	54.45
	BGH95	MTC	greatest length	2	I	-	198
	LBI95	MTC	distal width	2	10	50.4–64.4	54.09
	LBI95	MTC	greatest length	2	I	-	174.5
	BGH95	MTT	distal width	I	I	-	43.6
	BGH95	MTT	distal width	2	54	27.1–60.5	48.7
	BGH95	MTT	distal width	3	8	45.2–54.5	48.8
	BGH95	MTT	distal width	4	2	47.8–58.8	53.3
	BGH95	MTT	greatest length	2	3	195–250	221.66
	LBI95	MTT	distal width	2	15	43.4–64.9	50.76
	LBI95	MTT	greatest length	2	I	-	201
Sheep	BGH95	tibia	distal width	2	2	21.8–23.2	22.5
	BGH95	tibia	distal width	4	2	21.5–22.5	22.0
	BGH95	MTT	greatest length	2	3	127.2–142.5	133.67
	BGH95	MTT	distal width	2	3	22.2–24.6	23.2
Pig	BGH95	humerus	distal width	2	4	27.2–35.9	32.675
	BGH95	humerus	distal width	3	I	-	31.2
	LBI95	humerus	distal width	2	2	34.9–39.4	37.15
Horse	BGH95	radius	greatest length	2	I	-	330
Chicken	BGH95	femur	greatest length	2	2	75.2–79.9	77.55
	LBI95	femur	greatest length	2	6	67.8–85.4	75.78

Table 132 Selected metric measurements of animals recovered from Jubilee Line Extension sites

Age	Tooth sequence	Age class	Period I	2a	2b	2c	3	Total
I–6 months	MI erupting	A/B	0	I	0	0	0	I
15–26 months	M2 in wear, M3 unworn	C/D	0	0	0	0	0	0
26–30 months	M3 in wear;	E/F/G	I	6	3	7	2	19
3+ years	M3 in heavy wear	H/I	0	19	7	19	I	46
Total			I	26	10	26	3	66

Deciduous premolar dp4 present in 2 from 2a, I from 2b and I from 2c
Total number of mandibles = 66
Total number of loose mandibular teeth = 74

Table 133 Cattle tooth wear information from Borough High Street (BGH95)

Age	Bone fusion	Period I N	%F	2 N	%F	3 N	%F	4 N	%F
7–10 months	scapula, pelvis	I	100	56	91.07	7	100	3	100
12–18 months	hum d, radius p, Ph1, Ph2	I	100	134	94.78	15	100	12	100
24–36 months	mtc d, tibia d, mtt d	I	100	147	79.59	16	87.5	8	100
36–42 months	ulna, cal, fem p	I	100	37	72.97	9	77.5	4	75.00
42–48 months	rad d, hum p, fem d, tibia p	I	100	103	66.02	-	-	7	57.14

Period I: no infants
Period 3: infant mtt [2010], F/N skull frag [2010]

Age	Bone fusion	Period 2a N	%F	2b N	%F	2c N	%F
7–10 months	scapula, pelvis	34	88.24	5	100	17	94.12
12–18 months	hum d, radius p, Ph1, Ph2	68	97.06	13	100	53	90.57
24–36 months	mtc d, tibia d, mtt d	61	75.40	19	63.16	67	88.06
36–42 months	ulna, cal, fem p	26	69.23	2	100	9	77.78
42–48 months	rad d, hum p, fem d, tibia p	83	63.85	14	78.57	6	66.67

Period 2a: infant ulna [1845], F/N tibia [2220], Infant radius [4072], Infant scapula [4078]
Period 2b: no infants
Period 2c: infant humerus [1070]

Table 134a and b Cattle fusion information from Borough High Street (BGH95)

Age	Tooth sequence	Age class	Period I	2a	2b	2c	3	Total
1–6 months	M1 erupting	A/B	-	0	-	0	-	0
15–26 months	M2 in wear, M3 unworn	C/D	-	I	-	I	-	2
26–30 months	M3 in wear	E/F/G	-	5	I		-	6
3+ years	M3 in heavy wear	H/I	-	7	I	I	-	9
Total			-	13	2	2	-	17

Total number of mandibles = 13
Total number of loose mandibular teeth = 7

Table 135 Cattle tooth wear information from LBI95

Age	Bone fusion	Period I N	%F	2 N	%F	3/4 N	%F
7–10 months	scapula, pelvis	-	-	21	95.24	-	-
12–18 months	hum d, radius p, Ph1, Ph2	-	-	25	96.00	-	-
24–36 months	mtc d, tibia d, mtt d	-	-	32	87.50	I	100
36–42 months	ulna, cal, fem p	-	-	9	22.22	I	0
42–48 months	rad d, hum p, fem d, tibia p	-	-	7	85.71	-	-

Age	Bone fusion	Period 2a N	%F	2b N	%F	2c N	%F
7–10 months	Scapula, pelvis	13	92.3	6	100	2	100
12–18 months	hum d, radius p, Ph1, Ph2	14	100	8	87.5	3	100
24–36 months	mtc d, tibia d, mtt d	23	86.9	7	85.14	2	100
36–42 months	ulna, cal, fem p	7	14.28	0	0	2	50
42–48 months	rad d, hum p, fem d, tibia p	5	100	I	0	I	100

Period 2c: infant mtt [316]

Table 136a and b Cattle fusion information from LBI95

Age	Tooth sequence	Age class	Period I	2a	2b	2c	3	Total
1–6 months	M1 unworn	A	-	-	-	-	-	0
6–12 months	M1 worn, M2 unworn	B	-	-	-	I	-	I
12–24 months	M2 worn	C	-	4	3	I	-	8
2+ years	M3 worn	D		2		2	I	5
Total			0	6	3	4	I	14

No deciduous teeth present
Total number of mandibles = 14
Total number of loose teeth = 11

Table 137 Pig tooth wear information from Borough High Street (BGH95)

Age	Bone fusion	Period I N	%F	2 N	%F	3 N	%F	4 N	%F
Less than 1 year	scapula d, humerus d, radius p, pelvis ace	I	100	36	92.31	3	100	4	100
2–2.5 years	tibia d, Mtp d, phalange 1	-	-	37	24.32	8	25	I	0
3–3.5 years	humerus p, radius d, ulna p, femur (p&d), tibia p	I	0	21	38.09	2	0	I	0
Total		2		94		13		6	

Age	Bone fusion	Period 2a N	%F	2b N	%F	2c N	%F
Less than 1 year	scapula d, humerus d, radius p, pelvis ace	9	88.88	15	100	15	86.67
2–2.5 years	tibia d, Mtp d, phalange 1	20	20.00	6	33.33	11	27.27
3–3.5 years	humerus p, radius d, ulna p, femur (p&d), tibia p	16	43.75	-	-	5	20.00
Total		35		21		31	

Table 138a and b Pig fusion information from Borough High Street (BGH95)

Age	Tooth sequence	Age class	Period I	2a	2b	2c	3	Total
1–6 months	MI unworn	A	-	0	0	0	-	0
6–12 months	MI worn, M2 unworn	B	-	7	4	I	-	12
12–24 months	M2 worn	C	-	3	4	I	-	8
2+ years	M3 worn	D	-	4	3	0	-	7
Total			-	14	11	2	-	27

Some deciduous teeth present
Total number of mandibles = 27
Total number of Loose teeth = I

Table 139 Pig tooth wear information from LBI95

Age	Bone fusion	Period I		Period 2		Period 3	
		N	%F	N	%F	N	%F
Less than I year	scapula d, humerus d, radius p, pelvis ace	-	-	26	68	-	-
2–2.5 years	tibia d, Mtp d, phalange I	-	-	21	14.28	-	-
3–3.5 years	humerus p, radius d, ulna p, femur (p&d), tibia p	-	-	20	5.00	-	-
Total		-	-	67			

Age	Bone fusion	Period 2a		2b		2c	
		N	%F	N	%F	N	%F
Less than I year	scapula d, humerus d, radius p, pelvis ace	14	64.28	7	57.14	5	100
2–2.5 years	tibia d, Mtp d, phalange I	6	16.67	12	16.17	3	0
3–3.5 years	humerus p, radius d, ulna p, femur (p&d), tibia p	11	0	5	20.00	4	0
Total		31		24		12	

Period 2a: Mc3 infant [394], femur and humerus infant [403]

Table 140a and b Pig fusion information from LBI95

Discussion

Diet and status

The bulk of the diet at Borough High Street was supplied by cattle and accords with King's suggestion of the Romanisation of London being accompanied by the increasing popularity of cattle over pigs and sheep/goat (King 1984). This pattern is in line with recent findings at other Roman sites in London, namely Fennings Wharf (Rielly 2001) and Winchester palace (Rielly in prep b); however, it was reversed at LBI95. The same process for pigs as for cattle is cited by King to explain the dominance of the pigs at a small number of sites (King 1984). The high counts for pigs may be an indication of high status. Similar results have been found at Winchester Palace (Rielly in prep b) and a number of Roman bone assemblages within Italy (mostly villa sites) (King 1984).

The wild mammals consumed show much greater diversity at LBI95 than at Borough High Street, with much more frequent occurrences of red deer and hare. Only roe deer was slightly more common at Borough High Street than at LBI95. Species range and quantity of birds were also much more substantial at LBI95, including high-status species such as heron and swan.

LBI95 also showed a greater dependence on chicken, with approximately 30% more chicken recovered from this site than at Borough High Street.

Evidence for other high-status consumption was evident in the recovery of younger animals. A small number of younger individuals were present at Borough High Street, but at LBI95 there was strong evidence for the consumption of suckling pig, young lamb and also veal.

Economy

The majority of the meat evidence recovered from Borough High Street followed a pattern that was best illustrated at the butcher's shop and associated Open Area 11. A two-tier meat supply system was in operation; a small proportion of consumers were able to afford to eat cattle which had been bred specifically for their beef and were killed at the optimum meat return age so as to produce good quality meat. However, the majority of the cattle recovered were far beyond this age, many in excess of seven years old, from which the meat would have been of poor quality. In addition, meat was removed from all areas of the skeleton, indicating exploitation, and thus a market for, even the lowest quality

Age	Tooth sequence	Age class	Period I	2a	2b	2c	3	Total
0–6 months	M1 unworn	A/B		I				I
6–12 months	M1 in wear, M2 unworn	C	2		I			3
1–2 years	M2 in wear, M3 erupting	D					I	I
2–4 years	M3 in wear	E/F		I	I		2	4
4+ years	M3 in heavy wear	G/H/I		I			I	2
Total			2	3	2	0	4	10

No loose dp4s
Total number of mandibles = 8
Total number of loose teeth = 7

Table 141 Sheep/goat tooth wear information from Borough High Street (BGH95)

Age	Bone fusion	Period I N	%F	2 N	%F	3 N	%F	4 N	%F
3–10 months	*	-	-	35	51.43	2	50.00	2	00.0
15–24 months	tibia d, Mtt d, Mtc d.	-	-	21	23.81	2	00.00	1	100
3–3.5 years	Cal, femur (p&d), tibia p, ulna, radius d, humerus p	2	50.00	10	40.00	1	00.00	-	-
Total		2		66		5		3	

* bones fused by this age are scapula (distal), pelvis (acetabulum), humerus (distal), radius (proximal), phalanges 1 and 2

Age	Bone fusion	Period 2a N	%F	2b N	%F	2c N	%F
3–10 months	*	17	52.90	7	42.86	11	54.54
15–24 months	tibia d, Mtt d, Mtc d	14	14.28	3	33.33	4	50.00
3–3.5 years	cal, femur (p&d), tibia p, ulna, radius d, humerus p	4	75.00	3	00.00	3	33.33
Total		35		13		18	

Table 142a and b Sheep/goat fusion information from Borough High Street (BGH95)

beef. A high percentage of the bones were then further processed to facilitate the removal of marrow. The presence of these smashed and heavily butchered bones at the shop indicates that this stage of processing was carried out on the butcher's premises and the product was then sold on to consumers, rather than them doing it themselves, as is more common.

As the old age of the cattle and the butchery were consistent throughout the surrounding area of the butcher's shop, it is evident that there was a successful meat distribution network operating.

One question that arose during the analysis for this report was whether the butcher's shop was supplying the military. This proposition now seems highly unlikely. During prosperous times the military would probably have used the highest quality meat available to them, and during times of stress they would have had to settle for whatever was on offer. The butcher's shop represents prolonged exploitation of poor produce, while LBI95 indicates that higher quality meat was continually available in the vicinity.

Animals could have contributed secondary, non-meat products to the economy, both in life and after death. The large percentage of older cattle recovered from Borough High Street

indicates that they were not primarily bred for beef. Live cattle have two main uses other than meat: dairy and traction. They would only have been slaughtered for meat once their original usage became unproductive and/or uneconomical. The lack of gender information available for the cattle, due to heavily smashed and butchered fragments, limits useful discussion. However, a number of pathologies directly associated with stress on draught cattle were recorded, but these may only be a result of old age.

A small percentage of sheep were culled at maximum meat return point but the majority were slaughtered after they had reached maturity. The mature sheep could have been exploited for milk, but their primary value (if not meat) would have been for their wool. In both cases the animals were then imported 'on the hoof' to the sites to be killed.

There was limited evidence for on-site breeding. This is based on the small number of neonatal/foetal animals recovered, both cattle and pigs. As discussed above, it would have been easy and advantageous for a household to rear a small number of pigs. Chickens could also have been bred by a household, in order to provide meat and eggs; there is some evidence for this from the eggshell (below, 11.9).

Age	Tooth sequence	Age class	Period					Total
			I	2a	2b	2c	3/4	
0–6 months	MI unworn	A/B	-	0	0	I	0	I
6–12 months	MI in wear, M2 unworn	C	-	0	2	0	0	2
I–2 years	M2 in wear, M3 erupting	D	-	I	0	0	0	I
2–4 years	M3 in wear	E/F	-	I	0	I	I	3
4+ years	M3 in heavy wear	G/H/I	-	0	2	0	0	2
Total			-	2	4	2	I	9

No loose dp4s
Total number of mandibles = 9
Total number of loose teeth = I

Table 143 *Sheep/goat tooth wear information from LBI95*

Age	Bone fusion	Period					
		I		2		3/4	
		N	%F	N	%F	N	%F
3–10 months	*	-	-	8	0	-	-
15–24 months	tibia d, Mtt d, Mtc d.	-	-	15	13.33	-	-
3–3.5 years	cal, femur (p&d), tibia p, ulna, radius d, humerus p	-	-	15	33.33	-	-
Total		-		38		-	

* bones fused by this age are scapula (distal), pelvis (acetabulum), humerus (distal), radius (proximal), phalanges I and 2

Age	Bone fusion	Period					
		2a		2b		2c	
		N	%F	N	%F	N	%F
3–10 months	*	4	0	2	0	2	0
15–24 months	tibia d, Mtt d, Mtc d.	8	25.00	5	0	2	0
3–3.5 years	cal, femur (p&d), tibia p, ulna, radius d, humerus p	10	40.00	I	0	4	25
Total		22		8		8	

Period 2a: infant humerus, radius and tibia [428], scapula [444]

Table 144a and b *Sheep/goat fusion information from LBI95*

Industry

Strong evidence was present on Borough High Street for a number of craft industries. The assemblage recovered within Building 10 (the butcher's shop) was typical of the bones (the skull, horncores and feet) which would remain attached to the hide before its removal to the tanner's. These bones would have remained attached to the slippery hide to make it easier for the tanner to stretch the hide out to allow it to dry and further prepare the skin. It seems reasonable to assume that a butcher working with this quantity of animals would have a maintained a working relationship with the local tanner and passed the skins on to him. Further evidence for tanning was the recurring low quantity of phalanges recovered from bone dumps throughout the sites. Where phalanges were recovered they commonly had transverse knife marks consistent with the removal of hides.

There is a strong likelihood that, if a system for the removal of hides to tanneries was established, then a further network for the exploitation of horn would also have existed. There is no evidence for large-scale hornworking on the sites, but it seems likely that there was a 'horner's' in the near vicinity. However, there was evidence for the working of horn, both of sheep and cattle, on a small individual scale.

Like horn, bone had also been worked on an individual basis, with isolated examples being recovered from all areas and periods. For example, at Open Area 24 (BGH95) three worked cattle metatarsals were recovered; they had all been consistently sawn with a fine blade 35mm in from the proximal end.

Ritual

There was very limited evidence for any ritual activities involving animals on the sites falling within the confines of the project. Only one positive identification of such ritual activity was recovered. Building 5 from LBI95 contained a 'cooking pit' from which burnt remains of two very juvenile pig heads and a number of unidentified fish remains were recovered. The bones had been burnt to such a degree that it could not be considered the result of an accident. The usage of pig accords with recent findings by Lauwerier (cited in Sidell and Rielly 1998) during a study of Roman food offerings, where he found a dominance of chicken and pig bones. However, this deposit differs from his material in two ways. Firstly, most of his ritual deposits are associated with human burials, and secondly, they are thought to represent entire meals. Clearly this deposit is neither. A limited number of similar 'ritual' deposits, which are not associated with human remains, have been recovered from Roman London. A complete calcinated sheep skeleton was recovered from a posthole-like feature at Sommerton Way, Thamesmead (Rielly 1998) and a scattering of calcined sheep/goat remains were found within an early Roman ditch, which was possibly associated with a temple, at Franks' Sandpit, Betchworth (Pipe in prep b). A complete unburnt ox head was recovered from below the floor level at Courage's Brewery (Pipe in prep a), and most likely represents a foundation deposit. In view of the close association with Building 5 at LBI95, it is possible that this ritual deposit is a foundation deposit or a subsequent act designed to gain the favour of the gods.

An adult heron tarso-metatarsus was recovered from Open Area 9 at LBI95 (AD 100–20). It has been suggested that heron may have been associated with ritual activities during the Roman period at the east London Roman cemeteries site (Rielly 2000). However, at that site the heron was represented by an entire skeleton recovered alongside a dog skeleton, in conjunction with a noticeable absence of 'normal' domestic refuse. Heron bones have been found in London deposits of this period (West n d), in each case – like here – as part of a general dump.

11.9 The eggshell

Jane Sidell

Introduction

Assessment of the biological remains from samples collected during the excavations at Borough High Street indicated the presence of 16 samples of eggshell from well-stratified Roman deposits (Sidell 1997). Additionally, three assemblages from LBI95 (located close to the Ticket Hall site) were recovered. These are also dated to the Roman period, and are discussed here for convenience. Good potential was demonstrated for addressing research objective C (Drummond-Murray and Swain 1997) through analysis of the samples:

'What were the characteristics and functions of [the] buildings and other structures, through time?'

Methodology

The samples were immersed in water-filled flasks and placed in an ultrasonic tank to remove any soil adhering to the shell. The water was changed until no more soil was observed. Samples were rinsed, placed in petri dishes and air-dried. Each assemblage was scanned under a low-power binocular microscope at magnifications of x10–30. Preliminary groupings were made based on gross morphology and descriptions are given below in Table 145. Each fragment was assigned to a group and

representative fragments were then examined for pore count (external surface) and thickness measurement. These were made using an eyepiece graticule and calibrated to millimetres. Subsamples were taken from the groups and mounted on Cambridge type aluminium stubs with conductive carbon cement prior to scanning electron microscopy (SEM). The stubs were coated with gold under vacuum in an inert atmosphere to aid conductivity. These samples were subjected to image analysis using the SEM at magnifications of up to x1000. Counts of the mammillae on the internal surface were made using a magnification of x200. Photographs were made to assist identification, which was done with reference to a comparative collection (Sidell 1993). Further details of this technique may be found elsewhere (Sidell 1991).

Results

The descriptions of the preliminary groups identified may be found in Table 145. Table 146 shows the occurrence of these groups with the contextual information appended.

Discussion

BGH95

(See Table 146; Table 148)

IST CENTURY
Five deposits can be dated with certainty to the 1st century. These are, with one exception, from features in a series of open areas. The final one comes from the Boudican fire debris. The nature of the features suggests that the deposits are generally rubbish piles which had been utilised and accumulated in available space. Sample {416}, from the fill of a well, contains goose as well as chicken. Interestingly, several of the fragments of chicken egg show signs of having hatched. This indicates that chickens were being kept in this area for breeding as well as for their eggs. The goose is the only non-chicken identification made from Borough High Street. Although this may be significant and suggest that goose was preferred in the earlier period of occupation, the sample size is rather low. A further possibility is that the area was less developed before the Boudican revolt, and more open space was available for keeping birds, geese requiring more room than chickens.

2ND CENTURY
Nine samples come from the 2nd century, from a range of deposits; however, four of these are from the blacksmith's area. One of the samples again shows signs that eggs had hatched, and therefore indicates breeding as well as food production. A smithy is a rather unusual location for this, so it may simply be that rubbish deposits had accumulated here, in the occupation horizons. It is probable that the food waste may have derived from the occupants of the smithy, and was sufficiently small to be dropped on the floor and ignored; but the hatched material cannot have come into the deposit via this mechanism. One possibility is that the eggs were kept in the warm to assist incubation.

Type	Internal surface	External surface
A	White, crystalline, poorly defined mammillae	Flat, cream matt undulating with well defined pore openings
B	Yellow with well defined mammillae	Brown matt, rough with well defined pore openings

Table 145 Surface descriptions of eggshell

Context no.	Sample no.	Feature type	Date	Types
[446]	{26}	ditch fill OA8	AD 120–50	A
[1161]	{136}	occupation horizon B13	AD 70–160	A
[1265]	{153}	dump OA24	AD 140–60	A
[1337]	{159}	hearth spread S2 (blacksmith's)	2nd century AD	A
[1381]	{161}	pit fill OA24	2nd century AD	A
[1470]	{172}	dump OA45	2nd/3rd century AD	A
[1508]	{178}	occupation horizon S2 (blacksmith's)	mid 2nd century AD	A
[1508]	{183}	occupation horizon S2 (blacksmith's)	mid 2nd century AD	A
[1615]	{601}	occupation horizon S2 (blacksmith's)	AD 100–20	A
[1636]	{608}	pit fill B22	c AD 120	A
[1878]	{659}	Boudican burning OA10	AD 61	A
[1929]	{665}	pit fill OA11	AD 60–70	A
[2223]	{225}	ditch fill OA5	AD 50–60	A
[4136]	{416}	well fill OA19	AD 50–60	A, B
[4143]	{414}	pit fill OA8	AD 70–?	A
[6041]	{672}	dump OA2	AD 50–60	A

Table 146 Context details and types of eggshell present from BGH95

Context no.	Sample no.	Feature type	Date	Types
[322]	{109}	posthole fill B5	AD 100–20	A
[351]	{114}	pit fill OA10	AD 140+	A
[412]	{117}	dump OA9	AD 100–20	A, B

Table 147 Context details and types of eggshell present from LBI95

Context no.	Sample no.	Type	Thickness	Pore count	Identification
[446]	{26}	A	0.3mm	2/mm^2	Chicken
[1161]	{136}	A	0.3mm	1.56/mm^2	Chicken
[1265]	{153}	A	0.3mm	2.6/mm^2	Chicken
[1337]	{159}	A	0.3mm	1.9/mm^2	Chicken
[1381]	{161}	A	0.275mm	2.5/mm^2	Chicken
[1470]	{172}	A	0.3mm	1.9/mm^2	Chicken
[1508]	{178}	A	0.3mm	2/mm^2	Chicken
[1508]	{183}	A	0.3mm	2.25/mm^2	Chicken
[1615]	{601}	A	0.3mm	1.6/mm^2	Chicken
[1636]	{608}	A	0.325mm	1.8/mm^2	Chicken
[1878]	{659}	A	0.3mm	2.3/mm^2	Chicken
[1929]	{665}	A	0.275mm	2.1/mm^2	Chicken
[2223]	{225}	A	0.3mm	2.7/mm^2	Chicken
[4136]	{416}	A	0.3mm	2.25/mm^2	Chicken
[4136]	{416}	B	0.55mm	1.3/mm^2	Goose
[4143]	{414}	A	0.3mm	2/mm^2	Chicken
[6041]	{672}	A	0.3mm	1.9/mm^2	Chicken

Table 148 Identification table of eggshell samples from BGH95

The remaining samples come from a range of features, again indicating general waste disposal. Two of these are associated with buildings, Building 13 and Building 22. This may indicate that these buildings had people living, or at least eating, in them. All fragments were identified as chicken and none appear to be from hatched eggs. This shows that chicken eggs continued to be eaten throughout the 2nd century.

OTHER

One sample is from a deposit dated to the 2nd/3rd century, and one from later than AD 70. These both come from debris in open areas, again suggesting opportunistic food waste disposal of chicken eggshell.

LBI95

(See Table 147)

The three samples from this site date from the 2nd century, although the *terminus post quem* for [351] is uncertain. Sample {109} comes from a posthole associated with Building 5, and could therefore relate to the building's construction or destruction, either of which could have led to the deposition of material in a posthole. In either case, it is likely that the shell derives from food waste of the people associated with this building, whether they were constructing it, using it or living in it.

The other two samples come from deposits in the open areas, again waste disposal unfortunately not associated with buildings. However, both of these included goose eggshell, and some fragments of this were from hatched eggs. This suggests that goose breeding was taking place in an least one area of the site, and over a period of time in the 2nd century. One reason why breeding might have been relatively more prevalent at LBI95 than at BGH95 is the relative distance from the commercial centre and the consequently greater availability of space.

Conclusions

Eggshell was found in a range of deposits across the BGH95 and LBI95 sites. The majority of this was from 2nd-century contexts, although both 1st- and possibly 3rd-century features were also represented. Chicken eggshell was dominant, but goose was also present on both sites. The eggshell derived predominantly from cut features in open areas and is likely to be from general waste deposits. Several contexts are directly associated with buildings, most notably the smithy, from which four distinct assemblages were recovered. The evidence suggests that breeding of both chicken and geese was taking place in addition to egg production for food.

11.10 Archaeological conservation on the Jubilee Line Extension Project

Elizabeth Goodman

Introduction

Conservation has been involved with the Jubilee Line Extension excavations both in the field and at the post-excavation stages. Conservation involvement has been wide-ranging, providing advice on how to deal with freshly excavated material on site, carrying out specialised lifting techniques for especially large objects, and treating many of the finds in preparation for their study, display, or long-term storage. Detailed research on specific items has also been carried out.

Objects which have survived to the point of excavation have done so by reaching a relative equilibrium with their burial environment. With the disruption of this relatively stable state, artefacts are now perhaps at their most vulnerable. The artefacts from these excavations have therefore been stored, treated and packaged in accordance with best practice and with the Museum of London's archive guidelines (Museum of London 1998). Materials identification and investigative conservation were carried out using microscopic examination, X-radiography, and, in some cases, chemical spot test and/or by using sophisticated analytical

equipment such as X-ray fluorescence (XRF) or X-ray diffraction (XRD). Where these techniques have been carried out, the results have been incorporated into the catalogue and/or discussed in detail below. Conservation of selected objects was carried out with the aim of 'minimum intervention', wherever possible using reversible techniques. Objects were subsequently packed in archive-quality material and placed in suitable storage conditions.

Lifting of Mayor Sworder's Arches Roman mosaic floor

Virginia Neal and Kirsten Suenson-Taylor

It was decided that the mosaic floor (Fig 103) should be lifted and mounted by conservation in such a way that the mosaic could be used in temporary displays about the archaeology of the Jubilee Line Extension.

The surface of the mosaic was exposed, and soil and dirt removed. A layer of Bindflex (polyvinyl acetate emulsion) was brushed onto the tesserae and a layer of muslin laid over the top. A second layer of adhesive was then applied, and the edges of the mosaic were secured by the application of further adhesive and facing material. Since conditions on the site were damp, the adhesive was dried with the aid of a hot air blower.

When dry the mosaic was cut into sections, with care being taken to avoid straight cuts, which would have been visible when the mosaic was on display. Each section had to be manageable, and so they were all cut to a size no greater than one metre square. Metal sheets were eased under the bedding mortar to separate the tesserae from the mortar base. Each piece of mosaic was sandwiched securely between wooden boards and lifted out of the deep trench to be transported to the Museum of London. (For greater detail of this technique see Goodburn Brown 1992.)

In the laboratory the first task was to remove degraded mortar from the back of the tesserae. The remaining mortar was consolidated with Paraloid B72 and a synthetic filler was applied to the back of the tesserae as a replacement for the mortar which had been removed. This was followed by a layer of foaming epoxy resin, chosen because it is both lightweight and strong. The muslin facing material was then removed by the application of a solvent gel and minimal cosmetic work carried out.

Each mosaic section has been mounted onto Aerolam, a strong, rigid, lightweight fibreglass board developed for use in the aerospace industry. This has allowed the mosaic to be transported safely between temporary displays and the MoLAS stores. Once a permanent display location is decided upon, further cosmetic work may be carried out and the mount board painted as appropriate.

Conservation treatments

Of the nearly 2600 small finds recovered from the Jubilee Line excavations only 296 artefacts received some form of active conservation treatment. The treatment of only 11.5% of the registered finds is not unusual. It is standard practice to prioritise objects with the finds specialist at the assessment stage, and consequently only artefacts which may provide information that is important in the interpretation of a site will be treated. Within any given site, this prioritisation results in only 10–15% of the finds actually receiving active conservation treatment.

Metals

Copper alloy artefacts make up the bulk of the treated small finds archive. Most conservation work on metal artefacts begins with visual examination under a binocular microscope, with reference to X-radiographs, followed by mechanical cleaning using scalpel and other hand tools. Occasionally other mechanical devices such as air-abrasive and power-pen or mini-drill are used. Mechanical cleaning will reveal detail and a more uniform surface beneath often voluminous corrosion products, enabling the true shape and purpose of the artefact to be understood. During the removal of the corrosion it was apparent that a lot of organic remains were preserved within this voluminous mass. It would appear that such residues originated from the surrounding open areas and dumps. A possible reason for its inclusion in such quantities is that the metals corroded quickly once lost in the ground, acting as a bactericide and thus promoting ideal conditions for the preservation of organics. It is MoLAS policy to only partially clean, as necessary, coins and other metal objects if the treatment is intended for identification purposes only. This approach is more cost-effective, and since artefacts are not usually stripped of their corrosion and other burial deposits, these may be used in future research. However, this approach may set up instability problems for the future (Scott 1994).

After removal of soil and corrosion to reveal detail, copper alloys are stabilised with a corrosion inhibitor (benzotriazole) and coated with a protective acrylic lacquer also containing a corrosion inhibitor (Incralac). Ferrous artefacts are treated using an appropriate corrosion inhibitor (alkaline sulphite, tannic acid, TEA or Shell VPI), coated with an acrylic lacquer, and then stored in a desiccated environment.

Waterlogged materials

Only a small quantity of waterlogged material was recovered from the Jubilee Line excavations, the majority from a well on LBB95. This material had to be treated and dried, as wet material lacks strength and can be easily damaged. The stabilisation of the artefacts permits handling and study and thus conforms to the Museum of London archive transfer guidelines. In the case of wood, polyethylene glycol (PEG, molecular weights 200 and 4000) was used to bulk the wood, replacing burial water and protecting the cell structure during freeze-drying. Leather artefacts were treated using glycerol as a stabilising agent and cryogenic protector before freeze-drying.

Miscellaneous materials

Other materials such as glass, bone, ivory and shale were recovered from both aerobic and anoxic conditions. Those found in waterlogged environments also required special treatment before transfer to the archive to enable study. These materials were consolidated and/or dried using solvents.

The effect of burial conditions on preservation of copper alloy

It appears that much of the copper alloy from BGH95 and JSS92 is actively corroding in storage, and in the worst cases the object had disintegrated, resulting in total loss of information. At the assessment stage of the project, three of the identified small finds from BGH95 appeared to be actively disintegrating into a bright green powder. Six months later, at the beginning of the analysis phase, the number of copper alloy objects that had disintegrated had risen to at least six. Other objects from BGH95 and JSS92 were also exhibiting some signs of this corrosion product, including JSS92 [7] <1>, an object conserved and stabilised with benzotriazole at the beginning of 1992.

Samples of the bright green corrosion product from BGH95 [181] <2> (a possible armour fragment, of Roman date), and BGH95 [908] <799> (one of the disintegrated unidentified small finds), were sent to the Ancient Monuments Laboratory for analysis by XRD. It was found that the main constituent of the bright green powder was paratacamite, $Cu_2(OH)_3Cl$, which is the final product in a process sometimes called bronze disease. This product will promote further corrosion in a cyclical manner, actively causing the copper alloy to disintegrate. It is possible to actively treat this type of corrosion, but this would involve removing all corrosion products from the copper alloy, stabilising by immersion in benzotriazole and spot-treatment of active sites with silver oxide for all the copper alloy in the site archives. This is time-consuming and would not be cost-effective. Thus, if the copper alloy is to survive in the archive, a simple and cost-effective system must be devised to try and retard this process.

There is no simple way of preventing this deterioration but some steps can be taken to limit it. The great bulk of the archive appeared to be stable, but it was decided to deal with the whole of the Jubilee Line archive as a preventative measure. Corrosion mechanisms indicate that paratacamite is only active above a relative humidity (RH) of 35%; thus, by keeping RH down and fluctuations in temperature and RH to a minimum it is possible retard the rate of corrosion. All the copper alloy was first repacked using either Jiffy foam (polyethylene) or crystal boxes (polystyrene) containing acid-free tissue. This will act to support the artefacts whilst in storage, thereby minimising any physical damage. The objects were then placed in Stewart boxes (polyethylene) with desiccated silica gel. The desiccant was changed a fortnight later to ensure that the RH in the box was brought down to below 15%. This should ensure that the rate of corrosion is slowed and that further disintegration will not take place.

There have been only a few isolated cases of bronze disease in finds from MoLAS excavations in London. These sites from the Jubilee Line excavations can be considered to be unusual because of the high number of objects exhibiting signs of active corrosion and the poor preservation of the artefacts in general. The only sites that appear to be affected are BGH95, JSS92 and STU92 (only ten copper alloy artefacts were excavated from STU92; the corrosion is visually similar to BGH95 and one item is exhibiting similar corrosion to that confirmed as paratacamite). All three sites were situated beneath Borough High Street. This suggests that it may be the local burial environment under the road that is causing the copper alloy to decay in this manner. One possible explanation for the presence of chloride ions in the burial environment is that they are derived from the dissolution of rock salt, used for gritting the roads in winter. The chloride ions are then contained in rainwater running off the road, and could have gradually percolated through the soil into the burial environment. A fourth site, BTJ93, was also situated beneath Borough High Street, but as only two copper alloy items were recovered here the sample is too small to be considered significant.

FRENCH AND GERMAN SUMMARIES

Résumé

La construction de l'extension de la Jubilee Line a donné aux archéologues des services archéologiques du Musée de Londres l'occasion de rechercher l'archéologie des quartiers de Londres traversés par la nouvelle ligne de métro. Les tunnels passent bien au-dessous des niveaux archéologiques, mais chaque embranchement entre les tunnels et la surface – puits d'accès, cages d'ascenseurs, bouches d'aération, nouvelles stations – représentait un danger pour les restes. On a donc fait des recherches dans ces endroits entre 1991 et 1996.

Ce volume traite des résultats des travaux entrepris à l'intérieur et aux alentours de la gare de London Bridge sur des couches datant de l'époque romaine. Les fouilles principales ont porté sur la nouvelle aire de guichets donnant sur Borough High Street et ont été effectuées en 1995 durant six mois. Pendant la période préhistorique, la topographie du nord de Southwark était composée de plusieurs îles de sable peu élevées mais faisant saillie hors de portée des marées de la Tamise. On a pu étudier l'agencement de l'île située le plus au nord sur laquelle se trouvait la partie sud du premier pont de Londres construit par les romains. Sur le côté est de l'île, on a relevé en particulier la présence d'une anse jusque-là inconnue dans le Guy's Channel.

Les restes romains les plus anciens étaient constitués de plusieurs grandes fosses de carrières et de fossés d'évacuation. Les fosses servaient à l'extraction du gravier pour la construction de la route menant au pont, les fossés pour assécher les terrains inondables. Le tracé de la route menant au pont fut confirmé par les fouilles et on a également fouillé les premiers bâtiments en bois situés du côté est de cette route. L'un de ces bâtiments aurait pu être l'atelier d'un forgeron. Une allée étroite partait du côté est de la route principale. Tous les huit bâtiments placés le long de la route (sur une longueur de 60m) furent brûlés aux environs de 60 après J.-C. Cela représente sûrement un épisode du sac de Londres pendant la révolte de Boudica en 60/1 après J.-C. De petites surfaces de destruction datant de cette époque avaient été relevées à Southwark, ce qui suggère que l'agglomération au sud de la rivière avait été également détruite; cependant les fouilles extensives de la Jubilee Line ont fourni des éléments plus solides pour soutenir cette thèse.

Les bâtiments situés le long de la route ont été reconstruits peu après l'incendie. Un bâtiment en pierre fut construit sur le côté nord tandis que des bâtiments en bois ont été élevés le long du reste de la route. L'atelier d'un forgeron montrant plusieurs phases d'activité a été identifié et une boucherie fut aussi fouillée. Des allées étroites partant de l'est de la route principale nord–sud menant au pont furent trouvées ainsi que plusieurs canalisations en bois. Pendant la première partie du 2ème siècle une colonnade fut construite le long de la route, et un groupe de bâtiments en pierre formait peut-être un marché couvert de petite taille. Plus tard dans ce siècle un bâtiment contenant une grande quantité de grains de céréales – peut-être une boulangerie – fut placé le long de la route. Derrière ce bâtiment il y avait une surface à ciel ouvert comprenant des cours et des puits.

En retrait de la route, à l'est, un grand bâtiment en pierre construit à la fin du 1er siècle était peut-être un entrepôt. Il y avait aussi des traces d'assèchement des terres sur une grande échelle sur les bords est de l'île. Ce quartier est peut-être devenu un quartier résidentiel car un bâtiment de haut standing du 2ème siècle y a été fouillé; plus tard, au 3ème siècle, on y a construit un bâtiment garni de mosaïques.

A l'ouest de la route une autre partie de la *mansio* fouillée auparavant (Cowan 1992) fut retrouvée; elle avait des murs en plâtre peints de haute qualité. De plus amples informations sur le Southwark Street Channel qui séparait les îles nord et sud du Southwark romain furent aussi rassemblées ainsi que quelques tombes, bien qu'un véritable cimetière ne fut pas retrouvé.

Le programme archéologique fut entièrement financé, y compris les frais de publication, par London Underground Limited (le projet de prolongation de la Jubilee Line).

Zusammenfassung

Die Bauarbeiten an der Verlängerung der Jubilee Line gaben Archäologen des Museum of London Archaeology Service Gelegenheit, die Archäologie in den Gegenden Londons, die von der neuen Untergrundbahn durchquert sind, zu untersuchen. Die Tunnel selber liegen weit unterhalb jeglicher archäologischer Schichten. Jedoch jede Verbindung zwischen Tunnel und Erdoberfläche wie Notausgänge, Luft- und Rolltreppenschächte, sowie neue Stationen, stellten eine mögliche Bedrohung für die Archäologie dar. Alle diese Baumaßnahmen wurden zwischen 1991 und 1996 untersucht.

Der vorliegende Band behandelt die Arbeitsergebnisse für die römische Periode in und um den Bahnhof von London Bridge. Die Hauptausgrabung fand unter der neuen Fahrkartenschalterhalle in Borough High Street statt und dauerte sechs Monate im Jahr 1995. In vorgeschichtlicher Zeit bestand die Topographie im Norden von Southwark aus einer Reihe niedriger Sandinseln, die sich aus dem Tidefluß der Themse erhoben. Die Linienführung der nördlichsten Insel, auf der das südliche Ende der ersten römischen Londoner Brücke stand, wurde weiter aufgeklärt. Insbesondere wurde eine bisher unbekannte kleine Bucht des Guy's Channel auf der Ostseite der Insel festgestellt.

Die frühesten Funde aus römischer Zeit waren eine Anzahl großer Kiesgruben und Drainagegräben: erstere dienten der Kiesgewinnung für den Bau der Straße zur Brücke, letztere der Entwässerung des der Flut ausgesetzten Landes. Die Trassenführung der Straße zur Brücke wurde bestätigt und erste Fachwerkhäuser auf ihrer Ostseite ausgegraben. Eines der Häuser mag eine Schmiedewerkstatt gewesen sein. Eine schmale Gasse verlief von der Hauptstraße nach Osten. Alle acht Gebäude an der Straße (auf einer Strecke von 60m) brannten um 60 n.Chr. nieder. Die Ursache dafür ist fast sicher in der Plünderung *Londiniums* während des Boudica-Aufstandes um 61 n.Chr. zu suchen. Kleinere Zerstörungen diesen Datums hatte man in Southwark schon früher gefunden. Sie ließen vermuten, daß auch die Siedlung südlich des Flusses geplündert wurde. Das große Ausmaß der Jubilee-Ausgrabungen lieferte überzeugenden Nachweis hierfür.

Die Gebäude entlang der Straße wurden kurz nach dem Brand wieder aufgebaut. Ein Steingebäude wurde am Nordende errichtet, während die übrigen Häuser entlang der Straße wieder aus Fachwerk bestanden. Es wurde auch eine Schmiede mit mehreren Gebrauchsphasen und ein Schlachterladen gefunden. Schmale Gassen, die von der nord–südlich verlaufenden Brückenstraße nach Osten abzweigten, wurden freigelegt, wie auch eine Reihe von hölzernen Drainagen entlang der Straße. Im ersten Teil des 2. Jahrhunderts wurde eine Kollonade entlang der Straße errichtet und eine Anzahl Steinhäuser mögen zu einer kleinen Markthalle gehört haben. Ein Gebäude mit einer großen Menge an Getreideresten – möglicherweise eine Bäckerei – aus dem späteren Teil des Jahrhunderts wurde entlang der Straße gefunden. Hinter den Gebäuden war das Land unbebaut und enthielt Hofoberflächen und Brunnen.

Weiter von der Straße entfernt und östlich eines großen, im späten 1. Jahrhundert errichteten Steinhauses mag ein Speicher gestanden haben. Es gab auch Anzeichen für ausgedehnte Landgewinnung am Ostrand der Insel. Dort mag eine Wohngegend entstanden sein, da ein Gebäude aus dem 2. Jahrhundert mit Anzeichen für gehobenen sozialen Rang sowie ein jüngerer Gebäude aus dem 3. Jahrhundert mit Mosaikboden hier ausgegraben wurden.

Westlich der Straße wurde ein weiterer Teil des schon früher ausgegrabenen *Mansio* (Cowan 1992) mit hochwertiger Wandmalerei freigelegt. Weitere Informationen wurden zum Southwark Street Channel, der die Nord- und Südinseln voneinander trennte, aufgezeichnet. Auch wurden einige Bestattungen freigelegt, aber nichts, was man einen Friedhof nennen könnte.

Die gesamten archäologischen Arbeiten bis hin zur Publikation, wurden von London Underground Limited (Jubilee Line Extension Project) finanziert.

BIBLIOGRAPHY

Allason-Jones, L, 1985 Bell-shaped studs?, in *The production and distribution of Roman military equipment: proceedings of the Second Roman Military Equipment Research Seminar* (ed M C Bishop), BAR Int Ser 275, 95–108, Oxford

Allason-Jones, L, and Miket, R, 1984 *The catalogue of small finds from South Shields Roman fort*, Newcastle upon Tyne

Anderberg, A-L, 1994 *Atlas of seeds and small fruits of north-west European plant species: Part 4, Resedaceae–Umbelliferae*, Stockholm

Armitage, P L, 1982 A system for ageing and sexing the horn cores of cattle from British post medieval sites (17th to early 18th century) with special reference to unimproved British Longhorn cattle, in Wilson et al, 37–54

Atkinson, D, 1914 A hoard of samian ware from Pompeii, *J Roman Stud* 4, 27–64

Bailey, D M, 1988 *A catalogue of the lamps in the British Museum: III, Roman provincial lamps*, London

Baker, J, and Brothwell, D, 1980 *Animal diseases in archaeology*, London

Barber, B, and Bowsher, D, 2000 *The eastern cemetery of Roman London: excavations 1983–1990*, MoLAS Monogr Ser 4, London

Baudoux, J, 1998 Les Amphores à Strasbourg: fouilles récentes du tramway (Homme de Fer) et de la rue Hannong, in Laubenheimer, 91–105

Baudoux, J, Bocquet, A, Brulet, R, Laubenheimer, F, Marlière, E, and Vilvorder, F, 1998 La Production des amphores dans l'Est et le Nord des Gaules, in Laubenheimer, 11–48

Beal, J-C, and Feugère, M, 1983 Les Pyxides gallo-romaines en os de Gaule méridionale, *Documents d'Archéologie Méridionale* 6, 115–26

Beijerinck, W, 1947 *Zadenatlas der Nederlandsche flora*, Wageningen

Berggren, G, 1969 *Atlas of seeds and small fruits of north-west European plant species: Part 2, Cyperaceae*, Stockholm

Berggren, G, 1981 *Atlas of seeds and small fruits of north-west European plant species: Part 3, Saliaceae–Crucifereae*, Stockholm

Betts, I M, 1985 A scientific investigation of the brick and tile industry of York to the mid-eighteenth century, unpub PhD thesis, Univ Bradford

Betts, I M, 1987 Ceramic building material: recent work in London, *Archaeol Today* 9 26–8

Betts, I M, 1995 Procuratorial tile stamps from London, *Britannia* 26, 207–29

Betts, I M, and Foot, R, 1994 A newly identified late Roman tile group from southern England, *Britannia* 25, 21–34

Betts, I M, Black, E W, and Gower, J, 1994 A corpus of Roman relief-patterned tiles in Roman Britain, *J Roman Pottery Stud* 7, 1–167

Bird, D G, 1994 The origins of Roman London, *London Archaeol* 7(10), 268–70

Bird, J, Graham, A H, Sheldon, H L, and Townend, P (eds), 1978 *Southwark excavations 1972–74*, London Middlesex Archaeol Soc and Surrey Archaeol Soc Joint Pub 1, London

Bishop, M C, 1991 Soldiers and military equipment in the towns of Roman Britain, in *Roman Frontier Studies 1989: proceedings of the XVth International Congress of Roman Frontier Studies* (eds V A Maxfield and M J Dobson), 21–7, Exeter

Bishop, M C, and Coulston, J C N, 1993 *Roman military equipment*, London

Blagg, T F C, 1990 Building stone in Roman Britain, in *Stone quarrying and building in England: AD 43–1525* (ed D Parsons), 33–50, Chichester

Blows, J, 1998 Moulded stone from BSE94: report on the geological assessment of rock fragments for the Museum of London Archaeology Service, unpub MoLAS archive rep

Bluer, R, and Brigham, T, with Nielsen, R, in prep *Excavations at Lloyd's Register, London*, MoLAS Monogr Ser

Boardman, S, and Jones, G, 1990 Experiments on the effects of charring on cereal plant components, *J Archaeol Sci* 17, 1–11

Boersted, M den, 1956 *The bronze vessels in the Rijksmuseum G. M. Kam at Nijmegen*, Nijmegen

Borgard, P, 1994 L'Origine liparote des amphores 'Richborough 527' et la détermination de leur contenu, *SFECAG, Actes du Congrès de Millau*, 197–203

Boon, G, 1974 *Silchester: the Roman town of Calleva*, Newton Abbot

Branigan, K, and Dearne, M J, 1990 The Romano-British finds from Wookey Hole: an appraisal, *Proc Somerset Archaeol Natur Hist Soc* 134, 57–80

Brickley, M, and Miles, A, with Stainer, H, 1999 *The Cross Bones burial ground, Redcross Way, Southwark, London: archaeological excavations (1991–1998) for the London Underground Limited Jubilee Line Extension Project*, MoLAS Monogr Ser 3, London

Brigham, T, 1990 The late Roman waterfront in London, *Britannia* 21, 99–183

Brigham, T, Goodburn, D, and Tyers, I, with Dillon, J, 1995 A Roman timber building on the Southwark waterfront, London, *Archaeol J* 152, 1–72

Brigham, T, and Watson, B, in prep *Report on the excavations at Regis House, 1994–6*, MoLAS Monogr Ser

Brodribb, G, 1987 *Roman brick and tile*, Gloucester

Brown, A E, and Sheldon, H L, 1974 Highgate Wood: the pottery and its production, *London Archaeol* 2(9), 223–31

Burnham, B, and Wacher, J, 1990 *The small towns of Roman Britain*, Berkeley, Calif.

Butcher, K, 1992 The Maidenhatch Farm hoard of Constantinian copies, *Numis Chron* 152, 160–74

Callender, M, 1965 *Roman amphorae: with an index of stamps*, London

Carson, R A G, Hill, P V, and Kent, J P C, 1965 *Late Roman bronze coinage*, London

Castle, S A, 1972 A kiln of the potter Doinus, *Archaeol J* 129, 69–88

Clason, A T (ed), 1975 *Archaeological studies*, Amsterdam

Cohen, A, and Serjeantson, D, 1996 *A manual for the identification of bird bones from archaeological sites*, rev edn, London

Cool, H E M, and Price, J, 1995 *Roman vessel glass from excavations at Colchester, 1971–85*, Colchester Archaeol Rep 8, Colchester

Cowan, C, 1992 A possible mansio in Roman Southwark: excavations at 15–23 Southwark Street, 1980–86, *Trans London Middlesex Archaeol Soc* 43, 3–191

Cowan, C, in prep *The development of north-west Roman Southwark: excavations at Courage's Brewery, 1974–90*, MoLAS Monogr Ser

Cowan, C, Wheeler, L, and Westman, A, in prep *Roman Southwark: origins, development and economy*, MoLAS Monogr Ser

Crowley, N, 1992 Building material, in Cowan, 144–57

Crowley, N, in prep Building material, in Yule in prep

Crummy, N, 1983 *The Roman small finds from excavations in Colchester 1971–9*, Colchester Archaeol Rep 2, Colchester

Cunliffe, B, 1971 *Fishbourne: a Roman palace and its garden*, London

Dangréaux, B, and Desbat, A, 1988 Les Amphores du dépotoir Flavien du Bas-de-Loyasse à Lyon, *Gallia* 45, 115–53

Dannell, G B, 1971 The Samian pottery, in Cunliffe, B, *Excavations at Fishbourne 1961–1969: Vol 2, The finds*, Rep Res Soc Antiq London 27, London, 260–316

Dannell, G, Dickinson, B, and Vernhet, H, 1998 Ovolos on Dragendorff form 30 from the collections of F Hermet and D Rey, in *Form and fabric: studies in Rome's material past in honour of B R Hartley* (ed J Bird), Oxbow Monogr Ser 80, 69–109, Oxford

Davey, N, 1961 *A history of building materials*, London

Davey, N, and Ling, R, 1982 *Wall-painting in Roman Britain*, Britannia Monogr Ser 3, London

Davies, B J, 1992 Spot dates as quantitative data?, in *Interpretation of stratigraphy: a review of the art. Proceedings of a conference held on 18 June 1992* (ed K Steane), CLAU Archaeol Rep 31, 30–9, Lincoln

Davies, B J, 1993 Inter-site studies, in Milne and Wardle, 135–50

Davies, B J, Richardson, B, and Tomber, R S, 1994 *The archaeology of Roman London: Vol 5, A dated corpus of early Roman pottery from the City of London*, CBA Res Rep 98, London

Davis, A, 1995 An assessment of the plant remains from the Courage Brewery site, Southwark, unpub MoLAS archive rep

Davis, A, 2000 The plant remains, in Barber and Bowsher, 368–77

Dennis, G, 1978 1–7 St Thomas Street, in Bird et al, 291–422

Desbat, A, 1986, Céramiques romaines à glaçure plombifère des fouilles de Lyon (Hauts-de-Saint-Just, Rue des Farges, La Solitude), *Figlina* 7, 105–24

Desbat, A, and Savay-Guerraz, H, 1990, Note sur la découverte d'amphores Dressel 2/4 italiques, tardives, à Saint-Romain-en-Gal (Rhône), *Gallia* 47, 203–13

Detsicas, A, 1977 First century pottery manufacture at Eccles, Kent, in *Roman pottery studies in Britain and beyond: papers presented to John Gillam, July 1977* (eds J Dore and K Green), BAR Int Ser 30, 19–36, Oxford

Dodge, H, and Ward-Perkins, B (eds), 1992 *Marble in antiquity: collected papers of J B Ward-Perkins*, Archaeol Monogr Brit School Rome 6, London

Driesch, A von den, 1976 *A guide to the measurement of animal bones from archaeological sites*, Peabody Mus Bull 1, Cambridge, Mass.

Driesch, A von den, and Boessneck, J A, 1974 Kritische Anmerkungen zur Widerristhöhenberechnung aus Langenmassen vor- und frühgeschichtlicher Tierknochen, *Säugetierkundliche Mitteilungen* 22, 325–48

Drummond-Murray, J, and Swain, H, 1997 Excavations in advance of the Jubilee Line Extension in Southwark: updated project design for research and publication of Roman data, unpub MoLAS archive rep

Drummond-Murray, J, Thomas, C, and Siddell, J, with Miles, A, 1998 *The Big Dig*, London

Durand-Lefebvre, M, 1963 *Marques de potiers gallo-romains trouvées à Paris*, Paris

Edwards, J, 1984 *The Roman cookery of Apicius*, London

Evelein, M A, 1928 *De Romeinsche lampen*, Nijmegen

Farrar, R A H, 1981 The first Darfield hoard and the dating of black-burnished ware, in *Roman pottery research in Britain and North-West Europe: papers presented to Graham Webster* (eds A C Anderson and A S Anderson), BAR Int Ser 123, 417–30, Oxford

Ferretti, E, and Graham, A H, 1978 201–211 Borough High Street, in Bird et al, 53–176

Frere, S S (ed), 1972 *Verulamium excavations: Vol 1*, Rep Res Comm Soc Antiq London 28, London

Frere, S S (ed), 1984 *Verulamium excavations: Vol 3*, Oxford Univ Comm Archaeol Monogr 1, Oxford

Frere, S S, and St Joseph, J K, 1974 The Roman fortress at Longthorpe, Britannia 5, 1–129

Gillam, J P, 1953 Individual pieces from High House (milecastle 50TW), *Trans Cumberland Westmorland Antiq Archaeol Soc* 52, 34–7

Gillam, J P, 1976 Coarse Fumed ware in North Britain and beyond, *Glasgow Archaeol J* 4, 57–80

Giorgi, J, 1996 An assessment of the plant remains from the Jubilee Line sites, Southwark, unpub MoLAS archive rep

Giorgi, J, 1997 The plant remains from Fennings Wharf, Southwark, unpub MoLAS archive rep

Giorgi, J, in prep, The plant remains, in Seeley, D, in prep

Glasbergen, W, 1944 Versierde Claudisch–Neronische terra sigillata van Valkenburg ZH, in *De Romeinse castella in den dorpsheuvel te Valkenburg aan den Rijn (ZH)* (ed A E van Giffen), Jaarsverslag van de Vereeniging voor Terpenonderzoek 25/28, 206–17

Goffin, R, 1992, The wall plaster, in Cowan, 157–64

Goffin, R, in prep The wall plaster, in Yule in prep

Goodburn, D, 1991 A Roman timber-framed building tradition, *Archaeol J* 148, 182–204

Goodburn, R, 1984 Non-ferrous metal objects, in Frere 1984, 18–68

Goodburn Brown, D, 1992 The lifting of Roman floor and wall structures, in *Retrieval of objects from archaeological sites* (ed R Payton), 39–50, London

Gose, E, 1976 *Gefässtypen der römischen Keramik im Rheinland*, Cologne

Graham, A H, 1988a District heating scheme, in Hinton, 27–54

Graham, A H, 1988b 64–70 Borough High Street, in Hinton, 55–66

Graham, A H, and Hinton, P, 1988 The Roman roads in Southwark, in Hinton, 19–26

Grant, A, 1982 The use of tooth wear as a guide to the age of domestic ungulates, in Wilson et al, 91–108

Grant, M (trans), 1971 *Tacitus, The Annals of Imperial Rome*, rev edn, Harmondsworth

Gray-Rees, L, 1996 Assessment of the plant remains in environmental samples from Borough High Street (BGH95), Southwark, unpub MoLAS archive rep

Gray-Rees, L, 1997 Assessment of the plant remains in environmental samples from Regis House (KWS94),

City of London, unpub MoLAS archive rep

Gray-Rees, L, in prep Plant remains from Lloyd's Register, in Bluer and Brigham in prep

Green, M J, 1989 *Symbol and image in Celtic religious art*, London

Greene, K, 1979 *Report on the excavations at Usk, 1965–76: The pre-Flavian fine wares*, Cardiff

Greep, S, 1983 Early import of bone objects to south-east Britain, Britannia 14, 259–61

Greig, J, 1982 Garderobes, sewers, cesspits and latrines: their evidence for diet and health, *Current Archaeol* 8, 49–52

Greig, J, 1984 The palaeoecology of some British hay meadow types, in van Zeist and Casparie, 213–26

Groves, J, 1993 Ceramic studies, in Milne and Wardle, 114–50

Groves, J, in prep, The dating of the early groups, in Cowan in prep

Guido, M, 1978 *The glass beads of the prehistoric and Roman periods in Britain and Ireland*, Rep Res Comm Soc Antiq London 35, London

Guildhall Museum, 1908 *Catalogue of the London antiquities in the Guildhall Museum*, London

Hammer, F, in prep *Industry in north-west Roman Southwark: excavations at Courage's Brewery, 1984–8*, MoLAS Monogr Ser

Hammerson, M J, 1978 The Roman coins, in Bird et al, 587–600

Hammerson, M J, 1980 Romano-British copies of the coinage of AD 330–341, unpub MPhil thesis, Univ London

Hammerson, M J, 1988 Roman coins from Southwark, in Hinton, 417–26

Hammerson, M J, 1992 The coins, in Cowan, 137–44

Hammerson, M J, 1996 Problems of Roman coin interpretation in Greater London, in *Interpreting Roman London* (eds J Bird, A H Graham, and H L Sheldon), Oxbow Monogr 58, 153–64, Oxford

Hammerson, M, and Sheldon, H, 1987 Evidence for the Roman army in Southwark, in *Roman military equipment: the accoutrements of war* (ed M Dawson), BAR Int Ser 336, 167–74, Oxford

Harcourt, R A, 1974 The dog in prehistoric and early historic Britain, *J Archaeol Sci* 1, 151–75

Hartley, K F, 1972 The mortarium stamps, in Frere, 371–81

Hartley, K F, 1984 The mortarium stamps, in Frere, 280–91

Hartley, K F, 1985 The mortaria: discussion and conclusions, in Niblett, 92–6

Hartley, K F, 1988 Mortaria, in Hinton, 271–5

Hartley, K F, 1998 The incidence of stamped mortaria in the Roman Empire with special reference to imports to Britain, in *Form and Fabric: studies in Rome's material past in honour of B R Hartley* (ed J Bird), Oxbow Monogr 80, 199–217, Oxford

Hartley, K F, 1999 Stamps on Colchester and imported mortaria, in Symonds and Wade, 195–211

Hawkes, C F C, and Hull, M R, 1947 *Camulodunum: first report on the excavations at Colchester 1930–1939*, Rep Res Comm Soc Antiq London 14, London

Hayes, J W, 1972 *Late Roman pottery*, London

Heard, K, 1989 Preliminary report on excavations at 52–54 Southwark Street, unpub MoLAS archive rep

Heard, K, Sheldon, H, and Thompson, P, 1990 Mapping Roman Southwark, *Antiquity* 64, 608–19

Henig, M, 1970 The veneration of heroes in the Roman army, Britannia 1, 249–65

Henig, M, 1978 (1974) A corpus of Roman engraved gemstones from British sites, BAR Brit Ser 8, 2 edn, Oxford

Henig, M, 1979 The 'Alexander' gem from Caerleon, Bull Board Celtic Stud 28, 317–18

Henig, M, 1988 The chronology of Roman engraved gemstones, J Roman Archaeol 1, 142–52

Henig, M, 2000 Art in Roman London, in London under ground: the archaeology of a city (eds I Haynes, H Sheldon, and L Hanigan), 62–84, Oxford

Hermet, F, La Graufesenque, Paris

Hill, J, and Rowsome, P, in prep Excavations at 1 Poultry: Vol 1, The Roman sequence, MoLAS Monogr Ser

Hillman, G C, 1972 Distinguishing chaff remains of emmer and einkorn: summary of the criteria applied to the charred remains from Mycenae, unpub rep

Hillman, G C, 1981 Reconstructing crop husbandry practices from charred remains of crops, in Farming practice in British prehistory (ed R Mercer), 123–62, Edinburgh

Hinton, P (ed), 1988 Excavations in Southwark 1973–76, Lambeth 1973–79, London Middlesex Archaeol Soc and Surrey Archaeol Soc Joint Pub 3, London

Hodgson, G, 1976 The animals of Vindolanda, Haltwhistle

Holbrook, N, and Bidwell, P T, 1991 Roman finds from Exeter, Exeter Archaeol Rep 4, Exeter

Howe, M D, Perrin, J R, and Mackreth, D F, 1980 Roman pottery from the Nene Valley: a guide, Peterborough

Hull, M R, 1963 The Roman potters' kilns of Colchester, Rep Res Comm Soc Antiq London 21, Oxford

Isings, C, 1957 Roman glass from dated finds, Groningen

Jackson, R, 1985 Cosmetic sets from Late Iron Age and Roman Britain, Britannia 16, 165–92

Jackson, R, 1993 The function and manufacture of Romano-British cosmetic grinders: two important new finds from London, Antiq J 73, 165–9

Jackson, R, 1994 The surgical instruments, appliances and equipment in Celsus' De medicina, in La Médecine de Celse: aspects historiques, scientifiques et littéraires (eds G Sabbah and P Mudry), 167–209, Lyon

Jones, G E M, 1984 Interpretation of archaeological plant remains: ethnographic models from Greece, in van Zeist and Casparie, 43–61

Killock, D, 1997 Excavations at 51–53 Southwark Street, unpub Pre-Construct Archaeology archive rep

King, A C, 1984 Animal bones and the dietary identity of military and civilian groups in Roman Britain, Germany and Gaul, in Military and civilian in Roman Britain: cultural relationships in a frontier province (eds T Blagg and A King), BAR Brit Ser 136, 187–218, Oxford

King, C E, 1987 The Bicester hoard of folles, AD 317–348, Coin Hoards from Roman Britain II, London

Knorr, R, 1919 Töpfer und Fabriken verzierter Terra-Sigillata des ersten Jahrhunderts, Stuttgart

Knorr, R, 1952 Terra-Sigillata-Gefässe des ersten Jahrhunderts mit Töpfernamen, Stuttgart

Laubenheimer, F, 1992 Les Amphores en Gaule: production et circulation, Paris

Laubenheimer, F, 1998 Les Amphores en Gaule II: production et circulation, Paris

Laubenheimer, F, and Hénon, B, 1998 Les Amphores du Titelberg (Luxembourg), in Laubenheimer, 107–42

Lawrence, M J, and Brown, R W, 1973 Mammals of Britain: their tracks, trails and signs, London

Leblanc, O, and Desbat, A, 1992 Un Lot de céramiques du début du IIIe siècle à Saint-Romain-en-Gal (Rhône), Revue Archéologique de Narbonnaise 25, 125–50

Liversidge, J, 1969 Furniture and decoration, in The Roman villa in Britain (ed A L F Rivet), 127–72, London

Lowther, A W G, 1948 A study of patterns on Roman flue-tiles and their distribution, Surrey Archaeol Res Pap 1, London

Lyne, M A B, and Jefferies, R S, 1979 The Alice Holt/Farnham Roman pottery industry, CBA Res Rep 30, London

MacKenna, A S, 1993 The painted wall plaster from Redcross Way, unpub MoLAS archive rep

Mackinder, A, 1994 Flatiron Square grouting shaft, Union Street, unpub MoLAS archive rep

Mackinder, A, 2000 A Romano-British cemetery on Watling Street: excavations at 165 Great Dover Street, Southwark, London, MoLAS Archaeol Stud Ser 4, London

Maltby, M, 1979 Faunal studies from urban sites: the animal bones from Exeter 1971–1975, Exeter Archaeol Rep 2, Sheffield

Maltby, M, 1997 Domestic fowl on Romano-British sites: inter-site comparisons of abundance, Int J Osteoarchaeol 7, 402–14

Manning, W H, 1985 Catalogue of the Romano-British iron tools, fittings and weapons in the British Museum, London

Marlière, E, 1998 Les Amphores de Bavay, in Laubenheimer, 49–89

Marsden, P, 1965 A boat of the Roman period discovered on the site of New Guy's House, Bermondsey, Trans London Middlesex Archaeol Soc 21, 118–31

Marsden, P, 1980 Roman London, London

Marsden, P, 1994 Ships of the port of London: first to eleventh centuries AD, London

Marsh, G, 1978 Early 2nd-century fine wares in the London area, in Early fine wares in Roman Britain (eds P Arthur and G Marsh), BAR Brit Ser 57, 119–223, Oxford

Marsh, G, and Tyers, I, 1978 The Roman pottery from Southwark, in Bird et al, 535–82

Mattingly, H, Sydenham, E A, et al 1923ff Roman imperial coinage, London

Merrifield, R, 1983 London: city of the Romans, London

Miles, A, 1992 Redcross Way (REW92), unpub MoLAS archive rep

Millett, M, 1979 The dating of Farnham (Alice Holt) pottery, Britannia 10, 121–37

Mills, A, and McDonnell, J, 1992 The identification and analysis of the hammerscale from Burton Dassett, Warwickshire, unpub Engl Heritage Ancient Monuments Lab rep 47/92

Milne, G, 1985 The port of Roman London, London

Milne, G (ed), 1992 From Roman basilica to medieval market: archaeology in action in the City of London, London

Milne, G, 1995 English Heritage book of Roman London: urban archaeology in the nation's capital, London

Milne, G, and Wardle, A, 1993 Early Roman development at Leadenhall Court, London and related research, Trans London Middlesex Archaeol Soc 44, 23–169

Monaghan, J, 1987 Upchurch and Thameside Roman pottery: a ceramic typology for northern Kent, 1st to 3rd centuries AD, BAR Brit Ser 173, Oxford

Morris, J, 1982 Londinium: London in the Roman Empire, London

Museum of London, 1998 General standards for the preparation of archaeological archives deposited with the Museum of London, unpub MoL rep

Neal, D S, Wardle, A, and Hunn, J, 1990 Excavation of the Iron Age, Roman and medieval settlement at Gorehambury St Albans, Engl Heritage Archaeol Rep 14, London

Niblett, R, 1985 Sheepen: an early Roman industrial site at Camulodunum, CBA Res Rep 57, London

Oldenstein, J, 1976 Zur Ausrüstung römischer Auxiliareinheiten, Bericht der Römisch-Germanischen Kommission 57, 49–284

Olmer, F, 1998 Les Amphores de Mâlain-Mediolanum (Côte-d'Or), in Laubenheimer, 159–74

Orton, C R, Tyers, P A, and Vince, A G, 1993 Pottery in archaeology, Cambridge

Oswald, F, 1936–7 Index of figure-types on terra sigillata ('samian ware'), Annals Archaeol Anthropol 23.1–4, 24.1–4

Oswald, F, and Davies Pryce, T, 1920 An introduction to the study of terra sigillata, London

Peacock, D P S, and Williams, D F, 1986 Amphorae and the Roman economy, London

Pearson, E, and Giorgi, J, 1992 The plant remains, in Cowan, 165–70

Perring, D, 1991 Roman London, London

Picon, M, and Desbat, A, 1986 Note sur l'origine des céramiques à glaçure plombifère, généralement bicolore, des IIème et IIIème siècles, de Vienne et Saint-Romain-en-Gal, Figlina 7, 125–7

Picon, M, and Desbat, A, 1990 Appendice: étude en laboratoire, in Desbat and Savay-Guerraz, 212–13

Pipe, A, in prep a The animal bone, in Cowan in prep

Pipe, A, in prep b The animal bone, in D Williams in prep, Excavations at Franks' Sandpit, Betchworth, Surrey, Surrey Archaeol Collect

Pollard, R J, 1988 The Roman pottery of Kent, Kent Archaeol Soc Monogr 5, Maidstone

Precious, B J, 1997 An assessment of Roman pottery from 15–23 Southwark Street, London (FSS96), unpub Pre-Construct Archaeology archive rep

Pritchard, F A, 1986 Ornamental stonework from Roman London, Britannia 17, 169–89

Protocol Beuvray, 1998 Protocole de quantification des céramiques, in La quantification des céramiques: conditions et protocole (eds P Arcelin and M Tuffreau-Libre), 141–57, Glux-en-Glenne

Rackham, D J, 1986 Assessing the relative frequency of species by the application of a stochastic model to a zooarchaeological database, in van Wijngaarden-Bakker, 185–92

Rackham, D J, 1995 Skeletal evidence of medieval horses from London sites, in The medieval horse and its equipment c 1150–1450 (ed J Clark), HMSO Medieval Finds from Excavations in London Ser 5, 169–74, London

Rayner, L, in prep The Roman pottery, in Hill and Rowsome in prep

Rayner, L, and Seeley, F, 1996 Research aims for Roman pottery in Southwark, unpub MoLAS archive rep

Rayner, L, and Seeley, F, 1998 Pottery publications and research in Roman London, in Watson, 90–4

Rayner, L, and Seeley, F, in prep The Roman pottery, in Cowan et al in prep

Reece, R, 1987 Coinage in Roman Britain, London

Richardson, B, 1986 The pottery, in The Roman quay at St Magnus House, London: excavations at New French Wharf, Lower Thames Street, London, 1974–78 (ed T Dyson), London Middlesex Archaeol Soc Spec Pap 8, 96–138, London

Rielly, K, 1997 The assessment of the animal bones from the Jubilee Line Extension sites (Southwark), unpub MoLAS archive rep

Rielly, K, 1998 The animal bones from Sommerton Way, Thamesmead, SE28, London, Borough of Bexley (SNY97 and SWY97), unpub MoLAS archive rep

Rielly, K, 2000 The animal bone, in Barber and Bowsher, 366–8

Rielly, K, 2001 The animal bones from Fennings Wharf, in Watson et al, 214–20

Rielly, K, in prep a The animal bone, in Brigham and Watson in prep

Rielly, K, in prep b The animal bone, in Yule in prep

Rigby, V, 1989 Imports from Gallia Belgica, in Stead and Rigby, 121–37

Rogers, G B, 1974 Poteries sigillées de la Gaule centrale: I, Les motifs non figurés, Gallia Suppl 28, Paris

Rougemont, G M de, 1989 A field guide to the crops of Britain and Europe, London

Rouvier-Jeanlin, M, 1972 Les Figurines gallo-romaines en terre cuite au Musée des Antiquités Nationales, Gallia Suppl 24, Paris

Schmid, E, 1972 Atlas of animal bones, London

Schwab, I, 1978 106–114 Borough High Street, in Bird et al, 177–220

Scott, D, 1994 An examination of the patina and corrosion morphology of some Roman bronzes, J American Inst Conservation 33, 1–23

Sealey, P R, 1997 The Boudican revolt against Rome, Princes Risborough

Sealey, P R, in prep Ver. 1908 amphoras introduced, J Roman Pottery Stud 9

Sealey, P R, and Tyers, P A, 1989 Olives from Roman Spain: a unique amphora find in British waters, Antiq J 69, 53–72

Seeley, D, with Carlin, M, and Phillpotts, C, in prep Winchester Palace: excavations at the Southwark residence of the bishops of Winchester, MoLAS Monogr Ser

Seeley, F J, in prep The Roman pottery, in Bluer and Brigham in prep

Sheldon, H, 1974 Excavations at Toppings and Sun Wharves,

Southwark, 1970–1972, *Trans London Middlesex Archaeol Soc 25*, 1–116

Sheldon, H, 1978 The 1972–74 excavations: their contributions to Southwark's history, in Bird et al, 11–53

Shepherd, J D, 1992 The glass, in Cowan, 120–36

Shepherd, J D, 1993 The glass, in Milne and Wardle, 99–114

Sidell, E J, 1991 The identification of archaeological eggshell: a feasibility study, unpub MSc dissertation, Univ London

Sidell, E J, 1993 *A methodology for the identification of archaeological eggshell*, MASCA, the University Museum of Archaeology and Anthropology, University of Pennsylvania, Philadelphia, Suppl to Vol 10, Philadelphia, Pa.

Sidell, E J, 1997 Assessment of the eggshell from Borough High Street, London Borough of Southwark, unpub MoLAS archive rep

Sidell, E J, and Rielly, K, 1998 New evidence for the ritual use of animals in Roman London, in Watson, 95–109

Silver, I A, 1969 The ageing of domestic animals, in *Science in archaeology* (eds D Brothwell and E Higgs), 283–302, London

Sloane, B, Swain, H, and Thomas, C, 1995 The Roman road and the river regime: archaeological investigations in Westminster and Lambeth, *London Archaeol 7(14)*, 359–70

Stanfield, J A, and Simpson, G, 1958 *Central Gaulish potters*, London

Stead, I M, and Rigby, V, 1989 *Verulamium: the King Harry Lane site*, Engl Heritage Archaeol Rep 12, London

Straker, V, 1984 First and second century carbonised grain from Roman London, in van Zeist and Casparie, 323–9

Suggett, P G, 1954 Report on the excavations at Brockley Hill, Middlesex: March 1952 and May 1953, *Trans London Middlesex Archaeol Soc 113*, 259–76

Sutherland, C H V, 1935 *Romano-British imitations of bronze coins of Claudius I*, Amer Numis Soc, Numis Notes Monogr 65, New York

Symonds, R P, with Carreras-Monfort, C, 1993 Amphores romano-britanniques, in *SFECAG, Actes du Congrès de Versailles* (ed L Rivet), 281–91, Marseilles

Symonds, R P, 1997 Assessment of the Roman pottery from the JLE sites, unpub MoLAS archive rep

Symonds, R P, in prep a The Roman pottery, in Brigham and Watson in prep

Symonds, R P, in prep b The pottery, in Cowan in prep

Symonds, R P, and Tomber, R S, 1991 Late Roman London: an assessment of the ceramic evidence from the City of London, *Trans London Middlesex Archaeol Soc 42*, 59–99

Symonds, R P, and Wade, S M, 1999 *The Roman pottery from excavations in Colchester, 1971–86*, Colchester Archaeol Rep 10, Colchester

Teichert, M, 1975 Osteometrische Untersuchungen zur Berechnung der Widerristhöhe bei Schafen, in Clason, 51–69

Thomas, C, Sloane, B, and Phillpotts, C, 1997 *Excavations at the Priory and Hospital of St Mary Spital, London*, MoLAS Monogr Ser 1, London

Thomas, R, 1989, *Römische Wandmalerei aus Köln*, Cologne

Thompson, I, 1982 *Grog-tempered 'Belgic' pottery of south-eastern England*, BAR Brit Ser 108, Oxford

Thuault, M, and Vernhet, A, 1986 Le Rozier, in C Bémont and

J-P Jacob, La Terre sigillée gallo-romain: lieu de production du haut empire: implantations, produit, relations, *Documents d'Archéologie Française 6*, 110–13

Tomber, R, and Dore, J, 1998 *The National Roman Fabric Reference Collection: a handbook*, MoLAS Monogr Ser 2, London

Toynbee, J M C, 1962 *Art in Roman Britain*, London

Tyers, I, 1994, Dendrochronological dating of RWG94 Well 2, unpub MoLAS archive rep

Tyers, P, 1996 Late Iron Age and early Roman pottery traditions of the London region, in *Interpreting Roman London: papers in memory of Hugh Chapman* (eds J Bird, M Hassall, and H Sheldon), Oxbow Monogr Ser 58, 139–45, Oxford

Ulbert, G, 1969 Gladii aus Pompeiji, *Germania 47*, 97–128

Veen, M van der, 1992 *Crop husbandry regimes: an archaeological study of farming in northern England 1000 BC – AD 500*, Sheffield Archaeol Monogr 3, Sheffield

Vilvorder, F, Symonds, R P, Tomber, R S, and Rekk, S, in prep Les Amphores orientales en Gaule septentrionale et au sud-est de la Grande Bretagne, *RCRF Acta 36*

Wacher, J, 1995 *The towns of Roman Britain*, 2 edn, London

Walters, H B, 1908 *Catalogue of Roman pottery in the Department of Antiquities, British Museum*, London

Ward-Perkins, J, and Claridge, A, 1976 *Pompeii AD 79*, Roy Acad Arts exhibition catalogue, Bristol

Wardle, A, 1982 Musical instruments in the Roman world, unpub PhD thesis, Univ London

Wardle, A, in prep Accessioned finds, in Cowan et al in prep

Watson, B (ed), 1998 *Roman London: recent archaeological work*, J Roman Archaeol Monogr Suppl Ser 24, Portsmouth, RI

Watson, B, Brigham, T, and Dyson, T, 2001 *London bridge: 2000 years of a river crossing*, MoLAS Monogr Ser 8, London

Webster, P, 1996 *Roman samian pottery in Britain*, CBA Practical Handbooks in Archaeol 13, York

West, B, n d The Roman London Project, unpub MoLAS archive rep

Wheeler, R E M, 1930 *London in Roman times*, London Museum Catalogues No. 3, London

Wijngaarden-Bakker, L H van (ed), 1986 *Database management and zooarchaeology*, PACT (J European Study Grp Physical, Chemical, Biological, Mathematical Techniques applied to Archaeology) Res Vol 40, Amsterdam

Wilkinson K, 1996 An assessment of the sedimentological samples taken from Borough High Street, unpub Cotswold Archaeological Trust rep

Willis, S, in prep The character of Lyon ware distribution with particular attention to the evidence from northern Britain, *J Roman Pottery Stud*

Wilson, B, Grigson, C, and Payne, S (eds), 1982 *Ageing and sexing animal bones from archaeological sites*, BAR Brit Ser 109, Oxford

Wilson, C A, 1973 *Food and drink in Britain*, London

Wilson, C A, 1991 *Food and drink in Britain: from the Stone Age to recent times*, Harmondsworth

Wilson, M G, 1984 The other pottery, in Frere, 201–76

Wilson, R, 1990 Guy's Hospital redevelopment, St Thomas Street, SE1, in J Heathcote, Excavation round-up 1989: Part 2, London Boroughs, *London Archaeol 6(7)*, 193

Young, C J, 1977 *The Roman pottery industry of the Oxford region*, BAR Brit Ser 43, Oxford

Yule, B, 1982 A third century well group and the later Roman settlement in Southwark, *London Archaeol* 4(9), 243–9

Yule, B, 1988 Natural topography of north Southwark, in Hinton, 13–18

Yule, B, 1989 Excavations at Winchester Palace, Southwark, *London Archaeol* 6(2), 31–9

Yule, B, in prep *A prestigious Roman building complex on the Southwark waterfront*, MoLAS Monogr Ser

Yule, B, and Rankov, B, 1998 Legionary soldiers in 3rd-century Southwark, in Watson, 67–77

Zadoks-Josephus Jitta, A N, Peters, W J T, and Witteveen, A, 1973 *Description of the collections in the Rijksmuseum G. M. Kam at Nijmegen: VII, The figural bronzes*, Nijmegen

Zeist, W van, and Casparie, W A (eds), 1984 *Plants and ancient man: studies in palaeoethnobotany*, Rotterdam

Zohary, D, and Hopf, M, 1993 *Domestication of plants in the Old World: the origin and spread of cultivated plants in West Asia, Europe and the Nile Valley*, 2 edn, Oxford

INDEX

Compiled by Susanne Atkin

Page numbers in **bold** refer to illustrations
B Building
OA Open Area
S Structure